MACROECONOMIC THEORY
SECOND EDITION

This is a volume in

ECONOMIC THEORY, ECONOMETRICS, AND MATHEMATICAL
    ECONOMICS

Edited by Karl Shell, *Cornell University*

A complete list of titles in this series is available from the Publishers upon request.

MACROECONOMIC
THEORY
SECOND EDITION

THOMAS J. SARGENT

Hoover Institution
Stanford University
Stanford, California

and

Federal Reserve Bank
Minneapolis, Minnesota

ACADEMIC PRESS, INC.
Harcourt Brace Jovanovich, Publishers
Boston   San Diego   New York   Berkeley
London   Sydney   Tokyo   Toronto

ACADEMIC PRESS, INC.
San Diego, California 92101

United Kingdom Edition published by
ACADEMIC PRESS, INC. (London) Ltd.
24-28 Oval Road, London NW1 7DX

Library of Congress Cataloging-in-Publication Data

Sargent, Thomas J.
  Macroeconomic theory.

  (Economic theory, econometrics, and mathematical
economics)
  Includes bibliographies and indexes.
  1. Macroeconomics. I. Title. II. Series.
HB172.5.S27 1987   339′.01   86-28778
ISBN 0-12-619751-2 (alk. paper)

PRINTED IN THE UNITED STATES OF AMERICA
88 89 90 91   9 8 7 6 5 4 3 2

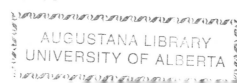

To Judy

CONTENTS

PREFACE TO THE SECOND EDITION

This is a revision of a book that was first published in 1979. In addition to some minor corrections and additions occurring throughout the text, the major changes consist in the deletion of one chapter of the old edition, the addition of three entirely new chapters, and substantial additions to three of the original chapters (those on difference equations, on stochastic difference equations, and on investment under uncertainty). I have also added an introductory section containing personal remarks about the history of some of the ideas in this book.

When the manuscript for the first edition of this book was sent to the publisher in 1977, I was only beginning to understand the ramifications of the cross-equation restrictions that the hypothesis of rational expectations imposes on an equilibrium stochastic process of a dynamic model. Some of those ramifications had leaked into the first edition of this book, but many more are present in this edition. A formula expressing these restrictions in linear models was published by Lars Hansen and me in 1980. That formula is applied repeatedly in this edition.

The first edition appeared at a time when discussions of the "policy ineffectiveness proposition" occupied much of the attention of macroeconomists. As work of John B. Taylor has made clear, the methodological and computational implications of the hypothesis of rational expectations for the theory of optimal macroeconomic policy far transcend the question of whether we accept or reject particular models embodying particular neutrality propositions. Indeed, relative to the simple early models of Barro and Sargent and Wallace, models in which government policy choices affect allocations require much more intricate exploitation of the cross-equation restrictions of rational expectations in optimally choosing government policy. The current edition contains many more examples of models in which a government faces a non-trivial policy choice than did the earlier edition.

I have completely rewritten the chapter on consumption and have added a new chapter on government debt and taxes, which analyzes the Barro tax-smoothing model, and a new chapter on dynamic optimal taxation, which analyzes the time inconsistency problem. I have also extended the treatment of both nonstochastic and stochastic linear difference equations. Applications of stochastic linear difference equations have become increasingly common in macroeconomics since the first edition appeared, with vector autoregressions and rational expectations econometrics becoming widespread. I have also added substantially to the chapter on investment under uncertainty.

I received helpful comments and criticisms on this material from many people. I would especially like to thank Charles Whiteman, Richard Todd, Shinichi Watanabe, Lawrence Christiano, Rao Aiyagari, Randall Wright, Richard Rogerson, Albert Marcet, Rodolfo Manuelli, Michael Stutzer, Will Roberds, and Eugene Yun for their comments. Wendy Williamson provided excellent research assistance and typing help, as well as discipline in meeting deadlines. For help in preparing graphs, I would like to thank Susan Mendesh, Steven Morus, George McCandless, and Robert Litterman. I would like to thank once more the Federal Reserve Bank of Minneapolis and the University of Minnesota for providing me with a wonderful environment for studying macroeconomics.

Christopher A. Sims and Neil Wallace taught me much of what is contained in this book.

July 1986

PREFACE TO THE FIRST EDITION

This book grew out of a series of lecture notes prepared for a first-year graduate course at the University of Minnesota. Part I is devoted to a presentation of some fairly standard nonstochastic macroeconomic analysis. Part II attempts to provide an introduction to some of the methods and issues in stochastic macroeconomics. This book does not purport to present a unified treatment of a single, widely received macroeconomic theory since the economics profession has not yet attached itself to any one such theory. On the contrary, one can concoct a large variety of plausible macroeconomic models at the level of rigor of the usual Keynesian model, models exhibiting very different responses to policy experiments. A partial aim of the first five chapters and the exercises given there is to exhibit the extent of this variety.

Part II uses a somewhat roundabout means of production and devotes some space to a treatment of some of the tools of modern macroeconomics: lag operators, linear least squares prediction, and stochastic difference equations. The chapter on stochastic difference equations is intended for browsing on the first reading, only parts of this chapter being required for understanding the sequel.

I received helpful comments from Thomas Doan, Preston Miller, Arthur Rolnick, Gary Skoog, Dale Henderson, Charles Whiteman, Rusdu Saracoglu, Neil Wallace, Mathew Canzoneri, and George McCandless. Special thanks are due to George McCandless who proofread and criticized the manuscript and prepared the Index.

I would like to thank the Research Department of the Federal Reserve Bank of Minneapolis for the support of my research and for permitting me to serve as an advisor for the past seven years. The Bank has provided an ideal environment for thinking about macroeconomics. Needless to say, the Federal Reserve Bank is not responsible for any of the opinions expressed in this work. Finally, I would like to thank the staff of Academic Press for their editorial assistance.

"A fellow may do many a crazy thing, and as long as he has no theory about it, we forgive him. But if there happens to be a theory behind his actions, everybody is down on him."

Gene Henderson, in *Henderson the Rain King* by Saul Bellow.

INTRODUCTION TO THE SECOND EDITION

This book was written gradually and continuously over the years 1970 to 1985. It amounts to a record of notes on lectures that I gave during those years in the graduate course in macroeconomic theory at the University of Minnesota. During those years there occurred revolutionary changes in the subject of macroeconomics. The fact that this book was written over a period of time that spanned this "rational expectations revolution" is evident from the book's structure.

The first five chapters, which I taught from 1970 to about 1974, describe the static analysis of various classical and Keynesian macroeconomic models. These chapters were written at a time when I was a devoted user of Keynesian economics and were heavily influenced by my studies of Tobin's work and his insistence on careful treatments of time and of stocks and flows. I was also very much influenced by papers by and discussions with my colleague Neil Wallace, who in those days was studying the foundations of Keynesian models. Two aspects of the looming rational expectations revolution are foreshadowed in these early chapters. First, following the ideas of Tobin and Wallace, these chapters stressed the important technical role played in these static analyses by the assumption that expectations of inflation are exogenous. It is that assumption that makes a static, or point-in-time, analysis capable of determining equilibrium values of all of the endogenous variables that have to be determined. Technically that assumption prevents the models from becoming dynamic ones in the forms of differential equations. Second, these early chapters contained an attempt to find "the people" underneath the schedules and to tell stories about the ends that their decisions were imagined to be serving. The stories in these chapters are not satisfactory by today's standards, for they are not fully coherent and cannot be made so by simple modifications. But it was thinking hard about precisely these models, about the hypothetical people in them and their objectives, and about the role of exogenous price expectations which led Neil

Wallace and me toward rational expectations macroeconomics. It is true that there were other, more elegant routes toward that end, through general equilibrium theory or optimal growth theory, but those were not the routes that Wallace and I took. (While Neil Wallace and I were struggling with Keynesian models, Robert E. Lucas, Jr., and Edward C. Prescott were mostly traveling along these alternative and more direct routes.) I preserve these first five chapters partly out of a desire not to obliterate or smooth out the trail which took me from Keynesian economics into rational expectations. Furthermore, it remains useful to study these models in their own right, both because a large part of the economics profession still has faith in them, and because they provide a concise introduction to some of the classic issues of the subject.

Keynesian and classical models of the type studied in the first five chapters consisted of collections of decision rules which were assumed to be fixed in the face of various policy interventions. By a decision rule is meant a function expressing an agent's decision about something as a function of the pertinent information that he possesses at the time he makes the decision. The consumption function, investment function, and demand schedule for money are all examples of decision rules in the Keynesian model. In Keynesian economics, policy experiments were conducted by holding these decision rules fixed while varying settings for government expenditures, taxes, and the money supply. Sometimes the adjective "structural" is used to denote the property of being invariant with respect to the class of policy interventions to be analyzed. Keynesian models treated decision rules as structural.

It turned out that thinking both about the exogeneity of expectations of inflation and about the purposes for which the hypothetical people in the model were making decisions undermined the notion that decision rules could be regarded as structural. Since expectations of inflation played an important role in these models, for example in analyses of the "Fisher effect," it was natural to seek to close the model by making them endogenous. Since the models were not random, and since they could be used to determine the path of future prices and thus actual inflation, essentially by repeating a static analysis for each successive point in time, it was also natural to impose that expected inflation equals actual inflation. In a perfectly certain environment, "perfect foresight" seems to be the most reasonable assumption. While this was a natural step, it was not an easy one to take or to see fully the consequences of. Chapter I already wrestles with this issue and indicates what Wallace and I perceived the difficulties to be in carrying out such an analysis, as of 1971 or so. Imposing perfect foresight on price expectations had the effect of converting a static model into a dynamic one which had to be analyzed using the tools of differential equations. Furthermore, the simple step of imposing perfect foresight meant that, expressed as functions of variables dated t and earlier, decision rules are not structural; with foresight, such decision rules would depend implicitly on the time paths or rules for setting paths of future government policy variables. This dependence would show up by making decision rules expressed as functions of variables dated t and earlier themselves functions of the rules or laws of motion imagined to govern the government policy variables. This theoretical observation is the basis for "Lucas's critique" stating that the decision rules of Keynesian models are not structural in the sense of being invariant with respect to changes in the time paths for government policy variables. This theoretical observation destroyed the scientific grounds for believing the policy conclusions drawn from Keynesian models. It also created a challenge to find methods for studying macroeconomic decision rules which respond systematically and predictably to the government's choice of strategy or time path for its policy variables. The remaining chapters of this book are devoted to describing such methods and a variety of sample models that were constructed by using such methods.

These remaining chapters contain a mixture of tools and models. The thoroughness with which methods and models are mixed may strike some readers as yielding a haphazard presentation. Again, this manner of presentation reflects the fact that the book was composed over a number of years, and that my own process of learning the subject has continually mixed technical tools and economic models. In this learning process, the desire to understand a particular economic model or phenomenon often prompted my learning to use some mathematical tool or other. More often than not, once that tool was possessed, it became clear how a further class of economic models or phenomena could be studied. This leap-frogging approach is reflected in this book. In retrospect, it would have been possible to smooth out the presentation of the material by isolating the purely technical material from that with economic content. I purposefully did not do so in order not to conceal what amounts to my own personal record of learning the subject. Also, to me it seems more fun to learn about the tools when applications are quickly mentioned to practice upon.

One example of a theoretical economic issue which required investment in mathematical tools has already been mentioned: the construction of models with foresight about future rates of inflation. The reason that it took Neil Wallace and me so long to understand this matter was that we didn't fully enough understand the structure of difference equations, even linear ones. Chapter IX summarizes much of what we needed to know in order to create models in which agents had foresight about the rate of inflation. However, once the tools of Chapter IX were in hand, other economic problems and the solutions to them readily suggested themselves. Thus, the variety of examples of tractable dynamic models suggested at the end of Chapter IX were easy to understand once the structure of difference equations was understood. This is only one illustration of the fact that as economic analysts we are directed by, if not prisoners of, the mathematical tools that we possess.

As another example of the same point, one of the main substantive economic motivations of my own studies has been to understand the connections between economic theories and econometric tests of those theories. A natural setting for creating an understandable relationship between the two is provided by random difference equations or "stochastic processes." Macroeconomists and applied time series econometricians very often report estimates of random difference equations. My initial goal in learning the material summarized in Chapter XI was to understand the structure of the linear stochastic difference equations that are often, if not usually, estimated in econometric studies. These were also the tools that Slutsky and Frisch had long ago forcefully commended to business cycle theorists. Furthermore, the theories of prediction of Wiener and Kolmogorov and the notions of causality proposed by Wiener, Granger, and Sims seemed potentially relevant for building stochastic models to understand phenomena in which foresight is important. In addition, stochastic difference equations formed the language used by John F. Muth in his two early articles on rational expectations. The material in Chapter XI had to be mastered in order fully to understand Muth's contributions and in order to be able to put his ideas to work in new contexts. This material turned out to provide insights and possess applications in a whole variety of directions of importance to macroeconomics. Key formulas for formulating rational expectations models (e.g., the formula for the expectation of a "geometric distributed lead"), the notion of "vector autoregressions," the structure of "leading indicators," and even the definition of the "business cycle" are among the economic dividends of the material in Chapter XI. It would not be much of an exaggeration to claim that Chapter XI introduces the "language of applied macroeconometrics" or at least one dialect. Furthermore, there turns out to be an intimate relationship between the classical linear prediction theory described in Chapter XI and the classical linear control theory described in Chapter IX.

When mastered, the tools of stochastic difference equations or stochastic processes prompt one to think about time series observations in terms of collections of (sample) moments with a linear structure that can be characterized by projections in various directions. Usually, these moments include the second moments of all pairs of variables under consideration at all leads and lags. This way of thinking affects both the way that we process observations and the way that we conceive "policy questions," whether we are proceeding formally or informally in an armchair. Once one begins to think about data in this way, it is natural to want economic models which produce stochastic difference equations as the outcome of the economic theorizing. It is desirable that these difference equations have free parameters that describe preferences and opportunities. This creates a framework in which the moments of the observable data can potentially be interpreted in terms of the economic parameters describing preferences and opportunities. There are many examples of this approach in this book. One key example is provided by the linear version of the Lucas-Prescott model of investment under uncertainty that is described in Chapter XIV. Linear stochastic difference equations lend themselves to the ready formulation and practical application of such models. In this book, the potential use of this idea is stressed in the context of a variety of versions of Lucas-Prescott models.

In terms of economic policy, thinking of stochastic processes promotes regarding policies as stochastic processes for the variables under the control of the policy maker. Rather than attempting to analyze the effects of one-time actions that are isolated in time, one is prompted to think of policy-making as a process producing a strategy which is to be used repeatedly over time and which results in a stochastic process for the policy maker's instrument of control. This is a good example of an area in which the tools that we are using influence the very questions that we ask and the way that we pose them. Thinking about policy in terms of repeated strategies or rules or regimes is natural for someone who thinks about dynamic economies in terms of stochastic processes.

I offer one more thought on the relationship between tools and models. I have mentioned the "rational expectations revolution," as the collection of developments in dynamic macroeconomics over the last fifteen years is sometimes called. Whether one wishes to refer to these developments as a "revolution" or as an evolution which proceeded continuously and inevitably out of Keynesian macroeconomics seems to be partly a matter of mood or taste. In the United States, macroeconomics since World War II has included a more or less continuous effort to discover microeconomic underpinnings behind the decision rules governing the Keynesian categories of consumption, investment, and money demand. Many of the celebrated contributions to macroeconomics in the post-war period were results of this effort, including the works of Friedman and Modigliani on consumption, Tobin, Baumol, and Samuelson on the demand for money, and Haavelmo, Jorgenson, Treadway, Gould, and Lucas on investment. This work was applauded by the profession in proportion to its sophistication and success in applying optimal control theory for understanding the decision in question. A widely agreed upon ultimate goal of such research was to combine the resulting decision rules obtained from these efforts to create ever more sophisticated Keynesian macroeconometric models. The Brookings Model emerged from an explicit attempt to accomplish just this.

From the viewpoint of this long line of research, exploring the implications of rational expectations was an inevitable step. The very same reasons that convinced economists that it is a good idea to analyze investment, consumption, and portfolio decisions by assuming expected utility maximizing agents who solve rich intertemporal problems, also commended the idea that agents would form their expectations optimally, i.e., "rationally." It is probably merely an intellectual coincidence that expectations about the future were the last domain to which macroeconomists applied the theory of optimizing agents: it just happened that economists in general and macroeconomists in particular learned the tools of optimal control (e.g., calculus of variations) somewhat before they learned the tools of optimal prediction and filtering. (I have already confessed the difficulties that Neil Wallace and I had in seeing how to build rational expectations into the Chapter I and II models, even after we decided that it was a desirable thing to do.)

There was another related strand of research in the Keynesian tradition that led inevitably toward rational expectations. This was the line of work, extending back to Tinbergen, which pursued the idea of applying optimal control theory to macroeconometric models in order to make precise quantitative statements about optimal monetary and fiscal policies. This line of thought, which was pursued by researchers such as Theil, Prescott, and Chow, prompted its advocates to think of a "policy" as a rule or repeated strategy to be chosen by the government to maximize an intertemporal objective function subject to "constraints" which took the form of an econometric model and which played the role of describing the "laws of motion" of the system that the government sought to control. In these policy experiments, the government was imagined to behave precisely as an agent with "rational expectations." In the early applications of this idea, the econometric model, consisting largely of hypothetical decision rules of private agents, was imagined to be fixed with respect to the choice of government policy rule (i.e., the econometric model was credited with being "structural"). In this work, the principle was discovered that the optimal monetary or fiscal policy rule for the government depended on the dynamic constraints faced by the government in the form of an econometric model. That is, it was discovered to be mistaken to expect there to be a single rule for monetary or fiscal policy that would be optimal over a range of alternative economies (econometric models). Technically, this finding was equivalent to the Lucas critique, only the names of the agents being different. It was inevitable that macroeconomists would eventually apply these ideas to private agents' decisions rules as well as those of the government. This would instill symmetry into these policy experiments by assuming that private agents, as well as the government agents, have "rational expectations" or, in other words, that private agents also solve dynamic optimization problems and take into account the constraints that they face, which include the laws of motion for policy variables that are chosen by the government. From the point of view of the evolution of this line of work, it is understandable that many of the earliest advocates and users of rational expectations in macroeconomics were originally Keynesian economists who had been interested in applying control theory for studying optimal monetary and fiscal policies.

The impulse to rational expectations theory was implicit in the agenda of Keynesian macroeconomics all along. However, the idea of rational expectations produced large and discontinuous changes in our conception of macroeconomic equilibria and in our methods for explaining observations. The idea also changed the way we think about optimal macroeconomic policy and about what features we believe a useful quantitative macroeconomic model will eventually have. Even the language that macroeconomists speak has changed. In this sense, there has been a rational expectations revolution.

PART I

Nonstochastic Macroeconomics

INTRODUCTION

These pages present static and dynamic analyses of some standard macro-economic models. By *static* analysis we mean the analysis of events assumed to occur at a point in time. In effect, statics studies the alternative point-in-time or momentary equilibrium values for a set of *endogenous variables* associated with alternative possible settings for the *exogenous variables* at the particular point in time under consideration. Endogenous variables are those determined by the model at hand, while exogenous variables are those given from outside the model.

The task of *dynamics* is to study the time paths of the endogenous variables associated with alternative possible time paths of the exogenous variables. Thus, in a dynamic analysis the behavior of a model is studied as time is permitted to pass. In contradistinction, in a static analysis attention is confined to events assumed to occur instantaneously, i.e., at a given moment.

A third kind of analysis, that of *stationary* states, is a limiting form of dynamic analysis, and is directed toward establishing the ultimate tendencies of certain endogenous variables, such as the capital–output ratio, as time passes without limit and as certain critical exogenous variables remain constant through time. Stationary analysis ought not to be confused with statics.

The distinguishing feature of a static analysis is that it is capable of determining alternative values of the endogenous variables, taking as given only the values of the exogenous variables at that point in time, which may include values of endogenous and exogenous variables that were determined in the past and are thus given or predetermined at the present moment. As we shall see, some models for which a dynamic analysis is possible simply cannot be subjected to static analysis. In order to perform static experiments it is necessary partly to divorce current events from future events so that what happens in the future does not affect what happens now. This requires restricting the way in which people are assumed to form expectations about the future, and in particular requires that people not possess perfect foresight.

Generally, our models will consist of n *structural* equations in n endogenous variables $y_i(t)$, $i = 1, \ldots, n$, and m exogenous variables $x_i(t)$, $i = 1, \ldots, m$:

$$g_i(y_1(t), y_2(t), \ldots, y_n(t), x_1(t), \ldots, x_m(t)) = 0, \qquad i = 1, \ldots, n. \tag{1}$$

A *structural equation* summarizes behavior, an equilibrium condition, or an accounting identity, and constitutes a building block of the model. In general, more than one and possibly all n endogenous variables can appear in any given structural equation. The system of equations (1) will be thought of as holding at each point in time t. Time itself will be regarded as passing continuously, so that t may be regarded as taking all values along the (extended) real line.

The exogenous variables $x_i(t)$, $i = 1, \ldots, m$, are assumed to be right-continuous functions of time, and furthermore are assumed to possess right-hand time derivatives of at least first and sometimes higher order at all points in time. By right-continuity of the functions $x_i(t)$ we mean

$$\lim_{t \to \bar{t}, \, t > \bar{t}} x_i(t) = x_i(\bar{t}),$$

so that $x_i(t)$ approaches $x_i(\bar{t})$ as t approaches $\bar{t}$ from above, i.e., from the future. However, the function $x_i(t)$ can jump at $\bar{t}$, so that we do *not* require

$$\lim_{t \to \bar{t}, \, t < \bar{t}} x_i(t) = x_i(\bar{t}).$$

For example, consider the function

$$x_i(t) = \begin{cases} 0, & t < \bar{t} \\ 1, & t \geq \bar{t}, \end{cases}$$

which is graphed in Figure 1. It is right-continuous everywhere even though it jumps, i.e., is discontinuous, at $\bar{t}$.

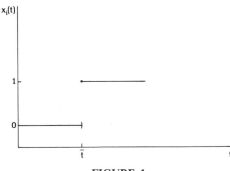

FIGURE 1

The right-hand time derivative of $x_i(t)$, which is assumed to exist everywhere, is defined as

$$\frac{d}{dt} x_i(\bar{t}) \equiv \lim_{t \to \bar{t}, t > \bar{t}} \frac{x_i(t) - x_i(\bar{t})}{t - \bar{t}}.$$

For the function graphed in Figure 1, the right-hand derivative is zero everywhere, even though the function jumps and hence is not differentiable at $t = \bar{t}$.

A model is said to be in static *equilibrium* at a particular moment if the endogenous variables assume values that assure that equations (1) are all satisfied. Notice that it is *not* an implication of this definition of equilibrium that the values of the endogenous variables are unchanging through time. On the contrary, since the values of the exogenous variables will in general be changing at some nonzero rates per unit time, the endogenous variables will also be changing over time.

Static analysis is directed toward answering questions of the following form. Suppose that one of the exogenous variables $x_i(t)$ takes a (small) jump at time $\bar{t}$, so that

$$\lim_{t \to \bar{t}, t < \bar{t}} x_i(t) \neq x_i(\bar{t}).$$

Then the question is to determine the responses of the endogenous variables at $\bar{t}$. The distinguishing characteristic of endogenous variables is that each of them is assumed to be able to jump discontinuously at any moment in time in order to guarantee that system (1) remains satisfied in the face of jumps in the $x_i(t)$. Thus, to be endogenous from the point of view of statics, a variable must be able to change instantaneously. Notice that it is possible for the right-hand time derivative of a variable to be endogenous, i.e., to be capable of jumping discontinuously, even though the variable itself must change continuously through time (Figure 2 gives an example). One way to view the difference

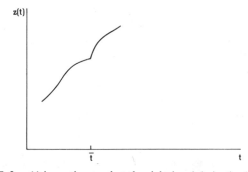

FIGURE 2 $z(t)$ is continuous, but the right-hand derivative jumps at $\bar{t}$.

between the classical and Keynesian models is that in the former the money wage is an endogenous variable in static experiments, while in the latter the right-hand time derivative of the money wage is an endogenous variable but the level of the money wage is exogenous.

To answer the typical question addressed in statics the *reduced form* equations corresponding to the system (1) must be found. The reduced form equations are a set of equations, each expressing one $y_i(t)$ as a function of only the $x_i(t)$:

$$y_i(t) = h_i(x_1(t), x_2(t), \ldots, x_m(t)), \qquad i = 1, \ldots, n. \tag{2}$$

We shall generally assume that the functions $g_i(\ )$ in the structural equations (1) are continuously differentiable in all directions, that the n structural equations were satisfied at all moments immediately preceding the moment we are studying, and that the Jacobian determinant

$$\left| \frac{\partial g}{\partial y} \right| = \begin{vmatrix} \partial g_1/\partial y_1 & \partial g_1/\partial y_2 & \cdots & \partial g_1/\partial y_n \\ \partial g_2/\partial y_1 & & \cdots & \partial g_2/\partial y_n \\ \vdots & & & \\ \partial g_n/\partial y_1 & & \cdots & \partial g_n/\partial y_n \end{vmatrix}$$

does not vanish when evaluated at the immediately preceding values of all variables. That is, we shall assume the hypotheses of the implicit function theorem.[1] Under these hypotheses there exist continuously differentiable functions of the reduced form (2) that hold for the $x_i(t)$ sufficiently close to the initial (prejump) values of the $x_i(t)$. If these equations (2) are satisfied, we are guaranteed that the structural equations (1) are satisfied. For jumps in $x_i(t)$ sufficiently small, i.e., within the neighborhood identified in the implicit function theorem, the equations (2) hold and can be used to answer the characteristic question posed in static analysis. In particular, the reduced form partial derivative

$$\frac{\partial y_i(t)}{\partial x_j(t)} = \frac{\partial h_i}{\partial x_j(t)} (x_1(t), \ldots, x_m(t)) \tag{3}$$

gives the response of $y_i(t)$ to a jump in $x_j(t)$ that occurs at t. We are generally interested in the sign of the partial derivative of the reduced form.

Rather than using the implicit function theorem directly to calculate the reduced form partial derivatives (3), it will be convenient to use the following alternative technique that always gives the correct answer. First, take the differential of all equations in (1) to obtain

$$\frac{\partial g_i}{\partial y_1} dy_1 + \cdots + \frac{\partial g_i}{\partial y_n} dy_n + \frac{\partial g_i}{\partial x_1} dx_1 + \cdots + \frac{\partial g_i}{\partial x_m} dx_m = 0, \qquad i = 1, \ldots, n, \tag{4}$$

[1] See, e.g., A. E. Taylor and W. R. Mann, *Advanced Calculus*, 2nd ed., p. 363 (Lexington, Massachusetts: Xerox, 1972).

all partial derivatives being evaluated at the initial values of the x_i and y_j. Then by successive substitution eliminate $dy_2, \ldots, dy_n$ from the above system (4) of linear equations to obtain an equation of the form

$$dy_1 = f_1{}^1 \, dx_1 + f_2{}^1 \, dx_2 + \cdots + f_m{}^1 \, dx_m, \tag{5}$$

where the $f_j{}^1$ are functions of the partial derivatives that appear in (4). Now Equation (5) is the total differential of the reduced form for y_1 since dy_1 is a function of only $dx_1, \ldots, dx_m$. Taking the differential of the first equation of (2) gives

$$dy_1 = \frac{\partial h_1}{\partial x_1} \, dx_1 + \cdots + \frac{\partial h_1}{\partial x_m} \, dx_m. \tag{6}$$

From (6) and (5) it therefore follows that

$$f_j{}^1 = \partial h_1 / \partial x_j \qquad \text{for} \quad j = 1, \ldots, n,$$

so that the $f_j{}^1$ are the reduced form partial derivatives. Successive substitution in the system (4) will also, of course, yield the differentials of the reduced forms for the other endogenous variables, thereby enabling us to obtain the corresponding reduced form partial derivatives. The reduced form partial derivatives are often called "multipliers" in macroeconomics.

CHAPTER I

THE "CLASSICAL" MODEL

Our model describes the determination of an economy's rate of output and the uses to which it is put. The economy produces a single good, which is produced at a rate per unit time of Y. This rate of output is divided among a real rate of consumption C, a real rate of investment I, a real rate of government purchases G, and a real rate of depreciation of capital δK:

$$Y = C + I + G + \delta K. \tag{1}$$

Equation (1) is the national income identity linking aggregate output and its components.

The economy is organized into three sectors. *Firms* employ capital and labor to produce output. The *government* collects taxes and purchases goods, issues money and bonds, and conducts open-market operations. *Households* own the government's money and bond liabilities and all of the equities of firms. They make both a saving decision and a decision to allocate their portfolios of paper assets among bonds, equities, and money.

1. FIRMS

The economy consists of a large number of n perfectly competitive firms, each of which produces the same single good subject to the same production function. The rate of output of the ith firm at any instant is described by the instantaneous production function

$$Y_i = F(K_i, N_i), \qquad i = 1, \dots, n, \tag{2}$$

where Y_i is the output of the ith firm per unit time, K_i is the stock of capital employed by the ith firm, and N_i is employment of the ith firm.[1] The variables Y_i, K_i, and N_i should each be thought of as functions of time. We have omitted a subscript i from the function F because it is assumed that all firms share the

---

[1] Capital is measured in units of the one good in the economy, labor in number of men.

same production function. The production function is assumed to be characterized by positive though diminishing marginal products of capital and labor and a direct dependence of the marginal product of capital (employment) on employment (capital):

$$F_K, F_N > 0, \qquad F_{KK}, F_{NN} < 0, \qquad F_{KN} > 0.$$

The production function F is assumed to be linearly homogeneous in K_i and N_i, so that

$$\lambda F(K_i, N_i) = F(\lambda K_i, \lambda N_i), \qquad \lambda > 0.$$

By virtue of Euler's theorem on homogeneous functions we have

$$Y_i = \frac{\partial F}{\partial K_i}(K_i, N_i)K_i + \frac{\partial F}{\partial N_i}(K_i, N_i)N_i.$$

Also, by virtue of the linear homogeneity of F we have

$$\frac{\partial}{\partial K_i} F(K_i, N_i) = \frac{\partial F}{\partial \lambda K_i}(\lambda K_i, \lambda N_i);$$

setting $\lambda = 1/N_i$, we have

$$\frac{\partial}{\partial K_i} F(K_i, N_i) = \frac{\partial F}{\partial (K_i/N_i)}\left(\frac{K_i}{N_i}, 1\right),$$

so that the marginal product of capital depends only on the ratio of capital to labor. Similarly, the marginal product of labor depends only on the ratio of capital to labor.

In this one-good economy capital represents the accumulated stock of the one good that is available to assist in production. We assume that at any moment the stock of capital is fixed both to the economy and to each individual firm. Assuming that capital is fixed to the economy amounts to ruling out once-and-for-all gifts of physical capital from abroad or from heaven and once-and-for-all decreases in the capital stock due to natural or human disasters. Assuming that capital is fixed to each firm at each moment in time amounts to ruling out the existence of a perfect market in the existing stock of capital in which individual firms can purchase or sell (or rent) capital, and so effect a discrete change in their stock of capital at a moment in time. The absence of a market in existing capital might be rationalized by positing that once in place capital becomes completely specialized to each firm. Firms simply have no use for the existing capital of another firm, so that there is no opportunity for making a market in existing capital.[2] Regardless of how the assumption is

---

[2] Alternatively, it is often posited that there are costs of adjusting the capital stock that are internal to the firm and that rise at an increasing rate with increases in the absolute value of the rate of investment. As we shall see in Chapter VI, this can give rise to a Keynesian investment demand schedule of the form assumed in this chapter. In effect, the role of the costs of adjustment is to prevent firms from wanting to make discrete adjustments in their stocks of capital at a point in time.

rationalized, ruling out trading of existing stocks of capital is a fundamental feature of the class of "classical" and "Keynesian" models that we shall be describing. It is the feature that makes flow aggregate demand play such an important role. In contradistinction, in Tobin's "dynamic aggregative model," which we study in Chapter III and in which there *is* a perfect market in which firms trade *stocks* of capital, flow aggregate demand plays no role in determining the level of output at a point in time.

While firms cannot trade capital at a point in time, they are assumed to be able to vary employment instantaneously. Firms operate in a competitive labor market in which at any moment they can hire all the labor they want at the going money wage w measured in dollars per man per unit of time. Firms are perfectly competitive in the output market also, and each can sell output at any rate it wishes at the price of the one good in the model, p measured in dollars per good.

The typical firm's profits Π_i are defined by

$$\Pi_i = pF(K_i, N_i) - wN_i - (r + \delta - \pi)pK_i, \tag{3}$$

where r is the instantaneous rate of interest on government bonds, δ is the instantaneous rate of physical depreciation of capital, and π is the anticipated rate of increase in the price of (newly produced) capital goods. In a sense to be defined below $r + \delta - \pi$ is the appropriate cost of capital that should be used to define the firm's profits. Were there a rental market in capital, $(r + \delta - \pi)p$ would be the rental rate, expressed in dollars per unit time.

Each firm maximizes its profits per unit time with respect to the employment of labor, taking its capital stock as fixed momentarily. The firm's employment is then described by the first-order condition for maximization of (3),

$$\partial \Pi_i / \partial N_i = pF_{N_i}(K_i, N_i) - w = 0,$$

or

$$F_{N_i}(K_i, N_i) = w/p, \tag{4}$$

which states that the firm equates the marginal product of labor to the real wage. Equation (4) is in the nature of a firm's demand function for labor which, given K_i, relates the firm's demand for employment inversely to the real wage. For each firm, Equation (4) determines a capital–labor ratio, which is identical for all firms since all face a common real wage. At any moment the n firms have amounts of capital $K_i, i = 1, \ldots, n$, which might differ across firms. Employment of labor then varies proportionately with K_i across firms.

Our assumptions about the identity of firms' production functions and their profit-maximizing behavior in the face of perfectly competitive markets for output and labor imply that there is a useful sense in which there exists an aggregate production function. The total rate of output of the one good in the economy is Y, defined by

$$Y = \sum_{i=1}^{n} Y_i = \sum_{i=1}^{n} F(K_i, N_i).$$

By Euler's theorem we have

$$\sum_{i=1}^{n} Y_i = \sum_{i=1}^{n} (F_{K_i}(K_i, N_i)K_i + F_{N_i}(K_i, N_i)N_i).$$

But since the marginal products of capital and labor depend only on the capital–labor ratio and since that ratio is the same for all firms, the marginal products of capital and of labor, respectively, are the same for all firms. Thus, we can write

$$\sum_{i=1}^{n} Y_i = F_K\left(\frac{K_j}{N_j}, 1\right) \sum_{i=1}^{n} K_i + F_N\left(\frac{K_j}{N_j}, 1\right) \sum_{i=1}^{n} N_i.$$

Since the ratios K_i/N_i are the same for all n firms, they must be equal to the ratio of capital to employment for the economy $\sum_{i=1}^{n} K_i / \sum_{i=1}^{n} N_i$. Consequently, we have

$$Y = F_K(K/N, 1)K + F_N(K/N, 1)N,$$

where $K = \sum_{i=1}^{n} K_i$ and $N = \sum_{i=1}^{n} N_i$. But by applying Euler's theorem to F the above expression for Y can be written as the aggregate production function

$$Y = F(K, N). \tag{5}$$

Moreover, notice that $\partial F/\partial N$ equals the marginal product of labor for each firm, while $\partial F/\partial K$ equals the marginal product of capital for each firm. This fact makes it legitimate to carry out our subsequent analysis solely in terms of the aggregate production function (5) and the equality between the real wage and $\partial Y/\partial N$:

$$F_N(N, K) = w/p. \tag{6}$$

Equation (6) could be derived by maximizing economy-wide profits with respect to employment.

Notice that (5) is a valid description of the aggregate production relationship among Y, N, and K only for a certain distribution of the N_i across firms, the one predicted by Equation (4). That distribution is one that maximizes Y for any given N, given the fixed distribution of the K across firms. If some other distribution of the N_i across firms is imposed, one that violates (4), then Equation (5) will not describe the relationship among aggregate output Y, aggregate employment N, and the aggregate capital stock K. For our work, however, it is sufficient that (5) hold only in the sense described above.

It remains to describe the behavior of firms with respect to the accumulation of capital over time. If there were a perfect market in which firms could trade capital at each moment, firms would want to purchase (sell) capital instantaneously as long as the marginal product of capital exceeded (was less than) the real cost of capital $r + \delta - \pi$. However, such trading of capital has been ruled out. In its place we posit a Keynesian investment demand function on the part of firms. This function relates firms' demand to accumulate newly produced capital at some finite rate per unit time directly to the gap between the marginal product of capital and the cost of capital:

$$\frac{dK}{dt} \equiv I = I\left(\frac{F_K - (r + \delta - \pi)}{r - \pi}\right), \qquad I' > 0, \tag{7}$$

where dK/dt is interpreted as a right-hand derivative. According to (7), firms invest at a higher rate the higher is the marginal product of capital and the lower is the real interest rate $r - \pi$. Equation (7) describes aggregate investment demand for the economy and is assumed to have been derived from individual firms' investment demand functions of the same form. We shall find it convenient to write (7) in the compact form

$$I = I(q - 1), \qquad I' > 0, \tag{7'}$$

where q is defined by

$$q = \frac{F_K - (r + \delta - \pi)}{r - \pi} + 1 \equiv q(K, N, r - \pi, \delta). \tag{8}$$

We shall presently provide an interpretation of q as an important relative price that might plausibly govern firms' demand to accumulate capital. Notice that q is a function of K and N by virtue of the dependence of the marginal product of capital on the labor–capital ratio.

2. ASSETS OWNED BY HOUSEHOLDS

There are three paper assets that households alone own: money, bonds, and equities. Money, the quantity of which is denoted by M, measured in dollars, is a paper asset that is supposed to be used as the medium of exchange. It is issued by the government and bears a nominal yield that is fixed at zero. By *nominal yield* we mean the yield of the asset in percent per unit time that can be obtained while leaving the nominal quantity of the asset intact. By the *real yield* of an asset we mean the yield in percent per unit time that can be obtained while setting aside enough resources to keep the real stock (i.e., the stock measured in terms of its command over goods) of the asset held intact over time. The nominal yield on money is fixed at zero because holding money gives rise to no payments of interest. However, the real yield on money in general is not zero. The real quantity of money is M/p, a quantity measured in units of output. The time derivative of M/p is[3]

$$\frac{d(M/p)}{dt} = \frac{p\dot{M} - M\dot{p}}{p^2} = \frac{\dot{M}}{p} - \frac{M}{p}\frac{\dot{p}}{p}.$$

To keep M/p intact over time it is necessary to set the above derivative equal to zero, which gives

$$\frac{\dot{M}}{p} = \frac{M}{p}\frac{\dot{p}}{p} \qquad \text{or} \qquad \frac{\dot{M}}{M} = \frac{\dot{p}}{p}.$$

Thus to keep real money balances M/p intact, it is necessary to add to nominal money balances at the rate $\dot{p}/p$. Consequently, money has a real yield of $-\dot{p}/p$. That is, with $\dot{M}$ equal to zero, real balances depreciate at the rate $\dot{p}/p$ per unit time. People do not necessarily perceive the rate $\dot{p}/p$ at which prices are depreciating since that would in general require perfect foresight. We denote the rate per unit time at which people expect the price level to increase as π, which can differ from $\dot{p}/p$. The expected real rate of yield on money then equals $-\pi$.

The second asset is a variable-coupon bond that is issued by the government. The bond is essentially a savings deposit, changes in the interest rate altering the coupon but leaving the dollar value of bonds outstanding unchanged. We denote the nominal value of bonds outstanding by B, which is measured in dollars. The bonds bear a nominal yield of r in percent per unit time. Thus the bonds throw off a stream of interest payments of rB, which is measured in dollars per unit time. The *real yield* on bonds is defined as r minus the percentage real rate at which households must buy bonds to keep their real value B/p intact. Like money, the real value of a fixed nominal quantity of bonds depreciates at the rate $\dot{p}/p$. Thus, the expected real rate of return associated with holding bonds is $r - \pi$.

The third paper asset consists of equities, which are issued by firms in order to finance investment. We assume that firms issue no bonds and retain no earnings, so that all investment is financed by issuing equities. Only households hold, buy, and sell equities. By assuming that there is no market in which firms can purchase or sell physical capital we are obliged also to rule out the possibility that firms trade equities, which are the financial counterpart of physical capital. We assume also that households regard equities and bonds as perfect substitutes. This implies that their expected real yields will be equal, an equality enforced by investors' refusing to hold the lower yielding asset should the equality not hold. It follows that the nominal bond rate of interest is the pertinent yield for discounting expectations of firms' net cash flow (which equals

---

[3] Dots above variables will be taken to denote derivatives with respect to time, in general right-hand time derivatives.

expected aggregate dividends) in order to determine the value of firms' equities. At instant s firms pay out a flow of dividends

$$p(s)F(K(s), N(s)) - w(s)N(s) - \delta p(s)K(s),$$

measured in dollars per unit time. Then the nominal value of firms' equities at instant t, denoted by $V(t)$, is

$$V(t) = \int_t^\infty [p(s)F(K(s), N(s)) - w(s)N(s) - \delta p(s)K(s)]e^{-r(s-t)} \, ds.$$

We assume that firms and households expect the price level and wage rate to be following the paths

$$p(s) = p(t)e^{\pi(s-t)}, \qquad w(s) = w(t)e^{\pi(s-t)},$$

where π is the anticipated rate of inflation. We further assume that the public expects the real rate of dividends to remain unchanged over time at the current rate. Then $V(t)$ can be written

$$V(t) = [p(t)F(K(t), N(t)) - w(t)N(t) - p(t)\delta K(t)] \int_t^\infty e^{-(r-\pi)(s-t)} \, ds$$

or

$$V(t) = \frac{p(t)Y(t) - w(t)N(t) - p(t)\delta K(t)}{r - \pi}.$$

It is easy to see that $V(t)$ can be rewritten as

$$V(t) = \frac{p(t)(Y(t) - (w(t)/p(t))N(t) - F_K(t)K(t))}{r - \pi}$$

$$+ \frac{(F_K - (r + \delta - \pi))p(t)K(t)}{r - \pi} + p(t)K(t).$$

But by the marginal productivity condition for employment and Euler's theorem the first term in this expression equals zero, so that we have the following expression for the nominal value of equities:

$$V(t) = \left(\frac{F_K - (r + \delta - \pi)}{r - \pi} + 1\right)p(t)K(t). \tag{9}$$

The value of equities varies directly with the gap between the marginal product of capital and the cost of capital. It is interesting to compute the ratio of the nominal value of equities to the nominal value of the capital stock evaluated at the price of newly produced capital p:

$$\frac{V(t)}{p(t)K(t)} = \frac{F_K - (r + \delta - \pi)}{r - \pi} + 1 \equiv q,$$

which is the argument that appears in the aggregate investment schedule, Equation (8). Thus, our investment demand schedule is one that relates firms' demand for capital accumulation directly to the ratio of the value of equities to the replacement value of the capital stock q. This is the way Tobin formulates the Keynesian investment schedule (Tobin, 1969).

Notice that the dividend-price ratio, which equals the earning-price ratio, is

$$\frac{pY - wN - p\delta K}{V} = r - \pi,$$

which is the expected real rate of interest on bonds and equities. If we add the expected rate of appreciation in the nominal value of existing equities π to the earnings-price ratio, we obtain the nominal yield on equities r. It is interesting also to calculate the time derivative of $V(t)$. Writing $V(t)$ as $p(t)K(t)q(t)$, we have by logarithmic differentiation with respect to time

$$\frac{\dot{V}(t)}{V(t)} = \frac{\dot{p}(t)}{p(t)} + \frac{\dot{K}(t)}{K(t)} + \frac{\dot{q}(t)}{q(t)}.$$

Suppose q is constant over time, so that $\dot{q} = 0$. Then the nominal value of equities changes for two reasons. First, existing equities appreciate in nominal value at the rate $\dot{p}/p$, while investment leads to the issuing of new equities at the rate $\dot{K}/K$.

At each moment in time households allocate their existing wealth between, on the one hand, bonds and equities which they view as perfect substitutes, and on the other hand, money. Households' total real wealth is denoted W and defined by

$$(V + B + M)/p = W. \tag{10}$$

Households desire a division of their wealth between M and $B + V$ that is described by the pair of asset demand functions:

$$M^{\mathrm{D}}/p = m(r, Y, W), \tag{11}$$

$$(B^{\mathrm{D}} + V^{\mathrm{D}})/p = b(r, Y, W), \tag{12}$$

where D superscripts denote desired quantities. The demand schedules are constructed in such a way that at each value of r, Y, and W, total wealth is allocated between M and $B + V$, so that

$$(B^{\mathrm{D}} + V^{\mathrm{D}} + M^{\mathrm{D}})/p = W \tag{13}$$

for all r, Y, and W. This implies that the partial derivatives of (11) and (12) are related in certain definite ways.[4] Thus, take the total differential of Equation (11) and add it to the total differential of Equation (12):

$$d((M^{\mathrm{D}} + B^{\mathrm{D}} + V^{\mathrm{D}})/p) = (m_r + b_r)\, dr + (m_Y + b_Y)\, dY + (m_W + b_W)\, dW.$$

[4] Tobin has emphasized this. See Tobin (1969).

Subtract the total differential of Equation (13) from the above expression to obtain

$$0 = (m_r + b_r) \, dr + (m_Y + b_Y) \, dY + (m_W + b_W - 1) \, dW.$$

This equality can hold for all values of dr, dY, and dW if and only if

$$m_r + b_r = 0, \qquad m_Y + b_Y = 0, \qquad \text{and} \qquad m_W + b_W = 1.$$

We shall assume that these restrictions characterize the asset demand functions (11) and (12).

Portfolio equilibrium requires that households be satisfied with the division of their portfolios between bonds and equities, on the one hand, and money on the other:

$$M^D/p = M/p \qquad \text{and} \qquad (B^D + V^D)/p = (B + V)/p.$$

But notice that (10) and (13) together imply that either one of the above equations is sufficient to describe portfolio equilibrium. For suppose that

$$M/p = M^D/p.$$

Then subtracting this equality from (13) gives

$$\frac{B^D + V^D}{p} = W - \frac{M}{p} = \frac{B + V}{p},$$

so that the demand for the stock of bonds and equities equals the supply. This is an example of Walras' law: if demand functions build in balance-sheet constraints and if individuals are content with their holdings of all assets but one, then they must be satisfied with their holdings of that last asset too.

We choose to characterize portfolio equilibrium by equality between the supply and demand for money balances:

$$M/p = M^D/p = m(r, Y, W).$$

We assume that $m_r < 0$, $m_Y > 0$, and $m_W = 0$. It follows that $b_r > 0$, $b_Y < 0$, and $b_W = 1$, so that at given r and Y households desire to hold any increments in real wealth entirely in the form of bonds and equities. We can write our condition for portfolio equilibrium as

$$M/p = m(r, Y), \qquad m_r < 0, \quad m_Y > 0. \tag{14}$$

Real output Y enters (14) as a proxy for the rate of transacting in the economy. We posit that the higher the rate of transacting, the higher is the demand for real money balances. The nominal interest rate r equals the difference between the real yield on bonds and equities $r - \pi$ and the real yield on money $-\pi$. We posit that the larger the difference between those real yields, the greater is the incentive to economize on money balances in order to hold one of the higher yielding assets.

We can summarize the portfolios of the three sectors of the economy with the following three balance sheets:

Government		Firms		Households	
Assets	Liabilities	Assets	Liabilities	Assets	Liabilities
	B	qpK	V	V	
	M			B	
	Net worth			M	Net worth

Firms hold neither bonds nor money, while the government owns neither capital nor equities. Households own only paper assets.

3. THE GOVERNMENT

The government collects taxes net of transfers at the real rate T per unit time and makes expenditures at the real rate G per unit time. It will be assumed that government purchases share with consumption the characteristic that they lead to no accumulation of stocks. Goods purchased by the government are used up immediately and do not augment the capital stock. Real taxes net of transfers T are assumed to be collected in a way that makes T independent of real income and the price level.[5] The government sets T and G subject to the flow budget constraint

$$G = T + \frac{\dot{B}}{p} + \frac{\dot{M}}{p}, \tag{15}$$

where G, T, $\dot{M}/p$, and $\dot{B}/p$ are all measured in goods per unit time.

The government also conducts open-market operations, which are once-and-for-all exchanges of bonds for money at a moment. These exchanges are made subject to the constraint

$$dM = -dB. \tag{16}$$

It bears emphasizing that we have defined T as real tax collections net of transfers, and that we include interest payments on the stock of government bonds B as part of those transfer payments. To elaborate this point, let T_0 be real tax collections net of all transfers *except* real interest paid on the government debt. Then T and T_0 are linked by

$$T = T_0 - (r - \pi)\frac{B}{p}, \tag{17}$$

[5] For alternative and more complicated methods of parametrizing tax collections, see Henderson and Sargent (1973).

where $(r - \pi)$ is the real rate of interest paid on the interest bearing part of the debt. The government budget constraint (15) can then be written

$$G + (r - \pi)\frac{B}{p} - T_0 = \frac{\dot{B}}{p} + \frac{\dot{M}}{p}. \tag{18}$$

The difference $G + (r - \pi)(B/p) - T_0$ is called the gross-of-interest government deficit, while $G - T_0$ is called the net-of-interest government deficit. In various experiments, analysts sometimes mean by a "constant fiscal policy" that they are holding the net-of-interest deficit $G - T_0$ constant (Sargent and Wallace, 1981). By specifying a constant fiscal policy, other analysts intend to hold constant the gross-of-interest deficit $G - T = G + (r - \pi)(B/p) - T_0$ (McCallum, 1984). This book always adopts the latter interpretation, something important to remember when interpreting our results.

Our choosing to specify fiscal policy in terms of G and T in this way means that when the government conducts an open market operation subject to (16) with G and T held fixed, it is being assumed that tax collections T_0 are adjusted by just enough to offset the altered interest payments associated with the altered value of B/p in the hands of the public. For example, when the open-market authority contracts the stock of M subject to (16) thereby increasing the stock of B in the hands of the public and also increasing the flow of real interest payments on that debt due to the public (if $r - \pi > 0$), it is assumed that the government simultaneously raises taxes T_0 by just enough to cover those added interest payments.[6]

4. HOUSEHOLDS

Households make two distinct sets of decisions. First, given their stock of wealth at any point in time, they decide how they wish to allocate it among alternative assets. This decision is described by the portfolio equilibrium condition (14). Secondly, they make a distinct decision about how fast they wish their wealth to grow, i.e., they choose a saving rate. This decision determines how they divide their disposal income between consumption and saving.[7]

Household's perceived disposable income represents the rate of income they receive that they expect to be able either to consume or save. Consumption leads to no accumulation of stocks, while saving causes households' wealth in the form of paper assets to grow at some rate per unit time. Households' demand for

[6] This assumption makes the open-market authority more powerful vis-à-vis the fiscal authority than was assumed by Sargent and Wallace (1981).

[7] Distinguishing sharply between households' saving and portfolio decisions is a hallmark of Keynesian macroeconomics. However, that distinction is *not* one that can in general be derived from microeconomic foundations with price-taking households. See Merton (1971). Under special assumptions, as Merton shows, the household's portfolio balance decision does separate from its saving decision.

consumption is summarized by a consumption function[8] that relates their intended real consumption C directly to their perceived real disposable income Y_D and inversely to the real interest rate on bonds and equities:

$$C = C(Y_D, r - \pi), \qquad 1 > C_1 > 0, \quad C_2 < 0, \tag{19}$$

where consumption plus saving equals perceived real disposable income:

$$S + C = Y_D.$$

The terms C_1 and C_2 in (19) denote the partial derivatives of C with respect to the first and second arguments, respectively. It is assumed that C_1, the marginal propensity to consume out of perceived real disposable income, is positive but less than unity. Desired consumption is posited to decrease in response to an increase in the real rate of interest.

Perceived real disposable income Y_D is equal to the real value of wage payments *plus* dividend payments (which equal economy-wide firms' net cash flow since firms retain no earnings) *minus* total real tax collections net of government transfer payments *minus* the perceived rate of capital loss on the real value of the public's net claims on the government *plus* the rate at which the real value of equities is increasing *minus* the real rate at which firms are issuing equities to finance investment. The real rate of wage payments is $wp^{-1}N$. Firms' real dividends are paid at the rate $Y - wp^{-1}N - \delta K$. The anticipated rate of capital loss on the real value of government debt is $(M + B)p^{-1}\pi$. Firms issue equities at the real rate $\dot{K}$ to finance their investment, while the real value of equities actually increases at the rate $q\dot{K} + K\dot{q}$. We shall assume that $\dot{q}$ is expected to be zero,[9] so that the real value of equities is expected to increase at the rate $q\dot{K}$. Then perceived real disposable income is

$$Y_D = Y - \delta K - T - \frac{M + B}{p}\pi + (q - 1)\dot{K}. \tag{20}$$

This concept of disposable income turns out to equal the rate at which society expects that it could consume while leaving its real wealth defined by (10) intact. To show this we differentiate (10) with respect to time to obtain

$$\dot{W} = \frac{\dot{M} + \dot{B}}{p} - \frac{M + B}{p}\frac{\dot{p}}{p} + q\dot{K} + K\dot{q}.$$

---

[8] As Robert Clower has emphasized, confronting households with a disposable income, which they must then decide to consume or save, is very different from the microeconomist's procedure of confronting households with wages, prices, and interest rates on the basis of which they allocate their labor and consumption over time. Clower and Robert Barro and Herschel Grossman have explored setups that might rationalize the consumption function. See Clower (1965) and Barro and Grossman (1971).

[9] As we shall see, the public's expectation of $\dot{q}$ and $\dot{p}$ must be exogenously set at some values in order to do static analysis.

Next replace $\dot{p}/p$ with the public's expectation of it, and replace $\dot{q}$ with the value the public expects it to be, which we have assumed is zero. We obtain

$$\dot{W}_e = \frac{\dot{M} + \dot{B}}{p} - \frac{M + B}{p}\pi + q\dot{K},$$

where $\dot{W}_e$ is the rate of change of wealth expected by the public. By virtue of the government's flow budget constraint $(\dot{M} + \dot{B})/p = G - T$, while by virtue of the national income identity $G = Y - \dot{K} - \delta K - C$. Using these equalities, $\dot{W}_e$ can be written

$$\dot{W}_e = Y - \delta K - T - \frac{M + B}{p}\pi + (q - 1)\dot{K} - C.$$

Using (20), the above equation can be written as

$$C + \dot{W}_e = Y_D,$$

which verifies that the concept of disposable income Y_D corresponds to the rate at which households can consume while expecting that their real wealth is being left intact (i.e., that $\dot{W}_e = 0$).

5. LABOR SUPPLY

We have now set down enough equations to determine the six endogenous variables Y, N, C, I, p, and r in our Keynesian model, a model that views the money wage rate w as exogenous at a point in time. In our classical model, on the other hand, w is a variable that must be determined by the model at each moment; so we stand in need of one more equation. The classical model includes a labor supply curve that describes the labor–leisure preferences of workers:

$$N^S = N(w/p), \qquad N' > 0, \tag{21}$$

where N^S is the volume of employment offered by workers at instant t. It is postulated that the supply of labor is an increasing function of the real wage. The description of the workings of the classical labor market is completed by imposing the condition that actual employment N must equal to volume of employment forthcoming at the existing real wage N^S. Substituting actual employment N for N^S in (21) then yields

$$N = N(w/p). \tag{22}$$

6. THE COMPLETE MODEL

The classical model can now be summarized as consisting of equations (1), (5), (6), (7′), (14), (19), and (22), seven equations potentially able to determine seven variables at any moment. For convenience we write down these equations here, renumbering them:

$$w/p = F_N(K, N) \tag{I}$$

$$N = N(w/p) \tag{II}$$

$$Y = F(K, N) \tag{III}$$

$$C = C\left(Y - T - \delta K - \frac{M + B}{p}\pi + (q(K, N, r - \pi, \delta) - 1)I, r - \pi\right) \tag{IV}$$

$$I = I(q(K, N, r - \pi, \delta) - 1) \tag{V}$$

$$Y = C + I + G + \delta K \tag{VI}$$

$$M/p = m(r, Y). \tag{VII}$$

We have replaced the variable q in Equations (IV) and (V) with the function $q(K, N, r - \pi, \delta)$ which equals q by Equation (8). The model then consists of seven equations which we shall view as determining the seven variables N, w/p, Y, C, I, r, and p. All of these variables are permitted to jump discontinuously as functions of time in order to satisfy the seven equations at each moment. The parameters of the model consist of the exogenous variables T, G, K, π, M and the additional parameters determining the shapes of the underlying functions. Notice that the anticipated rate of inflation, which is assumed to be unanimously held, is one of the parameters and that in particular it is *not* a variable that depends on the actual rate of inflation. Were π to depend on $\dot{p}/p$, defined as the right-hand time derivative of the logarithm of p, then the above seven equations would involve eight variables—$\dot{p}$ would be the eighth—and would not form a complete model. For similar reasons, we have assumed that the public's expectation of $\dot{q}$ is exogenous, and more particularly equal to zero. If the expected $\dot{q}$ were a function of the actual $\dot{q}$, we would have to determine the actual right-hand time derivative of q in order to determine the values of our other variables at any moment—more of this later. For now, we simply assume that π and the expected $\dot{q}$ are both exogenous and note that on this assumption the model possesses the same number of equations as variables it must determine at a point in time.[10]

We begin our analysis of the classical model by in effect linearizing the system of Equations (I)—(VII) around initial equilibrium values of the vari-

---

[10] As we shall see later, equality between the number of equations and the number of variables to be determined is not sufficient to guarantee that the model possesses a unique equilibrium.

ables. We assume that such an initial equilibrium exists. (Later we shall consider some problems posed by Keynesians that may call into question the existence of an equilibrium in a classical model like ours.) Then to obtain a linear system we proceed to obtain the total differentials of Equations (I)–(VII), the differentials being understood as representing deviations from initial equilibrium values of the variables:

$$d(w/p) = F_{NN}\, dN + F_{NK}\, dK \tag{i}$$

$$dN = N'\, d(w/p) \tag{ii}$$

$$dY = F_N\, dN + F_K\, dK \tag{iii}$$

$$dC = C_1\, dY - C_1\, dT - C_1\delta\, dK - C_1 \frac{M + B}{p}\, d\pi$$

$$- C_1\pi\left(\frac{dM + dB}{p} - \frac{M + B}{p}\frac{dp}{p}\right) + C_1[(q - 1)\, dI + Iq_N\, dN$$

$$+ Iq_K\, dK + Iq_{r-\pi}\, dr - Iq_{r-\pi}\, d\pi] + C_2\, dr - C_2\, d\pi \tag{iv}$$

$$dI = I'q_N\, dN + I'q_K\, dK + I'q_{r-\pi}\, dr - I'q_{r-\pi}\, d\pi \tag{v}$$

$$dY = dC + dI + dG + \delta\, dK \tag{vi}$$

$$\frac{dM}{p} - \frac{M}{p}\frac{dp}{p} = m_r\, dr + m_Y\, dY. \tag{vii}$$

We have assumed that δ is always constant, so $d\delta = 0$. The derivatives of q with respect to N, K, and $r - \pi$, which appear in (iv) and (v), are obtained by differentiating Equation (8):

$$dq = \frac{(F_{KN}\, dN + F_{KK}\, dK - (dr - d\pi))(r - \pi) - (F_K - (r + \delta - \pi))(dr - d\pi)}{(r - \pi)^2}$$

$$= \frac{1}{r - \pi}(F_{KN}\, dN + F_{KK}\, dK - q(dr - d\pi)).$$

Thus, we have

$$q_N = \frac{1}{r - \pi} F_{KN} > 0, \qquad q_K = \frac{1}{r - \pi} F_{KK} < 0, \qquad q_{r-\pi} = \frac{-q}{r - \pi} < 0;$$

so q is an increasing function of employment and a decreasing function of capital and the real rate of interest.

Notice that Equation (iv) can be simplified somewhat due to the constraint on open-market operations, $dM + dB = 0$. It is then of some interest to write Equations (i)–(vii) in the following matrix form:

$$
\begin{bmatrix}
1 & -F_{NN} & 0 & 0 & 0 & 0 & 0 \\
-N' & 1 & 0 & 0 & 0 & 0 & 0 \\
0 & -F_N & 1 & 0 & 0 & 0 & 0 \\
0 & -C_1 I q_N & -C_1 & 1 & -C_1(q-1) & -(C_1 I q_{r-\pi} + C_2) & -C_1 \pi(M+B)/p^2 \\
0 & -I' q_N & 0 & 0 & 1 & -I' q_{r-\pi} & 0 \\
0 & 0 & 1 & -1 & -1 & 0 & 0 \\
0 & 0 & m_Y & 0 & 0 & m_r & M/p^2
\end{bmatrix}
\begin{bmatrix}
d(w/p) \\
dN \\
dY \\
dC \\
dI \\
dr \\
dp
\end{bmatrix}
$$

$$
=
\begin{bmatrix}
F_{NK}\, dK \\
0 \\
F_K\, dK \\
[\; C_1 dT - C_1 \delta\, dK - C_1((M+B)/p)\, d\pi + I q_K\, dK \\
-(C_1 I q_{r-\pi} + C_2)\, d\pi] \\
I' q_K\, dK - I' q_{r-\pi}\, d\pi \\
dG + \delta\, dK \\
dM/p
\end{bmatrix}.
$$

Inspection of the 7×7 matrix on the left-hand side of the above equation reveals a peculiar characteristic of the classical model, a characteristic that is very important. In particular, note that only two variables appear in the first two equations: $d(w/p)$ and dN. All of the other variables have zero coefficients in the first two equations. As a consequence, these two equations form an independent subset that determines $d(w/p)$ and dN, no contribution being made by the remaining variables to the determination of these two. Similarly, the first three equations also form an independent subset capable of determining dY as well as dN and $d(w/p)$ independently of the other four equations in the model. The above system is an example of a "block recursive" system of equations. In such a system interdependence is not general, the system being solvable sequentially since at least one subset of equations involves an independent subset of the variables. However, once the variables in the subset are determined, they may influence, though not be influenced by, the remaining variables.[11] The fact that the classical model has this property is very important.

We solve the subsystem formed by Equations (i) and (ii) by substituting (ii) into (i), which yields

$$d(w/p) = F_{NN} N' \, d(w/p) + F_{NK} \, dK$$

or

$$d(w/p) = \frac{F_{NK}}{1 - F_{NN} N'} \, dK. \tag{23}$$

Since we have assumed that $F_{NK} > 0$, $F_{NN} < 0$, $N' > 0$, it follows that $F_{NK}/(1 - F_{NN} N') > 0$. Equation (23) states that a change in the capital stock at a point in time, could it occur, would drive the real wage upward.

Substituting (23) into (ii) yields

$$dN = N' \frac{F_{NK}}{1 - F_{NN} N'} \, dK. \tag{24}$$

Since $N' > 0$, (24) implies that an increase in the capital stock at a point in time would increase employment. It would do so by causing an increase in the demand for labor, in turn causing an increase in the real wage, which would increase the quantity of labor supplied.

Substituting (24) into (iii), the total differential of the production function, yields

$$dY = \left(\frac{F_N N' F_{NK}}{1 - F_{NN} N'} + F_K \right) dK. \tag{25}$$

Since F_K and F_N are both positive, it follows that a once-and-for-all increase in capital would produce an increase in the rate of output, both because the marginal product of capital is positive and because the increase in capital would increase both the marginal product of capital and the number of workers employed.

Equations (23)–(25) show that given the production function and the labor supply schedule, only a once-and-for-all change in the capital stock can bring

[11] A system of equations is said to be block recursive if it can be written in the form $Ax = b$ where

$$A = \begin{bmatrix} A^{11} & A^{12} & \cdots & A^{1N} \\ A^{21} & A^{22} & \cdots & A^{2N} \\ \vdots & & & \\ A^{N1} & A^{N2} & \cdots & A^{NN} \end{bmatrix}, \qquad x = \begin{bmatrix} x^1 \\ x^2 \\ \vdots \\ x^N \end{bmatrix}, \qquad b = \begin{bmatrix} b^1 \\ b^2 \\ \vdots \\ b^N \end{bmatrix}$$

where A^{IJ} are matrices; and where $A^{IJ} = 0$ for all $I = 1, \ldots, N$ and $J > I$. In the case of the classical model, A^{12} would consist of the 3×4 matrix in the upper right-hand corner of the matrix in the text. Then the first three variables can be determined from

$$x^1 = (A^{11})^{-1} b^1.$$

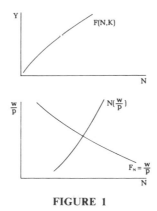

FIGURE 1

about a once-and-for-all change in the rate of output: K is the only exogenous variable that enters into the determination of the levels of output, employment, and the real wage at a point in time. Other exogenous variables may affect the time rates of change of those three variables, but not their levels at a point in time. We shall assume from now on that capital can be accumulated only by investing, thus ruling out once-and-for-all jumps in the capital stock. From this it follows that given the production function and the labor supply schedule, output, employment, and the real wage are constants at a point in time, independent of what government policy and the public's expectations are.

The situation is depicted in Figure 1, which shows the production function, its derivative with respect to employment, which is the demand schedule for employment, and the supply schedule for labor. Employment and the real wage are determined at the intersection of the demand and supply schedules for labor, while output is determined by substituting the equilibrium level of employment into the production function.

Equations (i)–(iii) may be thought of as determining aggregate supply. The remaining four equations play the role of ensuring that aggregate demand is made equal to aggregate supply, aggregate demand doing all of the adjusting. In most discussions of the classical model it is only Equations (iv)–(vi) that are involved in equilibrating aggregate demand and supply, the money market equilibrium equation (vii) playing no role. This requires that dp not appear in Equations (iv)–(vi) since only then will those three equations form an independent subset in dC, dI, and dr, given the values of dY, $d(w/p)$, and dN that emerge from the aggregate supply subset.[12] This condition will be met only if it happens that the coefficient of dp in Equation (iv), which is $-C_1\pi(M + B)/p^2$, happens to equal zero. This will be so either if π happens to be zero or if $M + B$ is zero, B being negative and representing government loans to the public.

---

[12] Alternatively, notice that if the coefficients of dp are all zero, the formal requirements for block recursiveness with respect to dC, dI, and dr are fulfilled.

Since it is commonly assumed that real consumption is independent of the price level, we begin our analysis by tentatively assuming that $M + B = 0$ initially. Then substituting (iv) and (v) into (vi) and setting $dK = dY = dN = 0$,[13] we have

$$-C_1 \, dT + [C_1 Iq_{r-\pi} + C_2 + (1 + C_1(q-1))I'q_{r-\pi}] \, dr$$
$$-[C_1 Iq_{r-\pi} + C_2 + (1 + C_1(q-1))I'q_{r-\pi}] \, d\pi + dG = 0.$$

Solving for dr, we have

$$dr = \frac{C_1}{H} \, dT - \frac{1}{H} \, dG + d\pi \tag{26}$$

where $H = C_1 Iq_{r-\pi} + C_2 + (1 + C_1(q-1))I'q_{r-\pi}$.

We assume that the partial derivative of disposable income with respect to the interest rate obeys

$$\frac{-C_2}{C_1} > Iq_{r-\pi} + (q-1)I'q_{r-\pi} = \left. \frac{\partial Y_D}{\partial r} \right|_{dT = dY = d\pi = dp = 0},$$

which requires that, if it is positive, it not be too large in absolute value. This condition is sufficient, although not necessary, to guarantee that H is negative. As we shall see below, H must be negative if the model is to be "stable." The magnitude H has a straightforward interpretation. It is the total derivative of aggregate demand $C + I + G + \delta K$ with respect to the interest rate. Manipulation of (26) then produces the following expression for the partial derivatives of r with respect to the exogenous variables T, G, and π:

$$\partial r / \partial T = C_1 / H < 0, \qquad \partial r / \partial G = -1/H > 0, \qquad \partial r / \partial \pi = 1.$$

These are partial derivatives of the "reduced form" for r, which express r solely in terms of the exogenous variables, the endogenous variables all having been eliminated by substitution. The interest rate rises in response to an increase in government purchases or a decrease in the rate of tax collections. If π rises, r rises by the same amount, leaving $r - \pi$ unaltered.[14]

To determine the effect of changes in T, G, and π on net investment I we substitute (26) into (v) and solve for the reduced form partial derivatives of I with respect to those exogenous variables:

$$\frac{\partial I}{\partial T} = I'q_{r-\pi} \frac{\partial r}{\partial T} > 0,$$

$$\frac{\partial I}{\partial G} = I'q_{r-\pi} \frac{\partial r}{\partial G} < 0,$$

$$\frac{\partial I}{\partial \pi} = I'q_{r-\pi} \frac{\partial r}{\partial \pi} - I'q_{r-\pi} = 0.$$

---

[13] We know from solving (i)–(iii) that $dY = dN = 0$ if $dK = 0$.

[14] This outcome plays an important role in Friedman's (1968) article.

We see that net investment I is stimulated by an increase in taxes or a decrease in government expenditures. A change in π leaves the real rate of interest $r - \pi$ unaltered and so has no effect on investment.

The effects of changes in T, G, and π on consumption can be studied by substituting (26) into (iv) and computing the following reduced form partial derivatives:

$$\frac{\partial C}{\partial T} = -C_1 + (C_2 + C_1 Iq_{r-\pi} + C_1(q - 1)I'q_{r-\pi})\frac{\partial r}{\partial T}$$

$$\frac{\partial C}{\partial G} = (C_2 + C_1 Iq_{r-\pi} + C_1(q - 1)I'q_{r-\pi})\frac{\partial r}{\partial G}$$

$$\frac{\partial C}{\partial \pi} = (C_2 + C_1 Iq_{r-\pi} + C_1(q - 1)I'q_{r-\pi})\frac{\partial r}{\partial \pi}$$

$$-(C_2 + C_1 Iq_{r-\pi} + C_1(q - 1)I'q_{r-\pi}) = 0.$$

If q is not too much smaller than 1, then $C_2 + C_1 Iq_{r-\pi} + C_1(q - 1)I'q_{r-\pi}$ is negative, and $\partial C/\partial G$ is negative while $\partial C/\partial T$ is also negative. The expression $Iq_{r-\pi} + (q - 1)I'q_{r-\pi}$ is the partial derivative of disposable income with respect to the interest rate. We have assumed that this derivative satisfies

$$-C_2/C_1 > Iq_{r-\pi} + (q - 1)I'q_{r-\pi},$$

so that the derivative of disposable income with respect to the interest rate is less than $-C_2/C_1$, which guarantees that $\partial C/\partial G < 0$. It also follows that $\partial C/\partial T < 0$.

In this version of the classical model—in which $M + B$ is equal to zero initially—the interest rate bears the entire burden of adjusting the level of aggregate demand, so that it equals the aggregate supply of output determined by Equations (I)-(III). We have already seen that given the capital stock, aggregate supply is independent of the other exogenous variables. If from a position of initial equilibrium, one of the exogenous variables changes in such a manner that it induces an increase in aggregate demand at the initial interest rate, the interest rate must rise to diminish desired consumption and investment by enough to restore equality between aggregate demand and the unchanged rate of aggregate supply determined by (I)-(III). That is why the interest rate must rise, for example, in response to increases in aggregate demand induced by increases in government expenditures or reductions in taxes. The rise in the interest rate in turn generally induces changes in rates of capital accumulation and consumption. Only in the case of a change in π does the net effect of the change fail to affect investment and consumption. That is because a change in π produces an equivalent change in r which leaves $r - \pi$, the real rate of interest, unaltered.

The determination of the interest rate in the classical model is easily illustrated graphically. First note that since disposable income is allocated between saving and consumption, we have

$$S + C = Y - T - \delta K + (q - 1)I.$$

Substituting the national income identity (VI) into the above equation and rearranging yields an alternative form of the equilibrium condition between aggregate demand and aggregate supply,

$$G + qI = S + T. \tag{27}$$

Equation (27) states that in equilibrium real government expenditures plus real investment evaluated at the stock market value of equities must equal saving plus the rate of tax collections. A version of (27) is sometimes interpreted as stating that "injections" $(G + qI)$ must equal "leakages" $(S + T)$ if the economy is to be in equilibrium.

The role of the interest rate in making aggregate demand equal to the predetermined aggregate supply is shown graphically in Figure 2, which depicts $S + T$ as an increasing function of interest and $qI + G$ as varying inversely with the interest rate. We know that qI is inversely related to the interest rate since

$$\frac{\partial q(K, N, r - \pi)I(q(K, N, r - \pi))}{\partial r} = q_{r-\pi}I + qI'q_{r-\pi} < 0,$$

as long as $I > -qI'$, which we assume is true.

We have depicted saving plus exogenous tax collections as varying directly with the interest rate, which need not be true. For saving is defined by

$$S = Y_D - C(Y_D, r - \pi).$$

The derivative of saving with respect to the interest rate is

$$\frac{\partial S}{\partial r} = \frac{\partial Y_D}{\partial r} - C_1 \frac{\partial Y_D}{\partial r} - C_2 = \frac{\partial Y_D}{\partial r}(1 - C_1) - C_2.$$

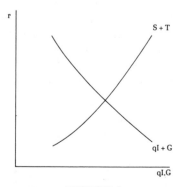

FIGURE 2

We have assumed that $\partial Y_D/\partial r$ obeys $-C_2/C_1 > \partial Y_D/\partial r$, which implies only that

$$\frac{\partial S}{\partial r} < -\frac{C_2}{C_1}(1 - C_1) - C_2 \quad \text{or} \quad \frac{\partial S}{\partial r} < -\frac{C_2}{C_1}.$$

So our assumptions do not rule out a saving schedule that depends inversely on the rate of interest.

Both $S + T$ and $G + qI$ also depend on output since I varies with employment and S with output. But output is predetermined from the point of view of interest rate determination, and it will not vary in response to variations in G or T. The equilibrium interest rate is determined at the intersection of the $qI + G$ and the $S + T$ curves. Using Figure 2, it is easy to verify that increases in government expenditures drive the interest rate upward, while increases in tax collections drive it downward. An increase in π is easily verified[15] to shift both the $S + T$ curve and the $G + qI$ curve upward by the amount of the increase in π. The result is that r rises by the increase in π, the equilibrium $G + qI$ being left unchanged.

An equivalent "loanable-funds" interpretation can readily be placed on the process of interest rate determination. Substituting the government's flow budget constraint into Equation (27) yields the alternative form of that equation

$$qI + \frac{\dot{M}}{p} + \frac{\dot{B}}{p} = S.$$

The left-hand side of this equation is the actual time rate of growth of the economy's real stock paper assets, money, bonds, and equities. The right-hand side is the rate at which the public desires to add to its stocks of assets, i.e., desired saving. In equilibrium the actual rate of growth of the economy's paper assets must just equal the rate at which the public wishes to add to its assets. The actual real growth rate of government issued financial assets $(\dot{M} + \dot{B})/p$ is equal to the government's deficit. Given that rate and given total taxes T, the interest rate adjusts to ensure that desired saving exceeds the expected rate of increase in the real value of equities qI exactly by the real rate at which the government is expanding the public's claims upon it in the form of financial assets. Thus, for example, given real tax receipts T, an increase in government expenditures raises $(\dot{M} + \dot{B})/p$; in order for equilibrium to be restored, the interest rate must rise, thus diminishing investment and therefore the rate of issuing equities and stimulating saving, to such a point that the new higher real rate of addition to

---

[15] For example, given $G + qI$, how much must r change in order to stay on the $G + qI$ curve when π changes? Taking the differential of the $G + qI$ schedule and setting $d(G + qI) = dN = dK = 0$, we have

$$(Iq_{r-\pi} + qI'q_{r-\pi})\,dr = (Iq_{r-\pi} + qI'q_{r-\pi})\,d\pi$$

or $dr = d\pi$, which establishes that the $qI + G$ curve shifts upward by the amount of the increase in π.

government-issued financial assets is consistent with the public's saving and investment plans. The above equation succinctly summarizes the traditional rationale for levying taxes as opposed to financing government expenditures by printing bonds or money: it is to protect the rate of growth of physical capital by limiting the extent to which private saving is diverted to accumulating claims on the government instead of (claims on) physical capital.

The differentials of the interest rate and output having been determined in Equations (i)–(vi), the role of Equation (vii) is simply to determine the differential of the price level:

$$\frac{dp}{p} = \frac{dM}{M} - m_r \frac{p}{M} dr - m_Y \frac{p}{M} dY. \tag{28}$$

Thus, if the money supply is the only exogenous variable that changes, only the price level is affected, and it changes proportionately with the money supply. On the other hand, the price level does respond to the changes in output and the interest rate that emerge from Equations (i)–(iv), increases in the interest rate driving the price level upward, while increases in output drive it downward. However, as long as neither dp nor dM appears in Equations (i)–(vi), "money is a veil," having no effects on output, employment, the real wage, consumption, investment, or the interest rate. Recall that in order to eliminate dp from the equation for dC we assumed that $M + B$ was zero initially.

7. STABILITY

It is important to verify that the equilibrium positions we have described are stable, i.e., that there is a tendency to return to them if the system is displaced from them. Otherwise the comparative static exercises we have performed are of little practical interest. The need to examine the stability of static equilibria is the heart of Samuelson's *correspondence principle* (Samuelson, 1963, pp. 257–269).

In the classical model it is usual to argue that the commodity price level adjusts when there is a discrepancy between aggregate demand and supply of goods, while the interest rate adjusts when there is inequality between the supply of real balances and the demand. We summarize this by the following two differential equations, where s is a "time" index:

$$\frac{dp}{ds} = \sigma(C(Y_D, r - \pi) + I(q - 1) + G + \delta K - F(K, N)),$$

$$\sigma' > 0 \quad \sigma(0) = 0;$$

$$\frac{dr}{ds} = \beta\left(m(r, Y) - \frac{M}{p}\right), \quad \beta' > 0, \quad \beta(0) = 0.$$

The first equation states that the price level rises when flow aggregate demand exceeds flow aggregate supply, while the second states that the interest rate rises when the demand for real balances exceeds the supply, or, what is the same, when the real supply of bonds and equities exceeds the demand for them. Taking the first-order part of the Taylor's expansion of these equations around equilibrium values of the variables gives the approximation:

$$\frac{dp}{ds} = \sigma'\{C_2 + I'q_{r-\pi} + C_1[(q-1)I'q_{r-\pi} + Iq_{r-\pi}]\}(r - r_0)$$

$$\frac{dr}{ds} = \beta'm_r(r - r_0) + \beta'\frac{M}{p^2}(p - p_0)$$

where zero subscripts denote initial equilibrium values and where we continue to assume that $M + B$ equals zero initially, so that changes in the price level do not affect Y_D. This system can be written in matrix form as

$$\begin{bmatrix} dp/ds \\ dr/ds \end{bmatrix} = \begin{bmatrix} 0 & \sigma'H \\ \beta'M/p^2 & \beta'm_r \end{bmatrix} \begin{bmatrix} p - p_0 \\ r - r_0 \end{bmatrix}$$

where, as in (26), H is defined by

$$H = C_2 + I'q_{r-\pi} + C_1q_{r-\pi}((q-1)I' + I).$$

This system is an example of a linear differential equation of first order of the form $dx/ds = Ax$ where x is an $n \times 1$ vector, A is an $n \times n$ matrix. The solution of the system has the general form

$$x_j(s) = \sum_{h=1}^{n} k_{jh}e^{\lambda_h s}$$

where $x_j(s)$ is the value of the jth component of x at instant s, the k_{jh} are constants, and the λ_h, $h = 1, \ldots, n$, are the roots of the characteristic equation

$$|A - \lambda I| = 0$$

where the vertical bars denote the determinant. The system will be stable if the eigenvalues, the λ's, have negative real parts. For our system, the characteristic equation is

$$\begin{vmatrix} -\lambda & \sigma'H \\ \beta'M/p^2 & \beta'm_r - \lambda \end{vmatrix} = 0,$$

$$\lambda^2 - \beta'm_r\lambda - \sigma'\beta'(M/p^2)H = 0.$$

Necessary and sufficient conditions that the eigenvalues have negative real parts are that the coefficients on λ and the constant term both be positive. (Samuelson, 1963, pp. 430–431.) Thus, necessary and sufficient conditions for stability are

$$\beta'm_r < 0, \qquad \sigma'\beta'(M/p^2)H < 0.$$

Since σ', β', and M/p^2 all exceed zero, our stability conditions are

$$m_r < 0, \qquad H = C_2 + I'q_{r-\pi} + C_1 q_{r-\pi}((q-1)I' + 1) < 0.$$

The interest elasticity of the demand for money must be negative, while the interest slopes of the consumption and investment schedules must sum to a negative number.

Notice that if $m_r = 0$, the model is not stable. If m_r equals zero, the characteristic equation becomes

$$\lambda^2 - \sigma'\beta'(M/p^2)H = 0$$

whose solution is

$$\lambda = \pm\sqrt{\sigma'\beta'H(M/p^2)}.$$

Since H is negative, the two roots are conjugate imaginary numbers, i.e., the real part of the roots are zero. Consequently, where $\lambda_1 = bi$, $\lambda_2 = -bi$, the solution for $r(s) - r_0$, for example, will have the form

$$\begin{aligned}
r(s) - r_0 &= k_{11}e^{bis} + k_{12}e^{-bis} \\
&= k_{11}(\cos bs + i \sin bs) + k_{12}(\cos bs - i \sin bs) \\
&= (k_{11} + k_{12})\cos bs + (k_{11} - k_{12})i \sin bs.
\end{aligned}$$

Where the roots are complex, as in the present case, it can be shown that $k_{12} = k_{11}^*$, where the asterisk denotes complex conjugation. Letting $k_{11} = x + iy$, we have $k_{12} = x - iy$. Thus, our solution for r becomes

$$r(s) - r_0 = 2x \cos bs - 2y \sin bs.$$

The solution consists of a nondamped, nonexplosive sinusoidal function. There is no tendency for the system to approach equilibrium as "time" passes, regardless of the adjustment speeds.[16] Remember, however, that it is a linear approximation to the actual dynamic system which possesses this borderline instability with nondamped but nonexplosive oscillations. In this case the

----

[16] The role of real and imaginary parts of the roots in governing convergence to equilibrium can be seen by rewriting the solution of $x_j(s)$ as

$$x_j(s) = \sum_{h=1}^{n} k_{jh}e^{(a_h + b_h i)s}$$

where $\lambda_h = a_h + b_h i$. Then

$$x_j(s) = \sum_{h=1}^{n} k_{jh}e^{a_h s}(\cos b_h s + i \sin b_h s).$$

If all $a_h < 0$, the oscillations of the system (if any) are damped. If all $a_h = 0$, there is no damping.

behavior of the system itself, as opposed to the linear approximation, may be either stable or unstable. The character of the nonlinearities of the system is what will determine whether the system is stable. The appropriate way to analyze the matter is to consider higher order terms in the Taylor's series approximation to the dynamic system.

The possible instability of the model where $m_r = 0$ means that comparative static exercises that are performed assuming $m_r = 0$ must be interpreted carefully. On the correspondence principle, such exercises make sense only if we interpret them as describing how the system will behave as m_r approaches zero from below.

The differential equations set out above should not be construed as describing the actual evolution of the system in calendar time. For as we have already pointed out, the endogenous variables are assumed to jump instantaneously to satisfy the equilibrium conditions continuously through time. Consequently, we shall interpret the adjustment processes described above as processes in which σ' and β' both approach infinity. Under this interpretation the stability calculations retain their sense, while we can keep the view that adjustments of the variables of the model occur instantaneously.

8. THE MODEL WITH $M + B \neq 0$

Up to now we have assumed that $M + B$ initially equals zero, implying that expected real disposable income and consumption are both independent of the price level. We now investigate the implications of abandoning that special assumption, and assume $M + B > 0$. Inspection of Equations (i)–(vii) indicates that, given dY, dN, and $d(w/p)$ determined by Equations (i)–(iii), Equations (iv)–(vii) form an interdependent system that determines dC, dI, dr, and dp. Consequently, we should expect dM, which appears in (vii), now to influence dI, dr, and dC.

To solve the system, we first substitute (iv) and (v) into (vi) to obtain the differential of the r-p locus that makes aggregate demand equal to aggregate supply:

$$0 = -C_1 \, dT + dG + \frac{M + B}{p} C_1 \pi \frac{dp}{p} + H \, dr - \left(H + C_1 \frac{M + B}{p} \right) d\pi, \quad (29)$$

where, as in Equation (26), H is defined by

$$H = C_2 + C_1 I q_{r-\pi} + [1 + C_1(q - 1)] I' q_{r-\pi} < 0.$$

Notice that the slope in the p-r plane of the locus of points that make aggregate demand equal to aggregate supply depends on the sign of $(M + B)\pi$.

Equation (28) gives the differential of the locus of points that make the demand for real balances equal to the supply. Substituting (28) into (29) gives an equation that is the differential of the reduced form equation for r:

$$\left(H - m_r \frac{M + B}{M} C_1 \pi \right) dr = C_1\, dT - dG - \frac{M + B}{p} C_1 \pi \frac{dM}{M}$$

$$+ \left(H + C_1 \frac{M + B}{p} \right) d\pi. \qquad (30)$$

We assume that

$$H - m_r \frac{M + B}{M} C_1 \pi < 0,$$

a condition that guarantees that aggregate demand falls in response to an increase in r. This is a condition required for stability. We use (30) to compute the following reduced form partial derivatives:

$$\frac{\partial r}{\partial G} = \frac{-1}{H - m_r((M + B)/M)C_1\pi} > 0,$$

$$\frac{\partial r}{\partial T} = \frac{C_1}{H - m_r((M + B)/M)C_1\pi} < 0,$$

$$\frac{\partial r}{\partial \pi} = \frac{H + C_1((M + B)/p)}{H - m_r((M + B)/M)C_1\pi}.$$

We note that if $M + B$ is set equal to zero, the above expressions agree with our earlier expressions for these three partial derivatives. We note that if $M + B$ exceeds zero and π is positive, an increase in government expenditures or a decrease in taxes will increase the rate of interest more than if $M + B$ were zero provided that $H - m_r((M + B)/M)C_1\pi < 0$, as we have assumed. Thus, suppose government expenditures rise. This tends to increase the interest rate, which in turn, through Equation (vii), causes the price level to rise. But the rise in the price level in turn reduces the real value of government debt, and given an exogeneous, positive π also reduces the anticipated rate of real capital loss on those assets. Hence expected real disposable income increases, which in turn increases the desired rate of consumption, driving the interest rate up even further. A similar explanation holds for the response of the interest rate to an increase in taxes. It is clear that the signs of those effects ought to depend on the signs of π and $(M + B)/p$ since if one of them is negative, an increase in p will produce a decrease in expected real disposable income.

Next notice that an increase in π no longer leads to an equivalent increase in the interest rate. This is due to the effect of changes in π on expected real disposable income. It is possible for the interest rate to rise more or less than the given rise in π.

We now evaluate the reduced form partial derivative of r with respect to M:

$$\frac{\partial r}{\partial M} = \frac{-((M + B)/p)C_1\pi}{MH - m_r(M + B)C_1\pi}.$$

If $M + B$ or π equals zero, we see that an increase in the money supply has no effect on the interest rate, as before. If π and $M + B$ are both positive, however, then an increase in M drives r upward. The increase in money drives prices upward, which reduces the real value of anticipated capital losses on paper assets, thus raising perceived real disposable income, driving intended consumption upward. The real interest rate must then rise to equate aggregate demand with aggregate supply. Thus money has ceased to be a veil, being capable of affecting the real interest rate and hence the rate of capital accumulation. That in turn gives the monetary authority some control over the economy's rate of growth over time. But clearly, money remains impotent as far as concerns determining the level of output at a point in time.

9. THE MODEL WITH $\pi = \dot{p}/p$[17]

Up to now we have always taken as exogenous those expectations that pertain to the future values of some of the endogenous variables. In doing so we have ruled out the existence of "perfect foresight" or for that matter the existence of any systematic relationships between expectations and the actual subsequent behavior of those endogenous variables about which expectations are being formed. We have done so in spite of the fact that, given assumed paths of the exogenous variables over future time, the model is supposed to be capable of determining the value of the endogenous variables at each moment. Here we show that making the assumption that expectations of future endogenous variables are exogenous is necessary in order to perform comparative static exercises, i.e., exercises that involve computing alternative equilibrium values of endogenous variables at one and only one point in time.

Suppose that we have a model that can be summarized by the system of m reduced form equations in T exogenous variables:

$$\begin{aligned}
z_1(t) &= f_1(x_1(t), \ldots, x_T(t)) \\
z_2(t) &= f_2(x_1(t), \ldots, x_T(t)) \\
&\vdots \\
z_m(t) &= f_m(x_1(t), \ldots, x_T(t))
\end{aligned} \tag{31}$$

[17] This is our first brush with the idea of rational expectations. The subject of this section was studied in the context of a continuous time version of Cagan's (1956) model of hyperinflation by Sargent and Wallace (1973a). Econometric implications of that model were pursued in the context of a discrete time model by Sargent and Wallace (1973b), Sargent (1977), and Hansen and Sargent (1983). Hansen and Sargent (1983) studied the implications for discrete time data of a continuous time version of Cagan's model.

where $z_j(t)$ is the value of the jth endogenous variable at instant t and $x_i(t)$ is the value of the ith exogenous variable at time t. The exogenous variables do not respond to movements of the endogenous variables at a point in time, but may depend on past values of the endogenous variables. For example, the capital stock is related to past rates of investment by

$$K(t) = \int_{t_0}^{t} I(s) \, ds + K(t_o), \qquad t > t_0; \tag{32}$$

but the current capital stock is independent of the current rate of investment, as long as the latter is finite. The evolution of the capital stock over time is thus determined by the model, but at each moment the capital stock is predetermined.

The system of equations (31) determines the values of the endogenous variables at any given moment. Furthermore, if we specify arbitrary time paths for the exogenous variables or, where appropriate, laws of motion over time that, like Equation (32), link exogenous variables to past values of endogenous variables, then the system of equations (31) is capable of determining the endogenous variables at each moment over some time interval. The model thus describes the "dynamic" behavior of the endogenous variables, despite the fact that we have heretofore restricted ourselves to comparing alternative equilibrium positions at a point in time. Those static exercises were meaningful since the model was capable of determining the equilibrium values of the variables at a given moment, taking into account only the values of the exogenous variables at that moment.

Now suppose we append to Equations (31) the relationship

$$x_1(t) = \dot{z}_m(t) \equiv \lim_{\varepsilon \to 0, \varepsilon > 0} \frac{z_m(t + \varepsilon) - z_m(t)}{\varepsilon} \tag{33}$$

where $x_1(t)$ is a variable, previously treated as exogenous, that equals the public's expectation of the time rate of change of $z_m(t)$ over the immediate future. For example, z_m might be the logarithm of the price level, so that $x_1(t)$ would correspond to the anticipated rate of inflation. Notice that the derivative in (33) is a right-hand derivative, so that (33) embodies a notion of "perfect foresight."

If Equation (33) is added to (31), we have a system that is no longer capable of determining the values of the endogenous variables at a single point in time, given the remaining exogenous variables $x_2(t), \ldots, x_T(t)$ at that point in time. For in order to determine any endogenous variable at a point in time it is necessary also to determine $\dot{z}_m(t)$, the right-hand derivative of z_m, at that same moment in time. But to determine $\dot{z}_m$ requires in effect that we determine z_m over at least a small interval of the future. The equation for $z_m(t)$ is found by substituting (33) into the last equation of (31):

$$z_m(t) = f_m(\dot{z}_m(t), x_2(t), \ldots, x_T(t)). \tag{34}$$

At any given moment in time this equation determines only a locus of $z_m(t)$, $\dot{z}_m(t)$ combinations that satisfy it. So long as both $z_m(t)$ and $\dot{z}_m(t)$ are viewed as being determined by the model at the current instant, we are not able to arrive at a solution.

It might be thought that a way out of our problem is to differentiate (34) with respect to time in the right-hand direction in order to get an equation that determines $\dot{z}_m(t)$. But this yields

$$\dot{z}_m(t) = \frac{\partial f_m}{\partial x_1} \ddot{z}_m(t) + \frac{\partial f_m}{\partial x_2} \dot{x}_2(t) + \cdots + \frac{\partial f_m}{\partial x_T} \dot{x}_T(t) \tag{35}$$

where all time derivatives are right-hand ones. Equation (35) only determines a locus of $\dot{z}_m$, $\ddot{z}_m$ combinations that solve the equation, given values of $\dot{x}_2(t), \ldots, \dot{x}_T(t)$. Following this line of reasoning will then lead us to follow an infinite progression calculating higher and higher order time derivatives of z_m. In order to determine z_m under assumption (34), it is necessary to determine right-hand derivatives of *all* orders at time t.

Equivalently, Equation (34) is a differential equation in $z_m(t)$, one that might possibly be solved for a time path of $z_m(t)$ over a time interval $t_0 \le t \le t_n$ where t_n could be arbitrarily large. To compute a particular solution a terminal condition on z_m would have to be supplied. Then z_m might be able to be expressed as a function of (expected) future values of the exogenous variables, e.g.,

$$z_m(t) = g\left(\int_t^{t_n} W_2(s-t)x_2(s)\, ds, \ldots, \int_t^{t_n} W_T(s-t)x_T(s)\, ds, z_m(t_n) \right) \tag{36}$$

for $t_0 \le t \le t_n$ where $W_2(\ ), \ldots, W_T(\ )$ are coefficients that are functions of the parameters of the equation system (31). Equation (36) expresses the current value of z_m over time in terms of the (expected) paths of the exogenous variables. In order to determine the equilibrium value of z_m at any one moment in time it is necessary to calculate an equilibrium time path of z_m over some portion of the future.

To do the point-in-time comparative static exercises we have performed it is necessary to divorce equilibrium values of the endogenous variables at one moment from any dependence on equilibrium values of those variables in subsequent moments. To do that it is necessary to deny the existence of any relationships that, like Equation (33), produce a dependence of current endogenous variables on subsequent values of endogenous variables. This explains why we have maintained that the public's expectations do not embody perfect foresight or do not depend systematically on actual subsequent values for any endogenous variables. Instead, we have viewed them as exogenous at any moment.

To illustrate the point, consider the classical model described above in which it is assumed that $M + B$ equals zero initially, so that "money is a veil." In that model $\bar{Y}$, N, w/p, C, I, and r are all independent of the level of the money supply. In addition, the real rate of interest $r - \pi$ was seen to be independent of the rate of expected inflation and the money supply. We could write this as

$$r = (r - \pi) + \pi, \qquad r = \rho + \pi,$$

where ρ equals $r - \pi$ and is independent of π and M. Given r and Y, the job of Equation (VII) is to determine the price level:

$$M/p = m(r, Y)$$

or

$$M/p = m(\rho + \pi, Y). \qquad \text{(VII')}$$

Given M, Y, ρ, and π, Equation (VII') is capable of determining a unique price level.

But suppose that we require that $\pi = \dot{p}/p$ where $\dot{p}$ is interpreted as a right-hand derivative. The variable $\dot{p}/p$ is viewed as being determined by the model. The equation

$$M/p = m(\rho + \dot{p}/p, Y),$$

with Y, M, and ρ given, is capable of determining only a locus of $(p, \dot{p}/p)$ combinations that guarantee portfolio balance. In particular, higher $\dot{p}/p$'s are compatible with higher p's at a moment in time, so that the momentary $(\dot{p}/p, p)$ locus determined by (VII') is like the one shown in Figure 3. The value of the exogenous variables at a point in time and the restrictions in Equations (I)–(VII) do not contain enough information to determine both p and $\dot{p}/p$ at that point in time.

It is useful to pursue this illustration using a concrete example of the model that was proposed by Cagan (1956). Ignoring the role of income and the real interest rate, Cagan assumed that the demand for money obeyed the equation

$$\ln[M(t)/p(t)] = \alpha\pi(t) \qquad \text{where} \quad \alpha < 0.$$

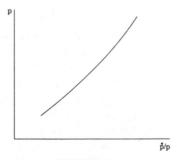

FIGURE 3

We suppose that the public's expectation $\pi(t)$ equals the right-hand derivative $(d/dt\ p(t))/p(t) = (d/dt)(\ln\ p(t))$. It is convenient to use the operator D defined by

$$Dx(t) = dx(t)/dt, \qquad D^n x(t) = d^n x(t)/dt^n.$$

For many purposes, it is legitimate to manipulate D like an algebraic symbol, which accounts for its utility. So the above equation can be rearranged to read

$$D \ln p(t) + \alpha^{-1} \ln p(t) = \alpha^{-1} \ln M(t). \tag{37}$$

We think of M as being the exogenous variable, so that this is a one-equation model that is supposed to determine p.

Given only the value of M at a point in time, Equation (37) is incapable of determining either p or Dp at that point in time. That is because Equation (37) is in effect one equation in two variables, p and Dp, at each point in time.

Rewrite (37) as

$$(D + \alpha^{-1}) \ln p(t) = \alpha^{-1} \ln M(t),$$

then

$$\ln p(t) = \frac{\alpha^{-1}}{\alpha^{-1} + D} \ln M(t) \tag{38}$$

or

$$\ln p(t) = \frac{1}{1 + \alpha D} \ln M(t). \tag{38'}$$

Now recall the geometric expansion $1/(1 - \lambda) = 1 + \lambda + \lambda^2 + \cdots$, for $|\lambda| < 1$. Similarly, it is appropriate (see Agnew, 1960) to interpret $1/(1 + \alpha D)$ as the analogous expansion $1/(1 + \alpha D) = 1 - \alpha D + \alpha^2 D^2 - \alpha^3 D^3 + \cdots$, where $-\alpha D$ is treated as if it were λ in the above formula for the geometric expansion. So we have

$$\ln p(t) = [1 - \alpha D + \alpha^2 D^2 - \alpha^3 D^3 + \cdots] \ln M(t)$$
$$\ln p(t) = \ln M(t) - \alpha D \ln M(t) + \alpha^2 D^2 \ln M(t) - \cdots, \tag{39}$$

which expresses $\ln p(t)$ in terms of an infinite number of right-hand derivatives of $\ln M(t)$ with respect to time at t. Equation (39) can be derived directly, without use of the D operator, by repeatedly differentiating the demand schedule for money with respect to time and eliminating successively higher derivatives of $\ln p(t)$. This indicates that to determine $\ln p(t)$ it is necessary simultaneously to determine time derivatives of all orders of $\ln p(t)$, which requires taking into account time derivatives of $\ln M(t)$ of all orders at time t. But if we know time derivatives of all orders of $\ln p(t)$ at t, does the logic behind Taylor's series expansions imply that we know the values of $\ln p(s)$ for $s \geq t$ also? The answer is yes, as the following alternative interpretation of the solution (38) readily shows. Notice that[18]

$$\frac{\alpha^{-1}}{\alpha^{-1} + D} = -\frac{1}{\alpha} \int_t^\infty e^{(s-t)(\alpha^{-1}+D)} \, ds = -\frac{1}{\alpha} \left[\frac{e^{(s-t)(\alpha^{-1}+D)}}{\alpha^{-1} + D} \right]_{s=t}^{s=\infty}.$$

So (38) can be written

$$\ln p(t) = \left[-\frac{1}{\alpha} \int_t^\infty e^{(s-t)(\alpha^{-1}+D)} \, ds \right] \ln M(t). \tag{40}$$

Now consider $e^{(s-t)D}$. Taking its Taylor's series expansion about $(s - t)D = 0$, we have

$$e^{(s-t)D} = 1 + (s - t)D + \frac{(s - t)^2 D^2}{2!} + \cdots.$$

So we have

$$e^{(s-t)D}x(t) = x(t) + (s - t)Dx(t) + \frac{(s - t)^2 D^2}{2!} x(t) + \cdots = x(t + s - t) = x(s),$$

so long as $x(t)$ has a convergent Taylor's series expansion, which we shall assume. We exploit the above equality in order to write (40) as

$$\ln p(t) = -\frac{1}{\alpha} \int_t^\infty (e^{(s-t)/\alpha})(e^{(s-t)D} \ln M(t)) \, ds.$$

Since $e^{(s-t)D}M(t) = M(s)$, the above equation can be written as[19]

$$\ln p(t) = -\frac{1}{\alpha} \int_t^\infty e^{(s-t)/\alpha} \ln M(s) \, ds. \tag{41}$$

---

[18] On the right-hand side of the expression, we are treating D as a fixed number and assuming that $(1/\alpha + D) < 0$, so that the integral is convergent. The reader interested in a more rigorous treatment of the operational calculus used here is directed to any good reference on Laplace transforms, for example, Gabel and Roberts (1973).

[19] Notice that if $(1/\alpha + D) > 0$, we can write

$$\frac{\alpha^{-1}}{\alpha^{-1} + D} = \frac{1}{\alpha} \int_{-\infty}^t e^{(s-t)(\alpha^{-1}+D)} \, ds.$$

Then repeating the argument in the text that led to (41) gives

$$\ln p(t) = \frac{1}{\alpha} \int_{-\infty}^t e^{(s-t)/\alpha} \ln M(s) \, ds,$$

which expresses $p(t)$ in terms of *past* values of $M(s)$. However, since $1/\alpha < 0$, on the right-hand side is not a convergent integral, for example, for the money supply process $M(s) = \bar{M} = a$ constant. For this same money supply process, the integral in Equation (41) *is* convergent. This illustrates a general point: differential equations with forcing functions can generally be solved in terms of past values of the forcing variables or alternatively in terms of future values of the forcing variables. If the solution in one direction is convergent, the solution in the other direction is in general not convergent. Here and in what follows, we adopt the procedure of choosing the convergent solution, a procedure that can be rationalized as a variant of Samuelson's "correspondence principle."

It can be verified by differentiation that (41) is a solution to the differential equation (37) where D is interpreted as a right-hand derivative operator. Equation (41) is the particular solution of (37) corresponding to the "forcing" function $M(t)$. As always, we must add to (41) the solution to the homogeneous equation

$$(D + \alpha^{-1}) \ln p(t) = 0,$$

which is easily verified to be $ce^{-t/\alpha}$ where c is an arbitrary constant chosen to satisfy some condition. If we impose the "reasonable" condition that the public expects inflation to occur only if the money supply is increasing, this has the effect of making $c = 0$, so that (41) is the appropriate solution.

According to Equation (41), the value of $\ln p(t)$ at t depends on the value of the entire money supply path from t until forever. So values of the endogenous variable $p(t)$ cannot be determined solely from the values of the exogenous variables at t. Instead, the entire time path of $M(s)$ for $s \geq t$ must be supplied. We simply cannot do static or point-in-time exercises. We are thrust into a dynamic analysis. Of course, a dividend of this is that we do have the solution for the entire time paths of the endogenous variables.

One way to specify the evolution of the money supply is to assume that its logarithm is described by an nth order linear differential equation, which we express as

$$\theta(D) \ln M(t) = 0 \tag{42}$$

where $\theta(D) = \theta_n D^n + \theta_{n-1} D^{n-1} + \cdots + \theta_0, \theta_n \neq 0$, subject to n initial conditions in the forms of values of $D^j \ln M(t)$ for $j = 0, \ldots, n-1$ at some particular time t. In order that the integral on the right side of (41) converges, it is sufficient to assume that the real parts of the solutions s_0 to the polynomial equation $\theta(s_0) = 0$ are less than $-\alpha^{-1}$. Under this assumption, Hansen and Sargent (1981) have established the following formulas:

$$\int_t^\infty e^{(s-t)/\alpha} \ln M(s)\, ds = \left[\frac{\theta^{-1}(-\alpha^{-1})\theta(D) - 1}{D + \alpha^{-1}} \right] \ln M(t)$$

$$= \theta(-\alpha^{-1})^{-1} \sum_{j=0}^{n-1} D^j \sum_{k=j}^{n-1} \theta_{k+1}(-\alpha^{-1})^{k-j} \ln M(t). \tag{43}$$

Thus, the solution (41) has a representation

$$\ln p(t) = -\alpha^{-1}\theta^{-1}(-\alpha^{-1}) \sum_{j=0}^{n-1} D^j \sum_{k=j}^{n-1} \theta_{k+1}(-\alpha^{-1})^{k-j} \ln M(t). \tag{44}$$

For example, in the special first-order case in which $\theta(D) = D + \theta_0$, (44) becomes

$$\ln p(t) = [1/(1 - \alpha\theta_0)] \ln M(t).$$

Two things are noteworthy about representation (44). First, the logarithm of the price level is asserted to depend on the path of the logarithm of the money supply with coefficients that depend on the θ_j's in (42), parameters that describe the money supply process. The reason for this is readily understandable, since (41) indicates that the price level depends on expected future values of the money supply. How these future values are related to past and present values of the money supply depends on the parameters θ_j governing the money supply process. The dependence of the parameters in (44) on those in (42) is our first encounter with a general principle of dynamic economic theory that equations like (44) which depict an observable relationship of endogenous and exogenous variables are themselves functions of the law (e.g., (42)) governing the motion of the exogenous variables. This principle has sweeping implications, as we shall see later in more detail. The present example is enough to see that this theory argues against searching for a single relationship between prices and the money supply of the form (44) that is to hold for all times and places (i.e., for any settings of $\theta(D)$).

Second, we note that the number of derivative components on the right side of (44) is $(n - 1)$, one less than the order of the differential equation governing $\ln M(t)$.

10. AN ALTERNATIVE DEFINITION OF DISPOSABLE INCOME[20]

Under the definition of disposable income used up to now it has "mattered," in the sense of affecting the equilibrium values of some of the variables at a point in time, how the government finances its expenditures G as between taxes on the one hand and printing bonds and money on the other. At the same time it has not mattered in what proportion the government finances its deficit $p(G - T)$ —by printing bonds or money.[21] (We know that the division between $\dot{M}$ and $\dot{B}$ has not mattered because, while G and T both appeared in the system of Equations (I)–(VII), neither $\dot{M}$ nor $\dot{B}$ did.) These features of our model stem directly from the definition of expected real disposable income that we have employed. Here we show how these aspects of the model are altered when an alternative and more "illusion-free" concept of disposable income is utilized.

The alternative definition of disposable income is derived from a definition of wealth that subtracts the discounted value of future interest payments on the

---

[20] A more advanced and general treatment of the issues raised in this section is given by Robert Barro (1974).

[21] Of course, the rate of growth over time of $M + B$ is equal to the nominal deficit per unit time. How the deficit is financed affects the evolution of M and B over time and may matter once time is permitted to elapse, depending on whether the monetary authority subsequently undertakes offsetting open-market operations.

current stock of government debt from the definition of wealth used to derive our previous disposable income concept. That definition of real wealth was

$$W = qK + \frac{M}{p} + \frac{B}{p}.$$

Our new definition is

$$W_1 = qK + \frac{M}{p} + \frac{B}{p} - \frac{DTL}{p}$$

where DTL denotes the present value of the future interest payments on the current interest-bearing government debt. The rationale behind this definition is that these debt service charges are ultimately charges that the public is liable to pay through higher taxes in the future. The flow of interest payments (in dollars per unit time) on the current government debt is rB. The present value of future interest charges on the current debt is

$$DTL = \int_{t_0}^{\infty} rBe^{-r(t-t_0)} \, dt = B.$$

Thus, W_1 can now be written as $W_1 = qK + (M/p)$. Expected real disposable income is now defined as the rate at which households can consume while expecting to leave real wealth W_1 intact. The following definition of disposable incomes satisfies this definition:

$$Y_D' = Y - T - \delta K - \frac{\dot{DTL}}{p} - \frac{M}{p}\pi + (q-1)I$$

$$= Y - T - \delta K - \frac{\dot{B}}{p} - \frac{M}{p}\pi + (\dot{q}-1)I.$$

Substituting the national income identity and the government budget constraint into the above definition of disposable income yields

$$Y_D' = C + qI + \frac{\dot{M}}{p} - \frac{M}{p}\pi,$$

which verifies that Y_D' is the amount individuals can consume while expecting that they are leaving their real wealth W_1 intact.

The concept Y_D' differs from Y_D in two ways: it excludes expected capital losses on the interest-bearing portion of the public debt since interest-bearing government debt is not a part of wealth; and it deducts $\dot{B}/p$, which equals the real rate of increase of discounted tax liabilities that results from printing bonds at the rate $\dot{B}$ per unit time.

Now consider the effects of replacing Y_D with Y_D' in the consumption function (IV). The consumption function is the only relationship in which T appeared in the earlier version of our model. We immediately notice an important change that results from using our new definition of disposable income. In the old version of the model neither $\dot{M}$ nor $\dot{B}$ appeared in any of the equations determining the levels of our seven variables. That is what sufficed to show that it did not matter how the government financed its deficit. Now, however, $\dot{B}$ appears in our new version of Equation (IV)

$$C = C\left(Y - T - \delta K - \frac{\dot{B}}{p} - \frac{M}{p}\pi + (q - 1)I, r - \pi\right). \qquad \text{(IV')}$$

We can immediately show that now, given the level of G, it does not matter whether the government uses taxes or bond printing to finance its expenditures. If it offsets a change in taxes of dT by a change in bond-printing just sufficient to continue financing the current level of G, there is no effect on disposable income, and so no change in aggregate demand, given $r - \pi$. For holding G and $\dot{M}/p$ constant, we have from the government budget constraint

$$dT = -d(\dot{B}/p).$$

Such a simultaneous change in taxes and bond-printing is easily seen to leave disposable income Y_D' unaltered, and so to leave aggregate demand unaffected. It follows that none of our seven variables is affected by changes in the extent to which government expenditures are financed by T on the one hand or $\dot{B}/p$ on the other.

   Under certain very special additional conditions it is possible to show that a more general conclusion follows, namely that it does not matter whether the government finances its expenditures by collecting taxes, printing bonds, or printing money. In particular, we assume that the interest elasticity of the demand for money is zero, i.e., $m_r = 0$. We also assume that at each instant $\pi = \dot{p}/p$. From our discussion in Section 9, we know that this last assumption cannot be made lightly. We shall proceed by assuming that while $\pi = \dot{p}/p$ at any moment, people expect this same rate of inflation to prevail over the indefinite future. This means that we do not equate the expected magnitude $\dot{\pi}$ with the right-hand time derivative of $\dot{p}/p$. Instead, we simply assume that $\dot{\pi}$ is zero. Thus people are assumed to foresee the first time derivative of the logarithm of the price level, but not the second time derivative. This assumption makes $\dot{\pi}$ exogenous and permits us to determine both p and $\dot{p}/p$ at an instant, given the exogenous variables and their right-hand time derivatives.

   Differentiating the portfolio balance condition with respect to time and solving for $\dot{p}/p$, we have

$$\frac{\dot{p}}{p} = \frac{\dot{M}}{M} - \frac{m_Y}{M/p}\dot{Y}.$$

The system that we describe is one in which $\dot{Y}$ can be viewed as being determined by the right-hand time derivatives of Equations (I)–(III). In addition, the system is one in which $\dot{K}$, which is determined by Equations (IV)–(VI), is independent of π. It then follows that $\dot{Y}$ will be independent of π and $\dot{M}/M$. Taking the total differential of the above equation for $\dot{p}/p$, which equals π, gives

$$d\pi = d\left(\frac{\dot{M}}{M}\right) - \frac{m_Y((M/p)\,d\dot{Y} - \dot{Y}m_r\,d\pi)}{(M/p)^2}.$$

Since $d\dot{Y}$ will always be zero for the experiments that we shall describe and since $m_r = 0$, we write the above differential as

$$d\pi = d\left(\frac{\dot{M}}{M}\right) = \frac{d\dot{M}}{M} - \frac{\dot{M}}{M}\frac{dM}{M}.$$

Since we shall be studying a case in which $dM = 0$, we have $d\pi = d\dot{M}/M$. Now we seek to evaluate the effect on disposable income Y_D' of an increase in money creation that results from financing more of government expenditures by money creation and less by taxes and bond-printing. One effect on disposable income comes about as the result of the higher rate of expected inflation that accompanies the higher actual rate of inflation that is caused by the higher rate of money creation. The effect on disposable income of the higher rate of money creation is found by evaluating $d((M/p)\pi)$, which is the differential of the expected capital loss on the real money supply. We have

$$d\left(\frac{M}{p}\,\pi\right) = \pi m_r\,dr + \frac{M}{p}\,d\pi = \pi m_r\,d\pi + \frac{M}{p}\,d\pi = \pi m_r\,\frac{d\dot{M}}{M} + \frac{d\dot{M}}{p}.$$

But since we are assuming that $m_r = 0$, we have $d((M/p)\pi) = d\dot{M}/p$. Now note that

$$d\left(\frac{\dot{M}}{p}\right) = \frac{d\dot{M}}{p} - \frac{\dot{M}}{p}\frac{dp}{p}$$

and that, since $m_r = 0$, the rise in π does nothing to cause p to change. Thus we have that $d((M/p)\pi) = d(\dot{M}/p)$. Taking the total differential of the government budget constraint gives

$$dG = dT + d\left(\frac{\dot{M}}{p}\right) + d\left(\frac{\dot{B}}{p}\right);$$

or, since $d((M/p)\pi) = d(\dot{M}/p)$, $dG = dT + d(\dot{B}/p) + d((M/p)\pi)$. It follows that on our assumptions disposable income is not affected by changing from one means of financing government expenditures to another, given the level of government expenditures, for

$$dY_d' = d(Y + (q - 1)I - \delta K) - dT - d\left(\frac{\dot{B}}{p}\right) - d\left(\frac{M}{p}\,\pi\right)$$
$$= d(Y + (q - 1)I - \delta K) - dG.$$

Thus it does not matter how the government finances its expenditures, whether by taxes, money creation, or bond creation.

This is a system in which the traditional rationale for taxing rather than printing bonds and money breaks down. That is, an increase in taxes, holding G constant, does not affect the rate of capital accumulation. For notice that since $S + C = Y_D'$, we have

$$S + C = Y - \delta K - T + (q - 1)I - \frac{M}{p}\pi - \frac{\dot{B}}{p}.$$

Substituting the national income identity and the government budget constraint into the above equation and rearranging yields

$$S = qI + \frac{\dot{M}}{p} - \frac{M}{p}\pi.$$

Since $d(\dot{M}/p) = d((M/p)\pi)$, it follows that $dS = q\, dI$, i.e., that saving equals investment at the margin, in the sense that, holding G constant, changes in S at a point in time are accompanied by equal changes in qI, regardless of the setting for T. Whether or not the government finances its expenditures by taxing has no impact on the economy's rate of capital accumulation and hence its rate of physical growth.

11. NEUTRALITY

Macroeconomic models like the one we have been studying possess a characteristic known as neutrality. Suppose we have a macroeconomic model that consists of m structural equations relating m endogenous variables $z_1, \ldots, z_m$ and n exogenous variables $x_1, \ldots, x_n$. Suppose the first m_1 endogenous variables are expressed in units involving the monetary unit of account, e.g., dollars or dollars per unit of output or dollars per man hour. The remaining $m - m_1$ endogenous variables are measured in "real" units, units not involving the monetary unit of account. Similarly suppose that the first n_1 exogenous variables are measured in units of money, while the remaining $n - n_1$ are not. The system of m structural equations can be written as

$$g_1(z_1, \ldots, z_m, x_1, \ldots, x_n) = 0$$

$$g_2(z_1, \ldots, z_m, x_1, \ldots, x_n) = 0$$

$$\vdots \tag{45}$$

$$g_m(z_1, \ldots, z_m, x_1, \ldots, x_n) = 0.$$

Suppose that for the particular values of the exogenous variables $x_1{}^0, \ldots, x_n{}^0$ the system is in equilibrium provided that the endogenous variables assume the particular values $z_1{}^0, \ldots, z_m{}^0$. Those values of the z's and the x's satisfy the system of equations (45). The model is said to possess the property of *neutrality* if the particular values $\lambda z_1^0, \ldots, \lambda z_{m_1}^0$, $z_{m_1+1}^0, \ldots, z_m^0$ and $\lambda x_1^0, \ldots, \lambda x_{n_1}^0$, $x_{n_1+1}^0, \ldots, x_n^0$ for any scalar $\lambda > 0$ also satisfy the equilibrium conditions (45). That is, the system is a neutral one if, on starting from an initial position of equilibrium, multiplying all those endogenous and exogenous variables that are measured in the monetary unit by a positive scalar leaves the system in equilibrium.

It is easily verified that the model we have been studying possesses the property of neutrality. Thus, consider the model formed by Equations (I)–(VII). Multiply all variables measured in nominal or dollar units by the scalar λ. If the system was initially in equilibrium at a price level of p_0 and a wage rate of w_0, it will now have an equilibrium with price λp_0 and wage λw_0, while the equilibrium values of Y, N, C, I, and r are unchanged.

A system will possess the property of neutrality if it can be written so that each equation involves only magnitudes measured in dollar-free "real" units. Thus, if everywhere there appears a dollar-denominated magnitude, like the stock of money or bonds or the wage rate, it is divided through by another dollar-denominated variable, like the price level or the wage rate, then the model is one that describes relations among real magnitudes. If this is true, then doubling or tripling the nominal magnitudes cannot have any influence on the equilibrium values of those real variables. The system formed by Equations (I)–(VII) is an example of one in which variables measured in dollars never appear except where they are divided by the price level. Consequently multiplying M, B, w, and p by any $\lambda > 0$ does not change the equilibrium values of the real variables determined by that system. The real variables determined by the model are Y, N, C, I, r, w/p, and M/p.

12. DICHOTOMY

A macroeconomic model is said to dichotomize if a subset of equations can determine the values of all real variables with the level of the money supply playing no role in determining the equilibrium value of any real variable. Given the equilibrium values of the real variables, the level of the money supply helps determine the equilibrium values of all nominal variables that are endogenous but cannot influence any real variable. In a system that dichotomizes the equilibrium values of all real variables are independent of the absolute price level. In such a system "money is a veil."

As we have seen, the system formed by Equations (I)–(VII) does not dichotomize unless $M + B$ equals zero initially. Now consider the system discussed in Section 10, which is formed by replacing (IV) with (IV'), which we repeat here for convenience:

$$C = C\left(Y - T - \delta K - \frac{\dot{B}}{p} - \frac{M}{p}\pi + (q-1)I, r - \pi \right). \tag{IV'}$$

Substituting $m(r, Y)$ for M/p in (IV′) gives

$$C = C\left(Y - T - \delta K - \frac{\dot{B}}{p} - \pi m(r, Y) + (q - 1)I, r - \pi\right). \qquad \text{(IV″)}$$

The system formed by Equations (I)–(III), (IV″), (V)–(VII) is one that dichotomizes under certain assumptions about financing the government debt. To take a simple special case first, suppose $\dot{B}$ equals zero, so that the deficit is financed by printing money. Then Equations (I)–(III), (IV″), (V), and (VI) alone are capable of determining all real variables, it not being necessary to know the money supply and the price level in order to determine the equilibrium values of the real variables. More generally, suppose that M and $\dot{M}$ always vary proportionately, so that, for example, a doubling of the level of the money supply is accompanied by a doubling of the right-hand time derivative of the money supply. Under this constraint, the system under study does dichotomize. This can be seen most easily if the government flow budget constraint is used to rewrite (IV″) as

$$C = C\left(Y - T - \delta K - (G - T) + \frac{\dot{M}}{p} - m(r, Y)\pi + (q - 1)I, r - \pi\right).$$

Suppose the system is initially in equilibrium. Then doubling M, $\dot{M}$, p, and w and keeping all real variables unchanged leaves the system in equilibrium. No change in aggregate demand at the initial r and Y is induced by such proportional changes in M, $\dot{M}$, p, and w.

Obviously, "neutrality" and "dichotomy" are distinct concepts. A system in which there is neutrality need not dichotomize, while a system in which "money is a veil" need not be one that satisfies our definition of a neutral system. To take an (admittedly artificial) example of a system that dichotomizes but in which neutrality fails, consider the system that consists of Equations (I)–(III), (V)–(VII), and the following replacement for (IV):

$$C = C(Y - T - \delta K + (q - 1)I, r - \pi, M + B),$$
$$1 > C_1 > 0, C_2 < 0, C_3 > 0. \qquad \text{(IV″)}$$

Under the constraint on open-market operations, this is a system that dichotomizes. Increasing the money supply subject to $dM + dB = 0$ increases the price level and money wage proportionately but leaves all real variables unaffected. The differentials of the first six equations involve only the differentials of real variables, which is what yields the dichotomy. On the other hand, neutrality is not a characteristic of the system since increasing M, B, w, and p proportionately will not leave the system in equilibrium if we start from a position of equilibrium. Instead, the increase in $M + B$ increases intended consumption, causing the interest rate to rise and the price level and money wage to rise more than proportionately with the increase in the stocks of money and bonds.

13. CONCLUSIONS

In the classical model the level of employment is determined in the labor market. The assumption of perfectly flexible money wages and prices permits the labor market to "clear," a real wage being determined at which the quantity of labor demanded by firms exactly equals that which workers are willing to supply. There can be no involuntary unemployment since the volume of employment is always equal to the labor supply forthcoming at the prevailing real wage. Everyone who wants to work at the existing real wage is employed. If for some reason unemployment were to emerge because of deficient aggregate demand, the unemployed workers would bid down the *money* wage. Since firms are competitive, this would lead in the first instance to proportionate reductions in the price level, which would in itself leave the real wage unchanged and do nothing to alleviate unemployment. But the reduction in the price level would increase the supply of real balances, causing the interest rate to fall. That would increase the level of aggregate demand for goods and services and cause the level of employment to rise.

Aggregate demand plays no role in determining the volume of employment and output, although it does affect their rates of growth over time. Instead, exogenous changes in aggregate demand cause whatever adjustments in the interest rate that are necessary to bring the demand for goods into equality with the supply of goods, which is determined in the labor market. The interest rate plays the role of totally alleviating any "Keynesian" problems of deficient aggregate demand.

Finally, the role of money depends on the precise definition of perceived real disposable income. Whatever that definition, however, the money supply plays no role in determining the levels of employment and output, although, as we have seen, under some circumstances it may affect their rates of growth over time.

REFERENCES

Agnew, R. P. (1942) *Differential Equations*, 1st ed. New York: McGraw-Hill.
Barro, R. J. (1974). "Are Government Bonds Net Wealth?" *Journal of Political Economy*, Vol. 82, No. 6, pp. 1095–1117.
Barro, R. J. and Grossman, H. J. (1971). "A General Disequilibrium Model of Income and Employment." *American Economic Review*, Vol. LXI, No. 1, pp. 82–93.
Cagan, P. (1956). "The Monetary Dynamics of Hyperinflation." In *Studies in the Quantity Theory of Money* (M. Friedman, ed.). Chicago, Illinois: Univ. of Chicago Press.
Clower, R. (1965). "The Keynesian Counterrevolution: A Theoretical Appraisal." In *Theory of Interest Rates, Conference on the Theory of Interest and Money, Royaumont, France, 1962.* (Hahn, F. H. and Breckling, F. P. R. eds.). London: Macmillan, and New York: St. Martin's.
Friedman, M. (1968). "The Role of Monetary Policy." *American Economic Review*, Vol. LVIII, No. 1, pp. 1–17.
Gabel, R. A. and Roberts, R. A. (1973). *Signals and Linear Systems*. New York: Wiley.

Hansen, L. P. and T. J. Sargent (1981), "Formulating and Estimating Continuous Time Rational Expectations Models." *Federal Reserve Bank of Minneapolis, Staff Report #75*, Oct.

Hansen, L. and Sargent, T. J. (1983). "Aggregation Over Time and the Inverse Optimal Predictor Problem for Adaptive Expectations in Continuous Time." *International Economic Review*, Vol. 24, No. 1, pp. 1–20.

Henderson, D. W. and Sargent, T. J. (1973). "Monetary and Fiscal Policy in a Two-Sector Aggregate Model." *American Economic Review*, Vol. 63, No. 3, pp. 345–365.

McCallum, B. T. (1984). "Are Bond-Financed Deficits Inflationary? A Ricardian Analysis." *Journal of Political Economy*, Vol. 92, No. 1, pp. 123–135.

Merton, R. C. (1971). "Optimum Consumption and Portfolio Rules in a Continuous Time Model." *Journal of Economic Theory*, Vol. 3, No. 4, p. 373–413.

Samuelson, P. A. (1963). *Foundations of Economic Analysis*. Cambridge, Massachusetts: Harvard Univ. Press.

Sargent, T. J. and Wallace, N. (1973a). "Rational Expectations and the Dynamics of Hyperinflation." *International Economic Review*, Vol. 63, No. 3, pp. 328–350.

Sargent, T. J. and Wallace, N. (1973b). "The Stability of Money and Growth with Perfect Foresight." *Econometrica*, Vol. 41, No. 6, pp. 1043–1048.

Sargent, T. J. and Wallace, N. (1981). "Some Unpleasant Monetarist Arithmetic." *Federal Reserve Bank of Minneapolis Quarterly Review*, Vol. 5, No. 3, pp. 1–17.

Sargent, T. J. (1977). "The Demand for Money During Hyperinflations Under Rational Expectations, I." *International Economic Review*, Vol. 18, No. 1, pp. 59–82.

Taylor, A. E. and Mann, W. R. (1972). *Advanced Calculus*, 2nd ed. Lexington, Massachusetts: Xerox.

Tobin, J. (1969). "A General Equilibrium Approach to Monetary Theory." *Journal of Money, Credit, and Banking*, Vol. 1, No. 1, pp. 15–29.

CHAPTER II

THE KEYNESIAN MODEL

1. GENERAL ANALYSIS

The standard "Keynesian" model has as its outstanding characteristics that the full employment of labor is not automatic and that the volume of employment at a point in time is in part determined by monetary and fiscal policies. These features stand in sharp contrast to those of the classical model, in which full employment is guaranteed and fiscal and monetary variables have no impact on output and employment at a point in time, though they may influence the growth rates of employment and output.

We shall consider the Keynesian model as consisting of the following six equations:

$$Y = F(K, N) \tag{1}$$

$$w/p = F_N \tag{2}$$

$$C = C\left(Y - T - \delta K - \frac{M + B}{p}\pi, r - \pi\right) \tag{3}$$

$$I = I(q(K, N, r - \pi, \delta) - 1) \tag{4}$$

$$C + I + G + \delta K = Y \tag{5}$$

$$M/p = m(r, Y). \tag{6}$$

There are two differences, one inessential and the other essential, between this Keynesian model and the classical model presented above. To take the inessential difference first, the consumption function in the above model incorporates a simpler concept of disposable income than the one used in our classical model. In particular, the disposable income concept

$$Y - T - \delta K - ((M + B)/p)\pi$$

ignores any effects of discrepancies between the equity-market and reproduction-cost value of the stock of capital, i.e., it ignores the effects of movements of q

away from unity. In effect, the disposable income concept used here corresponds to a wealth concept $W = ((M + B)/p) + K$, in the sense that it is the rate that individuals perceive they can consume while leaving intact their real wealth so defined. We use this simplified definition of disposable income to streamline the presentation somewhat. Little harm is thereby done since the ingredients for analyzing things under the more complicated definition of income have been presented with the classical model.

The essential difference between the classical model and the Keynesian model is the absence from the latter of the classical labor supply curve combined with the labor market equilibrium condition. Since there is one fewer equation in the Keynesian model, it can determine only six endogenous variables instead of the seven that are determined in the classical model. To close the Keynesian model, the money wage w is regarded as an exogenous variable, one that at a point in time can be regarded as being given from outside the model, perhaps from the *past* behavior of itself and other endogenous or exogenous variables. While w is regarded as a datum, unaffected contemporaneously by changes in the other parameters of the model, we need not assume that it is constant through time. The time derivative dw/dt can be nonzero and might very well itself be functionally related to the variables of the model.[1] All that we require is that the value of dw/dt implied by any such relationship be finite so that w cannot jump at a point in time as a result of its interactions with other endogenous and exogenous variables.

It bears emphasizing that the equation that we have deleted in moving from the classical to the Keynesian model, $N = N^S(w/p)$, is a combination of the two equations

$$N^S = N^S(w/p) \qquad \text{and} \qquad N = N^S,$$

the first being a supply schedule, the second an equilibrium condition. Note that we continue to require that employment satisfy the labor demand schedule (2). We shall think of the labor supply schedule $N^S = N^S(w/p)$ as being satisfied and helping to determine the unemployment rate. But since N^S nowhere appears in Equations (1)–(6), it plays no role in determining the equilibrium position of the model. The force of removing the classical equation $N = N^S(w/p)$ should be thought of as removing the labor market equilibrium condition. Indeed, so long as we do not require the equality $N = N^S$, the labor supply schedule $N^S = N^S(w/p)$ can be appended as a seventh equation of the Keynesian model, one that is easily seen not to interact with the first six equations. Usually, the model is assumed to reach equilibrium in a position satisfying $N < N^S$, so that there is an excess supply of labor.

Removing the labor schedule—labor market equilibrium condition and making the money wage exogenous are the essential changes that must be made

---

[1] The Phillips curve is an example of what we have in mind.

in the classical model in order to arrive at the Keynesian model. The asset structure, the constraints on the behavior of the government, and the assumptions underlying the remaining six equations are all as they were in the classical model. Thus, the Keynesian model consists of six equations in the six endogenous variables p, Y, N, r, C, and I. The exogenous variables are w, M, G, T, π, δ, and K as well as the parameters determining the shapes of the various schedules.

We begin our analysis of the model by totally differentiating Equations (1)–(6). In what follows we shall assume $dK = d\delta = 0$. Then we obtain the following system of six equations in the differentials of our six variables:

$$dY = F_N \, dN \tag{i}$$

$$\frac{dw}{w} - \frac{dp}{p} = \frac{F_{NN}}{F_N} \, dN \tag{ii}$$

$$dC = C_1 \, dY - C_1 \, dT - C_1 \frac{M + B}{p} \, d\pi$$

$$- C_1 \pi \left(\frac{dM + dB}{p} - \frac{dp \, (M + B)}{p^2} \right) + C_2 \, dr - C_2 \, d\pi \tag{iii}$$

$$dI = I'q_N \, dN + I'q_{r-\pi} \, dr - I'q_{r-\pi} \, d\pi \tag{iv}$$

$$dC + dI + dG = dY \tag{v}$$

$$\frac{dM}{p} - \frac{dp}{p} \frac{M}{p} = m_r \, dr + m_Y \, dY. \tag{vi}$$

The differential of the consumption function can be simplified by recalling the constraint on open market operations, $dM + dB = 0$. The system can then be written as the following matrix equation:

$$
\begin{bmatrix}
1 & -F_N & 0 & 0 & 0 & 0 \\
0 & F_{NN}/F_N & 0 & 0 & 0 & 1/p \\
-C_1 & 0 & 1 & 0 & -C_2 & -C_1\pi(M + B)/p^2 \\
0 & -I'q_N & 0 & 1 & -I'q_{r-\pi} & 0 \\
1 & 0 & -1 & -1 & 0 & 0 \\
m_Y & 0 & 0 & 0 & m_r & M/p^2
\end{bmatrix}
\begin{bmatrix}
dY \\
dN \\
dC \\
dI \\
dr \\
dp
\end{bmatrix}
$$

$$
=
\begin{bmatrix}
0 \\
dw/w \\
-C_1 \, dT - (C_2 + C_1((M + B)/p)) \, d\pi \\
-I'q_{r-\pi} \, d\pi \\
dG \\
dM/p
\end{bmatrix}
$$

Inspection of the matrix on the left reveals that the system is *not* block recursive. That is, it is impossible to find an independent subset of equations that determines a subset of variables. Instead, interdependence is general, interactions occurring among all six variables. As a consequence, we should expect that a change in any one parameter will in general affect the equilibrium values of all of the variables at a point in time.

In order to solve the system we shall utilize Hicks's (1937) IS-LM curve apparatus. This simply entails adopting the strategy of collapsing Equations (i)–(iv) into a system of two equations in dY and dr, this being accomplished by eliminating dN, dp, dC, and dI by substitution. First we obtain the total differential of the IS curve, a schedule that shows the locus of combinations of the interest rate and output that satisfy Equation (5), the aggregate demand–aggregate supply equality, as well as satisfying the consumption, investment, and production schedules. Substituting (iii) and (iv) into (v) yields

$$C_1 \, dY - C_1 \, dT - C_1 \frac{M+B}{p} \, d\pi + C_1\pi \frac{M+B}{p} \frac{dp}{p} + C_2 \, dr - C_2 \, d\pi$$

$$+ I'q_N \, dN + I'q_{r-\pi} \, dr - I'q_{r-\pi} \, d\pi + dG = dY. \tag{7}$$

Solving (i) for dN and (ii) and (i) for dp/p yields

$$dN = \frac{1}{F_N} \, dY, \qquad \frac{dp}{p} = \frac{dw}{w} - \frac{F_{NN}}{F_N{}^2} \, dY.$$

Substituting these two expressions into (7) yields

$$C_1 \, dY - C_1 \, dT - C_1 \frac{M+B}{p} \, d\pi + C_1\pi \frac{M+B}{p}\left(\frac{dw}{w} - \frac{F_{NN}}{F_N{}^2} \, dY\right)$$

$$+ C_2 \, dr - C_2 \, d\pi + I' \frac{q_N}{F_N} \, dY + I'q_{r-\pi} \, dr - I'q_{r-\pi} \, d\pi + dG = dY,$$

which is the total differential of the IS curve. Rearranging yields

$$\left(1 - C_1 - I' \frac{q_N}{F_N} + C_1\pi \frac{M+B}{p} \frac{F_{NN}}{F_N{}^2}\right) dY$$

$$= -C_1 \, dT + dG + (C_2 + I'q_{r-\pi}) \, dr$$

$$+ \left(-I'q_{r-\pi} - C_2 - C_1 \frac{M+B}{p}\right) d\pi + C_1\pi \frac{M+B}{p} \frac{dw}{w}. \tag{8}$$

As with our analysis of the classical model, we shall begin by assuming that $M + B$ equals zero. Then (8) simplifies to

$$\left(1 - C_1 - I' \frac{q_N}{F_N}\right) dY = -C_1 \, dT + dG + (C_2 + I'q_{r-\pi}) \, dr - (I'q_{r-\pi} + C_2) \, d\pi. \tag{9}$$

The slope of the IS curve is given by

$$\frac{dr}{dY}\bigg|_{IS} = \frac{1 - C_1 - I'q_N/F_N}{C_2 + I'q_{r-\pi}}. \tag{10}$$

The denominator of the right-hand side is negative, while the numerator may be of either sign. It is positive if

$$1 - C_1 > I'q_N/F_N.$$

Now $1 - C_1$ is the marginal propensity to save out of disposable income. The expression $I'q_N/F_N$ represents the marginal propensity to invest out of income; to see this differentiate the investment schedule partially with respect to Y:

$$\frac{\partial I}{\partial Y} = \frac{\partial I}{\partial q}\frac{\partial q}{\partial N}\frac{\partial N}{\partial Y} = I'q_N\frac{1}{F_N}.$$

Accordingly, the IS curve will be downward sloping only if the marginal propensity to save exceeds the marginal propensity to invest out of income. We shall henceforth assume that this condition is satisfied. (The model can be stable even if this condition is violated, provided at least that the IS curve is less steep than the LM curve.)

To determine how the IS curve shifts when the parameters T, G, and π change, we use (9) to evaluate the partial derivatives of r with respect to each parameter, dY being set equal to zero:

$$\frac{\partial r}{\partial T}\bigg|_{IS} = \frac{C_1}{C_2 + I'q_{r-\pi}} < 0, \qquad \frac{\partial r}{\partial G}\bigg|_{IS} = \frac{-1}{C_2 + I'q_{r-\pi}} > 0, \qquad \frac{\partial r}{\partial \pi}\bigg|_{IS} = 1.$$

The IS curve shifts upward when taxes decrease or government expenditures increase; when anticipated inflation increases, the IS curve shifts upward by the amount of the increase in anticipated inflation.

The LM curve depicts the combinations of interest rates, and output that assure equality between the demand and supply for real balances, the production function and marginal condition for employment assumed to be satisfied. The differential of the LM curve is derived by using (i) and (ii) to eliminate dp from (vi). Thus,

$$\frac{dp}{p} = \frac{dw}{w} - \frac{F_{NN}}{F_N^2}dY.$$

Substituting the expression on the right for dp/p in (vi) yields

$$\frac{dM}{p} - \frac{M}{p}\frac{dw}{w} + \frac{M}{p}\frac{F_{NN}}{F_N^2}dY = m_r\,dr + m_Y\,dY.$$

Solving for dr yields

$$dr = \frac{1}{m_r}\left(\frac{dM}{p} - \frac{M}{p}\frac{dw}{w} + \left(\frac{F_{NN}}{F_N^2}\frac{M}{p} - m_Y\right)dY\right). \tag{11}$$

The slope of the LM curve is thus given by

$$\left.\frac{dr}{dY}\right|_{LM} = \frac{1}{m_r}\left(\frac{F_{NN}}{F_N^2}\frac{M}{p} - m_Y\right) > 0.$$

Notice that as m_r approaches zero, the LM curve approaches a vertical position; while as $m_r \to -\infty$, as is supposed in the case of the "liquidity trap," the slope of the LM curve approaches zero. By using (11) it is easily established how the LM curve shifts when w or M changes. Thus, setting $dY = 0$ in (11) and solving for dr we have

$$dr = \frac{1}{m_r}\left(\frac{dM}{p} - \frac{M}{p}\frac{dw}{w}\right).$$

This expression establishes that for a given level of income, if the money supply rises, the interest rate must fall (provided $-\infty < m_r$) in order to maintain equilibrium between the demand and supply for money. Similarly, when money wages fall, the interest rate must also fall, again provided $-\infty < m_r$, in order to keep the money market in equilibrium.

An interest rate and an income level that satisfy the six equations of the model are determined at the intersection of the IS and LM curves, as depicted in Figure 1. So long as the IS curve is downward sloping and the LM curve is upward sloping, we are assured that the equilibrium is unique (if it exists). Using our knowledge of how the IS and LM curves shift when the various parameters of the model change, it is easy to ascertain the effects of those changes on the equilibrium rate of output and rate of interest. For example, if the level of government expenditures rises, the IS curve shifts upward and to the right, while

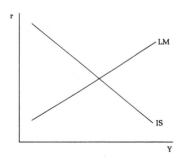

FIGURE 1

the LM curve is left unchanged. This drives both income and the interest rate upward, provided that the LM curve is not vertical—in which case the interest rate alone rises—or horizontal—in which case only the rate of output rises. An increase in the money supply shifts the LM curve toward the right, which drives the interest rate down and output upward, provided that the LM curve is not horizontal.

We can solve the system analytically by substituting (11) into (9). We obtain

$$\left(1 - C_1 - I' \frac{q_N}{F_N}\right) dY = -C_1 \, dT + dG - (C_2 + I'q_{r-\pi}) \, d\pi$$

$$+ \frac{C_2 + I'q_{r-\pi}}{m_r} \left(\frac{dM}{p} - \frac{M}{p} \frac{dw}{w} + \left(\frac{F_{NN}}{F_N^2} \frac{M}{p} - m_Y\right) dY\right)$$

or

$$\left(1 - C_1 - I' \frac{q_N}{F_N} - \frac{C_2 + I'q_{r-\pi}}{m_r}\left(\frac{F_{NN}}{F_N^2} \frac{M}{p} - m_Y\right)\right) dY$$

$$= -C_1 \, dT + dG - (C_2 + I'q_{r-\pi}) \, d\pi + \frac{C_2 + I'q_{r-\pi}}{m_r}\left(\frac{dM}{p} - \frac{M}{p} \frac{dw}{w}\right).$$

$$(12)$$

This is the total differential of the reduced form of Y. On our assumption that $1 - C_1 > I'q_N/F_N$, the coefficient on dY is positive (notice that it may be positive even if that condition is violated). Let H now stand for the coefficient on dY in (12). Then the reduced form partial derivatives of Y with respect to T, G, π, M, and w are given by:

$$\frac{\partial Y}{\partial T} = \frac{-C_1}{H} \le 0, \qquad \frac{\partial Y}{\partial G} = \frac{1}{H} \ge 0$$

$$\frac{\partial Y}{\partial \pi} = \frac{-(I'q_{r-\pi} + C_2)}{H} \ge 0, \qquad \frac{\partial Y}{\partial M} = \frac{C_2 + I'q_{r-\pi}}{m_r pH} \ge 0,$$

$$\frac{\partial Y}{\partial w} = \frac{-(C_2 + I'q_{r-\pi})M}{m_r pwH} \le 0.$$

Notice that as $m_r \to 0$, $H \to \infty$, so that $\partial Y/\partial G$, $\partial Y/\partial T$, and $\partial Y/\partial \pi$ approach zero. On the other hand, as $m_r \to -\infty$, $\partial Y/\partial M$ and $\partial Y/\partial w$ both approach zero. Also, if $C_2 = I' = 0$, then $\partial Y/\partial M = \partial Y/\partial w = 0$. Thus, if neither consumption nor investment expenditures respond to variations in the interest rate, changes in the money supply and the money wage have no effects on output. All of those special cases are easy to analyze graphically using the IS and LM curves.[2] More generally, we might characterize the relative potency of monetary and fiscal policy by a "bang-per-buck ratio" namely

$$\frac{\partial Y}{\partial G} \bigg/ \frac{\partial Y}{\partial M} \, p,$$

or the ratio of the derivative of real output with respect to real government expenditures to the derivative of real output with respect to the nominal money supply divided by the price level. This ratio is given by

$$\frac{\partial Y}{\partial G} \bigg/ \frac{\partial Y}{\partial M} \, p = \frac{m_r}{C_2 + I' q_{r-\pi}}.$$

Under this definition, changes in real government expenditures are relatively more potent the more responsive to the interest rate is the demand for real balances and the less responsive to real interest are consumption and investment demand. (Our bang-per-buck measure of the relative potency of monetary and fiscal policies is of very little practical use since what is important for policy-making in the real world is the relative uncertainty associated with using the two kinds of policy. We are ignoring uncertainty here and hence, except in certain limiting cases, cannot say anything about the relative merits of relying on monetary as opposed to fiscal policy to achieve desired real output and price objectives.[3])

Having determined the equilibrium interest rate and output, the equilibrium levels of N, p, C, and I are easily determined. Thus, N is determined from (1), p from (2), I from (4), and C from (3).

---

[2] Notice that if $m_r = -\infty$, from (12) we have

$$\frac{\partial Y}{\partial G} = \frac{1}{1 - C_1 - I'(q_N/F_N)} \quad \text{and} \quad \frac{\partial Y}{\partial T} = \frac{-C_1}{1 - C_1 - I'(q_N/F_N)}.$$

The expression for $\partial Y/\partial G$ is the "super-multiplier" of Hicks, the reciprocal of the difference between the marginal propensity to save and the marginal propensity to invest out of income. If I' equals zero, so that investment does not respond to variations in income, the above expressions are identical with the standard simple Keynesian multiplier formulas. Also, notice that if I' equals zero, the response of output to a change in government expenditures matched by an equal change in taxes is given by

$$\frac{\partial Y}{\partial G}\bigg|_{dT = dG} = 1,$$

which is a version of the so-called balanced-budget multiplier.

[3] Optimal policy in the presence of uncertainty is studied in Chapter XVII.

2. STABILITY

As in the classical model, it is usual to posit that if aggregate demand exceeds aggregate supply, the price level is bid up; while if the demand for real balances exceeds the supply, the interest rate is bid up. In the Keynesian model, however, output varies with the price level as the system moves along the aggregate supply schedule

$$p = p(Y, w, K),$$

the schedule that we implicitly derived above by eliminating N from Equations (1) and (2). As shown above, the partial derivative of p with respect to Y along this curve is given in

$$\frac{dp}{p} = -\frac{F_{NN}}{F_N{}^2} dY$$

or

$$dY = -\frac{w}{p^2} \frac{F_N}{F_{NN}} dp. \tag{13}$$

During the adjustment to equilibrium, we shall insist that the system remain continuously on the aggregate supply curve, so that (13) is satisfied continuously.

We posit the following differential equations for p and r, where s is a "time" index:

$$dp/ds = \alpha[C(Y - T - \delta K, r - \pi) + I(q(N, K, r - \pi, \delta) - 1) + G + \delta K - Y],$$
$$\alpha' > 0, \quad \alpha(0) = 0$$

$$dr/ds = \beta[m(r, Y) - M/p], \qquad \beta' > 0, \quad \beta(0) = 0.$$

Taking a linear approximation to these equations around equilibrium values and using (13), we have

$$\frac{dp}{ds} = \alpha'\left(1 - C_1 - I'\frac{q_N}{F_N}\right)\frac{w}{p^2}\frac{F_N}{F_{NN}}(p - p_0) + \alpha'(C_2 + I'q_{r-\pi})(r - r_0),$$

$$\frac{dr}{ds} = \beta'\left(\frac{M}{p^2} - m_Y\frac{w}{p^2}\frac{F_N}{F_{NN}}\right)(p - p_0) + \beta'm_r(r - r_0),$$

where zero subscripts denote initial equilibrium values. This is a first-order differential equation whose characteristic equation is

$$\begin{vmatrix} a - \lambda & b \\ c & d - \lambda \end{vmatrix} = \lambda^2 - (a + d)\lambda + (ad - bc) = 0,$$

where

$$a = \alpha'\left(1 - C_1 - I'\frac{q_N}{F_N}\right)\frac{w}{p^2}\frac{F_N}{F_{NN}}, \qquad b = \alpha'(C_2 + I'q_{r-\pi}),$$

$$c = \beta'\left(\frac{M}{p^2} - m_Y\frac{w}{p^2}\frac{F_N}{F_{NN}}\right), \qquad d = \beta'm_r.$$

Necessary and sufficient conditions for the system to be stable (i.e., have roots with negative real parts) are $-(a + d) > 0$ and $ad - bc > 0$ (see Samuelson, 1963, pp. 430–431). The first condition can be written

$$\alpha'\left(1 - C_1 - I'\frac{q_N}{F_N}\right)\frac{w}{p^2}\frac{F_N}{F_{NN}} + \beta'm_r < 0, \tag{14}$$

while the second condition is

$$m_r\left(1 - C_1 - I'\frac{q_N}{F_N}\right)\frac{w}{p^2}\frac{F_N}{F_{NN}} - (C_2 + I'q_{r-\pi})\left(\frac{M}{p^2} - m_Y\frac{w}{p^2}\frac{F_N}{F_{NN}}\right) > 0,$$

which is equivalent with

$$\frac{1 - C_1 - I'q_N/F_N}{C_2 + I'q_{r-\pi}} - \frac{1}{m_r}\left(\frac{M}{w}\frac{F_{NN}}{F_N} - m_Y\right) < 0 \tag{15}$$

or

$$\left.\frac{\partial r}{\partial Y}\right|_{IS} - \left.\frac{\partial r}{\partial Y}\right|_{LM} < 0,$$

so that a necessary condition for stability is that the LM curve is steeper than the IS curve. This condition is automatically satisfied when the LM curve is upward sloping and the IS curve is downward sloping. It can still be satisfied if the IS curve is upward sloping, provided that the LM curve is more steeply sloped. Since α' and β' are both positive, condition (14) will be satisfied so long as $1 - C_1 - I'q_N/F_N > 0$, which is our condition for the IS curve to be downward sloping. If $1 - C_1 - I'q_N/F_N < 0$, condition (14) can still be satisfied, but it will depend then on the relative sizes of the adjustment speeds α' and β'.

As before, these differential equations do *not* literally describe the evolution of p and r in real time t. For the model already determines p, r, and the other endogenous variables at each point in time, and hence determines their evolution through time. As earlier, we shall interpret the differential equations of this section as describing the pressure toward adjustment, the adjustments themselves occurring instantaneously. Thus, we regard the differential equations of this section as holding with the adjustment speeds α' and β' being driven toward infinity.

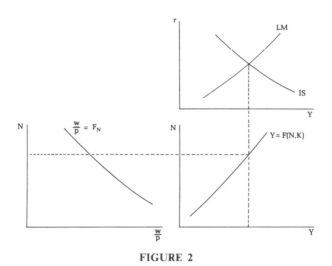

FIGURE 2

Some Experiments

We utilize a graphical apparatus (Figure 2) with IS-LM curves in the upper panel, the production function in the lower right panel, and the demand schedule for labor in the lower left panel. Equilibrium output and interest are determined at the intersection of the IS and LM curves. The production function then determines employment; then given N the demand schedule for labor determines the real wage w/p. Since w is exogenous, p is thereby determined.

We analyze the effects of several shocks.

An increase in government expenditures: An increase in G shifts the IS curve outward, sparking an upward movement along the LM curve, thereby in general causing both r and Y to increase. The rise in Y requires a larger N, which in turn requires a lower real wage and therefore, with w fixed, a higher price level.

Our stability analysis suggests that the following adjustment pressures materialize to propel the system (instantaneously) from the initial equilibrium to the new one. At the initial values of r and Y, the rise in G causes aggregate demand $C(\quad) + I(\quad) + G + \delta K$ to exceed aggregate supply $F(K, N)$. That causes the price level p to be bid upward, causing the real wage to fall since w is fixed, and thereby causing employers to expand employment N. So output is driven up. At the initial r and the expanded Y and p, the demand for nominal balances rises, creating an excess demand for money. Households attempt to acquire more money by disposing of bonds and equities, but in the aggregate they cannot since the quantities of money, bonds, and equities are fixed. What happens then is that the interest rate r is bid upward until households are satisfied with the amount of money in existence. The rise in r causes I and C to fall, which helps reduce aggregate demand and moderate the magnitude of the increase in Y required to reestablish equilibrium.

An increase in the money supply: An increase in M shifts the LM curve downward, sparking a movement downward along the IS curve, causing r to fall and Y to rise. The increase in Y means that N must rise, w/p must fall, and p must rise. Both C and I rise, due to the effects of the lower interest rate and higher income.

The adjustment pressures can be described as follows. At the initial r, Y combination, the open market operation disturbs portfolio balance, leaving households with more money than they want. Consequently, they attempt to move into bonds and equities and out of money. The effect is to bid the interest rate down. But that in turn stimulates I and C, causing flow aggregate demand to exceed flow aggregate supply. This causes the price level to be bid up, forcing a fall in the real wage and creating incentives for entrepreneurs to expand employment. As N increases, so does output Y.

An increase in the money wage (the Keynes effect): An increase in w causes the LM curve to shift to the left, causing a movement upward along the IS curve. This means that r must rise and Y must fall. Then from the production function N must fall, and from the demand schedule for labor w/p must rise. From the portfolio equilibrium condition

$$M/p = m(r, Y)$$

we know that p must rise since the rise in r and fall in Y cause $m(r, Y)$ to fall; p must rise to cause M/p to fall; C and I both fall, both because of the fall in Y and the rise in r.

The adjustment pressures work as follows. At the intial Y, r combination, the rise in w causes a proportional increase in p, as competitive producers simply pass on the wage increase. The rise in p stimulates the demand for nominal balances, thereby upsetting portfolio equilibrium and leaving an excess demand for money. The interest rate is bid upward as households attempt to dispose of bonds and equities and acquire money. The rise in r in turn restricts I and C, causing aggregate demand to be less than aggregate supply. This causes prices to start falling, causing the real wage to rise, employment to fall, and output to decrease.

Thus, an increase in the money wage works very much like a decrease in the money supply. The adverse effect of an increase in the money wage on employment and output is commonly known as the "Keynes effect."

The reader is invited to analyze the effects of changes in other exogenous variables and to analyze the adjustment pressures driving the system toward the new equilibrium in each case.

3. ANALYSIS OF "COST-PUSH" AND "DEMAND-PULL" INFLATION

It should be apparent that we could easily have solved the system (i)–(vi) by collapsing it into two equations in another pair of variables, for example dp and dY. Thus, the solution of (1) and (2) can be taken to represent the aggregate

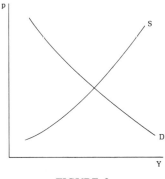

FIGURE 3

supply schedule in the p-Y plane. Its differential, derived from (i) and (ii), is given by

$$dY = \frac{F_N^2}{F_{NN}} \frac{dw}{w} - \frac{F_N^2}{F_{NN}} \frac{dp}{p}.$$

Aggregate supply is seen to vary directly with the price level; at a given price level aggregate supply increases when the money wage falls. A typical aggregate supply schedule is depicted in Figure 3. An aggregate demand schedule in the p-Y plane can be derived from Equations (3)–(6). Its differential, derived from (iii)–(vi), is given by

$$dY\left(1 - C_1 - I'\frac{q_N}{F_N} + \frac{C_2 + I'q_{r-\pi}}{m_r} m_Y\right)$$
$$= -C_1\,dT + dG - (C_2 + I'q_{r-\pi})\,d\pi$$
$$+ \frac{(C_2 + I'q_{r-\pi})}{m_r}\frac{dM}{p} - \frac{(C_2 + I'q_{r-\pi})}{m_r}\frac{M}{p^2}\,dp.$$

On our usual assumptions, the slope of the aggregate demand schedule is negative, such as is true of the one in Figure 3. The slope of the aggregate demand schedule is

$$\left.\frac{dp}{dY}\right|_{Dd} = -\frac{1 - C_1 - I'\dfrac{q_N}{F_N} + \dfrac{C_2 + I'q_{r-\pi}}{m_r} m_Y}{\dfrac{C_2 + I'q_{r-\pi}}{m_r}\dfrac{M}{p^2}}$$

$$= -\frac{[m_r(1 - C_1 - I'q_N/F_N) + (C_2 + I'q_{r-\pi})m_Y]p^2}{(C_2 + I'q_{r-\pi})M}.$$

It is interesting to compute the following limits:

$$\lim_{m_r \to 0} \frac{dp}{dY}\Big|_{Dd} = -m_Y \frac{p^2}{M}, \qquad \lim_{m_r \to -\infty} \frac{dp}{dY}\Big|_{Dd} = -\infty,$$

$$\lim_{C_2 + I'_{qr} - \pi \to 0} \frac{dp}{dY}\Big|_{Dd} = -\infty.$$

As $m_r \to -\infty$, the aggregate demand curve becomes vertical in the p-Y plane. In this "liquidity trap" case decreases in the money wage, which shift the aggregate supply curve outward in the p-Y plane, do nothing to stimulate real output. Except in limiting cases, increases in G, π, and M and decreases in T will in general shift aggregate demand upward and/or outward in the p-Y plane.

The equilibrium levels of income and prices are determined at the intersection of the aggregate demand and supply curve, as depicted in Figure 3. We leave it to the reader to analyze the effects of changes in various parameters by making use of this graphical device. Needless to say, the apparatus will produce the same results as those produced by the IS-LM analysis.

The apparatus consisting of the aggregate demand curve and aggregate supply curve in the p-Y plane can readily be used to explain the distinction between increases in the price level caused by "demand-pull," on the one hand, and "cost-push" on the other. The aggregate supply curve, being the locus of p-Y combinations that solves Equations (1) and (2), depends on the capital stock, the money wage, and the parameters of the production function. Changes in these elements of supply, most particularly the money wage rate, are what are called "cost-push" factors that can cause the price level to move. Thus, an exogenous increase in the money wage will shift the aggregate supply curve upward, in general driving the price level up as well as the real wage and the interest rate, while causing employment, output, and firms' real profits to fall. We know that real profits Π_0 fall since

$$\Pi_0 = Y - (w/p)N - (r + \delta - \pi)K;$$

taking the total differential gives

$$d\Pi_0 = (F_N - (w/p))\, dN - N\, d(w/p) - K\, dr = -(N\, d(w/p) + K\, dr).$$

We know that both the real wage and interest rate rise when w increases, thus assuring that profits decrease. So do dividends.

"Demand-pull" causes of price changes stem from changes in parameters that affect the position of aggregate demand in the p-Y plane. These parameters include π as well as the government policy variables T, G, and M. Increases in G and M and decreases in T shift aggregate demand upward in the p-Y plane, causing output, employment, the price level, and real dividends to rise while the real wage falls. To see that real dividends rise, recall that real dividends are

$$\text{div} = Y - (w/p)N - \delta K.$$

Then

$$d(\text{div}) = (F_N - (w/p))\, dN - N\, d(w/p) = -N\, d(w/p),$$

and so dividends move inversely with the real wage. When demand-pull factors push the price level up, the interest rate will rise if the cause is a rise in π or G or a decline in T, while it will fall if a rise in M is what causes the jump in p. Similarly, how real profits move depends on the particular source of demand-pull. For notice that real profits are

$$\Pi_0 = Y - (w/p)N - (r + \delta - \pi)K$$
$$= Y - (w/p)N - F_K K + (F_K - (r + \delta - \pi))K.$$

By Euler's theorem and the marginal productivity condition for labor, we have

$$\Pi_0 = (F_K - (r + \delta - \pi))K.$$

Whether real profits rise or fall depends on what happens to the gap between the marginal product of capital and the real cost of capital. When that gap increases, as will happen when the money supply is increased, profits rise as does investment. But an increase in government expenditures will generally narrow that gap and cause profits and investment to fall.

It is clear that while both "cost-push" and "demand-pull" factors can cause the price level to rise, they do produce effects of opposite sign on the real wage, output, employment, and dividends. It is those differences that could in principle be used to identify particular inflationary episodes as being of the "cost-push" or "demand-pull" variety (Phelps, 1961).

4. THE MODEL WITH $(M + B)\,\pi \neq 0$

Thus far, our analysis of the Keynesian model has been conducted on the assumption that $M + B$ equals zero, or alternatively on the assumption that perceived real capital gains on the public's holdings of government debt should not be a component of perceived real disposable income. If we relax that assumption, we see from Equation (8) that the position of the IS curve will depend on the money wage. Thus, setting dY in (8) equal to zero, we find that dr must satisfy

$$dr = -\frac{C_1 \pi((M + B)/p)}{C_2 + I' q_{r-\pi}} \frac{dw}{w}$$

if all the other exogenous variables are constant and if the equality between aggregate demand and supply is to be maintained when money wages change. The denominator of this expression is negative, while the numerator may be positive or negative depending on the signs of π and $M + B$. If π and $M + B$ are both positive, dr is positively related to dw, the IS curve thus shifting upward when w rises. That is because, given output, an increase in money wages leads to an increase in prices which depreciates the real value of anticipated capital losses on the public's holdings of bonds and money, thus *raising* disposable income and aggregate demand. Under these conditions, then, an increase in money wages causes both the IS curve and the LM curve to shift upward. Interest rates are bound to rise, but what happens to output depends on the relative shifts and relative slopes characterizing the IS and LM curves.

To determine the solution analytically when $\pi(M + B)$ does not necessarily equal zero, we substitute (11) into (8) to obtain

$$\left(1 - C_1 - I'\frac{q_N}{F_N} + C_1\pi\frac{M + B}{p}\frac{F_{NN}}{F_N^2}\right)dY$$

$$= -C_1\,dT + dG - \left(I'q_{r-\pi} + C_2 + C_1\frac{M + B}{p}\right)d\pi + C_1\pi\frac{M + B}{p}\frac{dw}{w}$$

$$+ \frac{C_2 + I'q_{r-\pi}}{m_r}\left(\frac{dM}{p} - \frac{M}{p}\frac{dw}{w} + \left(\frac{F_{NN}}{F_N^2}\frac{M}{p} - m_Y\right)dY\right)$$

or

$$\left(1 - C_1 - I'\frac{q_N}{F_N} + C_1\pi\frac{M + B}{p}\frac{F_{NN}}{F_N^2} - \frac{C_2 + I'q_{r-\pi}}{m_r}\left(\frac{F_{NN}}{F_N^2}\frac{M}{p} - m_Y\right)\right)dY$$

$$= -C_1\,dT + dG - \left(I'q_{r-\pi} + C_2 + C_1\frac{M + B}{p}\right)d\pi$$

$$+ \left(C_1\pi\frac{M + B}{p} - \frac{C_2 + I'q_{r-\pi}}{m_r}\frac{M}{p}\right)\frac{dw}{w} + \frac{C_2 + I'q_{r-\pi}}{m_r}\frac{dM}{p}.$$

Even provided that π is small, so that the coefficient of dY is positive—a requirement of stability—an increase in w is seen to have ambiguous effects on output when $\pi(M + B)$ is positive since the coefficient of dw may be either positive or negative. This conclusion is consistent with our analysis of the effects on the IS and LM curves of changes in w.

5. THE CLASSICAL MODEL AGAIN

Suppose that we now relax the assumption that wages are fixed at a point in time, allowing wages to change instantaneously in response to deviations of employment from its full-employment level. This can be accomplished by reinstating the labor market equilibrium condition of the classical model, $N = N(w/p)$. Once these changes are made we are back with the classical model. In terms of the IS-LM apparatus, the workings of the classical model are depicted in Figure 4. Since the IS and LM curves are based on six of the equations in the classical model, they continue to describe the locus of r, Y

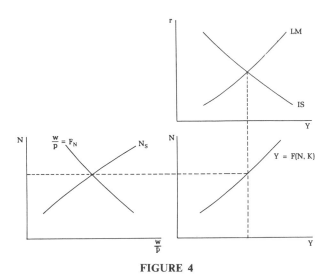

FIGURE 4

combinations that equilibrate aggregate demand and supply and the demand and supply for real balances, respectively, *given* an assumed money wage. Let us assume that $\pi(M + B)$ equals zero, so that the IS curve is independent of the money wage.[4] Then the model works as follows. The levels of output, employment, and the real wage are determined by the supply and demand functions for labor and the production function, as depicted by the bottom two diagrams in Figure 4. The equilibrium interest rate is determined by substituting the equilibrium level of output into the IS curve in order to find the interest rate that is required to call forth an aggregate demand that just equals the aggregate supply. The LM curve thus plays no role in determining the equilibrium interest rate. Instead, given the equilibrium interest rate and rate of output, the LM curve is used to solve for the equilibrium money wage. Thus, the money wage adjusts to such a level that the LM curve always goes through the r, Y combination determined in the aggregate supply and aggregate demand sectors of the model. Of course, given the equilibrium wage rate, it is very easy to solve for the price level since real wages have already been determined in the labor market. Hence, it seems that there cannot be an underemployment equilibrium in the classical model since flexible wages will assure us that the IS and LM curves intersect at the level of output determined on the supply side.

Notice, however, that the analysis above depends on the "good behavior" of the IS and LM curves. In particular, the analysis breaks down in the case in which $m_r = -\infty$ at some positive interest rate since then changes in w are incapable of changing the interest rate that at a given level of income

---

[4] The reader is invited to figure out how things work when this specification is dropped.

FIGURE 5

equilibrates the money market. The situation is depicted in Figure 5. There the level of income determined on the aggregate supply side, which we indicate by the vertical line at Y_F, is not the same as the level of income determined at the intersection of the IS and LM curves. No amount of wage deflation is capable of driving the LM curve downward, so that it intersects an IS curve at r_0, the interest rate that is sufficiently low that it generates an aggregate demand equal to Y_F. As we approach a regime in which the Keynesian liquidity trap is relevant, the flexibility of the interest rate becomes limited by the willingness of the public to hold virtually any quantity of money at the ruling interest rate. Injecting more real balances into the system, either through open-market operations or money wage decreases, fails to drive the interest rate downward. Thus, the interest rate is prevented from playing its crucial role of equilibrating aggregate supply and demand. Formally, the rate of output Y is overdetermined in this system, one solution for the output rate being determined by the labor market and the production function, another by the intersection of the IS and LM curves. There is no device to reconcile the two solutions for output. The other side of the coin is that the money wage is underdetermined since the model in no way restricts the level of w (the model can be written in a form in which w nowhere appears).

A response to this argument was advanced by Pigou (1943). Pigou argued that even in the face of a liquidity trap, full employment in the classical system would be guaranteed if the consumption function were amended to include the real net wealth of the public as an independent argument. In our model the public's real net wealth consists of the sum of the capital stock K and the real debt of the governnment $(M + B)/p$. Then, following Pigou, suppose we replace (3) with the consumption function

$$C = C\left(Y - T - \delta K - \pi\frac{M + B}{p}, r - \pi, \frac{M + B}{p} + K\right) \qquad (3a)$$

where C_3 is assumed to be positive, an increase in the public's net wealth raising consumption at given levels of real perceived disposable income and the real interest rate. If this consumption function replaces (3), the differential of the IS curve, Equation (8), must be amended to

$$
\left(1 - C_1 - I' \frac{q_N}{F_N} + C_1\pi \frac{M+B}{p} \frac{F_{NN}}{F_N^2} - C_3 \frac{M+B}{p} \frac{F_{NN}}{F_N^2} \right) dY
$$

$$
= -C_1\, dT + dG + (C_2 + I'q_{r-\pi})\, dr - \left(I'q_{r-\pi} + C_2 + C_1 \frac{M+B}{p} \right) d\pi
$$

$$
+ \left(C_1\pi \frac{M+B}{p} - C_3 \frac{M+B}{p} \right) \frac{dw}{w}. \tag{8'}
$$

As before, we assume that the coefficient of dY is positive. To simplify things we also assume that π equals zero, an assumption that is usually made in discussions of the "Pigou effect." Then, we can determine the effect of money wage changes on the IS curve by setting all differentials except dr and dw equal to zero in (8'). We find that

$$
\left. \frac{\partial r}{\partial w} \right|_{IS} = \frac{C_3((M+B)/pw)}{C_2 + I'q_{r-\pi}},
$$

an expression that is negative so long as $M + B$ exceeds zero. Hence an increase in the money wage shifts the IS curve downward. By causing prices to rise, an increase in the money wage diminishes the real value of the debt owed the public by the government, thus tending to reduce the intended rate of consumption. Since we assumed that π is zero, there can occur no countervailing effects on perceived disposable income that could conceivably offset the effect of the changed level of wealth on consumption. (On the other hand, if π and $M + B$ were both positive, an increase in money wages would tend to *increase* consumption through its effect on perceived real disposable income. This could offset part or all of the "wealth effect.")

In the context of the Keynesian dilemma depicted in Figure 5 the Pigou effect provides a means of salvaging the automatic nature of full employment in a regime of perfectly flexible money wages. Even if a drop in money wages fails to shift the LM curve downward via the "Keynes effect," it will drive the IS curve outward due to the wealth or "Pigou effect." Provided that this effect is sufficiently potent, eventually the IS curve will be driven far enough out that aggregate demand will be equal to the full employment output Y_F, even at the rate of interest determined at the liquidity trap.

It is important to realize that this argument depends on several critical assumptions. Most important, there must occur no effects on perceived disposable income that could offset the wealth effect when wages change. If π is positive, these could conceivably offset the effects on consumption of real wealth changes stemming from jumps in the price level.

6. A DIGRESSION ON WEALTH, SAVING, AND THE RATE OF INTEREST IN THE CLASSICAL MODEL

In "Wealth, Saving, and the Rate of Interest," Lloyd Metzler (1951) argued that incorporating the Pigou effect into the classical macroeconomic model meant that money ceased to be a "veil." Instead a change in the money supply could effect the rate of interest and the rate of capital accumulation. Metzler pointed out that whether or not a change in the money supply had such effects depended on whether it was engineered through an open-market operation or whether it was dropped from the sky, like manna from heaven. While Metzler's version of the classical model was somewhat different from the one dealt with here, his basic point can be established from an analysis of our classical model.

We assume that π equals zero, so that we can ignore perceived real capital gains on the public's net holdings of financial assets as a component of perceived disposable income. Then the Pigouvian consumption function (3a) becomes

$$C = C\left(Y - T - \delta K, r - \pi, \frac{M + B}{p} + K\right), \qquad C_1 > 0, \quad C_2 \le 0, \quad C_3 > 0.$$

In a classical model with such a consumption function, the equilibrium interest rate and price level are determined simultaneously by the aggregate demand–aggregate supply equality and the equilibrium condition for real money balances:

$$C\left(Y - T - \delta K, r - \pi, \frac{M + B}{p} + K\right)$$

$$+ I(q(K, N, r - \pi, \delta) - 1) + G + \delta K = Y,$$

$$\frac{M}{p} = m(r, Y).$$

Taking the total differentials of these two equations and setting $dY = dK = dN = d\delta = 0$ yields

$$(C_2 + I'q_{r-\pi})\, dr - (C_2 + I'q_{r-\pi})\, d\pi + C_3\left(\frac{dM + dB}{p}\right)$$

$$- C_3 \frac{M + B}{p} \frac{dp}{p} + dG - C_1\, dT = 0$$

$$\frac{dp}{p} = \frac{dM}{M} - m_r \frac{p}{M}\, dr.$$

Substituting the second expression into the first and rearranging yields

$$\left(C_2 + I'q_{r-\pi} + C_3 \frac{M+B}{M} m_r \right) dr - (C_2 + I'q_{r-\pi}) \, d\pi$$

$$+ C_3 \left(\frac{dM + dB}{p} \right) - C_3 \frac{M+B}{p} \frac{dM}{M} + dG - C_1 \, dT = 0, \qquad (16)$$

an equation expressing dr in terms of the differentials of the parameters π, M, B, T, and G, so that it is the differential of the reduced form for r. Now consider the effects on the interest rate of a change in the money supply engineered through an open-market purchase of bonds, so that $dM + dB = 0$. Then $\partial r / \partial M$ is given by

$$\left. \frac{\partial r}{\partial M} \right|_{dM = -dB} = \frac{C_3 \dfrac{M+B}{p} \dfrac{1}{M}}{C_2 + I'q_{r-\pi} + C_3 \dfrac{M+B}{M} m_r}.$$

So long as $M + B > 0$, the above derivative is negative. An increase in the money supply accomplished through open-market operations raises the price level, thereby reducing the real wealth of the public's net holdings of financial assets, reducing real wealth, stimulating saving, and lowering the rate of interest. Such a change in the money supply consequently has effects on the real variables of the economy.

On the other hand, consider a change in the money supply accomplished not through open-market exchanges, but by simply engaging in a once-and-for-all giveaway of money *and* bonds, the giveaway being effected in such a fashion that the proportion of nominal money to nominal bonds remains unaltered. The increment in money and bonds can be thought of as a once-and-for-all "bonus" that is dispensed by the government. Thus, we no longer retain the constraint on open-market operations, instead substituting the condition that

$$d\left(\frac{M+B}{M} \right) = 0.$$

which is simply the requirement that the gift of bonds and money is not to alter the proportion of money to bonds. Writing out the above differential, we have

$$\frac{dM + dB}{M} - \frac{dM}{M} \left(\frac{M+B}{M} \right) = 0.$$

Multiplying both sides of this equation by M/p yields

$$\frac{dM + dB}{p} - \frac{dM}{M} \left(\frac{M+B}{p} \right) = 0,$$

an equality that holds for gift operations satisfying our stipulation that the relative quantities of bonds and money must not be altered by the gift. Substituting this equality into (16) yields

$$\left(C_2 + I'q_{r-\pi} + C_3 \frac{M + B}{M} m_r\right) dr - (C_2 + I'q_{r-\pi}) d\pi + dG - C_1 dT = 0,$$

which is the differential of the reduced form for the interest rate. Since dM does not appear in the equation, it follows that a change in the money supply accomplished by an operation that does not alter the ratio of money to bonds has no effect on the interest rate. The reason is that such a once-and-for-all increase in money and bonds has no effect on real wealth.

The conclusion of this analysis is that in a classical system incorporating a Pigouvian consumption function, the effects of a change in the nominal money supply depend on the nature of accompanying changes in the nominal stock of bonds. Only in the special case in which the ratio of money to bonds is constant does a change in the money supply produce no effect on the interest rate, and hence on the rates of consumption and investment.

7. KEYNESIAN ECONOMICS AND WALRAS'S LAW

Walras's law states that where excess demand functions have been constructed so that they obey the pertinent budget constraints, the dollar sum of all excess demands must be zero. This means that an excess supply in one market must be balanced by offsetting excess demands elsewhere.

It is frequently asserted that an important aspect of the Keynesian model is that it violates Walras's law: there is an excess supply of labor that is nowhere balanced by an offsetting excess demand (see, e.g., Clower, 1965). Since Walras's law is frequently misinterpreted in analyses of Keynesian models, the subject bears some attention.

It should first be noted that households face two sorts of constraints, the satisfaction of each of which will give rise to a form of Walras's law. First, households face the (stock) balance sheet constraint

$$\frac{B^D + V^D + M^D}{p} = \frac{B + V + M}{p} \quad (= W),$$

which says that they must allocate their entire wealth, but no more, among bonds, equities, and money. Satisfaction of this constraint gives rise to the cross-equation restrictions on the slopes of the asset demand schedules $b_r = -m_r$, $b_Y = -m_Y$, $b_W + m_W = 1$. Furthermore, note that the constraint can be rearranged to read

$$\frac{M^D}{p} - \frac{M}{p} = \frac{B - B^D}{p} + \frac{V - V^D}{p},$$

which states that the excess demand for money equals the sum of the excess supplies for bonds and equities. This is the form of Walras's law for stocks of paper assets in our model.

In addition to the balance sheet constraint, households face the flow budget constraint

$$C + S = Y_D,$$

which says that they can allocate their disposable income between consumption and saving. Let us ignore the term $((M + B)/p)\pi$, say by assuming that π is zero. Stockholders receive as real dividends $Y - (w/p)N - \delta K$, where Y and N are actual quantities of output and employment, respectively. Here Y and N are determined via the aggregate supply curve and labor demand schedules, respectively, as functions of w/p. At a real wage of w/p, workers would like to supply an amount of labor $N^S(w/p)$. Consequently, as a function of w/p, "desired" disposable income is

$$Y_D^* = Y - \frac{w}{p}N - \delta K + \frac{w}{p}N^S\left(\frac{w}{p}\right) - T$$

$$= Y - \frac{w}{p}\left(N - N^S\left(\frac{w}{p}\right)\right) - \delta K - T,$$

where by "desired" we mean the amount of income consistent with firms and households being able to transact whatever quantities they wish at the going real wage w/p. Suppose we equate Y_D^* to $C + S$, a step *not* taken in the Keynesian model. This gives

$$C = Y - \frac{w}{p}\left(N - N^S\left(\frac{w}{p}\right)\right) - \delta K - T - S.$$

Aggregate demand Y_A is then

$$Y_A = C + \dot{K} + G + \delta K = Y - \frac{w}{p}\left(N - N^S\left(\frac{w}{p}\right)\right) - T - S + G + \dot{K},$$

which by virtue of the government budget constraint $(p(G - T) = \dot{M} + \dot{B})$ implies

$$Y_A - Y = \frac{w}{p}\left(N^S\left(\frac{w}{p}\right) - N\right) + \left(\dot{K} + \frac{\dot{M}}{p} + \frac{\dot{B}}{p} - S\right), \tag{17}$$

which is Walras's law for flows. It states that the excess aggregate demand for goods $(Y_A - Y)$ equals the sum of the excess supply of labor weighted by the real wage and the excess of the actual real rate of accumulation of assets $\dot{K} + \dot{M}/p + \dot{B}/p$ over the desired rate of accumulation S, i.e., the excess flow supply of real assets.

Such a law does *not* hold in the Keynesian model. In the Keynesian model, in equilibrium $N^S(w/p) > N$, while at the same time $Y_A = Y$ and $S = \dot{K} + (\dot{M} + \dot{B})/p$. The reason for this apparent violation of Walras's law is that the Keynesian model does not impose a flow budget constraint of the form

$$C + S = Y_D^*,$$

the form needed to derive the above form of Walras's law. Instead of constraining $C + S$ to equal *desired* disposable income Y_D^*, the Keynesian model constrains $C + S$ to equal *actual* disposable income Y_D, where actual disposable income is defined by taking the labor component of income to be $(w/p)N$ where N is the amount of actual employment, given by the labor demand schedule. Dividend income continues to be $Y - (w/p)N - \delta K$, so that actual disposable income is

$$Y_D = Y - \frac{w}{p}N - \delta K + \frac{w}{p}N - T = Y - \delta K - T.$$

Equating $C + S$ to Y_D gives

$$C = Y - \delta K - T - S,$$

so that aggregate demand must satisfy

$$Y_A = C + \dot{K} + G + \delta K = Y - T + G - S + \dot{K},$$

which by virtue of the government budget constraint implies

$$Y_A - Y = \left(\dot{K} + \frac{\dot{M}}{p} + \frac{\dot{B}}{p} - S \right). \tag{18}$$

This states that excesss aggregate demand for goods equals the excess flow supply of assets, a form of Walras's law that deletes the labor market. The labor market's deletion is effected by using actual labor income and not desired (supplied) labor times the real wage in defining disposable income. Equation (18) is the form of Walras's law implicit in the Keynesian model. It is what lies behind the equivalence of $C + I + G + \delta K = Y$ and $S = \dot{K} + \dot{M}/p + \dot{B}/p$ as descriptions of flow equilibrium in the Keynesian model.

According to some economists, it is important that for the Keynesian model, Walras's law in the sense of Equation (17) does not hold. The argument is that because the pertinent concept of labor income is less than workers desire it to be and this constrains workers' flow demands, excess supply in the labor market is prevented from generating offsetting, and presumably expansionary, excess demands in the flow market for goods or paper assets. But clearly it still remains rigidity of the money wage that causes the system to settle at an equilibrium with unemployment. Downward movements in the money wage rate cause outward shifts in the aggregate supply curve in the p, Y plane, causing movements downward along the demand schedule in the p, Y plane (the Keynes effect), thus causing output and employment to rise.

EXERCISES

1. Take a simple version of the Keynesian model described above, one with $\pi(M + B)/p$ excluded from the consumption function.

A. Describe the behavior of the model (i.e., the response of all endogenous variables to jumps in each of the exogenous variables) where the endogenous variables are taken to be Y, N, C, I, r, and M, while the exogenous variables are G, T, π, w, p, and K.

B. Describe the behavior of the model where the endogenous variables are Y, N, C, I, p, and M and the exogenous variables are G, T, K, π, w, and r.

2. Take a simple version of the classical model. Describe the behavior of the model where the endogenous variables are Y, N, C, I, w, r, and M, while the exogenous variables are G, T, π, p, and K.

3. Consider an economy described by the following equations:

$$Y/K = A(N/K)^{1.10} \qquad \text{(production function. Bodkin and Klein, 1967)}$$
$$N/K = \beta_0(w/p)^{\beta_1} \qquad \beta_1 < 0 \text{ (demand function for labor)}$$
$$I = I(r) \qquad I' < 0$$
$$C = C(Y - T) \qquad 0 < C' < 1$$
$$C + I + G = Y$$
$$M/p = m(r, Y, W) \qquad m_r < 0, \quad m_Y > 0, \quad m_W = 1$$
$$W = ((M + B)/p) + K.$$

The endogenous variables are:

$Y = \text{GNP}$	$C = \text{consumption}$	$N = \text{employment}$
$r = \text{interest rate}$	$p = \text{the price level}$	$W = \text{real wealth held by the public}$
$I = \text{investment.}$		

The exogenous variables are:

$K = \text{the capital stock}$	$M = \text{the money stock, a liability of the government}$
$w = \text{the money wage}$	$B = \text{stock of government interest bearing bonds}$
$T = \text{tax collections}$	$G = \text{government expenditures, a flow.}$

Government bonds are like savings deposits, having a variable interest rate and fixed nominal value. Describe the effects on Y, N, P, and r of:

A. An increase in the money supply brought about by an open-market operation, i.e., $dM = -dB$.

B. A once-and-for-all increase in the money supply caused by a one-time government money bonus to veterans, i.e., $dM > 0, dB = 0$.

C. A once-and-for-all increase in the stock of outstanding government bonds, caused by a one-time gift of some new government bonds to veterans, i.e., $dB > 0, dM = 0$.

4. Consider the following macroeconomic model:

$$Y = F(K, N) \qquad F_K, \quad F_N > 0, \quad F_{KK}, F_{NN} < 0, \quad F_{KN} > 0$$
$$w/p = F_N$$
$$N^S = N^S\left(\frac{w}{p}, r - \pi\right) \qquad N^S_{w/p} > 0, \quad N^S_{r-\pi} > 0$$
$$N = N^S$$
$$I = I(r - \pi) \qquad I' < 0$$
$$C = C(Y - T) \qquad 1 > C' > 0$$
$$C + I + G = Y$$
$$M/p = m(r, Y) \qquad m_r < 0, \quad m_Y > 0$$

where Y is GNP, K is the capital stock, N is employment, w is the money wage, N^S is the supply of labor, p is the price level, r is the interest rate, π is the anticipated inflation rate, I is investment, C is consumption, G is government expenditure, T is taxes net of transfers. The endogenous variables are Y, N, N^S, w, p, r, C, and I. The exogenous variables are M, K, G, T, and π.

A. Describe the effects on Y, p, r, and N of: (1) an increase in M, (2) an increase in G with T constant, and (3) an increase in π. Does an increase in π leave the real rate of interest unchanged?

B. Suppose that the government finances its deficit by printing bonds and/or money. At the equilibrium values of the variables that satisfy the above equations are we assured that the public will be willing to accumulate new "bonds and/or money" at exactly the rate at which the government is creating it? Explain.

5. Consider an economy described by the IS-LM diagram in Figure 6.

FIGURE 6

Here (Y_e, r_e) is an equilibrium output–interest rate pair. Consider now the situation at (Y_e, r_1).

A. Is there an excess supply or an excess demand for money at (Y_e, r_1)?

B. Is there an excess supply or an excess demand for output at (Y_e, r_1)?

C. Are your answers to (A) and (B) consistent with Walras' law?

6. Assume an economy in which money matters; the monetary authority can influence the interest rate, real output and employment, and the price level at any moment in time. Also, the firms of this economy are price takers, at least in the labor market, so the marginal product of labor and the real wage are equal at every moment. Now, suppose that a constant-purchasing-power law is passed, a law that requires all firms to compensate employees for any change in the commodity price level by increasing money wages proportionately. What is the significance of this new law for the monetary authority? Is it still able to influence real output and employment, the interest rate, and the price level?

7. There is a country whose government is financing all of its expenditures by means of money creation. All money is the liability of the government, there being no commercial banks. The government acts to keep its rate of real expenditures G constant over time at the real rate $G = \bar{G}$. Accordingly, money creation is governed by

$$\frac{dM}{dt} \bigg/ p(t) = \bar{G}$$

where M is the money supply and p the price index. Suppose that real output is constant over time and that actual and expected inflation at each moment both equal $(dM/dt)/M(t)$. Since $\bar{G}$ is a nonnegligible proportion of the country's GNP, this country has been experiencing a high rate of inflation. It also happens that the government has prohibited residents of this country from holding money and other assests of any foreign countries.

A. How would you find the maximum rate of real expenditures that the government can finance by money creation?

B. Assume that $\bar{G}$ is initially lower than the maximum G described in (A), and that the rate of money creation is correspondingly lower than the rate needed to maximize G. Explain whether abandoning the restriction on holding of foreign assets would make it easier or harder for the government to finance its expenditures at the same real rate $\bar{G}$ by money creation.

C. Assuming that it would still be possible to finance $\bar{G}$ solely by money creation if the prohibition on holding foreign assets were eliminated, would the equilibrium rate of inflation be higher or lower than initially?

8. Consider the following model of a small country:

$$Y = F(N, K) \qquad F_N, F_K, F_{NK} > 0, \quad F_{NN}, F_{KK} < 0 \quad \text{production function}$$

$$w/p = F_N \qquad \text{marginal equality for employment}$$

$$I = I(r) \qquad I' < 0 \quad \text{investment schedule}$$

$$X = X(t) \qquad X_t < 0 \quad \text{export schedule}$$

$$t = \frac{e \cdot p}{p^*} \qquad \text{definition of terms of trade}$$

$$C = c(Y - T) \qquad 1 > c' > 0 \quad \text{consumption function}$$

$$C + I + G + X = Y \qquad \text{equilibrium condition in market for domestic good}$$

$$M/p = m(r, Y) \qquad m_r < 0, \quad m_Y > 0 \quad \text{portfolio equilibrium condition.}$$

Here Y is GNP, N is employment, K is capital, I investment, C consumption, X exports, M the money supply, r the interest rate, p the price level in this country (measured in dollars per unit domestic good), p^* the price level in the rest-of-the-world (measured in pounds per unit rest-of-the-world good), t the terms of trade (measured in rest-of-the-world good per unit domestic good), and e is the exchange rate measured in pounds per dollar (it is the price of dollars measured in foreign currency). Notice that exports decline when t rises. The domestic interest rate r must equal the world interest rate and hence is *exogenous*. The other exogenous variables are K, w, p^*, G, T, and *either M or e*. The endogenous variables are Y, N, p, I, C, X, t, and *either e or M*.

A. Consider a regime in which the government pegs the exchange rate e at some arbitrary level, so that e is exogenous and M is endogenous. In this fixed exchange-rate regime, analyze the effects on the endogenous variables of:

    (i) an increase in G;

    (ii) an increase in the exchange rate e;

    (iii) an increase in w.

B. Consider a flexible exchange rate regime in which the government sets M exogenously and permits e to be endogenous. Analyze the effects on the endogenous variables of:

    (i) an increase in G;

    (ii) an increase in M;

    (iii) an increase in w.

9. What are the units of the following variables: π w, N, p, Y, C, I, G, K, M, B, $(M + B)/p$, $((M + B)/p)\pi$?

10. Keynes liked to measure real GNP in terms of "wage units," i.e., he liked to work with the variable pY/w. What are the units of this variable?

11. Some classical economists assert that there can be no such thing as "cost-push" inflation. Discuss.

REFERENCES

Clower, R. (1965). "The Keynesian Counterrevolution: A Theoretical Appraisal." In *Theory of Interest Rates. Conference on the Theory of Interest and Money. Royaumont, France 1962* (F. H. Hahn and F. P. R. Brechling, eds.). London: Macmillan, and New York: St. Martin's.

Hicks, J. R. (1937). "Mr. Keynes and the 'Classics'; a Suggested Interpretation." *Econometrica*, Vol. 5, No. 1, pp. 147–159.

Leijonhufvud, A. (1968). *On Keynesian Economics and the Economics of Keynes*. London and New York: Oxford Univ. Press.

Metzler, L. (1951). "Wealth, Savings and the Rate of Interest." *Journal of Political Economy*, Vol. LIX, No. 2, pp. 93–116.

Phelps, E. S. (1961). "A Test for the Presence of Cost Inflation in the United States, 1955-57." *Yale Economic Essays*, Vol. 1, No. 1, pp. 28–69.

Pigou, A. C. (1943). "The Classical Stationary State." *Economic Journal*, Vol. LIII, pp. 343–351.

Samuelson, P. A. (1963). *Foundations of Economic Analysis*. Cambridge, Massachusetts: Harvard Univ. Press.

CHAPTER III

TOBIN'S DYNAMIC AGGREGATIVE MODEL

One of the most important features of the "classical" and "Keynesian" models presented above is that they incorporate an investment demand schedule, a schedule that in a sense permits discrepancies between firms' actual and desired capital stocks at any moment. In those models firms were not permitted to adjust their capital stocks instantaneously, for it was assumed that there was no "perfect" market in existing stocks of capital. Thus, a firm faced with a discrepancy between the marginal productivity of capital and the marginal cost of capital could respond only by investing or disinvesting at some finite rate per unit time.

In this chapter we investigate the model that emerges when we replace the "Keynesian" flow investment demand function with the assumption that there is a perfect market in existing capital, one in which firms can purchase or sell (or rent) all the capital they want at a point in time. A major reason for performing this exercise is to highlight the important role played by firms' investment demand function in the standard "Keynesian" model. Another rationale for undertaking the exercise is that it forces us to face some difficult questions about the adequacy of the standard one-sector "Keynesian" model as a vehicle for representing the major doctrines in Keynes's *General Theory*.

1. THE FIRM'S OPTIMIZATION PROBLEM

We now assume that the typical firm can purchase or sell all the capital it wants at any point in time at the price of the one good in the model p. Except where noted, all other characteristics of firms, households, and the government are as described in the previous chapters. Thus, among other things, we continue to assume that firms issue no bonds, although this assumption could easily be relaxed.

The object of the firm is to maximize its present value, which is simply the discounted value of its net cash flow. The ith firm's net cash flow at time t is

$$p(t)F(K_i(t), N_i(t)) - w(t)N_i(t) - p(t)(\dot{K}_i(t) + \delta K_i(t))$$

where i subscripts denote variables corresponding to the ith firm. The first term $p(t)Y_i$ is the firm's revenue, the second term $w(t)N_i$ is the firm's payroll, and the third term $p(t)(\dot{K}_i + \delta K_i)$ is the firm's current expenditures on capital goods. It pays out $p(t)\delta K_i$ to maintain its capital stock intact and $p(t)\dot{K}_i$ to add its capital stock at the rate $\dot{K}_i$ per unit time.

We assume that bonds and equities are perfect substitutes from the viewpoint of wealth-holders, which implies that the nominal interest rate on bonds is the appropriate rate for discounting the firm's cash flow. Thus, the firm's present value at time 0 is

$$V(K_i, N_i, \dot{K}_i, t)$$
$$= \int_0^\infty e^{-rt}[p(t)F(K_i(t), N_i(t)) - w(t)N_i(t) - p(t)(\dot{K}_i(t) + \delta K(t))]\, dt. \quad (1)$$

Following our practice with the previous models, we assume that the firm expects the price $p(t)$ and the wage $w(t)$ to follow the paths

$$p(t) = pe^{\pi t}, \qquad w(t) = we^{\pi t}$$

where π is the anticipated rate of inflation. Then (1) becomes

$$V(K_i, N_i, \dot{K}_i, t) = \int_0^\infty e^{-(r-\pi)t}[pF(K_i, N_i) - wN_i - p(\dot{K}_i + \delta K_i)]\, dt \quad (1')$$

where K_i and N_i are understood as functions of time. Expression (1') is of the form

$$g(y, X, \dot{X}, t) = \int_0^\infty f(y, X, \dot{X}, t)\, dt.$$

Among the necessary conditions for this to obtain an extremum are the following "Euler equations" (see Intriligator, 1971, Chapter 12):

$$\frac{\partial f}{\partial y} = 0, \quad t \in [0, \infty); \qquad \frac{\partial f}{\partial X} - \frac{d}{dt}\frac{\partial f}{\partial \dot{X}} = 0, \quad t \in [0, \infty).$$

For expression (1') to obtain a maximum, we thus require that at each point in time

$$e^{-(r-\pi)t}\left(p\frac{\partial F}{\partial N_i} - w\right) = 0 \quad \text{and} \quad e^{-(r-\pi)t}\left(p\frac{\partial F}{\partial K_i} - p(r + \delta - \pi)\right) = 0.$$

These conditions simply state that the marginal product of each input must be equated to the appropriate real rental at each point in time:

$$\partial F/\partial N_i = w/p, \quad (2)$$

$$\partial F/\partial K_i = (r + \delta - \pi). \quad (3)$$

Expression (3) implies that $r + \delta - \pi$ ought to be regarded as the real cost of capital, just as w/p is the real wage of labor. Moreover, this is the cost of capital that ought to be used in defining the firm's profits. For then the firm's profits are

$$\Pi_i = p(t)F(K_i, N_i) - w(t)N_i - (r + \delta - \pi)p(t)K_i(t). \qquad (4)$$

Notice that maximizing profits at each point in time is then equivalent to maximizing the firm's present value, i.e., it leads to the same marginal conditions, (2) and (3). The equivalence of the two approaches—profit maximization and present value maximization—is a consequence of using the appropriate cost of capital in calculating the firm's profits. The "cost of capital" is thus a derived concept: it is the rental, when imputed to capital, that makes present value maximization equivalent with profit maximization at each moment.

The following is a more direct way of verifying the equivalence of present value maximization and profit maximization. In (1′) use integration by parts to evaluate the term

$$\int_0^\infty e^{-(r-\pi)t}\dot{K}\, dt.$$

Set $du = \dot{K}\, dt$, $u = K$, $v = e^{-(r-\pi)t}$, and $dv = -(r - \pi)e^{-(r-\pi)t}\, dt$ and use the integration by parts formula

$$\int v\, du = uv - \int u\, dv$$

to obtain

$$\int_0^\infty e^{-(r-\pi)t}\dot{K}\, dt = K(t)e^{-(r-\pi)t}\Big|_0^\infty + \int_0^\infty K(r - \pi)e^{-(r-\pi)t}\, dt$$

$$= -K(0) + \int_0^\infty e^{-(r-\pi)t}(r - \pi)K\, dt$$

where we are assuming $\lim_{t \to \infty} e^{-(r-\pi)t}K(t) = 0$. Substituting the above expression into (1′) gives

$$V(K_i, N_i, \dot{K}_i, t) = pK(0) + \int_0^\infty e^{-(r-\pi)t}[pF(K_i, N_i) - w_i N_i$$

$$-(r - \pi + \delta)pK_i]\, dt,$$

which says that the value of the firm equals the reproduction value of its initial capital stock plus the discounted present value of its profits. The integral on the right-hand side is maximized by maximizing $pF - wN - (r + \delta - \pi)\rho K$ at each instant. Here $V(K_i, N_i, \dot{K}_i, t)$ is to be regarded as a function of the entire time paths $K_i(t)$, $N_i(t)$, $\dot{K}_i(t)$, and t for t going from zero to infinity.

By virtue of the linear homogeneity of $F(K, N)$, F_K and F_N are both homogeneous of degree zero in K and N, i.e., they depend only on the ratio of N to K. Indeed, use the linear homogeneity of F to write

$$\mu Y = F(\mu K, \mu N).$$

Set $\mu = 1/K$ to obtain

$$Y/K = F(1, N/K) \equiv f(\lambda)$$

where $\lambda \equiv N/K$. It follows that

$$Y = Kf(N/K)$$

and that

$$\frac{\partial Y}{\partial N} = Kf'\left(\frac{N}{K}\right)\frac{1}{K} = f'\left(\frac{N}{K}\right) > 0,$$

which shows that the marginal product of labor depends only on the ratio of N/K. It is straightforward to show that $f''(N/K) < 0$, so that the marginal product of employment varies inversely with the employment capital ratio.

We calculate the marginal product of capital as

$$\frac{\partial Y}{\partial K} = \frac{\partial}{\partial K}\left(Kf\left(\frac{N}{K}\right)\right) = f\left(\frac{N}{K}\right) + Kf'\left(\frac{N}{K}\right)\left(-\frac{N}{K^2}\right) = f\left(\frac{N}{K}\right) - \frac{N}{K}f'\left(\frac{N}{K}\right),$$

which shows that the marginal product of capital depends only on the employment capital ratio. It is easy to show that the marginal product of capital varies directly with the employment capital ratio.

Given fixed w, p, and $r + \delta - \pi$, Equations (2) and (3) imply two independent solutions for the firm's employment–capital ratio, solutions that will in general be different. So long as the solutions are different, it is possible to show that the firm's profits are either positive or negative, so that there are incentives either for the firm to expand without bound or else shut down.[1] As a result of these incentives the model as a whole will contain forces that reconcile the labor–capital ratios that solve (2) and (3). In particular, p and r will adjust so that (2) and (3) hold at the same labor–capital ratio.

---

[1] See Henderson and Quandt (1971) for an analysis of a competitive firm with a linearly homogeneous production function and variable factors of production.

In any event, since (2) and (3) determine only a labor–capital ratio, the size of the firm, as indexed by Y or N or K, is indeterminate, as is its rate of growth over time. This is a consequence of the assumptions of a linearly homogeneous production function and perfectly variable factors of production.

For convenience, let us arbitrarily resolve this indeterminacy in the scale of the firm and its growth rate by assuming that $\dot{K}_i = 0$ for all time. At the optimal N_i/K_i, this setting for $\dot{K}_i$ delivers a present value as great as can be achieved by any other path, so that the assumption is harmless. (We invite the reader to carry out analogous computations for the case in which $\dot{K}_i > 0$.) Assuming that $\dot{K}_i = 0$, (1') becomes

$$V = [pF(K_i, N_i) - wN_i - \delta pK_i] \int_0^\infty e^{-(r-\pi)t}\, dt$$

$$= \frac{pF(K_i, N_i) - w_iN_i - \delta pK_i}{r - \pi}$$

$$= \frac{pF(K_i, N_i) - w_iN_i - (r + \delta - \pi)pK_i}{r - \pi} + \frac{r - \pi}{r - \pi}pK_i$$

$$= \frac{p[F(K_i, N_i) - F_N N_i - F_K K_i]}{r - \pi} + pK_i.$$

But since F is linearly homogeneous in N_i and K_i, the expression in brackets is zero, so that the value of the firm is the reproduction value of its capital stock $V = pK_i$. Since the firm has no bonds outstanding, V equals the nominal value of the owners' equity in the firm. Thus q equals unity always. The nominal yield on equity ρ equals net cash flow (earnings) per value of equity *plus* the anticipated capital gain on equity:

$$\rho = \frac{pY_i - wN_i - p\delta K_i}{pK_i} + \frac{\dot{V}}{pK_i}$$

$$= \frac{pY_i - wN_i - (r + \delta - \pi)pK_i}{pK_i} + (r - \pi) + \frac{\dot{p}K_i + \dot{K}_i p}{pK_i}.$$

Setting $\dot{K}_i$ equal to zero, as we have above, and replacing $\dot{p}/p$ with the relevant anticipated magnitude π yields

$$\rho = r - \pi + \pi = r,$$

which confirms that the nominal yield on equities equals the bond rate.

We now assume that all firms in the economy maximize their present value, so that (3) holds at each moment for each firm. As a consequence, we assume that the marginal productivity condition for capital also holds for the entire economy, so that

$$F_K(K, N) = r + \delta - \pi \tag{5}$$

at each instant. This equality is held to be enforced by firms' trading existing capital at each moment in time. If $F_K > r + \delta - \pi$, firms bid for more capital; while if $F_K < r + \delta - \pi$, firms all attempt to dispose of capital instantaneously.

A version of Tobin's "dynamic aggregative model" (Tobin, 1955) is derived by replacing our "Keynesian" investment function with the marginal equality (5). The rest of the model we will deal with is identical with our "Keynesian" model. Thus, our model consists of the following six equations:

$$Y = F(K, N) \tag{I}$$

$$w/p = F_N \tag{II}$$

$$(r + \delta - \pi) = F_K \tag{III}$$

$$M/p = m(r, Y) \tag{IV}$$

$$C = c(Y - \delta K - T - ((M + B)/p)\pi, r - \pi) \tag{V}$$

$$C + I + G + \delta K = Y. \tag{VI}$$

The endogenous variables of the model are Y, N, C, I, r, and p. The exogenous variables are w, K, π, δ, G, T, B, and M. The constraints on the government and the behavior of holders of paper assets are all assumed to be the same as they are in the Keynesian model.

Studying the behavior of the model is facilitated by writing down the total differentials of Equations (I)–(VI):

$$dY = F_N \, dN + F_K \, dK \tag{i}$$

$$\frac{dw}{p} - \frac{w}{p}\frac{dp}{p} = F_{NN} \, dN + F_{NK} \, dK \tag{ii}$$

$$dr - d\pi = F_{KN} \, dN + F_{KK} \, dK \tag{iii}$$

$$\frac{dM}{p} - \frac{M}{p}\frac{dp}{p} = m_r \, dr + m_Y \, dY \tag{iv}$$

$$dC = c_1 \, dY - c_1 \delta \, dK - c_1 \, dT - c_1 \frac{M + B}{p} \, d\pi$$

$$+ c_1 \pi \frac{M + B}{p}\frac{dp}{p} + c_2 \, dr - c_2 \, d\pi \tag{v}$$

$$dC + dI + dG + \delta \, dK = dY. \tag{vi}$$

The system can be displayed compactly in the following matrix equation:

$$
\begin{bmatrix}
1 & -F_N & 0 & 0 & 0 & 0 \\
0 & -F_{NN} & -\dfrac{w}{p^2} & 0 & 0 & 0 \\
0 & -F_{KN} & 0 & 1 & 0 & 0 \\
m_Y & 0 & \dfrac{M}{p^2} & m_r & 0 & 0 \\
-c_1 & 0 & -c_1 \pi \dfrac{M+B}{p^2} & -c_2 & 1 & 0 \\
1 & 0 & 0 & 0 & -1 & -1
\end{bmatrix}
\begin{bmatrix}
dY \\ dN \\ dp \\ dr \\ dC \\ dI
\end{bmatrix}
$$

$$
=
\begin{bmatrix}
F_K \, dK \\
-dw/p + F_{NK} \, dK \\
d\pi + F_{KK} \, dK \\
dM/p \\
-c_2 \, d\pi - c_1 \delta \, dK - c_1 \, dT - c_1 \dfrac{M+B}{p} \, d\pi \\
dG + \delta \, dK
\end{bmatrix}.
$$

Inspection of the matrix on the left-hand side of the equation reveals that the system is block recursive: there is a 4×2 matrix of zeros in the upper right-hand portion of that matrix, which implies that the first four equations of the model form an independent subset that determines Y, N, p, and r. Given those variables, the fifth equation determines consumption (note that 5×1 matrix of zeros in the upper right-hand portion of our matrix, which means that the first five equations form an independent subset in Y, N, p, r, and C). Finally, the last equation determines investment.

To solve the system, our strategy will be to collapse the four equations (i)–(iv) into two equations in two unknowns. Tobin himself collapsed the system into two equations in p and N. For ease of comparison with our earlier models, we shall collapse it into two equations in r and Y. The first equation is the LM curve, which is identical with the LM curve of the "Keynesian" model. Its total differential, derived by substituting (i) and (ii) into (iv), is

$$
dr = \frac{1}{m_r} \left(\frac{dM}{p} - \frac{M}{p} \frac{dw}{w} + \left(\frac{F_{NN}}{F_N^2} \frac{M}{p} - m_Y \right) dY \right). \tag{6}
$$

FIGURE 1

The LM curve depicts the combinations of the interest rate and output that equate the demand and supply of real balances as well as satisfying the production function and the marginal condition for employment.

The second schedule depicts the combinations of output and the interest rate that satisfy the marginal productivity condition for capital. It is thus in the nature of a capital market equilibrium curve, which depicts the combinations of r and Y that make firms content to hold the existing stock of capital. The curve is derived from Equations (III) and (I). Its differential is derived by substituting (i) into (iii):

$$dr = d\pi + F_{KN}\, dN, \qquad dr = d\pi + (F_{KN}/F_N)\, dY. \tag{7}$$

Since F_{KN} is positive, the capital equilibrium curve is upward sloping in the r-Y plane. We assume, however, that its slope is less steep than is that of the LM curve, which will be seen to be a necessary condition required for stability.[2]

The model is summarized graphically in Figure 1, which depicts an LM curve intersecting an upward sloping "capital-equilibrium" curve, which we have labeled KE. The intersection of those two curves determines an r and Y that solve our model.

To illustrate the workings of the model, we shall consider the response of output and the interest rate to changes in the money supply and the wage rate, which influence the position of the LM curve, and changes in the anticipated rate of inflation, which shift the KE curve. An increase in the money supply will shift the LM curve toward the right, just as in our Keynesian model. At the old equilibrium level of output portfolio balance would require a decrease in the interest rate since wealth-holders would be content to hold more money and fewer bonds only at a lower interest rate. But such a decrease in the interest rate would disturb the equality between the net marginal product of capital and the real rate of interest, so that firms would want to acquire more capital. They would attempt to do so, but since the quantity of capital in existence is fixed, the

---

[2] Tobin's article analyzes how the model might behave if the stability conditions were not to be fulfilled in a certain region.

result would be a rise in the price of existing capital, which in our model is the price of the one good in the model. The rise in the price level would lower real wages, inducing employers to hire more employees and to produce more output. That would in turn increase the marginal productivity of capital, thus increasing the interest rate at which firms would be content to hold just the existing capital stock. However, the increases in the price level and the rate of output also increase the interest rate needed to achieve portfolio balance. If the rate at which the portfolio-balancing interest rate rises with output exceeds the rate of which the capital-balancing interest rate rises with output, as will be true if the LM curve is steeper than the KE curve,[3] the system will be driven to equilibrium at a higher output and interest rate than characterized the initial equilibrium. The situation is depicted in Figure 1.

A fall in the money wage works in very much the same way since it also produces a shift of the LM curve to the right. The fall in wages induces a fall in prices, which reduces the interest rate required for portfolio balance at the initial income level. That in turn disturbs capital market equilibrium, causing firms to bid for capital, raising the price level, stimulating output, and finally reversing the tendency for the interest rate to fall through the effects of rising output on the demand for money and the marginal product of capital. Thus a fall in the money wage causes both output and the interest rate to rise.

The effect of an increase in the anticipated rate of inflation π is depicted in Figure 2. The effect is to shift the KE curve upward by the amount of the increase in π. Such a change disturbs the marginal productivity equality for capital at the old output level, causing firms to bid for more capital, which in turn causes the price level and output to rise. But that raises the marginal product of capital, which means that the interest rate must eventually rise by more than the increase in π in order to restore equilibrium.

The model can be solved analytically by equating (6) and (7), and then solving for dY. This yields the differential of the reduced form for Y

$$\left[\frac{1}{m_r} \left(\frac{F_{NN}}{F_N^2} \frac{M}{p} - m_Y \right) - \frac{F_{KN}}{F_N} \right] dY = d\pi - \frac{1}{m_r} \frac{dM}{p} + \frac{1}{m_r} \frac{M}{p} \frac{dw}{w}. \tag{8}$$

If the stability conditions are satisfied, the coefficient on dY is positive. This guarantees that Y varies directly with π and M and inversely with w.

As expression (8) reveals, fiscal policy has no impact on the level of output at a point in time. Neither dG nor dT appears in (8). In addition, the consumption function, and so by implication also the Keynesian multiplier, play no role in determining the rate of output. On the other hand, monetary policy is seen to play an important role in determining output, one that depends not at all on its

---

[3] This is a necessary but not a sufficient condition for stability. The reader is invited to determine the stability conditions following the procedures of Chapters I and II. Assume that prices rise when $F_K > r + \delta - \pi$, and that interest rises when $m(r, Y) > M/p$.

FIGURE 2

influencing the desired flow of expenditures for consumption or investment, the only way money acquired potency in our one-sector "Keynesian" model. Instead, money works by disturbing equilibrium in the market for existing capital. That causes firms to try to purchase or sell capital, which in turn causes the price changes that are the prerequisite for output changes with a fixed money wage.

Once output and the interest rate are determined by (6) and (7), employment and the price level are easily calculated from Equations (I) and (IV). Then consumption is determined by Equation (V). Finally, investment is determined by Equation (VI). Note that fiscal policy is important as a determinant of $\dot{K}$, and hence the economy's rate of growth over time, even though it is incapable of influencing the levels of output, employment, price, and the interest rate at a point in time.[4]

2. INTERPRETATION AS A SPECIAL TWO-SECTOR MODEL

How is it that an increase in government purchases or a decrease in taxes fails to affect aggregate employment and output at a point in time? The best way to explain the mechanism that denies any potency to such changes in fiscal policy is to consider Tobin's model as a special case of a two-sector model in which there are different consumption and investment goods. Production of the investment good Y_I, satisfies the linearly homogeneous production function

$$Y_I = I(K_I, N_I), \qquad I_K, I_N, I_{KN} > 0, \qquad I_{NN}, I_{KK} < 0$$

---

[4] Guillermo Calvo (1980) has pointed out how sensitively the results described in this section depend on the assumption that expectations about the rate of inflation are exogenous. Calvo drops the exogeneity of π and assumes instead perfect foresight, or equivalently in this nonstochastic model, rational expectations for π. Under rational expectations, Calvo finds that with money wages less than perfectly flexible, government fiscal operations affect output and employment.

where K_I is capital employed in the investment goods industry, and N_I is employment in the investment good industry. Output of consumption goods Y_c, satisfies the linearly homogeneous production function

$$Y_c = C(K_c, N_c), \qquad C_K, C_N, C_{KN} > 0, \qquad C_{NN}, C_{KK} < 0$$

where K_c and N_c are capital and employment in the consumption goods industry, respectively.

The price of capital goods is $p_1 p$, while the price of consumption goods is p. Firms in each industry can hire all the labor they want at the money wage w, can purchase all the capital they want at the price $p_1 p$, and can sell all the output they want at their respective product price. There are thus perfect markets in capital and employment. Firms in each industry maximize profits with respect to variations in both employment and capital. Profits in the capital goods industry are

$$\Pi_I = p_1 p I(K_I, N_I) - w N_I - (r + \delta - \pi) p_1 p K_I,$$

which implies the marginal conditions

$$I_K = r + \delta - \pi, \qquad I_N = \frac{1}{p_1} \frac{w}{p}.$$

Profits in the consumer goods industry are

$$\Pi_c = p C(K_c, N_c) - w N_c - (r + \delta - \pi) p_1 p K_c,$$

which implies the marginal conditions

$$C_K = p_1(r + \delta - \pi), \qquad C_N = w/p.$$

In addition to having the above marginal conditions hold, we require that the market in existing capital clear, i.e. $K_I + K_c = K$, where K is the amount of capital in existence.

Our assumptions about households' portfolio and saving behavior remain as before, where $Y = p_1 Y_I + Y_c$, GNP measured in consumption goods, appears in the portfolio equilibrium schedule and the consumption function.

Collecting the equations of our model, we have

$$Y = p_1 Y_I + Y_c \tag{9}$$

$$Y_I = I(K_I, N_I) \tag{10}$$

$$Y_c = C(K_c, N_c) \tag{11}$$

$$I_K = r + \delta - \pi \tag{12}$$

$$I_N = \frac{1}{p_1} \frac{w}{p} \tag{13}$$

$$C_K = p_1(r + \delta - \pi) \tag{14}$$

$$C_N = \frac{w}{p} \tag{15}$$

$$K_1 + K_c = K \tag{16}$$

$$Y_c = c\left(Y - \delta K - T - \frac{M + B}{p}\pi; r - \pi\right) + G \tag{17}$$

$$\frac{M}{p} = m(r, Y), \tag{18}$$

which is a system of ten equations in the ten endogenous variables Y, Y_1, Y_c, N_1, N_c, K_1, K_c, r, p_1, and p. The exogenous variables are w, M, T, G, K, B, and π. Notice that we have assumed that the government purchases consumption goods at the rate G. (For an analysis of this model, see Henderson and Sargent, 1973.)

We now consider the special case in which the production functions $I(\ ,\ )$ and $C(\ ,\ )$ are identical, so that

$$I(K, N) = C(K, N) = F(K, N).$$

Using (12) and (13), we have

$$\frac{F_K}{F_N} = \frac{I_K}{I_N} = \frac{p_1(r + \delta - \pi)}{w/p}. \tag{19}$$

Using (14) and (15), we have

$$\frac{F_K}{F_N} = \frac{C_K}{C_N} = \frac{p_1(r + \delta - \pi)}{w/p}. \tag{20}$$

By virtue of the linear homogeneity of $F(K, N)$, we have

$$F_K(K, N) = F_K(K/N, 1) \qquad \text{and} \qquad F_N(K, N) = F_N(K/N, 1),$$

so that F_K/F_N is a function of K/N with derivative

$$\frac{d(F_K/F_N)}{d(K/N)} = \frac{F_N F_{KK} - F_K F_{NK}}{F_N{}^2} < 0. \tag{21}$$

An increase in the capital–labor ratio thus lowers F_K/F_N. Inequality (21) implies that we can invert the above relation to obtain the capital–labor ratio as a function of F_K/F_N,

$$\frac{K}{N} = \xi\left(\frac{F_K}{F_N}\right), \qquad \xi' = \left(\frac{F_N{}^2}{F_N F_{KK} - F_K F_{NK}}\right) < 0. \tag{22}$$

Now by virtue of Equations (19) and (20), we have

$$\frac{F_K(K_1, N_1)}{F_N(K_1, N_1)} = \frac{F_K(K_c, N_c)}{F_N(K_c, N_c)} = \frac{p_1(r + \delta - \pi)}{w/p}.$$

In combination with Equation (22) this implies

$$\frac{K_I}{N_I} = \frac{K_c}{N_c} = \xi\left(\frac{p_1(r + \delta - \pi)}{w/p}\right),$$

so that the capital–labor ratios are identical in the two industries. Taking the ratio of (15) to (13), we have

$$C_N/I_N = p_1.$$

But since $K_I/N_I = K_c/N_c$, we have $C_N = I_N$, so that the above equality implies that $p_1 = 1$.

Now notice that by virtue of Euler's theorem, we have

$$\begin{aligned}
Y &= p_1 Y_I + Y_c \\
&= p_1(F_K K_I + F_N N_I) + (F_K K_c + F_N N_c) \\
&= (p_1 F_K K_I + F_K K_c) + (p_1 F_N N_I + F_N N_c) \\
&= F_K\left(\frac{K}{N}, 1\right)K + F_N\left(\frac{K}{N}, 1\right)N \\
&= F(K, N)
\end{aligned} \tag{23}$$

where $N = N_c + N_I$. Moreover, notice that since

$$\frac{K_I}{N_I} = \frac{K_c}{N_c} = \frac{K_I + K_c}{N_I + N_c},$$

we have

$$F_K(K_c, N_c) = F_K(K_I, N_I) = F_K(K, N), \tag{24}$$

$$F_N(K_c, N_c) = F_N(K_I, N_I) = F_N(K, N). \tag{25}$$

Notice that since $Y = F(K, N)$ and $p_1 = 1$, we have

$$Y_I + Y_c = F(K, N),$$

which is the "transformation curve" between Y_I and Y_c, a straight line with slope -1 and intercept $F(K, N)$. This curve gives the maximum Y_I (or Y_c) that the economy can produce for given values of K, N, and Y_c(or Y_I). To find the transformation curve, we can maximize $Y_I = F(K_I, N_I)$ subject to $\bar{Y}_c = F(K - K_I, N - N_I)$, which is accomplished by unconstrained maximization of

$$J = F(K_I, N_I) + \lambda(\bar{Y}_c - F(K - K_I, N - N_I)),$$

where λ is a Lagrange multiplier. The first-order conditions are

$$\frac{\partial J}{\partial K_I} = F_{K_I} + \lambda F_{K_c} = 0, \qquad \frac{\partial J}{\partial N_I} = F_{N_I} + \lambda F_{N_c} = 0,$$

$$Y_c = F(K - K_I, N - N_I).$$

Dividing the first marginal condition by the second gives

$$F_{K_I}/F_{N_I} = F_{K_c}/F_{N_c},$$

which by virtue of the linear homogeneity of $F(\ )$ implies

$$K_I/N_I = K_c/N_c = K/N,$$

which, again by the linear homogeneity of F, implies that

$$F_{K_I}(K_I, N_I) = F_{K_c}(K_c, N_c) = F_K(K, N),$$
$$F_{N_I}(K_I, N_I) = F_{N_c}(K_c, N_c) = F_N(K, N).$$

Euler's theorem then implies that

$$
\begin{aligned}
Y_I + Y_c &= F_{K_c}(K_c, N_c)K_c + F_{N_c}(K_c, N_c)N_c + F_{K_I}(K_I, N_I)K_I + F_{N_I}(K_I, N_I)N_I \\
&= F_K(K, N)K + F_N(K, N)N \\
&= F(K, N).
\end{aligned}
$$

Since the transformation curve has a slope of -1, it follows that p_1 must equal unity so long as the marginal equalities for the factors of production are in force and both Y_I and Y_c are positive.

As a result of (23)–(25) and the fact that $p_1 = 1$ we have that for the special case in which the production functions in the two industries are identical, the model consisting of Equations (9)–(18) can be collapsed to the following system:

$$Y = F(K, N)$$

$$r + \delta - \pi = F_K(K, N)$$

$$w/p = F_N(K, N)$$

$$Y = Y_c + Y_I$$

$$Y_c = c\left(Y - T - \delta K - \frac{M + B}{p}\pi, r - \pi\right) + G$$

$$M/p = m(r, Y),$$

which consists of six equations in the endogenous variables Y, N, r, p, Y_c, and Y_I and the exogenous variables M, w, B, π, G, T, and K. This system is identical with Tobin's dynamic aggregative model.

We are now in a position to analyze the forces that prevent changes in G from having any effects on the aggregate levels of output and employment. Suppose G increases by dG. The model predicts that Y_c will rise by dG, while Y_I will fall by dG, so that holdings of capital and employment in the two industries will change according to

$$dN_c = \frac{N_c}{Y_c} dG = \frac{N_I}{Y_I} dG = -dN_I, \qquad dK_c = \frac{K_c}{Y_c} dG = \frac{K_I}{Y_I} dG = -dK_I.$$

These changes occur at fixed values of p_1, p, w, and r, so that labor–output and capital–output ratios remain unchanged. Notice that $N_c/Y_c = N_I/Y_I$, and $K_c/Y_c = K_I/Y_I$ by virtue of the assumption of identical production functions in the two industries.

What market forces prompt producers of capital goods to release just the amounts of capital and labor that producers of consumer goods need to meet the increased demand for their output? At the initial equilibrium values of Y, Y_I, and Y_c, the increased demand for consumer goods caused by the increase in G produces a slight tendency for p to rise, while $p_1 p$ remains constant. The rise in p induces a rise in the profits of consumer goods producers, while profits of investment goods producers remain unchanged:

$$\left.\frac{d\Pi_I}{dp}\right|_{d(p_1 p) = 0} = 0, \qquad \left.\frac{d\Pi_c}{dp}\right|_{d(p_1 p) = 0} = Y_c > 0.$$

The rate of return on capital in the consumer goods industry thus rises, exceeding that in the investment goods industry. This causes firms in the consumer good industry to bid for capital, which firms in the investment industry are willing to sell or rent to them in order to obtain the highest possible rate of return on their capital. How much of a rise in p is required to bring about such changes in the distribution of capital and employment? The slightest upward movement in p (or downward movement in p_1) is sufficient to bring about arbitrarily large required changes in the distribution of capital and employment across industries. That is, a drop in p_1 below unity causes the system to move along a transformation curve to the corner where all resources are devoted to producing consumption goods. Consequently, in equilibrium p and p_1 remain at their initial levels, as do Y and M. For if p_1 were to fall below unity, all resources would be devoted to producing consumption goods, which would surely not be an equilibrium situation provided that the initial value of Y_I exceeds the new level of G.

3. INVESTMENT AND SAVING

We notice that the economy's rate of net investment is determined as a "residual" in Equation (VI). By substituting the definition of disposable income into Equation (VI), it can be written in the equivalent form

$$I + G = S + T + \frac{M + B}{p} \pi.$$

Assume now that the government's budget is balanced, so that G equals T, and that the anticipated rate of inflation π is zero. Then we have

$$I = S, \tag{26}$$

which is the familiar statement that "investment equals saving." After the publication of Keynes's *General Theory* there was a good deal of controversy about the meaning of this equality, which is of course present in the "classical" and "Keynesian" models as well as the model being studied here. In particular, some controversy centered about whether or not the investment rate appearing in (26) ought to be interpreted as "intended" or *ex ante* investment, and whether the equality should be interpreted as an equilibrium condition or as a statement of necessary relationships between *ex post* quantities. These old controversies are of some interest in the light of Tobin's model since the model contains no *ex ante* investment demand schedule. Consequently here (26) ought not to be interpreted as an equilibrium relationship between *ex ante* concepts. Instead, (26) states that saving intentions are realized and that these, together with the government's fiscal policies, govern the economy's rate of capital accumulation. In this sense investment is determined entirely on the "supply side," i.e., by the flow of resources that consumers and the government are willing not to consume. Notice also that the model contains a device for reconciling firms to whatever rate of investment is determined by this process. The rate of investment determines subsequent levels of the capital stock. The model will generate time paths of prices, the interest rate, and output which guarantee that firms are content to hold just the existing capital stock at each moment in time. Thus, in this model no useful purpose is served by introducing a distinction between intended and realized investment.[5]

The model is obviously quite "monetarist" in its predictions. Fiscal policy matters not at all, while changes in the money supply produce effects on output at a point in time. Moreover, money acquires this potency not by its effects on desired flows of consumption and investment, as is true in the Keynesian model. Instead, money impinges on the economy by producing effects in the market for existing physical assets. It is from that market that pressures on the price level emerge, and it is changes in the price level that permit output to be affected at a point in time. In view of these properties of the model it is not surprising that monetarists have on occasion emphasized the important role played by markets in stocks of physical assets in the process by which the effects of money supply changes are transmitted (for example, see Friedman and Meiselman, 1963, especially pp. 217–222).

The impotence of fiscal policy in this model may seem peculiar in the light of Keynes's doctrine of the marginal efficiency of capital, which seems to indicate that the formal model of Keynes's *General Theory* contains a perfect market in which firms can always purchase and sell existing physical capital goods (see

---

[5] It is a defensible position that the model under consideration more faithfully reflects Keynes's views of the determinants of capital accumulation than does our "Keynesian" model. As a consequence, it helps rationalize some of Keynes's views on the saving-equals-investment controversies just discussed.

Keynes, 1937, especially pp. 221-222 in the Clower reprint). The marginal efficiency of capital was defined as that rate of discount which equates the present value of the stream of returns associated with a given capital good to the purchase price of the good. Keynes asserted that firms would purchase capital goods until the marginal efficiency of capital equals the rate of interest. As Keynes pointed out, this is equivalent to assuming that firms maximize their present value.[6] In terms of the one-sector model we are studying here note that the present cost of an additional unit of capital is simply the current price of the one good p. The flow of net returns associated with an additional unit of capital at time t is $p(t)F_K - p(t)\delta$. Thus the marginal efficiency of capital ξ is defined as that rate of discount satisfying the equation

$$p = \int_0^\infty e^{-\xi t}[p(t)F_K - \delta p(t)]\, dt.$$

Assuming that $p(t)$ is expected to follow the path $p(t) = pe^{\pi t}$, the above equation simplifies to

$$p = (pF_K - p\delta)\int_0^\infty e^{-(\xi - \pi)t}\, dt, \qquad p = \frac{pF_K - p\delta}{\xi - \pi}.$$

Thus the marginal efficiency of capital is $\xi = F_K + \pi - \delta$. Keynes asserted that firms will purchase or sell capital goods until ξ equals r: $r = \xi = F_K + \pi - \delta$, which can be written $F_K = r + \delta - \pi$, which is equivalent with the marginal condition for capital that springs from present value maximization.

EXERCISES

1. Consider an economy described by the following equations:

$Y = F(K, N)$ with $F_K, F_N, F_{KN} > 0;\ F_{NN}, F_{KK} < 0$

$w/p = F_N$

$r = F_K$

$C = C(Y - T)$ with $0 < C' < 1$

$Y = C + I + G$

$M/p = H(r, C + I)$ with $H_r < 0,\ H_{C+I} > 0.$

Here Y is GNP, N employment, K capital, w the money wage, p the price level, C consumption, I investment, T taxes net of transfers, G government purchases, and M the money supply. The exogenous variables are K, M, G, T, and w. The endogenous variables are Y, N, C, I, r, and p. Describe the effects on all six endogenous variables of:

    A. an increase in M achieved via an open-market operation;
    B. an increase in T;
    C. an increase in G.

---

[6] Keynes pointed out that his marginal efficiency of capital was identical with Irving Fisher's "rate of return over cost." See *General Theory*, Chapter 11. For analyses of the concept of internal rate of return see Alchian (1955).

2. Consider an economy described by the following equations.

$$Y = F(K, N) \quad \text{with} \quad F_K, F_N, F_{KN} > 0; \quad \text{and} \quad F_{NN}, F_{KK} < 0 \quad \text{(production function)}$$
$$w/p = F_N \quad \text{(marginal equality for employment)}$$
$$r = F_K \quad \text{(marginal equality for capital)}$$
$$C = C(Y_D) \quad \text{with} \quad 0 < C' < 1 \quad \text{(consumption function)}$$
$$Y_D = Y - T$$
$$C + I + G = Y$$
$$M/p = m(r, Y_D) \quad \text{with} \quad m_r < 0, m_{Y_D} > 0 \quad \text{(portfolio equilibrium condition)}.$$

The endogenous variables are:

Y = GNP C = consumption

N = employment r = interest rate

p = the price level Y_D = disposable income

I = investment.

The exogenous variables are:

K = the capital stock M = the money stock, a liability of the government

w = the money wage G = government expenditures

T = tax collections.

Describe the effects on the endogenous variables of:

    A. an increase in the money wage;
    B. an increase in government expenditure;
    C. an increase in tax collections.

REFERENCES

Alchian, A. A. (1955). "The Rate of Interest, Fisher's Rate of Return Over Cost and Keynes' Internal Rate of Return." *The American Economic Review*, Vol. XLV, No. 5, pp. 938–942.

Calvo, G. (1980). "Tax-Finance Government Spending in a Neoclassical Model with Sticky Wages and Rational Expectations." *Journal of Economic Dynamics and Control*, Vol. 2, No. 1, pp. 61–78.

Friedman, M., and Meiselman, D. (1963). "The Relative Stability of Monetary Velocity and the Investment Multiplier in the United States, 1897–1958." *Stabilization Policies*, pp. 217–222. Commission on Money Credit, Englewood Cliffs, New Jersey: Prentice-Hall.

Henderson, D. W., and Sargent, T. (1973). "Monetary and Fiscal Policy in a Two-Sector Aggregative Model." *American Economic Review*, Vol. LXIII, No. 3, pp. 345–365.

Henderson, J. M., and Quandt, R. E. (1971). *Microeconomic Theory*, 2nd ed. New York: McGraw-Hill.

Hirshleifer, J. (1958). "On the Theory of Optimal Investment Decision." *The Journal of Political Economy*, Vol. LXVI, No. 4, pp. 329–352.

Intriligator, M. D. (1971). *Mathematical Optimization and Economic Theory*, Chapter 12. Englewood Cliffs, New Jersey: Prentice-Hall.

Keynes, J. M. (1937). "The General Theory of Employment." *The Quarterly Journal of Economics*, Vol. LI, No. 2, pp. 209–223. Reprinted in R. Clower, ed. (1969). *Monetary Theory*, pp. 215–225. Baltimore, Maryland: Penguin Book Ltd.

Tobin, J. (1955). "A Dynamic Aggregative Model." *The Journal of Political Economy*, Vol. LXIII, No. 2, pp. 103–115.

CHAPTER IV

MISCELLANEOUS TOPICS

1. THE "REAL BILLS" DOCTRINE

Up to now we have taken the money supply as a parameter, one which is somehow determined by the government. It happens, however, that the government has not always viewed the money supply as a thing it ought to control, even when it has had the tools needed to control it. Instead, it has often been argued that the proper function of the monetary authorities is to set the interest rate at some reasonable level, allowing the money supply to be whatever it must be to ensure that the demand for money at that interest rate is satisfied. Such a rule was actually written into the original act that established the Federal Reserve System in the U.S. The rule was known as the "real bills" doctrine. It was alleged that the quantity of money would automatically be properly regulated if the monetary authorities ensured that banks always had enough reserves to meet the demand for loans intended to finance "real" (as opposed to "speculative") investments at an interest rate set "with a view of accommodating commerce and business."

Here we analyze the effect of such a rule in the context of the "classical" model discussed above. The effect of the rule is to make the interest rate an exogenous variable, one determined by the monetary authorities, and the money supply endogenous. The monetary authority simply conducts whatever open-market operations that are required to make the interest rate what it wants it to be. The authority stands ready to buy or sell whatever quantities of government bonds are offered at the announced interest rate.

We consider the version of the classical model discussed in Chapter I, which consists of the following seven equations:

$$Y = F(K, N) \tag{1}$$

$$w/p = F_N(K, N) \tag{2}$$

$$N = N^S(w/p) \tag{3}$$

$$C = c\left(Y - T - \delta K - \frac{M + B}{p}\,\pi, r - \pi \right) \tag{4}$$

$$I = I(q(K, N, r - \pi) - 1) \tag{5}$$

$$C + I + G + \delta K = Y \tag{6}$$

$$M/p = m(r, Y). \tag{7}$$

The endogenous variables are Y, N, p, w, C, I, and M, while the exogenous variables are G, T, K, π and r. The monetary authority is assumed to peg r by permitting the money supply to be whatever it must be to equal the demand for money at that interest rate.

The system is block recursive, Equations (1)–(3) determining Y, N, and w/p. Equations (4)–(6) are then three equations that, given the previously determined value of Y, can determine the three endogenous variables C, I, and p. Once these three variables have been determined, the last equation determines M, given the previously determined values of p and Y.

The workings of the model can be illustrated with Figure 1. The authority pegs the interest rate at $\bar{r}$. The first three equations determine output at its full employment level, which we denote by Y_F. The next three equations determine a level of aggregate demand which equals Y_F at the pegged interest rate $\bar{r}$. Since $\bar{r}$ cannot adjust to make aggregate demand equal aggregate supply, the entire burden falls on the price level, which influences consumption through its effect on perceived real disposable income. The price level adjusts to make the IS curve pass through the intersection of $\bar{r}$ and Y_F. Finally, the portfolio balance equation determines the money supply. To peg the interest rate, the government must issue enough money to guarantee that the LM curve passes through the intersection of Y_F and $\bar{r}$.

To illustrate how the model works, suppose that there is an increase in government expenditures. Since the interest rate and output are fixed, the price level must adjust to diminish perceived disposable income and consumption by

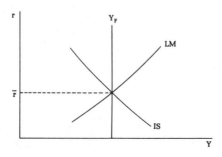

FIGURE 1

just enough to offset the increase in G. In particular, the change in p and the change in G must obey

$$dG = -c_1 \left(\frac{M + B}{p^2} \pi \right) dp.$$

If $M + B$ and π are both positive, prices must fall in order to increase the real value of the government's debt to the public and the anticipated real capital losses on that debt, thereby decreasing disposable income and consumption. The fall in p in turn causes a fall in M through the portfolio balance equation.

Notice that the "stability" of the system in response to a change in G depends on the sign of $((M + B)/p)\pi$. For if G rises, at the initial r, p, and Y, there is an excess demand for goods, which we usually posit leads to rising prices. But if $((M + B)/p)\pi$ is positive, a fall in p is required to restore equilibrium, so that the system is driven away from equilibrium. On the other hand, if $((M + B)/p)\pi$ is negative, the system is stable.

Suppose now that $\pi(M + B) = 0$, so that p no longer appears in the consumption function. Then the fourth, fifth, and sixth equations of our system are three equations in only two variables, C and I, since p no longer appears. These three equations in general "overdetermine" the two variables I and C. The investment equation can be viewed as determining I, while the consumption function determines C. But in general the values of C and I so determined will violate the national income equation, where Y has been determined by (1)–(3).

While the model overdetermines C and I, p and M are "underdetermined." Each of these two variables appear only in the seventh equation, which is not capable of determining their values.

The problem with the model is illustrated by Figure 2. The first three equations determine Y_F, while the second three determine an IS curve. There is nothing to guarantee that the IS curve passes through the point $(Y_F, \bar{r})$. The model posits too many independent relationships between r and Y to enable equilibrium to be determined.

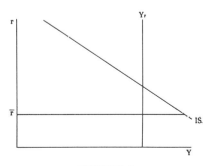

FIGURE 2

Nor can the problem be avoided by pegging r at the "correct" level, i.e., at the intersection of the Y_F line and the IS curve. It is true that if r is pegged at that level, the solution for Y from the labor market and production function agrees with that from the IS curve. But it remains true that the portfolio balance curve determines only the ratio $\cdot M/p$ and cannot determine the level of either M or p. So even if r is pegged at the "correct" level, the price level and the money supply are indeterminate.

This model illustrates the danger of naive "equation counting" as a technique supposedly capable of determining whether a model possesses a unique equilibrium. Our model consists of seven equations in seven variables. The equality between the number of equations and number of variables does not suffice to guarantee that the equations have a solution. The problem is in the last four equations, which given Y, N, and w/p, form a system of four equations in the four variables C, I, p, and M. But the system decomposes in an unfortunate way, the fourth, fifth, and sixth equations forming an independent subset involving only I and C, while the seventh is an independent equation involving both p and M.

The standard criticisms made of the "real bills" doctrine are based on the analysis above. The argument is that any attempt to peg the interest rate is destabilizing, to say the least. For example, Wicksell (1965) argued that pegging the interest rate too low would set off increases in the price level and money supply of indefinitely large magnitudes. The model itself possesses no equilibrium when the monetary authorities peg the interest rate at such a level, but "stability conditions" do imply that the price level and money supply will rise, and rise by indefinitely large amounts, if the monetary authorities pursue such a policy.[1]

It should be clear that the criticism of the "real bills" doctrine based on the classical analysis described above is formally correct only in a system that contains neither a Pigou effect nor nonzero perceived real capital gains on the government's debt to the public. This is another illustration of Metzler's point that assigning a role to the Pigou effect fundamentally alters some important aspects of the classical macroeconomic system.

The model discussed above is important in the history of economic thought. Through analysis of such an overdetermined system, Wicksell (1965) performed some early "Keynesian" economic analysis.

---

[1] The representation and criticism of the real bills doctrine reported in this section are standard ones, but are not universally accepted. Sargent and Wallace (1982) provide a defense of a version of the real bills doctrine, interpreted as an instruction to the open market authority to implement unfettered intermediation of safe government and private debt through either open market policy or financial deregulation. Sargent and Wallace's analysis rests on a different model of the demand for money than the one that is used in the first five chapters of this book. In particular, their paper uses a model of the demand for money which builds on some ideas of Tobin and Modigliani and Miller which we shall study in Chapter VII.

2. "INSIDE" AND "OUTSIDE" MONEY[2]

Up to now we have assumed that firms have no bonds outstanding, issuing equities to finance all of their investment. We have also assumed that the government does not own any of the liabilities of firms. We now abandon these assumptions in order to provide a framework for understanding the distinctions some economists have made between "inside money" and "outside money."

We shall work with a version of Tobin's (1955) "dynamic aggregative model." We now assume that firms issue both variable-coupon bonds, whose nominal value is B_f, and equities, whose nominal value is V. Households regard firms' bonds and equities as perfect substitutes when their real yields are equal. They also regard firms' bonds as perfect substitutes for those of the government. These assumptions imply that government bonds, bonds issued by firms, and equities will all bear the same perceived real rate of return: $r - \pi$. The value of owners' equity equals the capitalized value of firms' net cash flow after paying off bond holders,

$$V(t) = \int_t^\infty [p(s)Y(s) - w(s)N(s) - \delta p(s)K(s) - r(s)B_f(s)]e^{-r(s-t)}\, ds.$$

Assume that the variables Y, N, K, B_f, and r are expected to remain at their current values, while w and p are expected to follow the paths

$$w(s) = w(t)e^{\pi(s-t)}, \qquad p(s) = p(t)e^{\pi(s-t)}.$$

Then $V(t)$ becomes

$$V(t) = [pY - wN - \delta pK] \int_t^\infty e^{-(r-\pi)(s-t)}\, ds - rB_f(t) \int_t^\infty e^{-r(s-t)}\, ds$$

$$= \frac{pY - wN - \delta pK}{r - \pi} - B_f(t).$$

From the linear homogeneity of F and the profit-maximization conditions for K and N this becomes

$$V(t) = p(t)K(t) - B_f(t).$$

Thus, the value of owners' and creditors' claims on firms, $V(t) + B_f(t)$, equals the market value of firms' physical capital. Firms' consolidated balance sheet is as follows:

Assets	Liabilities
pK	B_f
	V

[2] A good paper on the topic of this section is Patinkin (1961).

The household sectors' balance sheet is now:

Assets	Liabilities
$B_f(h)$	
B_G	
V	
M	Net worth

Here $B_f(h)$ denotes the nominal quantity of firms' bonds held by the household section, while B_G denotes the nominal quantity of government bonds, which are all held by households. Households continue to own all equities and all money in the system.

The government issues debt in the form of money and government bonds, the total quantity outstanding being B_G. The government also owns a quantity of firms' bonds denoted by $B_f(G)$. The government's balance sheet is thus:

Assets	Liabilities
$B_f(G)$	M
	B_G
	Net worth

Notice that $B_f = B_f(h) + B_f(G)$. The government conducts open market operations subject to $dM + dB_G = dB_f(G)$.

The economy is assumed to be described by the following "classical" version of Tobin's (1955) "dynamic aggregative model":

$$Y = F(K, N) \tag{8}$$

$$w/p = F_N \tag{9}$$

$$N = N^S\left(\frac{w}{p}\right) \tag{10}$$

$$r = F_K - \delta \tag{11}$$

$$M/p = m(r, Y) \tag{12}$$

$$C = C(Y - T - \delta K, r, W), \qquad C_3 > 0 \tag{13}$$

$$C + I + G + \delta K = Y. \tag{14}$$

We have assumed that π equals zero. We have added a classical labor supply curve, Equation (10), to Tobin's model. Households' real wealth W is given by

$$W = \frac{M + V + B_G + B_f(h)}{p}.$$

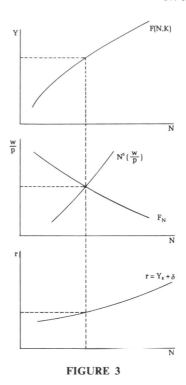

FIGURE 3

Equation (13) is a Pigouvian consumption function, real consumption varying directly with households' real wealth.

As in the classical model, Equations (8)–(10) form an independent subset that determines Y, w/p, and N. Equation (11) then determines r. Equation (12) determines p. Equations (13) and (14) then determine the division of Y into C and I, and hence influence the economy's rate of growth over time. The determination of Y, N, w/p, and r is illustrated in Figure 3.

We shall now examine the circumstances under which money is a "veil" in this model, having no effects on the real variables of the model. We already know that at a point in time, Y, w/p, and N are determined by Equations (8)–(10) and hence cannot be influenced by changes in the government's balance sheet. However, it is possible that C and I, and hence the economy's growth rate, can be influenced by such changes. Whether or not monetary policy affects C and I depends entirely on whether or not it is able to affect consumers' wealth, thereby influencing consumption.

We first consider a regime in which all money is "inside" money. In this regime the government issues no bonds and holds a volume of firms' bonds equal to the value of the money supply:

$$M = B_f(G) \qquad \text{and} \qquad B_G = 0.$$

All money is matched or "backed" by government holdings of private debt. Such money is called "inside" money because it does not represent a net claim of the private sector, i.e., firms and households, against an outside sector. The claims that the money represents are just offset by government claims against firms. In such a regime households' wealth is

$$W = \frac{M + V}{p} + \frac{B_f - B_f(G)}{p} = \frac{M + V}{p} + \frac{B_f - M}{p}$$

$$= \frac{V + B_f}{p} = K.$$

Households' real wealth equals the real value of the capital stock. It follows that an open-market operation, i.e., a government exchange of money for firms' bonds, will have no influence on households' real wealth, and will not affect either C or I. The only effect will be to produce a proportional change in the price level.

Now consider a regime in which all money is "outside" money. That is, the government owns no bonds issued by firms so that $B_f(G) = 0$. All money thus represents a net claim of households against an outside sector, the government. In this regime, households' real wealth is

$$W = \frac{M + B_G + V + B_f}{p} = \frac{M + B_G}{p} + K.$$

The constraint on open-market operations is now $dM = -dB_G$ since we assume $B_f(G)$ remains at zero. Recall that by virtue of Equations (8)–(12), $dM/M = dp/p$. Now calculate the differential of W:

$$dW = \frac{p(dM + dB_G) - dp(M + B_G)}{p^2} = \frac{dM + dB_G}{p} - \frac{M + B_G}{p}\frac{dM}{M}. \quad (15)$$

If the change in money is accomplished via open-market operations,

$$dW = -\frac{M + B_G}{p}\frac{dM}{M},$$

so that an increase in the money supply decreases the real wealth of households: it leaves $M + B_G$ unchanged, but causes an increase in the price level. The change in wealth will affect consumption through Equation (13) and capital accumulation through Equation (14). Thus in a regime of all "outside" money changes in the money supply accomplished through open-market operations affect some "real" variables.

To establish the conditions under which changes in money will have no effects in such a regime we set dW equal to zero in (15) and rearrange to arrive at the condition:

$$dM/M = dB_G/B_G.$$

This states that to have no real effects, changes in the money supply must be accompanied by equiproportional changes in government bonds. In order to have no real effects changes in money must not alter the proportion of government bonds to money held by households.

Now consider a regime in which all money is "inside" money, so that it is always true that $M = B_f(G)$. Suppose that there are also government bonds outstanding, so that $B_G > 0$. The government only conducts open-market operations in firms' bonds, so that $dM = dB_f(G)$. Households' real wealth is then

$$W = \frac{M + V}{p} + \frac{B_G + B_f - M}{p} = \frac{V + B_f}{p} + \frac{B_G}{p} = K + \frac{B_G}{p}.$$

The differential of W is

$$dW = \frac{p\, dB_G - B_G\, dp}{p^2} = \frac{dB_G}{p} - \frac{B_G}{p} \frac{dM}{M}.$$

This expression will equal zero only if

$$dB_G/B_G = dM/M,$$

i.e., only if changes in money are accompanied by equiproportional changes in government bonds. Such a change could not be accomplished by open-market operations, but would have to occur as a result of a government giveaway program, for example, issuing a veterans' bonus. Under the regime considered here, changes in money engineered via open-market operations affect W and hence C and I.

3. UNIONS AND REAL WAGES

Here we present a "classical" analysis of the impact of unions on real wages and other aggregate variables. We assume that there are two kinds of jobs with skilled employment of N men and unskilled employment of n men. The total labor supply equals $N + n = \overline{N}$ men, which we assume is fixed. There is a union for skilled workers that sets a fixed money wage W_N for skilled workers. The union sets the wage for skilled workers so that it always exceeds the wage for unskilled labor and so that there are always some skilled workers who cannot find skilled jobs. If a person who is skilled cannot find work as a skilled worker, he joins the unskilled labor force and takes an unskilled job at wage W_n. There he can always find a job because the market for unskilled labor is competitive and has a market-determined money wage W_n.

There is one good in the model produced subject to the production function

$$Y = F(N, n, K), \qquad F_N, F_n, F_K > 0, \quad F_{NN}, F_{nn}, F_{KK} < 0,$$

$$F_{Nn} = F_{NK} = F_{nK} = 0. \tag{16}$$

The rest of the model is

$$W_N/p = F_N \qquad\qquad \text{marginal condition for skilled labor} \qquad (17)$$

$$W_n/p = F_n \qquad\qquad \text{marginal condition for unskilled labor} \qquad (18)$$

$$N + n = \bar{N} \qquad\qquad \text{full employment condition} \qquad (19)$$

$$C = C(Y - T), \quad 1 > C' > 0 \qquad \text{consumption function} \qquad (20)$$

$$I = I(r - \pi), \qquad I' < 0 \qquad \text{investment schedule} \qquad (21)$$

$$C + I + G = Y \qquad\qquad\qquad (22)$$

$$M/p = m(r, Y), \qquad m_r < 0 < m_Y \quad \text{portfolio balance schedule.} \qquad (23)$$

The model consists of eight equations in the eight endogenous variables $Y, N, n, C, I, r, p,$ and W_n. The exogenous variables are $M, G, T, \pi, K, W_N,$ and $\bar{N}$.

Equations (20)–(22) define an IS curve in the r, Y plane. Equations (16), (17), and (19) define an aggregate supply curve in the p, Y plane, which can be combined with the portfolio balance schedule (23) to form an LM curve.

To derive the differential of the aggregate supply curve, compute the differential of (16) and (19):

$$dY = F_N \, dN + F_n \, dn + F_K \, dK, \qquad dN + dn = d\bar{N} = 0,$$

or

$$dn = -dN.$$

So we have

$$dY = (F_N - F_n) \, dN + F_K \, dK. \qquad (24)$$

Since we assume that the union manages to keep W_N greater than W_n, it follows that

$$F_N = W_N/p > W_n/p = F_n \qquad \text{or} \qquad F_N - F_n > 0,$$

so that from (24) output rises as skilled employment rises and unskilled employment falls. This occurs because of the greater productivity of unskilled labor at the margin.

Computing the total differential of (17) gives

$$\frac{dp}{p} = \frac{-F_{NN}}{F_N} \, dN + \frac{dW_N}{W_N}.$$

Substituting the above equation into (24) gives the total differential of the aggregate supply curve

$$\frac{dp}{p} = \frac{-F_{NN}}{F_N} \frac{1}{F_N - F_n} \, dY + \frac{F_K F_{NN}}{F_N(F_N - F_n)} \, dK + \frac{dW_N}{W_N}, \qquad (25)$$

which has positive coefficients on dY and dW_N, and a negative coefficient on dK. The supply curve is upward sloping in the p, Y plane because in order for Y to increase, N must increase at the expense of n. This can occur if p rises, permitting W_N/p and hence F_N to fall. Substituting the differential of the aggregate supply curve (25) into the differential of the portfolio balance schedule gives

$$
dr = \frac{1}{m_r} \frac{dM}{p} - \frac{1}{m_r} \left(m_Y - \frac{F_{NN}}{F_N} \frac{M}{p} \frac{1}{F_N - F_n} \right) dY - \frac{1}{m_r} \frac{M}{p} \frac{F_{NN}}{F_N}
$$
$$
\times \frac{F_K}{F_N - F_n} dK - \frac{1}{m_r} \frac{M}{p} \frac{dW_N}{W_N},
$$

which is the total differential of the LM curve. The LM curve is upward sloping in the r, Y plane, and shifts downward when M or K increases and when W_N decreases.

The equilibrium of the system occurs at the intersection of the IS and LM curves. To illustrate how the model works, consider the effects of an increase in government expenditures G, which we know shifts the IS curve outward and so drives both the interest rate and output up. The increase in aggregate demand causes the price level to rise, which with W_N fixed causes the real wage of skilled workers to fall, creating incentives to hire more of them. Employment of unskilled labor falls because the money wage W_n rises more than proportionately with the price level. Notice that the model predicts that periods of high output are associated with a narrowing of the difference in wage rates between high-skill and low-skill workers.[3]

When the labor union imposes an increase in W_N, we have an example of "cost-push" inflation. The LM curve shifts back, driving output down and the interest rate up. Since output falls, we know that employment of unskilled labor rises. From the portfolio balance condition and the fact that r has risen while Y has fallen we know that $m(r, Y)$ has fallen; so M/p must also fall, meaning p must rise. This rise in p helps achieve the reduction in W_n/p required to stimulate employment of unskilled workers. From Equation (18) we have that the differential of W_n obeys

$$
\frac{dW_n}{p} = \frac{dp}{p} \frac{W_n}{p} + F_{nn} \, dn.
$$

Since $dn > 0$ and $dp > 0$, it is impossible to determine whether W_n rises or falls. Upward pressure on W_n is exerted by the increase in the price level p; but downward pressure is exerted by the increase in the number of workers seeking unskilled jobs because of the union's action in raising W_N.

In summary, then, the effect of the union's imposition of an increase in W_N is to raise the skilled real wage, but to decrease the unskilled real wage. The effect

---

[3] Wachter has pointed to a tendency for interindustry wage differentials to narrow during periods of high output. See Wachter (1970).

on "average" real wages in the economy is ambiguous. Similarly, the effect of the increase in W_N on some average money wage level is also ambiguous.

There is a literature on the question of whether unions have acted to affect the average level of real wages in the American economy. The sort of model described here is perhaps potentially relevant for this question since in the American economy only about one-quarter of the labor force is unionized.

4. LANGE'S CRITIQUE OF THE CLASSICAL DICHOTOMY

In a famous but confusing line of reasoning, Oscar Lange criticized classical models that dichotomize as being inconsistent with Walras' law.[4] We ought immediately to be suspicious of such a criticism since we have seen above that the models that we have constructed obey versions of Walras' law, even those models that dichotomize.

Lange characterized the real sector by the equations

$$q_i = d_i(p_1, \ldots, p_n) = d_i(\lambda p_1, \ldots, \lambda p_n), \qquad i = 1, \ldots, n, \tag{26}$$

$$0 = q_i - q_i^\circ = e_i(p_1, \ldots, p_n)$$

$$= e_i(\lambda p_1, \ldots, \lambda p_n), \qquad i = 1, \ldots, n, \quad \lambda > 0. \tag{27}$$

Here p_i is the price of the ith good, measured in dollars per unit of the ith good; q_i° is the exogenous rate of output of the ith good, q_i is the rate of demand for the ith good. Equations (26) are a set of n demand functions that are homogeneous of degree zero in all prices, while Equations (27) are a set of equilibrium conditions requiring that excess demands $q_i - q_i^\circ$, which are also homogeneous of degree zero in all prices, all equal zero.[5] Equations (26) and (27) are viewed as determining the rates of consumption q_i, $i = 1, \ldots, n$, and the $n - 1$ relative prices p_i/p_1, $i = 2, \ldots, n$. The supplies q_i° are taken as exogenous, so that this is a "pure exchange" economy. The demand and excess demand schedules are assumed to build in budget constraints of the form $\sum_{i=1}^n p_i(q_i - q_i^\circ) = 0$, where q_i°, $i = 1, \ldots, n$, are quantities supplied. Then one of the excess demand equations is redundant (can be deduced from the others), so that the system (26) and (27) consists of $2n - 1$ independent equations for determining the n quantities q_i, $i = 1, \ldots, n$, and the $n - 1$ relative prices p_i/p_1, $i = 2, \ldots, n$. The absolute prices $p_1, \ldots, p_n$ remain undetermined.

Now suppose that we add to this real system a single asset, money, the stock of which is denoted by M. Individuals are supposed to be satisfied with their holdings of this asset when the following quantity theory equation holds:

$$M \bigg/ \sum_{i=1}^n \delta_i p_i = k \sum_{i=1}^n \sigma_i q_i, \qquad k > 0, \tag{28}$$

---

[4] Lange (1944). While differing substantially in various details, the message of this section is basically Archibald and Lipsey's (1958).

[5] For a description of general equilibrium systems, see Henderson and Quandt (1971).

where the δ_i and σ_i are fixed (index number) weights, M is an exogenous variable, and k is a parameter. Now notice that the system formed by (26)–(28) is capable of determining absolute prices $p_1, \ldots, p_n$ as well as the quantities $q_1, \ldots, q_n$. The role of Equation (28) is only to determine the aggregate price index $\sum_{i=1}^{n} \delta_i p_i$, which given the relative prices $p_2/p_1, \ldots, p_n/p_1$ determined by (26) and (27), pins down the absolute prices $p_1, \ldots, p_n$. So the system "dichotomizes."

Lange's criticism of that dichotomy was this. Suppose the system is initially in equilibrium, Equations (26)–(28) holding for a set of values $\bar{p}_1, \ldots, \bar{p}_n, \bar{q}_1, \ldots, \bar{q}_n$. Now increase the money supply. At the initial prices and quantities, there is an excess supply of money since Equation (28) is now violated. But notice that at the initial prices and quantities Equations (26) and (27) continue to be satisfied. We thus encounter a situation in which there is an excess supply of money that is nowhere balanced by offsetting excess demands. Lange took this to mean that Walras' law was violated, interpreting that as a flaw in the classical dichotomy. An excess supply of money seems not to set up any pressures for the absolute prices of the n individual commodities to change.

There are two problems with this analysis. First, the q_i are flows, while $M/\sum \delta_i p$ is a stock, so that the excess demands and supplies referred to in the above argument are not comparable. Second, it is misleading simply to set down equations for excess demands and expect Walras' law to hold unless care has been taken to ensure that the demand functions are jointly determined so as to satisfy a budget constraint.

In the above model there is only one stock, money. There is therefore no portfolio problem facing individuals, there being no alternative assets for them to hold. So Equation (28) is *not* a portfolio balance schedule, though it formally resembles some of the portfolio balance schedules that we encountered earlier. Instead, Equation (28) must be interpreted as giving target wealth or a target wealth–income ratio. When actual wealth $M/\sum \delta_i p_i$ deviates from desired wealth $k \sum \sigma_i q_i$, it is reasonable to posit that individuals respond by accumulating or decumulating money at some rate per unit time. Thus suppose we posit the ad hoc accumulation schedule

$$\frac{\dot{M}}{\sum \delta_i p_i} = \phi \cdot \left[k \sum \sigma_i q_i - \frac{M}{\sum \delta_i p_i} \right], \qquad \phi > 0.$$

At the same time we must also modify the budget constraint facing individuals to be

$$\sum_{i-1}^{n} p_i(q_i - q_i^\circ) + \dot{M} = 0$$

or

$$\sum_{i=1}^{n} p_i(q_i - q_i^\circ) + \phi \sum_{i=1}^{n} \delta_i p_i \left[k \sum_{i=1}^{n} \sigma_i q_i - M \middle/ \sum_{i=1}^{n} \delta_i p_i \right] = 0. \qquad (29)$$

For a system of excess demand equations for the n goods constructed subject to the budget constraint (29), an "excess supply" of money clearly will always be accompanied by offsetting excess demands for goods as individuals attempt to decumulate money balances, making the demand for goods exceed available supplies. But notice that it is the stock excess supply of money *times* the factor $\phi \sum \delta_i p_i$ that equals the excess demand for goods.

Demand and excess demand schedules constructed subject to (29) might be written in the form

$$q_i = d_i(p_1, \ldots, p_n, \phi \sum \delta_i p_i[k \sum \sigma_i q_i - M/\sum \delta_i p_i])$$
$$= d_i(\lambda p_1, \ldots, \lambda p_n, \lambda\phi \sum \delta_i p_i[k \sum \sigma_i q_i - M/\sum \delta_i p_i]), \qquad \lambda > 0 \quad (26')$$
$$0 = q_i - q_i^{\circ} = e_i(p_1, \ldots, p_n, \phi \sum \delta_i p_i[k \sum \sigma_i q_i - M/\sum \delta_i p_i])$$
$$= e_i(\lambda p_1, \ldots, \lambda p_n, \lambda\phi \sum \delta_i p_i[k \sum \sigma_i q_i - M/\sum \delta_i p_i], \qquad \lambda > 0,$$
$$(27')$$

which are homogeneous of degree zero in all arguments (not just prices alone). Equations (26'), (27'), and (28) now form a system capable of determining $p_1, \ldots,$ p_n and $q_1, \ldots, q_n$. Walras' law obtains for this system.

Notice that the comparative statics of this system is formally identical with that of the system formed by Equations (26)–(28). That is, the system dichotomizes. Substituting Equation (28) into (26') and (27') gives

$$q_i = d_i(p_1, \ldots, p_n, 0), \qquad 0 = q_i - q_i^{\circ} = e_i(p_1, \ldots, p_n, 0),$$

which determine the q_i and $n - 1$ relative prices. Equation (28) then determines the absolute price level.

The following experiment shows the forces that propel the system formed by (26'), (27'), and (28) from one equilibrium position to another. Suppose that the system is initially in equilibrium. Then a jump occurs in the money supply (a gift from heaven–for there cannot be any open-market operations in a world with only one asset). At the initial prices and quantities, that upsets Equations (26'), (27'), and (28) since individuals have larger wealth than they desire. They attempt to dispose of some of their money at a finite rate per unit time by purchasing additional goods at some rate per unit time. This causes prices to be bid up, which continues until the price level $\sum \delta_i p_i$ has increased proportionately with the money supply, all relative prices and quantities being the same as in the initial equilibrium. So the effect of a jump in the money supply is an instantaneous jump in all absolute prices with all real variables being left unaltered.

The subject of this section produced a large and tortuous literature, often characterized by careless treatment of distinctions between stocks and flows. Most of that literature concerned a model with only one asset, money, a model that therefore requires no theory of portfolio balance. That model is therefore quite different from the models that we have described in earlier sections.

5. THE LOANABLE FUNDS EQUATION

Consider a version of our classical model in which π is zero, in order to justify failing to carry around capital gains nuisance terms. The classical theory of interest asserts that (in the absence of a Pigou effect) the IS curve determines the interest rate. (In the presence of a Pigou effect or a nonzero π the IS curve and portfolio balance condition mutually determine interest and the price level.) The classical theory of interest is thus often summarized by the statement that the interest rate adjusts to equate saving plus taxes to investment plus government expenditures. Disposable income Y_D satisfies

$$C + S = Y_D = Y - T - \delta K.$$

Substituting for Y from the national income identity gives

$$C + S = C + I + G + \delta K - T - \delta K$$

or

$$S + T - I + G. \tag{30}$$

We can write the saving function as

$$S = Y - T - \delta K - C(Y - T - \delta K, r - \pi)$$

$$\equiv s(Y - T - \delta K, r - \pi), \qquad 1 > s_1 > 0, \quad s_2 > 0, \tag{31}$$

which follows from the definition of disposable income and the consumption function. The investment schedule as before is

$$I = I(q(K, N, r - \pi) - 1). \tag{32}$$

Equations (30)–(32) determine I, S, and r. Substituting (31) and (32) into (30), we obtain the IS curve

$$s(Y - T - \delta K, r \quad \pi) + T = I(q(K, N, r - \pi)) + G, \tag{33}$$

which since Y and N are predetermined by the labor market and production function, is one equation in the endogenous variable r. This is the usual presentation of the classical theory of interest, and it is logically consistent if somewhat simplified by the special assumptions ruling out Pigou effects and complicating movements in capital gains on the government debt.

The famous "loanable funds" equation is often used in discussing the classical theory of interest. While the loanable funds equation is itself valid, these expositions of the classical theory are usually erroneous.

To derive the loanable funds equation, we note that in the classical model, portfolio balance obtains continuously. It follows that

$$\dot{M}/p = \dot{M}^{D}/p \tag{34}$$

where the dots denote right-hand time derivatives and the D superscript indicates demand. Adding (30) and (34) we obtain the famous "loanable funds" equation

$$S + \frac{\dot{M}}{p} = I + (G - T) + \frac{\dot{M}^{D}}{p}, \tag{35}$$

which says that real saving plus money creation equals investment plus "hoarding" plus the government deficit. This equation in effect says that the flow supply of bonds and equities equals the flow demand for bonds and equities. To see this notice that saving satisfies

$$S = \frac{\dot{M}^{D}}{p} + \frac{(\dot{B} + \dot{V})^{D}}{p},$$

where $(\dot{B} + \dot{V})^{D}$ is households' total flow demand for firms' equities and the government's interest bearing debt. Substituting the above equation and the government's budget constraint into (35) gives

$$\frac{\dot{M}^{D}}{p} + \frac{(\dot{B} + \dot{V})^{D}}{p} + \frac{\dot{M}}{p} = I + \frac{\dot{M} + \dot{B}}{p} + \frac{\dot{M}^{D}}{p}$$

or

$$\frac{(\dot{B} + \dot{V})^{D}}{p} = I + \frac{\dot{B}}{p}, \tag{36}$$

which states the equality of the flow demand for bonds and equities with the flow supply (firms are issuing equities at the real rate I per unit time). Thus Equation (36) states a condition that is equivalent with the "loanable funds" equation (35).

Loanable funds theorists claim that (35), in conjunction with (31), (32) and supplementary equations for $\dot{M}$ and $\dot{M}^{D}$, determines the interest rate. But this cannot be in a classical model since (30)–(32) are sufficient to determine S, I, and r. In the standard classical model the portfolio balance condition then determines p. The loanable funds equation (35) holds, but it plays no independent role itself, being merely the sum of (30) and (34). It serves only to verify that the "flow" supply of bonds and equities equals the flow demand, and just shows that the accounting has been done correctly.

After the publication of Keynes's *General Theory*, a large and often confused literature developed about the relationship of the loanable funds theory of interest to Keynes's liquidity preference theory. The literature is full of stock–flow errors and failures to recognize that especially in Keynes's model, but also in the classical model, the theory of interest is macroeconomic and not of the character of partial equilibrium.

6. IN DEFENSE OF KEYNESIAN ANALYSES THAT "IGNORE" THE GOVERNMENT'S BUDGET CONSTRAINT

Recently it has been common to hear the textbook Keynesian model criticized for ignoring the fact that the government has a budget constraint. Christ (1968) and others have claimed that various Keynesian multiplier formulas are mistaken because they ignore the government's budget constraint. The assertion is that the government's budget constraint plays a role which Keynesian economists overlooked, and which alters some of the substantive conclusions of Keynesian models. Here we describe the sense in which the textbook Keynesian model is immune from that charge.

Consider the following standard Keynesian macroeconomic model:

$$Y = F(N, K) \qquad F_N, F_K, F_{NK} > 0; \quad \text{production}$$
$$F_{KK}, F_{NN} < 0 \qquad \text{function} \qquad (37)$$

$$w/p = F_N(N, K) \qquad \qquad \text{marginal equality for labor} \qquad (38)$$

$$I = I(F_K(N, K) \qquad I' > 0 \qquad \text{investment}$$
$$- (r - \pi)) \qquad \qquad \text{schedule} \qquad (39)$$

$$C = C(Y - T) \qquad 1 > C' > 0 \qquad \text{consumption schedule} \qquad (40)$$

$$C + I + G = Y \qquad \qquad \text{national income identity} \qquad (41)$$

$$M/p = m(r, Y) \qquad m_r < 0, \quad m_Y > 0 \qquad \text{portfolio balance condition} \qquad (42)$$

$$\frac{\dot{w}}{w} = f\left(\frac{N^S - N}{N^S}\right) + \alpha\pi \quad f' < 0, \quad 0 \le \alpha \le 1 \quad \text{Phillips curve} \quad (43)$$

$$\dot{K} = I \qquad (44)$$

$$\dot{M} + \dot{B} = p(G - T). \qquad (45)$$

Here Y is real GNP, N employment, K the capital stock, w the money wage, p the price level, I real investment, C real consumption, G real government purchases, T real tax collections, M the stock of money (a government liability), r the interest rate, π the expected rate of inflation, N^S the labor supply, and B is the stock of government bonds held by the public. The variables Y, C, I, G, and T are all real flows measured in goods per unit time; M and B are stocks measured in dollars; N, N^S, and K are stocks; π and r are pure numbers per unit time. Each of the variables appearing in the system of Equations (37)–(45) should be regarded as a function of time. We shall assume that time passes continuously.[6]

The model is usually manipulated like this.[7] One feeds into the model paths of the exogenous variable $G(t)$, $T(t)$, $M(t)$, $N^S(t)$, and $\pi(t)$ over the time interval $[t_0, t_1)$, $t_1 > t_0$, where t_1 may be infinity. In addition, one must specify initial conditions for K, w, and B in the form of their values at time t_0, namely the single values $K(t_0)$, $w(t_0)$, and $B(t_0)$. Given these inputs, the model consisting of Equations (37)–(45) will generate entire time paths over the interval $[t_0, t_1)$ for the endogenous variables Y, N, p, r, C, and I, and paths over the interval (t_0, t_1) for the remaining three endogenous variables K, w, and B.

Two kinds of analysis are commonly carried out with this model. *Comparative dynamics* examines the alternative time paths of the endogenous variables associated with alternative time paths of the exogenous variables. *Comparative statics* freezes time and asks how the endogenous variables at one single point in time would differ in response to differing assumed values of the exogenous variables at that point in time. It is important to note that some variables that are endogenous from the dynamic point of view, in particular K, w, and $M + B$ in this model, are exogenous from a static point of view, in the sense that they are inherited from the past and cannot jump at a point in time in order to equilibrate the model in response to assumed jump discontinuities in the exogenous variables at a point in time. That is, w, K, and $M + B$ are determined by the solutions of the differential Equations (43), (44), and (45) and are therefore continuous functions of time and are given from the point of view of a static or point-in-time analysis. On the other hand, the variables Y, N, p, r, C, and I are free to exhibit jump discontinuities in order to equilibrate the model. Consequently, these six variables are endogenous both from the dynamic and static points of view.

Now consider the following two propositions:

Proposition 1: The time path of M matters in the sense of affecting some of the endogenous variables Y, N, p, r, C, and I.

Proposition 2: For determining the paths of Y, N, p, r, C, and I, it is important to take into account Equation (45), the government budget constraint.

---

[6] The exogenous variables M, G, T, π, and N^S are assumed to be right continuous functions of time which possess right-hand time derivatives everywhere. A dot over a variable denotes a right-hand time derivative. Notice that a variable, say $M(t)$, can have a discontinuity from the left at t and still possess a right-hand time derivative.

[7] This is the standard regime to impose on the model, but is not the only possible one. By a regime we mean a categorization of variables into exogenous and endogenous classes.

Proposition 1 has long been acknowledged in competent presentations of the Keynesian model (see, e.g., Ackley (1961) and Bailey (1962)). Now various writers have advanced Proposition 2 as a truth seemingly over and above Proposition 1, and have criticized the Keynesian analysis for failing to take into account. However, at best Proposition 2 is a restatement of part of Proposition 1. At worst, it is just plain wrong.

First, notice that from a static point of view, Equations (37)–(42) form a subset of equations that determines Y, N, p, r, C, and I at a point in time, given the exogenous variables K, M, G, T, and π at that point in time. In particular, notice that Y, N, p, r, C, and I are determined prior to and independently of $\dot{M} + \dot{B}$, which is determined by (45). From a static point of view, then, it is perfectly legitimate to ignore (45) in determining Y, N, p, r, C, and I because $\dot{M} + \dot{B}$ does not appear in Equations (37)–(42).

So Proposition 2, if it is saying anything, must be about dynamics. But it seems wrong even as a statement about dynamics.[8] This unfavorable interpretation of Proposition 2 is obtained by noticing that our model is dynamically recursive with respect to B. Equation (45), the government budget constraint, determines only the path of $B(t)$, for t on the interval (t_0, t_1). Removal of Equation (45) from the system, as is often done in textbook analyses of Keynesian models, in no way limits the ability of the model to determine time paths of the "interesting" endogenous variables Y, N, p, r, C, and I.

The most favorable interpretation that can be put on Proposition 2 is as follows. Suppose that one wants to manipulate the model under a regime[9] in which $B(t) = B(t_0)$ for all t in $[t_0, t_1)$. Under this regime, all that the model user is free to specify exogenously about the path of M is the initial condition $M(t_0)$. Under the constraint $B(t) = B(t_0)$, Equation (45) will determine $\dot{M}$ and ultimately an entire time path of M on the open interval (t_0, t_1). The time path of $M(t)$ so determined will be continuous, by virtue of being the solution of the differential equation (45). Notice that this regime rules out open-market

---

[8] The subject of this section is taken up more fully and in more modern and complete dynamic models by McCallum (1984) and Sargent and Wallace (1981). McCallum specifies a path for fiscal policy that holds constant through time the gross-of-interest government deficit. Under that specification, McCallum shows that it is feasible for the real value of the stock of interest bearing government debt per capita to grow without bound, provided that the government has access to lump sum taxes. Sargent and Wallace (1981) specify a path for fiscal policy that holds constant the net-of-interest government deficit. Under this specification, the stock of interest bearing government debt per capita is bounded, a restriction that limits the ability of a monetary authority to fight inflation without help from the fiscal authority. McCallum's monetary authority needs less help from the fiscal authority than Sargent and Wallace's because like the monetary authority of the present book, McCallum's monetary authority has been granted more power than Sargent and Wallace's by virtue of the specification that his fiscal authority is setting the gross-of-interest government deficit.

[9] The other exogenous variables continue to be time paths of G, T, and π over $[t_0, t_1)$ and initial conditions $K(t_0)$ and $w(t_0)$.

operations in the form of jump discontinuities in M that leave $M + B$ a continuous function of time. In this special regime Proposition 2 is true because things have been set up so that Equation (45) determines the time path of M—something that it generally does not do in a regime that permits open-market operations. But notice that Proposition 2 adds absolutely nothing to what has already been asserted in Proposition 1. So in this special case Proposition 2 is correct but innocuous. It is not correct to criticize users of the Keynesian model, who readily grant Proposition 1, for failing to mention Proposition 2.

One way that might seem to salvage some meaning for Proposition 2 is to amend the system by replacing (40) and (42) with

$$C = c\left(Y - T - \frac{M + B}{p}\pi\right) \qquad 1 > c' > 0 \tag{40'}$$

$$\frac{M}{p} = m\left(r, Y, \frac{M + B}{p} + K\right) \qquad m_r < 0, \quad m_Y > 0$$

$$1 > m_{(M + B)/p) + K} > 0. \tag{42'}$$

Here we have entered the real value of government debt to the public in the definition of disposable income and in the portfolio balance schedule in the usual ways. In the model formed by replacing (40) and (42) with (40') and (42'), not only the division of government debt between M and B, but also the total stock of government debt $M + B$ matters in the sense of affecting the variables Y, N, p, r, C, and I. Since Equation (45) determines the path of $M + B$ over time, it is important to take it into account. This is true, but is subsumed in the following version of Proposition 1, which is appropriate for a system in which equations like (40') or (42') replace (40) or (42):

Proposition 1': The time paths of M and $M + B$ matter in the sense of affecting some of the endogenous variables Y, N, p, r, C, and I.

This proposition was long accepted in presentations of the Keynesian model, as illustrated in the extensive literature on the Pigou effect and the burden of the debt (for example, see Metzler (1951)).[10]

---

[10] Christ (1968) has noted that static Keynesian multiplier formulas, versions of which we described in Chapter II, are not what he obtains when he calculates long-run dynamic multipliers while imposing some arbitrary limiting conditions, including that the government deficit converge to zero as a function of time. The Keynesian static multiplier formulas pertain to point-in-time exercises, and are not comparable with the multipliers calculated by Christ. Notice that Christ's long-run multipliers ignore capital accumulation and price and wage dynamics, and so do not correspond with dynamic multipliers that would emerge, à la Chapter V, from a solution to the sort of Keynesian model described in Chapter II. For a discussion of some of these matters, see Wallace (1971).

REFERENCES

Ackley, G. (1961). *Macroeconomic Theory.* New York: Macmillan.

Archibald, G. C. and Lipsey, R. C. (1958). "Monetary and Value Theory: A Critique of Lange and Patinkin." *Review of Economic Studies,* Vol. 26(1), No. 69, 1–22.

Bailey, M. J. (1962). *National Income and the Price Level.* New York: McGraw-Hill.

Christ, C. F. (1968). "A Simple Macroeconomic Model with a Government Budget Restraint." *Journal of Political Economy,* Vol. 76, January–February.

Henderson, J. M. and Quandt, R. E. (1971). *Microeconomic Theory,* 2nd ed. New York: McGraw-Hill.

Lange, O. R. (1944). *Price Flexibility and Employment.* Bloomington, Indiana: The Principia Press.

McCallum, B. T. (1984). "Are Bond-Financed Deficits Inflationary? A Ricardian Analysis." *Journal of Political Economy,* Vol. 92, No. 1, pp. 123–135.

Metzler, L. (1951). "Wealth, Saving, and the Rate of Interest." *Journal of Political Economy,* Vol. LIX, No. 2, pp. 93–116.

Patinkin, D. (1961). "Financial Intermediaries and the Logical Structure of Monetary Theory," *American Economic Review,* Vol. 51, No. 1, pp. 95–116.

Sargent, T. J. and Wallace, N. (1981). "Some Unpleasant Monetarist Arithmetic." *Federal Reserve Bank of Minneapolis Quarterly Review,* Vol. 5, No. 3, pp. 1–17.

Sargent, T. J. and Wallace, N. (1982). "The Real Bills Doctrine vs. the Quantity Theory of Money: A Reconsideration." *Journal of Political Economy.* Vol. 90, No. 6, pp. 1212–1236.

Tobin, J. (1966). *National Economic Policy.* New Haven, Connecticut: Yale Univ. Press.

Wachter, M. L. (1970). "Cyclical Variation in the Interindustry Wage Structure." *American Economic Review,* Vol. 60, No. 1, pp. 75–84.

Wallace, N. (1971). "A Static Nonstationary Analysis of the Interaction Between Monetary and Fiscal Policy." *University of Minnesota, Center for Economic Research, Discussion Paper No. 9,* August.

Wicksell, K. (1965). *Interest and Prices.* New York: Augustus Kelly.

CHAPTER V

DYNAMIC ANALYSIS OF A KEYNESIAN MODEL

This chapter describes the dynamics of the Keynesian macroeconomic model under two alternative assumptions about the formation of expectations of inflation.[1] One assumption is that expectations of inflation are formed "adaptively," so that π is governed by the differential equation

$$D\pi = \beta\left(\frac{Dp}{p} - \pi\right), \qquad \beta > 0$$

where D is the right-hand time derivative operator.[2] The solution of the above differential equation is[3]

$$\pi(t) = \pi(t_0)e^{-\beta(t-t_0)} + \beta \int_{t_0}^{t} e^{-\beta(t-s)} \frac{Dp}{p}(s)\, ds,$$

[1] The analysis in this chapter was inspired by my efforts in 1970 and 1971 to formalize for students the relationships among the various hypotheses advanced in Milton Friedman's AEA presidential address (1968). In particular, I wanted to convey the sense in which the "natural unemployment rate hypothesis" and Irving Fisher's theory about the relationship between interest rates and inflation were two sides of the same coin. While working with adaptive expectations (Section 1 of this chapter), one obtains only weak or "long-run" versions of Friedman's hypotheses. Switching to rational expectations (or "perfect foresight") leads to much more precise and more immediate versions of Friedman's hypotheses. Struggling with models like the one in this chapter led Neil Wallace and me to produce Sargent and Wallace (1975) and Sargent (1973b). Robert E. Lucas (1972) was approaching related results via a distinct road. See also Sargent (1973a) for a use of the adaptive expectations version of the model of this chapter in an effort to understand the "Gibson Paradox." This chapter assumes familiarity with Solow (1956).

[2] The adaptive expectations hypothesis $D\pi = \beta(Dp/p - \pi)$ was introduced by Cagan (1956) and Friedman (1956).

[3] That this is the solution can be verified by applying Leibniz's rule, which follows. Let $\varphi(t)$ be defined on $[c, d]$ by

$$\varphi(t) = \int_{\alpha(t)}^{\beta(t)} f(x, t)\, dx$$

where f and f_t are continuous and α and β are differentiable on $[c, d]$. Then φ has a derivative at each point in $[c, d]$ which is given by

$$\varphi'(t) = f(\beta(t), t)\beta'(t) - f(\alpha(t), t)\alpha'(t) + \int_{\alpha(t)}^{\beta(t)} f_t(x, t)\, dx.$$

For a derivation of the rule, see Bartle (1964, pp. 307–308).

so that $\pi(t)$ is formed as a geometric "distributed lag" of past actual rates of inflation. The other assumption under which the model will be analyzed is that of perfect foresight, so that $\pi = Dp/p$. Changing from the first to the second assumption about expectations will be seen to convert the particular model that we analyze from a Keynesian one to a classical one, even though the "structural" equations of the model remain the same.

1. THE MODEL WITH ADAPTIVE EXPECTATIONS

The model is identical with the Keynesian model described above, except that it is augmented with a Phillips curve. We shall take advantage of the linear homogeneity of the production function and write it in the intensive form

$$Y/K = F(1, N/K) = f(N/K)$$

or

$$y = f(\lambda), \qquad f'(\lambda) > 0, \quad f''(\lambda) < 0, \tag{1}$$

where $y = Y/K$ and $\lambda = N/K$.

The marginal product condition for employment can be written

$$\frac{w}{p} = f'(\lambda) \quad \left(= \frac{\partial}{\partial N} Kf\left(\frac{N}{K}\right) = \frac{\partial}{\partial N} F(K, N) \right). \tag{2}$$

The Keynesian investment schedule will be written in the intensive form

$$\dot{K}/K = I(F_K - (r + \delta - \pi)), \qquad I' > 0,$$

or

$$i = I/K = I(f(\lambda) - \lambda f'(\lambda) - (r + \delta - \pi)). \tag{3}$$

Notice that

$$F_K(K, N) = \frac{\partial}{\partial K}\left(Kf\left(\frac{N}{K}\right)\right) = f\left(\frac{N}{K}\right) + Kf'\left(\frac{N}{K}\right)\left[-\frac{N}{K^2}\right] = f(\lambda) - \lambda f'(\lambda).$$

The consumption function is assumed to be linear and "proportional," which permits us to write it in the capital intensive form

$$\frac{C}{K} = z\left[\frac{Y}{K} - \frac{T}{K} - \frac{\delta K}{K}\right], \qquad 0 < z < 1$$

or

$$c = z(y - \bar{t} - \delta) \tag{4}$$

where $\bar{t} = T/K$. The parameter z is the marginal propensity to consume.

We write the national income identity as

$$y = c + i + g + \delta \tag{5}$$

where $g = G/K$ and $c = C/K$.

The portfolio equilibrium condition is assumed to take the form

$$M/pK = m(r, y), \tag{6}$$

which can be rationalized by assuming the demand for money $m(r, Y)$ is homogeneous of degree one in output.

We posit that the evolution of the money wage is governed by the Phillips curve

$$\frac{Dw}{w} = h\left(\frac{N}{N^S}\right) + \pi, \qquad h' > 0, \quad h(1) = 0, \tag{7}$$

where N^S is the labor supply. Given π, Equation (7) depicts a trade-off between the rate of employment relative to the labor supply and the rate of wage inflation. An increase in π shifts the Phillips curve upward by the amount of that increase.

The labor supply is exogenous and is governed by

$$N^S(t) = N^S(t_0)e^{n(t - t_0)} \tag{8}$$

where n is the proportionate rate of growth of the labor supply.

The model is completed by specifying that expectations of inflation obey the adaptive scheme

$$\pi(t) = \pi(t_0)e^{-\beta(t - t_0)} + \beta \int_{t_0}^{t} e^{-\beta(t - s)} \frac{Dp(s)}{p(s)} \, ds. \tag{9}$$

Collecting equations, the complete model is:

$$y = f(\lambda) \tag{1}$$

$$\frac{w}{p} = f'(\lambda) \tag{2}$$

$$i = I(f(\lambda) - \lambda f'(\lambda) - (r + \delta - \pi)) = \dot{K}/K \tag{3}$$

$$c = z(y - \tilde{t} - \delta) \tag{4}$$

$$y = c + i + g + \delta \tag{5}$$

$$\frac{M}{pK} = m(r, y) \tag{6}$$

$$\frac{Dw}{w} = h\left(\frac{\lambda K}{N^S}\right) + \pi \tag{7}$$

$$N^S(t) = N^S(t_0)e^{n(t - t_0)} \tag{8}$$

$$\pi(t) = \pi(t_0)e^{-\beta(t - t_0)} + \beta \int_{t_0}^{t} e^{-\beta(t - s)} \frac{Dp(s)}{p(s)} \, ds \tag{9}$$

$$K(t) = K(t_0) + \int_{t_0}^{t} i(s)K(s) \, ds.$$

Given the initial conditions $w(t_0)$, $\pi(t_0)$, $K(t_0)$, and given time paths for the exogenous variables M, g, and $\tilde{t}$ for $t \geq t_0$, the model will generate time paths of the endogenous variables y, λ, K, c, w, p, r, and π. Notice that even though w, π, and K are fixed or "exogenous" at a point in time, being inherited from the past according to (3), (7), and (9), they are endogenous variables from the point of view of our dynamic analysis. The analysis determines their evolution over time.

The momentary equilibrium of our system can be determined by solving Equations (1)–(6) for IS and LM curves. The IS curve gives the combinations of r and y that make the demand for output equal to the supply. It is derived by substituting (3) and (4) into (5):

$$y = z(y - \tilde{t} - \delta) + I(f(\lambda) - \lambda f'(\lambda) - (r + \delta - \pi)) + g + \delta. \qquad (10)$$

Since $f'(\lambda) > 0$, we can invert (1) and obtain

$$\lambda = \lambda(y), \qquad \lambda'(y) = \frac{1}{f'(\lambda)} > 0, \qquad \lambda''(y) = \frac{-f''(\lambda)\lambda'(y)}{f'(\lambda)^2} > 0.$$

Substituting this into (10) yields the IS curve:

$$y = z(y - \tilde{t} - \delta) + I\left(y - \frac{\lambda(y)}{\lambda'(y)} - (r + \delta - \pi)\right) + g + \delta.$$

The slope of the IS curve in the r-y plane is given by

$$\frac{dy}{dr}\bigg|_{\text{IS}} = \frac{-I'}{1 - z - I'(\lambda(y)\lambda''(y)/\lambda'(y)^2)},$$

which is of ambiguous sign since $\lambda''(y) > 0$. The denominator of the above expression is Hicks's "supermultiplier," the term $I'\lambda\lambda''/\lambda'^2$ being the marginal propensity to invest out of income. We shall assume that this term is less than the marginal propensity to save, so that the IS curve is downward sloping. The position of the IS curve depends on the parameters g, $\tilde{t}$, and π in the usual way. An increase in π shifts the IS curve upward by the amount of that increase.

We can write the marginal productivity condition for labor as

$$p = w\lambda'(y).$$

Substituting the expression for p into (6) yields the LM curve

$$M = w\lambda'(y)Km(r, y),$$

the slope of which is easily verified to be positive in the r-y plane. The LM curve shows the combinations of r and y that guarantee portfolio balance. Its position depends on M, w, and K, all of which are parameters at a point in time.

The momentary equilibrium of the system is determined at the intersection of the IS and LM curves. That equilibrium will in general be a nonstationary one, the interest rate, the real wage, and the capital–labor ratio possibly changing over time. However, given fixed values of g, $\bar{t}$, and $\dot{M}/M$, the system may over time approach a steady state in which the interest rate, real wage, and employment–capital ratio are fixed, while prices and wages change at a rate equal to $\dot{M}/M$ minus n. We shall use two curves to characterize the steady-state growth path in the r-y plane. The first is simply a vertical line at the steady-state output–capital ratio, which we denote by y^*. From (5) the rate of growth of capital is

$$i = y - z(y - \bar{t} - \delta) - g - \delta.$$

Since $D(K/N)/(K/N) = DK/K - DN/N = i - n$, we have

$$\frac{D(K/N)}{K/N} = y - z(y - \bar{t} - \delta) - g - \delta - n.$$

Setting $D(K/N)$ to zero and solving for y yields the value of y^*:

$$y^* = \frac{n + g + \delta(1 - z) - z\bar{t}}{1 - z}.$$

This is the value of the output–capital ratio at which the capital–labor ratio is stationary, i.e., unchanging through time. We show y^* as a vertical line in Figure 1. On our assumptions the steady-state value of y is independent of the interest rate.

If firms are to be content to increase the capital stock at the steady-state rate n, so that $i - n$ equals zero, we require

$$I\left(y - \frac{\lambda(y)}{\lambda'(y)} - (r + \delta - \pi)\right) - n = 0, \tag{11}$$

which is implicitly an equation that tells us what $r + \delta - \pi$ must be if the system is to be in a steady-state equilibrium at a given y. Taking the total differential of the above equation and rearranging gives

$$\frac{d(r + \delta - \pi)}{dy} = \frac{\lambda''\lambda}{\lambda'^2} > 0$$

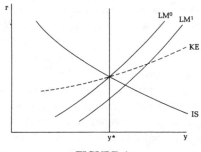

FIGURE 1

as the slope of the locus of points in the r, y plane along which (11) is satisfied. The slope is positive, reflecting the direct dependence of the marginal product of capital on the output–capital ratio. We call (11) the capital–market equilibrium curve and label it KE. Note that an increase in π causes the KE curve to shift upward by the full amount of the increase.

The determination of momentary and steady-state equilibrium can be illustrated with Figure 1. Notice that the IS curve has been drawn so that it intersects the KE curve at y^*, the steady-state output–capital ratio. That this must be so can be verified as follows. Along the KE curve, Equation (11) is satisfied. Substituting for $I(\quad)$ from (11) into the IS curve gives

$$y = z(y - \tilde{t} - \delta) + n + g + \delta \qquad \text{or} \qquad y = \frac{n + g + \delta(1 - z) - z\tilde{t}}{1 - z},$$

which is identical with our expression for y^*. A steady state is determined at the intersection of the KE and IS curves. Momentary equilibrium is determined at the intersection of the IS and LM curves. If the IS and LM curves intersect at an $r - y$ combination below the KE curve, capital is growing more rapidly than n at that moment. The model possesses mechanisms propelling over time the intersection of the IS and LM curves toward the intersection of the IS and KE curves. The dynamics of capital and the money wage are the key elements in the mechanism.

To illustrate how the model works suppose that the system is initially in a full, steady-state equilibrium, the IS, LM, and KE curves all intersecting at y^*, as in Figure 1. Suppose that $\dot{M}/M = n$, so that the equilibrium rate of inflation is zero. We know this because in the steady-state r and y and therefore $m(r, y)$ are constant through time. Therefore, M/pK must be constant through time, so that $\dot{M}/M - \dot{p}/p - \dot{K}/K = 0$ or $\dot{M}/M - \dot{p}/p - n = 0$. The system is in a steady state so that the LM, IS, and KE curves are unchanging through time. Since in that steady state $\dot{w}/w = \dot{p}/p = \pi = \dot{M}/M - n = 0$, we know from the Phillips curve that N/N^S must equal unity. Now suppose that at some point in time there occurs a once-and-for-all jump in M, engineered via an open-market operation that leaves $\dot{M}/M$ unaltered. To simplify matters we shall suppose that π remains fixed at zero, its steady-state value, during the movement to a new steady-state. So we temporarily suspend (9) and substitute $\pi(t) = 0$. We also assume that g and $\tilde{t}$ are constant over time. The immediate effect of the jump in the money supply is to shift the LM curve to the right, say to LM^1, in Figure 1. The result is an instantaneous jump in employment and the output–capital ratio. Employment now exceeds the labor supply, causing the money wage to adjust upward over time, as described by the Phillips curve (7). In addition, the nominal interest rate has fallen, creating a larger discrepancy between the marginal product of capital, which has risen, and the real rate of interest. Firms respond by adding to the capital stock at a rate exceeding n—this occurs at each moment the momentary solution is at an r-y combination below the KE curve. Since capital is growing faster than the money supply and since money wages are rising over time, the LM curve shifts upward over time, from LM^1 toward LM^0 in Figure 1. To show this notice that, for fixed values of y, logarithmic differentiation of the LM curve with respect to time yields

$$\dot{r}\big|_{LM} = \frac{m(r,\,y)}{m_r} \left[\frac{\dot{M}}{M} - \frac{\dot{K}}{K} - \frac{\dot{w}}{w} \right]. \tag{12}$$

If the expression in brackets is negative, then at each value of y, the r that maintains portfolio balance is increasing over time. Now when enough time has passed to move the LM back to LM^0, so that y and r are back at their initial values, the adjustment is not yet complete. When the LM curve has shifted back to LM^0, the values of y and λ are at their initial values. But since $\dot{K}/K$ exceeded n all during the intervening period, we know that N/N^S, which had the initial value of unity, since $\dot{w}/w = 0$ initially, now exceeds unity. For $N/N^S = \lambda K/N^S$; λ has returned to its initial value, but K has grown faster than n at each intervening moment, so that N/N^S must now exceed unity. The Phillips curve therefore implies that $\dot{w}/w > 0$, implying that the LM curve continues to shift up over time (see (12)) since $\dot{M}/M - \dot{K}/K - \dot{w}/w$ is still less than zero even though $\dot{K}/K$ has returned to its steady-state value once the LM curve has come back to its initial position. The system must therefore "overshoot," having y fall below y^* as wages rise and the LM curve moves to an intersection with the IS curve above the KE curve. During moments when such an intersection occurs, $DK/K < n$, which in itself helps to increase $\dot{M}/M - \dot{K}/K - \dot{w}/w$, and thus tends to reverse the direction of movement of the LM curve over time. Given stability, eventually this effect dominates the tendency of rising wages to shift the LM curve to the left, so that the LM curve starts moving back toward the right. Furthermore, as λ falls and the ratio K/N^S falls with the passage of time (notice that K is growing more slowly than N^S so long as the LM curve intersects the IS curve above the KE curve), N/N^S and hence Dw/w fall over time. Depending on the particular parameter values, it is possible, though not necessary, that N/N^S actually falls below unity, in which case Dw/w becomes negative. This means that w has "overshot" its new steady-state value and must rise again, which requires another "boom" period during which $N/N^S > 1$. If w is falling (and $N/N^S < 1$) when the LM curve again shifts back to its original, pre-open-market-operation position, it follows that the LM curve continues shifting toward the right, inducing a y above y^* again. Thus, it is possible that the approach back to the steady state is an oscillatory one, characterized by alternating periods of boom and recession. The model thus has implicit in it, depending on the particular parameter values, a theory of the business cycle.

The alternative possibility is that following the initial jump in y, y overshoots the steady-state value y^* only once. As the LM curve shifts leftward and passes an intersection with the IS curve at y^*, it can happen that w rises continuously toward its new steady-state value and fails to overshoot it, so that $N/N^S \geq 1$ throughout the adjustment process. In this lucky state of affairs the "boom" is followed by no bust. Notice that in this case the "stabilizing" force is provided by the fact that $DK/K < n$ when the LM curve intersects the IS curve above the KE curve, tending to drive the LM curve rightward, toward the steady state.

The adjustment process in response to the once-and-for-all jump in M would be even more complex if we were to permit π to respond to the occurrence of actual inflation, say by restoring our Equation (9). For then the IS curve and the KE curve would shift upward during the early part of the transition as π increases in response to the emergence of inflation. It is easily verified that when π changes, the IS curve continues to intersect the KE curve at y^*. The result of allowing π to depend on past values of $\dot{p}/p$ is to accentuate the "overshooting" or cyclical phenomenon. Following the original jump in M, the LM curve will now be shifting toward an intersection of y^* with an IS curve associated with a positive rate of expected inflation since inflation has occurred during the transition up to that moment. Since π is positive and, as we verified earlier, $N/N^S > 1$ at the moment the LM curve has shifted back enough to intersect an IS curve at y^*, wages are rising even faster at that moment than they would have been had π been zero throughout the transition. Assuming that the system is dynamically stable, the final resting place for all variables will be the same as if π had remained at its steady-state value of zero throughout the adjustment process; but the path to steady-state equilibrium may be much different.

The final effect of the once-and-for-all jump in M, once the system has returned to its steady state, is to leave all real variables unaltered and to increase the price level and money wage proportionately with the money supply. The variables r and y have steady-state values determined at the intersection of the IS and KE curves, which are not affected by the jump in M. In the new steady state $\dot{w}/w$ must be zero, which means that N/N^S must be unity, which means since λ is at its initial steady-state value, that K/N^S must be at its initial steady-state value. This means that once enough time has elapsed after the open-market operation occurred, $K(t)$ is what it would have been had no open-market operation occurred. In other words, the open-market operation redistributes investment over time, but does not affect the capital stock in moments far into the future. Since $M/pK = m(r, y)$ is not moved from its steady-state value, and K eventually returns to the path it would have followed without the open-market operation, p must eventually have increased proportionately with the initial jump in M.

Though this model is clearly Keynesian in its momentary or point-in-time behavior, its steady-state or long-run properties are "classical" in the sense that real variables are unaffected by the money supply. The real variables are determined at the intersection of the KE and IS curves which are determined by propensities to save and invest and the government's fiscal policies. In the steady state the price level must adjust so that the LM curve passes through the intersection of the IS and KE curves.[4]

2. PERFECT FORESIGHT $(\pi = Dp/p)$

We now abandon Equation (9) and for it substitute the assumption of perfect foresight or "rationality":

$$\pi(t) = Dp(t)/p(t), \tag{9'}$$

where we continue to interpret D as the right-hand time derivative operator. Equation (9') asserts that people accurately perceive the right-hand time derivative of the log of the price level, the rate at which inflation is proceeding.

The dynamics of the model in response to shocks are very much different when (9') replaces (9). To solve the model, we begin by substituting (9') into (7) obtain

$$\frac{Dw}{w} = h\left(\frac{\lambda K}{N^S}\right) + \frac{Dp}{p}. \tag{13}$$

Differentiating (2) logarithmically with respect to time gives

$$\frac{Dw}{w} = \frac{f''(\lambda)}{f'(\lambda)} D\lambda + \frac{Dp}{p}. \tag{14}$$

Equating (13) with (14) gives

$$h\left(\frac{\lambda K}{N^S}\right) = \frac{f''(\lambda)}{f'(\lambda)} D\lambda \quad \text{where} \quad \frac{f''(\lambda)}{f'(\lambda)} < 0. \tag{15}$$

Now (15) is a differential equation in the employment–capital ratio λ, which may be solved for λ in terms of past values of K and N^S. To illustrate, suppose that $f(\lambda)$ is Cobb–Douglas, so that

$$y = f(\lambda) = A\lambda^{1-\alpha}.$$

Then we have

$$f'(\lambda) = A(1-\alpha)\lambda^{-\alpha}, \quad f''(\lambda) = -\alpha(1-\alpha)A\lambda^{-\alpha-1}, \quad \frac{f''(\lambda)}{f'(\lambda)} = \frac{-\alpha}{\lambda}.$$

Also suppose that $h(\lambda K/N^S)$ takes the form

$$h\left(\frac{\lambda K}{N^S}\right) = \gamma \ln \frac{N}{N^S} = \gamma \ln N - \gamma \ln N^S, \quad \gamma > 0,$$

---

[4] Models have been described in which the monetary growth rate does affect the steady-state capital–output ratio. See Tobin (1965). For a model in which the monetary growth rate does not affect the steady-state capital–output ratio, see Sidrauski (1967).

where ln denotes the natural logarithm. Then (15) becomes

$$\gamma \ln N - \gamma \ln N^S = -\alpha \frac{\dot{\lambda}}{\lambda} = -\alpha D \ln N + \alpha D \ln K. \tag{16}$$

Rearranging, we have

$$(\gamma + \alpha D) \ln N = \gamma \ln N^S + \alpha D \ln K$$

or

$$\left(\frac{\gamma}{\alpha} + D\right) \ln N = \frac{\gamma}{\alpha} \ln N^S + D \ln K.$$

This is a linear, first-order differential equation in ln N. To find its solution, divide through by $\gamma/\alpha + D$ to get

$$\ln N = \frac{1}{D + (\gamma/\alpha)} \left[\frac{\gamma}{\alpha} \ln N^S + D \ln K \right].$$

Notice that

$$\frac{1}{D + (\gamma/\alpha)} = \frac{e^{(s-t)((\gamma/\alpha) + D)}}{(\gamma/\alpha) + D} \Big|^t_{s = -\infty}$$

$$= \int_{-\infty}^t e^{(s-t)((\gamma/\alpha) + D)} \, ds = \int_{-\infty}^t e^{(s-t)(\gamma/\alpha)} e^{(s-t)D} \, ds.$$

Recalling that $e^{(s-t)D} x(t) = x(s)$, we have

$$\ln N(t) = \int_{-\infty}^t e^{(s-t)(\gamma/\alpha)} e^{(s-t)D} \left[\frac{\gamma}{\alpha} \ln N^S(t) + D \ln K \right] ds$$

$$\ln N(t) = \frac{\gamma}{\alpha} \int_{-\infty}^t e^{(s-t)(\gamma/\alpha)} \ln N^S(s) \, ds + \int_{-\infty}^t e^{(s-t)(\gamma/\alpha)} \frac{DK(s)}{K(s)} \, ds. \tag{17}$$

Equation (17) is the solution to Equation (16) and expresses ln N at t as distributed lags of past values of the labor supply and capital stock. Since these are predetermined at time t, we immediately know that employment and hence output will not respond at t to the imposition of shocks to the system at t.

   Given the value of N at t determined from some version of (17) and given the quantity of K inherited from the past, output is determined by Equation (1), the real wage by (2), and c by (4). Given c and y, (5) then determines i. Given i and λ, Equation (3) determines $r - \pi$ at t. Equation (7) determines $Dw/w - Dp/p$.

   Notice that given entire time paths from now until forever for the fiscal variables g and $\bar{t}$, the model determines entire time paths of the real variables without using the portfolio balance equation. In effect, then, this model dichotomizes.

   All real variables have now been determined and it remains only to determine the values of p and Dp/p at instant t. They are determined by the portfolio balance condition in the manner indicated in Chapter I. To illustrate, suppose the portfolio balance equation (6) assumes the special form

$$M/pK = e^{\beta r} y, \qquad \beta < 0. \tag{18}$$

We know that in this system, r is determined by (3), which we express by inverting (3) and writing

$$r = f(\lambda) - \lambda f'(\lambda) - \delta + \pi + \xi(i), \qquad \xi' < 0.$$

Substituting this into (18) gives

$$M/pK = y \exp \beta(f(\lambda) - \lambda f'(\lambda) - \delta + \pi + \xi(i))$$

or

$$\ln M - \ln p - \ln K = \ln y + \beta[f(\lambda) - \lambda f'(\lambda) - \delta + \pi + \xi(i)].$$

Substituting Dp/p for π and rearranging gives

$$\left[\frac{1}{\beta} + D\right] \ln p = \frac{1}{\beta} [\ln M - \ln K - \ln y - \beta[f(\lambda) - \lambda f'(\lambda) - \delta + \xi(i)]].$$

Pursuing a line of reasoning identical to that in Chapter I, it is verified that the solution of this differential equation is

$$\ln p(t) = -\frac{1}{\beta} \int_t^\infty e^{(s-t)/\beta} [\ln M(s) - \ln K(s) - \ln y(s)$$
$$- \beta[f(\lambda(s)) - \lambda(s) f'(\lambda(s)) - \delta + \xi(i(s))]] \, ds. \tag{19}$$

(We are again imposing a terminal condition that suppresses the term $ce^{-t/\beta}$ that should be added to the above solution.) Equation (19) expresses the current price level as a function of the entire *future* paths of the money supply, the capital stock, the employment–capital ratio λ, and the rate of investment. The value of π is also determined by (19), and can be obtained by differentiating the path given by (19) with respect to time from the right. Notice that in this model, the entire time paths of the variables appearing on the right-hand side of (19) can all be determined before the current price level is determined. That is, we showed how (17) determines the values of N and λ at t, and how this readily enables us to calculate the rate of growth of capital, i. This enables us to update the capital stock and so to determine subsequent values of N. Proceeding in this way, given the exogenous fiscal policy variables, the entire time paths of all the real variables can be determined before determining the price level at any moment.

Since all of the structural equations remain the same, the model continues to be characterized by the IS, LM, and KE curves. The steady state is determined at the intersection of the IS and KE curves. But now the instantaneous value of y is determined by substituting the value of λ determined by the solution to (15),

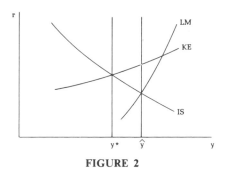

FIGURE 2

e.g., (17), into the production function. The momentary equilibrium value of y so determined, call it $\hat{y}$, depicted in Figure 2, when substituted into the IS curve gives the momentary value of $r - \pi$. The LM curve must pass through the intersection of the IS curve and the vertical line at $\hat{y}$; jumps in the price level occur to assure this.

If we return to the experiment performed earlier under adaptive expectations, we shall see how radically the substitution of (9′) for (9) alters the adjustment dynamics. We assume that the system is initially in a steady state and that $\dot{M}/M = n$, so that $\dot{w}/w = \dot{p}/p = \pi = 0$. At the current moment there occurs an *unexpected* jump in M that leaves the right-hand derivative DM/M unchanged.[5] The only result is an instantaneous jump in p and w proportional to the jump in M with all real variables unaltered. Since the solution to (15), e.g., (17), implies that y will not jump in response to the jump in M, the price level must jump to keep the LM curve passing through the intersection of the KE and IS curves. To show this explicitly for the sample portfolio balance equation that leads to (19) as the solution for the price level, suppose that the initial path of the log of the money supply was expected to be

$$\ln M(s), \qquad s \geq t.$$

After the once-and-for-all jump in the money supply that leaves DM/M unaltered, the new path of the log of the money supply is expected to be

$$\phi + \ln M(s), \qquad s \geq t, \quad \phi > 0.$$

[5] If the jump in M that occurs at some moment t had previously been expected to occur, it would not cause a jump in p at t. This follows from Equation (19), which implies that $p(s)$ will be a continuous function of time at t, even if there is a discontinuity in $M(s)$ at t or anywhere else. However, $\pi(t)$ will jump at t in response to a previously anticipated jump in M. By contrast, the experiment that we are performing here is one in which the monetary authority at t suddenly and unexpectedly moves from a previously planned money supply path of $M(s)$, $s \geq t$, to a new planned path of $e^{\phi}M(s)$ for $s \geq t$.

The new price level $p'(t)$ differs from the initial price level given by (19) according to

$$\ln p'(t) - \ln p(t) = -\frac{1}{\beta} \int_t^\infty e^{(s-t)/\beta} [\ln M(s) + \phi] \, ds + \frac{1}{\beta} \int_t^\infty e^{(s-t)/\beta} \ln M(s) \, ds$$

$$= -\frac{1}{\beta} \int_t^\infty \phi e^{(s-t)/\beta} \, ds = \phi.$$

So the price level jumps by the same multiplicative factor ϕ as does the money supply. Notice that in the above calculations we use the fact that the paths of the variables $K(s)$, $\lambda(s)$, and $i(s)$ will be unaltered when the money supply jumps.

Now consider the response of the system to a jump in M which had previously been anticipated. Suppose that the money supply follows the path

$$\ln M(s) = \ln M(t_0) + n(s - t_0), \qquad t_0 + \theta > s,$$

$$\ln M(s) = \ln M(t_0) + \phi + n(s - t_0), \qquad t_0 + \theta \le s,$$

so that the money supply is expected to and does jump at $t_0 + \theta$. Using (19) and ignoring the terms in the real variables, we compute the price path for $t < t_0 + \theta$ as

$$\ln p(t) = -\frac{1}{\beta} \int_t^{t_0+\theta} e^{(s-t)/\beta} n(s - t_0) \, ds - \frac{1}{\beta} \int_{t_0+\theta}^\infty e^{(s-t)/\beta} (n(s - t_0) + \phi) \, ds$$

$$+ \text{ other terms}, \qquad t_0 \le t \le t_0 + \theta$$

$$= -\frac{1}{\beta} \int_t^\infty e^{(s-t)/\beta} n(s - t_0) \, ds - \frac{\phi}{\beta} \int_{t_0+\theta}^\infty e^{(s-t)/\beta} \, ds + \text{ other terms}$$

$$= -\frac{1}{\beta} \int_t^\infty e^{(s-t)/\beta} n(s - t_0) \, ds + \phi e^{(t_0+\theta-t)/\beta}$$

$$+ \text{ other terms}, \qquad t_0 \le t \le t_0 + \theta.$$

For $t \ge t_0 + \theta$, the solution for the price level is

$$\ln p(t) = -\frac{1}{\beta} \int_t^\infty e^{(s-t)/\beta} n(s - t_0) \, ds + \phi + \text{ other terms}.$$

The jump in the money supply at $t_0 + \theta$ is reflected in earlier values of the price level. The above calculations show that the price level is continuous at $t_0 + \theta$, so that no jump occurs in p at the moment when M jumps. However, the expected rate of inflation π does jump at $t_0 + \theta$. For, notice that

$$\frac{d}{dt} \phi e^{(t_0+\theta-t)/\beta} = -\phi/\beta \exp((t_0 + \theta - t)/\beta).$$

At $t_0 + \theta$, therefore, the left-hand derivative of the log of the price level exceeds the right-hand derivative by $-\phi/\beta > 0$. So there is a sudden fall in π at $t_0 + \theta$. It is this downward jump in π, leading to a downward jump in r, that stimulates the demand for money enough at $t_0 + \theta$ to guarantee that portfolio balance is maintained in the face of the jump in M that occurs at that moment.

The two experiments just performed show how essential it is to distinguish between jumps in policy variables that are anticipated and unanticipated in the model with perfect foresight.

The effect of substituting the perfect foresight assumption (9′) for the adaptive expectations mechanism (9) has been to convert the model from one with Keynesian momentary behavior to one with classical momentary behavior. In the system with perfect foresight, (9′), money is a "veil," momentarily as well as in the long run. Jumps in the money supply do not cause any real movements of the sort that they do in the system with adaptive expectations.

The distinction between the models under (9) and (9′) is mathematically subtle. Under the adaptive expectations scheme (9) the model must be manipulated under the "Keynesian" assumption that the money wage does not jump at a point in time, so that the Phillips curve (7) gives the time derivative of the wage (= the right-hand time derivative = the left-hand time derivative). Essentially, this is because at any moment t, Equations (8) and (9) make $N^S(t)$ and $\pi(t)$ predetermined from past variables. Of course $K(t)$ is also inherited from the past. Equations (1)–(7) then form a system of seven equations in the seven endogenous variables $y(t)$, $\lambda(t)$, $i(t)$, $c(t)$, $p(t)$, $r(t)$, and $Dw(t)/w(t)$. The model is incapable of restricting any additional variables, in particular $w(t)$, at the moment t. So $w(t)$ must be regarded as fixed and inherited from the past at each point in time.

However, in the system with $\pi = Dp/p$, it is employment that is predetermined at any moment in time by the differential equation (15). Since employment is predetermined at t, say by (17), y, λ, and w/p are also predetermined and constrained to change continuously as functions of time. They cannot jump at a point in time. But if w/p cannot jump, and neither can K or y, then if M jumps at a point in time, we know that p and w must jump in order to satisfy the portfolio balance equation at each moment.

EXERCISES

1. Under both adaptive expectations and perfect foresight, perform a dynamic analysis of Tobin's dynamic aggregative model, formed by substituting for Equation (3) the equation

$$r + \delta - \pi = f(\lambda) - \lambda f'(\lambda).$$

Now instantaneous equilibrium occurs at the intersection of the KE and LM curves, while steady-state equilibrium occurs at the intersection of the KE curve and y^* line.

2. For both adaptive expectations and perfect foresight, analyze the dynamics of the model when the Phillips curve is modified to assume the form

$$\dot{w}/w = h(N/N^S) + \alpha\pi, \quad h' > 0, \quad h(1) = 0, \quad 0 < \alpha < 1.$$

REFERENCES

Bartle, R. G. (1964). *The Elements of Real Analysis*, pp. 307–308. New York: Wiley.

Cagan, P. (1956). "The Monetary Dynamics of Hyperinflation." In *Studies in the Quantity Theory of Money* (M. Friedman, ed.). Chicago: University of Chicago Press.

Friedman, J. (1968). "The Role of Monetary Policy." *American Economic Review*, Vol. 58, No. 1, pp. 1–17.

Friedman, M. (1956). *A Theory of the Consumption Function*. New York: National Bureau of Economic Research.

Lucas, R. E. Jr. (1972). "Expectations and the Neutrality of Money." *Journal of Economic Theory*, Vol. 4, No. 2, pp. 103–124.

Sargent, T. J. (1973a). "Interest Rates and Prices in the Long Run: A Study of the Gibson Paradox." *Journal of Money, Credit and Banking*, Vol. 5, No. 1, Part 2, pp. 385–449.

Sargent, T. J. (1973b). "Rational Expectations, The Real Rate of Interest, and the Natural Rate of Unemployment." *Brookings Papers on Economic Activity*, 1973:2, pp. 429–472. (Correction in *BPEA*, 1973:3).

Sargent, T. J. and Wallace, N. (1975). "Rational Expectations, the Optimal Monetary Instrument, and the Optimal Money Supply Rule." *Journal of Political Economy*, Vol. 83, No. 2, pp. 241–254.

Sidrauski, M. (1967). "Rational Choice and Patterns of Growth in a Monetary Economy." *American Economic Review*, Vol. 57, No. 2, pp. 534–544.

Solow, R. M. (1956). "A Contribution to the Theory of Economic Growth." *Quarterly Journal of Economics*, Vol. 70, No. 1, pp. 65–94.

Tobin, J. (1965). "Money and Economic Growth." *Econometrica*, Vol. 33, No. 4, pp. 671–684.

CHAPTER VI

THE INVESTMENT SCHEDULE

1. THE COST-OF-CHANGE MODEL

As a comparison of the Keynesian model with Tobin's dynamic aggregative model reveals, whether or not it is assumed that there exists a market in stocks of capital at each moment has drastic theoretical implications, particularly about the potency of fiscal policy as a device for inducing short-run movements in output and employment. The structure of the Keynesian model depends sensitively on ruling out a perfect market in existing stocks of capital and instead positing a demand schedule on the part of firms for a finite rate of addition per unit time to their capital stocks. That element of the Keynesian model is perhaps its most essential piece, ruling out as it does the instantaneous movements of capital across firms and industries that thwart fiscal policy in Tobin's model; at the same time, the investment schedule is the weakest part of the Keynesian model from a theoretical viewpoint, being defended (at least until recently) on a very ad hoc basis.

This chapter describes the most successful attempt to rationalize the Keynesian investment schedule, a line of work due to Eisner and Strotz (1963), Lucas (1967), Gould (1968), and Treadway (1969). The key to the theory is the assumption that there are costs associated with adjusting the capital stock at a rapid rate per unit of time and that these costs increase rapidly with the absolute rate of investment, so rapidly that the firm never attempts to achieve a jump in its capital stock at any moment. These adjustment costs occur at a rate per unit of time (measured in capital goods per unit of time) described by the twice differentiable function $C(\dot{K})$, which obeys

$$C'(\dot{K}) \gtreqless 0 \quad \text{as} \quad \dot{K} \gtreqless 0, \qquad C''(\dot{K}) > 0, \qquad C(0) = 0.$$

See Figure 1. Costs of adjusting the capital stock are nonnegative and increase at an increasing rate with the absolute value of investment. The firm's discounted net cash flow net of costs of adjustment is defined to be

$$f(N(t), K(t), \dot{K}(t), t) = e^{-rt}[p(t)F(K(t), N(t)) - w(t)N(t) - J(t)\delta K(t) \\ - J(t)\dot{K}(t) - J(t)C(\dot{K})]$$

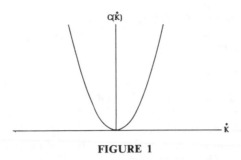

FIGURE 1

where $J(t)$ is the price of capital goods at time t and r is the instantaneous interest rate, assumed constant over $[0, \infty)$. We continue to assume that $F(K, N)$ is linearly homogeneous in K and N. The firm chooses paths of N and K over time to maximize its present value over the time interval $[0, \infty)$, which is

$$PV = \int_0^\infty f(N(t), K(t), \dot{K}(t), t)\, dt$$

subject to $K(0) = K_0$, where K_0 is given. The firm operates in competitive markets for output and labor, being able to rent all the labor it desires at the wage w and to sell all the output it wants at the price p. The firm starts out with capital stock $K(0)$.

Among the necessary conditions for an extremum for present value are the "Euler equations" (see Intriligator, 1971, Chapter 12)

$$\frac{\partial f}{\partial N} = 0, \qquad t \in [0, \infty),$$

$$\frac{\partial f}{\partial K} - \frac{d}{dt}\frac{\partial f}{\partial \dot{K}} = 0, \qquad t \in [0, \infty).$$

Evaluating these derivatives, we have

$$\frac{\partial f}{\partial N} = e^{-rt}\left[p(t)\frac{\partial F}{\partial N} - w(t) \right],$$

$$\frac{\partial f}{\partial K} = e^{-rt}\left[p(t)\frac{\partial F}{\partial K} - J(t)\delta \right],$$

$$\frac{\partial f}{\partial \dot{K}} = -e^{-rt}[J(t) + J(t)C'(\dot{K})],$$

$$\frac{d}{dt}\frac{\partial f}{\partial \dot{K}} = -e^{-rt}[\dot{J}(t) + \dot{J}(t)C'(\dot{K}) + J(t)C''(\dot{K})\ddot{K}]$$

$$+ re^{-rt}[J(t) + J(t)C'(\dot{K})].$$

So for our problem the Euler equations become

$$p(t)\frac{\partial F}{\partial N} - w(t) = 0 \qquad \text{or} \qquad \frac{\partial F}{\partial N} = \frac{w(t)}{p(t)} \tag{1}$$

and

$$p\frac{\partial F}{\partial K} - J\delta - rJ + \dot{J} - (rJ - \dot{J})C'(\dot{K}) + JC''(\dot{K})\ddot{K} = 0. \tag{2}$$

Equation (1) requires that the marginal product of labor equal the real wage at each moment, an equation that determines the labor–capital ratio at each moment (since $F(K, N)$ is linearly homogeneous). Equation (2) is a differential equation that determines the (finite) rate of growth of the capital stock at each moment. To simplify the problem we now assume that firms expect the prices $J(t)$, $p(t)$, and $w(t)$ to grow over time at the *same* constant rate per unit time π over the entire horizon of our problem. This makes $\dot{J}/J = \dot{p}/p = \dot{w}/w = \pi$ for all t, and leaves relative prices and wages constant over time. We assume that $r - \pi > 0$. Furthermore, assume for simplicity that the cost-of-change function is quadratic, so that

$$C(\dot{K}) = \tfrac{1}{2}\gamma\dot{K}^2, \qquad \gamma > 0.$$

On this assumption Equation (2) becomes

$$p\frac{\partial F}{\partial K} - J\delta - rJ + \dot{J} - (rJ - \dot{J})\gamma\dot{K} + J\gamma\ddot{K} = 0.$$

Dividing by J and solving for $\ddot{K}$ gives

$$\ddot{K} = \frac{1}{\gamma}\left(r + \delta - \frac{\dot{J}}{J} - \frac{p}{J}F_K\right) + \left(r - \frac{\dot{J}}{J}\right)\dot{K}. \tag{3}$$

On our assumptions, since all relative prices are constant over time and since r and $\dot{J}/J$ are constant over time, the above equation is a fixed coefficient, linear differential equation in $\dot{K}$:

$$\frac{d\dot{K}}{dt} = A + B\dot{K} \quad \text{where} \quad A = \frac{1}{\gamma}\left(r + \delta - \pi - \frac{p}{J}F_K\right), \quad B = r - \pi > 0. \tag{4}$$

We assume that $A \leq 0$. Since w/p is constant over time, so is N/K, making F_K and therefore A constant over time. The differential equation (4) has the solution

$$\dot{K} = \alpha e^{Bt} - (A/B) \tag{5}$$

where α is a constant chosen to ensure that an initial condition or terminal condition is satisfied. If $\alpha = 0$, then $\dot{K} = -A/B$ for all t. But if $\alpha \neq 0$, $\dot{K}$ follows an exponential path in which (after a time) the absolute value of investment increases at an exponential rate. (See Figure 2.) Given that the time path of $\dot{K}$ is described by Equation (5), the time path of K itself is described by

$$K(t) = \frac{\alpha}{B}e^{Bt} - \frac{A}{B}t + K(0) - \frac{\alpha}{B}. \tag{6}$$

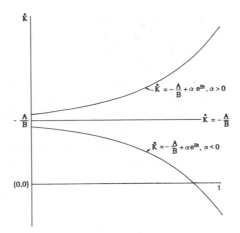

FIGURE 2

Given expressions (5) and (6) we can compute the firm's discounted net cash flow $f(\ )$ as

$$f(N(t), K(t), \dot{K}(t), t) = e^{-rt}\left(p\frac{F}{K} - w\frac{N}{K} - J\delta\right)K(t) - e^{-rt}J\dot{K} - e^{-rt}J\frac{\gamma}{2}\dot{K}^2$$

$$= e^{-(r-\pi)t}D\left[-\frac{A}{B}t + \frac{\alpha}{B}e^{Bt} + K(0) - \frac{\alpha}{B}\right]$$

$$- e^{-(r-\pi)t}J(0)\left(\alpha e^{Bt} - \frac{A}{B}\right) - e^{-(r-\pi)t}\left(\alpha e^{Bt} - \frac{A}{B}\right)^2\frac{\gamma}{2}J(0)$$

where $D = [p(0)F/K - w(0)N/K - J(0)\delta]$ and $p(t) = e^{\pi t}p(0)$, $w(t) = e^{\pi t}w(0)$, and $J(t) = e^{\pi t}J(0)$. Noting that $B = r - \pi$, we have

$$f(\ ) = e^{-Bt}D\left[-\frac{A}{B}t + \frac{\alpha}{B}e^{Bt} + K(0) - \frac{\alpha}{B}\right] - e^{-Bt}J(0)\left(\alpha e^{Bt} - \frac{A}{B}\right)$$

$$- e^{-Bt}\left[\alpha^2 e^{2Bt} - 2\alpha\frac{A}{B}e^{Bt} + \left(\frac{A}{B}\right)^2\right]J(0)\frac{\gamma}{2},$$

$$f(N(t), K(t), \dot{K}(t), t) = D\left\{-\frac{A}{B}te^{-Bt} + \frac{\alpha}{B} + \left(K(0) - \frac{\alpha}{B}\right)e^{-Bt}\right\}$$

$$- J(0)\left\{\alpha - \frac{A}{B}e^{-Bt}\right\}$$

$$- J(0)\frac{\gamma}{2}\left\{\alpha^2 e^{Bt} - 2\alpha\frac{A}{B} + \frac{A^2}{B^2}e^{-Bt}\right\}.$$

As $t \to \infty$, the first term in braces approaches α/B; the second term in braces approaches α, while the third term in braces approaches ∞ unless $\alpha = 0$, in which case it approaches zero. These calculations imply that as t becomes large, the discounted net cash flow $f(\ )$ becomes a larger and larger negative number (since the last term in braces is multiplied by $-\gamma/2$) unless $\alpha = 0$. This occurs because the rate of investment is increasing approximately exponentially, causing costs of adjustment to rise at an even faster exponential rate. These costs of adjustment become so large eventually that they swamp the firm's revenue, and lead to large negative net returns. That makes present value a very large negative number. Clearly, such paths are not optimal ones for the firm to follow, even though they satisfy the Euler equations. To rule out such paths, the condition $\alpha = 0$ must be met, implying that the pertinent solution of our differential equation (4) is

$$\dot{K} = -A/B$$

or

$$\dot{K} = \frac{1}{\gamma}\left[\frac{pJ^{-1}F_K - (r + \delta - \pi)}{r - \pi}\right]. \tag{7}$$

Notice that in the context of a one-sector model, $p = J$, so that (7) is a version of our Keynesian investment schedule

$$\dot{K} = I(q - 1), \qquad I' > 0,$$

where $q = (F_K - (r + \delta - \pi))/(r - \pi) + 1$.

The condition $\alpha = 0$ for our infinite horizon problem is in the nature of a "transversality condition." It is a boundary condition that makes us choose that solution of (5) maximizing present value. We can briefly consider the case in which the firm has a finite horizon and maximizes

$$PV = \int_0^T f(N(t), K(t), \dot{K}(t), t)\, dt$$

subject to $K(0) = K_0$ where the discounted net cash $f(N, K, \dot{K}, t)$ is defined as above. For this problem, the necessary conditions for a maximum are the Euler equations

$$\frac{\partial f}{\partial N} = 0, \qquad t \in [0, T],$$

$$\frac{\partial f}{\partial K} - \frac{d}{dt}\frac{\partial f}{\partial \dot{K}} = 0, \qquad t \in [0, T],$$

and the transversality condition,[1]

$$\frac{\partial f}{\partial \dot{K}}(T)K(T) = 0, \qquad \frac{\partial f}{\partial \dot{K}}(T) \leq 0.$$

For our problem, the transversality condition is

$$-e^{-rT}J(T)[1 + C'(\dot{K}(T))]K(T) = 0, \qquad -[1 + C'(\dot{K}(T))] \leq 0,$$

or simply

$$[1 + C'(\dot{K}(T))]K(T) = 0, \qquad 1 + C'(\dot{K}(T) \geq 0.$$

In our specific example with quadratic costs of adjustment and fixed expected relative prices, which led to (5), the condition becomes

$$[1 + \gamma\dot{K}(T)]K(T) = 0.$$

This condition instructs us to choose α in (5) according to the following principle. First, consider choosing α to set $1 + \gamma\dot{K}(T) = 0$. Then check to make sure that with this choice of α, $K(T) \geq 0$. If not, then choose α so that according to (6), $K(T) = 0$.

We shall study the case in which $K(T) \geq 0$ with α chosen to make $1 + \gamma\dot{K}(T) = 0$, leaving the alternative case to the reader. We require from (5) that

$$\dot{K}(T) = \alpha e^{BT} - \frac{A}{B} = -\frac{1}{\gamma} \qquad \text{or} \qquad \alpha = e^{-BT}\left(\frac{A}{B} - \frac{1}{\gamma}\right).$$

Notice that since $B > 0$, the α given by this formula approaches zero as $T \to \infty$. (Of course, to check that the formula is valid for a given T, we must check that with that choice of α, $K(T) \geq 0$ in (6).) The path of investment followed is depicted in Figure 3. Notice that since we have assumed $B > 0$, $A < 0$, it follows that $\alpha < 0$. The solution for investment has the following "turnpike" property: for T sufficiently large, the rate of investment $\dot{K}$ spends most of the time within an arbitrarily small neighborhood of the infinite horizon investment rate $-A/B$. The solution of the infinite horizon problem is the limit of the solution of the finite horizon problem as $T \to \infty$.

---

[1] See Arrow and Kurz (1970, pp. 37–38, Propositions 1 and 3). To match up our notation with that of Arrow and Kurz, set $U(x, v, t) = f(N, K, \dot{K}, t)$, where the vector $x = (N, K)$, and where the "control" $v = \dot{K}$. Then for K, condition (b) of Arrow and Kurz becomes $\partial f/\partial \dot{K} + \lambda = 0$ or $\lambda = -\partial f/\partial \dot{K}$. (Here we have substituted λ for Arrow and Kurz's p in order to avoid confusion with p as used in the text.) Using this condition together with Arrow and Kurz's condition $\dot{\lambda} = -\partial f/\partial K$ then gives our Euler equation for K, namely $(d/dt)\partial f/\partial \dot{K} = \partial f/\partial K$. Since $\lambda = -\partial f/\partial \dot{K}$, Arrow and Kurz's condition (d) is the transversality condition given in the text.

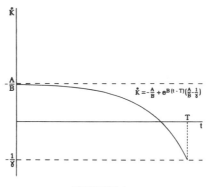

FIGURE 3

It bears emphasizing that we were able to deduce the Keynesian investment schedule (7)

$$I = \frac{1}{\gamma}\left[\frac{pJ^{-1}F_K - (r + \delta - \pi)}{r - \pi}\right] \tag{7}$$

only by severely restricting the paths of the processes for $w(t)$, $p(t)$, and $J(t)$ which the firm is assumed to expect to hold in the future. In particular, we assumed that the firm expects w, p, and J each to inflate at the common rate π, so that no relative price changes are expected by the firm. The upshot of this is that (7) *cannot* be expected to describe investment demand for *arbitrary* paths of $w(t)$, $p(t)$, and $J(t)$ which the firm believes itself to be confronted with. The firm's optimal capital accumulation plan will in general not obey a simple law like (7) but will depend intricately on the form of the paths for w, p, and J that it expects to face. Below, we shall consider a stochastic setup that makes explicit the dependence of the firm's optimal decision rule on its views of the (stochastic) processes governing the prices it faces.

Derivations of the Keynesian investment schedule along the lines sketched above seem to provide the most satisfactory theoretical foundations yet laid down for that schedule. The theory obviously depends critically on the assumption that costs of adjustment increase at an increasing rate with the absolute value of investment ($C'' > 0$).

2. AN ALTERNATIVE REPRESENTATION

The Keynesian investment schedule can be represented in an alternative form to that given above, which the following heuristic derivation serves to highlight. Let the real present value of the firm, measured in consumption goods, be at time 0

$$V(K(0)) = \int_0^\infty e^{-rt}\left[F(K, N) - \frac{w}{p}N - \delta\frac{J}{p}K - \frac{J}{p}\dot{K} - \frac{J}{p}C(\dot{K})\right]dt,$$

which for $0 < \varepsilon < \infty$ can be represented as

$$V(K(0)) = \int_0^\varepsilon e^{-rt} \left[F(K, N) - \frac{w}{p} N - \delta \frac{J}{p} K - \frac{J}{p} \dot{K} - \frac{J}{p} C(\dot{K}) \right] dt$$
$$+ e^{-r\varepsilon} V(K(\varepsilon)).$$

We are letting $V(K(t))$ denote the real value of the firm at time t, expressed as a function of the capital stock at t, $K(t)$. For small ε, the above equality is well approximated as

$$V(K(0)) = \varepsilon \left[F(K, N) - \frac{w}{p} N - \delta \frac{J}{p} K - \frac{J}{p} \dot{K} - \frac{J}{p} C(\dot{K}) \right]$$
$$+ e^{-r\varepsilon} V(K(\varepsilon))$$

where the term in brackets is evaluated at some point $0 \le t < \varepsilon$, say $t = 0$.

We can interpret $V(K(0))$ as being the value of the firm at $t = 0$, as reflected in the stock market. In making investment decisions, the firm is assumed to maximize the discounted future value of present stockholders' equity in the company. For moment $\varepsilon > 0$, the discounted future value of the company is $e^{-r\varepsilon} V(K(\varepsilon))$. But part of this total will be owned by the stockholders who finance whatever new capital the firm buys between time 0 and ε by purchasing equity newly issued by the firm. Between time 0 and ε, the firm will purchase capital goods in the (approximate) amount $\varepsilon I(0)$, and will have to issue new equities valued in consumption goods at $\varepsilon[Jp^{-1}I(0) + Jp^{-1}C(I(0))]$ in order to invest at this rate. (Remember that the cost of investing at the rate $\dot{K}$ is $J\dot{K} + JC(\dot{K})$.) So the discounted future value of the equity of present owners of the firm is given by

$$e^{-r\varepsilon} V(K(\varepsilon)) - \varepsilon \left[\frac{J}{p} I(0) + \frac{J}{p} C(I(0)) \right],$$

which it is convenient to write as

$$e^{-r\varepsilon} V(K(0) + \varepsilon I(0)) - \varepsilon \left[\frac{J}{p} I(0) + \frac{J}{p} C(I(0)) \right]. \tag{8}$$

Assume that $V(K(t))$ is a differentiable function (see Benveniste and Scheinkman [1979] for a way to prove that V is differentiable). The firm chooses $I(0)$ to maximize (8). The first order necessary condition for this maximation is

$$e^{-r\varepsilon} \frac{dV}{dK} (K(0) + \varepsilon I(0)) = \frac{J}{p} (1 + C'(I(0))).$$

Evaluating this equality at $\varepsilon = 0$ gives the condition

$$\frac{dV}{dK} (K(0)) = \frac{J}{p} (1 + C'(I(0))).$$

Since $C'' > 0$, this equation can be inverted to yield the investment schedule

$$I(0) = g\left(\frac{p}{J}\frac{dV}{dK}(K(0)) - 1\right) \tag{9}$$

where $g' = C''^{-1}$. This is an example of what Hayashi (1982) calls a "marginal q" representation of an investment schedule.

Hayashi (1982) shows how the specification of adjustment costs can be altered in order to yield an "average q" theory of investment, that is, one in which "marginal q", dV/dK, equals "average q", $V(K)/K$. This is accomplished by replacing the adjustment cost function $C(\dot{K})$ with the different specification $Kh(\dot{K}/K)$, where h satisfies $h' \gtrless 0$ as $\dot{K}/K \gtrless 0$, $h'' > 0$. With $C(\dot{K})$ replaced by adjustment costs $Kh(\dot{K}/K)$, the firm's current period return function is linearly homogenous in $(K, N, \dot{K})$. Hayashi shows that this specification makes $V(K)$ linearly homogenous in K, so that $V'(K) = V(K)/K$. Hayashi describes the sense in which this is a desirable specification for empirical work, because data on $V(K)/K$ are presumably directly observable from observations on the prices of the firm's outstanding debt and equity.

REFERENCES

Arrow, K. J., and Kurz, M. (1970). *Public Investment, The Rate of Return and Optimal Fiscal Policy.* Baltimore, Maryland: Johns Hopkins Press.

Benveniste, L. M. and Scheinkman, J. A. (1979). "On the Differentiability of the Value Function in Dynamic Models of Economics." *Econometrica*, Vol. 47, No. 3, pp. 727–732.

Eisner, R. and Strotz, R. H. (1963). "Determinants of Business Investment." Research Study Two in *Impacts of Monetary Policy*. Englewood Cliffs, New Jersey: Prentice-Hall.

Gould, J. P. (1968). "Adjustment Costs in the Theory of Investment of the Firm." *The Review of Economic Studies*, Vol. XXXV (1), No. 101, pp. 47–56.

Hayashi, F. (1982). "Tobin's Marginal q and Average q: A Neoclassical Interpretation." *Econometrica*, Vol. 50, No. 1, pp. 213–224.

Intriligator, M. D. (1971). *Mathematical Optimization and Economic Theory*, Chapter 12, Englewood Cliffs, New Jersey: Prentice-Hall.

Lucas, R. E. Jr. and Prescott, E. C. (1971). "Investment Under Uncertainty." *Econometrica*, Vol. 39, No. 5, pp. 659–681.

Lucas, R. E. Jr. (1967). "Adjustment Costs and the Theory of Supply." *The Journal of Political Economy*, Part 1, Vol. 75, No. 4, pp. 321–334.

Treadway, A. B. (1969). "On Rational Entrepreneurial Behavior and the Demand for Investment." *The Review of Economic Studies*, Vol. XXXVI (2), No. 106, pp. 227–240.

PART II

Introduction to Stochastic Macroeconomics

CHAPTER VII

BEHAVIOR UNDER UNCERTAINTY[1]

1. THE STATE PREFERENCE MODEL

This chapter describes the elements of the state-preference analysis of choice under uncertainty, and several of its applications that are of interest to macroeconomists. Among the applications studied will be Tobin's analysis of the diversification demand for money, the Modigliani–Miller theorem, and, in the next chapter, Azariadis' analysis of labor contracts and "sticky wages." The originator of the state preference approach was Arrow (1964).

We assume that the individual's preferences can be described by a utility function that makes utility depend on the amount of the one good that the individual consumes. So we write

$$\text{utility} = U(C) \tag{1}$$

where C is the amount of the good consumed. We assume that $U(C)$ is twice continuously differentiable, increasing in consumption, $U'(C) > 0$; that the marginal utility of consumption, though positive, decreases with increases in C, $U''(C) < 0$; and that $U(C)$ is bounded for $C \in [0, \infty)$.[2]

We assume that the individual is making plans for the future, which we initially think of as collapsed to a single date in the future. To incorporate the existence of uncertainty, we assume that there are n mutually exclusive states of the world, indexed by $\theta = 1, 2, \ldots, n$. The individual has a set of subjective probabilities $\pi(\theta) \geq 0$ giving the probability that he assigns to the occurrence of state θ.

---

[1] The reader is urged to study two articles by Hirshleifer (1965, 1966). Also see Friedman and Savage (1948) reprinted in Stigler and Boulding (1952).

[2] We can dispense with the boundedness assumption under certain conditions: see pp. 152–155.

An individual's claim to future consumption goods will in general depend on the state of nature that happens to occur. We let $C(\theta)$ denote his consumption if state θ occurs. The individual is assumed to maximize his expected utility[3]

$$v = \sum_{\theta=1}^{n} \pi(\theta)U(C(\theta)),$$

subject to certain constraints.

Suppose that there are only two states of the world, so that $n = 2$. The individual's expected utility is then

$$v = \pi(1)U(C(1)) + \pi(2)U(C(2)).$$

Along lines of constant expected utility (indifference curves) we have

$$dv = 0 = \pi(1)U'(C(1))\,dC(1) + \pi(2)U'(C(2))\,dC(2),$$

which implies that

$$\left.\frac{dC(2)}{dC(1)}\right|_{dv=0} = -\frac{\pi(1)U'(C(1))}{\pi(2)U'(C(2))}. \tag{2}$$

Expression (2) gives the slope of the indifference curve. The concavity of the indifference curve is found by differentiating (2):

$$\frac{d^2C(2)}{dC(1)^2} = -\frac{\pi(1)U''(C(1))}{\pi(2)U'(C(2))} + \frac{\pi(1)U'(C(1))U''(C(2))\,dC(2)/dC(1)}{\pi(2)U'(C(2))^2} > 0.$$

The slope of the indifference curves increases as $C(1)/C(2)$ increases, implying that they are convex.

Next notice that for $C(1) = C(2)$, we have

$$\left.\frac{dC(2)}{dC(1)}\right|_{dv=0,\,C(1)=C(2)} = -\frac{\pi(1)}{\pi(2)}. \tag{3}$$

Bundles of $C(1)$, $C(2)$ for which $C(1) = C(2)$ correspond to certain claims since regardless of the state that occurs, the individual is able to consume the same amount. A 45° line through the origin in the $C(1)$, $C(2)$ plane thus contains all certain bundles (see Figure 1), so it is appropriately called the certainty line. Along the certainty line, the slope of the indifference curves equals $-\pi(1)/\pi(2)$, independently of the form of the utility function—so long as the form of the utility function does not itself depend on the state of nature that occurs. The certainty line is thus an "expansion path."

Consider an individual whose initial endowment consists of a certain claim on Y_0 units of consumption goods. The individual is then confronted with a bet that he can undertake in any amount α so long as $\alpha \le Y_0$. If $\alpha > 0$ units of the

---

[3] See Luce and Raiffa (1957, Chapter 2) for a discussion of the restrictions on preferences needed to rationalize this assumption.

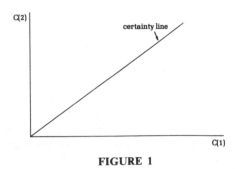

FIGURE 1

bet are taken, the individual will receive an additional $\alpha X(1)$ units of the consumption good if state 1 occurs, but must sacrifice α units of output if state 2 occurs. Thus the payoff/cost $(dC(1), dC(2))$ associated with taking α goods worth of the bet is $(\alpha X(1), -\alpha)$. The bet is said to be "favorable" if its expected value in terms of goods is positive. The expected value of the bet's net payoff stream is

$$\pi(1)\alpha X(1) - \pi(2)\alpha = \pi(1)\alpha X(1) - (1 - \pi(1))\alpha = \pi(1)\alpha(X(1) + 1) - \alpha.$$

The bet is then favorable if $\pi(1)\alpha(X(1) + 1) - \alpha > 0$ or

$$\pi(1) > \frac{1}{X(1) + 1}. \tag{4}$$

The bet is said to be "fair" if the above inequality is replaced by an equality.

If the individual undertakes α units of the bet, his claims to consumption across states of nature become

$$C(1) = Y_0 + \alpha X(1), \qquad C(2) = Y_0 - \alpha,$$

from which we can deduce that by varying the amount of the bet taken, α, the individual can substitute $C(1)$ for $C(2)$ at the (constant) rate

$$dC(2)/dC(1) = -1/X(1). \tag{5}$$

So $-1/X(1)$ is the slope of the "budget line" through (Y_0, Y_0) along which the individual can trade claims to consumption in state 1 for claims to consumption in state 2. If $\alpha = 0$, the individual's claims remain (Y_0, Y_0). If $\alpha = Y_0$, the individual's claims become $(Y_0 X(1) + Y_0, 0)$. The straight line connecting these two points is the individual's budget line (see Figure 2).

As long as the slope of the budget line exceeds the slope of the individual's indifference curve at Y_0, Y_0, the individual can increase his expected utility by undertaking at least a small part of the bet. This requires that

$$-\frac{1}{X(1)} > -\frac{\pi(1)}{\pi(2)} = -\frac{\pi(1)}{1 - \pi(1)},$$

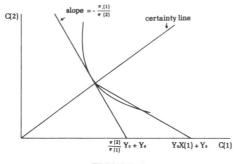

FIGURE 2

from Equations (3) and (5). The above inequality can be rearranged to read

$$\pi(1) > \frac{1}{X(1) + 1},$$

which is identical with inequality (4), the condition that the bet be favorable. For our special case, we have thus proved Arrow's proposition that an individual will always take at least a small part of a favorable bet (Arrow, 1971, p. 100).

Within this framework we now consider securities that entitle the individual to alternative patterns of consumption across our two states of nature. Consider a security, one unit of which entitles the owner to receive $X(1)$ units of the consumption good if state 1 occurs and $X(2)$ units if state 2 occurs. If the individual buys α units of the security, he is entitled to receive a pattern of returns $(\alpha X(1), \alpha X(2))$ across states of nature. In Figure 3 one unit of the security gives the returns labeled by point A. Suppose that the security costs the individual S_X units of current output per unit of security. If the individual has an investment portfolio worth Y_0 units of current output, he could then buy Y_0/S_X units of the security and obtain a pattern of returns $(Y_0 X(1)/S_X, \ Y_0 X(2)/S_X)$ across states of nature. Point B in Figure 3 depicts such a pattern of returns.

FIGURE 3

Now suppose that there is a second security, one unit of which gives a pattern of returns $(Z(1), Z(2))$ across states of nature, where $Z(1)$ and $Z(2)$ are both denominated in consumption goods. If one unit of the security costs S_Z, the individual could purchase Y_0/S_Z units of the security if he put his whole portfolio of Y_0 current goods into that security. Then his pattern of returns across states of nature would be $(Y_0 Z(1)/S_Z, Y_0 Z(2)/S_Z)$. Such a pattern of returns across states is labeled D in Figure 3. We suppose that the two vectors of returns across states $[X(1)/S_X, X(2)/S_X]$ and $[Z(1)/S_Z, Z(2)/S_Z]$ are linearly independent, which means that the only scalars b_1 and b_2 for which

$$b_1 \begin{bmatrix} X(1)/S_X \\ X(2)/S_X \end{bmatrix} + b_2 \begin{bmatrix} Z(1)/S_Z \\ Z(2)/S_Z \end{bmatrix} = 0$$

are $b_1 = b_2 = 0$. This assumption rules out the situation in which the points $(X(1)/S_X, X(2)/S_X)Y_0$ and $(Z(1)/S_Z, Z(2)/S_Z)Y_0$ in Figure 3 both lie along a line through the origin.

Now suppose that the individual considers putting a percentage λ of his portfolio into security X, and $1 - \lambda$ into security Z. He would then purchase $\lambda Y_0/S_X$ units of security X and $(1 - \lambda)Y_0/S_Z$ units of security Z. His pattern of returns across states of nature would then be

$$(C(1), C(2)) = Y_0 \left(\lambda \frac{X(1)}{S_X} + (1 - \lambda) \frac{Z(1)}{S_Z}, \lambda \frac{X(2)}{S_X} + (1 - \lambda) \frac{Z(2)}{S_Z} \right). \qquad (6)$$

Such points are linear combinations of $(X(1), X(2))Y_0/S_X$ and $(Z(1), Z(2))Y_0/S_Z$, and so lie on the straight line connecting points D and B in Figure 3. A change in λ brings changes in the consumption stream across states according to

$$dC(1) = \left[\frac{X(1)}{S_X} - \frac{Z(1)}{S_Z} \right] Y_0 \, d\lambda, \qquad dC(2) = \left[\frac{X(2)}{S_X} - \frac{Z(2)}{S_Z} \right] Y_0 \, d\lambda,$$

so that the "budget line" along which the consumer can alter the pattern of claims to the consumption good across states of nature has slope

$$\frac{dC(2)}{dC(1)} = \left(\frac{X(2)}{S_X} - \frac{Z(2)}{S_Z} \right) \bigg/ \left(\frac{X(1)}{S_X} - \frac{Z(1)}{S_Z} \right).$$

For this slope to be negative, the numerator and denominator must be of opposite sign, which means that one security must not dominate another. That is, one unit of current output's worth of security X must offer more consumption in state 1 if it offers less in state 2 than does one unit of current output's worth of security 2. In effect, the ratio

$$\frac{dC(2)}{dC(1)} = \left(\frac{X(2)}{S_X} - \frac{Z(2)}{S_Z} \right) \bigg/ \left(\frac{X(1)}{S_X} - \frac{Z(1)}{S_Z} \right)$$

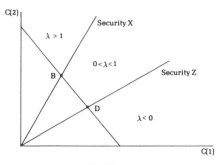

FIGURE 4

measures the relative price at which the individual can exchange $C(1)$ for $C(2)$ by trading security X for security Z.

By suitably choosing λ (which need not be between 0 and 1) the individual is able to obtain any combination of $C(1)$ and $C(2)$ in the nonnegative quadrant satisfying Equation (6). A negative λ or one exceeding unity indicates that one security or the other is being sold short or being issued by the individual (see Figure 4). Notice that by choosing his portfolio suitably, the individual can set $C(1)$ equal to $C(2)$, so that he need bear no risk, if that is his desire.

The individual chooses his portfolio so as to maximize his expected utility subject to the budget constraint (6). Usually, this involves choosing λ so that it corresponds to a point of tangency between an indifference curve and the budget line. As always, however, corner solutions are possible.

Suppose now that a third security, security Y, is added to our setup. The security has returns across states $(Y(1)/S_Y,\ Y(2)/S_Y)$ measured in consumption goods in states 1 and 2, respectively, per unit of current consumption good; S_Y is the price of one unit of the security in terms of current consumption goods. If the individual initially uses his entire investment portfolio to purchase X or Y or Z he will obtain the $C(1)$, $C(2)$ combination denoted by point x, y, or z in Figure 5.

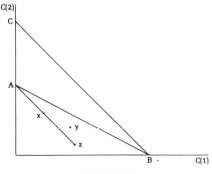

FIGURE 5

The assumption that the return vectors of securities X and Z are linearly independent across states implies, since there are only two states, that the return vector of security Y is a linear combination of the return vectors for X and Z:

$$\begin{bmatrix} Y(1)/S_Y \\ Y(2)/S_Y \end{bmatrix} = \alpha \begin{bmatrix} X(1)/S_X \\ X(2)/S_X \end{bmatrix} + \beta \begin{bmatrix} Z(1)/S_Z \\ Z(2)/S_Z \end{bmatrix}$$

where α and β are scalars. Where there are two (n) states of the world, there can be at most two (n) securities whose vector of returns across states are linearly independent. Now since there are three securities and since individuals are assumed to be perfect competitors in buying, selling, and issuing these securities, there are three ratios that summarize how individuals can exchange $C(1)$ for $C(2)$. One ratio refers to exchanging $C(1)$ for $C(2)$ by trading X for Z; a second by trading X for Y; a third by trading Y for Z. These three ratios are

$$\frac{dC(2)}{dC(1)} = \left(\frac{X(2)}{S_X} - \frac{Z(2)}{S_Z}\right) \bigg/ \left(\frac{X(1)}{S_X} - \frac{Z(1)}{S_Z}\right) \qquad X \text{ for } Z,$$

$$\frac{dC(2)}{dC(1)} = \left(\frac{X(2)}{S_X} - \frac{Y(2)}{S_Y}\right) \bigg/ \left(\frac{X(1)}{S_X} - \frac{Y(1)}{S_Y}\right) \qquad X \text{ for } Y,$$

$$\frac{dC(2)}{dC(1)} = \left(\frac{Y(2)}{S_Y} - \frac{Z(2)}{S_Z}\right) \bigg/ \left(\frac{Y(1)}{S_Y} - \frac{Z(1)}{S_Z}\right) \qquad Y \text{ for } Z.$$

Unless these three ratios are equal, arbitrage possibilities are present. By this we mean that by capitalizing on the discrepancies among the ratios, individuals can execute a sequence of transactions that provides a certain return of unbounded magnitude. For example, consider the situation depicted in Figure 5 where the three ratios above are not equal since points x, y, and z fail to lie along a straight line. Suppose the individual initially puts his entire investment portfolio into security X, and then issues security Z and buys security X with the proceeds so as to move from point X to point A in Figure 5. Next suppose that he moves along line AB to point B by selling security X and purchasing security Y. Once at point B he can move to point C by selling security Z and buying more X. Once at C, he can become even better off by issuing more X and buying more Y, and so on. There is thus no limit to the ($C(1)$, $C(2)$) combination that the individual can command by executing such transactions. Notice that the individual, if he chooses, can obtain an indefinitely large but perfectly certain ($C(1) = C(2)$) consumption stream by exploiting these opportunities. This illustrates how pure arbitrage transactions involve no risk.

The upshot of course is that the three exchange ratios $dC(2)/dC(1)$ listed above must be equal. That is, all three points x, y, and z in Figure 5 must lie along the same straight line. In the example above, presumably investors' attempts to exploit the arbitrage possibilities would cause the prices $S_X, S_Z,$ and

S_Y to change so that x, y, and z would lie along a straight line. To show this formally, let

$$x(j) = X(j)/S_X, \qquad y(j) = Y(j)/S_Y, \qquad z(j) = Z(j)/S_Z, \qquad \text{for} \quad j = 1, 2.$$

Equality of the three exchange ratios means

$$\frac{x(2) - z(2)}{x(1) - z(1)} = \frac{x(2) - y(2)}{x(1) - y(1)} = \frac{y(2) - z(2)}{y(1) - z(1)}.$$

From the linear dependence of $(y(1), y(2))$ upon $(x(1), x(2))$ and $(z(1), z(2))$ we have

$$y(1) = \alpha x(1) + \beta z(1), \qquad y(2) = \alpha x(2) + \beta z(2).$$

Substituting these two equations into our exchange rate equalities with some rearranging gives the condition $\alpha + \beta = 1$, which is the condition that in Figure 5 the point y must lie on a straight line connecting the points x and z.

There are really only two goods in the preceding example, $C(1)$ and $C(2)$. The securities X, Y, and Z have value only because they represent claims to $C(1)$, $C(2)$ bundles. In effect, having three securities with return vetors that do not lie along a straight line implies that three prices obtain for those two goods, raising the arbitrage possibilities discussed above. To exhibit the logic of this and other problems, it is sometimes analytically convenient to work with "pure" securities that pay off one unit of consumption in state i and nothing in any other state. Such securities were introduced by Arrow and are known as Arrow–Debreu contingent securities. The return vector for such a security lies along one of the axes. Thus, in our two-state example, one unit of a state 1 contingent security offers a return vector $(1, 0)$, while one unit of a state 2 security offers a return vector $(0, 1)$ (see Figure 6).

Even where such contingent securities do not literally exist, it is possible effectively to "trade" them and to compute implicit prices for them where the number of ordinary securities equals or exceeds the number of states of nature. For example, consider our two-state example where securities X and Z exist.

FIGURE 6   Payoff vector of a state 1 Arrow–Debreu pure security.

Security X derives its value from the value that consumers attach to the consumption stream the security delivers. Let $p(i)$ be the amount of current output an individual would sacrifice to obtain one more unit of consumption in state i. Then it must be so that

$$S_X = X(1)p(1) + X(2)p(2),$$
$$S_Z = Z(1)p(1) + Z(2)p(2),$$

(7)

i.e., the price of each real security must reflect the value of the consumption streams that the security represents a claim on. The above equations can be solved for $p(1)$, $p(2)$, the implicit prices of the contingent securities, so long as $X(1)Z(2) - Z(1)X(2) \neq 0$, so long as the returns on securities X and Z are not linearly dependent.

Dividing both sides of the above equations by S_X and S_Z, respectively, gives

$$1 = \frac{X(1)}{S_X} p(1) + \frac{X(2)}{S_X} p(2) = x(1)p(1) + x(2)p(2),$$

$$1 = \frac{Z(1)}{S_Z} p(1) + \frac{Z(2)}{S_Z} p(2) = z(1)p(1) + z(2)p(2).$$

Solving for $p(1)$, $p(2)$ gives

$$\begin{bmatrix} p(1) \\ p(2) \end{bmatrix}_{x,z} = \begin{bmatrix} z(2) & -x(2) \\ -z(1) & x(1) \end{bmatrix} \Big/ [x(1)z(2) - x(2)z(1)] \cdot \begin{bmatrix} 1 \\ 1 \end{bmatrix}$$

where as before $x(i) = X(i)/S_X$, etc. Now if there is a third security Y, we could also solve for $p(1)$, $p(2)$ using the system of equations

$$1 = x(1)p(1) + x(2)p(2),$$
$$1 = y(1)p(1) + y(2)p(2).$$

The solution for $p(1)$, $p(2)$ is

$$\begin{bmatrix} p(1) \\ p(2) \end{bmatrix}_{x,y} = \begin{bmatrix} y(2) & -x(2) \\ -y(1) & x(1) \end{bmatrix} \Big/ [x(1)y(2) - y(1)x(2)] \cdot \begin{bmatrix} 1 \\ 1 \end{bmatrix}.$$

Now the "law of one price" requires that

$$\begin{bmatrix} p(1) \\ p(2) \end{bmatrix}_{x,y} = \begin{bmatrix} p(1) \\ p(2) \end{bmatrix}_{x,z} = \begin{bmatrix} p(1) \\ p(2) \end{bmatrix}_{y,z}.$$

By using the explicit solutions for $(p(1), p(2))$ it is straightforward to verify that the arbitrage condition $\alpha + \beta = 1$ above is equivalent with the law of one price. That is, the implicit value placed on a unit of return in state i must be the same regardless of the particular securities used to synthesize that return.

More generally, suppose there are n states of the world. Suppose that markets for the n contingent securities do not actually exist and that claims promising one dollar if state θ occurs never are traded. Instead, as in the real world, there are n' different companies each selling claims entitling the owner to share in the company's profits. Under a certain rank condition, so long as there are more companies than states of nature, it is as if there existed markets in n contingent securities since by buying and selling actual securities in the proper fashion, the individual can obtain any desired pattern of returns across states of nature.

We suppose that the ith firm's returns across states of nature are given by $x_i(\theta)$, $\theta = 1, \ldots, n$. Suppose that it is possible to select n such firms each of whose patterns of returns across states of nature are not linearly dependent on the returns of the remaining $n - 1$ firms. That is, for each $i = 1, \ldots, n$, the vector $(x_i(1), x_i(2), \ldots, x_i(n))$ cannot be written as a linear combination of the $n - 1$ vectors $(x_j(1), x_j(2), \ldots, x_j(n))$ for $j \neq i$. Let the market values of our n firms be $V_1, V_2, \ldots, V_n$. If there were n contingent securities, each promising to pay one dollar in state θ and having price $p(\theta)$, the values of the n firms would have to obey

$$V_1 = \sum_{\theta=1}^{n} x_1(\theta)p(\theta), \qquad V_2 = \sum_{\theta=1}^{n} x_2(\theta)p(\theta), \qquad \ldots, \qquad V_n = \sum_{\theta=1}^{n} x_n(\theta)p(\theta),$$

or in compact notation

$$V = xp \qquad (8)$$

where

$$V = \begin{bmatrix} V_1 \\ \vdots \\ V_n \end{bmatrix}, \qquad x = \begin{bmatrix} x_1(1) & x_1(2) \cdots x_1(n) \\ \vdots & \\ x_n(1) & x_n(2) \cdots x_n(n) \end{bmatrix}, \qquad p = \begin{bmatrix} p(1) \\ \vdots \\ p(n) \end{bmatrix}.$$

Since x is of full rank, (8) can be used to solve for p, giving

$$p = x^{-1}V. \qquad (9)$$

Equation (9) tells us how to unscramble the implicit prices of the n implicit contingent securities from the market values of n firms and the patterns of their returns across states of nature.

2. LIQUIDITY PREFERENCE AS BEHAVIOR TOWARD RISK

Tobin's (1958) explanation of the demand for money as emerging partly as a result of wealthholders' desire to diversify their holdings can be viewed as an application of the theory just described. Suppose that there are two states of the world and that there are two assets: a risky asset that pays off $x(\theta)$ in state $\theta = 1$, 2 for each unit of current output's worth of the asset; and a riskless asset called "money" that pays off one unit of current output, regardless of state, for each unit of current output invested in it. From our preceding dicussion we know that the household will hold at least a little of the risky asset provided that the expected rate of return is positive, i.e., provided that holding the risky security amounts to undertaking a favorable bet. By investing one sure unit of output ("money") in the risky asset, the investor obtains an expected return of $\pi(1)x(1) + \pi(2)x(2)$, which must exceed unity if the security is to offer the individual a favorable bet. Notice that for money to be held, it must be so that either $x(1) < 1$ or $x(2) < 1$, or else the risky asset would dominate money. The expected rate of return on the risky asset, denoted by r, is given by

$$r = \pi(1)x(1) + \pi(2)x(2) - 1.$$

It is easy to show that if we start from a position in which $r = 0$, an increase in r, i.e., an increase in either $x(1)$ or $x(2)$, will cause the investor to increase his holdings of the risky asset and decrease his holdings of money. (This is an example of Arrow's proposition that at least a small part of a favorable bet will be undertaken. We leave it to the reader to work out the details.) Clearly, by risk aversion, if $r = 0$, the investor will hold his entire portfolio in terms of money. Notice that we have established that at low enough interest rates, the investor's holdings of money will vary inversely with the interest rate on the risky asset.

At higher interest rates, an increase in r (i.e., in $x(1)$ or $x(2)$) may or may not cause holdings of money to contract. As usual, there are two effects: a substitution effect inducing a movement along an indifference curve, an effect that leads to lower money holdings; and a wealth or income effect, which may or may not offset the substitution effect, depending on the shape of the investor's indifference curves.

Notice that it is possible that the investor will want to hold no money (though if $r > 0$, he will always want to hold some of the risky asset). This will occur if the rate of return on the risky asset is so high that the situation is as depicted in Figure 7 where the budget line is flatter than the indifference curve even where the investor's entire portfolio is in the risky asset.

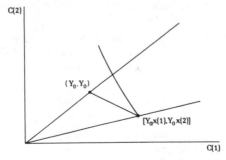

FIGURE 7 (Y_0, Y_0) = returns vector if whole portfolio held in money. $(Y_0x(1), Y_0x(2))$ = returns vector if whole portfolio held in risky asset.

The theory described above has often been embodied in a somewhat different form, the famous "mean–variance analysis" set forth by Tobin. As above, the individual is assumed to maximize expected utility

$$v = \sum_{\theta=1}^{n} \pi(\theta)U(C(\theta)).$$

If we know $C(\theta)$ and $\pi(\theta)$ for each θ, it is straightforward to deduce a probability distribution $g(C)$ that gives the probability that consumption will obtain the value C. In particular,

$$g(\tilde{C}) = \left[\sum_{\theta \in T} \pi(\theta), \; T = \{\theta \,|\, C(\theta) = \tilde{C}\} \right].$$

In the finite-state case currently under discussion $g(\tilde{C})$ will obtain a nonzero, positive value at only a finite number of $n' \leq n$ values of consumption C. Denote these values of consumption as $C_1, C_2, \ldots, C_{n'}$. Then expected utility v can be written as

$$v = \sum_{i=1}^{n'} U(C_i)g(C_i) \tag{10}$$

where $\sum_{i=1}^{n'} g(C_i) = 1$.

In a setup with a continuum of states of the world and where consequently C is allowed to take on any real value, the probability associated with consumption occurring in a neighborhood of width ε around C is approximately given by $\varepsilon f(C; B)$ where $f(C; B)$ is the probability density function associated with C, and B is a list of parameters determining that distribution. In this case expected utility v is

$$v = v(B) = \int_{-\infty}^{\infty} U(C)f(C; B)\, dC. \tag{11}$$

Given $U(C)$, expected utility is a function only of the parameters B determining the distribution of consumption. If there is only one parameter in B, as would be true if C were distributed according to the Poisson distribution, then expected utility would depend only on the value of that one parameter. If there are p parameters in B, then expected utility depends on all p of them.

The theory has been developed for distributions $f(C; B)$ that can be characterized by two parameters—one measuring mean or central tendency, the other measuring dispersion. The normal distribution is an example of such a distribution, being completely characterized by the mean and variance of the distribution. Members of the class of stable distributions of Paul Lévy are also characterized by two parameters.

It greatly facilitates the analysis also to assume that $f(C; B)$ is a "stable" distribution. A variate Z with density $f(Z; B_Z)$ is said to be stable if when another variate y with the same form of density $f(y; B_y)$, perhaps with $B_z \neq B_y$, is added to Z, the result is to produce a variate $X = Z + y$ obeying the same probability law $f(X; B_X)$. Assuming that the distribution $f(C; B)$ is stable is natural because stable distributions are the only distributions that serve as the limiting distribution in central limit theorems. The normal distribution is the best known of stable distributions. The Cauchy distribution is another. The central limit property of stable distributions is useful here because the random variable C is often thought of as representing a linear combination of a large number of independently distributed returns on various investments, implying that it will approximately follow a stable distribution.[4]

Assuming that $f(C; B)$ has the two parameters mean μ_C and standard deviation σ_C and that it is also a stable distribution amounts to assuming that it is a normal distribution.[5] That is because the normal distribution is the only (symmetric) stable distribution for which the standard deviation exists. Then expected utility v is

$$v(\mu_C, \sigma_C) = \int_{-\infty}^{\infty} U(C) f(C; \mu_C, \sigma_C) \, dC.$$

Defining the standardized variable Z as $Z = (C - \mu_C)/\sigma_C$, we have that $C = \mu_C + \sigma_C Z$. Then

$$v = v(\mu_C, \sigma_C) = \int_{-\infty}^{\infty} U(\mu_C + \sigma_C Z) f(Z; 0, 1) \, dZ$$

where $f(Z; 0, 1)$ is the standard, unit variance normal distribution. Since expected utility $v(\mu_C, \sigma_C)$ depends only on the two parameters μ_C, σ_C, we can define indifference curves in the μ_C, σ_C plane, i.e., combinations of μ_C and σ_C that yield constant levels of expected utility. Along such curves we have

$$dv = 0 = d\mu_C \int_{-\infty}^{\infty} U'(\mu_C + \sigma_C Z) f(Z; 0, 1) \, dZ$$

$$+ d\sigma_C \int_{-\infty}^{\infty} Z U'(\mu_C + \sigma_C Z) f(Z; 0, 1) \, dZ,$$

---

[4] A good reference on stable laws and central limit theorems is Feller (1966, Vol. II, 1st ed).
[5] The density function for the normal distribution is

$$f(C; \mu_C, \sigma_C) = \frac{1}{\sigma_C \sqrt{2\pi}} \exp\left(-\frac{(C - \mu_C)^2}{2\sigma_C^2} \right).$$

With this distribution, for expected utility to be defined, the utility function $U(C)$ must satisfy

$$|U(C)| \leq A e^{BC^2}, \qquad A > 0, \quad B > 0,$$

for some A and B. See Chipman (1973).

so that the slope of the indifference curves in the μ_C, σ_C plane is

$$\frac{d\mu_C}{d\sigma_C} = -\frac{\int_{-\infty}^{\infty} ZU'(\mu_C + \sigma_C Z)f(Z;0,1)\,dZ}{\int_{-\infty}^{\infty} U'(\mu_C + \sigma_C Z)f(Z;0,1)\,dZ} \tag{12}$$

Since $U'' < 0$ while $f(Z;0,1)$ is symmetric, the numerator on the right is negative so long as $\sigma_C > 0$ (negative Z's being multiplied by larger U''s than positive Z's); the denominator is positive since $U' > 0$. Thus the slope (12) is positive. To find the concavity of the indifference curves we differentiate (12) with respect to σ_C to obtain

$$\frac{d^2\mu_C}{d\sigma_C^2} = -\frac{\int_{-\infty}^{\infty} (Z + d\mu_C/d\sigma_C)^2 U''(\mu_C + \sigma_C Z)f(Z;0,1)\,dZ}{\int_{-\infty}^{\infty} U'(\mu_C + \sigma_C Z)f(Z;0,1)\,dZ},$$

which is positive since $U'' < 0$ and $U' > 0$. This shows that each indifference curve has a slope that increases as we move upward along a curve. An example of a map of such curves is depicted in Figure 8.

It is convenient to use Equation (12) to compute the slope of the indifference curves at zero standard deviation. We have

$$\left.\frac{d\mu_C}{d\sigma_C}\right|_{\sigma_C=0} = -\frac{\int ZU'(\mu_C)f(Z;0,1)\,dZ}{\int U'(\mu_C)f(Z;0,1)\,dZ} = \frac{-\int Zf(Z;0,1)\,dZ}{\int f(Z;0,1)\,dZ} = \frac{-E(Z)}{1} = 0.$$

The numerator equals zero since the normal distribution is symmetric about $Z = 0$ and since $U'(\mu_C)$ is independent of Z. Thus the indifference curves have zero slope for $\sigma_C = 0$. This property of the indifference curves will be seen to reflect that an individual will always take at least a small part of a favorable risk.

To take a specific example, suppose $U(C) = -e^{-\lambda C}$, $\lambda > 0$. Notice that

$$U'(C) = \lambda e^{-\lambda C} > 0 \qquad \text{for} \quad C \in (-\infty, \infty),$$
$$U''(C) = -\lambda^2 e^{-\lambda C} < 0 \qquad \text{for} \quad C \in (-\infty, \infty).$$

The density function for the normal distribution is

$$f(C; \mu, \sigma) = \frac{1}{\sigma\sqrt{2\pi}} \exp\left(-\frac{(C-\mu)^2}{2\sigma^2}\right).$$

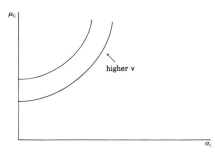

higher v

μ_c

σ_c

FIGURE 8

Consequently expected utility is given by

$$E(U(C)) = \frac{1}{\sigma\sqrt{2\pi}}\int_{-\infty}^{\infty} -e^{-\lambda C}\exp\left(-\frac{(C-\mu)^2}{2\sigma^2}\right)dC$$

$$= \frac{1}{\sigma\sqrt{2\pi}}\int_{-\infty}^{\infty} -\exp\left[-\left(\lambda C + \frac{(C-\mu)^2}{2\sigma^2}\right)\right]dC. \qquad (13)$$

Notice that

$$\lambda C + \frac{(C-\mu)^2}{2\sigma^2} = \frac{2\lambda C\sigma^2 + C^2 - 2\mu C + \mu^2}{2\sigma^2}$$

$$= \frac{[C-(\mu-\lambda\sigma^2)]^2 + 2\lambda\mu\sigma^2 - \lambda^2\sigma^4}{2\sigma^2}$$

$$= \frac{[C-(\mu-\lambda\sigma^2)]^2}{2\sigma^2} + \lambda(\mu - \tfrac{1}{2}\lambda\sigma^2).$$

Substituting the above expression into (13) gives

$$E[U(C)] = -e^{-\lambda(\mu-(1/2)\lambda\sigma^2)}\frac{1}{\sigma\sqrt{2\pi}}\int_{-\infty}^{\infty}\exp\left(-\frac{(C-(\mu-\lambda\sigma^2))^2}{2\sigma^2}\right)dC.$$

But we know that

$$\frac{1}{\sigma\sqrt{2\pi}}\int_{-\infty}^{\infty}\exp\left(-\frac{(C-\mu')^2}{2\sigma^2}\right)dC = 1$$

for any μ' and $\sigma > 0$. So we have

$$E[U(C)] = -\exp(-\lambda(\mu - \tfrac{1}{2}\lambda\sigma^2)).$$

Along curves of constant expected utility we require

$$\mu - \tfrac{1}{2}\lambda\sigma^2 = \text{constant}.$$

So the mean, standard deviation indifference curves satisfy

$$d\mu - \lambda\sigma\, d\sigma = 0,$$

so that their slope is

$$d\mu/d\sigma = \lambda\sigma > 0 \qquad \text{for} \quad \sigma > 0$$

and their concavity is

$$d^2\mu/d\sigma^2 = \lambda > 0.$$

This concludes our analysis of our specific example for $U(C)$.

Having characterized the individual's preferences, we now describe his opportunities. Suppose that there is available to the individual a safe asset that has the property that if he puts his entire portfolio into this asset, he will obtain a consumption stream characterized by mean C_0 and standard deviation zero. Suppose there is also an alternative asset (or maybe a portfolio of other assets) such that if the individual uses his entire portfolio to purchase this asset he obtains consumption goods in an amount $C_0 X$ where X is a normally distributed random variable with mean μ_X and variance σ_X^2. If the individual invests a proportion $1 - \lambda$ in the risky asset and λ in the safe asset, $0 \leq \lambda \leq 1$, he receives consumption

$$C = \lambda C_0 + (1 - \lambda)C_0 X.$$

Then the mean of his consumption would be

$$\mu_C = \lambda C_0 + (1 - \lambda)C_0 \mu_X. \tag{14}$$

Notice that $C - \mu_C = (1 - \lambda)C_0(X - \mu_X)$, so that

$$\sigma_C = (1 - \lambda)C_0 \sigma_X. \tag{15}$$

Solving (15) for λ, substituting into (14) and rearranging we obtain

$$\mu_C = C_0 + \left(\frac{\mu_X - 1}{\sigma_X}\right)\sigma_C, \qquad 0 \leq \sigma_C \leq C_0 \sigma_X, \tag{16}$$

which gives the locus of combinations of μ_C, σ_C attainable by varying λ. The mean μ_C rises linearly with the standard deviation σ_C, the slope being $(\mu_X - 1)/\sigma_X$. Of course, the expected rate of return $\mu_X - 1$ must exceed zero for the opportunity locus to have a positive slope. This is the condition that the risk be favorable. Such an opportunity locus is depicted in Figure 9.

As we have seen, the slope of the indifference curves at $\sigma_C = 0$ is zero. That means that if $\mu_X - 1 > 0$, the individual will always take at least a small part of the risk since then the opportunity locus through $(0, C_0)$ has a positive slope, permitting the individual to move to a higher level of expected utility by taking

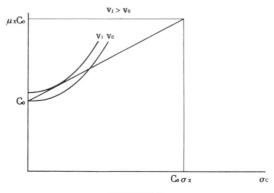

FIGURE 9

some risk. It follows that beginning from a situation where $\mu_X - 1 = 0$, an increase in the rate of return on the risky asset, $\mu_X - 1$, will lead to a decrease in the amount held in the safe asset and an increase in holdings of the risky asset. Thus, for a low enough rate of return on the risky asset, an increase in that rate does cause a decrease in the investor's demand for the safe asset. For higher values of the rate of return on the risky asset, however, an increase in that rate will not necessarily lead to a decrease in holdings of the safe asset, there being offsetting substitution and wealth effects. We leave it to the reader to study these offsetting effects in the context of the present graphical formulation of the theory. Needless to say, all of these features of the analysis have their counterparts in the state-preference version of the theory which we summarized above.

There are several unsatisfactory aspects of the theory that we have just sketched. For the formulation cast in terms of the mean and standard deviation of consumption, we have to assume that consumption is normally distributed, which requires that we act as if consumption can be an unbounded negative number. It is difficult to imagine negative consumption. If to circumvent this difficulty we restrict consumption to be nonnegative, we must pay for this by adopting a probability function for consumption that lacks the statistical property of stability, and so greatly weakens the appeal of the theory. But as we have seen above, the essence of the theory can be cast in terms of the state-preference analysis where the assumption that consumption has a normal distribution need play no role.

As a theory of the demand for money, the theory is of somewhat limited applicability. For one thing, the occurrence of unforeseen price level changes makes money a risky asset in terms of goods, so that the "money" in the model above does not really correspond with the asset called money in the real world. For another thing, money is dominated by assets like treasury bills and savings deposits that are as risk-free as money but offer positive nominal yields. The above theory is really at best one about the demand for such assets, not money. To explain the demand for money it seems essential to take into account the presence of transactions costs.[6]

3. THE MODIGLIANI-MILLER THEOREM

Throughout these pages we have assumed that firms have no bonds outstanding, that they retain no earnings, and so they finance all of their investment by issuing equities. It is an implication of the Modigliani-Miller theorem that our assumptions about these matters are not restrictive (Modigliani and Miller, 1958). In particular, Modigliani and Miller's analysis implies that in the absence of a corporate income tax, the firm's cost of capital is

---

[6] For starters, see Baumol (1952), and Tobin (1956).

independent of whether the firm raises the funds by retaining earnings, issuing bonds, or issuing equities. Moreover, Modigliani and Miller's theorem was proved in the context of a model that explicitly recognized the existence of uncertainty. This section sketches the reasoning of Modigliani and Miller by using the state-preference presentation of Stiglitz (1969).

We collapse the entire future into a single point in the future. We assume that there is a finite number n of possible future states of the world, each state representing an entire constellation of possible outcomes of all sorts of events in the future. We let $\theta = 1, 2, \ldots, n$ be an index over the possible states. For example, $\theta = 1$ might correspond to a complicated event such as "on January 1, 1990 it rains one inch in Eugene, Oregon, Minnesota is playing California in the Rose Bowl, a Democrat is President," and so on. States $\theta = 2, \ldots, n$ correspond to different outcomes of such events. An individual's happiness, indexed by U, in the event that state θ prevails depends in the usual way on the amounts of m goods that he consumes:

$$U = U(q_1(\theta), \ldots, q_m(\theta)), \qquad \partial U / \partial q_i(\theta) > 0, \quad U(\ ) \text{ concave},$$

where $q_i(\theta)$ is the amount of the ith good consumed by the individual in state θ, $i = 1, \ldots, m$. We have assumed that the form of the utility function $U(\ )$ is independent of the state θ.

The consumer's notions about the likelihood of various states of the world occurring are supposed to be summarized by a set of subjective probabilities $\pi(1), \pi(2), \ldots, \pi(n)$ that obey $\sum_{\theta=1}^n \pi(\theta) = 1$, where $\pi(\theta)$ is the probability that the consumer assigns to state θ occurring. Individuals are assumed to maximize expected utility v:

$$v = \sum_{\theta=1}^n \pi(\theta) U(q_1(\theta), \ldots, q_m(\theta)). \tag{17}$$

The consumer is assumed to come into a certain endowment $q_i{}^0(\theta)$ of claims to goods, $i = 1, \ldots, m$, should state θ occur, $\theta = 1, \ldots, n$. It is assumed that there exist competitive futures markets in which individuals trade claims to the ith good in state θ prior to the occurrence of the state. The individual faces a price $p_i(\theta)$ at which he can buy or sell whatever claims he wishes on the ith good contingent on state θ occurring. The value of the consumer's endowment is

$$\sum_{\theta=1}^n \sum_{i=1}^m p_i(\theta) q_i{}^0(\theta).$$

The consumer maximizes expected utility v subject to

$$\sum_{\theta=1}^n \sum_{i=1}^m p_i(\theta) q_i{}^0(\theta) = \sum_{\theta=1}^n \sum_{i=1}^m p_i(\theta) q_i(\theta), \tag{18}$$

which states that the market value of his endowment equals the market value of the bundle of contingent commodities that he purchases. Where λ is an undetermined Lagrange multiplier, the consumer's problem can be formulated as optimizing

$$J = \sum_{\theta=1}^{n} \left\{ \pi(\theta) U(q_1(\theta), \ldots, q_m(\theta)) + \lambda \left(\sum_{i=1}^{m} p_i(\theta)(q_i(\theta) - q_i^{0}(\theta)) \right) \right\}.$$

The first-order conditions are

$$\pi(\theta) \frac{\partial U}{\partial q_i(\theta)} + \lambda p_i(\theta) = 0, \qquad i = 1, \ldots, m, \quad \theta = 1, \ldots, n. \tag{19}$$

$$\frac{\partial J}{\partial \lambda} = 0.$$

Dividing (19) for θ and i by (19) for $\tilde{\theta}$ and j, we have

$$\frac{\partial U/\partial q_i(\theta)}{\partial U/\partial q_j(\tilde{\theta})} = \frac{\pi(\tilde{\theta})}{\pi(\theta)} \frac{p_i(\theta)}{p_j(\tilde{\theta})}, \tag{20}$$

which is the analogue of the familiar static marginal equality for the household. From (20) and the budget constraint (18) demand curves for the nm contingent commodities can be derived. By aggregating these demand curves over the set of all consumers, market demand schedules can be obtained, which together with total market endowments permit computing a general equilibrium in which the prices $p_i(\theta)$, $i = 1, \ldots, m$, $\theta = 1, \ldots, n$ are determined.

Arrow (1964) has shown that consumers are just as well off where these nm markets in m commodities contingent on state θ ($= 1, \ldots, n$) occurring are replaced by n markets in "contingent securities," with one security for each state. Each security promises to pay one "dollar" should state θ occur. Following the occurrence of a state, consumers then trade the m goods as described by the standard static model.

We consider a competitive model in which there exists a complete set of n markets for the n contingent securities, each promising to pay one dollar if state θ occurs in the future. The model is assumed to possess a general equilibrium in which the equilibrium price of a claim to one dollar in state θ is $p(\theta)$. The units of $p(\theta)$ are (sure) dollars now per unit of a dollar in state θ. Notice that the price of a sure dollar next period is $\sum_{\theta=1}^{n} p(\theta)$, which can be interpreted as the reciprocal of one plus the risk-free rate of interest. The assumption that there exist perfect markets in the contingent securities for all n states of the world means that it is possible to ensure against any risk. Individuals need bear no risks if that is their preference.

We shall assume no taxes are present. Now consider a firm whose prospective returns, net of labor and materials costs, but gross of capital costs, are $X(\theta)$ dollars in state θ. Suppose that the firm issues an amount of B dollars worth of bonds. The firm now promises to pay $(r + 1)B$ dollars to its bond holders next period, provided that it does not go bankrupt, i.e., provided that $X(\theta) \geq (r + 1)B$. If the firm does go bankrupt, i.e., if $X(\theta) \leq (r + 1)B$, then the bond holders receive only $X(\theta)$. Thus the realized rate of return on bonds $r(\theta)$ depends on the state of the world:

$$r(\theta) + 1 = \begin{cases} r + 1 & \text{if } X(\theta) \geq (r + 1)B \\ X(\theta)/B & \text{if } X(\theta) < (r + 1)B. \end{cases}$$

Only if $X(\theta) \geq (r + 1)B$ for all θ is $r(\theta)$ equal to the promised coupon rate r for all θ.

The value of the firm's bonds must equal the sum of the values of the contingent securities that the bond implicitly consists of. For each state in which the firm does not go bankrupt, the bonds will in total pay off $(r + 1)B$. The present value of those returns is

$$(r + 1)B \sum_{\theta \in S} p(\theta) \qquad \text{where} \quad S = \{\theta | X(\theta) \geq (r + 1)B\}.$$

For states θ in $S' = \{\theta | X(\theta) < (r + 1)B\}$, in which the firm goes bankrupt, the bonds pay off $X(\theta)$. So the present value of payments in those states is

$$B \sum_{\theta \in S'} \frac{X(\theta)}{B} p(\theta).$$

The total present value of the firm's bonds B must thus satisfy

$$B = (r + 1)B \sum_{\theta \in S} p(\theta) + B \sum_{\theta \in S'} \frac{X(\theta)}{B} p(\theta).$$

Dividing by B and solving for $r + 1$, we obtain

$$r + 1 = \frac{1 - \sum_{\theta \in S'} X(\theta)B^{-1}p(\theta)}{\sum_{\theta \in S} p(\theta)}, \tag{21}$$

which tells us that the rate of return that a firm's bonds must bear depends on the firm's probability of defaulting, and so on the number of bonds it has issued. Notice that if there is zero probability of the firm's going bankrupt, S' being empty, r equals the risk-free rate of interest.

The firm's equities bear a payout stream across states of nature given by

$$X(\theta) - (r + 1)B \qquad \text{if } X(\theta) \geq (r + 1)B,$$
$$0 \qquad \text{if } X(\theta) < (r + 1)B.$$

As with bonds, the value of the firm's equities must equal the sum of the values of the contingent securities that the equities implicitly represent. So we have that the present value of equities E is

$$E = \sum_{\theta \in S} (X(\theta) - (r + 1)B)p(\theta). \tag{22}$$

Substituting for $r + 1$ from (21) in the above expression gives

$$E = \sum_{\theta \in S} p(\theta)X(\theta) - B\left(\frac{1 - \sum_{\theta \in S'} X(\theta)B^{-1}p(\theta)}{\sum_{\theta \in S} p(\theta)}\right) \sum_{\theta \in S} p(\theta)$$

$$= \sum_{\theta \in S} p(\theta)X(\theta) - B + \sum_{\theta \in S'} X(\theta)p(\theta)$$

$$= \sum_{\theta \in S \cup S'} p(\theta)X(\theta) - B \tag{23}$$

or

$$E + B = \sum_{\theta \in S \cup S'} p(\theta)x(\theta). \tag{24}$$

Equation (24) states that the total value of the firm's debt plus equity equals the present value of the firm's return across states of nature, evaluated at the price of claims to one dollar contingent on the associated states of nature. The total value $E + B$ is therefore independent of the ratio of debt to equity. This is the Modigliani–Miller theorem.

Now assume that the firm is contemplating a project that costs C sure dollars today, and that will cause the firm's returns to change by $d\,X(\theta)$ in state θ. The value of stockholders' equity if the project is not undertaken is given by (23). If the project is undertaken, the value of the original stockholders' equity will be

$$E' = \sum_{\theta} p(\theta)X(\theta) - B + \sum_{\theta} p(\theta)\,dX(\theta) - C.$$

The value of the original stockholders' equity is increased by undertaking the project so long as

$$\sum_{\theta} p(\theta)\,dX(\theta) - C > 0;$$

the project ought to be undertaken by the firm so long as the above inequality is met because it will increase the value of the equity of initial stockholders. This is true regardless of whether the project is financed by issuing bonds or more equities. In particular, notice that the rate of interest r on the firm's bonds, which depends on the volume of bonds that the firm has outstanding, is not pertinent in helping the firm determine whether or not to undertake the project.

To be more specific, suppose that the project is financed by issuing bonds. If the project is not undertaken, the value of the firm is

$$E^0 + B^0 = \sum_{\theta} p(\theta)X^0(\theta).$$

If the project is undertaken the value of the firm will be

$$E' + B' = \sum_{\theta} p(\theta)(X^0(\theta) + dX(\theta)).$$

Therefore

$$E' + B' = E^0 + B^0 + \sum_\theta p(\theta)\, dX(\theta)$$

or

$$E' - E^0 = \sum_\theta p(\theta)\, dX(\theta) - (B' - B^0).$$

If the firm finances by issuing bonds, $B' - B^0 = C$, the cost of the project. Thus the value of equities, depending on whether the project is undertaken, varies according to

$$E' - E^0 = \sum_\theta p(\theta)\, dX(\theta) - C,$$

which should exceed zero in order that the project be undertaken.

If the project is financed by issuing equities, $B' = B^0$, implying that

$$E' = E^0 + \sum_\theta p(\theta)\, dX(\theta).$$

To finance the project, the firm must issue C dollars worth of new equities. The new value of the equities of the original stockholders will be $E' - C$, which is obtained by subtracting C from both sides of the above equation:

$$E' - C = E^0 + \sum_\theta p(\theta)\, dX(\theta) - C.$$

It follows that $E' - C$ will exceed E^0 if $\sum_\theta p(\theta)\, dX(\theta) - C$ exceeds zero.

4. EFFECTS OF A CORPORATE INCOME TAX

We now suppose that the firm's profits net of interest payments to bond holders are taxed at a corporate profits tax rate t_K. The returns to stockholders then equal $(1 - t_K)(X(\theta) - (r + 1)B)$ for states in S, i.e., states satisfying $X(\theta) \geq (r + 1)B$, and zero for states in which bankruptcy occurs. The interest rate r on the firm's bonds continues to obey (21). The value of the firm's equities is now given by

$$E = \sum_{\theta \in S} (1 - t_K)(X(\theta) - (r + 1)B)p(\theta).$$

Substituting for r from (21) in the above equation and rearranging gives

$$E = (1 - t_K) \sum_{\theta=1}^{n} X(\theta)p(\theta) - B + t_K B. \tag{25}$$

For $t_K > 0$, the value of the firm, $E + B$, varies directly with the stock of bonds outstanding. Equation (25) thus predicts that it is in stockholders' interest to have the firm levered an indefinitely large amount. The presence of the corporate income tax implies that there is an optimal debt–equity ratio for the firm (one indefinitely large) and thus causes the Modigliani–Miller theorem to fail to hold.

To elaborate, suppose that the firm initially has B bonds outstanding and that the value of the outstanding equities is given by E in (25). Now suppose that the firm contemplates issuing an additional amount of bonds $B' - B > 0$ and retiring outstanding equities with the proceeds. As before, we assume that the distribution of returns $X(\theta)$ and prices $p(\theta)$ across states are independent of the firm's financing decision. Then using (25) to calculate the value of outstanding equities when B' bonds are outstanding gives

$$E' = E - (B' - B) + t_K(B' - B)$$

or

| value of equity remaining stockholders | = | original value of equity of owners still holding equities after the repurchase | + | $t_k \cdot$(amount of equities bought out). |

Here E is the original value of outstanding equities, while $B' - B$ is the volume of equities bought out, so that $E - (B' - B)$ is the original value of equity owners left in the firm after some owners have been bought out.

We should note that matters become much more complex when individual income taxes with different rates for interest income and capital gains are included in the analysis.

REFERENCES

Arrow, K. (1964). "The role of securities in the optimal allocation of risk bearing." *Review of Economic Studies*, Vol. 31, pp. 91–96.

Arrow, K. J. (1971). *Essays in the Theory of Risk Bearing*, p. 100, Chicago, Illinois: Markham Publishing Company.

Baumol, W. J. (1952). "The transactions demand for cash: An inventory theoretic approach." *The Quarterly Journal of Economics*, Vol. LXVI, No. 4, pp. 545–556.

Chipman, J. S. (1973). "The ordering of portfolios in terms of mean and variance." *The Review of Economic Studies*, Vol. XL (2), No. 122, pp. 167–190.

Feller, W. (1966). *An Introduction to Probability Theory and Its Applications*, Vol. II, 1st ed., New York: Wiley.

Friedman, M., and Savage, L. J. (1948). "The utility analysis of choices involving risk." *The Journal of Political Economy*, Vol. LVI, No. 4, pp. 279–304.

Hirshleifer, J. (1965). "Investment decision under uncertainty-choice-theoretic approaches." *The Quarterly Journal of Economics*, Vol. LXXIX, No. 4, pp. 509–536.

Hirshleifer, J. (1966). "Investment decision under uncertainty: Applications of the state-preference approach." *The Quarterly Journal of Economics*, Vol. LXXX, No. 2, pp. 252–277.

Luce, R. D., and Raiffa, H. (1957). *Games and Decisions*, New York: Wiley.

Modigliani, F., and Miller, M. H. (1958). "The cost of capital, corporation finance and the theory of investment." *American Economic Review*, Vol. 48, No. 63, pp. 261–297.

Stigler, G. J. and Boulding, K. E. (1952). *Readings in Price Theory*. Chicago, Illinois: American Economic Association, R. D. Irwin.

Stiglitz, J. E. (1969). "A re-examination of the Modigliani–Miller theorem." *American Economic Review*, Vol. 59, No. 5, pp. 784–793.

Tobin, J. (1956). "The interest-elasticity of transactions demand for cash." *The Review of Economics and Statistics*, Vol. 38, No. 3, pp. 241–247.

Tobin, J. (1958). "Liquidity Preference as Behavior Towards Risk." *The Review of Economic Studies*, Vol. 25 (2), No. 7, pp. 65–86.

CHAPTER VIII

IMPLICIT LABOR CONTRACTS AND STICKY WAGES

1. INTRODUCTION

This chapter provides practice in applying the state preference approach that was described in Chapter VII. The application to be studied is a version of the "implicit contract" model of Azariadis (1976). A related model was constructed by Martin Baily (1974). The original work by Azariadis and Baily fostered the development of an extensive literature on implicit contracts, which is surveyed by Sherwin Rosen (1985)[1].

The model to be studied in this chapter is a one-period, partial model of a firm confronting a body of workers. The firm is subject to demand uncertainty, and must contract to hire a number of workers *before* the demand uncertainty is resolved. The workers have access to opportunities outside the firm which are fully sumarized by a market-determined level of expected utility available elsewhere. The risk-sharing and work-sharing opportunities open to the workers are exogenously limited in such a way that the workers find it in their interest to accept an "implicit contract" entailing exposure to a positive probability of being unemployed and payment by the firm of a real wage that is independent of the state of demand.

The present model does not deliver results that can be interpreted as the *dynamically* inflexible *money* wages assumed in Keynesian models. Instead, the model delivers *real* wages that are fixed across states of nature at a given point in time.

2. EMERGENCE OF STATE-INDEPENDENT WAGES

We consider a competitive firm that will be able to sell all that it wants of a perishable output in period t at the price $p(\theta)$. The price $p(\theta)$ depends on the

---

[1] The model described in this chapter is a much simplified version of the one developed by Azariadis (1976), although the setup here is not exactly identical with his.

state of the world θ that prevails at date t. For date t, we assume that there are two states of the world, indexed by $\theta = 1, 2$, and that $p(1) > p(2)$. The firm and its workers share a common view of the probabilities of states 1 and 2 emerging, denoted by $\pi(1)$ and $\pi(2)$, respectively. We assume that $0 < \pi(1) < 1$; of course $\pi(1) + \pi(2) = 1$.

The firm's output in state θ is given by $f(n(\theta))$ where $n(\theta) \geq 0$ is the firm's employment, measured in number of men, in state θ. The production function f satisfies $f' > 0$, $f'' < 0$; the marginal product of labor is positive but diminishing. We further assume that $\lim_{n \to 0} f'(n) = \infty$ and that $\lim_{n \to \infty} f'(n) = 0$.

The firm pays workers a money wage $w(\theta)$ in state θ. The wage may be dependent on state θ. The firm's profits in state θ are then given by

$$p(\theta)f(n(\theta)) - w(\theta)n(\theta).$$

The firm's objective is to maximize the expected value of its profits:

$$V = \sum_{\theta=1}^{2} \pi(\theta)(p(\theta)f(n(\theta)) - w(\theta)n(\theta)).$$

Positing that the firm maximizes expected profits means that the firm has a neutral attitude toward risk and is willing to accept fair bets in unlimited amounts.[2]

The representative worker possesses a utility function that gives his happiness as a function of the wages that he receives and his leisure. It is assumed that a worker either works full time, in which case his level of leisure is $L = L_0$, or else he is unemployed, in which case he has leisure $L_1 > L_0$. There is no part-time or overtime work.[3] The worker's happiness is given by the utility function

$$U = g(w(\theta), L), \qquad g_1 > 0, g_{11} < 0, \quad g_2 \geq 0, g_{22} \leq 0,$$

which is assumed to be concave and to possess continuous second partial derivatives. If the worker is employed, his utility can be written solely as a function of his wage

$$U = U(w(\theta)) = g(w(\theta), L_0)$$

since L_0 is a parameter. Our assumptions on g imply that $U' > 0$, $U'' < 0$, so that the worker is assumed to be risk averse. We let r denote the pecuniary value the worker attaches to having leisure L_1 rather than L_0, i.e., it is the amount he

---

[2] That is, it is as if the firm were trying to maximize its expected utility of profits, but that its utility function is linear in profits.

[3] This turns out to be a critical assumption. See the exercise at the end of this chapter.

would have to be paid to make him indifferent between working and not working. So r is defined by the equality

$$g(0, L_1) = g(r, L_0) = U(r).$$

The worker's pecuniary income is thus $w(\theta)$ in state θ if he is employed in state θ, and r if he is unemployed. The worker maximizes expected utility which, given our definition of r, can be written as a function only of the distribution of his pecuniary income across states.

The firm employs $n(1)$ workers in state 1 and $n(2)$ workers in state 2. Its procedure is to offer jobs to a number $\max(n(1), n(2))$ workers, and then to lay workers off in a random fashion in the state for which $n(\theta) < \max(n(1), n(2))$. In our case, since $p(1) > p(2)$, there is a presumption that the firm will set $n(1) > n(2)$, so that $\max(n(1), n(2)) = n(1)$. Workers are aware of the firm's policy on this matter, and consequently realize that if state 2 occurs in a given period, only $n(2)/n(1)$ of the workers having jobs with the firm will actually be employed. Since the firm lays off workers randomly, the worker believes that should state 2 occur his chances of working are $n(2)/n(1)$ while his chances of being laid off are $(n(1) - n(2))/n(1)$. Laid off workers receive no wages from the firm.

The worker seeks to maximize his expected utility, which is

$$v = \pi(1)U(w(1)) + \pi(2)\frac{n(2)}{n(1)}U(w(2)) + \pi(2)\left(1 - \frac{n(2)}{n(1)}\right)U(r).$$

The firm is assumed to be able to hire as large a labor force as it wants subject to the restraint that its jobs offer workers a level of expected utility v at least as great as $\bar{v}$, where $\bar{v}$ is a market-determined level of expected utility that workers can obtain by accepting jobs with other firms. The firm's problem is thus to maximize expected profits

$$\pi(1)(p(1)f(n(1)) - w(1)n(1)) + \pi(2)(p(2)f(n(2)) - w(2)n(2)) \qquad (1)$$

subject to the constraint

$$\bar{v} = \pi(1)U(w(1)) + \pi(2)\frac{n(2)}{n(1)}U(w(2)) + \pi(2)\left(1 - \frac{n(2)}{n(1)}\right)U(r). \qquad (2)$$

The firm chooses $w(1)$, $w(2)$, $n(1)$, $n(2)$ so as to maximize (1) subject to (2).[4] The firm's problem is thus to choose a wage and layoff policy to maximize its profits subject to the constraints imposed by the labor market. Notice that according to (2), workers are willing to sacrifice some wages in state 2 for more security of

---

[4] In effect, the firm chooses and announces in advance a "contingency plan" for setting w and n as a function of the state (i.e., price) that will occur.

employment, i.e., a higher $n(2)/n(1)$. Maximization of (1) subject to (2) is carried out through unconstrained maximization of

$$J(n(1), n(2), w(1), w(2), \lambda) = \pi(1)(p(1)f(n(1)) - w(1)n(1))$$
$$+ \pi(2)(p(2)f(n(2)) - w(2)n(2))$$
$$+ \lambda \left[\bar{v} - \pi(1)U(w(1)) - \pi(2)\frac{n(2)}{n(1)} \right.$$
$$\left. \cdot U(w(2)) - \pi(2)\left(1 - \frac{n(2)}{n(1)}\right)U(r) \right] \qquad (3)$$

where λ is an undetermined Lagrange multiplier. The first-order conditions for a maximum of (3) are:

$$\frac{\partial J}{\partial n(1)} = \pi(1)p(1)f'(n(1)) - \pi(1)w(1) + \lambda\pi(2)\frac{n(2)}{n(1)^2}(U(w(2)) - U(r)) = 0, \qquad (4)$$

$$\frac{\partial J}{\partial n(2)} = \pi(2)p(2)f'(n(2)) - \pi(2)w(2) - \lambda\pi(2)\frac{1}{n(1)}(U(w(2)) - U(r)) = 0, \qquad (5)$$

$$\frac{\partial J}{\partial w(1)} = -\pi(1)n(1) - \lambda\pi(1)U'(w(1)) = 0, \qquad (6)$$

$$\frac{\partial J}{\partial w(2)} = -\pi(2)n(2) - \lambda\pi(2)\frac{n(2)}{n(1)}U'(w(2)) = 0, \qquad (7)$$

$$\frac{\partial J}{\partial \lambda} = \bar{v} - \pi(1)U(w(1)) - \pi(2)\frac{n(2)}{n(1)}U(w(2)) - \pi(2)\left(1 - \frac{n(2)}{n(1)}\right)U(r) = 0. \qquad (8)$$

Equation (6) can be written $n(1) = -\lambda U'(w(1))$, while Equation (7) can be written $n(1) = -\lambda U'(w(2))$. Both of these equations can be satisfied only if

$$U'(w(2)) = U'(w(1)). \qquad (9)$$

But since $U'(w)$ is a strictly decreasing function of w—recall that we have assumed that $U'' < 0$—Equation (9) can be satisfied only if

$$w(1) = w(2) = w. \qquad (10)$$

According to (10), the wage rate should be independent of the state that occurs. The firm should offer a fixed wage w and not adjust it, say, downward in state 2 simply because $p(1) > p(2)$.

To indicate the forces that lead to the wage being constant across states of nature, we study the worker's and the firm's indifference curves with respect to $w(1)$ and $w(2)$. Holding expected utility v and $n(2)/n(1)$ both constant, $w(1)$ and $w(2)$ can vary so long as they satisfy

$$0 = dv = \pi(1)U'(w(1))\,dw(1) + \pi(2)\frac{n(2)}{n(1)}U'(w(2))\,dw(2).$$

Hence, in the $w(1)$, $w(2)$ plane, the slope of the worker's indifference curve is

$$\frac{dw(2)}{dw(1)} = -\frac{\pi(1)\,n(1)}{\pi(2)\,n(2)}\,\frac{U'(w(1))}{U'(w(2))} < 0.$$

Differentiating the above equation with respect to $w(1)$ gives

$$\frac{d^2w(2)}{dw(1)^2} = -\frac{\pi(1)\,n(1)}{\pi(2)\,n(2)}\,\frac{U''(w(1))}{U'(w(2))} - \left(\frac{\pi(1)\,n(1)}{\pi(2)\,n(2)}\right)^2\frac{U'(w(1))^2 U''(w(2))}{U'(w(2))^3} > 0,$$

which shows that the indifference curves are convex.

Holding both expected profits V and $n(1)$ and $n(2)$ constant, the firm is content with movements in $w(1)$ and $w(2)$ that satisfy

$$-\pi(1)n(1)\,dw(1) - \pi(2)n(2)\,dw(2) = dV = 0$$

or

$$\frac{dw(2)}{dw(1)} = -\frac{\pi(1)\,n(1)}{\pi(2)\,n(2)} < 0,$$

which gives the slope of the firm's indifference curves in the $w(1)$, $w(2)$ plane, along which expected profits are constant. Differentiating the above equation with respect to $w(1)$ gives $d^2w(2)/dw(1)^2 = 0$, which shows that the firm's indifference curves are straight lines, a consequence of the firm's neutral attitude toward risk. Higher expected profits correspond to firm indifference curves closer to the origin, while higher expected utility for workers corresponds to indifference curves further from the origin. (See Figure 1.) The firm maximizes its expected profits subject to a fixed level of v by equating the slope of its iso-expected profit line to the slope of the worker's indifference curve:

$$\frac{-\pi(1)\,n(1)}{\pi(2)\,n(2)} = -\frac{\pi(1)\,n(1)}{\pi(2)\,n(2)}\,\frac{U'(w(1))}{U'(w(2))},$$

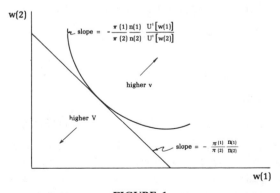

FIGURE 1

or

$$U'(w(1)) = U'(w(2)).$$

The above condition can only be satisfied where $w(1) = w(2)$ Thus, given $n(1)$ and $n(2)$, the firm maximizes its expected profits subject to a constant level of v by eliminating any risk that the wage depend on the state of demand for the firm's product (i.e., on $p(\theta)$).

3. EXISTENCE OF LAYOFFS

We now turn to analyzing the determinants of $n(1)$ and $n(2)$, and so the probability of employment, $n(2)/n(1)$. To start with an interesting extreme case, we begin by assuming that $r = 0$, so that workers derive no additional utility from their additional leisure when unemployed. Under this assumption it happens that $n(2) = n(1)$, so that employment is constant across states and the probability of employment is unity. To show this in a convenient way, suppose on the contrary that the firm employs $n(\theta)^\circ$ men in state θ, where $n(2)^\circ < n(1)^\circ$, and pays a wage of w° that is fixed across states of nature. Then expected profits are

$$(V)^\circ = \pi(1)p(1)f(n(1)^\circ) + \pi(2)p(2)f(n(2)^\circ) - n(1)^\circ w^\circ(\pi(1) + \pi(2)n(2)^\circ/n(1)^\circ).$$

Since workers are risk-averse, they prefer a certain wage of

$$\tilde{w} = w^\circ\left(\pi(1) + \pi(2)\frac{n(2)^\circ}{n(1)^\circ}\right) < w^\circ,$$

to the uncertain wage packet of w° with probability $\pi(1) + \pi(2)n(2)^\circ/n(1)^\circ$ and zero with probability $\pi(2)(1 - n(2)^\circ/n(1)^\circ)$. So if the firm employs $n(1)^\circ$ workers in each state, paying them the reduced wage $\tilde{w}$, workers are better off. The firm's expected wage bill is unchanged since the new expected wage bill is

$$n(1)^\circ\tilde{w} = n(1)^\circ w^\circ(\pi(1) + \pi(2)n(2)^\circ/n(1)^\circ).$$

The firm's expected profits with $n(1) = n(1)^\circ$, $n(2) = n(1)^\circ$ and the certain money wage $\tilde{w}$ are given by

$$(V)' = \pi(1)p(1)f(n(1)^\circ) + \pi(2)p(2)f(n(1)^\circ) - n(1)^\circ\tilde{w}.$$

Subtracting $(V)^\circ$ from $(V)'$ gives

$$(V)' - (V)^\circ = \pi(2)p(2)(f(n(1)^\circ) - f(n(2)^\circ)),$$

which is positive so long as $n(1)^\circ > n(2)^\circ$. Thus, the firm's expected profits are greater and workers are happier with $n(2) = n(1)^\circ$, so that in a sense additional workers in state 2 are free to the firm so long as $n(2)^\circ < n(1)^\circ$. Since workers have a positive marginal product, it pays the firm to set $n(1) = n(2)$.

So with $r = 0$, employment, output, and the wage rate are each constant across states, this in spite of the fact that the price of the firm's ouput varies across states. Evidently, then, the firm's supply curve is vertical, while its demand for workers is independent of the real wage in terms of the firm's own good. Notice that the equilibrium in which $w(1) = w(2)$ and $n(1) = n(2)$ is one in which the worker bears no risk since he or she receives a certain wage of $w(1)$. The firm bears all the risk. This is a consequence of the firm's risk neutrality and the worker's risk aversion. The firm is willing to accept whatever fair bets are offered to it, while the worker attempts to avoid any fair bets. There is thus incentive for the firm and individuals to trade risks so that the firm accepts whatever risks must be borne. The character of our results stems directly from the asymmetrical attitudes toward risk that we have attributed to the firm, on the one hand, and to the worker on the other.

We now examine the case in which $r > 0$. We begin by taking the total differential of the firm's expected profits,

$$d(V) = -(\pi(1)n(1) + \pi(2)n(2))\,dw + \pi(1)[p(1)f'(n(1)) - w]\,dn(1)$$
$$+ \pi(2)[p(2)f'(n(2)) - w]\,dn(2).$$

Assume that $n(1) = n(2)$ initially and hold $n(1)$ fixed (i.e., set $dn(1) = 0$). Then we have

$$d(V) = -n(1)\,dw + \pi(2)[p(2)f'(n(2)) - w]\,dn(2).$$

The firm is willing to bear variations in w and $n(2)$ so long as expected profits remain unchanged, $(d(V) = 0)$, i.e., so long as the variations of w and $n(2)$ satisfy

$$dw = \pi(2)(p(2)f'(n(2)) - w)\,dn(2)/n(1). \qquad (11)$$

Since $p(2)f'(n(2)) - w < 0,$[5] the firm is willing to increase w if it can decrease $n(2)$. Notice that

$$d\left(\frac{n(2)}{n(1)}\right) = \frac{dn(2)}{n(1)} - \frac{n(2)}{n(1)}\frac{dn(1)}{n(1)}, \qquad (12)$$

so that if $dn(1) = 0$, as we are assuming, then $d(n(2)/n(1)) = dn(2)/n(1)$.

Where $r > 0$, is it still true that contracts will be written so that $n(2) = n(1)$? The worker's expected pecuniary income is

$$E(\tilde{w}) = \pi(1)w + \pi(2)\frac{n(2)}{n(1)}w + \pi(2)\left(1 - \frac{n(2)}{n(1)}\right)r,$$

---

[5] The marginal conditions (6) and (7) imply $\lambda = -n(1)/U'(w)$. Substituting this into marginal condition (5) gives

$$p(2)f'(n(2)) - w = -\left(\frac{U(w) - U(r)}{U'(w)}\right) < 0$$

since $U(w) - U(r) > 0$ and $U'(w) > 0$.

where now $r > 0$. Taking the total differential of the above equation and setting $n(2)/n(1) = 1$, we have

$$dE(\tilde{w}) = dw + \pi(2)[w - r]\, d\left(\frac{n(2)}{n(1)}\right). \tag{13}$$

Now if $n(2) = n(1)$ initially, firms are just willing to raise wages and decrease $n(2)$ so long as dw and $dn(2)$ obey (11), which with use of (12) can be written as

$$dw = \pi(2)(p(2)f'(n(2)) - w)\, d(n(2)/n(1)). \tag{14}$$

The effects on the expected income of the worker of such a variation in an initial w and $n(2)$, starting from a position where $n(1) = n(2)$, are found by substituting (14) into (13):

$$dE(\tilde{w}) = \pi(2)[p(2)f'(n(2)) - r]\, d(n(2)/n(1)). \tag{15}$$

Now if $p(2)f'(n(2)) - r < 0$, the worker's expected pecuniary income will increase as a result of a *lowering* of $n(2)/n(1)$ since then sign $dE(\tilde{w}) = -\text{sign}$ $d(n(2)/n(1))$. This means that if $p(2)f'(n(2)) - r < 0$ and $n(2)/n(1) = 1$, the firm, in effect, is in a position to offer the worker a favorable bet. By bearing a little uncertainty, i.e., accepting a decrease in $n(2)/n(1)$ below unity, the worker can increase his expected pecuniary income. As we have seen above, a risk-averse individual who behaves as our worker does will always take at least a small part of a favorable bet (this is Arrow's proposition, which we have encountered in several guises already). This means that the workers will be anxious to get, and the firm willing to offer, a contract in which $n(2)/n(1) < 1$. Thus, if $p(2)f'(n(2)) - r < 0$, $n(2)/n(1)$ cannot equal unity; some workers will be unemployed in state 2.

4. INCENTIVES FOR "UNEMPLOYMENT COMPENSATION"

The following considerations provide a heuristic way of understanding what is going on here. Suppose we begin from a situation where $n(2)/n(1) = 1$. Since $p(2)f'(n(2)) - w < 0$, given w, the firm would have higher expected profits if $n(2)$ were smaller. By lowering $n(2)$ by $dn(2)$, the firm's expected profits would increase by $(p(2)f'(n(2)) - w)\, dn(2)$. So the firm would actually be willing to pay unemployment compensation in an amount up to $-[p(2)f'(n(2)) - w]$ per man in order to have $dn(2)$ fewer people working in state 2; i.e., the firm would be willing to pay this much in order to have some people not work. In order not to work in state 2, a worker would want the firm to pay him at least $w - r$, the excess of his pecuniary income when he is working over that when he is not. Then the firm is willing to pay the worker not to work more than he requires to be induced not to work if

$$w - p(2)f'(n(2)) - (w - r) > 0, \qquad r - p(2)f'(n(2)) > 0, \tag{16}$$

which is our condition for $n(2)/n(1)$ to be less than unity. In our setup the firm is constrained from actually paying unemployment compensation, but part of the "surplus" available when condition (16) is met is distributed to workers in the form of the firm's offering workers what amounts to a favorable bet for them. In our setup workers can share in the "surplus" only by bearing some risk. That is, we have ruled out the possibility that the firm directly offers to insure workers against unemployment, offering to pay them some amount when they are unemployed. Since workers are risk averse, there seems to be an incentive for such an institution to emerge.

To show that this indeed can be the case, suppose that firms now consider paying workers an amount per worker of $w(3)$ for not working in state 2. The firm's expected profits are then

$$V = \pi(1)(p(1)f(n(1)) - w(1)n(1)) + \pi(2)(p(2)f(n(2))$$
$$- w(2)n(2)) - \pi(2)w(3)(n(1) - n(2))$$

where $n(1) - n(2)$ is the number of men in state 2 receiving unemployment compensation from the firm. The worker's expected utility is

$$v = \pi(1)U(w(1)) + \pi(2)\frac{n(2)}{n(1)}U(w(2)) + \pi(2)\left(1 - \frac{n(2)}{n(1)}\right)g(w(3), L_1).$$

The firm's problem can then be formulated as the unconstrained optimization of

$$J = \pi(1)(p(1)f(n(1)) - w(1)n(1)) + \pi(2)(p(2)f(n(2))$$
$$- w(2)n(2)) - \pi(2)w(3)(n(1) - n(2))$$
$$+ \lambda\left[\bar{v} - \pi(1)U(w(1)) - \pi(2)\frac{n(2)}{n(1)}U(w(2)) - \pi(2)\left(1 - \frac{n(2)}{n(1)}\right)g(w(3), L_1)\right]$$

where λ is again a Lagrange multiplier. The marginal conditions for $w(1)$ and $w(2)$ are identical with (6) and (7), which can be written as

$$n(1) = -\lambda U'(w(1)), \tag{6'}$$

$$n(1) = -\lambda U'(w(2)). \tag{7'}$$

Equating to zero the partial derivative of J with respect to $w(3)$ gives

$$-\pi(2)(n(1) - n(2)) - \lambda\pi(2)\left(\frac{n(1) - n(2)}{n(1)}\right)\frac{\partial g(w(3), L_1)}{\partial w(3)} = 0$$

or

$$n(1) = -\lambda\frac{\partial g(w(3), L_1)}{\partial w(3)}. \tag{17}$$

Together, Equations (6'), (7'), and (17) imply

$$U'(w(1)) = U'(w(2)) = \partial g(w(3), L_1)/\partial w(3). \tag{18}$$

Given the strictly decreasing nature of $U'(\ )$, the above equality implies that $w(1) = w(2)$.

Consider now the particular utility function

$$U = g(w, L) = h(w + BL), \qquad B > 0; \quad h' > 0, \quad h'' < 0. \qquad (19)$$

This utility function is characterized by straight-line indifference curves between wages and leisure, so that wages and leisure are perfect substitutes. Given this utility function, $U(w)$ is given by

$$U(w) = h(w + BL_0);$$

r is defined by $h(r + BL_0) = h(BL_1)$ or

$$r + BL_0 = BL_1, \qquad r = B(L_1 - L_0).$$

Notice that

$$g(w(3), L_1) = h(w(3) + BL_1) = h(w(3) + r + BL_0)$$
$$= g(w(3) + r, L_0) = U(w(3) + r).$$

This implies that

$$\partial g(w(3), L_1)/\partial w(3) = U'(w(3) + r).$$

Given the above equality, Equation (18) becomes

$$U'(w(1)) = U'(w(2)) = U'(w(3) + r),$$

which together with the strictly decreasing nature of $U'(\ )$ implies

$$w(1) = w(2) = w(3) + r = w.$$

Then if at $n(2) = n(1)$, $r > p(2)f'(n(2))$, condition (16), the firm will set $n(2) < n(1)$ but pay unemployment compensation at the rate $w(3) = w - r$. In this fashion, for the particular utility function (19), the labor contract is fashioned so that workers bear no risks, trading them all to the firm.

For utility functions not of the form (19), it will not in general be true that $w(3) + r = w(1) = w(2)$. Still, for many utility functions, it will be true that (19) can be satisfied with $w(3) > 0$, so that the firm will opt to set $n(1) > n(2)$ and pay unemployment compensation if condition (16) is met. Evidently, this institutional arrangement is Pareto superior to the one posited at the beginning of this chapter, which had the effect of preventing the firm from offering workers unemployment insurance, thereby ruling out a certain "market."

5. CONCLUSIONS

The model described in this chapter is one example of a line of work which instructs caution in interpreting data on observed wage rates. The present model is one in which the observed wage rate reflects a process of equilibration *across* states of nature, and cannot be interpreted correctly solely in terms of the single state of nature (demand) which is actually observed. Interpreting wage observations in dynamic models grows even subtler, for in such models wage processes equilibrate across time as well as across states of nature.[6]

EXERCISE

(Work sharing) In the setup above each worker must work $L_1 - L_0$ in either state 1 or 2. So no shortening of hours per man was permitted, only layoffs in state 2. Suppose instead that the firm offers jobs to $n(1)$ workers *all* of whom work $L_1 - L_0$ hours in state 1 but only $\alpha(L_1 - L_0)$ hours in state 2 where $\alpha < 1$.

A. Describe how α, $w(1)$, and $w(2)$ are determined.

B. Would this arrangement be better or worse than the setup in the text? Are there any incentives for the arrangement of this problem to emerge and replace the setup of the text? (*Hint*: given an exogenous, market-determined level of workers' expected utility, calculate the firm's expected profits under each kind of policy.)

REFERENCES

Azariadis, C. (1976). "On the incidence of unemployment." *Review of Economic Studies*, Vol. XLIII (1), No. 133, pp. 115–126.

Baily, M. N. (1974). "Wages and Employment under Uncertain Demand." *Review of Economic Studies*, Vol. 41, No. 1, pp. 37–50.

Hansen, G. D. (1985). "Indivisible Labor and the Business Cycle." *Journal of Monetary Economics*, Vol. 16, No. 3, pp. 309–327.

Jovanovic, B. (1979). "Job Matching and the Theory of Turnover." *Journal of Political Economy*, Vol. 87, No. 5, Pt. 1, pp. 972–990.

Rosen, S. (1985). "Implicit Contracts: A Survey." *Journal of Economic Literature*, Vol. 23, No. 3, pp. 1144–1175.

[6] Jovanovic (1979) has analyzed a dynamic model of job matching which has this feature, and which highlights the difficulty of interpreting time series on wage rates. (The equilibrium wage process in Jovanovic's model is not known to be unique.) See Gary Hansen (1985) for an equilibrium model of unemployment, in which there are potentially a variety of distinct decentralization schemes and associated wage processes that support the same equilibrium allocation.

CHAPTER IX

DIFFERENCE EQUATIONS AND LAG OPERATORS[1]

Linear difference equations underlie much work in macroeconomics and applied economic dynamics. Lag operators provide a powerful tool for solving systems of linear difference equations, and for gaining insights about their structure. Lag operators constitute a language which much of macroeconomics and dynamic econometrics takes for granted. This chapter provides an introduction to the analysis of nonstochastic difference equations via lag operators. While a variety of economic examples occur in this chapter, additional examples continue to occur throughout the remainder of this book.

1. LAG OPERATORS

The backward shift or lag operator is defined by

$$LX_t = X_{t-1}$$
$$L^n X_t = X_{t-n} \qquad \text{for} \quad n = \cdots, -2, -1, 0, 1, 2, \ldots. \tag{1}$$

Multiplying a variable X_t by L^n thus gives the value of X shifted back n periods. Notice that if $n < 0$ in (1), the effect of multiplying X_t by L^n (more precisely, the effect of "operating on X_t with L^n") is to shift X *forward* in time by $-n$ periods.[2] This language is loose. Actually, we are starting out with a *sequence* $\{X_t\}_{t=-\infty}^{\infty}$ which associates a real number X_t with each integer t. We are operating on the

---

[1] It would be useful for the reader to be familiar with the material on difference equations in Allen (1960) and Baumol (1959).

[2] This chapter aims to teach the reader to manipulate lag operators, while devoting little or no attention to describing their mathematical foundations. The key Riesz–Fischer theorem which justifies these methods is discussed briefly in Chapter XI, pp. 249–253. The reader interested in increasing his proficiency with these techniques is urged to consult Gabel and Roberts (1973, Chapter 4).

sequence $\{X_t\}$ with the operator L^n to obtain the new sequence $\{y_t\}_{t=-\infty}^{\infty} = \{X_{t-n}\}_{t=-\infty}^{\infty}$. Formally, the operator L^n maps one sequence into another sequence.

We shall consider polynomials in the lag operator

$$A(L) = a_0 + a_1 L + a_2 L^2 + \cdots = \sum_{j=0}^{\infty} a_j L^j$$

where the a_j's are constants and $L^0 \equiv 1$. Operating on X_t with $A(L)$ yields a moving sum of X's:

$$A(L)X_t = (a_0 + a_1 L + a_2 L^2 + \cdots)X_t$$

$$= a_0 X_t + a_1 X_{t-1} + a_2 X_{t-2} + \cdots = \sum_{j=0}^{\infty} a_j X_{t-j}.$$

It is generally convenient to work with polynomials $A(L)$ that are "rational," meaning that they can be expressed as the ratio of two (finite order) polynomials in L:

$$A(L) = B(L)/C(L)$$

where

$$B(L) = \sum_{j=0}^{m} b_j L^j, \qquad C(L) = \sum_{j=0}^{n} c_j L^j$$

where the b_j and c_j are constants. Assuming that $A(L)$ is rational amounts to imposing a more economical and restrictive parametrization on the a_j.

To take the simplest example of a rational polynomial in L, consider[3]

$$A(L) = \frac{1}{1 - \lambda L}. \tag{2}$$

For the scalar $|C| < 1$, we know that

$$\frac{1}{1 - C} = 1 + C + C^2 + \cdots. \tag{3}$$

Thus suggests treating λL of (2) exactly like the C of (3) to get

$$\frac{1}{1 - \lambda L} = 1 + \lambda L + \lambda^2 L^2 + \cdots, \tag{4}$$

---

[3] Actually, we should write $A(L) = I/(I - \lambda L)$ where I is the identity lag operator defined by $I \equiv 1 + 0L + 0L^2 + \cdots$. So I satisfies $Ix_t = x_t$, and thus acts like unity.

an expansion which is sometimes only "useful" so long as $|\lambda| < 1$. To motivate the equality (4), assume that $|\lambda| < 1$ and operate on both sides of (4) with $1 - \lambda L$ to obtain

$$\frac{1 - \lambda L}{1 - \lambda L} = 1 = (1 + \lambda L + \lambda^2 L^2 + \cdots) - \lambda L(1 + \lambda L + \lambda^2 L^2 + \cdots) = 1.$$

The reason that we say that (4) is sometimes "useful" only if $|\lambda| < 1$ derives from the following argument. We intend often to multiply $1/(1 - \lambda L)$ by X_t to obtain the infinite moving sum

$$\frac{1}{1 - \lambda L} X_t = (1 + \lambda L + \lambda^2 L^2 + \cdots)X_t = \sum_{i=0}^{\infty} \lambda^i X_{t-i}. \tag{5}$$

Consider this sum for a path of X that is constant over time, so that $X_{t-i} = \bar{X}$ for all i and all t. Then the sum (5) becomes

$$\frac{1}{1 - \lambda L} X_t = \bar{X} \sum_{i=0}^{\infty} \lambda^i.$$

The sum $\sum_{i=0}^{\infty} \lambda^i$ equals $1/(1 - \lambda)$ if $|\lambda| < 1$. But if $|\lambda| \geq 1$ that sum is unbounded, being $+\infty$ if $\lambda \geq 1$. We shall sometimes (though not always) be applying the polynomial in the lag operator (4) in situations in which it is appropriate to go infinitely far back in time; and we sometimes find it necessary to insist that in such cases the infinite sum in (5) exist where X has been constant through time. This is what leads to the requirement sometimes imposed that $|\lambda| < 1$ in (4). As we shall see, however, in standard analyses of difference equations, which take the starting point of all processes as some point only finitely far back into the past, the requirement that $|\lambda| < 1$ need not be imposed in (4).

It is useful to note that there is an alternative expansion for the "geometric" polynomial $1/(1 - \lambda L)$. For notice that formally

$$\frac{1}{1 - \lambda L} = \frac{-(\lambda L)^{-1}}{1 - (\lambda L)^{-1}} = \frac{-1}{\lambda L}\left(1 + \frac{1}{\lambda}L^{-1} + \left(\frac{1}{\lambda}\right)^2 L^{-2} + \cdots\right)$$

$$= \frac{-1}{\lambda}L^{-1} - \left(\frac{1}{\lambda}\right)^2 L^{-2} - \left(\frac{1}{\lambda}\right)^3 L^{-3} - \cdots, \tag{6}$$

an expansion which is especially "useful" where $|\lambda| > 1$, i.e., where $|1/\lambda| < 1$. So (6) implies that

$$\frac{1}{1 - \lambda L} X_t = -\frac{1}{\lambda} X_{t+1} - \left(\frac{1}{\lambda}\right)^2 X_{t+2} - \cdots = -\sum_{i=1}^{\infty} \left(\frac{1}{\lambda}\right)^i X_{t+i},$$

which shows $(1/(1 - \lambda L))X_t$ to be a geometrically declining weighted sum of *future* values of X. Notice that for this infinite sum to be finite for a constant time path $X_{t+i} = \bar{X}$ for all i and t, the series $-\sum_{i=1}^{\infty} (1/\lambda)^i$ must be convergent, which requires that $|1/\lambda| < 1$.

More generally, let $\{x_t\}_{t=-\infty}^{\infty}$ be any bounded sequence of real numbers, i.e., for some $M > 0$, $|x_t| < M$ for all t. Then applying the operator $1/(1 - \lambda L)$ to the sequence $\{x_t\}_{t=-\infty}^{\infty}$ can be taken to give either the sequence $\{y_t\}_{t=-\infty}^{\infty}$ where

$$y_t = \frac{1}{1 - \lambda L} x_t = \sum_{j=0}^{\infty} \lambda^j x_{t-j}$$

or the sequence $\{z_t\}_{t=-\infty}^{\infty}$ where

$$z_t = \frac{-(\lambda L)^{-1}}{1 - (\lambda L)^{-1}} x_t = -\sum_{j=1}^{\infty} \left(\frac{1}{\lambda}\right)^j x_{t+j}.$$

In general, $\{y_t\}$ is a bounded sequence if $|\lambda| < 1$, while $\{z_t\}$ is a bounded sequence if $|\lambda| > 1$. In many (though not all) contexts, we want application of $(1 - \lambda L)^{-1}$ to map all bounded sequences into bounded sequences, so that we choose the "backward" expansion if $|\lambda| < 1$ and the forward expansion if $|\lambda| > 1$.

To illustrate how polynomials in the lag operator can be manipulated, consider the difference equation

$$Y_t = \lambda Y_{t-1} + bX_t + a, \qquad t = -\infty, \ldots, 0, 1, 2, \ldots, \tag{7}$$

where X_t is an exogenous variable and Y_t is an endogenous variable and $\lambda \neq 1$. Here, X_t is a sequence of real numbers $t = \cdots, -1, 0, 1, 2, \ldots$. Write the above equation as

$$(1 - \lambda L)Y_t = a + bX_t.$$

Operating on both sides of this equation by $(1 - \lambda L)^{-1}$ gives

$$Y_t = \frac{a}{1 - \lambda L} + \frac{b}{1 - \lambda L} X_t + c\lambda^t$$

$$= \frac{a}{1 - \lambda} + b \sum_{i=0}^{\infty} \lambda^i X_{t-i} + c\lambda^t, \tag{8}$$

since $a/(1 - \lambda L) = a \sum_{i=0}^{\infty} \lambda^i = a/(1 - \lambda)$. Here c is any constant. The reason that we must include the term $c\lambda^t$ in (8) is that for any constant c, $(1 - \lambda L)c\lambda^t = c\lambda^t - c\lambda\lambda^{t-1} = 0$.[4] Therefore, it follows that application of $1 - \lambda L$ to both sides of (8) gives Equation (7) once again. Consequently, (8) is the general "solution" of the difference equation (7) and describes the entire time path of Y associated with a given time path of X. In order to get a "particular solution" we must be able to tie down the constant c. This requires an additional bit of information in the form of a specified value of Y_t at some particular time or some conditions on

---

[4] Technically, we are free to add to the solution any function of time $f(t)$ for which $(1 - \lambda L)f(t) = 0$. It can be proved that $f(t) = c\lambda^t$ is the only such function.

the path of $\{Y_t\}$ such as boundedness. Notice that for the Y_t defined by (8) to be finite, $\lambda^i X_{t-i}$ must be "small" for large i. More precisely, we require

$$\lim_{n \to \infty} \sum_{i=n}^{\infty} \lambda^i X_{t-i} = 0 \qquad \text{for all } t. \tag{9}$$

For the case of X constant for all time, $X_{t-i} = \bar{X}$ all i and t, this condition requires $|\lambda| < 1$. Notice also that the infinite sum $a \sum_{i=0}^{\infty} \lambda^i$ in (8) is finite only if $|\lambda| < 1$, in which case it equals $a/(1 - \lambda)$, or if $a = 0$, in which case it equals zero regardless of the value of λ. We tentatively assume that $|\lambda| < 1$.

For analyzing difference equations with arbitrary initial conditions given, it is convenient to rewrite (8) for $t > 0$ as

$$Y_t = a \sum_{i=0}^{t-1} \lambda^i + a \sum_{i=t}^{\infty} \lambda^i + b \sum_{i=0}^{t-1} \lambda^i X_{t-i} + b \sum_{i=t}^{\infty} \lambda^i X_{t-i} + c\lambda^t$$

$$= \frac{a(1 - \lambda^t)}{1 - \lambda} + \frac{a\lambda^t}{1 - \lambda} + b \sum_{i=0}^{t-1} \lambda^i X_{t-i} + b\lambda^t \sum_{i=0}^{\infty} \lambda^i X_{0-i} + c\lambda^t,$$

$$Y_t = \frac{a(1 - \lambda^t)}{1 - \lambda} + b \sum_{i=0}^{t-1} \lambda^i X_{t-i} + \lambda^t \left\{ \frac{a}{1 - \lambda} + b \sum_{i=0}^{\infty} \lambda^i X_{0-i} + c\lambda^0 \right\}, \qquad t \geq 1. \tag{10}$$

The term in braces equals Y_0, as reference to expression (8) will confirm. So (10) becomes

$$Y_t = \frac{a(1 - \lambda^t)}{1 - \lambda} + b \sum_{i=0}^{t-1} \lambda^i X_{t-i} + \lambda^t Y_0$$

or

$$Y_t = \frac{a}{1 - \lambda} + \lambda^t \left(Y_0 - \frac{a}{1 - \lambda} \right) + b \sum_{i=0}^{t-1} \lambda^i X_{t-i}, \qquad t \geq 1. \tag{11}$$

Now textbooks on difference equations often analyze the special case in which $X_t = 0$ for all $t \geq 0$. Under this special circumstance (11) becomes

$$Y_t = \frac{a}{1 - \lambda} + \lambda^t \left(Y_0 - \frac{a}{1 - \lambda} \right), \tag{12}$$

which is the solution of the first-order difference equation $Y_t = a + \lambda Y_{t-1}$ subject to the initial condition that Y equals the arbitrary given value Y_0 at time 0. Notice that if $Y_0 = a/(1 - \lambda)$, then (12) implies $Y_t = Y_0$ for all $t \geq 0$, which shows $a/(1 - \lambda)$ to be a "stationary point" or long-run equilibrium value of Y. Notice also that if, as we are assuming, $|\lambda| < 1$, then (12) implies that

$$\lim_{t \to \infty} Y_t = \frac{a}{1 - \lambda},$$

which shows that the system is "stable," tending to approach the stationary point as time passes.

Now consider the first-order system (7) under the assumption that $a = 0$, so that $a \sum_{i=0}^{\infty} \lambda^i$ equals zero regardless of the value of λ. Then the appropriate counterpart to (10) is

$$Y_t = b \sum_{i=0}^{t-1} \lambda^i X_{t-i} + \lambda^t \left\{ b \sum_{i=0}^{\infty} \lambda^i X_{0-i} + c\lambda^0 \right\}.$$

Assuming that condition (9) is met even where $|\lambda| > 1$ (so that the second term in the equation is finite), the above equation becomes

$$Y_t = b \sum_{i=0}^{t-1} \lambda^i X_{t-i} + \lambda^t Y_0, \qquad t \geq 1.$$

As before we analyze the special case where $X_t = 0$ for all $t > 0$. Then the above equation becomes

$$Y_t = \lambda^t Y_0, \qquad t \geq 1.$$

The stationary point of this solution is zero since if $Y_0 = 0$, Y will remain equal to zero forever, regardless of the value of λ. However, if $|\lambda| > 1$, the system will diverge farther and farther from this stationary point if either $Y_0 > 0$, or $Y_0 < 0$. If $\lambda > 1$, Y_t will tend toward $+\infty$ as $t \to \infty$ provided $Y_0 > 0$; Y_t will tend toward $-\infty$ as $t \to \infty$ if $Y_0 < 0$. If $\lambda < -1$, Y_t will display explosive oscillations of periodicity two time periods.

We can also solve the difference equation (7) by applying the "forward inverse" of $1 - \lambda L$ to get the general solution

$$Y_t = \frac{-\lambda^{-1}L^{-1}}{1 - \lambda^{-1}L^{-1}} a + b \left(\frac{-\lambda^{-1}L^{-1}}{1 - \lambda^{-1}L^{-1}} \right) X_t + d\lambda^t,$$

$$Y_t = \frac{a}{1 - \lambda} - b \sum_{i=0}^{\infty} \left(\frac{1}{\lambda} \right)^{i+1} X_{t+i+1} + d\lambda^t, \tag{8'}$$

where d is a constant to be determined from some side condition on the path of Y_t, such as an initial condition or terminal condition. If $a = 0$, then for *any* value of $\lambda \neq 1$, in general (8) and (8') *both* represent solutions of the difference equation (7). They are simply alternative representations of the solution in the sense that for any given initial condition or other side condition, one can generally find values of d and c which guarantee that both (8) and (8') satisfy (7). The equivalence of the solutions (8) and (8') will hold whenever $(b/(1 - \lambda L))X_t$ and $(b\lambda^{-1}L^{-1}/(1 - \lambda^{-1}L^{-1}))X_t$ are both finite for all t.

It often happens, however, that either $(b/(1 - \lambda L))X_t$ or

$$\frac{b\lambda^{-1}L^{-1}}{1 - \lambda^{-1}L^{-1}} X_t$$

fails to be finite, i.e., the infinite sum fails to converge. In this case, one or the other of the representations (8) or (8') breaks down, i.e., fails to give a Y_t sequence that is finite for all finite t. For example, if the sequence $\{X_t\}$ is bounded, this is sufficient to imply that $\{(b/(1 - \lambda L))X_t\}$ is a bounded sequence if $|\lambda| < 1$, but not sufficient to imply that

$$\frac{b\lambda^{-1}L^{-1}}{1 - \lambda^{-1}L^{-1}} X_t$$

is a convergent sum for all t. Similarly, if $|\lambda| > 1$, boundedness of the sequence $\{X_t\}$ is sufficient to imply that

$$\left\{ \frac{b\lambda^{-1}L^{-1}}{1 - \lambda^{-1}L^{-1}} X_t \right\}$$

is a bounded sequence, but fails to guarantee finiteness of $(b/(1 - \lambda L))X_t$. In instances where one of $(b/(1 - \lambda L))X_t$ or

$$\frac{b\lambda^{-1}L^{-1}}{1 - \lambda^{-1}L^{-1}} X_t$$

is always finite and the other is not we shall take as our solution to (7) either (8) where the backward sum in X_t is finite, or (8') where the forward sum in X_t is finite. This procedure assures us that we shall find the unique solution of (7) that is finite for all finite t, provided that such a solution exists. Such a solution is guaranteed to exist where $\{X_t\}$ is a bounded sequence.

Now if we desired to impose that the $\{Y_t\}$ sequence given by (8) or (8') is bounded—as we are free to do if no other side condition has been imposed —then it is evident that we must set $c = 0$ in (8) or $d = 0$ in (8'). This is necessary since if $\lambda > 1$ and $c > 0$,

$$\lim_{t \to \infty} c\lambda^t = \infty;$$

while if $\lambda < 1$ and $c > 0$,

$$\lim_{t \to -\infty} c\lambda^t = \infty.$$

It follows that Y_t will be bounded for all t only if c or d is zero. For the solution in the forward direction to be finite for all finite t, we clearly require a condition analogous to (9)

$$\lim_{n \to \infty} \sum_{i=n}^{\infty} \left(\frac{1}{\lambda}\right)^i X_{t+i} = 0. \tag{9'}$$

The principle of solving "stable roots" ($|\lambda| < 1$) backward and "unstable roots" ($|\lambda| > 1$) forward was encountered in Chapter I. It is a device designed to ensure that the solution of the differential (or difference) equation maps bounded functions (or sequences) as driving processes into bounded functions (or sequences). Below, we shall see that a formal justification for this procedure is sometimes available in the context of difference equations that emerge from optimum problems.

2. SECOND-ORDER DIFFERENCE EQUATIONS

Consider the second-order difference equation

$$Y_t = t_1 Y_{t-1} + t_2 Y_{t-2} + a + bX_t, \tag{13}$$

where $\{X_t\}$ is again an exogenous sequence of real numbers for $t = \cdots, -1, 0, 1, \ldots$. Using lag operators, (13) can be written as

$$(1 - t_1 L - t_2 L^2)Y_t = a + bX_t.$$

A solution to this difference equation is given by

$$Y_t = \frac{a}{1 - t_1 L - t_2 L^2} + \frac{b}{1 - t_1 L - t_2 L^2} X_t \tag{14}$$

where we have temporarily ignored the terms analogous to $c\lambda^t$ which appeared in the general solution of the first-order equation. By long division it is easy to verify that

$$\frac{b}{1 - t_1 L - t_2 L^2} = \sum_{i=0}^{\infty} w_i L^i \tag{15}$$

where $w_0 = b$, $w_1 = bt_1$, and

$$w_j = t_1 w_{j-1} + t_2 w_{j-2} \quad \text{for} \quad j \geq 2.$$

That is,

$$
\begin{array}{r}
1 + t_1 L + (t_2 + t_1{}^2)L^2 + (t_1(t_2 + t_1{}^2) + t_1 t_2)L^3 + \cdots \\
\hline
1 - t_1 L - t_2 L^2 \overline{\smash{\big)}\,1} \\
\underline{1 - t_1 L - t_2 L^2} \\
t_1 L + t_2 L^2 \\
\underline{t_1 L - t_1{}^2 L^2 \qquad\quad - t_1 t_2 L^3} \\
(t_2 + t_1{}^2)L^2 + t_1 t_2 L^3 \\
\underline{(t_2 + t_1{}^2)L^2 - t_1(t_2 + t_1{}^2)L^3 - t_2(t_2 + t_1{}^2)L^4} \cdots.
\end{array}
$$

Notice that the weights in (15) follow a geometric pattern if $t_2 = 0$, as we would expect, since then (13) collapses to a first-order equation.

It is convenient to write the polynomial $1 - t_1 L - t_2 L^2$ in an alternative way, given by the *factorization*

$$
\begin{aligned}
1 - t_1 L - t_2 L^2 &= (1 - \lambda_1 L)(1 - \lambda_2 L) \\
&= 1 - (\lambda_1 + \lambda_2)L + \lambda_1 \lambda_2 L^2,
\end{aligned}
\tag{16}
$$

so that $\lambda_1 + \lambda_2 = t_1$ and $-\lambda_1\lambda_2 = t_2$. To see how λ_1 and λ_2 are related to the *roots* or *zeros* of $1 - t_1 z - t_2 z^2$, notice that

$$(1 - \lambda_1 z)(1 - \lambda_2 z) = \lambda_1\lambda_2\left(\frac{1}{\lambda_1} - z\right)\left(\frac{1}{\lambda_2} - z\right).$$

Therefore the equation

$$0 = (1 - \lambda_1 z)(1 - \lambda_2 z) = \lambda_1\lambda_2\left(\frac{1}{\lambda_1} - z\right)\left(\frac{1}{\lambda_2} - z\right)$$

is satisfied at the two roots $z = 1/\lambda_1$ and $z = 1/\lambda_2$. Given the polynomial $1 - t_1 z - t_2 z^2$, the roots $1/\lambda_1$ and $1/\lambda_2$ are found from solving the *characteristic equation*

$$1 - t_1 z - t_2 z^2 = 0 \qquad \text{or} \qquad t_2 z^2 + t_1 z - 1 = 0$$

for two values of z. The roots are given by the quadratic formula

$$z = \frac{-t_1 \pm \sqrt{t_1^2 + 4t_2}}{2t_2}. \tag{17}$$

Formula (17) enables us to obtain the reciprocals of λ_1 and λ_2 for given values of t_1 and t_2.

We assume that $\lambda_1 \neq \lambda_2$, $\lambda_1 \neq 1$. Then without loss of generality we can write the second-order difference equation as

$$(1 - \lambda_1 L)(1 - \lambda_2 L)Y_t = a + bX_t.$$

The general solution to this difference equation is

$$Y_t = \frac{a}{(1 - \lambda_1 L)(1 - \lambda_2 L)} + \frac{b}{(1 - \lambda_1 L)(1 - \lambda_2 L)}X_t + c_1\lambda_1^t + c_2\lambda_2^t \tag{18}$$

where c_1 and c_2 are any constants. To see that (18) solves the difference equation for any values of c_1 and c_2, operate on both sides of (18) with

$$(1 - \lambda_1 L)(1 - \lambda_2 L)$$

and notice that

$$(1 - \lambda_1 L)(1 - \lambda_2 L)c_1\lambda_1^t = (1 - \lambda_1 L)(1 - \lambda_2 L)c_2\lambda_2^t = 0.$$

In order to determine a particular solution to the difference equation, we now need two side conditions on the path of Y_t. For example, two initial conditions in the forms of given values for Y at time 0 and 1 are sufficient to determine c_1 and c_2.

Notice that since $\lambda_1 \neq \lambda_2$,

$$\frac{1}{(1 - \lambda_1 L)(1 - \lambda_2 L)} = \frac{1}{\lambda_1 - \lambda_2}\left(\frac{\lambda_1}{1 - \lambda_1 L} - \frac{\lambda_2}{1 - \lambda_2 L}\right),$$

which can be verified directly. Thus (18) can be written

$$
Y_t = \frac{a}{(1 - \lambda_1)(1 - \lambda_2)} + \frac{\lambda_1 b}{\lambda_1 - \lambda_2} \frac{1}{1 - \lambda_1 L} X_t
$$

$$
- \frac{\lambda_2 b}{\lambda_1 - \lambda_2} \frac{1}{1 - \lambda_2 L} X_t + c_1 \lambda_1{}^t + c_2 \lambda_2{}^t
$$

$$
= a \sum_{i=0}^{\infty} \lambda_1{}^i \sum_{j=0}^{\infty} \lambda_2{}^j + \frac{\lambda_1 b}{\lambda_1 - \lambda_2} \sum_{i=0}^{\infty} \lambda_1{}^i X_{t-i}
$$

$$
- \frac{\lambda_2 b}{\lambda_1 - \lambda_2} \sum_{i=0}^{\infty} \lambda_2{}^i X_{t-i} + c_1 \lambda_1{}^t + c_2 \lambda_2{}^t \tag{19}
$$

where we are making use of the fact that for a constant a

$$
H(L)a = \sum_{i=0}^{\infty} h_i L^i a = a \sum_{i=0}^{\infty} h_i = aH(1).
$$

Notice that

$$
\frac{1}{1 - \lambda_1 L} \frac{1}{1 - \lambda_2 L} = \sum_{i=0}^{\infty} \lambda_1{}^i L^i \sum_{j=0}^{\infty} \lambda_2{}^j L^j,
$$

so that the sum of the distributed lag weights $\sum_{i=0}^{\infty} \lambda_1{}^i \sum_{i=0}^{\infty} \lambda_2{}^i$ is finite and equals $1/((1 - \lambda_1)(1 - \lambda_2))$ provided that both $|\lambda_1| < 1$, $|\lambda_2| < 1$. So in writing (19) we require either that both $|\lambda_1|$ and $|\lambda_2|$ be less than unity or that $a = 0$, so that $a \sum_{i=0}^{\infty} \lambda_1{}^i \sum_{j=0}^{\infty} \lambda_2{}^j$ is defined. Furthermore, we require that

$$
\lim_{n \to \infty} \sum_{i=n}^{\infty} \lambda_j{}^i X_{t-i} = 0, \qquad \text{all } t,
$$

hold for $j = 1, 2$, so that the geometric sums in (19) are both finite.

Suppose that $a = 0$. On this assumption write (19) for $t \geq 1$ as

$$
Y_t = \frac{\lambda_1 b}{\lambda_1 - \lambda_2} \sum_{i=0}^{t-1} \lambda_1{}^i X_{t-i} - \frac{\lambda_2 b}{\lambda_1 - \lambda_2} \sum_{i=0}^{t-1} \lambda_2{}^i X_{t-i}
$$

$$
+ \frac{\lambda_1 b}{\lambda_1 - \lambda_2} \sum_{i=t}^{\infty} \lambda_1{}^i X_{t-i} - \frac{\lambda_2 b}{\lambda_1 - \lambda_2} \sum_{i=t}^{\infty} \lambda_2{}^i X_{t-i} + c_1 \lambda_1{}^t + c_2 \lambda_2{}^t
$$

or

$$
Y_t = \frac{\lambda_1 b}{\lambda_1 - \lambda_2} \sum_{i=0}^{t-1} \lambda_1{}^i X_{t-i} - \frac{\lambda_2 b}{\lambda_1 - \lambda_2} \sum_{i=0}^{t-1} \lambda_2{}^i X_{t-i} + \lambda_1{}^t \theta_0 + \lambda_2{}^t \eta_0, \quad t \geq 1, \tag{20}
$$

where

$$
\theta_0 = \left\{ c_1 + \frac{b \lambda_1}{\lambda_1 - \lambda_2} \sum_{i=0}^{\infty} \lambda_1{}^i X_{0-i} \right\} \quad \text{and} \quad \eta_0 = \left\{ c_2 - \frac{b \lambda_2}{\lambda_1 - \lambda_2} \sum_{i=0}^{\infty} \lambda_2{}^i X_{0-i} \right\}.
$$

The case in which $X_t = 0$ for $t \geq 1$ is often analyzed, as for the first-order case. On this assumption (20) becomes

$$Y_t = \lambda_1{}^t\theta_0 + \lambda_2{}^t\eta_0, \qquad t \geq 1. \tag{21}$$

If $\theta_0 = \eta_0 = 0$, $Y_t = 0$ for all $t \geq 1$, regardless of the values of λ_1 and λ_2. So $Y = 0$ is the stationary point or long-run equilibrium value of (21).

If λ_1 and λ_2 are real, then $\lim_{t \to \infty} Y_t$ will equal zero if and only if both $|\lambda_1| < 1$ and $|\lambda_2| < 1$, regardless of the values of the parameters θ_0 and η_0, so long as they are finite.

If $\lambda_1 > 1$, $|\lambda_2| < |\lambda_1|$, and $\theta_0 > 0$, then $\lim_{t \to \infty} Y_t = +\infty$. If $\lambda_1 > 1$, $|\lambda_2| < |\lambda_1|$, and $\theta_0 < 0$, then $\lim_{t \to \infty} Y_t = -\infty$. Thus, Y will tend toward the stationary point zero as time passes provided that both $|\lambda_1| < 1$ and $|\lambda_2| < 1$. If one or both of the λ's exceed one in absolute value, the behavior of Y will eventually be "dominated" by the term in (21) associated with the λ that is larger in absolute value; i.e., eventually Y will grow approximately as $\lambda_m{}^t$, where λ_m is the λ_j with the larger absolute value.

Now suppose that the roots are complex. If the roots are complex, they will occur as a complex conjugate pair, as the quadratic formula (17) verifies. So assume that the roots are complex, and write them as

$$\lambda_1 = re^{iw} = r(\cos w + i \sin w), \qquad \lambda_2 = re^{-iw} = r(\cos w - i \sin w)$$

where the real part is $r \cos w$ and the imaginary part is $\pm r \sin w$. Notice that

$$\lambda_1 - \lambda_2 = r(e^{iw} - e^{-iw}) = 2ri \sin w. \tag{22}$$

Equation (21) becomes

$$\begin{aligned} Y_t &= \theta_0(re^{iw})^t + \eta_0(re^{-iw})^t \\ &= \theta_0(r^t e^{iwt}) + \eta_0(r^t e^{-iwt}) \\ &= \theta_0 r^t[\cos wt + i \sin wt] + \eta_0 r^t[\cos wt - i \sin wt] \\ &= (\theta_0 + \eta_0)r^t \cos wt + i(\theta_0 - \eta_0)r^t \sin wt. \end{aligned} \tag{23}$$

Since Y_t must be a real number for all t, it follows that $\theta_0 + \eta_0$ must be real and $\theta_0 - \eta_0$ must be imaginary. Therefore, θ_0 and η_0 must be complex conjugates, say $\theta_0 = pe^{i\theta}$, $\eta_0 = pe^{-i\theta}$. Therefore we can write

$$Y_t = pe^{i\theta}r^t e^{iwt} + pe^{-i\theta}r^t e^{-iwt} = pr^t[e^{i(wt+\theta)} + e^{-i(wt+\theta)}]$$

$$= 2pr^t \cos(wt + \theta). \tag{24}$$

This is the solution of the "unforced" (i.e., $X_t = 0$ for all t) second-order difference equation with complex roots. The parameters p and θ are chosen to satisfy two side conditions on the path of Y_t, say two initial conditions. The path of Y_t oscillates with a frequency determined by w. The "damping factor" r^t is determined by the amplitude r of the complex roots. The value $Y_t = 0$ is the stationary point of the difference equation, which will be approached at $t \to \infty$ for arbitrary initial conditions if $r < 1$. If $r > 1$, the path of Y_t displays explosive oscillations, unless the initial conditions are, say, $Y_0 = 0$, $Y_1 = 0$, so that Y starts out at the stationary point for two successive values. If $r < 1$, the system displays damped oscillations provided $w \neq 0$, which is so when the roots are complex. If $r = 1$, Y_t displays repeated oscillations of unchanging amplitude, and the solution is "periodic."

If λ_1 and λ_2 are complex, the distributed lag weights of (19) are easily shown to oscillate. For we have

$$\frac{b}{\lambda_1 - \lambda_2} \sum_{j=0}^{\infty} (\lambda_1^{j+1} - \lambda_2^{j+1}) X_{t-j} = \frac{b}{re^{iw} - re^{-iw}} \sum_{j=0}^{\infty} [(re^{iw})^{j+1} - (re^{-iw})^{j+1}] X_{t-j}$$

$$= \frac{b}{2ri \sin w} \sum_{j=0}^{\infty} 2r^{j+1} i \{\sin w(j+1)\} X_{t-j} = b \sum_{j=0}^{\infty} r^j \frac{\sin w(j+1)}{\sin w} X_{t-j}.$$

Since the roots are complex, $\sin w \neq 0$. Notice that the damping factor weighting the sine curve is r^j, so that the amplitude of the lag weights decreases as j increases, provided that $r < 1$.

As noted above, the roots λ_1 and λ_2 are the reciprocals of the roots of the polynomial

$$1 - t_1 z - t_2 z^2 = 0. \tag{25}$$

For we know that $1 - t_1 z - t_2 z^2 = (1 - \lambda_1 z)(1 - \lambda_2 z)$, with roots $1/\lambda_1$ and $1/\lambda_2$. Alternatively, multiply the above equation by z^{-2} to obtain

$$z^{-2} - z^{-1} t_1 - t_2 = 0 = (z^{-1} - \lambda_1)(z^{-1} - \lambda_2)$$

or

$$s^2 - t_1 s - t_2 = 0 \tag{26}$$

where $s = z^{-1}$. Notice that the roots of (26) are the reciprocals of the roots of (25). Thus, λ_1 and λ_2 are the roots of (26).

It is interesting to know what values of t_1 and t_2 yield complex roots. Using the quadratic formula we have that the roots of (26) are

$$\lambda_i = s = \frac{t_1 \pm \sqrt{t_1^2 + 4t_2}}{2}.$$

For the roots to be complex, the term whose square root is taken must be negative, i.e.,

$$t_1^2 + 4t_2 < 0, \tag{27}$$

which implies that $t_2 < 0$. In case (27) is satisfied, the roots are

$$\lambda_1 = \frac{t_1}{2} + \frac{i\sqrt{-(t_1^2 + 4t_2)}}{2} = a + bi, \qquad \lambda_2 = \frac{t_1}{2} - \frac{i\sqrt{-(t_1^2 + 4t_2)}}{2} = a - bi.$$

To write $a + bi$ in polar form we recall that

$$a + bi = r \cos w + ri \sin w = re^{iw}$$

where $r = \sqrt{a^2 + b^2}$ and where $\cos w = a/r$. Thus we have that

$$r = \sqrt{\left(\frac{t_1}{2}\right)^2 - \frac{(t_1^2 + 4t_2)}{4}} = \sqrt{-t_2}.$$

We also have that

$$\cos w = \frac{t_1}{2\sqrt{-t_2}} \qquad \text{or} \qquad w = \cos^{-1}\left(\frac{t_1}{2\sqrt{-t_2}}\right).$$

For the oscillations to be damped we require that $r = \sqrt{-t_2} < 1$, which requires that $-t_2 < 1$.

The periodicity of the oscillations is $2\pi/\cos^{-1}(t_1/2\sqrt{-t_2})$; i.e., this is the number of periods from peak to peak in the oscillations.

If the roots are real, movements will be damped if both roots are less than one in absolute value. That requires

$$-1 < \frac{t_1 + \sqrt{t_1^2 + 4t_2}}{2} < 1 \qquad \text{and} \qquad -1 < \frac{t_1 - \sqrt{t_1^2 + 4t_2}}{2} < 1.$$

The condition $\frac{1}{2}(t_1 + \sqrt{t_1^2 + 4t_2}) < 1$ implies

$$\sqrt{t_1^2 + 4t_2} < 2 - t_1, \qquad t_1^2 + 4t_2 < 4 + t_1^2 - 4t_1,$$

$$t_1 + t_2 < 1. \tag{28}$$

The condition $\frac{1}{2}(t_1 - \sqrt{t_1^2 + 4t_2}) > -1$ implies that

$$-\sqrt{t_1^2 + 4t_2} > -2 - t_1, \qquad \sqrt{t_1^2 + 4t_2} < 2 + t_1,$$

$$t_1^2 + 4t_2 < t_1^2 + 4 + 4t_1,$$

$$t_2 < 1 + t_1. \tag{29}$$

Conditions (28) and (29) must be satisfied for the roots, if real, to be less than unity in absolute value.

Notice that both roots are negative and real if

$$t_1^2 + 4t_2 > 0 \qquad \text{and} \qquad \frac{t_1 + \sqrt{t_1^2 + 4t_2}}{2} < 0,$$

which implies

$$t_1 < -\sqrt{t_1^2 + 4t_2}, \qquad t_1^2 > t_1^2 + 4t_2, \qquad 0 > t_2.$$

Figure 1 depicts regions of the t_1, t_2 plane for which conditions (27), (28), or (29) are or are not satisfied. The graph shows combinations of t_1 and t_2 that give rise to damped oscillations, explosive oscillations, etc.

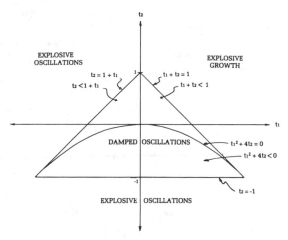

FIGURE 1 (Source: W. Baumol, *Economic Dynamics*, 2nd ed., p. 221, New York: Macmillan. Copyright 1959 by Macmillan Publishing Co., Inc.)

A. An Example

Maybe the most famous second-order difference equation in economics is the one associated with Samuelson's multiplier accelerator model (see Samuelson, 1944). Samuelson posited the model

$$C_t = cY_{t-1} + \alpha, \qquad 1 > c > 0 \quad \text{(consumption function)}$$

$$I_t = \gamma(Y_{t-1} - Y_{t-2}), \qquad \gamma > 0 \quad \text{(accelerator)}$$

$$C_t + I_t = Y_t,$$

FIGURE 2

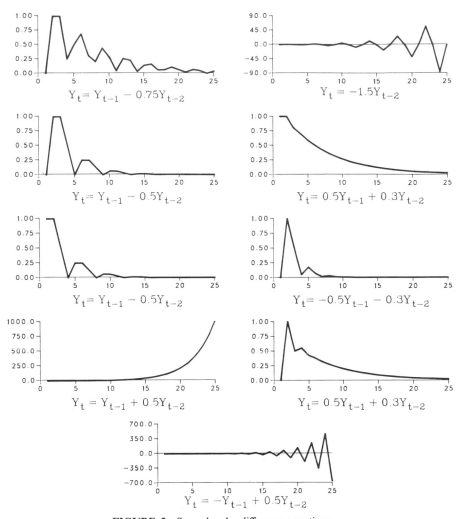

FIGURE 3 Second-order difference equations.

where C_t is consumption and I_t is investment. Substituting the first two equations into the third gives

$$Y_t = (c + \gamma)Y_{t-1} - \gamma Y_{t-2} + \alpha$$

or

$$Y_t = t_1 Y_{t-1} + t_2 Y_{t-2} + \alpha$$

where $t_1 = c + \gamma$, $t_2 = -\gamma$. Notice that $t_1 + t_2 = c$. So increases in the parameter γ move the parameters t_1 and t_2 downward and to the right along the line

$t_1 + t_2 = c$ in Figure 2. Using Figure 2, the values of c and γ compatible with damped oscillations, explosive oscillations, and so on, can easily be determined.

Figure 3 shows some realizations of second-order difference equations for various values of t_1 and t_2. In each case the values Y_1 and Y_2 were the two initial conditions which we specified arbitrarily. The reader can check that the behavior of these realizations matches that predicted by Figure 1.

3. SECOND-ORDER DIFFERENCE EQUATIONS (EQUAL ROOTS)

The preceding treatment assumed that $\lambda_1 \neq \lambda_2$. (Notice that we divided by $\lambda_1 - \lambda_2$ to obtain (19).) If $\lambda_1 = \lambda_2$, then the polynomial we must study is

$$\frac{1}{(1 - \lambda L)(1 - \lambda L)} = \frac{1}{1 - \lambda L}(1 + \lambda L + \lambda^2 L^2 + \cdots)$$

$$= (1 + \lambda L + \lambda^2 L^2 + \cdots) + \lambda L(1 + \lambda L + \lambda^2 L^2 + \cdots)$$

$$+ \lambda^2 L^2(1 + \lambda L + \lambda^2 L^2 + \cdots) + \cdots$$

$$= 1 + 2\lambda L + 3\lambda^2 L^2 + \cdots,$$

$$\frac{1}{(1 - \lambda L)^2} = \sum_{i=0}^{\infty} (i + 1)\lambda^i L^i. \tag{30}$$

The lag distribution generated by the polynomial in (30) is called a second-order Pascal lag distribution. It is the lag operator product or "convolution" of two geometric lag distributions with the same decay parameter[5] λ.

With the aid of (30) we can study the solution to difference equations of the form

$$(1 - \lambda L)^2 Y_t = a + bX_t.$$

The general solution is

$$Y_t = a \sum_{i=0}^{\infty} (i + 1)\lambda^i + b \sum_{i=0}^{\infty} (i + 1)\lambda^i X_{t-i} + c_1\lambda^t + c_2 t\lambda^t \tag{31}$$

where c_1 and c_2 are any real constants. To verify that (31) is the solution, operate on both sides by $(1 - \lambda L)^2$ and verify that $(1 - \lambda L)^2\{c_1\lambda^t + c_2 t\lambda^t\} = 0$ for any choices of c_1 and c_2. To get a particular solution, we require two side conditions on the path of Y_t to determine the two constants c_1 and c_2. For $a\sum_{i=0}^{\infty}(1 + i)\lambda^i$ to be finite either $|\lambda| < 1$ or $a = 0$ must be satisfied.

Assume that $a = 0$ and notice that (31) can be rewritten for $t \geq 1$ as

$$Y_t = b \sum_{i=0}^{t-1} (1 + i)\lambda^i X_{t-i} + b \sum_{i=t}^{\infty} (1 + i)\lambda^i X_{t-i} + c_1\lambda^t + c_2 t\lambda^t. \tag{32}$$

---

[5] Let $w(L) = \sum_{j=-\infty}^{\infty} w_j L^j$, $v(L) = \sum_{j=-\infty}^{\infty} v_j L^j$. The *convolution* of the two sequences $\{w_j\}_{j=-\infty}^{\infty}$, $\{v_j\}_{j=-\infty}^{\infty}$ is the sequence whose jth element is $h_j = \sum_{k=-\infty}^{\infty} w_k v_{j-k}$. The reader should verify that $\sum_{j=-\infty}^{\infty} h_j L^j = h(L) = w(L)v(L) = v(L)w(L)$.

The second sum can be written as

$$b \sum_{j=0}^{\infty} (j + 1 + t)\lambda^{t+j}X_{0-j} = b\lambda^t \sum_{j=0}^{\infty} (j + 1)\lambda^j X_{0-j} + bt\lambda^t \sum_{j=0}^{\infty} \lambda^j X_{0-j}.$$

Therefore (32) becomes

$$Y_t = b \sum_{i=0}^{t-1} (1 + i)\lambda^i X_{t-i} + \lambda^t\theta_0 + t\lambda^t\eta_0 \tag{33}$$

where

$$\theta_0 = \left\{ c_1 + b \sum_{j=0}^{\infty} (j + 1)\lambda^j X_{0-j} \right\} \quad \text{and} \quad \eta_0 = \left\{ c_2 + b \sum_{j=0}^{\infty} \lambda^j X_{0-j} \right\}.$$

As for our earlier cases, (33) displays the solution for $t \geq 1$ as the sum of the distributed lag in $X_1, X_2, \ldots, X_t$ and two initial conditions. If $X_t = 0$ for $t \geq 1$, the sequence Y_t will approach its stationary value of zero if $|\lambda| < 1$. If $|\lambda| > 1$, the sequence Y_t will diverge from the stationary point of zero unless $\theta_0 = \eta_0 = 0$.

4. Nth-ORDER DIFFERENCE EQUATIONS (DISTINCT ROOTS)

Consider a rational polynomial with nth-order denominator:

$$A(L) = \frac{F(L)}{G(L)} = \frac{F(L)}{(1 - \lambda_1 L)(1 - \lambda_2 L)\cdots(1 - \lambda_n L)}.$$

We assume that the degree of the numerator polynomial is less than the degree of the denominator polynomial. The zeros of $G(z) = 0$ are $z_1 = 1/\lambda_1$, $z_2 = 1/\lambda_2, \ldots, \ldots, z_n = 1/\lambda_n$ since each of these values for z satisfies the equation

$$G(z) = (1 - \lambda_1 z)(1 - \lambda_2 z)\cdots(1 - \lambda_n z) = 0.$$

Suppose the n roots are distinct. Now the method of partial fractions enables us to express $A(L)$ as

$$\frac{F(L)}{(1 - \lambda_1 L)\cdots(1 - \lambda_n L)} = \frac{A_1}{1 - \lambda_1 L} + \frac{A_2}{1 - \lambda_2 L} + \cdots + \frac{A_n}{1 - \lambda_n L} \tag{34}$$

where $A_1, A_2, \ldots, A_n$ are constants to be determined. To determine them, multiply both sides of the above equation by $(1 - \lambda_1 L)\cdots(1 - \lambda_n L)$ to get

$$F(L) = A_1(1 - \lambda_2 L)\cdots(1 - \lambda_n L) + A_2(1 - \lambda_1 L)(1 - \lambda_3 L)\cdots(1 - \lambda_n L)$$
$$+ \cdots + A_n(1 - \lambda_1 L)\cdots(1 - \lambda_{n-1}L).$$

Evaluating the above equation at $L = 1/\lambda_1$, the first root of $G(L) = 0$, gives

$$A_1 = \frac{F(1/\lambda_1)}{(1 - (\lambda_2/\lambda_1))\cdots(1 - (\lambda_n/\lambda_1))}.$$

For the general term A_i, we obtain

$$A_i = \frac{F(1/\lambda_i)}{(1 - (\lambda_1/\lambda_i))\cdots(1 - (\lambda_{i-1}/\lambda_i))(1 - (\lambda_{i+1}/\lambda_i))\cdots(1 - (\lambda_n/\lambda_i))}. \quad (35)$$

As an example, consider applying (34) to the second-order denominator polynomial

$$A(L) = \frac{1}{(1 - \lambda_1 L)(1 - \lambda_2 L)} = \frac{A_1}{1 - \lambda_1 L} + \frac{A_2}{1 - \lambda_2 L}.$$

We have

$$A_1 = \frac{1}{1 - (\lambda_2/\lambda_1)} = \frac{\lambda_1}{\lambda_1 - \lambda_2} \quad \text{and} \quad A_2 = \frac{1}{1 - (\lambda_1/\lambda_2)} = \frac{\lambda_2}{\lambda_2 - \lambda_1}.$$

Thus we obtain

$$\frac{1}{(1 - \lambda_1 L)(1 - \lambda_2 L)} = \frac{1}{\lambda_1 - \lambda_2}\left(\frac{\lambda_1}{1 - \lambda_1 L} - \frac{\lambda_2}{1 - \lambda_2 L}\right),$$

which we earlier used on the way to deriving (19).

Suppose we have an nth-order difference equation

$$(1 - \lambda_1 L)(1 - \lambda_2 L)\cdots(1 - \lambda_n L)Y_t = bX_t. \quad (36)$$

The general solution to (36) is obtained by "dividing"[6] by $(1 - \lambda_1 L)\cdots$ $(1 - \lambda_n L)$ to obtain

$$Y_t = \frac{b}{(1 - \lambda_1 L)\cdots(1 - \lambda_n L)}X_t + c_1\lambda_1{}^t + \cdots + c_n\lambda_n{}^t,$$

where $c_1, \ldots, c_n$ are any constants. That this is the solution can be verified by operating on both sides of the above equation with $(1 - \lambda_1 L)\cdots(1 - \lambda_n L)$. We now require n side conditions on the path of Y_t to determine the n constants $c_1, \ldots, c_n$. We suppose that the λ_j are all distinct. Then application of (34) to the above equation gives

$$Y_t = b\sum_{r=1}^{n}\left(\frac{A_r}{1 - \lambda_r L}\right)X_t + \sum_{j=1}^{n}c_j\lambda_j{}^t, \quad (37)$$

which shows that Y_t can be expressed as the weighted sum of n geometric distributed lags with decay coefficients $\lambda_1, \lambda_2, \ldots, \lambda_n$.

---

[6] That is, "operating on both sides with the operator inverse of

$$(1 - \lambda_1 L)(1 - \lambda_2 L)\cdots(1 - \lambda_n L)."$$

Given n initial values of Y, and assuming $X_t = 0$ always, it is possible to start up difference equation (36) finitely far back in the past and to obtain a solution of the form

$$Y_t = \lambda_1{}^t \eta_1 + \lambda_2{}^t \eta_2 + \cdots + \lambda_n{}^t \eta_n$$

where $\eta_1, \ldots, \eta_n$ are constants chosen to satisfy the n initial values. The above equation can be derived from (37) by applying calculations analogous to those applied above in the first- and second-order cases.

5. Nth-ORDER DIFFERENCE EQUATIONS (N EQUAL ROOTS)

Consider the nth-order difference equation

$$(1 - \lambda L)^n Y_t = b X_t, \tag{38}$$

which has the solution

$$Y_t = \frac{b}{(1 - \lambda L)^n} X_t + c_1 \lambda^t + c_2 t \lambda^t + \cdots + c_n t^{n-1} \lambda^t.$$

The polynomial $1/(1 - \lambda L)^n$ is the one associated with an nth-order Pascal lag distribution, which is formed by multiplying (convolving) n geometric lag distributions with the same decay parameter λ. We have already studied the second-order Pascal distribution. The binomial expansion with negative exponent is

$$(1 - x)^{-n} = 1 + nx + \frac{n(n + 1)}{2!} x^2 + \frac{n(n + 1)(n + 2)}{3!} x^3 + \cdots$$

$$+ \frac{n(n + 1) \cdots (n + i - 1)}{i!} x^i + \cdots, \qquad |x| < 1.$$

Notice that $n(n + 1) \cdots (n + i - 1) = (n + i - 1)!/(n - 1)!$ The coefficient on x in the above expansion is thus

$$\binom{n + i - 1}{i} \equiv \frac{(n + i - 1)!}{i!(n - 1)!}.$$

Therefore, the expansion can be written

$$(1 - x)^{-n} = \sum_{i=0}^{\infty} \binom{n + i - 1}{i} x^i.$$

Consequently, for a lag-generating function[7] with n equal roots, we have

$$\frac{1}{(1 - \lambda L)^n} = \sum_{i=0}^{\infty} \binom{n + i - 1}{i} \lambda^i L^i, \tag{39}$$

which agrees with our earlier formulas for the special cases $n = 1$ and $n = 2$.
To arrive at (39) in an alternative way, write

$$f(\lambda L) = \frac{1}{(1 - \lambda L)} = \sum_{i=0}^{\infty} (\lambda L)^i.$$

Differentiating with respect to λL gives

$$f'(\lambda L) = \frac{1}{(1 - \lambda L)^2} = \sum_{i=0}^{\infty} i(\lambda L)^{i-1} = \sum_{i=0}^{\infty} (i + 1)(\lambda L)^i,$$

which is (39) with $n = 2$. Differentiating again with respect to λL gives

$$f''(\lambda L) = \frac{2}{(1 - \lambda L)^3} = \sum_{i=0}^{\infty} i(i - 1)(\lambda L)^{i-2}$$

or

$$\frac{1}{(1 - \lambda L)^3} = \sum_{i=0}^{\infty} \frac{(i + 1)(i + 2)}{2} (\lambda L)^i = \sum_{i=0}^{\infty} \binom{i + 2}{i} (\lambda L)^i,$$

which is (39) with $n = 3$.
With the aid of (39), the solution to (38) can be written

$$Y_t = b \sum_{i=0}^{\infty} \binom{n + i - 1}{i} \lambda^i X_{t-i} + c_1 \lambda^t + c_2 t \lambda^t + \cdots + c_n t^{n-1} \lambda^t.$$

6. AN EXAMPLE OF A FIRST-ORDER SYSTEM

Consider the following model studied by Cagan (1956). Let m_t be the log of the money supply, p_t the log of the price level and p_{t+1}^e the log of the price expected to prevail at time $t + 1$ given information available at time t. The model is

$$m_t - p_t = \alpha(p_{t+1}^e - p_t), \qquad \alpha < 0, \tag{40}$$

which is a portfolio equilibrium condition. The demand for real balances varies inversely with expected inflation $p_{t+1}^e - p_t$. The variable m_t is exogenous.
Suppose first that

$$p_{t+1}^e - p_t = \gamma(p_t - p_{t-1}), \tag{41}$$

[7] A term synonymous with "polynomial in the lag operator."

so that the public expects inflation next period to be the current rate of inflation, $p_t - p_{t-1}$, multiplied by the constant γ. Then (40) becomes

$$m_t - p_t = \alpha\gamma p_t - \alpha\gamma p_{t-1}.$$

Using lag operators, this can be written as

$$[(\alpha\gamma + 1) - \alpha\gamma L]p_t = m_t$$

or

$$\left[1 - \frac{\alpha\gamma}{1 + \alpha\gamma}L\right]p_t = \frac{1}{1 + \alpha\gamma}m_t.$$

The solution can be written

$$p_t = \frac{1}{1 + \alpha\gamma}\sum_{i=0}^{\infty}\left(\frac{\alpha\gamma}{1 + \alpha\gamma}\right)^i m_{t-i} + \left(\frac{\alpha\gamma}{1 + \alpha\gamma}\right)^t c$$

where c is a constant to be determined by, say, a given value of p at some time. The solution for p_t will be finite for the time path $m_t = \bar{m}$ for all t, provided that

$$\left|\frac{\alpha\gamma}{1 + \alpha\gamma}\right| < 1.$$

The above inequality is in the spirit of the "stability condition" developed by Cagan in his paper. It is a condition that delivers a bounded p_t for all $t \geq 0$ for $\{m_t\}$ sequences that are bounded. Notice that

$$\frac{1}{1 + \alpha\gamma}\sum_{i=0}^{\infty}\left(\frac{\alpha\gamma}{1 + \alpha\gamma}\right)^i = \frac{(1 + \alpha\gamma)^{-1}}{1 - \alpha\gamma(1 + \alpha\gamma)^{-1}} = 1.$$

Thus, the long-run effect of a once-and-for-all jump in m is to drive p up by an equal amount (provided the above "stability condition" is met).

Returning to (40), let us abandon (41) and now assume perfect foresight:

$$p_{t+1}^e = p_{t+1}. \tag{42}$$

Substituting (42) into (40) gives

$$m_t - p_t = \alpha p_{t+1} - \alpha p_t \qquad \text{or} \qquad \alpha p_{t+1} + (1 - \alpha)p_t = m_t.$$

Write this as

$$\left(L^{-1} + \frac{1 - \alpha}{\alpha}\right)p_t = \frac{1}{\alpha}m_t$$

or

$$\left(1 - \frac{\alpha - 1}{\alpha}L\right)p_t = \frac{1}{\alpha}m_{t-1}. \tag{43}$$

Notice that since $\alpha < 0$, it follows that $(\alpha - 1)/\alpha > 1$. This fact is an invitation to solve (43) in the "forward" direction, i.e., to use (6). Dividing both sides of (43) by $(1 - ((\alpha - 1)/\alpha)L)$ gives

$$p_t = \left(\frac{\alpha^{-1}}{1 - (\alpha - 1)\alpha^{-1}L} \right) m_{t-1} + c\left(\frac{\alpha - 1}{\alpha} \right)^t$$

where c is any constant. Using (6), this becomes

$$p_t = \left(\frac{\alpha^{-1}(-\alpha(\alpha - 1)^{-1}L^{-1})}{1 - \alpha(\alpha - 1)^{-1}L^{-1}} \right) m_{t-1} + c\left(\frac{\alpha - 1}{\alpha} \right)^t$$

$$= -\frac{1}{\alpha - 1} \left(\sum_{i=0}^{\infty} \left(\frac{\alpha}{\alpha - 1} \right)^i L^{-i} \right) m_t + c\left(\frac{\alpha - 1}{\alpha} \right)^t,$$

$$p_t = \frac{1}{1 - \alpha} \sum_{i=0}^{\infty} \left(\frac{\alpha}{\alpha - 1} \right)^i m_{t+i} + c\left(\frac{\alpha - 1}{\alpha} \right)^t. \tag{44}$$

Notice that since $\alpha < 0$, $0 < \alpha/(\alpha - 1) < 1$, so that the sum of the lag weights is finite. Equation (44) expresses the log of the current price as a moving sum of current and *future* values of the log of the money supply. Notice that

$$\frac{1}{1 - \alpha} \sum_{i=0}^{\infty} \left(\frac{\alpha}{\alpha - 1} \right)^i = \frac{(1 - \alpha)^{-1}}{1 - \alpha(\alpha - 1)^{-1}} = 1,$$

so that p is a weighted *average* of current and future values of m. The solution for p_t given by (44) will be finite for all finite t if there is a constant $K > 0$ and an x, $1 \le x < (\alpha - 1)/\alpha$ such that $|m_t| < Kx^t$ for all t. This is a condition that the money supply not grow too fast. For the solution given by (44) to be bounded for money supply paths that are bounded, we would require that $c = 0$. This amounts to an arbitrary terminal condition that rules out the occurrence of runaway inflations in the absence of runaway growth in the money supply.

7. AN EXAMPLE OF A SECOND-ORDER SYSTEM

Consider the following model studied by Muth (1961). Let p_t be the price of a commodity at t, C_t the demand for current consumption, I_t the stock of inventories of the commodity, Y_t the output of the commodity, and p_t^e the price previously expected to prevail at time t; $\{X_t\}$ is a bounded sequence of real numbers that represents the effects of the weather on supply. The model is

$$C_t = -\beta p_t, \qquad \beta > 0 \qquad \text{(demand curve)}$$

$$Y_t = \gamma p_t^e + X_t, \qquad \gamma > 0 \qquad \text{(supply curve)}$$

$$I_t = \alpha(p_{t+1}^e - p_t), \qquad \alpha > 0 \qquad \text{(inventory demand)}$$

$$Y_t = C_t + (I_t - I_{t-1}) \qquad \text{(market clearing)}.$$

Let us suppose that there is perfect foresight so that $p_t^e = p_t$ for all t. Making this assumption and substituting the first three equations into the fourth gives

$$\gamma p_t + X_t = \alpha(p_{t+1} - p_t) - \alpha(p_t - p_{t-1}) - \beta p_t$$

or

$$\alpha p_{t+1} - (2\alpha + \beta + \gamma)p_t + \alpha p_{t-1} = X_t.$$

Dividing by α gives

$$p_{t+1} - \frac{2\alpha + \beta + \gamma}{\alpha} p_t + p_{t-1} = \alpha^{-1}X_t$$

or

$$(L^{-1} - \phi + L)p_t = \alpha^{-1}X_t$$

where $\phi = ((\beta + \gamma)/\alpha) + 2 > 0$. Multiplying by L gives

$$(1 - \phi L + L^2)p_t = \alpha^{-1}X_{t-1}. \tag{45}$$

We need to factor the polynomial $1 - \phi L + L^2$ as

$$1 - \phi L + L^2 = (1 - \lambda_1 L)(1 - \lambda_2 L) = 1 - (\lambda_1 + \lambda_2)L + \lambda_1\lambda_2 L^2$$

so that we require

$$\lambda_1 + \lambda_2 = \phi, \qquad \lambda_1\lambda_2 = 1.$$

The second equality establishes that $\lambda_1 = 1/\lambda_2$, so that the two roots appear as a reciprocal pair. So we can write

$$1 - \phi L + L^2 = (1 - \lambda L)(1 - \lambda^{-1}L)$$

where λ is chosen to satisfy $\lambda + \lambda^{-1} = \phi$. So (45) can be written

$$(1 - \lambda L)(1 - \lambda^{-1}L)p_t = \alpha^{-1}X_{t-1}. \tag{46}$$

Since $(\beta + \gamma)/\alpha > 0$, it follows that $\phi = ((\beta + \gamma)/\alpha) + 2 > 2$. That implies that λ does not equal 1 since $\lambda + \lambda^{-1} = \phi$. Notice that if $\lambda > 1$, $\lambda^{-1} < 1$. So one of our roots necessarily exceeds 1, the other necessarily is less than 1.

We divide both sides of (46) by $(1 - \lambda L)(1 - \lambda^{-1}L)$ to obtain

$$p_t = \frac{1}{\alpha}\frac{1}{(1 - \lambda L)(1 - \lambda^{-1}L)}X_{t-1} + c_1\lambda^t + c_2\left(\frac{1}{\lambda}\right)^t \tag{47}$$

where c_1 and c_2 are any constants. Without loss of generality, suppose $\lambda < 1$ and let $\lambda_2 = 1/\lambda$. Use (6) and (19) to write the solution as

$$
p_t = \frac{\alpha^{-1}\lambda}{\lambda - \lambda_2}\left(\frac{1}{1 - \lambda L}\right)X_{t-1} - \frac{\alpha^{-1}\lambda_2}{(\lambda - \lambda_2)}\left(\frac{-(\lambda_2 L)^{-1}}{1 - (\lambda_2)^{-1}L^{-1}}\right)X_{t-1} + c_1\lambda^t + c_2\left(\frac{1}{\lambda}\right)^t
$$

$$
= \frac{\alpha^{-1}\lambda}{\lambda - \lambda^{-1}}\left(\frac{1}{1 - \lambda L}\right)X_{t-1} + \frac{\alpha^{-1}\lambda^{-1}}{\lambda - \lambda^{-1}}\left(\frac{\lambda L^{-1}}{1 - \lambda L^{-1}}\right)X_{t-1} + c_1\lambda^t + c_2\lambda^{-t}
$$

$$
= \frac{\alpha^{-1}\lambda}{\lambda - \lambda^{-1}}\left(\frac{1}{1 - \lambda L}\right)X_{t-1} + \frac{\alpha^{-1}}{\lambda - \lambda^{-1}}\left(\frac{1}{1 - \lambda L^{-1}}\right)X_t + c_1\lambda^t + c_2\lambda^{-t},
$$

$$
p_t = \frac{\alpha^{-1}}{\lambda - \lambda^{-1}}\sum_{i=1}^{\infty}\lambda^i X_{t-i} + \frac{\alpha^{-1}}{\lambda - \lambda^{-1}}\sum_{i=0}^{\infty}\lambda^i X_{t+i} + c_1\lambda^t + c_2\lambda^{-t},
$$

$$
p_t = \frac{\alpha^{-1}}{\lambda - \lambda^{-1}}\sum_{i=-\infty}^{\infty}\lambda^{|i|} X_{t-i} + c_1\lambda^t + c_2\lambda^{-t}. \tag{48}
$$

The solution (48) expresses p_t as a "two-sided" distributed lag of X, i.e., as a weighted sum of past, present, and future values of X. In this model the current price depends on the entire path of exogenous shock X over the entire past *and* the entire future. As usual, the constants c_1 and c_2 are determined from two side conditions on the path of p_t. For example, if we were to impose the side conditions $\lim_{t \to -\infty}|p_t| < \infty$, $\lim_{t \to +\infty}|p_t| < \infty$, i.e., if we imposed boundedness on the p_t path for all bounded $\{X_t\}$ sequences, then we would require $c_1 = c_2 = 0$.

8. AN OPTIMIZATION EXAMPLE: SOLVING A SYSTEM OF EULER EQUATIONS

Thus far, our advice to solve stable roots backward and unstable roots forward has been to a certain extent arbitrary, being partly based on the desire to have solutions that are bounded. As it happens, when a linear difference equation emerges from a dynamic quadratic optimization problem, there are present additional necessary conditions for optimality which have precisely the effect of causing us to solve the stable root(s) backward and the unstable root(s) forward. We shall illustrate this for the case of a firm employing a single factor of production, labor, and facing a quadratic technology and quadratic costs of adjusting its labor force.

We consider a firm that at time t chooses employment to maximize its present value

$$
v_t = \sum_{j=0}^{\infty} b^j \left\{ (f_0 + a_{t+j})n_{t+j} - \frac{f_1}{2}n_{t+j}^2 - \frac{d}{2}(n_{t+j} - n_{t+j-1})^2 - w_{t+j}n_{t+j} \right\}, \tag{49}
$$

n_{t-1} given. Here $f_0, f_1, d > 0$ and the discount factor b obeys $0 < b < 1$. Here w_{t+j} is the real wage faced by the firm at time $t + j$, while n_{t+j} is the firm's employment at $t + j$. The firm faces a known sequence of $\{a_{t+j}\}_{j=0}^{\infty}$, a_{t+j} being a shock to the marginal product of labor at time $t + j$. We assume for all t that for some $K > 0$, $|w_t| < K(x)^t$, $|a_t| < K(x)^t$, where $1 \leq x < 1/\sqrt{b}$; sequences that satisfy these inequalities for some $K > 0$ and $1 \leq x < 1/\sqrt{b}$ will be termed of exponential order less than $1/\sqrt{b}$. The firm faces costs of adjusting its labor force rapidly, which we model by deducting the term $\frac{1}{2}d(n_{t+j} - n_{t+j-1})^2$ from real revenue each period. The firm faces known sequences $\{w_{t+j}\}_{j=0}^{\infty}$ and $\{a_{t+j}\}_{j=0}^{\infty}$ and is assumed to choose a sequence $\{n_{t+j}\}_{j=0}^{\infty}$ to maximize v_t.

In order to discover the appropriate solution to this problem it is convenient to consider the finite horizon problem: maximize

$$v_t^T = \sum_{j=0}^{T} b^j \left\{ (f_0 + a_{t+j})n_{t+j} - \frac{f_1}{2} n_{t+j}^2 - \frac{d}{2}(n_{t+j} - n_{t+j-1})^2 - w_{t+j}n_{t+j} \right\} \quad (50)$$

subject to n_{t-1} being given. This problem matches our infinite horizon problem when we drive T to infinity. If a sequence $\{n_{t+j}\}_{j=0}^{T}$ is to maximize (50), it must satisfy the following system of first-order necessary conditions, which we derive by differentiating (50) with respect to $n_t, n_{t+1}, \ldots, n_{t+T}$:

$$f_0 + a_{t+j} - w_{t+j} - f_1 n_{t+j} - d(n_{t+j} - n_{t+j-1})$$
$$+ db(n_{t+j+1} - n_{t+j}) = 0, \qquad j = 0, 1, \ldots, T - 1, \quad (51)$$
$$b^T[f_0 + a_{t+T} - w_{t+T} - f_1 n_{t+T} - d(n_{t+T} - n_{t+T-1})] = 0. \quad (52)$$

Equation (51) is a system of second-order linear difference equations known as the "Euler equations," which we write as

$$dbn_{t+j+1} - (f_1 + d(1 + b))n_{t+j} + dn_{t+j-1} = w_{t+j} - a_{t+j} - f_0$$

or

$$bn_{t+j+1} + \phi n_{t+j} + n_{t+j-1} = \frac{1}{d}(w_{t+j} - a_{t+j} - f_0), \qquad j = 0, 1, \ldots, T - 1,$$

$$\phi = -\left(\frac{f_1}{d} + (1 + b)\right). \quad (53)$$

To solve this second-order difference equation, we need two boundary conditions. One boundary condition is supplied by the historically given initial level of n_{t-1}, and the other by the terminal condition (52). That terminal condition is known as the transversality condition and is a necessary condition for optimality. To get the terminal condition in the infinite horizon problem, it is appropriate to take

$$\lim_{T \to \infty} b^T[f_0 + a_{t+T} - w_{t+T} - f_1 n_{t+T} - d(n_{t+T} - n_{t+T-1})]n_{t+T} = 0 \quad (54)$$

as the transversality condition. We obtain this condition by multiplying (52) by the terminal stock of employment n_{t+T}, and taking the limit of the resulting equation as $T \to \infty$. Sufficient conditions for the transversality condition (54) to hold are, first, that $\{a_{t+j}\}$ and $\{w_{t+j}\}$ be of exponential order less than $1/\sqrt{b}$, and, second, that the solution for $\{n_{t+j}\}$ be of exponential order less than $1/\sqrt{b}$. Thus, suppose that $\{w_t\}$, $\{a_t\}$, and $\{n_t\}$ are each of exponential order less than $1/\sqrt{b}$. Then notice that

$$|b^T[f_0 n_{t+T} + a_{t+T} n_{t+T} - w_{t+T} n_{t+T} - (f_1 + d)n^2_{t+T} + d(n_{t+T} n_{t+T-1})]|$$

$$\leq b^T f_0 |n_{t+T}| + b^T |a_{t+T} n_{t+T}| + b^T |w_{t+T} n_{t+T}|$$

$$+ b^T (f_1 + d)|n^2_{t+T}| + b^T d|n_{t+T} n_{t+T-1}| \leq b^T f_0 K x^{t+T}$$

$$+ b^T K x^{2(t+T)} + b^T K x^{2(t+T)} + b^T (f_1 + d)K x^{2(t+T)}$$

$$+ b^T d K x^{2(t+T)-1}$$

$$= f_0 K x^t b^T x^T + K(2 + f_1 + d)b^T x^{2T} x^{2t} + dK b^T x^{2T} x^{2t-1}.$$

From the definition of a sequence of exponential order less than $1/\sqrt{b}$, we have that $0 < x\sqrt{b} < 1$. This condition implies that $xb < \sqrt{b} < 1$. Therefore the limit as $T \to \infty$ of the expression above equals zero. This proves that the conditions that $\{a_t\}$, $\{w_t\}$ and $\{n_t\}$ are of exponential order less than $1/\sqrt{b}$ are sufficient to imply that the transversality condition (54) is satisfied. The necessary conditions for optimality for the infinite horizon problem are then satisfied if we can find a solution to the difference equation

$$bn_{t+j+1} + \phi n_{t+j} + n_{t+j-1} = d^{-1}(w_{t+j} - a_{t+j} - f_0)$$

subject to the transversality condition (54) and the known initial value of n_{t-1}.

To solve the difference equation, write it as

$$b\left(1 + \frac{\phi}{b}L + \frac{1}{b}L^2\right)n_{t+j+1} = \frac{1}{d}(w_{t+j} - a_{t+j} - f_0).$$

We seek a factorization

$$\left(1 + \frac{\phi}{b}L + \frac{1}{b}L^2\right) = (1 - \lambda_1 L)(1 - \lambda_2 L) = 1 - (\lambda_1 + \lambda_2)L + \lambda_1 \lambda_2 L^2.$$

Equating powers of L gives

$$-\phi/b = (\lambda_1 + \lambda_2), \qquad 1/b = \lambda_1 \lambda_2, \qquad \text{or} \qquad 1/\lambda_1 b = \lambda_2.$$

Thus we have that λ_1 must satisfy

$$-\frac{\phi}{b} = \left(\lambda_1 + \frac{1}{\lambda_1 b}\right) \qquad \text{or} \qquad \frac{f_1}{d} + (1 + b) = -\phi = \lambda_1 b + \frac{1}{\lambda_1}.$$

FIGURE 4

Figure 4 depicts the determination of λ_1 and λ_2. The function $\lambda b + \lambda^{-1}$ attains a minimum at $\lambda = \sqrt{1/b}$, attaining a value of $2\sqrt{b}$ there. For $0 < b < 1$, we have that $1 + b \geq 2\sqrt{b}$ with equality at $b = 1$, so that even with $f_1 = 0$, in which case $\phi = -(1 + b)$, we have $-\phi \geq 2\sqrt{b}$. This assures that with $f_1 > 0$ the solutions for λ_1 and λ_2 as depicted in Figure 4 are real and distinct. Without loss of generality, let λ_1 be the smaller root. Then notice that the preceding implies that $\lambda_1 < 1/\sqrt{b} < \lambda_2$. By using Figure 4 we can establish that $\lambda_1 < 1 < 1/b < \lambda_2$. From $-\phi = ((f_1/d) + 1 + b)$, we have that $-\phi > 1 + b$, since $f_1/d > 0$. Now if $-\phi$ were to equal $1 + b$, we would have λ_1 and λ_2 being determined from

$$1 + b = \lambda b + \lambda^{-1}$$

or

$$b\lambda^2 - (1 + b)\lambda + 1 = 0, \qquad (\lambda b - 1)(\lambda - 1) = 0,$$

so that $\lambda_1 = 1$, $\lambda_2 = 1/b$. Since $-\phi > 1 + b$, inspection of Figure 4 shows that unity must be an upper bound for λ_1 and $1/b$ a lower bound for λ_2.[8]

Having achieved this factorization, we write the difference equation as

$$b(1 - \lambda_1 L)(1 - \lambda_2 L)n_{t+j+1} = d^{-1}(w_{t+j} - a_{t+j} - f_0).$$

---

[8] A version of Figure 4 with $b = 1$ determines the intriguing golden ratio or golden section. The golden ratio is the unique positive number λ whose reciprocal equals itself plus unity: $\lambda^{-1} = 1 + \lambda$. This equation can be rearranged to read $\lambda^{-1} + \lambda = 1 + 2\lambda$. From the quadratic formula, the golden ratio equals $(\sqrt{5} - 1)/2 = 0.618034$ and is found as the intersection in the positive quadrant of the line $1 + 2\lambda$ with the curve $\lambda + \lambda^{-1}$. The golden ratio, which appears repeatedly in nature and mathematics, fascinated ancient people, and is reflected in the design of the Parthenon. One place that the number occurs in mathematics is as the limit as t goes to infinity of the ratio of successive terms in a Fibonacci sequence. A Fibonacci sequence is generated by the difference equation $x_{t+1} = x_t + x_{t-1}$ with initial conditions $x_0 = 1$, $x_{-1} = 0$. The characteristic polynomial $(1 - L - L^2)$ associated with this equation can be factored as $(\lambda - L)(\lambda^{-1} + L)$ where λ is the golden ratio. For more on the golden ratio, see "Math and Music: The Deeper Links," *The New York Times*, Sunday, August 29, 1982.

To satisfy the transversality condition, operate on both sides of this equation with the "forward" inverse of $1 - \lambda_2 L$ to get

$$(1 - \lambda_1 L)n_{t+j+1} = \frac{-(b\, d\lambda_2)^{-1}L^{-1}}{1 - \lambda_2^{-1}L^{-1}}(w_{t+j} - a_{t+j} - f_0) + c\lambda_2{}^t$$

where c is a constant. However, since $\lambda_2 > 1/b > 1/\sqrt{b}$, we must set $c = 0$ in order to satisfy the transversality condition, for otherwise $\{n_{t+j}\}$ would fail to be of exponential order less than $1/\sqrt{b}$. Setting $c = 0$ and observing that $1/\lambda_2 = b\lambda_1$, we have

$$n_{t+j+1} = \lambda_1 n_{t+j} - \frac{\lambda_1}{d} \sum_{i=0}^{\infty} \left(\frac{1}{\lambda_2}\right)^i (w_{t+j+1+i} - a_{t+j+1+i} - f_0), \qquad j = 0, 1, \ldots .$$

$$(55)$$

This is a demand schedule for employment that expresses current employment as a function of once-lagged employment and current and all future values of the real wage and the shock to productivity. Since $\lambda_2 > 1/b$, we have that $1/\lambda_2 < b$, so that the infinite weighted sum on the right-hand side of (55) converges for $\{a_{t+j}\}$ and $\{w_{t+j}\}$ sequences that are of exponential order of less than $1/b$. We have assumed the stronger condition that $\{a_t\}$, $\{w_t\}$ are sequences of exponential order less than $1/\sqrt{b}$, so that the infinite weighted sum on the right side of (55) converges.

It remains to show that (55) holds for $j = -1$ as well. To show this, take the solution (55) for $j = 0$ and use it to eliminate n_{t+1} from the Euler equation (53) for $j = 0$, thereby obtaining

$$\{b\lambda_1 + \phi\}n_t + n_{t-1} = z_t + \frac{b\lambda_1}{1 - \lambda_2^{-1}L^{-1}}z_{t+1}$$

where $z_t \equiv d^{-1}(w_t - a_t - f_0)$. Since $\lambda_1 + \lambda_2 = -\phi/b$ and $b\lambda_1 = \lambda_2^{-1}$, we can rearrange the above equation to read

$$n_t = \lambda_1 n_{t-1} - \frac{\lambda_1}{1 - \lambda_2^{-1}L^{-1}}z_t,$$

which asserts that (55) holds for $j = -1$. Thus, (55) gives the firm's optimal plan for setting n_{t+j+1} for $j = -1, 0, 1, \ldots .$

We have in effect imposed the transversality condition first by using the "unstable" root λ_2 to solve in the forward direction and second by setting $c\lambda_2{}^t = 0$ in (55). To see this, write (55) as

$$(1 - \lambda_1 L)n_{t+j+1} = \varepsilon_{t+j+1}, \qquad j = -1, 0, 1, 2, \ldots, \qquad (56)$$

where

$$\varepsilon_{t+j+1} \equiv -\frac{\lambda_1}{d} \frac{1}{1 - \lambda_2^{-1}L^{-1}}(w_{t+j+1} - a_{t+j+1} - f_0).$$

Since $\{w_{t+j}\}$ and $\{a_{t+j}\}$ are of exponential order less than $1/\sqrt{b}$, it follows[9] that the sequence $\{\varepsilon_{t+j+1}\}$ is of exponential order less than $1/\sqrt{b}$ and is finite for finite $t+j$. The solution of the difference equation (55) with n_{t-1} given is

$$n_{t+j+1} = \lambda_1^{j+2} n_{t-1} + \sum_{i=0}^{j+1} \lambda_1{}^i \varepsilon_{t+j+1-i}, \qquad j = -2, -1, 0, 1, \ldots. \qquad (57)$$

This is the unique solution to the Euler equation that satisfies the initial condition and the transversality condition (54). It is straightforward to verify that both the initial condition and the transversality condition are satisfied by this solution, the latter condition being satisfied by virtue of the exponential order being less than $1/\sqrt{b}$ for the $\{\varepsilon_{t+j}\}$ sequence and the fact that $|\lambda_1| < 1$. For notice that

$$\left| \sum_{i=0}^{j+1} \lambda_1{}^i \varepsilon_{t+j+1-i} \right| < \sum_{i=0}^{j+1} \lambda_1{}^i K(x)^{t+j+1-i} \leq K(x)^{t+j+1} \left(\frac{1}{1 - (\lambda_1/x)} \right),$$

which proves that $\sum_{i=0}^{j+1} \lambda_1{}^i \varepsilon_{t+j+1-i}$ is of exponential order less than $1/\sqrt{b}$. It follows that (57) implies that n_{t+j} is of exponential order less than $1/\sqrt{b}$, and therefore that the transversality condition (54) is satisfied.

It should be emphasized that the transversality condition compels us to solve the unstable root forward. If we had solved the unstable root λ_2 "backward," then eventually the solution for n_{t+j+1} would come to be dominated by terms of exponential order λ_2. Since $\lambda_2 > 1/\sqrt{b}$, that solution would violate the transversality condition (54).

In conclusion, the solution of our infinite horizon maximum problem is for the firm to set its employment according to the demand schedule or decision rule

$$n_{t+j+1} = \lambda_1 n_{t+j} - \frac{\lambda_1}{d} \frac{1}{1 - \lambda_2^{-1} L^{-1}} (w_{t+j+1} - a_{t+j+1} - f_0)$$

for $j = -1, 0, 1, 2, \ldots$.

9. A MORE GENERAL UNIVARIATE OPTIMIZATION PROBLEM

The problem of the preceding section is a special case of a more general quadratic optimization problem, one version of which follows. We define the polynomial in the lag operator,

$$d(L) = d_0 + d_1 L + \cdots + d_m L^m, \qquad (58)$$

---

[9] For example, since $|w_{t+j+1}| < K(x)^{t+j+1}$ for some $K > 0$ and for $1 \leq x < 1/\sqrt{b}$, we have

$$F_{t+j+1} \equiv \left| \sum_{i=0}^{\infty} \left(\frac{1}{\lambda_2} \right)^i w_{t+j+i+1} \right| < K \sum_{i=0}^{\infty} \left(\frac{1}{\lambda_2} \right)^i (x)^{t+j+i+1} = K \left(\frac{1}{1 - \lambda_2^{-1} x} \right) x^{t+j+1}$$

where $1/\lambda_2 < \sqrt{b}$ and $x < 1/\sqrt{b}$. Therefore, F is of exponential order less than $1/\sqrt{b}$.

where $d_0 \neq 0$, $d_m \neq 0$. We assume that g_t is a sequence of exponential order less than $1/\sqrt{b}$, where $0 < b < 1$. Then the problem is to choose a sequence $\{y_t, t \geq 0\}$ to maximize

$$\sum_{t=0}^{\infty} b^t \{g_t y_t - \tfrac{1}{2} h y_t^2 - \tfrac{1}{2}[d(L)y_t]^2\} \tag{59}$$

where $h > 0$, subject to $y_{-1}, y_{-2}, \ldots, y_{-m}$ given. The problem of Section 8 is a version of problem (59) with $g_t = (f_0 + a_t - w_t)$, $m = 1$, $y_t = n_t$, and $d(L) = \sqrt{d}(1 - L)$, $h = f_1$.

The Euler equation for this problem is

$$[d(bL^{-1})d(L) + h]y_t = g_t. \tag{60}$$

We invite the reader to verify that this is the Euler equation by differentiating (59) with respect to y_t and rearranging. Note that (53) is a special case of (60) with $d(L) = (1 - L)\sqrt{d}$, $h = f_1$, $g_t = (f_0 + a_t - w_t)$.

In addition to the Euler equation (60), the necessary and sufficient conditions for maximization of (59) are completed by the condition

$$\frac{h}{2} \sum_{t=0}^{\infty} b^t y_t^2 < +\infty. \tag{61}$$

Inspection of (59) reveals that any $\{y_t\}$ path that violates (61), even if it satisfies the Euler equation, gives a very bad outcome for the criterion function. Imposing conditions (61) is equivalent to imposing transversality conditions. Transversality conditions could be derived as in Section 8, by differentiating a finite T version of (59) with respect to $y_T, \ldots, y_{T-m+1}$, multiplying the resulting m expressions by $y_T, \ldots, y_{T-m+1}$, respectively, and setting the limits as $T \to \infty$ to zero. As do the transversality conditions, (61) forces the solution $\{y_t\}$ to be of exponential order less than $1/\sqrt{b}$.

We briefly describe how (60) is solved subject to (61). We first note a simple but important feature of the characteristic polynomial $h + d(bL^{-1})d(L)$ that appears in (60). This polynomial evaluated at any value z_0 equals the polynomial evaluated at bz_0^{-1}. In particular, if z_0 is a zero of this polynomial, then so is bz_0^{-1}. To prove this, suppose that z_0 is a zero, which means setting $L = z_0$ gives $h + d(bz_0^{-1}) d(z_0) = 0$. The claim is that this implies that setting $L = bz_0^{-1}$ will also set the polynomial to zero. Making this substitution gives $h + d(z_0) d(bz_0^{-1})$, which equals the characteristic polynomial evaluated at z_0, which equals zero by assumption. Thus, the zeros of the characteristic polynomial of the Euler equation come in pairs of the form $z_k, bz_k^{-1}, k = 1, \ldots, m$.

Let us assume that the zeros of the characteristic polynomial are distinct. (The reader can apply the methods of Section 5 to analyze the case of repeated zeros, if this becomes necessary.) There are $2m$ zeros of the polynomial $h + d(bz^{-1})d(z)$. Denote these zeros $z_1, z_2, \ldots, z_{2m}$. Without loss of generality, let the zeros be arranged in descending order according to their absolute value. Then we have that the zeros are ordered as $|z_1| \geq |z_2| \geq \cdots \geq |z_m| > |bz_m^{-1}| \geq |bz_{m-1}^{-1}| \geq \cdots \geq |bz_1^{-1}|$. (The weak inequalities leave open the possibility that there are complex roots.) Let us define $\lambda_k = 1/z_k$, $k = 1, \ldots, m$. Notice that the above ordering, and in particular $|z_m| > |bz_m^{-1}|$, implies that $|\lambda_k| < 1/\sqrt{b}$ for $k = 1, \ldots, m$. Then it is possible to factor the characteristic polynomial of the Euler equation as

$$h + d(bL^{-1})\, d(L) = c(bL^{-1})c(L) \tag{62}$$

where

$$c(L) = c_0(1 - \lambda_1 L)(1 - \lambda_2 L)\ldots(1 - \lambda_m L) \tag{63}$$

$$c_0 = [(-1)^m \lambda_0/(\lambda_1\lambda_2\ldots\lambda_m)] \tag{64}$$

and where λ_0 is a constant that is uniquely determined by h and $d(L)$.

Since $|\lambda_k| < 1/\sqrt{b}$ for $k = 1, \ldots, m$, (62)–(63) imply that $h + d(bL^{-1})d(L)$ has been factored into $c(bL^{-1})c(L)$, where the zeros of $c(z)$ exceed $\sqrt{b}$ in modulus, (from (63) the zeros of $c(z)$ are the $1/\lambda_k$'s) and where the zeros of $c(bz^{-1})$ are *less* than $\sqrt{b}$ in modulus.

Using factorization (62), the Euler equation (60) can be represented as

$$c(bL^{-1})c(L)y_t = g_t. \tag{65}$$

The unique solution of the Euler equation that satisfies (61) is given by

$$c(L)y_t = c(bL^{-1})^{-1}g_t. \tag{66}$$

or

$$(1 - \lambda_1 L)\ldots(1 - \lambda_m L)y_t = c_0^{-2}[(1 - \lambda_1 bL^{-1})\ldots(1 - \lambda_m bL^{-1})]^{-1}g_t. \tag{66}$$

A partial fraction representation of $c_0 c(bL^{-1})^{-1}$ is given by

$$[(1 - \lambda_1 bL^{-1})\ldots(1 - \lambda_m bL^{-1})]^{-1} = \sum_{k=1}^{m} \frac{A_k}{(1 - \lambda_k bL^{-1})} \tag{67}$$

where

$$A_k = \lim_{z \to \lambda_k b} (1 - \lambda_k bz^{-1})c_0/c(bz^{-1}). \tag{68}$$

Using (67), solution (66) can be represented as

$$(1 - \lambda_1 L)\ldots(1 - \lambda_m L)y_t = c_0^{-2} \sum_{k=1}^{m} \left(\frac{A_k}{1 - \lambda_k bL^{-1}}\right)g_t. \tag{69}$$

or

$$(1 - \lambda_1 L)\ldots(1 - \lambda_m L)y_t = c_0^{-2} \sum_{k=1}^{m} A_k \sum_{j=0}^{\infty} (b\lambda_k)^j g_{t+j}. \tag{70}$$

Since $|\lambda_k| < 1/\sqrt{b}$, $|b\lambda_k| < \sqrt{b}$. This condition, together with our having assumed that $\{g_t\}$ is of exponential order less than $1/\sqrt{b}$ guarantees that the right hand side converges, and that as a function of t it is itself of exponential order less than $1/\sqrt{b}$. It follows that the solution (70) starting from the given starting values $y_{-1}, \ldots, y_{-m}$ satisfies condition (61) and is therefore optimal.

We close this section with a remark on terminology. Consider solution (66), $c(L)y_t = c(bL^{-1})^{-1}g_t$. In the control literature, $c(L)y_t$ is called the "feedback part" of the solution for y, while $c(bL^{-1})^{-1} g_t$ is called the "feedforward part."

10. INTRODUCTION TO MULTIVARIATE DYNAMIC OPTIMIZATION

We now briefly describe a multivariate generalization of the problem of Section 9, and its solution. This section is a brief introduction to ideas described more fully in Hansen and Sargent [1981]. We define the matrix polynomial in the lag operator

$$D(L) = D_0 + D_1 L + \cdots + D_m L^m \tag{71}$$

where D_j is an $(n \times n)$ matrix. We let $\{G_t\}$ be a sequence of $(n \times 1)$ vectors, each component of which is a sequence of exponential order less than $1/\sqrt{b}$. We let H be an $(n \times n)$ positive definite matrix. Finally, we let $\{Y_t\}$ be a sequence of $(n \times 1)$ vectors of variables that are to be chosen for $t \geq 0$, with given initial values $Y_{-1}, Y_{-2}, \ldots, Y_{-m}$. The problem we are interested in is to choose $\{Y_t, t \geq 0\}$ to maximize

$$\sum_{t=0}^{\infty} b^t \{G_t' Y_t - \tfrac{1}{2} Y_t' H Y_t - \tfrac{1}{2}[D(L)Y_t]'[D(L)Y_t]\} \tag{72}$$

given $\{G_t, \ t \geq 0\}$ and $Y_{-1}, \ldots, Y_{-m}$. In (72), the prime (') denotes matrix transposition.

Necessary and sufficient conditions for a maximum of (72) are

$$\sum_{t=0}^{\infty} b^t Y_t' H Y_t < +\infty \tag{73}$$

and the Euler equations

$$\{H + D(bL^{-1})'D(L)\} Y_t = G_t. \tag{74}$$

That the Euler equations assume the form (74) can be proved using the method of Sections 8 and 9, namely by differentiating (72) with respect to Y_t, equating the result to a vector of zeros, and rearranging. Condition (73) is the correct generalization of (61), and is justified by similar reasoning.

The related-pairs property of the zeros of the characteristic polynomial of the Euler equation that held in the univariate case generalizes as follows.

If z_0 is a zero of $\det\{H + D(bz^{-1})'D(z)\}$ then so is bz_0^{-1}. Here "det" denotes the determinant of a matrix. The appropriate matrix analogue of the scalar polynomial factorization (62) is a matrix polynomial factorization $C(bL^{-1})'C(L)$, where the zeros of $\det C(z)$ exceed $\sqrt{b}$ in absolute value, while those of $\det C(bz^{-1})$ are less than $\sqrt{b}$ in absolute value. By a theorem on matrix polynomials of the form that appears in (74), there always exists a matrix factorization

$$H + D(bL^{-1})'D(L) = C(bL^{-1})'C(L) \tag{75}$$

where

$$C(L) = C_0 + C_1 L + \cdots + C_m L^m \tag{76}$$

and where the zeros of $\det C(z)$ exceed $\sqrt{b}$ in absolute value.

The solution of (74) satisfying (73) is then given by

$$C(L)Y_t = C(bL^{-1})'^{-1}G_t. \tag{77}$$

By the above mentioned property of the location of the zeros of $\det C(bz^{-1})$, we can represent $\det C(bL^{-1})'$, as

$$\det C(bL^{-1})' = \lambda_0(1 \quad \lambda_1 bL^{-1})\ldots(1 - \lambda_k bL^{-1})$$

where $|\lambda_j| < 1/\sqrt{b}$, $j = 1, \ldots, k$, where $k = mn$, and where we have assumed distinct zeros of $\det C(bz^{-1})$. Using a matrix version of partial fractions, $C(bL^{-1})'^{-1}$ can be represented as

$$C(bL^{-1})'^{-1} = \sum_{h=1}^{k} \frac{A_h}{(1 - \lambda_h bL^{-1})} \tag{78}$$

where

$$A_h = \lim_{z \to \lambda_h b} (1 - \lambda_h bz^{-1})C(bz^{-1})'^{-1}. \tag{79}$$

Note that each A_h is an $(n \times n)$ matrix. Using (78), (77) can be represented

$$C(L)Y_t = \sum_{h=1}^{k} A_h \sum_{j=0}^{\infty} (\lambda_h b)^j G_{t+j}. \tag{80}$$

Representation (80) is the vector generalization of (70).

Note in (77) a sort of symmetry in form between the "feedback part" $C(L)Y_t$ and the "feedforward part" $C(bL^{-1})'^{-1}G_t$ that generalizes a similar symmetry that we observed in the univariate problems.

A key step in solving problems of this sort is achieving the matrix factorization (75). Hansen and Sargent (1981) describe several methods for accomplishing this.

Example (i): Interrelated Factor Demand

   Consider the problem of a firm that maximizes

$$\sum_{t=0}^{\infty} b^t \left\{ q_t - w_t n_t - J_t k_t - \frac{d_1}{2}[(1-L)n_t]^2 - \frac{d_2}{2}[(1-L)k_t]^2 \right\}, \qquad 0 < b < 1,$$

(81)

subject to

$$q_t = f_1' \binom{n_t}{k_t} - \frac{1}{2}\binom{n_t}{k_t}' F \binom{n_t}{k_t},$$

(82)

where k_t is the stock of capital, n_t is the stock of labor, w_t is the real rental on labor, and J_t is the real rental on capital; f_1 is a (2×1) vector of positive constants, F is a positive definite matrix, and d_1 and d_2 are positive constants measuring adjustment costs. We assume that $\{J_t\}$ and $\{w_t\}$ for $t \ge 0$ are known sequences of exponential order less than $1/\sqrt{b}$. The problem is to choose sequences $\{k_t, n_t, t \ge 0\}$ to maximize (81) subject to (82), given initial values n_{-1}, k_{-1} and given sequences for w_t and J_t.

   Problem (81)–(82) is a special case of (72) with

$$G_t = f_1 - \begin{bmatrix} w_t \\ J_t \end{bmatrix},$$

$$D(L) = \begin{bmatrix} \sqrt{d_1}\,(1-L) & 0 \\ 0 & \sqrt{d_2}\,(1-L) \end{bmatrix},$$

and $H = F$. The solution (80) is an interrelated pair of decision rules for (n_t, k_t) of the form

$$C(L)\begin{bmatrix} n_t \\ k_t \end{bmatrix} = \sum_{h=1}^{2} A_h \sum_{j=0}^{\infty} (\lambda_h b)^j \left\{ f_1 - \begin{bmatrix} w_{t+j} \\ J_{t+j} \end{bmatrix} \right\}$$

(83)

where $C(L) = C_0 + C_1 L$. In (83) the decision rules for capital and labor interact in the sense that each of (n_t, k_t) depends on lagged values of the other, and that each depends on future rental rates for the other. This interdependence occurs so long as either F (or H) or $D(L)$ is not diagonal.

   Versions of this problem were studied and utilized by Nadiri and Rosen (1973), Hansen and Sargent (1981), and Eichenbaum (1983).

Example (ii): A Dynamic Nash Equilibrium[10]

   We consider a duopoly in an industry producing a single good. Demand is governed by a linear demand schedule,

$$p_t = A_0 - \frac{A_1}{2}(q_{1t} + q_{2t}) + u_t, \qquad A_0, A_1 > 0,$$

(84)

---

[10] A variety of linear quadratic dynamic games is analyzed by Hansen, Epple, and Roberds (1985). These authors use lag operator methods to obtain explicit solutions of their games, and to extract the econometric restrictions implied by their games.

where q_{it} is output of firm i at t, p_t is the price of output at t, and u_t is a given sequence of disturbances to demand of exponential order less than $1/\sqrt{b}$. Firm i maximizes

$$\sum_{t=0}^{\infty} b^t\{p_t q_{it} - q_{it}s_{it} - \tfrac{1}{2}[d_i(L)q_{it}]^2\}, \qquad 0 < b < 1, \tag{85}$$

where $d_i(L) = d_{i0} + \cdots + d_{im}L^m$, and where s_{it} is a sequence of shocks to costs of production of firm i, assumed to be a known sequence of exponential order less than $1/\sqrt{b}$. Here $[d_i(L)q_{it}]^2$ stands for costs of adjusting production rapidly. The maximization of (85) by i takes $\{s_{it}\}$, $\{u_t\}$, and $\{q_{jt}, j \neq i\}$ given for $t \geq 0$, and q_{it} given for $\{t = -m, \ldots, -1\}$, $i = 1, 2$. In particular, firm i is supposed to regard firm j's output sequence as given and beyond its influence.

Substituting (84) into (85) gives

$$\sum_{t=0}^{\infty} b^t \left\{\left[A_0 - \frac{A_1}{2}(q_{1t} + q_{2t}) + u_t\right]q_{it} - q_{it}s_{it} - \tfrac{1}{2}[d_i(L)q_{it}]^2\right\}. \tag{86}$$

The Euler equations for this problem for firms 1 and 2 are

$$\begin{bmatrix} (A_1 + d_1(bL^{-1})d_1(L)) & \dfrac{A_1}{2} \\[2mm] \dfrac{A_1}{2} & (A_1 + d_2(bL^{-1})d_2(L)) \end{bmatrix} \begin{bmatrix} q_{1t} \\ q_{2t} \end{bmatrix} \tag{87}$$

$$= \begin{bmatrix} A_0 + u_t - s_{1t} \\ A_0 + u_t - s_{2t} \end{bmatrix}.$$

We define a Nash equilibrium in the space of sequences of quantities q_{1t}, q_{2t} as a pair of sequences for q_{1t}, q_{2t}[11] that solve the interrelated Euler equations (87) and satisfy the boundary conditions

$$\sum_{t=0}^{\infty} b^t q_{it}^2 < +\infty \qquad \text{for} \quad i = 1, 2. \tag{88}$$

Equivalently, the Nash equilibrium is the pair of (q_{1t}, q_{2t}) sequences that satisfies the following conditions:

(i) Firm i's quantity sequence maximizes its present value (85), given firm j's sequence, for $(i, j) = (1, 2)$ and $(2, 1)$.

(ii) The output market clears, in the sense that (84) holds for all t.

Equation (87) is evidently in the form of a vector Euler equation in (q_{1t}, q_{2t}). The matrix polynomial on the left side of (87) can be factored into the form

---

[11] It is necessary to add the qualifier "in the space of sequences of quantities q_{1t}, q_{2t}" because different definitions of strategy spaces in general give rise to distinct Nash equilibria.

$C(bL^{-1})'C(L)$, where $C(L)$ is a (2×2) matrix polynomial with the zeros of det $C(z)$ exceeding $\sqrt{b}$ in absolute value. Then the Nash equilibrium can be represented

$$C(L)\begin{bmatrix} q_{1t} \\ q_{2t} \end{bmatrix} = C(bL^{-1})'^{-1}\begin{bmatrix} A_0 + u_t - s_{1t} \\ A_0 + u_t - s_{2t} \end{bmatrix}$$

where

$$C(L) = C_0 + C_1 L + \cdots + C_m L^m.$$

Note that the vector Euler equation (87) was discovered by our having solved an interrelated pair of univariate dynamic optimization problems. The resulting system of Euler equations (87) can itself be viewed as solving some vector optimization problem, since the matrix characteristic polynomial is expressible in the form $H + D(bL^{-1})'D(L)$. To seek the vector dynamic optimization problem that is implicitly solved by (87) is to pose a version of an "inverse optimal control problem:" given a system of difference equations, attempt to synthesize an optimum problem for which they are necessary conditions.[12,13]

11. ANOTHER EXAMPLE: LEARNING BY DOING

The following example is interesting from both a substantive and a technical point of view. From a technical point of view, the example will introduce a control problem in which a rational characteristic polynomial must be factored in order to solve the Euler equation.

We consider a monopolist who faces the linear law of demand

$$p_t = A_0 - (A_1/2)Q_t + u_t, \qquad A_0, A_1 > 0, \tag{89}$$

where p_t is price, Q_t is output, and u_t is a known sequence of shocks to demand, assumed to be of exponential order less than $1/\sqrt{b}$. The monopolist's total costs at t are given by

$$C(Q_t) = c_0 + c_1 Q_t + \frac{c_2}{2} Q_t^2 + c_3 Q_t s_t - c_4[h(L)Q_t]Q_t, \ c_0, c_1, c_2, c_3, c_4 > 0, \tag{90}$$

where s_t is a known sequence of shocks to marginal cost, assumed to be of exponential order less than $1/\sqrt{b}$, where $h(L) = \sum_{j=0}^{\infty} h_j L^j$. As an example of the

---

[12] We will encounter another "inverse optimal control problem" in Chapter XIV. There we will study the implicit social welfare criteria that are maximized by various versions of an equilibrium model of investment under uncertainty. In Chapter XI, we will study a technically related problem called the "inverse optimal predictor problem." Such a problem was posed by John F. Muth (1960). Given the expectations formation scheme utilized by Cagan (1956), Muth sought to discover a random environment which would render such a forecasting scheme optimum.

[13] In Chapter XV, we shall study a dominant player dynamic game in some detail.

sort of $h(L)$ that we have in mind, we shall later consider the special case $h(L) = 1/(1 - \rho L)$ where $\rho < 1$ but where ρ is close to one. Then (90) captures the notion that marginal costs of current output fall with cumulated past output. This is one version of a "learning-by-doing" cost structure.

The firm maximizes

$$\sum_{t=0}^{\infty} b^t \{ p_t Q_t - C(Q_t) \}, \ 0 < b < 1,$$

or using (89) and (90)

$$\sum_{t=0}^{\infty} b^t \left\{ \left[A_0 - \frac{A_1}{2} Q_t + u_t \right] Q_t - \left[c_0 + c_1 Q_t + \frac{c_2}{2} Q_t^2 + c_3 Q_t s_t - c_4 [h(L) Q_t] Q_t \right] \right\}.$$

$$(91)$$

The firm chooses a sequence $\{Q_t\}_{t=0}^{\infty}$ to maximize (91), taking as given Q_t for $t < 0$ and the sequences $\{u_t\}_{t=0}^{\infty}$, $\{s_t\}_{t=0}^{\infty}$. By using the preceding method, the Euler equation for the firm's problem is found to be, after some rearrangement,

$$[(A_1 + c_2) - c_4 h(L) - c_4 h(bL^{-1})] Q_t = A_0 + u_t - c_1 - c_3 s_t. \quad (92)$$

For convenience, set $c_1 = 0$. The boundary condition is

$$A_1 \sum_{t=0}^{\infty} b^t Q_t^2 < +\infty. \quad (93)$$

We shall now consider the special case of the model that emerges when we set $h(L) = 1/(1 - \rho L)$, $0 < \rho < 1$. In this case, the characteristic polynomial on the left side of the Euler equation (92) becomes the rational polynomial

$$k - \frac{c_4}{1 - \rho L} - \frac{c_4}{1 - \rho b L^{-1}}$$

where $k \equiv (A_1 + c_2)$. To solve the Euler equation (92) subject to boundary condition (93), the first step is to express the characteristic polynomial in terms of a common denominator, which gives

$$\frac{[k(1 + \rho^2 b) - 2c_4] - (k - c_4)\rho L - (k - c_4)b\rho L^{-1}}{(1 - \rho b L^{-1})(1 - \rho L)}. \quad (94)$$

Notice that the denominator is already factored, and that the zeros of the numerator come in the familiar pair $(z_0, b z_0^{-1})$. Our next step on the way to solving our problem is to factor the numerator. Note that the numerator is proportional to

$$\left[-L^{-1} + \left[\frac{k(1 + \rho^2 b) - 2c_4}{(k - c_4)\rho b} \right] - 1/bL \right] \equiv \frac{1}{\alpha b} (1 - \alpha b L^{-1})(1 - \alpha L) \quad (95)$$

where $1/\alpha$ is the zero of the characteristic polynomial that exceeds $1/\sqrt{b}$. Equating powers of L, as in section 8, shows that α must solve

$$\frac{1}{\alpha b} + \alpha = \left[\frac{k(1 + \rho^2 b) - 2c_4}{(k - c_4)\rho b}\right]. \tag{96}$$

We assume that the parameter $k \equiv A_1 + c_2, c_4, \rho, b$ are such that the right side exceeds $2\sqrt{b}$ in absolute value. This guarantees the existence of a real number α that solves (96). Note that for $\rho = b = 1$, the above equation has the solution $\alpha = 1/\alpha = 1$. By continuity of the solution in the arguments on the right hand side, for values of ρ and b sufficiently close to 1, α will be close to one.

Using (94) and (95), the Euler equation can be expressed

$$\frac{(1 - \alpha b L^{-1})(1 - \alpha L)}{(1 - \rho b L^{-1})(1 - \rho L)} Q_t = \frac{\alpha b}{(k - c_4)\rho b} [A_0 + u_t - c_3 s_t]. \tag{97}$$

The solution of the Euler equation (97) that satisfies boundary condition (93) can be expressed in "feedback-feedforward" form

$$\frac{(1 - \alpha L)}{(1 - \rho L)} Q_t = \frac{\alpha b}{(A_1 + c_2 - c_4)\rho b} \cdot \frac{(1 - \rho b L^{-1})}{(1 - \alpha b L^{-1})} [A_0 + u_t - c_3 s_t]. \tag{98}$$

Unless $\alpha = \rho$, Q_t feeds back on an infinite number of its own past values, reflecting the dynamics of the firm's optimally coping with the learning-by-doing cost structure. In general, $\rho \neq \alpha$. However, in the special limiting case $\rho = b = 1$, it can be verified that $\rho = \alpha$. In this special case, (98) collapses to the static decision rule

$$Q_t = \frac{1}{A_1 + c_2 - c_4} [A_0 + u_t - c_3 s_t],$$

despite the presence of the learning-by-doing cost structure.

12. A CONSUMPTION EXAMPLE

We begin with a technical remark. Suppose that we wish to differentiate with respect to x_t the expression

$$V = \sum_{t=0}^{\infty} b^t [a(L)z_t][d(L)x_t]$$

where $a(L) = \sum_{j=-\infty}^{\infty} a_j L^j$, $d(L) = \sum_{j=-\infty}^{\infty} d_j L^j$. We invite the reader to verify that

$$\frac{\partial V}{\partial x_t} = b^t d(bL^{-1})a(L)z_t. \tag{99}$$

We shall apply this formula in studying an optimal consumption problem.

A consumer is assumed to maximize

$$\sum_{t=0}^{\infty} b^t \left\{ u_0 + u_1 c_t - \frac{u_2}{2} c_t^2 \right\}, \qquad 0 < b < 1, \quad u_0, u_1, u_2 > 0, \qquad (100)$$

subject to

$$A_{t+1} = R[A_t + y_t - c_t], \qquad R \geq 1, \qquad (101)$$

and

$$A_t > B \qquad \text{for all} \quad t \geq 0, \qquad (102)$$

$$A_0 \quad \text{given.} \qquad (103)$$

Here c_t is consumption, y_t is labor income, A_t is nonhuman assets available at the beginning of period t, and R is the gross rate of return on nonhuman assets. We assume that $0 > B > -\infty$, so that (102) requires that assets be uniformly bounded from below. This condition rules out a strategy of consuming large amounts and financing it by borrowing along an increasing and unbounded path.

Use (101) to express c_t as

$$c_t = y_t - (R^{-1}L^{-1} - 1)A_t. \qquad (104)$$

Substituting (104) into (100) gives the criterion

$$J = \sum_{t=0}^{\infty} b^t \left\{ u_0 + u_1(y_t - (R^{-1}L^{-1} - 1)A_t) \right.$$

$$\left. - \frac{u_2}{2} \left(y_t^2 - 2y_t(R^{-1}L^{-1} - 1)A_t + [(R^{-1}L^{-1} - 1)A_t]^2 \right) \right\}, \qquad (105)$$

which is to be maximized by selecting a sequence for A_t, subject to the boundary conditions (102) and (103). Repeatedly applying formula (99), we find the Euler equation

$$-\frac{u_1}{u_2}(R^{-1}b^{-1} - 1) + (R^{-1}b^{-1}L - 1)y_t$$

$$- (R^{-1}b^{-1}L - 1)(R^{-1}L^{-1} - 1)A_t = 0 \qquad (106)$$

$$\text{for} \quad t = 1, 2, \dots.$$

The zeros of the characteristic polynomial in A_t are at $L = R^{-1} < 1$ and $L = Rb$. In order to satisfy the boundary conditions (102) and (103), the polynomial $(R^{-1}L^{-1} - 1)$ must be solved forwards, and the polynomial $(R^{-1}b^{-1}L - 1)$ solved backwards. Dividing (106) by $(R^{-1}L^{-1} - 1)$ gives

$$(R^{-1}b^{-1}L - 1)A_t = \frac{-u_1}{u_2} \frac{(R^{-1}b^{-1} - 1)}{(R^{-1} - 1)} + \left(\frac{R^{-1}b^{-1}L - 1}{R^{-1}L^{-1} - 1} \right) y_t$$

or

$$A_t = R^{-1}b^{-1}A_{t-1} + \frac{u_1}{u_2}\frac{(R^{-1}b^{-1}-1)}{(R^{-1}-1)} + \left(\frac{1 - R^{-1}b^{-1}L}{R^{-1}L^{-1}-1}\right)y_t. \quad (107)$$

Subtracting (107) from (101) lagged one period, namely,

$$A_t = R[A_{t-1} + y_{t-1} - c_{t-1}],$$

gives

$$0 = (R - R^{-1}b^{-1})A_{t-1} - \frac{u_1}{u_2}\frac{(R^{-1}b^{-1}-1)}{R^{-1}-1}$$

$$+ \frac{R(R^{-1}L^{-1}-1)}{(R^{-1}L^{-1}-1)}Ly_t - \frac{(1 - R^{-1}b^{-1}L)}{(R^{-1}L^{-1}-1)}y_t - Rc_{t-1}$$

or

$$c_{t-1} = (1 - R^{-2}b^{-1})A_{t-1} - \frac{u_1}{u_2}\frac{(R^{-1}b^{-1}-1)}{1-R} + \frac{(1 - R^{-2}b^{-1})}{1-L^{-1}R^{-1}}y_{t-1}. \quad (108)$$

Writing out the polynomial in L explicitly and shifting forward one period gives

$$c_t = (1 - R^{-2}b^{-1})\left[A_t + \sum_{j=0}^{\infty}R^{-j}y_{t+j}\right] - \frac{u_1}{u_2}\left(\frac{R^{-1}b^{-1}-1}{1-R}\right). \quad (109)$$

This is a certainty version of the permanent income theory of consumption. According to (109), consumption is a linear function of wealth, defined as the sum of nonhuman wealth A_t and the discounted present value of labor income, $\sum_{j=0}^{\infty}R^{-j}y_{t+j}$. In the special case that $bR = 1$, (109) collapses to

$$c_t = (1 - R^{-1})\left[A_t + \sum_{j=0}^{\infty}R^{-j}y_{t+j}\right].$$

It is also true that when $Rb = 1$, (109) and (101) imply that $c_t = c_0$ for all t, so that the model implies complete consumption smoothing. To convince oneself of this, the reader is invited to verify that the Euler equation of this model can be represented as

$$c_t = (Rb)^{-1}c_{t-1}.$$

Robert Hall [1978] pursued the empirical implications of a stochastic version of such an Euler equation. In Chapter XII below, we shall study this consumption example further.

13. NONANTICIPATIVE REPRESENTATIONS AND LUCAS'S CRITIQUE

We return to a version of the difference equation associated with Cagan's model of hyperinflation, which we studied in Section 6 above. In particular, we have

$$y_t = \lambda y_{t+1} + x_t, \qquad |\lambda| < 1,$$

where $\{x_t\}$ is a sequence of exponential order less than $1/\lambda$. The unique bounded solution of this equation is given by

$$y_t = \sum_{j=0}^{\infty} \lambda^j x_{t+j}. \tag{110}$$

This equation represents the solution for y_t in terms of an infinite number of future values of the "forcing variable" x_t. In practice, one often prefers a "nonanticipative" representation of a solution, in which y_t is expressed as a solution only of x's dated t and earlier. We now briefly show how representation (110) can be converted to an alternative representation expressing y_t as such a function of current and past x's only. Given (110), such a representation in terms of current and past x's can be attained by positing a specific difference equation for $\{x_t\}$ itself, using this difference equation to express x_{t+j} for $j \geq 1$ as functions of $\{x_t, x_{t-1}, \ldots\}$, and then using these functions to eliminate x_{t+j} for $j \geq 1$ from (110). The parameters of the representation for y_t as a function of current and past x's will depend on the parameters of the difference equation for x_t. This is so because the representation expressing y_t as a function of $\{x_t, x_{t-1}, \ldots\}$ incorporates the solution of the difference equation expressing $x_{t+j}, j \geq 1$, in terms of $\{x_t, x_{t-1}, x_{t-2}, \ldots\}$. For example, suppose that x_t is governed by the difference equation

$$x_t = \rho x_{t-1}, \qquad |\rho\lambda| < 1.$$

Then we have that

$$x_{t+j} = \rho^j x_t, \qquad j \geq 1.$$

Substituting this into (110) gives

$$y_t = \left(\frac{1}{1 - \lambda\rho}\right) x_t, \tag{111}$$

which is an expression for y_t in terms of x_t in which the parameter ρ of the difference equation for x_t appears.

More generally, assume that x_t is governed by the difference equation

$$a(L)x_t = 0 \tag{112}$$

where $a(L) = 1 - a_1 L - a_2 L^2 - \cdots - a_r L^r$ and where the zeros of $a(z)$ exceed $1/\lambda$ in absolute value. Then Hansen and Sargent (1980) show that the solution of (110) can be represented as

$$y_t = a(\lambda)^{-1} \left[1 + \sum_{j=1}^{r-1} \left(\sum_{k=j+1}^{r} \lambda^{k-j} a_k \right) L^j \right] x_t. \tag{113}$$

(We shall show how to derive this formula in Chapter XI.) Equation (113) is evidently a generalization of (111). That is, (111) is (113) for the case $r = 1$, $a_0 = 1$, $a_1 = \rho$.

Equations (112) and (113) display a hallmark of economic models incorporating foresight as in (110), namely the presence of cross-equation restrictions between, on the one hand, the parameters of the process $\{x_t\}$ of the forcing variables, and, on the other hand, the solution for y_t in terms of $\{x_t, x_{t-1}, \ldots\}$. This characteristic of models with foresight means that it will not be possible to find a representation expressing y_t as a function of $\{x_t, x_{t-1}, \ldots\}$ that is independent of the law of motion (difference equation) governing the forcing process $\{x_t\}$. Alterations in the law of motion for x_t will alter the *function* describing the dependence of y_t on current and past x's.

The presence of such cross-equation restrictions in models with foresight is the source of Robert E. Lucas's (1976) criticism of some econometric policy evaluation procedures of the past. Lucas criticized methods that took representations of a variable like y_t as a function of $\{x_t, x_{t-1}, \ldots\}$ and treated them as being invariant with respect to alterations in the difference equation generating the $\{x_t\}$ sequence.

EXERCISES

1. Verify that the presence of both *lagged* employment and *future* values of w_t and a_t on the right-hand side of the employment decision rule (55) (demand schedule) depends on having the adjustment cost parameter d strictly positive. (Set $d = 0$ and rework the firm's optimum problem.)

2. Determine the effect of an increase in d on the speed of adjustment parameters λ_1 and λ_2. Does a firm facing a small d adjust its labor force more or less quickly in response to current conditions than a firm facing a larger value of d? (*Hint:* use Figure 4.)

3. (*A Keynesian investment schedule*) A firm chooses a sequence of capital $\{k_{t+j}\}_{j=0}^{\infty}$ to maximize

$$v_t = \sum_{j=0}^{\infty} b^j \left\{ a_0 k_{t+j} - \frac{a_1}{2} k_{t+j}^2 - J_{t+j}(k_{t+j} - k_{t+j-1}) - \frac{d}{2}(k_{t+j} - k_{t+j-1})^2 \right\},$$

given $k_{t-1} > 0$, where $a_0, a_1, d > 0$ and where $\{J_{t+j}\}_{j=0}^{\infty}$ is a known sequence of the price of capital relative to the price of the firm's output. The sequence $\{J_{t+j}\}$ is of exponential order less than $1/b$, where $0 < b < 1$ is the discount factor (the reciprocal of one plus the real rate of interest).

   A. Derive the Euler equations and the transversality condition.

   B. Show that the optimum decision rule of the firm is of the form

$$k_{t+j+1} = \lambda_1 k_{t+j} + c_0 + \frac{c_1}{1 - \lambda_2^{-1} L^{-1}} (b J_{t+j+2} - J_{t+j+1}),$$

where $0 < \lambda_1 < 1 < \lambda_2$, and c_0 and c_1 are constants. Find c_0 and c_1; show how to find λ_1 and λ_2; and prove that the λ's obey the inequalities just stated.

4. (*Keynesian stabilization policy*) The reduced form for GNP (Y) is

$$Y_t = \alpha + BS_t + cg_t, \qquad B > 0, \quad c > 0,$$

where g is government purchases and S_t is exports, an exogenous variable outside the government's control. The sequence of exports $\{S_t\}_{t=0}^{\infty}$ is of exponential order less than $1/b$ where $0 < b < 1$. Suppose that the government sets g_t to minimize the loss function

$$T = \sum_{t=0}^{\infty} b^t \{(Y_t - Y_t^*)^2 + d(g_t - g_{t-1})^2\}, \qquad d \geq 0,$$

where $\{Y_t^*\}_{t=0}^{\infty}$ is a target sequence of GNPs that is of exponential order less than $1/b$, and d is non-negative and measures the cost of changing the setting of g from its previous value.

A. Derive an optimal rule for setting g_t under the assumption that $d = 0$.

B. Derive the optimal rule for setting g_t under the assumption that $d > 0$.

5. (*Cass–Koopmans optimum growth problem*) A planner wants to choose (consumption, capital) sequences that maximize

$$\sum_{t=0}^{\infty} \beta^t \left(u_0 c_t - \frac{u_1}{2} c_t^2 \right), \qquad u_0, u_1 > 0$$

subject to $c_t + k_{t+1} \leq f_0 k_t$, where k_0 is given and satisfies $0 < k_0 < (u_0/u_1)(1/(f_0 - 1))$. Here c_t is per capita consumption and k_t is per capita capital. Assume that $f_0 > 1/\beta > 1$, where β is the discount factor. The planner imposes the side condition that the $\{k_t\}$ sequence be bounded. (Actually, all we need is that k_t be required to be nonnegative, but boundedness does the job and is easier to handle technically.)

A. Find the Euler equation and the transversality condition. Interpret the transversality condition. (*Hint:* use the constraint to eliminate c_t from the objective function and differentiate with respect to successive k's.)

B. Solve the Euler equation for the steady state value of k, say $\bar{k}$. Find the steady-state value of $\bar{c}$. (*Hint:* you should get

$$\bar{k} = \left(\frac{1}{f_0 - 1} \right) \frac{u_0}{u_1}, \qquad \bar{c} = \frac{u_0}{u_1}.)$$

Interpret the steady-state value of $\bar{c}$.

C. Show that the optimal feedback rule for setting k is

$$k_{t+1} = \frac{1}{f_0 \beta} k_t - \left(\frac{1}{f_0 - 1} \right)\left(\frac{u_0}{u_1}\left(\frac{1}{\beta f_0} - 1 \right) \right). \tag{*}$$

(*Hint:* Solve the Euler equation.) Does this solution satisfy the transversality condition? If you had solved the "other" root backward, rather than forward, would the transversality condition be satisfied?

D. Prove that as $t \to \infty$ the solution for k_{t+1} in (∗) converges to $\bar{k}$.

E. Prove that consumption increases as capital increases toward its steady-state value.

6. A consumer is assumed to face the sequence of budget constraints

$$A_{t+1} = (1 + r)A_t + (1 + r)(y_t - c_t), \qquad t = 0, 1, 2, \ldots, \tag{†}$$

where A_t is his asset holdings at the beginning of period t, y_t is exogenous income, and c_t is consumption at t. Here $r > 0$ is the real rate of return on assets, assumed constant over time. The consumer earns (pays) each period $1 + r$ times his initial assets plus $1 + r$ times the addition (subtraction) to his assets made by consuming less (more) than his income. Assume that both c_t and y_t are of exponential order less than $1 + r$.

Suppose we impose upon the consumer the boundary condition

$$\lim_{t \to \infty} (1 + r)^{-t} A_t = 0.$$

Show that then the sequence of budget constraints (†) implies

$$A_t + \sum_{t=0}^{\infty} \frac{y_{t+i}}{(1 + r)^i} = \sum_{t=0}^{\infty} \frac{c_{t+i}}{(1 + r)^i}, \qquad t = 0, 1, 2, \ldots.$$

Interpret this result.

Assume that the consumer starts out with initial assets of A_0 at time 0. Show that the sequence of budget constraints (†) implies

$$A_t = \sum_{i=0}^{t-1} (1 + r)^{i+1}(y_{t-1-i} - c_{t-i-1}) + (1 + r)^t A_0.$$

Interpret this result.

7. Suppose that portfolio equilibrium is described by Cagan's equation:

$$m_t - p_t = -1(p_{t+1}^e - p_t), \qquad t = 0, 1, 2, \ldots,$$

where m_t is the log of the money supply, p_t the log of the price level at t, and p_{t+1}^e the public's expectation of p_{t+1}, formed at time t. Suppose that expectations are "rational," so that

$$p_{t+1}^e = p_{t+1}.$$

A. Suppose that $\{m_t\}$, $t = 0, 1, \ldots$, is given by

$$m_t = 10\lambda^t, \qquad t = 0, 1, 2, \ldots.$$

Compute the equilibrium value of p_t for $t = 0, 1, 2$, and $t = 5, 6$ for the following values of λ:
   (i) $\lambda = 1$;
   (ii) $\lambda = 1.5$;
   (iii) $\lambda = 2.0$.

B. Suppose that m_t follows the path

$$m_t = 10\lambda^t, \qquad t = 0, 1, 2, 3, 4$$

$$m_t = 11\lambda^t, \qquad t = 5, 6, 7, 8, \ldots.$$

Compute the equilibrium values of p_t for $t = 0, 1, 2, 3, 4, 5, 6$ assuming that $\lambda = 1.5$. How does this time path for $\{p_t\}$ compare with that computed in A(ii)? Graph the two paths.

8. (Advertising)
A monopolist faces the following demand curve for his product,

$$p_t = A_0 - A_1 Q_t + g(L)a_t + u_t, \qquad A_0, A_1 > 0,$$

where p_t is price, Q_t is output, a_t is advertising, u_t is a sequence of shocks to demand, and $g(L) = g_0 + g_1 L + \cdots + g_m L^m$, where $g_j > 0$ for $j = 0, \ldots, m$. The firm maximizes

$$\sum_{t=0}^{\infty} \beta^t \left\{ p_t Q_t - Q_t s_t - (1/2)[d(L)Q_t]^2 - \frac{\gamma}{2} a_t^2 - a_t w_t \right\}, \qquad 0 < \beta < 1, \tag{1}$$

where $d(L) = \sum_{j=0}^n d_j L^j$. In (1), s_t is a shock to costs, $\frac{1}{2}[d(L)Q_t]^2$ represents costs of rapid adjustment, and the marginal costs of advertising at t are $(w_t + \gamma a_t)$, where w_t is a known sequence. We assume that (u_t, s_t, w_t) are known sequences of exponential order less than $1/\sqrt{\beta}$. The criterion (1) is to be maximized over sequences for $\{Q_s, a_s, s \geq 0\}$ taking as given $\{Q_s, a_s, s < 0\}$.

A. Find the Euler equations for this problem.

B. Argue that the solution will be linear laws of motion for (Q_t, a_t) in which each of (Q_t, a_t) depends on lagged values of both Q and a, and current and future values of all of (u, s, w).

9. (Time to build with two processes)

Consider a monopolist whose output satisfies

$$Q_t = f(L)n_{1t} + g(L)n_{2t} \tag{1}$$

where

$$f(L) = \sum_{j=0}^{m} f_j L^j, \; g(L) = \sum_{j=0}^{r} g_j L^j, \qquad f_j \geq 0, \quad g_j \geq 0,$$

for all j. In (1), n_{1t} is the amount of labor at t that is assigned to process 1, while n_{2t} is the amount that is assigned to process 2. The idea is that output can be produced via two processes, with different timing characteristics, e.g., to represent the notion that the first process is fast but wasteful, while the other is efficient but time consuming, we might set $f(L) = L$, $g(L) = (\frac{1}{2})[L + L^2 + L^3 + L^4]$. The firm faces the demand curve

$$p_t = A_0 - A_1 Q_t + u_t, \qquad A_0, A_1 > 0, \tag{2}$$

where u_t is a known sequence of exponential order less than $1/\sqrt{\beta}$. The firm hires labor at the wage rate w_t, where w_t is a known sequence of exponential order less than $1/\sqrt{\beta}$. The firm's problem is to maximize

$$\sum_{t=0}^{\infty} \beta^t \{p_t Q_t - w_t(n_{1t} + n_{2t})\}, \qquad 0 < \beta < 1, \tag{3}$$

subject to (1) and (2), with $\{n_{1s}, s = -1, \ldots, -m\}$, $\{n_{2s}, s = -1, \ldots, -r\}$ given.

A. Find the Euler equations for this problem.

B. Indicate the form of the optimum decision rules for (n_{1t}, n_{2t}).

10. At time t, a farmer plants A_t units of land from which he produces $y_{t+1} = f_1 A_t$ units of output available to be sold at time $(t + 1)$ at price p_{t+1} where $f_1 > 0$. If A_t units of land are planted, the farmer's costs at time t are $c_0 A_t + (c_1/2)A_t^2 + c_2 A_t A_{t-1}$, where $c_0, c_1, c_2 > 0$. The term $c_2 A_t A_{t-1}$ reflects the wearing out of the land from two successive heavy plantings. The price of output p_t obeys the first-order difference equation

$$p_{t+1} = \alpha p_t$$

with p_0 given and $|\alpha| < 1/\sqrt{\beta}$. The farmer faces the p_t sequence as a price-taker. The farmer chooses $A_0, A_1, \ldots$ to maximize

$$\sum_{t=0}^{\infty} \beta^{t+1} p_{t+1}(f_1 A_t) - \sum_{t=0}^{\infty} \beta^t \left[c_0 A_t + \frac{c_1}{2} A_t^2 + c_2 A_t A_{t-1} \right], \qquad 0 < \beta < 1,$$

subject to A_{-1} given.

A. Obtain the first-order necessary conditions for optimization.

B. Assume that $c_1 = 5/2$, $c_2 = 1$, $\beta = 1$, $f_1 = 10$, and $c_0 = 1$. Find an optimal acreage plan for the farmer of the form

$$A_t = L(A_{t-1}, p_t, \text{constant})$$

where L is a linear function. Compute actual numerical values for the linear coefficients under the alternative assumptions $\alpha = 0.5$, $\alpha = 0$, and $\alpha = -0.5$.

C. Using your answer to B, describe how you would expect the farmer's supply of output next period, $y_{t+1} = f_1 A_t$, to vary with this period's price, p_t. When is supply y_{t+1} to vary inversely with p_t?

D. Use this example to illustrate the general observation that decision rules change whenever the economic environment changes.

11. A social planner wants to maximize the criterion

$$\sum_{t=0}^{\infty} b^t \{ u_1(c_t - a) - (\tfrac{1}{2})u_2(c_t - a)^2 - u_3 n_t - (\tfrac{1}{2})u_4 n_t^2 \},$$ (1)

$$0 < b < 1, \qquad u_1, u_2, u_3, u_4 > 0, \quad a > 0,$$

subject to

(a) $c_t + n_{t+1} + g = f n_t, \qquad g > 0, \quad f > 1, \quad fb > 1,$

(b) $n_0 > 0, \quad$ given. (2)

Here c_t is consumption, n_t is labor supplied, g is government purchases, which are fixed and outside the control of the planner, and a is a "bliss level" of consumption. (In the background in (1)–(2), it is understood that output at t equals $f \min(k_t, n_t)$ where k_t is capital at t. This fixed proportions technology makes it optimal to set $n_t = k_t$. We have substituted this into an original set of constraints to get (2).)

A. Show that the optimal path for $\{n_t\}$ converges as $t \to \infty$. Call the limit point the "stationary optimal value of n."

B. Give an explicit formula for the stationary optimal value of n, call it $\bar{n}$.

C. Stationary values of n_t must satisfy (2a) with $n_{t+1} = n_t = n$:

$$c + n + g = fn.$$ (3)

Consider the following "Golden rule" problem: to maximize

$$u_1(c - a) - (\tfrac{1}{2})u_2(c - a)^2 - u_3 n - (\tfrac{1}{2})u_4 n^2$$

subject to (3), by choice of c and n. (In words, find the utility maximizing sustainable levels of consumption and labor.) Solve this problem, finding an explicit formula for the "Golden rule" employment level, n_g.

D. Does $n_g = \bar{n}$, in general? If not, describe special settings of the parameter values for which $n_g = \bar{n}$. Interpret these special settings.

REFERENCES

Allen, R. G. D. (1960). *Mathematical Economics*, 2nd ed., London: Macmillan.

Baumol, W. J. (1959). *Economic Dynamics*, New York: Macmillan.

Cagan, P. (1956). "The monetary dynamics of hyperinflation." *Studies in the Quantity Theory of Money* (M. Friedman, ed.), Chicago: University of Chicago Press.

Eichenbaum, M. S. (1983). "A rational expectations equilibrium model of inventories of finished goods and employment." *Journal of Monetary Economics*, Vol. 29, No. 3, pp. 259–277.

Gabel, R. A. and Roberts, R. A. (1973). *Signals and Linear Systems*, New York: Wiley.

Hall, R. E. (1978). "Stochastic implications of the life cycle-permanent income hypothesis: theory and evidence." *Journal of Political Economy*, Vol. 86, No. 6, pp. 971–987, reprinted in *Rational Expectations and Econometric Practice* (R. E. Lucas, Jr. and T. J. Sargent, eds.), Minneapolis: University of Minnesota Press, 1981.

Hansen, L. P. and Sargent, T. J. (1980). "Formulating and estimating dynamic linear rational expectations models." *Journal of Economic Dynamics and Control*, Vol. 2, No. 1, pp. 7–46, reprinted in *Rational Expectations and Econometric Practice* (R. E. Lucas, Jr. and T. J. Sargent, eds.), Minneapolis: University of Minnesota Press, 1981.

Hansen, L. P. and Sargent, T. J. (1981). "Linear rational expectations models for dynamically interrelated variables." *Rational Expectations and Econometric Practice*, (R. E. Lucas, Jr. and T. J. Sargent, eds.), Minneapolis: University of Minnesota Press.

Hansen, L. P., Epple, D., and Roberds, W. (1985). "Linear quadratic models of resource depletion." *Energy, Foresight, and Strategy* (T. J. Sargent, ed.), Washington, DC: Resources for the Future.

Lucas, R. E. Jr. (1976). "Econometric policy evaluation: a critique." *The Phillips Curve and Labor Markets* (K. Brunner and A. Meltzer, eds.), Vol. 1, Carnegie-Rochester Conference Series on Public Policy, Amsterdam: North-Holland.

"Math and music: the deeper links." *New York Times*, Sunday, August 29, 1982.

Muth, J. F. (1960). "Optimal properties of exponentially weighted forecasts." *Journal of the American Statistical Association*, Vol. 55, No. 290, pp. 299-321.

Muth, J. F. (1961). "Rational expectations and the theory of price movements." *Econometrica*, Vol. 29, No. 3, pp. 315-335.

Nadiri, M. and Rosen, S. (1973). *A Disequilibrium Model of Demand for Factors of Production*, New York: Columbia University Press, for the NBER.

Samuelson, P. (1944). "Interaction between the multiplier analysis and the principle of acceleration." *Readings in Business Cycle Theory*, American Economic Association, New York: McGraw-Hill.

CHAPTER X

LINEAR LEAST SQUARES PROJECTIONS (REGRESSIONS)

The concept of linear regression has many important uses in macroeconomics, several of which we shall illustrate in subsequent chapters. One very important application will be its use in modeling the "signal extraction" problem faced by agents in an environment in which they have imperfect information about a variable affecting their welfare. By using a linear regression, agents can estimate that unobserved variable in a manner that is optimal, in a certain sense. Two leading applications of the signal extraction model in macroeconomics are Robert Lucas's model of the Phillips curve and Milton Friedman's theory of the consumption function. Another use we shall make of linear regression is to characterize and study the optimal control problem facing monetary and fiscal authorities.

1. LINEAR LEAST SQUARES REGRESSION: THE ORTHOGONALITY CONDITION

We consider a set of random variables $y, x_1, x_2, \ldots, x_n$. The population means of this list of random variables are denoted $Ey, Ex_1, \ldots, Ex_n$. We assume that these means are finite, as are the population second moments Ey^2, $Ex_1^2, \ldots, Ex_n^2$. By the Cauchy–Schwarz inequality the following cross second moments exist and are finite:

$$
\begin{array}{ccccc}
Eyx_1 & Ex_1^2 & Ex_1x_2 & \cdots & Ex_1x_n \\
Eyx_2 & Ex_2x_1 & Ex_2^2 & \cdots & Ex_2x_n \\
\vdots & \vdots & & & \\
Eyx_n & Ex_nx_1 & Ex_nx_2 & \cdots & Ex_n^2.
\end{array}
$$

Consider estimating the random variable y on the basis of knowing values only for the random variables $x_1, \ldots, x_n$ as well as knowing all of the means and

223

second moments listed above.[1] More specifically, suppose we restrict ourselves to estimating y by the linear function[2] of the x_i,

$$\hat{y} = a_0 + a_1 x_1 + \cdots + a_n x_n. \tag{1}$$

We seek to choose the a_i so that the random variable $\hat{y}$ is as "close" to y as possible, in the least squares sense that $E(y - \hat{y})^2$ is a minimum. Thus, our problem is to minimize

$$E(y - (a_0 + a_1 x_1 + \cdots + a_n x_n))^2 \tag{2}$$

with respect to $a_0, a_1, \ldots, a_n$. To facilitate the computations, let us define the new (trivial) random variable $x_0 \equiv 1$.

We are now in a position to state the *orthogonality principle*:

A necessary and sufficient set of conditions for $a_0, a_1, \ldots, a_n$ to minimize (2) is

$$E\{(y - (a_0 + a_1 x_2 + \cdots + a_n x_n))x_i\} = 0, \qquad i = 0, 1, \ldots, n. \tag{3}$$

Condition (3) says that $E(y - \hat{y})x_i = 0$ for all i. Two random variables w and z are said to be *orthogonal* if $E(wz) = 0$. Thus, (3) asserts that $y - \hat{y}$ is orthogonal to each x_i, $i = 0, \ldots, n$. The orthogonality principle asserts that the condition $E(y - \hat{y})x_i = 0$ for each i uniquely determines $\hat{y}$. (It will also uniquely determine the a_i if there is no linear dependence among the x_i.)

To prove the orthogonality principle, we proceed by minimizing

$$J = E\left(y - \sum_{i=0}^{n} a_i x_i\right)^2.$$

Differentiating J with respect to a_k gives

$$-\frac{\partial J}{\partial a_k} = 2E\left(y - \sum_{i=0}^{n} a_i x_i\right)x_k = 0, \qquad k = 0, 1, \ldots, n,$$

or

$$Eyx_k - \sum_{i=0}^{n} a_i Ex_i x_k = 0, \qquad k = 0, 1, \ldots, n. \tag{4}$$

---

[1] Luenberger (1969) and Naylor and Sell (1982) contain good treatments of inner product spaces, and of the technical results used in this chapter. The reader with some background in econometrics will note that we are *not* studying the "general linear model," (e.g., see Johnston, 1963, Chapter 4), which assumes that the right-hand side x variables are nonstochastic.

[2] The restriction to a linear function is in general a binding one. It is possible to show that to minimize $E\{y - g(x_1, \ldots, x_n)\}^2$ with respect to the choice of $g(x_1, \ldots, x_n)$, the optimal thing to do is to set $g(x_1, \ldots, x_n) = E[y|x_1, \ldots, x_n]$, the mathematical expectation of y conditional on $x_1, \ldots, x_n$. In general, the mathematical expectation $E[y|x_1, \ldots, x_n]$ is *not* a linear function of $x_1, \ldots, x_n$. In the special case that the variates $(y, x_1, \ldots, x_n)$ follow a multivariate normal distribution, the conditional mathematical expectation $E[y|x_1, \ldots, x_n]$ is linear in $x_1, \ldots, x_n$.

Clearly, these "normal equations" are equivalent with the orthogonality condition (3). Let x be the $1 \times (n + 1)$ row vector $x = (x_0, x_1, \ldots, x_n)$ and a the $(n + 1) \times 1$ column vector $a = (a_0, a_1, \ldots, a_n)'$. Then we can write the least squares normal equations (4) compactly as

$$Ex'y = (Ex'x)a.$$

Since $Ex'x$ is a nonnegative definite matrix, we are assured by the second-order conditions that the mean squared error J is minimized by choosing the a's to satisfy (4). This completes the proof of the orthogonality principle.

The orthogonality condition (3) in effect asserts that the "forecast error" $y - \sum_{i=0}^{n} a_i x_i$ is orthogonal to each of the x_i and therefore is also orthogonal to any linear combination of the x_i. Defining the forecast error as $\varepsilon = y - \sum_{i=0}^{n} a_i x_i$, we therefore have

$$y = \sum_{i=0}^{n} a_i x_i + \varepsilon \tag{5}$$

where $E(\varepsilon \sum_{i=0}^{n} a_i x_i) = 0$ and $E\varepsilon x_i = 0$ for $i = 0, 1, \ldots, n$.

Thus, (5) decomposes y into orthogonal parts. By virtue of the orthogonality of the random variables $\sum_{i=0}^{n} a_i x_i$ and ε we have the decomposition

$$Ey^2 = E\left(\sum_{i=0}^{n} a_i x_i\right)^2 + E\varepsilon^2.$$

The random variable $\sum_{i=0}^{n} a_i x_i$, where the a_i are chosen to satisfy the least squares orthogonality condition (3), is called the *projection* of y on $x_0, x_1, \ldots, x_n$. We shall find it convenient to denote the projection of y on $x_0, x_1, \ldots, x_n$ as

$$\sum_{i=0}^{n} a_i x_i \equiv P[y \mid 1, x_1, x_2, \ldots, x_n],$$

where remember that $x_0 = 1$ identically.

The orthogonality conditions (3) can be readily rearranged in the form of the familiar least squares normal equations. Write (3) explicitly for $i = 0, 1, \ldots, n$ to get the normal equations

$$\begin{bmatrix} Ey \\ Eyx_1 \\ Eyx_2 \\ \vdots \\ Exy_n \end{bmatrix} = \begin{bmatrix} 1 & Ex_1 & Ex_2 & \cdots & Ex_n \\ Ex_1 & Ex_1{}^2 & Ex_1 x_2 & \cdots & Ex_1 x_n \\ Ex_2 & Ex_1 x_2 & Ex_2{}^2 & \cdots & Ex_2 x_n \\ \vdots & & & & \\ Ex_n & Ex_1 x_n & Ex_2 x_n & \cdots & Ex_n{}^2 \end{bmatrix} \begin{bmatrix} a_0 \\ a_1 \\ a_2 \\ \vdots \\ a_n \end{bmatrix}. \tag{6}$$

Assuming that the $(n + 1) \times (n + 1)$ matrix above has an inverse, we have the following explicit equation for the a_i:

$$
\begin{bmatrix} a_0 \\ a_1 \\ \vdots \\ a_n \end{bmatrix} = [Ex_i x_j]^{-1} [Eyx_k] \tag{7}
$$

where $[Ex_i x_j]^{-1}$ is the inverse of the matrix with $(i + 1, j + 1)$th element $Ex_i x_j$, and $[Eyx_k]$ is the $(n + 1) \times 1$ vector with $(k + 1)$th element Eyx_k.

As an example, consider projecting y against a single variate x_1 (as well as the trivial variate $x_0 = 1$). Then (6) becomes

$$
\begin{bmatrix} Ey \\ Eyx_1 \end{bmatrix} = \begin{bmatrix} 1 & Ex_1 \\ Ex_1 & Ex_1{}^2 \end{bmatrix} \begin{bmatrix} a_0 \\ a_1 \end{bmatrix}.
$$

The solution of these two equations turns out to be

$$
a_0 = Ey - a_1 Ex_1, \qquad a_1 = \frac{E(y - Ey)(x_1 - Ex_1)}{E(x_1 - Ex_1)^2}.
$$

Denote the covariance between y and x_1 as $\sigma_{x_1 y} = E\{(y - Ey)(x_1 - Ex_1)\}$ and the variance of x_1 as $\sigma_{x_1}^2 = E\{(x_1 - Ex_1)^2\}$. Then the equations for a_1 and a_0 become the familiar

$$
a_0 = Ey - a_1 Ex_1, \qquad a_1 = \frac{\sigma_{x_1 y}}{\sigma_{x_1}^2}. \tag{8}
$$

2. RECURSIVE PROJECTION

It happens that the simple univariate formulas (8) can be used in a recursive way to assemble projections on many variables, e.g., $P[y|1, x_1, \ldots, x_n]$. This often affords a computational saving, and also carries insights about sequential learning.

Write the decomposition (5) for $n = 2$ as

$$
y = P[y|1, x_1, x_2] + \varepsilon, \qquad y = a_0 + a_1 x_1 + a_2 x_2 + \varepsilon \tag{9}
$$

where $E\varepsilon = 0$, $E\varepsilon x_1 = 0$, and $E\varepsilon x_2 = 0$. These three orthogonality conditions ensure that the a_i are the least squares parameter values. Now project both sides of (9) against 1 and x_1 to obtain the equation[3]

$$
P[y|1, x_1] = a_0 + a_1 x_1 + a_2 P[x_2|1, x_1]. \tag{10}
$$

---

[3] The projection operator is *linear* in the sense that for any two random variables y_1 and y_2 and any real constants c and d,

$$
P[cy_1 + dy_2|x_0, x_1, \ldots, x_n] = cP[y_1|x_0, x_1, \ldots, x_n] + dP[y_2|x_0, \ldots, x_n].
$$

To prove this equality, simply write out the normal equations for the projections on both sides of the asserted equality.

To get from (9) to (10) we have used the facts that

$$P[a_0|1, x_1] = a_0, \qquad P[x_1|1, x_1] = x_1, \qquad P[\varepsilon|1, x_1] = 0.$$

The first two came directly from application of the orthogonality principle to the problem of computing the indicated projection. More directly, it is clear that $E\{a_0 - t_0 - t_1 x_1\}^2$ is minimized by setting $t_0 = a_0$ and $t_1 = 0$. Similarly, $E\{x_1 - t_0 - t_1 x_1\}^2$ is minimized by setting $t_0 = 0$ and $t_1 = 1$. The last of the three equalities above comes from noting that from the orthogonality conditions in (9), $E\varepsilon = E\varepsilon x_1 = 0$. Substituting these into the least squares normal equations for $P[\varepsilon|1, x_1]$ shows that $P[\varepsilon|1, x_1] = 0$.

Subtracting (10) from (9) gives

$$y - P[y|1, x_1] = a_2(x_2 - P[x_2|1, x_1]) + \varepsilon \tag{11}$$

where we repeat that $E\varepsilon = E\varepsilon x_1 = E\varepsilon x_2 = 0$. Let $P[x_2|1, x_1] = b_0 + b_1 x_1$. The orthogonality conditions imply that

$$
\begin{aligned}
E[\varepsilon(x_2 - P[x_2|1, x_1])] &= E[\varepsilon(x_2 - b_0 - b_1 x_1)] \\
&= E\varepsilon x_2 - b_0 E\varepsilon - b_1 E\varepsilon x_1 = 0.
\end{aligned}
$$

Thus ε is orthogonal to $x_2 - P[x_2|1, x_1]$. The orthogonality principle therefore implies that $a_2(x_2 - P[x_2|1, x_1])$ must be the projection of $y - P[y|1, x_1]$ against $(x_2 - P[x_2|1, x_1])$. Thus, (11) can be rewritten

$$y = P[y|1, x_1] + P[(y - P[y|1,x_1])|(x_2 - P[x_2|1, x_1])] + \varepsilon. \tag{12}$$

Notice that by virtue of the orthogonality conditions on ε (12) implies

$$P[y|1, x_1, x_2] = P[y|1, x_1] + P[(y - P[y|1, x_1])|(x_2 - P[x_2|1, x_1])].$$

Let

$$P[y|1, x_1] = c_0 + c_1 x_1,$$
$$P[x_2|1, x_1] = b_0 + b_1 x_1,$$

$$P[(y - P[y|1, x_1])|(x_2 - P[x_2|1, x_1])] = d_0 + d_1(x_2 - b_0 - b_1 x_1).$$

(Actually, from (11), we know that $d_0 = 0$.) Then (12) can be written

$$
\begin{aligned}
y &= c_0 + c_1 x_1 + d_0 + d_1(x_2 - b_0 - b_1 x_1) + \varepsilon \\
&= (c_0 + d_0 - d_1 b_0) + (c_1 - b_1 d_1)x_1 + d_1 x_2 + \varepsilon.
\end{aligned} \tag{13}
$$

Comparing (9) with (13), we have

$$a_0 = (c_0 + d_0 - d_1 b_0) = (c_0 - d_1 b_0), \qquad a_1 = (c_1 - b_1 d_1), \qquad a_2 = d_1. \tag{14}$$

The relations (14) give the coefficients in the bivariate projection $P[y|1, x_1, x_2]$ in terms of the parameters of three univariate projections.

Equation (12) is a useful description of optimal least squares learning or sequential estimation. If at first we have data only on a variable x_1, the linear least squares estimates of y and x_2 are $P[y|1, x_1]$ and $P[x_2|1, x_1]$, respectively. If an observation x_2 subsequently becomes available, our estimate of y can be improved by adding to $P[y|1, x_1]$ the projection of the unobserved "forecast error" $y - P[y|1, x_1]$ on the observed forecast error $x_2 - P[x_2|1, x_1]$. So long as these forecast errors are correlated, the new observation on x_2 carries information useful for estimating y.

By induction (or by suitably interpreting x in (12) as a vector of random variables) it is straightforward to extend (12) to the vector form

$$P[y|\Omega, x] = P[y|\Omega] + P[(y - P[y|\Omega])|(x - P[x|\Omega])] \qquad (15)$$

where Ω is a list of random variables and x a random variable. The practical implication of (12) and (15) is that the multivariable regression (15) can be built up sequentially from a set of univariate regressions.

Somewhat more generally, where Ω is one vector of random variables and $x = (x_1, \ldots, x_n)$ is another vector of random variables there obtains the recursive projection formula[4]

$$P[y|\Omega, x] = P[y|\Omega] + P[y - P(y|\Omega)|x - P(x|\Omega)] \qquad (15')$$

where $x - P(x|\Omega)$ is the vector $x_1 - P(x_1|\Omega), \ldots, x_n - P(x_n|\Omega)$.

The recursive relation (15) is the foundation of *Kalman filtering*, a technique widely used by engineers. We shall see how the sequential learning mechanism in (15) was exploited by Lucas in obtaining his model of the Phillips curve.

3. THE LAW OF ITERATED PROJECTIONS

From (15) it is easy to deduce a fundamental relation which has been dubbed the *law of iterated projections*. In particular, project the random variable $P[y|\Omega, x]$ against the set of information Ω. Then this law states

$$P[P[y|\Omega, x]|\Omega] = P[y|\Omega].$$

To prove the law, write (15) as

$$P[y|\Omega, x] = P[y|\Omega] + a(x - P[x|\Omega])$$

where the fixed number a is given by

$$a = \frac{E(y - P[y|\Omega])(x - P[x|\Omega])}{E(x - P[x|\Omega])^2}.$$

---

[4] To prove that Equation (15') holds, note that by the orthogonality principle each element of the vector $x - P(x|\Omega)$ is orthogonal to each element of Ω. Further, the linear space spanned by (Ω, x) is the same linear space spanned by $(\Omega, x - P(x|\Omega))$. Therefore

$$P[y|\Omega, x] = P[y|\Omega] + P[y|x - P(x|\Omega)]. \qquad (*)$$

Since $P[P(y|\Omega)|x - P(x|\Omega)] = 0$ because $x - P(x|\Omega)$ is orthogonal to Ω and therefore to $P(y|\Omega)$, formula (15') follows by subtracting $0 = P[P(y|\Omega)|x - P(x|\Omega)]$ from $(*)$.

Project both sides of the above equation against Ω and note that by the orthogonality principle $P[(x - P[x|\Omega])|\Omega] = 0$, and of course $P[P[y|\Omega]|\Omega] = P[y|\Omega]$ since $P[y|\Omega]$ is a linear combination of elements in Ω. This proves the law.

4. THE SIGNAL-EXTRACTION PROBLEM

Suppose an agent wants to estimate a random variable s but only "sees" the random variable x which is related to s by

$$x = s + n$$

where $Esn = 0$; Es^2, $En^2 < \infty$; $Es = En = 0$. One interpretation is that x differs from s by the measurement error n. The linear least squares estimate of s is

$$P[s|1, x] = a_0 + a_1 x.$$

The least squares normal equations become

$$a_1 = \frac{E(xs)}{Ex^2} = \frac{E((s + n)s)}{E(s + n)^2}, \qquad a_1 = \frac{Es^2}{Es^2 + En^2}, \qquad a_0 = 0.$$

As a slightly richer example, consider a worker who wants to estimate (the log of) his real wage $w - p$. He "sees" the random variable w, but does not see the pertinent p at the time that he makes his decision to work. Suppose that the log wage w and log price p obey

$$w = z + u, \qquad p = z + v,$$

and $Ezu = Ezv = Euv = Eu = Ez = Ev = 0$. Here z represents neutral movements in the aggregate price level that leave the real wage unaltered. The variates u and v represent factors calling for real wage changes. The worker's linear least squares estimate of $w - p$ based on observing w and knowing the first and second moments of all random variables is

$$P[(w - p)|1, w] = a_0 + a_1 w.$$

We have

$$w - p = u - v, \qquad w = z + u.$$

So the normal equations imply

$$a_0 = 0, \qquad a_1 = \frac{E[(u - v)(z + u)]}{E[(z + u)^2]}, \qquad a_1 = \frac{Eu^2}{Ez^2 + Eu^2}.$$

Notice that $0 < a_1 < 1$, and that the greater is Eu^2/Ez^2, the closer to unity is a_1. That makes sense since the greater is Eu^2/Ez^2, the larger is the fraction of variance in w that is due to variation in the real-wage determining factor u.

5. SIGNAL EXTRACTION WITH DYNAMICS

We now use the recursive projection formula (15′) to solve a signal extraction problem that John Muth (1960) used to provide a rationalization for Milton Friedman's formula for permanent income. This will lead us to a version of the Kalman filter.[5]

We consider the structure

$$\theta_{t+1} = \rho\theta_t + \varepsilon_{t+1} \tag{16}$$

$$z_t = c\theta_t + u_t \tag{17}$$

where ρ and c are scalars, ε_{t+1} is a random variable satisfying $E\varepsilon_t = 0$ for all t, $E\varepsilon_t^2 = \sigma_\varepsilon^2$ for all t, and $E\varepsilon_t\varepsilon_{t-s} = 0$ for $s \neq 0$. We assume that u_t is a random variable satisfying $Eu_t = 0$ for all t, $Eu_t^2 = \sigma_u^2$ for all t, $Eu_tu_{t-s} = 0$ for $s \neq 0$ and $Eu_t\varepsilon_s = 0$ for all t, s. Equation (16) states that θ_t is governed by a first-order linear stochastic difference equation, while equation (17) states that z_t is a linear combination of θ_t and a "noise" u_t. Given this structure, consider the following problem that is to be solved by an agent who knows the values of $(c, \rho, \sigma_u^2, \sigma_\varepsilon^2)$. At time t, the agent is supposed to see $(z_t, z_{t-1}, \ldots, z_0)$, but not to have seen θ_t for any t. Thus θ_t is a "hidden variable." At time 0, before observing z_0, the agent is supposed to have an initial idea about the location of θ_0, which can be summarized by saying that he thinks it is distributed with mean $\hat{\theta}_0$ and variance about $\hat{\theta}_0$ of Σ_0. The agent's problem is to calculate $P[\theta_{t+1}|z_t, z_{t-1}, \ldots, z_0]$. Using (15′), we shall derive a convenient recursive formula for this projection.

We define $\hat{\theta}_{t+1} = P[\theta_{t+1}|z_t, z_{t-1}, \ldots, z_0]$. In (15′), at $t \geq 1$, we let $y = \theta_{t+1}$, $\Omega = (z_{t-1}, z_{t-2}, \ldots, z_0)$, $x = z_t$. Then in light of (16)–(17), and using $P[\varepsilon_{t+1}|z_t, z_{t-1}, \ldots, z_0] = 0$ and the orthogonality conditions assumed for (ε_{t+1}, u_t), (15′) becomes

$$P[\theta_{t+1}|z_t, z_{t-1}, \ldots, z_0] = P[\rho\theta_t|z_{t-1}, z_{t-2}, \ldots, z_0]$$
$$+ P[(\rho\theta_t - P[\rho\theta_t|z_{t-1}, \ldots, z_0])|(z_t - P[z_t|z_{t-1}, \ldots, z_0]).$$

or

$$\hat{\theta}_{t+1} = \rho\hat{\theta}_t + P[\rho(\theta_t - \hat{\theta}_t)|(c(\theta_t - \hat{\theta}_t) + u_t)] \tag{18}$$

where in the last line we use $z_t - P[z_t|z_{t-1}, \ldots, z_0] = c\theta_t + u_t - c\hat{\theta}_t$. Let us define

$$\Sigma_t = E(\theta_t - \hat{\theta}_t)^2. \tag{19}$$

Then we have that

$$P[\rho(\theta_t - \hat{\theta}_t)|c(\theta_t - \hat{\theta}_t) + u_t] = K_t[c(\theta_t - \hat{\theta}_t) + u_t] \tag{20}$$

---

[5] Anderson and Moore (1979) is a good source of results on recursive methods for solving prediction and filtering problems.

where

$$K_t = \frac{c\rho\Sigma_t}{c^2\Sigma_t + \sigma_u{}^2}. \tag{21}$$

In deriving (21), we use the orthogonality condition $Eu_t(\theta_t - \hat{\theta}_t) = 0$ which follows from (16)–(17) and the orthogonality conditions imposed on (ε_{t+1}, u_t). Substituting (20) into (18) and rearranging gives

$$\hat{\theta}_{t+1} = (\rho - K_t c)\hat{\theta}_t + K_t z_t. \tag{22}$$

Subtracting (22) from (16) and using (17) gives

$$\theta_{t+1} - \hat{\theta}_{t+1} = (\rho - K_t c)(\theta_t - \hat{\theta}_t) + \varepsilon_{t+1} - K_t u_t.$$

Computing variances gives

$$\Sigma_{t+1} = (\rho - K_t c)^2 \Sigma_t + \sigma_\varepsilon{}^2 + K_t{}^2 \sigma_u{}^2. \tag{23}$$

Equations (21), (22) and (23) are to be solved starting from the initial condition Σ_0 given. These three equations give a convenient recursive solution to our problem. The equations are a scalar version of the famous "Kalman filter."

By analyzing the pair of difference equations (21), (23), it is possible to establish the following two properties of the solution. First, for any value of ρ and for any value $c \neq 0$, starting the system from any $\Sigma_0 \geq 0$ leads to a Σ_t sequence that converges as $t \to \infty$. Second, for the same range of values of ρ and c, the parameter $(\rho - Kc)$, where $K = \lim_{t\to\infty} K_t$, is less than unity in absolute value. This implies that for the infinite history filtering problem, in which the agent is imagined to form $\hat{\theta}_{t+1} = P[\theta_{t+1}|z_t, z_{t-1}, \ldots]$ by projecting on an infinite record of current and past z's, the solution can be represented by the time invariant equation

$$\hat{\theta}_{t+1} = (\rho - Kc)\hat{\theta}_t + Kz_t \tag{24}$$

where $|(\rho - Kc)| < 1$, and K is the unique stationary solution of (21) and (23) that is associated with a stationary solution for which $\lim \Sigma_t = \Sigma > 0$. Equation (24) can be solved to give a version of Friedman and Cagan's formula

$$\hat{\theta}_{t+1} = K \sum_{j=0}^{\infty} (\rho - Kc)^j z_{t-j}. \tag{25}$$

Muth considered the case in which $c = 1$, $\rho = 1$. In this case, (25) becomes exactly the adaptive expectations mechanism that was used by Friedman and Cagan.

Note that the orthogonality conditions imposed on the (ε, u) process imply that

$$P[\theta_{t+j}|z_t, z_{t-1}, \ldots] = \rho^{j-1}\hat{\theta}_{t+1} \qquad \text{for} \quad j \geq 1. \tag{26}$$

6. THE TERM STRUCTURE OF INTEREST RATES

Meiselman's[6] error-learning model of the term structure of interest rates can be described quite compactly and motivated elegantly by using our results on recursive regression. The term structure of interest rates refers to interest rates on assets of similar quality but varying terms to maturity viewed as a function of the yield to maturity. The *yield curve* is a graph of yields to maturity against the maturity. The *yield to maturity* on a bond is defined as the (single) yield that makes the present value of the bond's (expected) stream of payments just equal to the present market price of the bond. The yield to maturity is seen to be equivalent with Keynes's "internal rate of return."

Let R_{nt} be the yield to maturity at time t on a bond that will mature at time $t + n$. Irving Fisher and John Hicks suggested viewing the n-period yield as an average of the current one-period yield and a sequence of one-period forward rates, which we approximate by the formula

$$R_{nt} = n^{-1}[R_{1t} + {}_{t+1}F_{1t} + {}_{t+2}F_{1t} + \cdots + {}_{t+n-1}F_{1t}], \qquad n = 1, 2, \ldots, \quad (27)$$

where ${}_{t+j}F_{1t}$ is the one-period forward rate that at time t pertains to one-period loans to be made at time $t + j$ and mature at time $t + j + 1$.[7] Equation (27) for $n = 1, 2, \ldots$ actually *defines* the forward rates ${}_{t+j}F_{1t}$ as functions of the observable yields $R_{1t}, R_{2t}, R_{3t}, \ldots$. Thus, using (27), we have

$$2R_{2t} = R_{1t} + {}_{t+1}F_{1t} \qquad \text{or} \qquad {}_{t+1}F_{1t} = 2R_{2t} - R_{1t}.$$

Similarly, we could calculate

$$_{t+j}F_{1t} = (j + 1)R_{j+1, t} - jR_{jt}, \qquad j = 1, 2, \ldots.$$

Now markets in forward loans (i.e., contracts executed at time t for loans to extend between some times $t + j$ to $t + k, k > j > 0$) do not literally exist, as futures markets do in some commodities like wheat and corn. Fisher and Hicks' point was that it was fruitful to decompose a given long rate into the implicit one-period forward rates composing it. Thus, a loan for two periods made at time t is viewed as a one-period (spot) loan made at time t plus a forward commitment entered into at time t to extend the loan for one additional period at time $t + 1$.

So far, all of this has been tautological since (27) is only a *definition* of forward rates. Hicks added content to (27) by adopting the expectations hypothesis, asserting that speculators would force forward yields into equality

---

[6] The present description of Meiselman's model is along the lines developed after Meiselman by Mincer, Pye, Diller, Shiller, and Nelson. For a useful survey of this literature, see Shiller (1978).

[7] This formula is an arithmetic approximation to Hicks's formula. Hicks's formula assumes discount bonds that have zero coupons. See Hicks (1939).

with the spot one-period rates that they expect to hold on the dates to which the forward rates pertain:

$$_{t+j}F_{1t} = \hat{R}_{1,t+j} \tag{28}$$

where $\hat{R}_{1t+j}$ is speculators' forecast of the one-period rate which, as of time t, they expect to prevail at time $t + j$. Hicks's argument was that unless (28) held speculators could always increase their expected returns by the appropriate combination of issuing and purchasing debts of various maturities. Thus, suppose that we have the following situation:

$$(R_{1t} = 0.05, R_{2t} = 0.04) \quad \Rightarrow \quad _{t+1}F_{1t} = 0.03;$$

$$\hat{R}_{1t+1} = 0.05.$$

Speculators expect one-period rates to remain stable between period one and two, but the two-period rate is below the one-period rate, indicating that the one-period forward rate is below the one-period spot rate. In this situation speculators could increase their expected returns, say by borrowing for two periods (at 0.04 per period for two periods) and putting the proceeds into a one-period bond the first period (at 0.05) and another one-period bond the second period (at a return that they expect to be 0.05). By executing this transaction, the speculator expects to get a net return of 0.01 of the amount borrowed each period. (Notice that the speculator need put up no money of his own. Notice also, however, that the speculator is undertaking a risky investment since the return is not a sure thing—the investor is not in an arbitrage situation where the returns are sure.) Hicks entertained the hypothesis that speculators would dominate the market and force (28) to hold.

To make (28) operational suppose we adopt a version of Muth's (1961) hypothesis of "rational expectations" and assume that $\hat{R}_{1t+j}$ is formed as the projection of R_{1t+j} against current and lagged spot rates $R_{1t}, R_{1t-1}, \ldots$. Then (28) becomes

$$_{t+j}F_{1t} = P[R_{1t+j}|1, R_{1t}, R_{1t-1}, \ldots]. \tag{29}$$

Applying our recursive regression formula (15), we have

$$P[R_{1t+j}|1, R_{1t+1}, R_{1t}, \ldots] = P[R_{1t+j}|1, R_{1t}, R_{1t-1}, \ldots]$$
$$+ b_j(R_{1t+1} - P[R_{1t+1}|1, R_{1t}, R_{1t-1}, \ldots]) \tag{30}$$

Substituting (29) into (30) gives

$$_{t+j}F_{1t+1} - {}_{t+j}F_{1t} = b_j(R_{1t+1} - {}_{t+1}F_{1t}). \tag{31}$$

Equation (31) is exactly the "error-learning" model proposed and implemented by Meiselman. Notice that (31) has no random disturbance, so that strictly speaking (31) should fit perfectly—the $\bar{R}^2$ statistic should be unity. In this sense high values of the $\bar{R}^2$ statistic confirm the theory. Meiselman estimated (31) for annual U.S. data over the period 1901–1954, found positive and statistically significant b_j, and found zero constant terms which (31) predicts (though as John Wood and Reuben Kessel pointed out, models other than Meiselman's might also be consistent with the zero intercept). Meiselman found moderately high values for the $\bar{R}^2$ statistics, though they were not all that close to unity (they ranged from 0.91 for $j = 1$ to 0.34 for $j = 8$).

It is straightforward to convert (31) into a regression equation with a disturbance. To illustrate how, suppose that speculators form their expectations at time t by projecting R_{1t+j} on a set $R_{1t}, R_{1t-1}, \ldots, y_t, y_{t-1}, \ldots$, where y_t is some random variable, distinct from R_{1t}, that is useful for forecasting R_{1t+j}. We can thus write

$$_{t+j}F_{1t} = P[R_{1t+j}|\Omega_t]$$

where $\Omega_t = R_{1t}, R_{1t-1}, \ldots, y_t, y_{t-1}, \ldots$. With little additional work, one can deduce the following bivariate version of our recursive learning formula (15):

$$P[R_{1t+j}|\Omega_{t+1}] - P[R_{1t+j}|\Omega_t] = \gamma_j(R_{1t+1} - P[R_{1t+1}|\Omega_t])$$
$$+ \beta_j(y_{t+1} - P[y_{t+1}|\Omega_t]), \qquad (32)$$

γ_j and β_j being the regression coefficients in the bivariate regression of $R_{1t+j} - P[R_{1t+j}|\Omega_t]$ regressed against $R_{1t+1} - P[R_{1t+1}|\Omega_t]$ and $y_{t+1} - P[y_{t+1}|\Omega_t]$.

Equation (32) is obviously in the same spirit as (15) and says that forecasts are revised according to the "surprising" information in the new observations y_{t+1} and R_{1t+1}. Equation (32) can be written

$$_{t+j}F_{1t+1} - {}_{t+j}F_{1t} = \gamma_j(R_{1t+1} - P[R_{1t+1}|\Omega_t]) + \beta_j(y_{t+1} - P[y_{t+1}|\Omega_t]). \quad (33)$$

Now simply project the right-hand side of the above equation against $R_{1t+1} - P[R_{1t+1}|\Omega_t]$ to get the representation

$$\gamma_j(R_{1t+1} - P[R_{1t+1}|\Omega_t]) + \beta_j(y_{t+1} - P[y_{t+1}|\Omega_t])$$
$$= \phi_j(R_{1t+1} - P[R_{1t+1}|\Omega_t]) + \varepsilon_{t+1} \qquad (34)$$

where

$$\phi_j = \frac{\beta_j E(R_{1t+1} - P[R_{1t+1}|\Omega_t])(y_{t+1} - P[y_{t+1}|\Omega_t])}{E(R_{1t+1} - P[R_{1t+1}|\Omega_t])^2} + \gamma_j$$

and where by the orthogonality principle ε_{t+1} is orthogonal to $R_{1t+1} - P[R_{1t+1}|\Omega_t]$. Substituting Equation (33) into Equation (34) gives

$$_{t+j}F_{1t+1} - {}_{t+j}F_{1t} = \phi_j(R_{1t+1} - {}_{t+1}F_{1t}) + \varepsilon_{t+1}, \qquad (35)$$

which is a regression equation that is in the form of Meiselman's error-learning model. The presence of the random term ε_{t+1} means that there is no implication that Equation (35) will bear a high $\bar{R}^2$ statistic.[8] High values of the $\bar{R}^2$ statistic would indicate that a large proportion of the information useful for forecasting interest rates is included in current and lagged one-period rates.

7. APPLICATION OF THE LAW OF ITERATED PROJECTIONS

Let us represent the expectations theory of the term structure in the form

$$_{t+j}F_{1t} = P[R_{1t+j}|\Omega_t], \qquad j = 1, 2, \ldots, \quad \text{all integer } t, \tag{36}$$

where $\Omega_t \supset \Omega_{t-1} \supset \Omega_{t-2} \supset \cdots$, so that Ω_t is an information set that includes all information available at time $t - 1$ and maybe some additional information. Applying the law of iterated projections to (36) gives

$$P[_{t+j}F_{1t}|\Omega_{t-1}] = P[P[R_{1t+j}|\Omega_t]|\Omega_{t-1}]$$
$$= P[R_{1t+j}|\Omega_{t-1}] = {}_{t+j}F_{t-1}$$

or

$$P[_{t+j}F_{1t}|\Omega_{t-1}] = {}_{t+j}F_{1t-1}. \tag{37}$$

A sequence of random variables

$$_{t+j}F_{1t-n}, \quad {}_{t+j}F_{1t-n+1}, \quad \cdots, \quad {}_{t+j}F_{1t} \tag{38}$$

with the property (37) is said to be a (weak) martingale with respect to Ω_{t-1}. It was Samuelson who first pointed out that the rational expectations theory of future markets implies that sequences of forward prices like (38) follow martingales (Samuelson, 1965).[9]

It is useful also to note that $P[(_{t+j}F_{1t} - {}_{t+j}F_{1t-1})|\Omega_{t-1}] = 0$ as a result of the law of iterated projections. This says that the revisions in the forecast of R_{1t+j} made between $t - 1$ and t cannot be predicted by a linear function of the information in Ω_{t-1}. This is a strong, testable implication of the theory.

8. CONCLUSIONS

The tools described in this chapter are workhorses in applied dynamic economics. We shall see in subsequent chapters how in the hands of Milton Friedman, John F. Muth, and Robert E. Lucas, Jr., the dynamic signal

[8] Further, notice that we have no restrictions on the signs of ϕ_j; they may be either positive or negative, depending on the various covariances among "surprises" that go into composing ϕ_j.

[9] Samuelson proved that a property analogous to (37) holds where linear projections are replaced by conditional mathematical expectations. A sequence that obeys that condition is called a martingale with respect to the conditioning information. For conditional expectations, there is a law of iterated expectations precisely paralleling the law of iterated projections. Given this law, Samuelson's theorem is proved in a similar fashion to the weak martingale theorem exhibited in the text.

extraction problem became an important tool for understanding the way "distributed lags" could arise in economic models.

The next chapter combines aspects of Chapters IX and X to study linear stochastic difference equations. The main idea is to discover a setting in which a sequence of dated scalar- or vector-valued variables, x_t, can be thought of as consisting of random variables, for which the second moments of x_t and x_s are defined for all possible t and s. In such a setting, the methods of this chapter can be used to calculate, say, the projection of x_t on $[x_{t-1}, \ldots, x_{t-n}]$ for each $n > 0$. Such a projection is known as a "vector autoregression," and is widely used for macroeconomic prediction, and also to create models of agents whose behavior is partly determined by their predictions.

EXERCISES[10]

1. Let the demand for money be governed by

$$m_t = p_t + ky + u_t$$

where $Eu_t = 0 = Eu_t m_t$. Here m_t is the log of the money supply, p_t the log of the price level, and y the constant level of the log of real income. Assume that Em_t^2 and Ep_t^2 exist.

Suppose that a researcher attempts to verify the absence of money illusion in this economy by estimating

$$m_t - \alpha p_t + \text{constant} + \text{residual}_t,$$

by least squares, and testing whether $\alpha = 1$. In arbitrarily large samples, will this procedure lead him to conclude the truth, namely that $\alpha = 1$? If this procedure is flawed provide a better one and defend it.

2. Suppose that the expectations theory of the term structure is correct and that

$$R_{2t} = \tfrac{1}{2}[R_{1t} + E_t R_{1t+1}]$$

where R_{nt} is the yield to maturity on an n-period bond and $E_t\{x\}$ is the mathematical expectation of x conditioned on information available at time t, assumed to include observations on past and present R_1 and R_2. Deduce the implications that the theory delivers for the population values of α, β, and λ in the following least squares regression

$$R_{2t} - \tfrac{1}{2}[R_{1t} + R_{1t+1}] = \alpha + \beta R_{2t-1} + \lambda R_{1t-1} + u_t$$

where u_t is a least squares residual obeying $Eu_t = Eu_t R_{2t-1} = Eu_t R_{1t-1} = 0$.

Use the following information to solve problems 3–8. Let Y and $X \equiv (x_0, x_1, \ldots, x_n)$ be random variables with known means and variances, with $x_0 \equiv 1$.

3. Prove that if $Ex_1 x_2 = 0$, then $P[Y|x_1, x_2] = P[Y|x_1] + P[Y|x_2]$.

4. Prove that if $E(x_1, x_2, \ldots, x_n) = (0, 0, \ldots, 0)$, then

$$P[Y|1, x_1, x_2, \ldots, x_n] = P[Y|1] + P[Y|x_1, x_2, \ldots, x_n].$$

5. Prove that if $Ex_1 x_2 = 0$, then $P[x_1|x_2] = 0$.

6. Let c, d be real numbers. Prove that $P[cY_1 + dY_2|X] = cP[Y_1|X] + dP[Y_2|X]$ where Y_1 and Y_2 are random variables.

---

[10] Exercises 6–10 were written by Charles Whiteman.

7. Use 3, 5, and 6 to prove the Kalman filter (recursive projection) formula, (15′):

$$P[Y|\Omega, X] = P[Y|\Omega] + P\{(Y - P[Y|\Omega])|(X - P[X|\Omega])\}$$

where Ω and X are random variables.

8. Interpret Y, Ω, and X as sets, and $P[Y|\Omega, X]$ as $Y(\Omega \ X)$. Derive the Kalman filter formula using Venn diagrams. (Interpret $Y - X$ as $Y \cap X^c$ where X^c is the complement of X.)

9. The labor supply schedule is given by

$$N_t = \gamma(w_t - \hat{E}p_t), \qquad \gamma > 0$$

where N_t is the logarithm of employment at time t, w_t is the logarithm of the money wage, and $\hat{E}p_t$ is the workers' perception of the average price of goods they will buy during period t. At the time that they see w_t and must make the decision to work or not, workers don't actually see the prices at which they will be able to buy goods. Instead, they must form their best guess about the average price at which they'll be able to buy things. Workers do know that the average price obeys

$$p_t = k + u_t$$

where k is a constant and u_t a serially uncorrelated random variable with mean zero and variance known by workers to be σ_u^2. The workers also know that w_t obeys

$$w_t = z_t + u_t$$

where z_t is a serially uncorrelated random variable with mean zero and variance σ_z^2. Assume also $Ez_t u_t = 0$. That is, u and z are uncorrelated. The variate z_t measures changes in actual real wages, while the variate u_t measures changes in w and p that actually leave the real wage unchanged. Workers know the value of w_t in each period and the parameters σ_u^2, σ_z^2, and k.

  A. Derive an operational labor supply schedule of the form

$$N_t = \phi w_t + h$$

where h is a constant, and derive explicit formulas linking h and ϕ to the parameters γ, σ_u^2 and σ_z^2.

  B. A researcher estimates the labor supply schedule, and finds $\phi > 0$ and a very high R^2. The researcher concludes that if the monetary authority wants to make N_t constant over time and equal to some high value N^*, it should follow a monetary policy that makes w constant over time at the value w that solves the equation

$$N^* = \phi w + h.$$

Is this a correct policy conclusion?

10. The consumption function is given by

$$C_t = c(Y_t - T_t^*)$$

where

$$C_t = \text{consumption at time } t$$

$$Y_t = \text{income at time } t$$

$$T_t^* = \text{consumers' perception of the taxes they will pay at time } t,$$

and c is the marginal propensity to consume out of (perceived) disposable income. At the time they make consumption decisions, agents do not know the taxes (T_t) they must pay at time t. Consumers do know that income is described by

$$Y_t = 3T_t + v_t$$

where v_t is a serially uncorrelated random variable with mean zero and variance σ_v^2. In addition, they know c, that $ET_t v_t = 0$ and the variance of T_t: $ET_t^2 = \sigma_T^2$.

A. Derive an operational consumption function of the form $C_t = \beta Y_t$ and give an explicit formula relating β to the parameters c, σ_v^2, and σ_T^2.

B. Suppose the Congress increases the volatility of taxes by an extraordinary amount. What happens to the consumption function?

REFERENCES

Anderson, B. D. O. and Moore, J. B. (1979). *Optimal Filtering*, Englewood Cliffs: Prentice-Hall.

Cagan, P. (1956). "The Monetary Dynamics of Hyperinflation." *Studies in the Quantity Theory of Money* (M. Friedman, ed.), Chicago, Illinois: University of Chicago Press.

Friedman, M. (1956). *A Theory of the Consumption Function*, Princeton, New Jersey: Princeton University Press.

Hicks, J. R. (1953). *Value and Capital*, London and New York: Oxford University Press.

Johnston, J. (1963). *Econometric Methods*, New York: McGraw-Hill.

Luenberger, D. G. (1969). *Optimization by Vector Space Methods*, New York: Wiley.

Meiselman, D. (1963). *The Term Structure of Interest Rates*, Englewood Cliffs, New Jersey: Prentice-Hall.

Muth, J. F. (1960). "Optimal Properties of Exponentially Weighted Forecasts." *Journal of the American Statistical Association*, Vol. 55, No. 290, pp. 299-306.

Muth, J. F. (1961). "Rational Expectations and the Theory of Price Movements." *Econometrica*, Vol. 29, No. 3, pp. 315-335.

Naylor, A. W. and Sell, G. R. (1982). *Linear Operator Theory in Engineering and Science*, 2nd ed., New York: Springer Verlag.

Samuelson, P. A. (1965). "Proof That Properly Anticipated Prices Fluctuate Randomly." *Industrial Management Review*, Vol. 6, No. 2, pp. 41-50.

Shiller, R. (1978). "Rational Expectations And the Dynamic Structure of Macroeconomic Models: A Critical Review." *Journal of Monetary Economics*, Vol. 4, No. 1.

CHAPTER XI

LINEAR STOCHASTIC DIFFERENCE EQUATIONS

1. INTRODUCTION

In Chapter IX, we studied linear difference equations of the form

$$(1 - a_1 L - \cdots - a_n L^n)y_t = x_t,\tag{1}$$

where $\{x_t\}_{t=-\infty}^{\infty}$ was taken to be a known sequence. We studied how to find the class of sequences $\{y_t\}$ that satisfy the difference equation and a set of prescribed boundary conditions on the $\{y_t\}$ sequence. Such a $\{y_t\}$ sequence was said to solve the difference equation.

The present chapter studies linear difference equations of the form (1) in which, rather than being a sequence of known numbers, $\{x_t\}$ is a sequence of independently and identically distributed random variables with known variance and mean. With this choice of mechanism for generating $\{x_t\}$, equation (1) is called a linear stochastic difference equation. A solution of such a difference equation is a sequence of random variables $\{y_t\}$. A sequence of random variables is called a stochastic process. While the x_t sequence is by assumption a stochastic process consisting of random variables that are independently and identically distributed over time, the y_t process that solves (1) will in general be correlated over time. That is, while the $\{x_t\}$ process by assumption satisfies

$$E(x_t - Ex_t)(x_{t+s} - Ex_{t+s}) = 0$$

for $s \neq 0$, for the y_t process in general $E(y_t - Ey_t)(y_{t+s} - Ey_{t+s}) \neq 0$ for $s \neq 0$. One way to characterize the solution of the difference equation is to summarize the second moments of the $\{y_t\}$ process and to describe how they depend on the a_j's of (1).

Stochastic difference equations provide a natural tool for interpreting and modeling economic time series. Macroeconomists spend much of their time interpreting sample first and second moments of observed time series. For example, for an observed sample on two variables $(y_t, z_t, t = 1, \ldots, T)$ we often calculate various of the sample moments

$$T^{-1} \sum_{t=1}^{T} y_t, \quad T^{-1} \sum_{t=1}^{T} z_t,$$

$$(T - k)^{-1} \sum_{t=k+1}^{T} y_t y_{t-k},$$

$$(T - k)^{-1} \sum_{t=k+1}^{T} y_t z_{t-k},$$

and

$$(T - k)^{-1} \sum_{t=k+1}^{T} z_t y_{t-k}$$

for various values of k. It is convenient to adopt a mathematical context in which these sample moments can be regarded as estimators of the population moments $Ey_t, Ez_t, Ey_t y_{t-k}, Ey_t z_{t-k}$, and $Ez_t y_{t-k}$, respectively, estimators which converge to these population moments as $T \to \infty$. Linear stochastic difference equations provide such a mathematical context. In studying how to solve stochastic difference equations, one of our intermediate goals is to learn how the coefficients a_j of (1) can be chosen in order to make the implied pattern of population moments $Ey_t y_{t-k}$ resemble $(T - k)^{-1} \sum_{t=k+1}^{T} y_t y_{t-k}$ as the lag k is varied.

Stochastic processes provide a natural context in which to formulate the problem of prediction. At time t, suppose that observations on a stochastic process $(y_{t+1}, y_{t+2}, \ldots)$ have not yet been revealed, but that observations on $(y_t, y_{t-1}, \ldots)$ are available. Suppose that the moments Ey_t and $Ey_t y_{t-k}$ are known for all t and k. Then what is the best way to predict $(y_{t+1}, y_{t+2}, \ldots)$ as a linear function of $(y_t, y_{t-1}, \ldots)$? This linear prediction problem was solved by Wiener and Kolmogorov in the late 1930s.

The linear prediction problem is of interest to macroeconomists for at least two reasons. First, macroeconomists are interested in modeling the behavior of agents who are operating in dynamic and uncertain contexts. Typically, the hypothesis of utility or profit maximization ends up confronting those agents with some version of a prediction problem that they must solve in order best to achieve their objective. As we shall see, by using prediction theory, it is possible to extend the solutions of the quadratic dynamic optimization problems that were encountered in Chapter IX to the case in which the forcing functions are stochastic processes whose future values are not known at the time when decisions must be made. Thus, prediction theory is an important tool in determining optimizing behavior under uncertainty.

Second, macroeconomists are interested in using their own models of economic time series (often a collection of estimated a_j's in (1) or estimated moments $Ey_t y_{t-k}$) in order to predict the future conditional on the past. When the econometric model occurs in the form of a vector version of (1), it is said to be a *vector autoregression*. Linear prediction theory applies directly to such a model.

One of the goals of much recent work in rational expectations economics has been to create models whose equilibria are vector stochastic difference equations. In these models, the outcome of the interaction of a collection of purposeful agents is a stochastic process for, say, prices and quantities whose evolution can be described by a (vector) stochastic difference equation. We shall study versions of such models in which the equilibria are described by linear stochastic difference equations, i.e., vector versions of (1). In such models, some of the a_j's become interpretable in terms of the purposeful behavior of the agents in the model; that is, they are functions of the parameters of people's objective functions and constraints. One goal of this line of research is to acquire the ability to predict how the equilibrium stochastic process (or difference equation) would change in response to hypothetical changes in particular aspects of the environment confronting the agents in the model.

The idea that low order linear stochastic difference equations could provide a useful model for business cycles can be traced back at least as far as Slutsky (1937) and Frisch (1933). We have seen in Chapter IX that low order nonstochastic linear difference equations with no forcing functions present (i.e., $x_t = 0$ for all t in (1)) result in solutions for y_t that are "smooth," being the weighted sum of a small number of geometric sequences. Such smooth sequences do not resemble observed economic time series. However, if a sufficiently erratic forcing sequence $\{x_t\}$ occurs in (1), the resulting $\{y_t\}$ sequence that solves (1) can be sufficiently erratic that it resembles observed economic time series. The idea of Slutsky was to make the $\{x_t\}$ sequence sufficiently erratic by choosing it as the realization of a sequence of independently and identically distributed random variables. The resulting realizations of the $\{y_t\}$ sequence that solves[1] (1) would be erratic enough to resemble observed time series. As we shall see, even first-order stochastic linear difference equations ($n = 1$ in (1)) can generate realizations that look like observed economic time series. Furthermore, the hypothesis that $\{x_t\}$ is a sequence of independently and identically distributed random variables in general implies that the future values $(y_{t+1}, y_{t+2}, \ldots)$ are at best imperfectly predictable from past values $(y_t, y_{t-1}, \ldots)$. It is desirable to have models in which both economic agents and econometricians confront uncertainty in this sense. This is one major reason that Slutsky's idea was adopted early on in dynamic econometrics, and why it has been retained and expanded upon in work on rational expectations.

---

[1] Here "solve" refers to the ordinary sense used in Chapter IX of finding a $\{y_t\}$ sequence that satisfies (1) given the realization of the $\{x_t\}$ sequence.

2. PRELIMINARY CONCEPTS[2]

A *stochastic process* is a collection of random variables, a collection indexed by a variable t. In our work we shall regard t as time and will require t to be an integer, so that we shall be working in discrete time. Thus, the stochastic process y_t is a collection of random variables $\ldots y_{-1}, y_0, y_1, y_2, \ldots$, there being one random variable for each point in time t belonging to the set T, which in our case is the set of integers. Alternatively, on each "drawing," we draw an entire *sequence* $\{y_k\}_{k=-\infty}^{\infty}$. We are interested in the probability distribution of such sequences. A single drawing of a sequence $\{y_k\}$ is called a *realization* of the stochastic process y_t.

We shall characterize the probability law governing the collection of random variables that make up the stochastic process by the list of means of y_t and by the covariances between y's at different points in time. (For a stochastic process that obeys the normal probability law, these parameters completely characterize the probability distribution. Even where y is not normal, the first and second moments contain much useful information, enough information to characterize the linear structure of the process.) In particular, we have that the mean of the process y_t is

$$Ey_t = \mu_t, \qquad t \in T,$$

where E is the mathematical expectation operator. The covariances are given by

$$E[(y_t - \mu_t)(y_s - \mu_s)] = \sigma_{t,s}.$$

A stochastic process is said to be wide-sense *stationary* (or covariance stationary or second-order stationary) if μ_t is independent of t and if $\sigma_{t,s}$ depends only on $t - s$. We shall henceforth deal with such stationary processes. The first and second moments of a stationary process are summarized by the mean μ and the *covariogram* $c(\tau)$ defined by

$$E[(y_t - \mu)(y_s - \mu)] = \sigma_{t,s} = E[(y_t - \mu)(y_{t-\tau} - \mu)] = \sigma_{t,t-\tau} \equiv c(\tau)$$

where $\tau = t - s$. The covariogram is easily verified to be symmetric, i.e., $c(\tau) = c(-\tau)$, and to obey $c(0) \geq |c(\tau)|$ for all τ, this inequality being an implication of the Schwarz inequality.

To find further restrictions on the covariogram let x_t be a covariance stationary stochastic process with mean zero and covariogram $c(\tau)$. Consider forming a weighted sum of x's at different dates

$$y = \sum_{j=1}^{n} a_j x_{t_j}$$

---

[2] The reader is assumed to be familiar with complex variables. The chapter on complex variables in Allen (1960) is a good place to start. See Churchill, Brown, and Verhey (1974) for a more extensive treatment.

where the a_j are fixed real numbers and $t_1, \ldots, t_n$ are integers. We must require that the random variable y have nonnegative variance, so that

$$Ey^2 = E\left(\sum_{j=1}^{n} a_j x_{t_j} \sum_{k=1}^{n} a_k x_{t_k} \right) = \sum_{j=1}^{n} \sum_{k=1}^{n} a_j a_k E x_{t_k} x_{t_j}$$

$$= \sum_{j=1}^{n} \sum_{k=1}^{n} a_j a_k c(t_k - t_j) \geq 0.$$

This last inequality is required to hold for any n, any list of a_j, and any selection of $(t_1, t_2, \ldots, t_n)$. A sequence $c(\tau)$ that satisfies this condition is said to be "nonnegative definite." The condition that $c(\tau)$ be nonnegative definite is a necessary and sufficient condition for a sequence $c(\tau)$ to be the covariogram of a well-defined stochastic process.[3]

A basic building block is the serially uncorrelated random process ε_t, which satisfies:

$$\begin{aligned} E(\varepsilon_t) &= 0 & \text{for all } t, \\ E(\varepsilon_t^{\,2}) &= \sigma_\varepsilon^{\,2} & \text{for all } t, \\ E(\varepsilon_t \varepsilon_{t-s}) &= 0 & \text{all } t \text{ and all } s \neq 0. \end{aligned} \tag{2}$$

This process is (wide-sense) stationary, each variate being uncorrelated with itself lagged $s = \pm 1, \pm 2, \ldots$ times, and is said to be serially uncorrelated. The process is also often referred to as "white noise." As we shall see, such a white-noise process can be viewed as the basic building block for a large class of stationary stochastic processes.

To illustrate how the white-noise process ε_t can be used to build up more complicated processes, consider the random process y_t

$$y_t = \sum_{j=0}^{\infty} b_j \varepsilon_{t-j} = B(L)\varepsilon_t \tag{3}$$

where $B(L) = \sum_{j=0}^{\infty} b_j L^j$, and where we assume $\sum_{j=0}^{\infty} b_j^{\,2} < \infty$, a requirement needed to assure that the variance of y is finite. We assume that the ε process is "white" and thus satisfies properties (2). Equation (3) says that the y process is a one-sided moving sum of a white-noise process ε.

We seek the covariogram of the y process, i.e., we seek the values of $c_y(k) = E(y_t y_{t-k})$ for all k. It will be convenient to obtain the *covariance generating function* $g_y(z)$, which is defined by

$$g_y(z) = \sum_{k=-\infty}^{\infty} c_y(k) z^k. \tag{4}$$

The coefficient on z^k in (4) is the kth lagged covariance $c_y(k)$.

---

[3] The condition turns out to be equivalent with the condition that the spectral density of x be nonnegative, a condition which also in effect stems from the requirement that the variance of every linear combination of x's at different points in time be nonnegative.

First notice that taking mathematical expectations on both sides of (3) gives

$$E(y_t) = \sum_{j=0}^{\infty} b_j E(\varepsilon_{t-j}) = 0 \qquad \text{for all } t.$$

It therefore follows that

$$c_y(k) = E\{(y_t - Ey_t)(y_{t-k} - Ey_{t-k})\} = Ey_t y_{t-k} \qquad \text{for all } k.$$

Since the $\{\varepsilon_t\}$ process is serially uncorrelated, it follows that

$$Ey_t y_{t-k} = E\left(\sum_{j=-\infty}^{\infty} b_j \varepsilon_{t-j} \cdot \sum_{h=-\infty}^{\infty} b_h \varepsilon_{t-k-h} \right) = \sigma_\varepsilon^2 \sum_{j=-\infty}^{\infty} b_j b_{j-k}$$

since only for $j = k + h$ (or $h = j - k$) is $E\varepsilon_{t-j}\varepsilon_{t-k-h}$ nonzero and equal to σ_ε^2. We have permitted the j and h indexes to run over negative values, though in our case $b_j = 0$ for $j < 0$. (The formula is correct even if $b_j \neq 0$ for $j < 0$.) The covariance generating function is then

$$g_y(z) = \sigma_\varepsilon^2 \sum_{k=-\infty}^{\infty} z^k \sum_{j=-\infty}^{\infty} b_j b_{j-k} = \sigma_\varepsilon^2 \sum_{j=-\infty}^{\infty} \sum_{k=-\infty}^{\infty} b_j b_{j-k} z^k.$$

Letting $h = j - k$ so that $k = j - h$, we have

$$g_y(z) = \sigma_\varepsilon^2 \sum_{j=-\infty}^{\infty} \sum_{h=-\infty}^{\infty} b_j b_h z^{j-h} = \sigma_\varepsilon^2 \sum_{j=-\infty}^{\infty} b_j z^j \sum_{h=-\infty}^{\infty} b_h z^{-h}.$$

The last equation gives the convenient expression

$$g_y(z) = \sigma_\varepsilon^2 B(z^{-1}) B(z) \tag{5}$$

where $B(z^{-1}) = \sum_{j=-\infty}^{\infty} b_j z^{-j}$, $B(z) = \sum_{j=-\infty}^{\infty} b_j z^j$. Equation (5) gives the covariance generating function $g_y(z)$ in terms of the b_j and the variance σ_ε^2 of the white noise ε.

To take an example that illustrates the usefulness of (5), consider the first-order process

$$y_t = \lambda y_{t-1} + \varepsilon_t \qquad \text{or} \qquad y_t = \left(\frac{1}{1 - \lambda L} \right) \varepsilon_t = \sum_{i=0}^{\infty} \lambda^i \varepsilon_{t-i}, \qquad |\lambda| < 1, \tag{6}$$

where, as always, ε is a white-noise process with variance σ_ε^2. We have

$$B(L) = \frac{1}{1 - \lambda L}, \qquad B(z) = \frac{1}{1 - \lambda z} = 1 + \lambda z + \lambda^2 z^2 + \cdots$$

$$B(z^{-1}) = \frac{1}{1 - \lambda z^{-1}} = 1 + \lambda z^{-1} + \lambda^2 z^{-2} + \cdots.$$

(Thus, $B(z)$ is found by replacing L in $B(L)$ by z.) So applying (5) we have

$$g_y(z) = \sigma_\varepsilon^2 \left(\frac{1}{1 - \lambda z^{-1}}\right)\left(\frac{1}{1 - \lambda z}\right). \tag{7}$$

From our experience with difference equations we know that the expression (7) can be written as a sum

$$g_y(z) = \frac{k_1 \sigma_\varepsilon^2}{1 - \lambda z} + \frac{k_2 \sigma_\varepsilon^2 z^{-1}}{1 - \lambda z^{-1}} \tag{8}$$

where k_1 and k_2 are certain constants. To find out what the constants must be, notice that (8) implies

$$g_y(z) = \sigma_\varepsilon^2 k_1(1 + \lambda z + \lambda^2 z^2 + \cdots) + \sigma_\varepsilon^2 k_2(z^{-1} + \lambda z^{-2} + \lambda^2 z^{-3} + \cdots),$$

so that $c_y(0) = k_1 \sigma_\varepsilon^2$ and $c_y(1) = \sigma_\varepsilon^2 \lambda k_1 = \sigma_\varepsilon^2 k_2 = c_y(-1)$. By direct computation using (6) we note that

$$Ey_t^2 = \sum_{i=0}^{\infty} \lambda^{i2} E\varepsilon_t^2 = \frac{\sigma_\varepsilon^2}{1 - \lambda^2},$$

$$Ey_t y_{t-1} = E \sum_{i=0}^{\infty} \lambda^i \varepsilon_{t-i} \sum_{j=1}^{\infty} \lambda^{j-1} \varepsilon_{t-j} = E \sum_{i=1}^{\infty} \lambda^i \lambda^{i-1} \varepsilon_{t-i}^2$$

$$= \sigma_\varepsilon^2 \lambda \sum_{i=1}^{\infty} \lambda^{2(i-1)} = \frac{\lambda \sigma_\varepsilon^2}{1 - \lambda^2}.$$

So for (8) to be correct, we require that

$$k_1 = \frac{1}{1 - \lambda^2}, \qquad k_2 = \frac{\lambda}{1 - \lambda^2}.$$

With these values of k_1 and k_2, we can verify directly that

$$\sigma_\varepsilon^2 \left[\frac{1/(1 - \lambda^2)}{1 - \lambda z} + \frac{z^{-1}(\lambda/(1 - \lambda^2))}{1 - \lambda z^{-1}}\right] = \sigma_\varepsilon^2 \frac{1}{1 - \lambda^2}\left[\frac{(1 - \lambda z^{-1}) + \lambda z^{-1} - \lambda^2}{(1 - \lambda z)(1 - \lambda z^{-1})}\right]$$

$$= \sigma_\varepsilon^2 \frac{1}{(1 - \lambda z)(1 - \lambda z^{-1})},$$

so that (7) and (8) are equivalent.

Expression (8) is the more convenient of the two expressions since it yields quite directly

$$g_y(z) = \sigma_\varepsilon^2 \frac{1}{1 - \lambda^2}\left[\frac{1}{1 - \lambda z} + \frac{\lambda z^{-1}}{1 - \lambda z^{-1}}\right]$$

$$= \sigma_\varepsilon^2 \frac{1}{1 - \lambda^2}[\{1 + \lambda z + \lambda^2 z^2 + \cdots\} + \{\lambda z^{-1} + \lambda^2 z^{-2} + \lambda^3 z^{-3} + \cdots\}].$$

Thus, we have that for the first-order Markov process (6)

$$c_y(k) = \frac{\sigma_\varepsilon^2}{1 - \lambda^2} \lambda^{|k|}, \qquad k = 0, \pm 1, \pm 2, \ldots.$$

The covariance declines geometrically with increases in $|k|$. We require $|\lambda| < 1$ in order that the y process have a finite variance.

To get this result more directly write the stochastic difference equation $y_t = \lambda y_{t-1} + \varepsilon_t$, then multiply y_t by y_{t-k}, $k > 0$, to obtain

$$y_t y_{t-k} = \lambda y_{t-1} y_{t-k} + \varepsilon_t y_{t-k}.$$

Taking the expected values on both sides and noting that $E\varepsilon_t y_{t-k} = 0$ gives the famous *Yule–Walker equation*

$$E(y_t y_{t-k}) = \lambda E(y_{t-1} y_{t-k}) \qquad \text{or} \qquad c_y(k) = \lambda c_y(k-1), \qquad k > 0,$$

which implies the solution

$$c_y(k) = \lambda^k c_y(0), \qquad k > 0.$$

From the symmetry of covariograms, it then follows that $c_y(k) = \lambda^{|k|} c_y(0)$ for all k. Notice that the covariogram obeys the solution of the nonrandom part of the difference equation with initial condition $c_y(0)$.

As a second example, consider the second-order process

$$y_t = \left(\frac{1}{1 - \lambda_1 L}\right)\left(\frac{1}{1 - \lambda_2 L}\right)\varepsilon_t, \qquad |\lambda_1| < 1, |\lambda_2| < 1, \quad \lambda_1 \neq \lambda_2, \qquad (9)$$

where ε_t is white noise with variance σ_ε^2. Multiply both sides of (9) by $(1 - \lambda_1 L)$ $(1 - \lambda_2 L)$ to get

$$y_t = t_1 y_{t-1} + t_2 y_{t-2} + \varepsilon_t \qquad (10)$$

where $t_1 = \lambda_1 + \lambda_2$ and $t_2 = -\lambda_1 \lambda_2$. Multiply (10) by y_{t-k} for $k > 0$ to get

$$y_t y_{t-k} = t_1 y_{t-1} y_{t-k} + t_2 y_{t-2} y_{t-k} + \varepsilon_t y_{t-k}.$$

Since $E\varepsilon_t y_{t-k} = 0$, we have

$$E(y_t y_{t-k}) = t_1 E(y_{t-1} y_{t-k}) + t_2 E(y_{t-2} y_{t-k}), \qquad k > 0,$$

which shows that $c_y(k)$ obeys the difference equation (the *Yule–Walker equation*)

$$c_y(k) = t_1 c_y(k-1) + t_2 c_y(k-2). \qquad (11)$$

So the covariogram of a second- (nth-) order process obeys the solution to the deterministic second- (nth-) order difference equation examined above. In particular, corresponding to (11) we consider the polynomial

$$1 - t_1 k - t_2 k^2 = 0, \qquad (12)$$

which has roots $1/\lambda_1$ and $1/\lambda_2$. (We know that $1 - t_1 k - t_2 k^2$ equals $(1 - \lambda_1 k)$ $(1 - \lambda_2 k)$, with roots $1/\lambda_1$ and $1/\lambda_2$.) Alternatively, multiply (12) by k^{-2} to obtain

$$k^{-2} - t_1 k^{-1} - t_2 = 0, \qquad x^2 - t_1 x - t_2 = 0 \qquad \text{where} \quad x = k^{-1}. \quad (13)$$

Notice that the roots of (13) are the reciprocals of the roots of (12), so λ_1 and λ_2 are the roots of (13).

The solution to the deterministic difference equation (11) is, as we have seen,

$$c_y(k) = \lambda_1^k z_0 + \lambda_2^k z_1, \qquad k \geq 0, \quad (14)$$

where z_0 and z_1 are certain constants chosen to make $c_y(0)$ and $c_y(1)$ equal the proper quantities. If the roots λ_1 and λ_2 are complex, we know from our work with deterministic difference equations and from the symmetry of covariograms that

$$c_y(k) = 2pr^k \cos(\omega k) \qquad \text{or} \qquad c_y(k) = c_y(0)r^k \cos(\omega k) \quad (15)$$

where $\lambda_1 = re^{i\omega}$ and $\lambda_2 = re^{-i\omega}$. According to (15), the covariogram displays damped (we require $r < 1$) oscillations with angular frequency ω. A complete cycle occurs as ωk goes from zero ($k = 0$) to 2π ($k = 2\pi/\omega$, if that is possible). The restrictions on t_1 and t_2 needed to deliver complex roots and so an oscillatory covariogram can be read directly from Figure 1 of Chapter IX.

Figure 1b displays a realization of a second-order process for values of t_1 and t_2 for which the roots are complex. Notice the tendency of this series to cycle, but with a periodicity that is somewhat variable from cycle to cycle. Figure 1a reports a realization of a first-order autoregressive process.

The foregoing suggests one tentative definition of a cycle in a single series: a series may be said to possess a "cycle" if its covariogram is characterized by (damped) oscillations. The typical "length" of the cycle can be measured by $2\pi/\omega$, where ω is the angular frequency associated with the damped oscillations in the covariogram (e.g., see (15)). To be labeled a business cycle the cycle should exceed a year in length. (Cycles of one year in length are termed *seasonals*.) We advance this only as a tentative definition of a cycle, and put off for a while discussing its adequacy.

3. THE CROSS COVARIOGRAM

Suppose we have two wide-sense stationary stochastic processes y_t and x_t. The processes are said to be *jointly wide-sense stationary* if the cross covariance $E(y_t - Ey_t)(x_{t-k} - Ex_{t-k})$ depends only on k and not on t. The *cross covariogram* is the list of these covariances viewed as a function of k. We denote it

$$c_{yx}(k) = E(y_t - Ey_t)(x_{t-k} - Ex_{t-k}).$$

Now suppose that y_t and x_t can be expressed as (perhaps two-sided) distributed lags of a single white-noise process ε_t:

$$y_t = B(L)\varepsilon_t, \qquad x_t = D(L)\varepsilon_t$$

where

$$B(L) = \sum_{j=-\infty}^{\infty} b_j L^j, \, D(L) = \sum_{j=-\infty}^{\infty} d_j L^j, \, \sum_{j=-\infty}^{\infty} b_j^2 < \infty, \, \sum_{j=-\infty}^{\infty} d_j^2 < \infty.$$

Since $E\varepsilon_t = 0$, we have

$$c_{yx}(k) = Ey_t x_{t-k} = E \sum_{j=-\infty}^{\infty} b_j \varepsilon_{t-j} \sum_{h=-\infty}^{\infty} d_h \varepsilon_{t-h-k}$$

$$= \sigma_\varepsilon^2 \sum_{j=-\infty}^{\infty} b_j d_{j-k}.$$

The cross-covariance generating function $g_{yx}(z)$ is defined by

$$g_{yx}(z) = \sum_{k=-\infty}^{\infty} c_{yx}(k) z^k.$$

In the present case, we have

$$g_{yx}(z) = \sigma_\varepsilon^2 \sum_{k=-\infty}^{\infty} \sum_{j=-\infty}^{\infty} b_j d_{j-k} z^k;$$

letting $h = j - k$ so that $k = j - h$, we have

$$g_{yx}(z) = \sigma_\varepsilon^2 \sum_{j=-\infty}^{\infty} \sum_{h=-\infty}^{\infty} b_j d_h z^{j-h} = \sigma_\varepsilon^2 \sum_{j=-\infty}^{\infty} b_j z^j \sum_{h=-\infty}^{\infty} d_h z^{-h}$$

$$= \sigma_\varepsilon^2 B(z) D(z^{-1}). \qquad (16)$$

This is a counterpart to Equation (5), and includes it as a special case.

Now suppose that we have the more general system

$$y_t = A(L)\varepsilon_t + B(L)u_t, \qquad x_t = C(L)\varepsilon_t + D(L)u_t, \qquad (17)$$

where ε_t and u_t are two mutually uncorrelated (at all lags) white-noise processes with variances σ_ε^2 and σ_u^2 respectively, and $Eu_t\varepsilon_{t-k} = 0$ for all k. By carrying out calculations analogous to those just completed, it is possible to express the cross-covariance generating function between y and x as

$$g_{yx}(z) = \sigma_\varepsilon^2 A(z) C(z^{-1}) + \sigma_u^2 B(z) D(z^{-1}). \qquad (18)$$

As it turns out, (17) is a very general representation for a bivariate stochastic process, including a large class of such processes.[4]

---

[4] Namely, all jointly wide-sense stationary, indeterministic processes.

We define $c_{xy}(k)$ and $g_{xy}(z)$ symmetrically. In particular, we define

$$c_{xy}(k) = E(x_t - Ex_t)(y_{t-k} - Ey_{t-k}) = c_{yx}(-k).$$

We define $g_{xy}(z)$ by

$$g_{xy}(z) = \sum_{k=-\infty}^{\infty} c_{xy}(k)z^k = \sum_{h=-\infty}^{\infty} c_{yx}(h)z^{-h}.$$

The particular system (17) implies that

$$g_{xy}(z) = \sigma_\varepsilon^2 A(z^{-1})C(z) + \sigma_u^2 B(z^{-1})D(z).$$

4. A MATHEMATICAL DIGRESSION ON FOURIER TRANSFORMS AND z TRANSFORMS[5]

The following theorem provides the foundation for the z transform, Fourier transform, and "lag operator" methods that we use repeatedly in these pages. The theorem, which we shall not prove,[6] is a version of the Riesz–Fischer theorem.

Theorem (Riesz–Fischer): Let $\{c_n\}_{n=-\infty}^{\infty}$ be a sequence of complex numbers for which $\sum_{n=-\infty}^{\infty} |c_n|^2 < \infty$. Then there exists a complex-valued function $f(\omega)$ defined for real ω's belonging to the interval $[-\pi, \pi]$, such that

$$f(\omega) = \sum_{j=-\infty}^{\infty} c_j e^{-i\omega j} \tag{19}$$

where the infinite series converges in the "mean square" sense that

$$\lim_{n\to\infty} \int_{-\pi}^{\pi} \left| \sum_{j=-n}^{n} c_j e^{-i\omega j} - f(\omega) \right|^2 d\omega = 0.$$

The function $f(\omega)$ is called the *Fourier transform of the c_k* and satisfies

$$\int_{-\pi}^{\pi} |f(\omega)|^2 d\omega < \infty$$

where the integral is a Lebesgue integral (i.e., "f belongs to $L_2[-\pi, \pi]$"). Given $f(\omega)$, the c_k can be "recovered" from the inversion formula

$$c_k = \frac{1}{2\pi} \int_{-\pi}^{\pi} f(\omega)e^{+i\omega k} d\omega. \tag{20}$$

---

[5] This section can be omitted on first reading.
[6] For a proof of the Reisz–Fischer theorem, see Apostol (1974, Chapter 11).

Finally, the function $f(\omega)$ and the c_k satisfy Parseval's relation

$$\frac{1}{2\pi} \int_{-\pi}^{\pi} |f(\omega)|^2 \, d\omega = \sum_{j=-\infty}^{\infty} |c_j|^2.$$

This completes the statement of the theorem.

Consider the space of all doubly infinite sequences $\{x_k\}_{k=-\infty}^{\infty}$ such that $\sum_{k=-\infty}^{\infty} |x_k|^2 < \infty$, i.e., the space of square summable sequences. We denote this space $l_2(-\infty, \infty)$. It is a *linear space* in the sense that it possesses the following two properties (among others)[7]:

(i) Let α be a scalar and let $\{x_t\}$ belong to $l_2(-\infty, \infty)$. Then $\{\alpha x_k\}$ belongs to $l_2(-\infty, \infty)$, i.e., $\sum_{k=-\infty}^{\infty} |\alpha x_k|^2 < \infty$.

(ii) Let $\{x_k\}$ and $\{y_k\}$ both belong to $l_2(-\infty, \infty)$. Then $\{x_k + y_k\}$ belongs to $l_2(-\infty, \infty)$, i.e., $\sum_{k=-\infty}^{\infty} |x_k + y_k|^2 < \infty$.

Now consider the space $L_2[-\pi, \pi]$ consisting of all functions $f(\omega)$ for which $\int_{-\pi}^{\pi} |f(\omega)|^2 \, d\omega < \infty$, i.e., the space of "square Lebesgue integrable functions" on $[-\pi, \pi]$. We denote this space $L_2[-\pi, \pi]$. This space is a *linear space* in the sense that it possesses the two properties (among some others):

(a) Let α be a scalar and let $f(\omega)$ belong to $L_2[-\pi, \pi]$. Then $\alpha f(\omega)$ belongs to $L_2[-\pi, \pi]$, i.e., $\int_{-\pi}^{\pi} |\alpha f(\omega)|^2 \, d\omega < \infty$.

(b) Let $f(\omega)$ and $g(\omega)$ both belong to $L_2[-\pi, \pi]$. Then $f(\omega) + g(\omega)$ belongs to $L_2[-\pi, \pi]$, i.e., $\int_{-\pi}^{\pi} |f(\omega) + g(\omega)|^2 \, d\omega < \infty$.

The spaces $l_2(-\infty, \infty)$ and $L_2[-\pi, \pi]$ are each *metric spaces* in the sense that each one possesses a well-defined metric or distance function. In particular, on $l_2(-\infty, \infty)$ the real-valued function

$$d_2(x, y) = \left[\sum_{k=-\infty}^{\infty} |x_k - y_k|^2 \right]^{1/2}$$

measures the distance between the two sequences $\{x_k\}$ and $\{y_k\}$. The function $d_2(\cdot, \cdot)$ is defined for all $\{x_k\}$ and $\{y_k\}$ in $l_2(-\infty, \infty)$ and is a "natural" measure of distance (it satisfies a triangle inequality $d(x, y) \leq d(x, z) + d(z, y)$ for all sequences x, y, and z in l_2). On $L_2[-\pi, \pi]$ the real-valued function

$$D_2(f, g) = \left\{ \frac{1}{2\pi} \int_{-\pi}^{\pi} |f(\omega) - g(\omega)|^2 \, d\omega \right\}^{1/2}$$

is a metric[8] that measures the "distance" between two functions $f(\omega)$ and $g(\omega)$. The metric $D_2(\cdot, \cdot)$ is defined for all $f(\omega)$ and $g(\omega)$ belonging to $L_2[-\pi, \pi]$.

---

[7] For a statement of the defining properties of linear spaces, see Naylor and Sell (1971).

[8] We adopt the usual convention that if $f = g$ except on a set of Lebesgue measure zero, we agree to say that the functions f and g are equal. On this convention $D_2(f, g)$ is a metric. See Naylor and Sell (1971) for more details.

Now consider the mapping from $l_2(-\infty, \infty)$ to $L_2[-\pi, \pi]$ defined by the Fourier transform

$$f(\omega) = \sum_{k=-\infty}^{\infty} c_k e^{-i\omega k}, \qquad \omega \in [-\pi, \pi]. \tag{19}$$

We also have the inverse mapping

$$c_j = \frac{1}{2\pi} \int_{-\pi}^{\pi} f(\omega) e^{+i\omega j} d\omega, \qquad j = 0, \pm 1, \pm 2, \ldots. \tag{20}$$

Now a converse of the Riesz–Fischer theorem is also true: let $f(\omega)$ belong to $L_2[-\pi, \pi]$. Then there exists a sequence $\{c_k\}$ such that $\sum |c_k|^2 < \infty$ and

$$f(\omega) = \sum_{k=-\infty}^{\infty} c_k e^{-i\omega k}$$

where

$$c_k = \frac{1}{2\pi} \int_{-\pi}^{\pi} f(\omega) e^{+i\omega k} d\omega$$

and where the infinite sum converges in the mean square sense. This converse theorem assures us that the mapping of $l_2(-\infty, \infty)$ into $L_2[-\pi, \pi]$ defined by (19) is *onto*. It is also one-to-one. The usefulness of the mapping (19) stems from the fact that it is an *isometric isomorphism* from $l_2(-\infty, \infty)$ to $L_2[-\pi, \pi]$; i.e., it is a *one-to-one* and *onto* transformation of points in $l_2(-\infty, \infty)$ into points in $L_2[-\pi, \pi]$ that preserves both linear structure (i.e., it is an *isomorphism*) and distance between "points" (i.e., it is an *isometric* mapping). That is, let $\{x_k\}$, $\{y_k\}$ belong to $l_2(-\infty, \infty)$, let α be a scalar, and let

$$x(\omega) = \sum_{k=-\infty}^{\infty} x_k e^{-i\omega k}, \qquad y(\omega) = \sum_{k=-\infty}^{\infty} y_k e^{-i\omega k}.$$

Then we have (as can be verified directly)

$$x(\omega) + y(\omega) = \sum_{k=-\infty}^{\infty} (x_k + y_k) e^{-i\omega k}, \qquad \alpha x(\omega) = \sum_{k=-\infty}^{\infty} \alpha x_k e^{-i\omega k}.$$

So "the Fourier transform of a sum of two sequences is the sum of their Fourier transforms" and "the Fourier transform of $\{\alpha x_k\}$ is α times the Fourier transform of $\{x_k\}$." This means that (19) is an isomorphism. We also have

$$\left\{ \frac{1}{2\pi} \int_{-\pi}^{\pi} |x(\omega) - y(\omega)|^2 d\omega \right\}^{1/2} = \left(\sum_{k=-\infty}^{\infty} |x_k - y_k|^2 \right)^{1/2}$$

or

$$D_2(x(\omega), y(\omega)) = d_2(x, y),$$

so that (19) is an isometric mapping.

The Fourier transformation (19) puts square summable sequences $\{x_k\}$ into one-to-one correspondence with square integrable functions $f(\omega)$ on $[-\pi, \pi]$. The transformation preserves linear structure and a measure of distance, as we have seen. The benefit from using the transformation is that operations that are complicated in one space are sometimes the counterparts of simple operations in another space. In particular, consider the *convolution* of two sequences $\{x_k\}$ and $\{y_k\}$ defined to be the new sequence

$$\{y * x_k\}_{k=-\infty}^{\infty} \equiv \left\{ \sum_{s=-\infty}^{\infty} y_s x_{k-s} \right\}_{k=-\infty}^{\infty} .$$

The Fourier transform of $(y * x)_k$ is given by

$$\sum_{k=-\infty}^{\infty} \sum_{s=-\infty}^{\infty} y_s x_{k-s} e^{-i\omega k} = \sum_{s=-\infty}^{\infty} y_s e^{-i\omega s} \sum_{k=-\infty}^{\infty} x_{k-s} e^{-i\omega(k-s)} = y(\omega) x(\omega)$$

where $y(\omega) = \sum_{k=-\infty}^{\infty} y_k e^{-i\omega k}$, $x(\omega) = \sum_{k=-\infty}^{\infty} x_k e^{-i\omega k}$. Thus the Fourier transform of the *convolution* of $\{x_k\}$ with $\{y_k\}$ is the *product* of the Fourier transforms of $\{x_k\}$ and $\{y_k\}$. The complicated convolution operation corresponds simply to multiplication of Fourier transforms.

All transform techniques exploit properties like the preceding one. The aim is to transform a problem from one space where it appears complicated to another isometrically isomorphic space where the operations are simpler, then to transform back to the original space using the inversion mapping such as (20) after the calculations have been performed.

By making the change of variable $z = e^{i\omega}$ in the Riesz–Fischer theorem, we obtain the following corollary which underlies our z-transform methods.

Corollary: Let $\{c_n\}_{n=-\infty}^{\infty}$ be a sequence of complex numbers for which $\sum_{n=-\infty}^{\infty} |c_n|^2 < \infty$. Then there exists a complex-valued function $g(z)$ with domain in the complex plane such that

$$g(z) = \sum_{j=-\infty}^{\infty} c_j z^j$$

where the infinite series converges in the mean square sense that

$$\lim_{n \to \infty} \int_{\Gamma} \left| \sum_{j=-n}^{n} c_j z^j - g(z) \right|^2 \frac{dz}{z} = 0$$

where Γ denotes the unit circle and the above integral is a contour integral. The function $g(z)$ is defined at least on the unit circle in the complex plane and satisfies

$$\left| \frac{1}{2\pi i} \int_{\Gamma} |g(z)|^2 \frac{dz}{z} \right| < \infty.$$

The function $g(z)$ is called the z *transform* of the sequence $\{c_k\}$. The c_k can be recovered from $g(z)$ by $c_k = (2\pi i)^{-1} \int_\Gamma g(z) z^{-k-1} \, dz$. This completes the corollary.

So long as we restrict ourselves to sequences satisfying $\sum |c_k|^2 < \infty$, the theorem and the corollary guarantee that the "z transforms" and Fourier transforms that we shall manipulate are well defined. The z transform in effect maps the sequence $\{c_k\}$ into a complex-valued function defined on the unit circle in the complex plane. The Fourier transform maps the sequence $\{c_k\}$ into a complex-valued function defined on the real line over the interval $[-\pi, \pi]$.

Notice that the complex-valued functions $e^{i\omega j}$, $j = 0, \pm 1, \pm 2, \ldots$ are an orthogonal set on the interval $[-\pi, \pi]$. That is, for $n \neq m$, we have

$$\frac{1}{2\pi} \int_{-\pi}^{\pi} e^{i\omega n} e^{-i\omega m} \, d\omega = \frac{1}{2\pi} \int_{-\pi}^{\pi} e^{i\omega(n-m)} \, d\omega = \frac{1}{2\pi i (n-m)} [e^{i\omega(n-m)}]_{-\pi}^{\pi}$$

$$= \frac{1}{2\pi i (n-m)} [e^{i\pi(n-m)} - e^{-i\pi(n-m)}]$$

$$= \frac{1}{\pi(n-m)} \sin \pi(n-m) = 0$$

since $\sin \pi(n-m) = 0$ for $n-m$ an integer.

For the most part, the Riesz–Fischer theorem and its corollary are sufficient for our needs. Below we shall briefly touch on a deterministic process for which the condition $\sum |c_k|^2 < \infty$ is violated (where the c_k depict the covariogram) so that the theorem will not suffice to define the Fourier transform of the c_k. It turns out that there is still a sense in which the Fourier transform of such "ill-behaved" $\{c_k\}$ sequences is defined, as we shall see.

5. EVALUATING THE INVERSE z TRANSFORM

In the previous section, we saw in the corollary to the Riesz–Fischer theorem that given a square summable sequence $\{c_j\}$, there exists a function $g(z)$, defined as

$$g(z) = \sum_{j=-\infty}^{\infty} c_j z^j$$

which is well defined at least on the unit circle ($z = e^{iw}$, $w \in [0, 2\pi]$). The function $g(z)$ is often called the "z-transform" of the sequence c_j. The function g maps points z in the complex plane into points $g(z)$ in the complex plane. Furthermore, we saw that the c_j can be recovered from the function $g(z)$ by the inversion formula

$$c_k = \frac{1}{2\pi i} \int_\Gamma g(z) z^{-k-1} \, dz, \qquad k = 0, \pm 1, \pm 2, \ldots \tag{21}$$

where the integral is a contour integral in the complex plane, and Γ denotes the unit circle. In this section, we give a pair of simple formulas for evaluating the integral on the right side of (21). Virtually no knowledge of complex analysis is required to use the formulas.[9]

As a prelude to giving this formula, we need to explain two concepts: that of a *pole* of the complex-valued function $g(z)$, and the *residue* that is associated with each pole.

Roughly speaking, a pole is a point in the complex plane, say z_0, such that $g(z)$ approaches infinity as z approaches z_0. In this book, we work almost entirely with functions $g(z)$ that are rational, that is, ratios of finite order polynomials in z. For this reason, the following test for poles of order m is sufficient to identify all of the poles of a function $g(z)$:

Test for poles: Given a function $g(z)$, suppose that for some positive integer m the function

$$\phi(z) = (z - z_0)^m g(z) \tag{22}$$

can be defined[10] so that $\phi(z_0) \neq 0$. Then $g(z)$ has a pole of order m at z_0.

To illustrate the concept of a pole, consider the important case in which $g(z)$ is a rational function, $g(z) = a(z)/b(z)$ where $a(z)$ and $b(z)$ are finite order polynomials in z with no zeros in common. Then according to the above test for poles, the poles of $g(z)$ are simply the zeros of $b(z)$. For one example, letting $g(z) = 1/(1 - \lambda z)^r$, r an integer, we find that $g(z)$ has a pole of order r at $z = \lambda^{-1}$.

We now turn to define the *residue* associated with a pole at z_0.

Definition of residue: Suppose that $g(z)$ has a pole of order m at $z = z_0$. Define the function $\phi(z) = (z - z_0)^m g(z)$. Then the *residue associated with z_0* is defined as

$$\operatorname{res}(z_0) = \frac{\phi^{(m-1)}(z_0)}{(m-1)!} \tag{23}$$

where $\phi^{(m-1)}(z_0)$ is the $(m-1)$th order derivative of ϕ evaluated at z_0. In the important special case in which $m = 1$, formula (23) reduces to $\operatorname{res}(z_0) = \phi(z_0)$ or

$$\operatorname{res}(z_0) = \lim_{z \to z_0} (z - z_0)g(z). \tag{24}$$

---

[9] Churchill, Brown, and Verhey (1974) is a good reference on the aspects of complex analysis being used in this section. Gabel and Roberts (1973) is a good reference on operational methods for linear dynamic systems.

[10] The function $\phi(z)$ must also be "analytic" at z_0, which means that its derivative exists at z_0 and at each point in the same neighborhood of z_0. In our examples, this requirement will routinely be satisfied.

We now give two convenient formulas for evaluating the inversion integral

$$c_j = \frac{1}{2\pi i} \int_\Gamma g(z) z^{-j-1} \, dz.$$

The formulas are given by

$$c_j = \frac{1}{2\pi i} \int_\Gamma g(z) z^{-j-1} \, dz$$

$$= \text{sum of residues of } g(z^{-1}) z^{j-1} \text{ at poles inside unit circle} \qquad (25)$$

$$= \text{sum of residues of } g(z) z^{-j-1} \text{ at poles inside unit circle}.$$

It is a good idea to use whichever of the two branches of (25) is most convenient to avoid the appearance of poles of order greater than one at zero.[11]

We now illustrate the utility of formulas (25) with some examples. For our first example, we take $g(z) = 1/(1 - \lambda z)$ with $|\lambda| < 1$. Using (25), we have that for $j > 0$, $c_j = $ sum of residues of $z^{j-1}/(1 - \lambda z^{-1})$ inside the unit circle. For $j > 0$, the function $z^{j-1}/(1 - \lambda z^{-1})$ has a single pole of order one at $z = \lambda$, with residue given by $\lim_{z \to \lambda} (z - \lambda) z^{j-1}/(1 - \lambda z^{-1}) = \lambda^j$. Therefore, for $j > 0$, $c_j = \lambda^j$. For $j < 0$ we use the second branch of (25) and find that the function $z^{-j-1}/(1 - \lambda z)$ has no poles inside the unit circle. Therefore, $c_j = 0$ for $j < 0$. Finally, for $j = 0$, we use the second branch of (25), and find that the function $z^{-j-1}/(1 - \lambda z)$ has a pole of order one at $z = 0$, which is the only pole inside the unit circle. The residue associated with this pole is $\lim_{z \to 0} (z - 0) z^{-1} (1 - \lambda z)^{-1} = 1$. Therefore $c_0 = 1$. Thus we have

$$c_j = \begin{cases} \lambda^j & j \geq 0 \\ 0 & j < 0. \end{cases}$$

Of course, these results could be more easily obtained simply by expanding $1/(1 - \lambda z)$ in a geometric sum. However, for some of the more complicated examples to be described below, the residue calculations are quicker than such an alternative method.

As a second example, consider the covariance generating function of the nth order autoregressive process

$$g_y(z) = \frac{1}{(1 - \lambda_1 z) \ldots (1 - \lambda_n z)(1 - \lambda_1 z^{-1}) \ldots (1 - \lambda_n z^{-1})}$$

$$= \frac{z^n}{(1 - \lambda_1 z) \ldots (1 - \lambda_n z)(z - \lambda_1) \ldots (z - \lambda_n)}$$

---

[11] The second representation in (25) is standard in texts on complex analysis (e.g., see Churchill, Brown and Verhey (1974).) The first is derived simply from the second as follows. Notice that $g(z^{-1}) = \sum_{n=-\infty}^{\infty} c_n z^{-n} = \sum_{j=-\infty}^{\infty} c_{-j} z^j = \sum_{j=-\infty}^{\infty} d_j z^j$ with $d_j = c_{-j}$. Using the second representation in (25) to calculate d_j, it follows that $c_j = $ sum of residues of $g(z^{-1}) z^{j-1}$ at poles inside the unit circle.

where $|\lambda_j| < 1$ for $j = 1, \dots, n$. Using formula (25) to evaluate

$$c_y(\tau) = \frac{1}{2\pi i} \int_\Gamma g_y(z) z^{-\tau - 1} \, dz,$$

we have

$$c_y(\tau) = \text{sum of residues of } \frac{z^{n - \tau - 1}}{(1 - \lambda_1 z) \dots (1 - \lambda_n z)(z - \lambda_1) \dots (z - \lambda_n)}$$
$$\text{at poles inside the unit circle}$$

$$\hspace{2.5cm} = \text{sum of residues of } \frac{z^{n + \tau - 1}}{(1 - \lambda_1 z) \dots (1 - \lambda_n z)(z - \lambda_1) \dots (z - \lambda_n)}$$
$$\text{at poles inside the unit circle.}$$

(26)

It is convenient to use the first line of (26) for $\tau \le 0$ and the second line for $\tau \ge 0$, in order to avoid poles of multiple order at $z = 0$. In each case, the function has poles of order one at $\lambda_1, \dots, \lambda_n$. For $\tau \ge 0$ the residue at pole λ_j is readily found to be

$$\text{res}(\lambda_j) = \frac{\lambda_j^{n + \tau - 1}}{\prod_{k=1}^{n} (1 - \lambda_k \lambda_j) \prod_{k=1, k \ne j}^{n} (\lambda_j - \lambda_k)}, \qquad \tau \ge 0.$$

It follows that

$$c_y(\tau) = \sum_{j=1}^{n} \frac{\lambda_j^{n + |\tau| - 1}}{\prod_{k=1}^{n} (1 - \lambda_k \lambda_j) \prod_{k=1, k \ne j}^{n} (\lambda_j - \lambda_k)}$$

(27)

where the absolute value sign in (27) follows either from the symmetry of the covariogram or from pursuing the implication of the second line of (26).

6. THE SPECTRUM

An alternative representation of the covariance generating function of y is the spectrum of the y process. Recall the covariance generating function of y defined in (4),

$$g_y(z) = \sum_{k=-\infty}^{\infty} c_y(k) z^k.$$

(4)

For the process $y_t = B(L)\varepsilon_t$, we have seen that

$$g_y(z) = B(z)B(z^{-1})\sigma_\varepsilon^2.$$

If we evaluate (4) at the value $z = e^{-i\omega}$, we have

$$g_y(e^{-i\omega}) = \sum_{k=-\infty}^{\infty} c_y(k) e^{-i\omega k}, \qquad -\pi < \omega < \pi.$$

(28)

Viewed as a function of angular frequency ω, $g_y(e^{-i\omega})$ is called the *spectrum* of y. The spectrum is the Fourier transform of the covariogram.

As we would expect from the inversion formula (20), the spectrum is itself a kind of covariance generating function. Given an expression for $g_y(e^{-i\omega})$ it is easy to recover the covariances $c_y(k)$ from the inversion formula (20). To motivate the inversion formula, we multiply (28) by $e^{i\omega h}$ and integrate with respect to ω from $-\pi$ to π:

$$\int_{-\pi}^{\pi} g_y(e^{-i\omega})e^{i\omega h}\, d\omega = \int_{-\pi}^{\pi} \sum_{k=-\infty}^{\infty} c_y(k)e^{i\omega(h-k)}\, d\omega = \sum_{k=-\infty}^{\infty} c_y(k) \int_{-\pi}^{\pi} e^{i\omega(h-k)}\, d\omega.$$

(29)

Now for $h = k$, we have

$$\int_{-\pi}^{\pi} e^{i\omega(h-k)}\, d\omega = \int_{-\pi}^{\pi} 1\, d\omega = 2\pi.$$

For $h \neq k$, we have

$$\int_{-\pi}^{\pi} e^{i\omega(h-k)}\, d\omega = \int_{-\pi}^{\pi} \cos \omega(h-k)\, d\omega + i \int_{-\pi}^{\pi} \sin \omega(h-k)\, d\omega$$

$$= +\sin \omega(h-k)]_{-\pi}^{\pi} - i \cos \omega(h-k)]_{-\pi}^{\pi} = 0.$$

Therefore, (29) becomes

$$\int_{-\pi}^{\pi} g_y(e^{-i\omega})e^{i\omega h}\, d\omega = 2\pi c_y(h).$$

Thus multiplying the spectrum by $e^{i\omega h}$ and integrating from $-\pi$ to π gives the hth lagged covariance times 2π. In particular, notice that for $h = 0$, we have

$$\int_{-\pi}^{\pi} g_y(e^{-i\omega})\, d\omega = 2\pi c_y(0),$$

so that the area under the spectrum from $-\pi$ to π equals 2π times the variance of y. This fact motivates the interpretation of the spectrum as a device for decomposing the variance of a series by frequency. The portion of the variance of the series occurring between any two frequencies is given by the area under the spectrum between those two frequencies.

Notice that from (28) we have

$$g_y(e^{-i\omega}) = \sum_{k=-\infty}^{\infty} c_y(k)e^{-i\omega k}$$

$$= c_y(0) + \sum_{k=1}^{\infty} c_y(k)(e^{i\omega k} + e^{-i\omega k})$$

$$= c_y(0) + 2 \sum_{k=1}^{\infty} c_y(k) \cos \omega k. \tag{30}$$

According to (30) the spectrum is real-valued at each frequency and is obtained by multiplying the covariogram of y by a cosine function of the frequency in question. Notice also that since $\cos x = \cos(-x)$, it follows from (30) that

$$g_y(e^{i\omega}) = g_y(e^{-i\omega}),$$

so that the spectrum is symmetric about $\omega = 0$.

Since $\cos(\omega + 2\pi k) = \cos(\omega)$, $k = 0, \pm 1, \pm 2, \ldots$, it follows that the spectrum is a periodic function of ω with period 2π. Therefore, we can confine our attention to the interval $[-\pi, \pi]$, or even $[0, \pi]$ by virtue of the symmetry of the spectrum about $\omega = 0$.

We now derive a fundamental formula linking the spectrum of one covariance stationary process y_t to the spectrum of another covariance stationary process x_t. We suppose that both $\{x_t\}$ and $\{y_t\}$ have zero mean and consider the projection equation

$$y_t = \sum_{j=-\infty}^{\infty} b_j x_{t-j} + \varepsilon_t \equiv B(L)x_t + \varepsilon_t$$

where $E\varepsilon_t x_{t-j} = 0$ for all j. Here $B(L)x_t$ is the projection of y_t on the entire x process, as is implied by the orthogonality principle. We then have that

$$y_t y_{t-j} = \left(\sum_{s=-\infty}^{\infty} b_s x_{t-s} \right) \left(\sum_{r=-\infty}^{\infty} b_r x_{t-j-r} \right)$$

$$+ \left(\sum_{s=-\infty}^{\infty} b_s x_{t-s} \right) \varepsilon_{t-j} + \left(\sum_{r=-\infty}^{\infty} b_r x_{t-j-r} \right) \varepsilon_t + \varepsilon_t \varepsilon_{t-j}.$$

Taking expected values of both sides and applying the orthogonality conditions gives

$$c_y(j) = E(y_t y_{t-j}) = \sum_{s=-\infty}^{\infty} \sum_{r=-\infty}^{\infty} b_s b_r c_x(j + r - s) + c_\varepsilon(j).$$

The spectrum of y is defined as

$$g_y(e^{-i\omega}) = \sum_{k=-\infty}^{\infty} c_y(k)e^{-i\omega k}$$

$$= \sum_{k=-\infty}^{\infty} \sum_{s=-\infty}^{\infty} \sum_{r=-\infty}^{\infty} b_r b_s c_x(k + r - s)e^{-i\omega k} + g_\varepsilon(e^{-i\omega}). \qquad (31)$$

Define the index $h = k + r - s$, so that $k = h - r + s$. Notice that

$$e^{-i\omega k} = e^{-i\omega(h-r+s)} = e^{-i\omega h}e^{-i\omega s}e^{i\omega r}. \qquad (32)$$

Substituting (32) into (31) gives

$$g_y(e^{-i\omega}) = \sum_{r=-\infty}^{\infty} b_r e^{i\omega r} \sum_{s=-\infty}^{\infty} b_s e^{-i\omega s} \sum_{h=-\infty}^{\infty} c_x(h) e^{-i\omega h} + g_\varepsilon(e^{-i\omega})$$

$$= B(e^{i\omega}) B(e^{-i\omega}) g_x(e^{-i\omega}) + g_\varepsilon(e^{-i\omega})$$

or

$$g_y(e^{-i\omega}) = |B(e^{-i\omega})|^2 g_x(e^{-i\omega}) + g_\varepsilon(e^{-i\omega}). \tag{33}$$

This is an important formula that shows how the spectrum of the "input" x is multiplied by the nonnegative real number $|B(e^{-i\omega})|^2$ in composing the spectrum of y.

Formula (33) can be used to analyze the effects of "filtering," in which we start with a covariance stationary random process x_t and *define* a new process

$$y_t = B(L)x_t, \tag{34}$$

so that formula (33) applies with $g_\varepsilon(e^{-i\omega}) \equiv 0$. We shall illustrate the usefulness of this formula in several contexts. To begin, formula (34) motivates the interpretation of the spectrum as decomposing the variance of y by frequency. Thus, suppose we could choose $B(e^{-i\omega})$ so that

$$B(e^{-i\omega}) = \begin{cases} 1 & \text{for } \omega \in [a, b] \cup [-b, -a], \quad 0 < a < b < \pi, \\ 0 & \text{otherwise.} \end{cases} \tag{35}$$

Thus, we are choosing a "filter," i.e., a set of b_j, that takes a random process x_t and transforms it into a random process y_t according to (34). A filter obeying (35) shuts off all the spectral power for frequencies not in the region $[a, b]$ or $[-b, -a]$. To determine a set of b_j that satisfies (35), we use the "inversion" formula seen earlier,

$$b_j = \frac{1}{2\pi} \int_{-\pi}^{\pi} B(e^{-i\omega}) e^{+i\omega j} \, d\omega = \frac{1}{2\pi} \int_{-b}^{-a} e^{i\omega j} \, d\omega + \frac{1}{2\pi} \int_a^b e^{i\omega j} \, d\omega$$

$$= \frac{1}{2\pi} \int_a^b (e^{i\omega j} + e^{-i\omega j}) \, d\omega = \frac{1}{2\pi} \int_a^b 2 \cos \omega j \, d\omega$$

$$= \frac{1}{\pi} \frac{1}{j} \sin \omega j \bigg]_a^b$$

$$= \frac{1}{\pi} \left(\frac{\sin jb - \sin ja}{j} \right), \qquad \text{for all integers } j. \tag{36}$$

Note that $b_j = b_{-j}$. With the b_j chosen in this way, the y process defined by

$$y_t = \sum_{j=-\infty}^{\infty} b_j x_{t-j}$$

has all of its variance occurring in the frequency bands $\omega \in [a, b]$, $\omega \in [-b, -a]$. The variance of y is given by

$$\frac{1}{2\pi} \int_{-\pi}^{\pi} g_y(e^{-i\omega}) \, d\omega = \frac{1}{2\pi} \int_{-b}^{-a} g_x(e^{-i\omega}) \, d\omega + \frac{1}{2\pi} \int_{a}^{b} g_x(e^{-i\omega}) \, d\omega.$$

In this sense $g_x(e^{-i\omega})$ gives a decomposition of the variance of x by frequency, the variance occurring over a given frequency band being found by integrating the spectrum over that band and dividing by 2π. We have already seen that by integrating the spectrum from $-\pi$ to π we obtain the variance of x times 2π. As we shall show presently, the decomposition of the variance of x by frequency that is reflected in the spectrum is one in which components at different frequencies can be regarded as orthogonal. More precisely, two components formed by applying two filters like (35) that let through power over disjoint frequency bands are mutually orthogonal at all lags.

Incidentally, the preceding calculations can be used to prove that the spectrum is always nonnegative. This can be done by proceeding by contradiction. Suppose that the spectrum $g_x(e^{-i\omega})$ is negative over a small band. Then choose a filter that shuts off all variance outside of this band. The result is to produce a new random process that has a negative variance, a contradiction. So the spectrum must be nonnegative.

Let us examine the spectra of some simple processes. First consider the white-noise process $y_t = \varepsilon_t$, ε_t white so that $c_y(0) = \sigma_\varepsilon^2$, $c_y(h) = 0$ for $h \neq 0$.

For this process, the covariance generating function is simply $g_y(z) = \sigma_\varepsilon^2$, so that the spectrum is

$$g_y(e^{-i\omega}) = \sigma_\varepsilon^2, \qquad -\pi \le \omega \le \pi.$$

The spectrum is flat, and equals σ_ε^2 at each frequency. Notice that

$$\int_{-\pi}^{\pi} g_y(e^{-i\omega}) \, d\omega = 2\pi\sigma_\varepsilon^2,$$

as expected. So a white noise has a flat spectrum, indicating that all frequencies between $-\pi$ and π are equally important in accounting for its variance.

Next consider the first-order process

$$y_t = B(L)\varepsilon_t = \frac{1}{1 - \lambda L} \varepsilon_t, \qquad -1 < \lambda < 1.$$

For this process the covariance generating function is

$$g_y(z) = \left(\frac{1}{1 - \lambda z}\right)\left(\frac{1}{1 - \lambda z^{-1}}\right)\sigma_\varepsilon^2.$$

Therefore, the spectrum is

$$g_y(e^{-i\omega}) = \left(\frac{1}{1 - \lambda e^{-i\omega}}\right)\left(\frac{1}{1 - \lambda e^{i\omega}}\right)\sigma_\varepsilon^2 = \frac{1}{1 - \lambda(e^{i\omega} + e^{-i\omega}) + \lambda^2}\,\sigma_\varepsilon^2$$

$$= \frac{1}{1 - 2\lambda \cos \omega + \lambda^2}\,\sigma_\varepsilon^2$$

Notice that

$$\frac{dg_y(e^{-i\omega})}{d\omega} = -(1 - 2\lambda \cos \omega + \lambda^2)^{-2}(2\lambda \sin \omega)\sigma_\varepsilon^2.$$

The first term in parentheses is positive. Since $\sin \omega > 0$ for $0 < \omega < \pi$, the second term is negative on $(0, \pi)$ if $\lambda < 0$ and positive on $(0, \pi)$ if $\lambda > 0$. Therefore, if $\lambda > 0$, the spectrum decreases on $(0, \pi)$ as ω increases; if $\lambda < 0$, the spectrum increases on $(0, \pi)$ as ω increases. Thus, if $\lambda > 0$, low frequencies (i.e., low values of ω) are relatively important in composing the variance of ω, while if $\lambda < 0$, high frequencies are the more important. It is easy to verify that the higher in absolute value is λ, the steeper is the spectrum. Notice that the first-order process can have a peak in its spectrum only at $\omega = 0$ or $\omega = \pm\pi$. A peak at $\omega = \pi$ corresponds to a periodicity of $2\pi/\omega = 2\pi/\pi = 2$ periods. A peak at $\omega = 0$ corresponds to a cycle with "infinite" periodicity, which is unobservable and hence not a cycle at all.

With quarterly data a business cycle corresponds to a peak in the spectrum at a periodicity of about 12 quarters. A first-order process is capable of having a peak only at two quarters or at "infinite" quarters, and so is not consistent with a business cycle in the sense of a peak in the spectrum at about twelve quarters. As we saw above, a first-order process cannot possess a covariogram with a periodicity other than two periods, and so with quarterly data cannot deliver a business cycle in the sense of an oscillatory covariogram.

A second-order process can have a peak in its spectrum inside the interval $(0, \pi)$. Consider the second-order process

$$y_t = \frac{1}{1 - t_1 L - t_2 L^2}\,\varepsilon_t,$$

ε_t white noise. For this process, the covariance generating function is

$$g_y(z) = \left(\frac{1}{1 - t_1 z - t_2 z^2}\right)\left(\frac{1}{1 - t_1 z^{-1} - t_2 z^{-2}}\right)\sigma_\varepsilon^2.$$

Therefore, the spectrum of the process is

$$g_y(e^{-i\omega}) = \left(\frac{1}{1 - t_1 e^{-i\omega} - t_2 e^{-2i\omega}} \right) \left(\frac{1}{1 - t_1 e^{i\omega} - t_2 e^{2i\omega}} \right) \sigma_\varepsilon^2$$

$$= \frac{\sigma_\varepsilon^2}{1 + t_1^2 + t_2^2 + (t_2 t_1 - t_1)(e^{i\omega} + e^{-i\omega}) - t_2(e^{-2i\omega} + e^{2i\omega})}$$

$$= \frac{\sigma_\varepsilon^2}{1 + t_1^2 + t_2^2 - 2t_1(1 - t_2)\cos\omega - 2t_2\cos 2\omega} = \frac{\sigma_\varepsilon^2}{h(\omega)}.$$

Differentiating with respect to ω, we have

$$\frac{dg_y(e^{-i\omega})}{d\omega} = -\sigma_\varepsilon^2 h(\omega)^{-2}(2t_1(1 - t_2)\sin\omega + 4t_2\sin 2\omega)$$

$$= -\sigma_\varepsilon^2 h(\omega)^{-2}((2\sin\omega)[t_1(1 - t_2) + 4t_2\cos\omega]).$$

We know that $h(\omega)^2 > 0$. For the above derivative to be zero at an ω belonging to $(0, \pi)$, we must have the term in brackets equal to zero:

$$t_1(1 - t_2) + 4t_2\cos\omega = 0 \qquad \text{or} \qquad \cos\omega = \frac{-t_1(1 - t_2)}{4t_2}, \qquad (37)$$

so that

$$\omega = \cos^{-1}\left(\frac{-t_1(1 - t_2)}{4t_2} \right). \qquad (38)$$

Equation (38) can be satisfied only if

$$\left| \frac{-t_1(1 - t_2)}{4t_2} \right| < 1 \qquad (39)$$

since $|\cos x| \leq 1$ for all x. By inspecting the second derivative of $g_y(e^{-i\omega})$ with respect to ω, it can be verified that at the ω given by (38) there is a peak in the spectrum if $t_2 < 0$ and a trough if $t_2 > 0$. Condition (39) is slightly more restrictive than the condition that the roots of the deterministic difference equation be complex so that the covariogram displays oscillations. Let us write (39) as

$$-1 < -t_1(1 - t_2)/4t_2 < 1. \qquad (40)$$

The boundaries of the region (40) are

$$-t_1(1 - t_2) = 4t_2 \qquad (41)$$

and

$$-t_1(1 - t_2) = -4t_2. \qquad (42)$$

The points $(t_1, t_2) = (0, 0)$ appear on both boundaries, while the point $(t_1, t_2) = (2, -1)$ appears on (41) and $(t_1, t_2) = (-2, -1)$ appears on (42). Differentiating (41) implicitly with respect to t_1 gives

$$dt_2/dt_1 = (t_2 - 1)/(4 - t_1)$$

so that along (41)

$$\left. \frac{dt_2}{dt_1} \right|_{t_1 = t_2 = 0} = -\frac{1}{4}$$

and

$$\left. \frac{dt_2}{dt_1} \right|_{t_1 = 2, t_2 = -1} = -1.$$

Differentiating (42) with respect to t_1 gives

$$dt_2/dt_1 = (1 - t_2)/(4 + t_1)$$

so that along (42)

$$\left. \frac{dt_2}{dt_1} \right|_{t_1 = t_2 = 0} = \frac{1}{4}, \quad \left. \frac{dt_2}{dt_1} \right|_{t_1 = -2, t_2 = -1} = 1.$$

Such calculations show that the boundaries of region (40) are as depicted in Figure 2. To be in region (40) with $t_2 < 1$ (a requirement of covariance stationarity) implies that the roots of the difference equation are complex. However, complex roots do not imply that (40) is satisfied. Consequently, the conditions for an oscillatory covariogram are not quite equivalent with those for a spectral peak.

To illustrate the ability of low-order stochastic difference equations to generate "realistic" data, Figures 1a and 1b show simulations of first- and second-order stochastic difference equations, while Figure 1c shows the solution of the deterministic part of the same second-order difference equation with initial conditions $y_0 = y_1 = 1$. Notice that even the first-order stochastic difference equation

$$y_t = 0.9y_{t-1} + \varepsilon_t,$$

ε_t a serially uncorrelated random term, appears to generate roughly alternating periods of boom and bust. This illustrates how stochastic difference equations can generate processes that "look like" they have business cycles even if their spectra do not have peaks on $(0, \pi)$ and even if their covariograms do not oscillate.

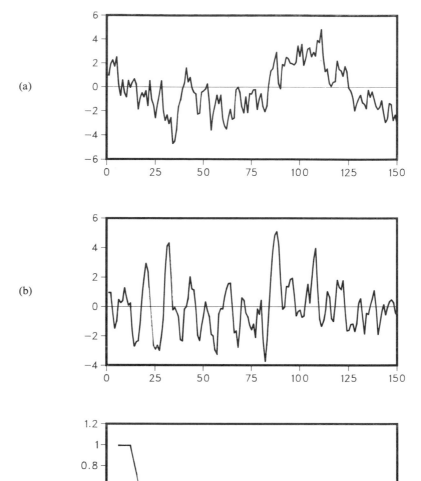

FIGURE 1 (a) $Y_t = 0.9Y_{t-1} + \varepsilon_t$; (b) $Y_t = Y_{t-1} - 0.5Y_{t-2} + \varepsilon_t$; (c) $Y_t = Y_{t-1} - 0.5Y_{t-2}$

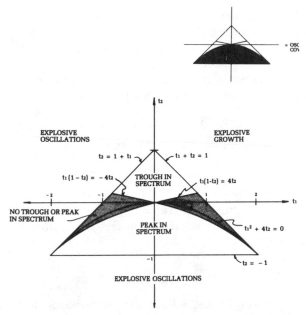

FIGURE 2 (Source: G. M. Jenkins and D. G. Watts, *Spectral Analysis and Its Applications*, p. 229, San Francisco: Holden-Day, 1969.)

7. THE CROSS SPECTRUM

An alternative representation of the cross covariogram is provided by the cross spectrum. Recall that the cross-covariance generating function between the jointly stationary processes y and x is defined by

$$g_{yx}(z) = \sum_{k=-\infty}^{\infty} c_{yx}(k)z^k.$$

If we evaluate $g_{yx}(z)$ at the value $z = e^{-i\omega}$, we have the cross spectrum

$$g_{yx}(e^{-i\omega}) = \sum_{k=-\infty}^{\infty} c_{yx}(k)e^{-i\omega k}.$$

Viewed as a function of angular frequency ω, $g_{yx}(e^{-i\omega})$ is called the cross spectrum between y and x.

The cross spectrum is of course a cross-covariance generating function. Given an expression for $g_{yx}(e^{-i\omega})$, it is possible to recover the cross covariances from the inversion formula

$$c_{yx}(k) = \frac{1}{2\pi} \int_{-\pi}^{\pi} g_{yx}(e^{-i\omega})e^{i\omega k}\, d\omega.$$

The validity of this inversion formula can be checked by following calculations analogous to those used to verify the inversion formula for the spectrum.

Unlike the spectrum, the cross spectrum is in general a complex number at each frequency, this being a consequence of the fact that $c_{yx}(k)$ is in general *not* symmetric ($c_{yx}(k)$ does *not* in general equal $c_{yx}(-k)$). In place of the symmetry property we have the readily verified property

$$g_{xy}(e^{-i\omega}) = \overline{g_{yx}(e^{-i\omega})} = g_{yx}(e^{+i\omega}) \qquad (43)$$

where the bar denotes complex conjugation and

$$g_{xy}(e^{-i\omega}) = \sum_{k=-\infty}^{\infty} c_{xy}(k)e^{-i\omega k}$$

and $c_{xy}(k) = Ex_t y_{t-k}$. Notice that $c_{xy}(k) = c_{yx}(-k)$.

Suppose that the stationary stochastic process y_t is related to the stochastic processes x_t and ε_t by

$$y_t = \sum_{j=-\infty}^{\infty} h_j x_{t-j} + \varepsilon_t \qquad (44)$$

where $E\varepsilon_t = Ex_t = 0$, and $E\varepsilon_t x_{t-s} = 0$ for all s, an orthogonality condition that characterizes $\sum h_j x_{t-j}$ as the projection of y_t on the space spanned by $\{x_{t-\infty}, \ldots, x_0, \ldots, x_{t+\infty}\}$. Then we have already seen that the spectrum of y satisfies

$$g_y(e^{-i\omega}) = |h(e^{-i\omega})|^2 g_x(e^{-i\omega}) + g_\varepsilon(e^{-i\omega})$$

where

$$h(e^{-i\omega}) = \sum_{j=-\infty}^{\infty} h_j e^{-i\omega j}.$$

To find the cross spectrum between y and x, first use (44) to calculate the kth lagged covariance as

$$Ey_t x_{t-k} = \sum_{j=-\infty}^{\infty} h_j E(x_{t-j} x_{t-k}), \qquad c_{yx}(k) = \sum_{j=-\infty}^{\infty} h_j c_x(k-j).$$

Thus the cross covariogram between y and x is the convolution of the sequence $\{h_j\}$ with the sequence $c_x(j)$. From the convolution property we immediately have

$$g_{yx}(e^{-i\omega}) = h(e^{-i\omega})g_x(e^{-i\omega})$$

since the Fourier transform of a convolution of two sequences is the product of the Fourier transforms of the two sequences. That is, taking Fourier transforms of each side (i.e., multiplying by $e^{-i\omega k}$ and summing over k) gives

$$\sum_{k=-\infty}^{\infty} c_{yx}(k)e^{-i\omega k} = \sum_{j=-\infty}^{\infty} \sum_{k=-\infty}^{\infty} h_j c_x(k-j)e^{-i\omega k}$$

Noting that $e^{-i\omega k} = e^{-i\omega(k-j)}e^{-i\omega j}$, the above can be written as

$$g_{yx}(e^{-i\omega}) = \sum_{j=-\infty}^{\infty} h_j e^{-i\omega j} \sum_{k=-\infty}^{\infty} c_x(k-j)e^{-i\omega(k-j)}$$

or

$$g_{yx}(e^{-i\omega}) = h(e^{-i\omega})g_x(e^{-i\omega}). \tag{45}$$

Notice that the covariance between y and x can be recovered from the inversion formula

$$c_{yx}(k) = \frac{1}{2\pi} \int_{-\pi}^{\pi} h(e^{-i\omega})g_x(e^{-i\omega})e^{i\omega k} \, d\omega.$$

Further, notice that given $g_{yx}(e^{-i\omega})$ and $g_x(e^{-i\omega})$, the h_k can be recovered from

$$h_k = \frac{1}{2\pi} \int_{-\pi}^{\pi} \frac{g_{yx}(e^{-i\omega})}{g_x(e^{-i\omega})} e^{i\omega k} \, d\omega.$$

Where estimators of $g_{yx}(e^{-i\omega})$ and $g_x(e^{-i\omega})$ are used in the above equation, the resulting estimator of the h_k is known as Hannan's inefficient estimator.

As an example, suppose that the jointly covariance stationary process (y, x) has covariance generating functions

$$g_x(z) = \sigma_\varepsilon^2 \left(\frac{1}{1 - 0.9z}\right)\left(\frac{1}{1 - 0.9z^{-1}}\right), \qquad g_y(z) = \sigma_u^2(1 - 0.8z)(1 - 0.8z^{-1})$$

$$g_{yx}(z) = \sigma_{u\varepsilon}(1 - 0.8z)(1 + 0.5z^{-1}).$$

Notice that this is equivalent with

$$g_x(e^{-i\omega}) = \sigma_\varepsilon^2 \frac{1}{(1 - 0.9e^{-i\omega})(1 - 0.9e^{+i\omega})} = \frac{\sigma_\varepsilon^2}{1.81 - 1.8 \cos \omega}$$

$$g_y(e^{-i\omega}) = \sigma_u^2(1.64 - 1.6 \cos \omega)$$

$$g_{yx}(e^{-i\omega}) = \sigma_{u\varepsilon}(0.6 - 0.8e^{-i\omega} + 0.5e^{+i\omega}).$$

Let us now use formula (45) to calculate the coefficient generating function $h(z)$ in the projection of y_t on the entire x process. Using z instead of $e^{-i\omega}$, formula (45) becomes

$$h(z) = g_{yx}(z)/g_x(z).$$

For our example this gives

$$g_{yx}(z)/g_x(z) = (\sigma_{u\varepsilon}/\sigma_\varepsilon^2)(1 - 0.8z)(1 + 0.5z^{-1})(1 - 0.9z^{-1})(1 - 0.9z).$$

The reader can easily multiply this polynomial in z and verify that $h_j = 0$ for $|j| > 2$ and that $h_j \neq 0$ for $j = -2, -1, 0, 1, 2$. Notice that, as in general, $h(z)$ is "two-sided," having nonzero coefficients on negative powers of z.

Now let us calculate the coefficients in the projection of x_t on the entire y process:

$$x_t = \sum_{j=-\infty}^{\infty} f_j y_{t-j} + \eta_t,$$

$E\eta_t y_{t-j} = 0$ for all j. Applying formula (45), exchanging the roles of y and x, gives

$$f(z) = g_{xy}(z)/g_y(z) = g_{yx}(z^{-1})/g_y(z).$$

In our example this gives

$$f(z) = \frac{\sigma_{u\varepsilon}(1 - 0.8z^{-1})(1 + 0.5z)}{\sigma_u^2(1 - 0.8z^{-1})(1 - 0.8z)} = \frac{\sigma_{u\varepsilon}}{\sigma_u^2} \frac{(1 + 0.5z)}{(1 - 0.8z)}.$$

It is readily verified that $f_j = 0$ for $j < 0$, so that $f(z)$ is "one-sided on the past and present."

We shall shortly study the conditions under which the projection of y on x or of x on y are "one-sided" or "two-sided."

Equation (16) can be generalized as follows. Let

$$y_{1t} = B_1(L)x_t, \qquad y_{2t} = B_2(L)x_t \qquad (46)$$

where x_t is a covariance stationary process and $B_1(L)$ and $B_2(L)$ arc the lag generating functions for square summable lag distributions. Then

$$g_{y_1 y_2}(e^{-i\omega}) = B_1(e^{-i\omega})B_2(e^{+i\omega})g_x(e^{-i\omega}). \qquad (47)$$

We invite the reader to verify this formula by using (46) to calculate $Ey_{1t}y_{2t-k}$, multiplying by $e^{-i\omega k}$, and summing over k. The derivation mimics the derivation of Equation (16) above.[12]

We now use formula (47) to show that the spectrum reflects a decomposition of x_t into processes that are orthogonal across frequencies. Thus let

$$y_{1t} = B_1(L)x_t, \qquad y_{2t} = B_2(L)x_t$$

where $B_1(L)$ and $B_2(L)$ are chosen to satisfy

$$B_1(e^{-i\omega}) = \begin{cases} 1, & \omega \in [-b, -a] \cup [a, b], \\ 0, & \omega \notin [-b, -a] \cup [a, b]; \end{cases}$$

$$B_2(e^{-i\omega}) = \begin{cases} 1, & \omega \in [-d, -c] \cup [c, d], \\ 0, & \omega \notin [-d, -c] \cup [c, d]. \end{cases}$$

To find the individual distributed lag coefficients, Equation (36) can be used. From (47), we note that if $[-b, -a] \cup [a, b]$ does not intersect the set of

---

[12] Alternatively, write x_t in terms of its moving average representation $x_t = c(L)\eta_t$ where $g_x(z) = \sigma_\eta^2 c(z)c(z^{-1})$. Then apply (16) to the system $y_{1t} = B_1(L)c(L)\eta_t$, $y_{2t} = B_2(L)c(L)\eta_t$.

frequencies $[-d, -c] \cup [c, d]$, then $B_1(e^{-i\omega})B_2(e^{i\omega}) = 0$ for all ω, so that $g_{y_1y_2}(e^{-i\omega}) = 0$. This in turn implies that y_1 and y_2 are processes that are orthogonal (uncorrelated) at all lags, as can be verified directly from the inversion formula. In this sense the spectrum $g_x(e^{-i\omega})$ decomposes the variance of x into a set of mutually orthogonal processes across frequencies.

The cross spectrum is a complex quantity that is usually characterized by real numbers in various ways. One characterization is in terms of its real and imaginary parts

$$g_{yx}(e^{-i\omega}) = \mathrm{co}(\omega) + i \, \mathrm{qu}(\omega)$$

where $\mathrm{co}(\omega)$ is called the cospectrum and $\mathrm{qu}(\omega)$ is called the quadrature spectrum. A more usual representation is the polar one

$$g_{yx}(e^{-i\omega}) = r(\omega)e^{i\theta(\omega)} \tag{48}$$

where

$$r(\omega) = \sqrt{\mathrm{co}(\omega)^2 + \mathrm{qu}(\omega)^2}, \qquad \theta(\omega) = \tan^{-1}\left[\frac{\mathrm{qu}(\omega)}{\mathrm{co}(\omega)}\right].$$

The phase statistic gives the lead of y over x at frequency ω, while the "gain" $r(\omega)$ tells how the amplitude in x is multiplied in contributing to the amplitude of y at frequency ω. Another interesting number is the coherence

$$\mathrm{coh}(\omega) = |g_{yx}(e^{-i\omega})|^2/(g_x(e^{-i\omega})g_y(e^{-i\omega})),$$

which, being essentially the ratio of a covariance squared to the product of two variances, is analogous to an R^2 statistic. It indicates the proportion of the variance in one series at frequency ω that is accounted for by variation in the other series.

Notice that from (45) and from the fact that the spectrum $g_x(e^{-i\omega})$ is real, the phase of the cross spectrum equals the phase of $h(e^{-i\omega}) = \sum h_j e^{-i\omega j}$, which is the Fourier transform of the h_j. That is, writing (45) and (48), we have

$$r(\omega)e^{i\theta(\omega)} = g_{yx}(e^{-i\omega}) = h(e^{-i\omega})g_x(e^{-i\omega})$$

or

$$h(e^{-i\omega}) = \frac{r(\omega)}{g_x(e^{-i\omega})}e^{i\theta(\omega)},$$

which shows that the phase of $g_{yx}(e^{-i\omega})$ equals the phase of $h(e^{-i\omega})$. For convenience, represent $h(e^{-i\omega})$ in polar form

$$h(e^{-i\omega}) = s(\omega)e^{i\theta(\omega)}$$

where $s(\omega) = r(\omega)/g_x(e^{-i\omega})$.

The following provides a heuristic device for interpreting $\theta(\omega)$. Suppose we consider as an input into the system (44) an x series consisting of a pure cosine wave of frequency ω:

$$x_t = 2 \cos \omega t = e^{i\omega t} + e^{-i\omega t}.$$

For this input path, suppressing the disturbance ε_t, (44) becomes

$$y_t = \sum h_j[e^{i\omega(t-j)} + e^{-i\omega(t-j)}] = e^{i\omega t} \sum h_j e^{-i\omega j} + e^{-i\omega t} \sum h_j e^{+i\omega j}.$$

But $\sum h_j e^{-i\omega j} = s(\omega)e^{i\theta(\omega)}$ and $\sum h_j e^{+i\omega j}$, being the complex conjugate of $\sum h_j e^{-i\omega j}$, equals $s(\omega)e^{-i\theta(\omega)}$. Therefore, we have

$$y_t = e^{i\omega t}s(\omega)e^{i\theta(\omega)} + e^{-i\omega t}s(\omega)e^{-i\theta(\omega)} = s(\omega)[e^{i(\omega t + \theta(\omega))} + e^{-i(\omega t + \theta(\omega))}]$$

$$= s(\omega)2 \cos(\omega t + \theta(\omega)).$$

Therefore, the response of (44) to an input in the form of a cosine wave of frequency ω is a cosine wave at the same frequency with amplitude multiplied by $s(\omega)$ and phase shifted by $\theta(\omega)$. The input cosine wave is at its peak at $t = 0$, while the output is at its peak at $\omega t + \theta(\omega) = 0$ or $t = -\theta(\omega)/\omega$ units of time. Thus, for $\theta(\omega) > 0$, the output *leads* the input by $-\theta(\omega)/\omega$ units of time (where we adopt the usual convention that $\theta(\omega)$ is constrained to be between $-\pi$ and $+\pi$, a convention needed to make the arctangent function single-valued).

While useful, the preceding interpretation of the phase has to be used cautiously. The reason is that the stochastic difference equations that we have been studying generate random processes with spectral power distributed across a continuum of frequencies between $-\pi$ and $+\pi$. It is really only over a nonnegligible *band* of frequencies that there occurs a positive contribution to variance. Thus, for such processes, there really do not occur input processes that are pure cosines, though this situation could be approached if the spectral density did display a very sharp peak at a given frequency. Processes with positive spectral power at a single given frequency do exist, and realizations of these processes do consist of (sums of) sine and cosine waves. But such processes are not generated by the stochastic difference equations that we are studying. (See pp. 289–290.)

It is interesting to note the following two facts about $h(e^{-i\omega})$. First, from the definition of $h(e^{-i\omega})$

$$h(e^{-i\omega}) = \sum_j h_j e^{-i\omega j},$$

we note that $h(e^{-i\omega})$ evaluated at $\omega = 0$ is the sum of the lag weights, i.e.,

$$h(e^{-i0}) = \sum h_j.$$

Notice that since

$$\sum h_j e^{-i\omega j} = \sum h_j \cos \omega j - i \sum h_j \sin \omega j$$

and that since sin 0 = 0, we have that

$$h(e^{-i0}) = s(0) = \sum h_j.$$

Since $h(e^{-i\omega})$ is real at zero frequency, the phase statistic $\theta(\omega)$ is zero at zero frequency, provided $\sum h_j \neq 0$:

$$\theta(\omega) = \tan^{-1}[-\sum h_j \sin \omega j/\sum h_j \cos \omega j], \qquad \theta(0) = \tan^{-1}[0] = 0. \quad (49)$$

Next, it is possible to show that the derivative of the phase statistic with respect to ω evaluated at $\omega = 0$ equals minus the mean lag. Recall that

$$\frac{d}{dx} \tan^{-1} u = \frac{1}{1 + u^2} \frac{du}{dx}.$$

Applying this to (49) gives

$$\theta'(\omega) = \frac{1}{1 + [-\sum h_j \sin \omega j/\sum h_j \cos \omega j]^2}$$
$$\times \left\{ \frac{-\sum h_j \cos \omega j \sum h_j j \cos \omega j - \sum h_j j \sin \omega j \sum h_j \sin \omega j}{(\sum h_j \cos \omega j)^2} \right\}.$$

Evaluating $\theta'(\omega)$ at $\omega = 0$ gives

$$\theta'(0) = -\sum h_j j/\sum h_j.$$

(Here we have used the facts that $\cos 0 = 1$, $\sin 0 = 0$.) The right-hand side of this equation is minus the "mean lag" of the lag distributed formed by the h's, a statistic often reported in econometric studies involving estimates of distributed lags.

8. A DIGRESSION ON LEADING INDICATORS

For years, the National Bureau of Economic Research (NBER) has employed a number of heuristic techniques designed to isolate "leading indicators" of business cycle movements, presumably as an aid in the early recognition and prediction of cyclical movements.[13] To translate into our vocabulary, essentially a good leading indicator displays a sizable phase lead at the low business cycle frequencies over some important "coincident" measures of the cycle, such as unemployment or GNP (as well as a large coherence with those coincident measures—so that the phase lead is not only large on average but is regular in its occurrence). While searching for leading indicators is perhaps an important thing to do in terms of categorizing data, it is important to recognize that a series y_t that displays a sizable phase lead over another series x_t, at the most important

---

[13] Leading indicators are published in *Business Conditions Digest*, published by the Department of Commerce.

business cycle frequencies does *not* necessarily help in predicting x_t any better than can be done by using past x's alone to predict x. We illustrate this fact with two examples.

First suppose we have the system governed by

$$x_t = \lambda x_{t-1} + u_t, \quad |\lambda| < 1, \quad y_t = h_0 x_t + h_1 x_{t-1} + \varepsilon_t \tag{50}$$

where $Eu_t = E\varepsilon_t = Eu_t\varepsilon_{t-s} = 0$ for all t and s, and where both u and ε are serially uncorrelated. The cross spectrum between y and x is given by

$$g_{yx}(e^{-i\omega}) = (h_0 + h_1 e^{-i\omega})g_x(e^{-i\omega}) = (h_0 + h_1 \cos \omega - ih_1 \sin \omega)g_x(e^{-i\omega})$$

$$= r(\omega)e^{i\theta(\omega)}g_x(e^{-i\omega})$$

where

$$r(\omega) = \sqrt{(h_0 + h_1 \cos \omega)^2 + (h_1 \sin \omega)^2}, \quad \theta(\omega) = \tan^{-1}\left[\frac{-h_1 \sin \omega}{h_0 + h_1 \cos \omega}\right].$$

Now by suitably choosing h_0 and h_1, at a given frequency $\theta(\omega)$ can be set arbitrarily in the interval $(-\pi, \pi)$. This is in spite of the fact that the model (50) implies that y_t is of no use in terms of predicting x_t, for x_t is governed by a pure "autoregression," and depends only on itself lagged and the unpredictable random term u_t. Thus, even if y_t leads x_t at the low business cycle frequencies, it is of no use in predicting x_t.

To specialize this example somewhat, suppose we have

$$x_t = \lambda x_{t-1} + u_t, \quad y_t = (x_t - x_{t-1}) + \varepsilon_t,$$

where as before u and ε are mutually orthogonal (at all lags) white-noise processes. Calculating $h(e^{-i\omega})$, we have

$$h(e^{-i\omega}) = 1 - e^{-i\omega} = e^{-i\omega/2}(e^{i\omega/2} - e^{-i\omega/2})$$

$$= e^{-i\omega/2}2i \sin(\omega/2) = 2e^{-i\omega/2}e^{i\pi/2} \sin(\omega/2)$$

$$= 2e^{i(\pi/2 - \omega/2)} \sin(\omega/2).$$

For $0 < \omega < \pi$, the phase angle is positive, implying that the output y leads x at all frequencies between zero and π. In spite of the fact that y leads at all of these frequency components, y is of no use in predicting x once lagged x's are taken into account.

As our second example, consider the system

$$y_t = \sum_{j=-\infty}^{\infty} h_j x_{t-j} + \varepsilon_t, \quad y_t = \lambda y_{t-1} + u_t$$

where we assume $E\varepsilon_t x_s = 0$ for all t, s, $Eu_t = 0$, and u_t is a white-noise stationary process. We further assume that

$$h_j = h_{-j} \quad \text{for all} \quad j \geq 1.$$

The cross spectrum between y and x is calculated to be

$$g_{yx}(e^{-i\omega}) = \{h_0 + h_1(e^{i\omega} + e^{-i\omega}) + h_2(e^{2i\omega} + e^{-2i\omega}) + \cdots\}g_x(e^{-i\omega})$$

$$= \left(h_0 + 2\sum_{j=1}^{\infty} h_j \cos \omega j\right)g_x(e^{-i\omega})$$

which is *real* for all ω. Therefore, the phase shift $\theta(\omega) = 0$ for all ω, so that y and x are perfectly in phase at all frequencies. Despite this, by using a theorem due to Sims (see pp. 314–324) it is possible to show that even given the past of x, past y does help predict present and future x's. This is a consequence of the lag distribution of the h_j being two-sided and of Sims's theorem 2, which we will describe in detail presently.

Taken together, these two examples illustrate the fact that displaying a phase lead is neither a necessary nor a sufficient condition for one series to be of use in predicting another.

9. ANALYSIS OF SOME FILTERS: THE SLUTSKY EFFECT AND KUZNETS'S TRANSFORMATIONS

Relation (33) can be used to show the famous "Slutsky effect" (1937). Slutsky considered the effects of starting with a white noise ε_t, taking a two-period moving sum n times, and then taking first differences m times. That is, Slutsky considered forming the series

$$Z_t = (1 + L)(1 + L)\cdots(1 + L)\varepsilon_t = (1 + L)^n\varepsilon_t$$

and

$$y_t = (1 - L)(1 - L)\cdots(1 - L)Z_t = (1 - L)^m Z_t = (1 + L)^n(1 - L)^m\varepsilon_t. \quad (51)$$

Applying (33) to (51), we have

$$g_y(e^{-i\omega}) = (1 + e^{i\omega})^n(1 + e^{-i\omega})^n(1 - e^{i\omega})^m(1 - e^{-i\omega})^m\sigma_\varepsilon^2$$

$$= [(1 + e^{i\omega})(1 + e^{-i\omega})]^n[(1 - e^{-i\omega})(1 - e^{i\omega})]^m\sigma_\varepsilon^2$$

$$= [2 + (e^{i\omega} + e^{-i\omega})]^n[2 - (e^{i\omega} + e^{-i\omega})]^m\sigma_\varepsilon^2$$

$$= \sigma_\varepsilon^2 2^n[1 + \cos \omega]^n 2^m[1 - \cos \omega]^m. \quad (52)$$

Consider first the special case where $m = n$. Then (52) becomes

$$g_y(e^{-i\omega}) = \sigma_\varepsilon^2 4^n[1 - \cos^2 \omega]^n = \sigma_\varepsilon^2 4^n[\sin^2 \omega]^n. \quad (53)$$

On $(0, \pi)$, the spectrum of y has a peak at $\omega = \pi/2$ since there $\sin \omega = 1$. Notice that since $\sin \omega \le 1$, (53) implies that as n becomes large, the peak in the spectrum of y at $\pi/2$ becomes sharp. In the limit, as $n \to \infty$, the spectrum of y becomes a "spike" at $\pi/2$, which means that y behaves like a cosine of angular frequency $\pi/2$.

Similar behavior results for fixed m/n as n becomes large where $m \neq n$. Consider (52) and set $dg_y(e^{-i\omega})/d\omega$ equal to zero in order to locate the peak in the spectrum:

$$dg_y/d\omega = \sigma_\varepsilon^2 2^{m+n}\{n[1 - \cos \omega]^m[1 + \cos \omega]^{n-1}(-\sin \omega)$$
$$+ m(1 - \cos \omega)^{m-1}(\sin \omega)[1 + \cos \omega]^n\}$$
$$= \sigma_\varepsilon^2 2^{m+n} \sin \omega\{(1 - \cos \omega)^{m-1}(1 + \cos \omega)^{n-1}$$
$$\cdot [m(1 + \cos \omega) - n(1 - \cos \omega)]\}.$$

This expression can equal zero on $(0, \pi)$ only if the expression in brackets equals zero:

$$m(1 + \cos \omega) - n(1 - \cos \omega) = 0,$$

which implies

$$\cos \omega = \frac{1 - (m/n)}{1 + (m/n)} \quad \text{or} \quad \omega = \cos^{-1}\left(\frac{1 - (m/n)}{1 + (m/n)}\right)$$

which tells us the frequency at which the spectrum of y attains a peak. For fixed m/n, the spectrum of y approaches a spike as $n \to \infty$. This means that as $n \to \infty$, y tends to behave more and more like a cosine of angular frequency $\cos^{-1}((1 - m/n)/(1 + m/n))$.

What Slutsky showed, then, is that by successively summing and then successively differencing a serially uncorrelated or "white-noise" process ε_t, a series with "cycles" is obtained.

Another use of (33) is in the analysis of transformations that have been applied to data. An example is Howrey's (1968) analysis of the transformations used by Kuznets. Data constructed by Kuznets have been inspected to verify the existence of "long swings," long cycles in economic activity of around twenty years. Before analysis, however, Kuznets subjected the data to two transformations. First, he took a five-year moving average:

$$Z_t = \tfrac{1}{5}[L^{-2} + L^{-1} + 1 + L + L^2]X_t \equiv A(L)X_t.$$

Then he took the centered first difference of the (nonoverlapping) five-year moving average:

$$y_t = Z_{t+5} - Z_{t-5} = [L^{-5} - L^5]Z_t = B(L)Z_t.$$

So we have that the y's are related to the X's by

$$y_t = \tfrac{1}{5}[L^{-5} - L^5][L^{-2} + L^{-1} + 1 + L + L^2]X_t - A(L)B(L)X_t.$$

The spectrum of y is related to the spectrum of X by

$$g_y(e^{-i\omega}) = A(e^{-i\omega})A(e^{i\omega})B(e^{-i\omega})B(e^{i\omega})g_x(e^{-i\omega}). \tag{54}$$

We have

$$A(e^{-i\omega}) = \frac{1}{5} \sum_{j=-2}^{2} e^{-i\omega j} = \frac{1}{5} \frac{e^{i\omega 2} - e^{-i\omega 3}}{1 - e^{-i\omega}}.$$

Thus,

$$A(e^{-i\omega})A(e^{i\omega}) = \frac{(\frac{1}{5})^2(e^{i\omega 2} - e^{-i\omega 3})(e^{-i\omega 2} - e^{i\omega 3})}{(1 - e^{-i\omega})(1 - e^{i\omega})}$$

$$= \frac{(\frac{1}{5})^2(2 - (e^{i\omega 5} + e^{-i\omega 5}))}{2 - (e^{i\omega} + e^{-i\omega})}$$

$$= \frac{(\frac{1}{5})^2 2(1 - \cos 5\omega)}{2(1 - \cos \omega)} = \frac{(\frac{1}{5})^2(1 - \cos 5\omega)}{1 - \cos \omega}.$$

Next, we have $B(e^{-i\omega}) = (e^{+i\omega 5} - e^{-i\omega 5})$, so that

$$B(e^{i\omega})B(e^{-i\omega}) = (e^{i\omega 5} - e^{-i\omega 5})(e^{-i\omega 5} - e^{i\omega 5})$$

$$= (2 - (e^{i\omega 10} + e^{-i\omega 10})) = 2(1 - \cos 10\omega).$$

So it follows from (33) that

$$g_y(e^{-i\omega}) = \frac{(\frac{1}{5})^2(1 - \cos 5\omega)2}{(1 - \cos \omega)}(1 - \cos 10\omega)g_x(e^{-i\omega}) = G(\omega)g_x(e^{-i\omega}),$$

where $G(\omega) = 2[(\frac{1}{5})^2(1 - \cos 5\omega)(1 - \cos 10\omega)/(1 - \cos \omega)]$. The term $G(\omega)$ is graphed in Figure 3. It has zeros at values where $\cos 5\omega = 1$ and where $\cos 10\omega = 1$. The first condition occurs on $[0, \pi]$ where

$$5\omega = 0, 2\pi, 4\pi, \qquad \omega = 0, \tfrac{2}{5}\pi, \tfrac{4}{5}\pi.$$

The condition $\cos 10\omega = 1$ on $[0, \pi]$ where

$$10\omega = 0, 2\pi, 4\pi, 6\pi, 8\pi, 10\pi \qquad \text{or} \qquad \omega = 0, \tfrac{1}{5}\pi, \tfrac{2}{5}\pi, \tfrac{3}{5}\pi, \tfrac{4}{5}\pi, \pi.$$

So $G(\omega)$ has zeros at $\omega = 0, \tfrac{1}{5}\pi, \tfrac{2}{5}\pi, \tfrac{3}{5}\pi, \tfrac{4}{5}\pi$, and π.

From the graph of $G(\omega)$, it follows that even if X_t is a white noise, a y series generated by applying Kuznets's transformations will have a large peak at a low frequency, and hence will seem to be characterized by "long swings." These long swings are clearly a statistical artifact; i.e., they are something induced in the data by the transformation applied and not really a characteristic of the economic system. With annual data, the biggest peak in Figure 3 corresponds to a cycle of about $20\tfrac{1}{4}$ years which is close to the 20-year cycle found by Kuznets. Howrey's observations naturally raise questions about the authenticity of the long swings identified by studying the data used by Kuznets.

$$G(\omega) = \left(\tfrac{1}{5}\right)^2 \frac{(1-\cos 5\omega) \cdot 2(1-\cos 10\omega)}{1-\cos \omega}$$

FIGURE 3

10. A SMALL KIT OF $h(e^{-i\omega})$'s

In order to provide some feel for the effects of various commonly used filters Figure 4 reports the amplitude and phase of $h(e^{-i\omega})$ for various $h(L)$ lag distributions.

We have already calculated that for $h(L) = 1 - L$,

$$h(e^{-i\omega}) = 2e^{i(\pi/2 - \omega/2)}\sin(\omega/2),$$

as the graphs confirm.

For $h(L) = 1 + L$, it is straightforward to calculate

$$h(e^{-i\omega}) - 1 + e^{-i\omega} = e^{-i\omega/2}(e^{+i\omega/2} + e^{-i\omega/2}) = 2e^{-i\omega/2}\cos(\omega/2),$$

which again agrees with our graphs.

Notice that for $h(L) = (1 - t_1 L - t_2 L^2)^{-1}$, we have chosen (t_1, t_2) in the regions of peaked spectra of our Figure 2. Notice that as required, $h(e^{-i\omega})$ is characterized by peaks. (See Figure 2.)

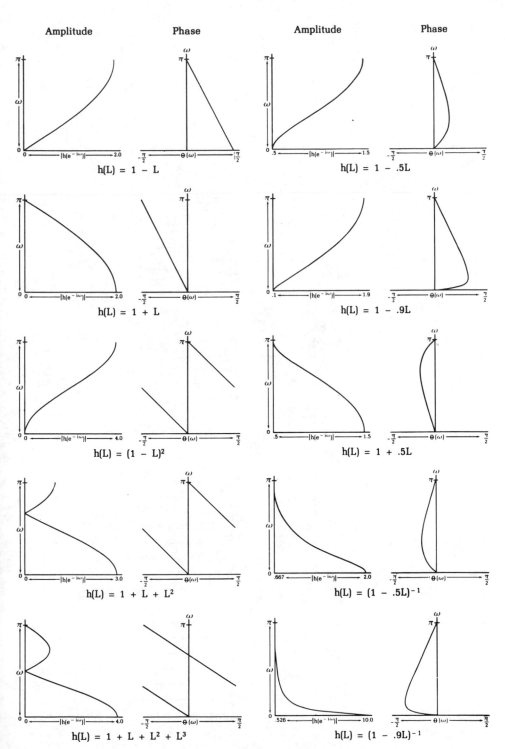

FIGURE 4 Frequency response functions.

277

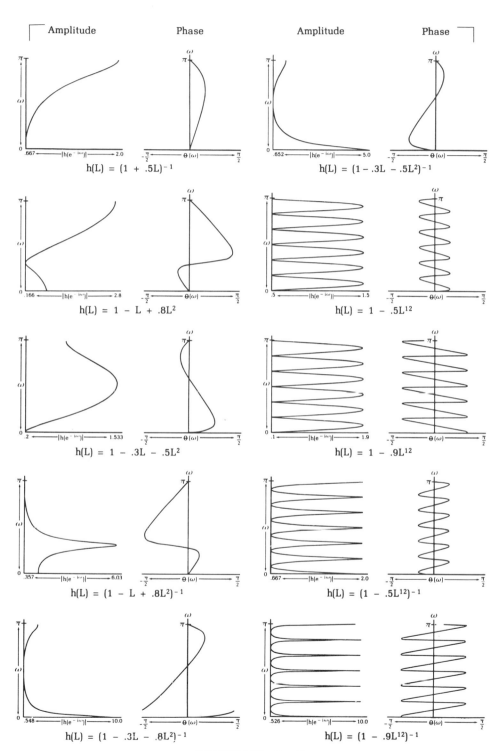

FIGURE 4 (*Continued*)

278

11. ALTERNATIVE DEFINITIONS OF THE BUSINESS CYCLE

We have already encountered two definitions of a cycle in a single series that is governed by a stochastic difference equation. According to the first definition, a variable possesses a cycle of a given frequency if its covariogram displays damped oscillations of that frequency, which is equivalent with the condition that the nonstochastic part of the difference equation has a pair of complex roots with argument (θ in the polar form of the root $re^{i\theta}$) equal to the frequency in question. A single series is said to contain a *business cycle* if the cycle in question has periodicity of from about two to four years (NBER minor cycles) or about eight years (NBER major cycles).

A second definition of a cycle in a single series is the occurrence of a peak in the spectral density of a series. As we have seen, this definition is not equivalent with the previous one, but usually leads to a definition of the cycle close to the first one.

It is probably correct however that neither one of these definitions is what underlies the concept of the business cycle that most experts have in mind. In fact, most economic aggregates have spectral densities that do not display pronounced peaks at the range of frequencies associated with the business cycle. The peaks that do occur in this band of frequencies tend to be wide and of modest height. The dominant feature of the spectrum of most economic time series is that it generally decreases drastically as frequency increases, with most of the power in the low frequency, high periodicity bands. This shape was dubbed by Granger (1966) the "typical spectral shape" of an economic variable.

Figure 5 contains a record of quarterly U.S. time series for seven series over the period 1947-1975. For each variable, the left panel plots the realization of

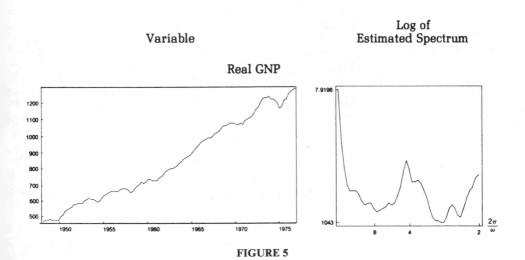

FIGURE 5

		Log of
	Variable	Estimated Spectrum

Unemployment Rate

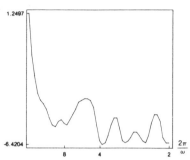

Interest Rate (Baa Bond Rate, NSA)

Change in Real Money Supply

FIGURE 5 (*Continued*)

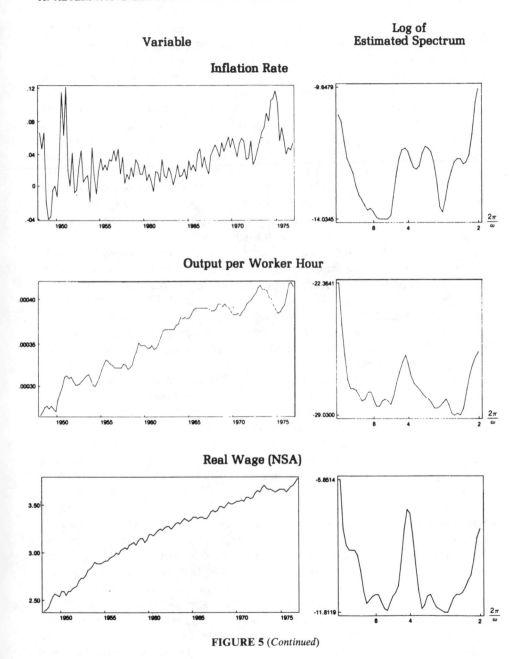

FIGURE 5 (*Continued*)

the time series, while the right panel records an estimate of the spectral density. We record these panels side by side partly in order to give the reader some practice in "reading" spectral densities, i.e., in picturing the kind of time series realizations that are typically associated with various spectral shapes. For example, Granger's concept of a "typical spectral shape" is illustrated by the logarithms of the spectral densities of real GNP, the unemployment rate, the real wage, the Baa rate, and output per man-hour in Figure 5. The generally downward sweeping spectrum is characteristic of a covariogram that is dominated by high, positive, low-order serial correlation. Notice that the inflation rate and change in the real money supply do not display the typical spectral shape, a characteristic that might have been anticipated from our study of the effects of applying the first difference filter $1 - L$. All of the series except the unemployment rate, which has been seasonally adjusted, display spectral peaks in the vicinity of four and two quarters, which is symptomatic of a seasonal pattern of serial correlation. "Seasonal adjustment" is a process of operating on a series with a filter $h(L)$ that is designed to diminish the seasonal frequencies near four and two quarters, while leaving the remaining frequencies as unaffected as possible. Notice how this procedure has "succeeded" for the unemployment rate and produced dips in the spectrum near four and two quarters (see Exercise 2). Notice how real GNP has no spectral peak in the business cycle range, while output per man-hour and the unemployment rate have only very modest peaks, this despite the fact that the sample paths of all three reflect "the business cycle." As mentioned earlier, the fact that a spectrum does not display a peak at the business cycle frequencies should not be taken to mean that the series did not experience any fluctuations associated with the business cycle. On the contrary, as Figure 1a indicated, a series could very well seem to move in sympathy with general business conditions, say as identified by the NBER, and yet have no spectral peak on the open interval $(0, \pi)$. This example cautions the reader against interpreting the lack of a peak in the spectrum at the business cycle frequencies as indicating the absence of any business cycle in the series.

What the preceding example does indicate is that our two preceding tentative possible definitions of the business cycle are deficient. The following definition seems to capture what experts refer to as the business cycle: the business cycle is the phenomenon of a number of important economic aggregates (such as GNP, unemployment, and layoffs) being characterized by high pairwise coherences at the low business cycle frequencies, the same frequencies at which most aggregates have most of their spectral power if they have "typical" spectral shapes. This definition captures the notion of the business cycle as being a condition symptomizing the common movements of a set of aggregates. Figure 6 reports estimated coherences for six variables over the period 1948I–1976IV. Notice the high pairwise coherences among the unemployment rate, real GNP, and output per man-hour at the low business cycle frequencies. In the next section we describe a statistical model that is capable of representing a collection of variables that satisfies the preceding definition of a

FIGURE 6 Coherences.

business cycle. This model helps convey the sense in which the preceding definition embodies ideas of Burns and Mitchell (1946).

12. INDEX MODELS

Let y_t be an ($n \times 1$) covariance stationary, linearly indeterministic stochastic process. The process y_t is said to satisfy an unobservable *index model*, in the sense of Sargent and Sims (1977), if it possesses a representation

$$y_t = \Lambda(L)f_t + D(L)\varepsilon_t \tag{55}$$

where f_t is a $(k \times 1)$ vector white noise, ε_t is an $(n \times 1)$ vector white noise, $\Lambda(L)$ is an $(n \times k)$ matrix of square summable polynomials in the lag operator, $D(L)$ is an $(n \times n)$ diagonal matrix of square summable polynomials in the lag operator, and the white noises f_t, ε_t satisfy the orthogonality conditions

$$E\begin{bmatrix} f_t \\ \varepsilon_t \end{bmatrix}\begin{bmatrix} f_{t-s} \\ \varepsilon_{t-s} \end{bmatrix}^T = \begin{bmatrix} \Sigma_f & 0 \\ 0 & \Sigma_\varepsilon \end{bmatrix}, \qquad s = 0 \tag{56}$$

$$= [0] \qquad s \neq 0$$

where Σ_f and Σ_ε are each diagonal matrices. Thus, each component of f_t and ε_t is orthogonal to every other component at all times, and to itself at all nonzero leads and lags. The model is restrictive when k is sufficiently smaller than n. Usually, it has been assumed that $k = 1$ or 2 in applied work.

Equations (55) and (56) imply that the covariance generating function of y_t satisfies

$$S_y(z) = \Lambda(z)\Sigma_f \Lambda(z^{-1})^T + D(z)\Sigma_\varepsilon D(z^{-1})^T \tag{57}$$

where T denotes transposition. Equation (57) states that the covariance generating function of y (or the spectral density matrix of y) is the sum of a matrix of rank k, namely $\Lambda(z)\Sigma_f \Lambda(z^{-1})^T$, and a diagonal matrix of rank n, namely $D(z)\Sigma_\varepsilon D(z^{-1})^T$. In other words, all of the covariance among distinct components of y is mediated through their common dependence on the k indexes f_t. Equation (57) is a frequency domain version of a "factor analysis" model, being a factor analytic model for each value of z. Geweke and Singleton (1981a,b) call (57) the "dynamic factor" model.

Following T. C. Koopmans (1947), Sargent and Sims (1977) proposed (55) with $k = 1$ as a statistical model that seemed consistent with the conception of the business cycle used by Arthur Burns and Wesley Claire Mitchell (1946) at the National Bureau of Economic Research. With $k = 1$, the covariances across distinct series entirely reflect their common dependence on the one-dimensional shock f_t.

Sargent and Sims (1977) described some macroeconomic models that would lead an index model like (55) to fit well. More recently, several researchers have applied stochastic optimal growth models which have assumed the form of a one unobservable index model. For example, see Kydland and Prescott (1982) and Altug (1985). The one index in these models is the innovation to a technology shock, while the components of ε_t are interpreted simply as mutually orthogonal measurement errors. Brock (1982) described a specification of preferences and technology in a stochastic growth model which could lead stock prices to exhibit an unobservable index structure.

A simple example of such a model can be obtained by adding mutually orthogonal measurement errors to the true series for y_{nt}, c_t, and $k_{t+1} - k_t$ in the linear stochastic growth model of Chapter XII, Section 9. The one index in this model is θ_t, the innovation to the technology shock.

13. REPRESENTATION THEORY

So far we have generally started with a white noise ε_t as a building block and considered constructing a stochastic process x_t via a transformation

$$x_t = B(L)\varepsilon_t.$$

In this section we reverse this procedure and start by assuming that we have a covariance stationary process x_t with covariogram $c(\tau)$. We then show that associated with every such process $\{x_t\}$ is a white-noise process $\{\varepsilon_t\}$ that is its fundamental building block. One purpose of this construction is to convey the sense in which the models we have been studying are quite general ones for covariance stationary processes.

Suppose that we have a covariance stationary stochastic process x_t with covariogram $c(\tau)$ and mean zero. We think of forming a sequence of linear least squares projections of x_t against a sequence of expanding sets of past x's, $\{x_{t-1}, x_{t-2}, \ldots, x_{t-n}\}$:

$$\hat{x}_t^n = \sum_{i=1}^n a_i^n x_{t-i} = P[x_t | x_{t-1}, \ldots, x_{t-n}] \qquad \text{or} \qquad x_t = \hat{x}_t^n + \varepsilon_t^n$$

where $E\varepsilon_t^n x_{t-i} = 0$ for $i = 1, \ldots, n$ by the orthogonality principle. These orthogonality conditions uniquely determine the projection $\hat{x}_t^n = \sum_{i=1}^n a_i^n x_{t-i}$. The population covariogram $c(\tau)$ contains all of the information necessary to calculate the a_i^n from the least squares normal equations.[14]

As n is increased toward infinity, it is possible to show that the sequence of projections $\{\hat{x}_t^n\}$ converges to a random variable $\hat{x}_t$ in the "mean square" sense that[15]

$$\lim_{n \to \infty} E(\hat{x}_t - \hat{x}_t^n)^2 = 0.$$

This means that for any $\delta > 0$, we can find an $N(\delta)$ such that

$$E(\hat{x}_t - \hat{x}_t^m)^2 < \delta$$

for all $m > N(\delta)$, so that in the mean square sense, we can approximate arbitrarily well the projection on the space spanned by the infinite set of lagged x's with the projection of x_t on a suitable finite set of lagged x's.[16] We write the projection of x_t on the space spanned by the infinite set $(x_{t-1}, x_{t-2}, \ldots)$ as

$$\hat{x}_t = P[x_t | x_{t-1}, x_{t-2}, \ldots]$$

---

[14] The a_i^n will be unique only if there are no linear dependencies across the x_{t-i}. The projection of x_t on the space spanned by $\{x_{t-1}, \ldots, x_{t-n}\}$ is unique even without that condition.

[15] It is not necessarily true that the sequence of a_i^n settles down nicely as $n \to \infty$, only that successive $\hat{x}_t^n$ get closer to each other and to $\hat{x}_t$ as $n \to \infty$.

[16] For a proof, see Anderson (1971, p. 419).

and have the decomposition of x_t as

$$x_t = P[x_t | x_{t-1}, x_{t-2}, \ldots] + \varepsilon_t \tag{58}$$

where ε_t is a least squares residual that obeys the orthogonality condition $E\varepsilon_t x_{t-i} = 0$ for all $i \geq 1$. In mean square ε_t is the limit as $n \to \infty$ of ε_t^n, i.e., $\lim_{n \to \infty} E(\varepsilon_t - \varepsilon_t^n)^2 = 0$.

We can now state an important decomposition theorem due to Wold.[17]

Theorem: Let $\{x_t\}$ be any covariance stationary stochastic process with $Ex_t = 0$. Then it can be written as

$$x_t = \sum_{j=0}^{\infty} d_j \varepsilon_{t-j} + \eta_t$$

where $d_0 = 1$ and where $\sum_{j=0}^{\infty} d_j^2 < \infty$, $E\varepsilon_t^2 = \sigma^2 \geq 0$, $E\varepsilon_t \varepsilon_s = 0$ for $t \neq s$ (so that $\{\varepsilon_t\}$ is serially uncorrelated), $E\varepsilon_t = 0$ and $E\eta_t \varepsilon_s = 0$ for all t and s (so that $\{\varepsilon\}$ and $\{\eta\}$ are processes that are orthogonal at all lags); and $\{\eta_t\}$ is a process that can be predicted arbitrarily well by a linear function of only past values of x_t, i.e., η_t is linearly deterministic. Furthermore, $\varepsilon_t = x_t - P[x_t | x_{t-1}, x_{t-2}, \ldots]$.

Proof: We let ε_t be the same ε_t as appears in (58), so that

$$\varepsilon_t = x_t - P[x_t | x_{t-1}, x_{t-2}, \ldots].$$

So ε_t is the error or "innovation" in predicting x_t from its own past. Now ε_t is orthogonal to $\{x_{t-1}, x_{t-2}, \ldots\}$, by the orthogonality principle. But ε_{t-s} is a linear combination of past x's:

$$\varepsilon_{t-s} = x_{t-s} - P[x_{t-s} | x_{t-s-1}, \ldots].$$

Therefore $E\varepsilon_t \varepsilon_{t-s} = 0$ for all t and s. So we have proved that $\{\varepsilon_t\}$ is a serially uncorrelated process.

Now think of projecting x_t against a sequence of sets spanned by $(\varepsilon_t, \varepsilon_{t-1}, \ldots, \varepsilon_{t-m})$ for successively larger m's. The typical projection of x_t on such a set is

$$\hat{x}_t^m = \sum_{j=0}^{m} d_j \varepsilon_{t-j}$$

where, since the ε_{t-j} are mutually orthogonal, the d_j are given by

$$d_j = (Ex_t \varepsilon_{t-j})/\sigma^2, \qquad \sigma^2 = E\varepsilon_t^2.$$

Notice that since $\varepsilon_t = x_t - P[x_t | x_{t-1}, x_{t-2}, \ldots]$ and since $E\varepsilon_t x_{t-i} = 0$ for all $i \geq 1$, we have $E\varepsilon_t^2 = Ex_t \varepsilon_t$. Thus, we have $d_0 = Ex_t \varepsilon_t / E\varepsilon_t^2 = 1$. Since the ε's are

---

[17] See Wold (1938). The proof given here parallels that given by Anderson (1971). The reader familiar with Hilbert spaces is urged to read Anderson at this point.

orthogonal, the d_j do not depend on m. Now calculate the variance of the prediction error, which is

$$E\left(x_t - \sum_{j=0}^{m} d_j \varepsilon_{t-j}\right)^2 = Ex_t^2 - 2\sum_{j=0}^{m} d_j Ex_t \varepsilon_{t-j} + E\left(\sum_{j=0}^{m} d_j^2 \varepsilon_{t-j}^2\right)$$

$$= Ex_t^2 - 2\sigma^2 \sum_{j=0}^{m}\left(\frac{Ex_t \varepsilon_{t-j}}{\sigma^2}\right)^2 + \sigma^2 \sum_{j=0}^{m}\left(\frac{Ex_t \varepsilon_{t-j}}{\sigma^2}\right)^2$$

$$= Ex_t^2 - \sigma^2 \sum_{j=0}^{m} d_j^2 \geq 0,$$

where the last inequality follows because the variance of the prediction error cannot be negative. Since $Ex_t^2 < \infty$, from the last inequality it follows that for all m

$$\sigma^2 \sum_{j=0}^{m} d_j^2 \leq Ex_t^2$$

so that $\sum_{j=0}^{\infty} d_j^2 < \infty$. It follows that $\sum_{j=0}^{\infty} d_j \varepsilon_{t-j}$ is well defined, i.e., it converges in the mean square sense.[18]

Now define the process η_t by

$$\eta_t = x_t - \sum_{j=0}^{\infty} d_j \varepsilon_{t-j}.$$

Notice that for $s \leq t$ we have

$$E\eta_t \varepsilon_s = Ex_t \varepsilon_s - E\sum_{j=0}^{\infty} d_j \varepsilon_s \varepsilon_{t-j} = Ex_t \varepsilon_s - d_{t-s} E\varepsilon_s^2$$

$$= Ex_t \varepsilon_s - Ex_t \varepsilon_s = 0.$$

In addition $E\eta_t \varepsilon_s = 0$ for all $s > t$ because ε_s is orthogonal to all x's dated earlier than s and by construction η_t is in the space spanned by x's dated t and earlier. Thus $\{\eta_t\}$ is orthogonal to $\{\varepsilon_t\}$ at all lags and leads. That is, the entire $\{\varepsilon\}$ process is orthogonal to the entire $\{\eta\}$ process.

---

[18] That is, the sequence of $\sum_{j=0}^{m} d_j \varepsilon_{t-j}$ is a Cauchy sequence. In particular, for $n > m$,

$$E\left(\sum_{j=0}^{m} d_j \varepsilon_{t-j} - \sum_{j=0}^{n} d_j \varepsilon_{t-j}\right)^2 = E\left(\sum_{j=m+1}^{n} d_j^2 \varepsilon_{t-j}^2\right)$$

$$= \sigma^2 \sum_{j=m+1}^{n} d_j^2.$$

Since $\sum_{j=0}^{\infty} d_j^2 < \infty$, it follows that we can choose an m big enough to drive $\sigma^2 \sum_{j=m+1}^{\infty} d_j^2$ arbitrarily close to zero.

Because η_t is orthogonal to ε_t, η_t must lie in the space spanned by $\{x_{t-1}, x_{t-2}, \ldots\}$ since square summable[19] linear combinations of $\{x_{t-1}, x_{t-2}, \ldots\}$ form the space of *all* random variables orthogonal to ε_t.[20] This implies that η_t can be predicted perfectly from lagged x's. More precisely, project $\eta_t = x_t - \sum_{j=0}^{\infty} d_j \varepsilon_{t-j}$ against $\{x_{t-1}, x_{t-2}, \ldots\}$ to get

$$P[\eta_t | x_{t-1}, \ldots] = P[x_t | x_{t-1}, \ldots] - \sum_{j=1}^{\infty} d_j \varepsilon_{t-j}$$

since $P[\varepsilon_t | x_{t-1}, \ldots] = 0$ and since $P[\varepsilon_{t-k} | x_{t-1}, \ldots] = \varepsilon_{t-k}$ for $k \geq 1$. Subtracting the above equation from the definition of η_t gives

$$\eta_t - P[\eta_t | x_{t-1}, \ldots] = (x_t - P[x_t | x_{t-1}, \ldots]) - d_0 \varepsilon_t = 0$$

since the one-step-ahead prediction error for x_t is $d_0 \varepsilon_t$. Thus, $\eta_t = P[\eta_t | x_{t-1}, \ldots]$, so that η_t can be predicted arbitrarily well (in the mean squared error sense) from past x's alone. More generally, we have

$$P[\eta_t | x_{t-k}, x_{t-k-1}, \ldots] = P[x_t | x_{t-k}, \ldots] - \sum_{j=k}^{\infty} d_j \varepsilon_{t-j}.$$

Subtracting this from the definition of η_t gives

$$\eta_t - P[\eta_t | x_{t-k}, \ldots] = (x_t - P[x_t | x_{t-k}, \ldots]) - \sum_{j=0}^{k-1} d_j \varepsilon_{t-j} = 0$$

since $\sum_{j=0}^{k-1} d_j \varepsilon_{t-j}$ is the k-step-ahead prediction error in predicting x_t from its own past. Thus, we have proved that η_t is (linearly) deterministic in the sense that it can be predicted arbitrarily well (in the mean squared error sense) arbitrarily far into the future from past x's only. This completes the proof of Wold's theorem.

The η_t process is termed the (linearly) deterministic part of x_t while $\sum_{j=0}^{\infty} d_j \varepsilon_{t-j}$ is termed the (linearly) indeterministic part. The reason for the adverb *linearly* is that the decomposition has been obtained by using linear projections.

Wold's theorem is important for us because it provides an explanation of the sense in which stochastic difference equations provide a general model for the indeterministic part of any univariate stationary stochastic process, and also the sense in which there exists a white-noise process ε_t that is the building block for the indeterministic part of x_t. Not surprisingly, the construction of the theorem can be extended to multivariate stochastic processes for which a corresponding orthogonal decomposition exists in which the deterministic and indeterministic parts are vectors.

[19] Those linear combinations $\sum_{j=1}^{\infty} f_j x_{t-j}$ for which $\sum_{j=1}^{\infty} f_j^2 < \infty$, so that the variance of the sum is finite.

[20] This is an implication of the orthogonality principle. See Anderson (1971).

As a particular example of a process that conforms to the representation given in Wold's decomposition theorem, consider the process

$$x_t = \sum_{j=0}^{\infty} d_j \varepsilon_{t-j} + \sum_{i=1}^{n} (a_i \cos \lambda_i t + b_i \sin \lambda_i t)$$

where ε_t is a covariance stationary, serially uncorrelated process with mean zero and variance σ_ε^2; $\sum_{j=0}^{\infty} d_j^2 < \infty$; a_i and b_i are random variables orthogonal to the entire ε process and satisfying $Ea_i = Eb_i = Ea_i b_j = 0$ for all i, j, $Ea_i a_j = Eb_i b_j = 0$ for all $i \neq j$, and $Ea_i^2 = Eb_i^2 = \sigma_i^2$; and the λ_i are fixed numbers in the interval $[-\pi, \pi]$. The process $\sum_{i=1}^{n} (a_i \cos \lambda_i t + b_i \sin \lambda_i t)$ is deterministic, is orthogonal to the process $\sum d_j \varepsilon_{t-j}$ at all lags, and is easily deduced[21] to have covariogram given by $\sum_{i=1}^{n} \sigma_i^2 \cos \lambda_i \tau$. As we have seen, the covariogram of $\sum_{j=0}^{\infty} d_j \varepsilon_{t-j}$ has generating function $\sigma_\varepsilon^2 d(z)d(z^{-1})$. The spectral density of the deterministic part turns out to be not well defined as an ordinary function. This can be seen by noting that the ordinary Fourier transform of the covariogram $\sigma^2 \cos \lambda_i \tau$ is

$$\sigma^2 \sum_{\tau=-\infty}^{\infty} \cos \lambda \tau e^{-i\omega\tau} = \sigma^2 \sum_{\tau=-\infty}^{\infty} \left(\frac{e^{i\lambda\tau} + e^{-i\lambda\tau}}{2} \right) e^{-i\omega\tau}$$

$$= \sigma^2 \sum_{\tau=-\infty}^{\infty} \left(\frac{e^{i(\lambda-\omega)\tau} + e^{-i(\lambda+\omega)\tau}}{2} \right).$$

Notice that the first term can be written

$$\sum_{\tau=-\infty}^{\infty} e^{i(\lambda-\omega)\tau} = 1 + \sum_{\tau=1}^{\infty} (e^{i(\lambda-\omega)\tau} + e^{-i(\lambda-\omega)\tau}) = 1 + 2 \sum_{\tau=1}^{\infty} \cos(\lambda - \omega)\tau.$$

The series $\sum_{\tau=1}^{\infty} \cos(\lambda - \omega)\tau$ is *not* a convergent series, so the spectrum of the deterministic part of our process is not well defined by the usual Fourier transformation.

However, it happens that there is a sense in which the spectrum of the deterministic part does exist, namely in the sense of a generalized function or "distribution." In particular, let $\delta(\omega)$ be the delta generalized function which has

---

[21] For example, let $x(t) = a \cos \lambda t + b \sin \lambda t$ where $Ea = Eab = Eb = 0$, $Ea^2 = Eb^2 = \sigma^2$. Then

$$Ex(t_1)x(t_2) = E\{a^2 \cos \lambda t_1 \cos \lambda t_2 + ab(\sin \lambda t_2 \cos \lambda t_1 + \cos \lambda t_2 \sin \lambda t_1)$$

$$+ b^2 \sin \lambda t_1 \sin \lambda t_2\}$$

$$= \sigma^2\{\cos \lambda t_1 \cos \lambda t_2 + \sin \lambda t_1 \sin \lambda t_2\}.$$

Since $\cos(\alpha - \beta) = \cos \alpha \cos \beta + \sin \alpha \sin \beta$, we have

$$Ex(t_1)x(t_2) = \sigma^2 \cos \lambda(t_1 - t_2) \quad \text{or} \quad Ex(t)x(t - T) = \sigma^2 \cos \lambda T.$$

These calculations can easily be extended to prove the assertion made in the text.

"infinite height and unit mass" at $\omega = 0$ and is zero everywhere else. That is, $\delta(\omega)$ is defined by

$$\int_{-\infty}^{\infty} \delta(\omega)g(\omega)d\omega = g(0),$$

which must hold for all "test functions" $g(\omega)$ that are continuous at $\omega = 0$. Then the spectral density of a process with covariogram $\sigma^2 \cos \lambda\tau$ is defined as

$$f(\omega) = 2\pi(\tfrac{1}{2}\sigma^2\delta(\omega - \lambda) + \tfrac{1}{2}\sigma^2\delta(\omega + \lambda)).$$

With the spectral density so defined, notice that the inversion formula holds, i.e.,

$$c(\tau) = \frac{1}{2\pi} \int_{-\infty}^{\infty} f(\omega)e^{i\omega\tau}d\omega = \frac{\sigma^2}{2}\left(\int_{-\infty}^{\infty} \delta(\omega - \lambda)e^{i\omega\tau}d\omega + \int_{-\infty}^{\infty} \delta(\omega + \lambda)e^{i\omega\tau}d\omega\right)$$

$$= \sigma^2\left(\frac{e^{i\lambda\tau} + e^{-i\lambda\tau}}{2}\right) = \sigma^2 \cos \lambda\tau.$$

Then the spectral density of the deterministic part of our process is

$$2\pi \sum_{i=1}^{n} \sigma_i^2\left(\frac{\delta(\omega - \lambda_i)}{2} + \frac{\delta(\omega + \lambda_i)}{2}\right),$$

so the spectral density function of the deterministic part is zero except for the singular points $\omega = \pm \lambda_i$, $i = 1, \ldots, n$, at which the spectrum has mass $\pi\sigma_i^2$. The spectral density thus has "spikes" at the points $\omega = \pm \lambda_i$.[22]

14. LINEAR LEAST SQUARES PREDICTION[23]

It is common in economics to assume that x_t is purely (linearly) indeterministic, which means that $\eta_t = 0$ for all t, or else that η_t has been removed.[24] Wold's theorem says that *any* indeterministic covariance stationary stochastic process x_t has the *moving average representation*

$$x_t = \sum_{j=0}^{\infty} d_j\varepsilon_{t-j}$$

or

$$x_t = d(L)\varepsilon_t, \qquad d(L) = \sum_{j=0}^{\infty} d_jL^j \qquad (59)$$

---

[22] There are essentially two ways in which a process can be deterministic. One is if its spectral density consists entirely of a number of "spikes" or delta functions. A second way is if its spectral density, even though having no spikes, is zero on some interval of ω's of positive length, or is "too close" to zero over such an interval. Heuristically, this second possible way of being deterministic is suggested by the Kolmogorov formula for the one-step-ahead prediction error variance $\sigma_\varepsilon^2 = \exp[(2\pi)^{-1} \int_{-\pi}^{\pi} \ln g(e^{-i\omega}) d\omega]$ where $g(e^{-i\omega})$ is the spectral density. See Whittle (1983, p. 26).

[23] A key reference on the subject of this section is Whittle (1983).

[24] For example, by suitable detrending and seasonal adjustment.

where $\{\varepsilon_t\}$ is the sequence of one-step-ahead linear least squares forecasting errors (innovations) in predicting x_t as a linear function of $\{x_{t-1}, x_{t-2}, \ldots\}$, i.e., $\varepsilon_t = x_t - P[x_t|x_{t-1}, x_{t-2}, \ldots]$. (As we have seen, it is natural to normalize $d(L)$ so that $d_0 = 1$, in which case $\sigma^2 = E\varepsilon_t^2$ is the variance of the one-step-ahead prediction error.)

Now suppose that $d(L)$ has an inverse that is one-sided in nonnegative powers of L. Where $d(L) = \sum_{j=0}^{n} d_j L^j$, a necessary and sufficient condition for $d(L)$ to have such a one-sided inverse is that the roots μ of $\sum_{j=0}^{n} d_j \mu^j = 0$ all lie outside the unit circle, i.e., all have absolute values exceeding unity. An inverse $a(L) \equiv d(L)^{-1}$ of $d(L)$ satisfies $a(L)d(L) = d(L)a(L) = I$ where I is the identity lag operator $I = 1 + 0L + 0L^2 + \cdots$. Operating on both sides of (59) with $a(L) = d(L)^{-1}$ gives

$$a(L)x_t = \varepsilon_t, \qquad a(L) = a_0 - \sum_{j=1}^{\infty} a_j L^j \tag{60}$$

or

$$a_0 x_t = a_1 x_{t-1} + a_2 x_{t-2} + \cdots + \varepsilon_t.$$

Since d_0 is unity, it turns out that a_0 is unity also. Equation (60) is termed the autoregressive representation for x_t. While every linearly indeterministic covariance stationary process has a moving average representation, not all of them have an autoregressive representation. Still, those that do have both a moving average and an autoregressive representation constitute a very wide class, and we shall henceforth assume that we are dealing with a member of this class.[25]

We now derive some formulas due to Wiener and Kolmogorov for linear least squares predictors. Let $P_{t-j}x_t$ be the linear least squares projection of x_t on the space spanned by $\{x_{t-j}, x_{t-j-1}, \ldots\}$, i.e.,

$$P_{t-j}x_t \equiv P[x_t|x_{t-j}, x_{t-j-1}, \ldots].$$

Now project both sides of (59) against $\{x_{t-1}, x_{t-2}, \ldots\}$ to get

$$P_{t-1}x_t = \sum_{j=0}^{\infty} d_j P_{t-1}\varepsilon_{t-j} = \sum_{j=1}^{\infty} d_j \varepsilon_{t-j},$$

[25] We remarked earlier that in general the sequence of the a_j^n in

$$P[x_t|x_{t-1}, \ldots, x_{t-n}] = \sum_{j=1}^{n} a_j^n x_{t-j}$$

does not converge as $n \to \infty$. However, under the roots condition given in the text, the a_j^n do converge. In particular, they converge to the a_j of Equation (60), so that $\lim_{n\to\infty} a_j^n = a_j$ for all $j = 1, 2, \ldots$.

which follows since $P_{t-1}\varepsilon_t = 0$, because ε_t is orthogonal to lagged x's; and since $P_{t-1}\varepsilon_{t-j} = \varepsilon_{t-j}$ for all $j \geq 1$, because ε_{t-j} is in the space spanned by $\{x_{t-1}, x_{t-2}, \ldots\}$. We write the above equation as

$$P_{t-1}x_t = (d(L)/L)_+ \varepsilon_{t-1}$$

where $(\quad)_+$ means "ignore negative powers of L," i.e., $(\sum_{j=-\infty}^{\infty} h_j L^j)_+ \equiv \sum_{j=0}^{\infty} h_j L^j$. Now assuming that x_t has an autoregressive representation, we can write $\varepsilon_{t-1} = a(L)x_{t-1} = d(L)^{-1}x_{t-1}$. Substituting this into the above equation gives

$$P_{t-1}x_t = \left(\frac{d(L)}{L}\right)_+ \frac{1}{d(L)} x_{t-1}, \tag{61}$$

which is a compact formula for the one-step-ahead linear least squares forecast of x_t based on its own past.

To get a formula for the general k-step-ahead linear least squares forecast, project both sides of (59) against $\{x_{t-k}, x_{t-k-1}, \ldots\}$ to get

$$P_{t-k}x_t = \sum_{j=k}^{\infty} d_j \varepsilon_{t-j} = (d(L)/L^k)_+ \varepsilon_{t-k}$$

$$P_{t-k}x_t = \left(\frac{d(L)}{L^k}\right)_+ \frac{1}{d(L)} x_{t-k} \tag{62}$$

which generalizes formula (61). Equation (62) is the Wiener–Kolmogorov formula for k-step-ahead linear least squares predictions.

A. Some Examples[26]

First-Order Markov: Consider the first-order autoregressive process $(1 - \lambda L)x_t = \varepsilon_t$, ε_t white noise, $|\lambda| < 1$, $\varepsilon_t = x_t - P[x_t|x_{t-1}, \ldots]$; we can write $x_t = (1/(1 - \lambda L))\varepsilon_t$. We have

$$P_{t-1}x_t = [L^{-1}(1 + \lambda L + \lambda^2 L^2 + \cdots)]_+ (1 - \lambda L)x_{t-1}$$

$$= (\lambda + \lambda^2 L + \cdots)(1 - \lambda L)x_{t-1}$$

$$= \left(\frac{\lambda}{1 - \lambda L}\right)(1 - \lambda L)x_{t-1} = \lambda x_{t-1}.$$

More generally,

$$P_{t-k}x_t = [L^{-k}(1 + \lambda L + \cdots)]_+ (1 - \lambda L)x_{t-k} = \lambda^k x_{t-k}.$$

---

[26] In these examples we continue to assume that $Ex_t = E\varepsilon_t = 0$. Modifying the formulas to account for a nonzero mean of x_t is trivial and involves adding constant terms to the formulas. Many more examples are worked out in Whittle (1983) and Nerlove (1967).

Thus we have

$$P_t x_{t+k} = \lambda^k x_t.$$

First-Order Moving Average: Suppose $x_t = (1 + \beta L)\varepsilon_t$, ε_t white, $|\beta| < 1$, $\varepsilon_t = x_t - P[x_t|x_{t-1}, \ldots]$. Then we have

$$P_{t-1}x_t = [L^{-1}(1 + \beta L)]_+\left(\frac{1}{1 + \beta L}\right)x_{t-1}, \qquad P_{t-1}x_t = \frac{\beta}{1 + \beta L}x_{t-1}.$$

We also have that for $k \geq 2$,

$$P_{t-k}x_t = [L^{-k}(1 + \beta L)]_+\left(\frac{1}{1 + \beta L}\right)x_{t-k} = 0,$$

which can also be seen directly by projecting on $\{x_{t-k}, x_{t-k-1}, \ldots\}$ both sides of $x_t = (1 + \beta L)\varepsilon_t$.

First-Order Moving Average, Autoregressive: Suppose we have

$$x_t = \left(\frac{1 + aL}{1 - \beta L}\right)\varepsilon_t, \qquad \varepsilon_t \text{ white}, \qquad |a| < 1, \quad |\beta| < 1,$$

$$\varepsilon_t = x_t - P[x_t|x_{t-1}, \ldots].$$

We then have

$$P_{t-1}x_t = \left(\frac{L^{-1}(1 + aL)}{(1 - \beta L)}\right)_+\left(\frac{1 - \beta L}{1 + aL}\right)x_{t-1}$$

$$= \left(\frac{L^{-1}}{1 - \beta L} + \frac{a}{1 - \beta L}\right)_+\left(\frac{1 - \beta L}{1 + aL}\right)x_{t-1}$$

$$P_{t-1}x_t = \left(\frac{\beta + a}{1 - \beta L}\right)\left(\frac{1 - \beta L}{1 + aL}\right)x_{t-1}, \qquad P_{t-1}x_t = \left\{\frac{a + \beta}{1 + aL}\right\}x_{t-1},$$

which expresses the forecast of x_t as a geometric distributed lag of past x's. The first-order mixed moving average, autoregressive model for x_t thus provides a rationalization for the familiar "adaptive expectations" model. As we let $\beta \to 1$ (from below, in order to assure that the roots condition $|\beta| < 1$ is met), $P_{t-1}x_t$ approaches

$$P_{t-1}x_t = \{(1 + a)/(1 + aL)\}x_{t-1},$$

which with $a < 0$ is equivalent with Cagan's (1956) adaptive expectations scheme

$$P_{t-1}x_t = \{(1 - \lambda)/(1 - \lambda L)\}x_{t-1},$$

with $a = -\lambda$. Notice that as $\beta \to 1$ (from below), we approach the situation in which $(1 - L)x_t = (1 + aL)\varepsilon_t$, so that the first difference of x_t follows a first-order moving average. The parameter a must be negative in order that $\lambda > 0$.

For the general case in which $k \geq 1$, we have

$$P_{t-k}x_t = \left(\frac{L^{-k}(1+aL)}{1-\beta L}\right)_+ \left(\frac{1-\beta L}{1+aL}\right)x_{t-k}$$

$$= \left(\frac{L^{-k}}{1-\beta L} + \frac{aL^{-k+1}}{1-\beta L}\right)_+ \left(\frac{1-\beta L}{1+aL}\right)x_{t-k}$$

$$= \left(\frac{\beta^k}{1-\beta L} + \frac{a\beta^{k-1}}{1-\beta L}\right)\left(\frac{1-\beta L}{1+aL}\right)x_{t-k} = \frac{\beta^{k-1}(\beta+a)}{(1+aL)}x_{t-k}.$$

We can write this alternatively as

$$P_t x_{t+k} = (\beta^{k-1}(\beta+a)/(1+aL))x_t.$$

Notice that as $\beta \to 1$ (from below) we approach the situation in which

$$P_t x_{t+k} = ((1+a)/(1+aL))x_t,$$

so that the same forecast is made for all horizons $k \geq 1$. In this sense there is a well-defined concept of "permanent x." This was first pointed out in the economics literature by Muth (1960), who showed that the hypothesis of rational expectations in conjunction with the model for income $(1-L)x_t = (1+aL)\varepsilon_t$ provides a rationalization both for the concept of permanent income and the geometric distributed lag formula that Friedman had earlier used to estimate permanent income in empirical work.

15. DERIVING A MOVING AVERAGE REPRESENTATION

The univariate prediction formulas given above assume that one has in hand a moving average representation for the covariance stationary stochastic process $x_t = d(L)\varepsilon_t$, in which ε_t lies in the linear space spanned by current and lagged x_t's. Suppose that one starts with a covariogram $c(\tau)$ of x_t and wishes to obtain such a moving average representation. We show how to accomplish this, beginning with a special case of a first-order moving average process.

Suppose that $c(\tau) = 0$ for $|\tau| \geq 2$. We seek a first order moving average process

$$x_t = d_0\varepsilon_t + d_1\varepsilon_{t-1} \tag{63}$$

where ε_t is a white noise that can be expressed as a square summable linear combination of $\{x_t, x_{t-1}, \ldots\}$. If representation (63) is correct, then we must have

$$c(0) = (d_0^2 + d_1^2)\sigma_\varepsilon^2$$
$$c(1) = d_0 d_1 \sigma_\varepsilon^2. \tag{64}$$

The idea is now to solve (64) for $(d_0, d_1, \sigma_\varepsilon^2)$ as a function of $c(0)$, $c(1)$. It is evident that we can solve (64) while normalizing by setting $d_0 = 1$. Solving the second equation for $\sigma_\varepsilon^2 = c(1)/d_1$ and substituting into the first equation of (64) gives the "Euler equation"

$$d_1^{-1} - \frac{c(0)}{c(1)} + d_1 = 0.$$

We call this an Euler equation because the coefficient on d_1^{-1} equals that on d_1. To solve this equation, we can express it as

$$\left(1 - \frac{c(0)}{c(1)} d_1 + d_1{}^2\right) = 0. \tag{65}$$

We seek to solve this for values of d_1. The roots of (65) come in a reciprocal pair. As in Chapter IX, let λ be one root and λ^{-1} be the other. Then we want to solve

$$\left(1 - \frac{c(0)}{c(1)} d_1 + d_1{}^2\right) = (1 - \lambda d_1)\left(1 - \frac{1}{\lambda} d_1\right).$$

Equating powers of d_1, we find that we must solve the equation

$$\lambda + \frac{1}{\lambda} = \frac{c(0)}{c(1)}.$$

A version of Figure 4 of Chapter IX can be used to solve this equation graphically (see Figure 7). Since $|\lambda + 1/\lambda| \geq 2$, it follows that we must have $|c(0)/c(1)| \geq 2$, or $2|c(1)| \leq c(0)$ in order that there exist real values of d_1 that solve (65).[27]

Alternatively, applying the quadratic formula to (65), we obtain

$$d_1 = \frac{\frac{c(0)}{c(1)} \pm \sqrt{\left(\frac{c(0)}{c(1)}\right)^2 - 4}}{2}.$$

Again, we require that $2|c(1)| \leq c(0)$ in order for a real solution to exist.

Once d_1 is found, σ_ε^2 is found from the equation $\sigma_\varepsilon^2 = c(1)/d_1$.

We have that for $2|c(1)| < c(0)$, there is a pair of solutions, one with $|d_1| > 1$, the other with $|d_1| < 1$. Thus, there are two representations of the form (63). Notice that from the formula $\sigma_\varepsilon^2 = c(1)/d_1$, the solution with the smaller absolute value of d_1 (the one that is less than unity in absolute value) is the one associated with the larger error variance. This suggests that associated with our two solutions are distinct ε_t processes. Our calculations so far have not yet built

---

[27] The spectral density for this x_t process is given by

$$g_x(e^{-iw}) = c(0) + 2c(1) \cos w.$$

We require that $2|c(1)| < c(0)$ in order that the spectral density be nonnegative, or equivalently, in order that $c(\tau)$ be a nonnegative definite sequence.

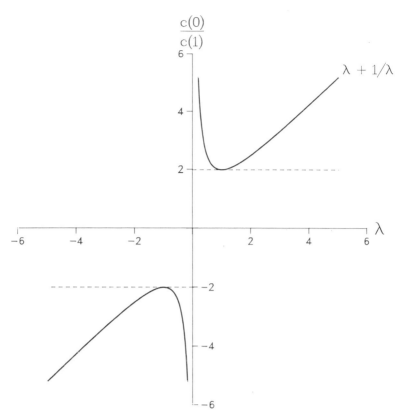

FIGURE 7 Factoring the "Euler equation" associated with a first order moving average process.

in the requirement that ε_t lies in the space spanned by current and lagged x_t's. This requirement is imposed by selecting the solution with $|d_1| < 1$. Since

$$x_t = \varepsilon_t + d_1 \varepsilon_{t-1},$$

we have

$$(1 + d_1 L)\varepsilon_t = x_t.$$

For $|d_1| < 1$, we have that ε_t can be expressed as a square summable linear combination of current and lagged x_t's:

$$\varepsilon_t = \sum_{j=0}^{\infty} (-d_1)^j x_{t-j}. \tag{66}$$

However, when $|d_1| > 1$, the right side of representation (66) is not square summable. When $|d_1| > 1$, the ε_t in (63) lies in the linear space spanned by square summable linear combinations of *future* x_t's and can be be expressed as

$$\varepsilon_t = \sum_{j=1}^{\infty} \left(\frac{1}{d_1}\right)^j x_{t+j}.$$

Thus, to obtain the representation in which ε_t lies in the linear space spanned by $\{x_t, x_{t-1}, \ldots\}$, we select $|d_1| < 1$. Since $\sigma_\varepsilon^2 = c(1)/d_1$, this selection results in selecting from among moving average representations that satisfy (64) the one for which σ_ε^2 is maximal. For the representation chosen in this way, σ_ε^2 is the variance of $(x_t - P[x_t|x_{t-1}, \ldots])$. The white noise process ε_t chosen by this procedure is said to be a *fundamental* white noise for x_t, meaning that it equals the process of one-step ahead errors in predicting x_t from its own past values.[28]

16. FINDING A WOLD REPRESENTATION: *m*th ORDER MOVING AVERAGE

More generally, suppose that we are given a process x_t with finite order moving average representation

$$x_t = a(L)u_t$$

where

$$a(L) = \sum_{j=0}^{m} a_j L^j,$$

and where u_t is a white noise that is not fundamental for x_t, i.e., $u_t \neq x_t - P[x_t|x_{t-1} \ldots]$. For convenience, we assume that the zeros of the polynomial $a(z)$ are distinct. The covariance generating function of x_t is given by

$$g_x(z) = a(z)a(z^{-1})\sigma_u^2. \tag{67}$$

We know that this process also possesses a Wold moving average representation

$$x_t = d(L)\varepsilon_t, \qquad d_0 = 1, \tag{68}$$

where $\varepsilon_t = x_t - P[x_t|x_{t-1}, \ldots]$. The condition that ε_t lie in the linear space spanned by $\{x_t, x_{t-1}, \ldots\}$ is equivalent with the condition that the zeros of $d(z)$ not be less than unity in absolute value. To see this heuristically, represent $d(L)$ as

$$d(L) = (1 - \lambda_1 L) \cdots (1 - \lambda_m L) \tag{69}$$

---

[28] One sometimes encounters an alternative condition that serves to select the moving average representation with a fundamental white noise. This is the "minimum phase condition," which in our example requires that the solution of (64) be selected in which the phase of $d(e^{-iw}) = 1 + d_1 e^{-iw}$ is smallest. For our example, the phase of $d(e^{-iw})$ is given by $\theta(w) = \tan^{-1}(-d_1 \sin w/(1 + d_1 \sin w))$. For low frequency, this is minimized in absolute value when the solution with $|d_1| < 1$ is selected.

where λ_j is the reciprocal of the jth zero of $d(z)$. Represent $d(L)^{-1}$ as

$$d(L)^{-1} = \sum_{j=1}^{m} \frac{A_j}{(1 - \lambda_j L)}. \tag{70}$$

Then (68) and (70) imply

$$\varepsilon_t = \sum_{j=1}^{m} A_j \sum_{k=0}^{\infty} \lambda_j^k x_{t-k}. \tag{71}$$

The geometric sums on the right side fail to converge if $|\lambda_j| > 1$. Imposing that $|\lambda_j| \leq 1$ for $j = 1, \ldots, m$ is necessary and sufficient for ε_t to lie in the space spanned by current and lagged x's. (This argument fails to reveal why when $|\lambda_j| = 1$ for some j, ε_t lies in the space spanned by current and lagged x_t's. When $|\lambda_j| = 1$ for some j, then although x_t possesses a moving average representation, it possesses no autoregressive representation. In this case, although ε_t is in the closure of the linear space spanned by $\{x_t, x_{t-1}, \ldots\}$, it can be expressed in the form $\sum_{j=0}^{\infty} w_j x_{t-j}$ for no square summable sequence of w_j's, but only as the limit of a sequence of such expressions.)

To find a fundamental moving average representation, we note that (68) and (69) imply that $g_x(z) = \sigma_\varepsilon^2 (1 - \lambda_1 z) \cdots (1 - \lambda_m z)(1 - \lambda_1 z^{-1}) \cdots (1 - \lambda_m z^{-1})$. Then we equate this to $g_x(z)$ given by (67) to get

$$\sigma_u^2 a(z) a(z^{-1}) = \sigma_\varepsilon^2 \, d(z) \, d(z^{-1})$$

or

$$\sigma_u^2 a(z) a(z^{-1}) = \sigma_\varepsilon^2 (1 - \lambda_1 z) \cdots (1 - \lambda_m z)(1 - \lambda_1 z^{-1}) \cdots (1 - \lambda_m z^{-1}). \tag{72}$$

Equation (72) asserts that $d(z)d(z^{-1})\sigma_\varepsilon^2$ is a symmetric *factorization* of $\sigma_u^2 a(z) a(z^{-1})$ in which the zeros of $\sigma_u^2 a(z) a(z^{-1})$ that are not inside the unit circle are placed in $d(z)$, while those that are not outside are put into $d(z^{-1})$. (Note that since $\sigma_u^2 a(z) a(z^{-1})$ evaluated at z_0 equals its value at z_0^{-1}, the zeros of $\sigma_u^2 a(z) a(z^{-1})$ come in reciprocal pairs. Thus, it is reminiscent of the characteristic polynomial of an Euler equation in the undiscounted case, when $b = 1$.)

The preceding tells us how to achieve a Wold moving average representation for a finite-order moving average process. First, find the zeros of $g_x(z)$. By the reciprocal pairs properties of these roots, half will not be outside the unit circle, while half will not be inside the unit circle. (Excuse the cumbersome wording, which is designed to cover the case of roots on the unit circle.) Let $\lambda_1, \ldots, \lambda_m$ be the roots that are not outside the unit circle. Set

$$d(L) = (1 - \lambda_1 L) \cdots (1 - \lambda_m L). \tag{73}$$

Then to find σ_ε^2, solve equation (72) at $z = 1$ to get

$$\sigma_\varepsilon^2 = \frac{g_x(1)}{d(1)^2}. \tag{74}$$

Hansen and Sargent (1980, p. 102) give a quick but equivalent method of finding $d(L)$. Given $\sigma_u^2 a(z) a(z^{-1})$, the problem is to find $\sigma_\varepsilon^2 d(z) d(z^{-1})$, where the zeros of $d(z)$ are not inside the unit circle. Let $z_1, \ldots, z_k$ be the zeros of $a(z)$ that are inside the unit circle, where $0 \leq k \leq m$. Then $d(z)$ satisfies

$$\frac{\sigma_\varepsilon}{\sigma_u} d(z) = a(z) \prod_{j=1}^{k} \frac{(1 - z_j z)}{(z - z_j)}. \tag{75}$$

For example, suppose $x_t = (1 + 2L)u_t$, where $\sigma_u^2 = 1$ and where u_t is a white noise. Then application of (75) gives the Wold moving average representation $x_t = (1 + (1/2)L)\varepsilon_t$, with $\sigma_\varepsilon = 2$, where ε_t is a fundamental white noise for $\{x_t\}$.

17. FINDING A WOLD REPRESENTATION: AN mth ORDER MOVING AVERAGE, nth ORDER AUTOREGRESSION

The following problem is a useful input into solving an interesting class of "signal extraction" problems.

Consider a covariance stationary process x_t with representation

$$x_t = \frac{a(L)}{b(L)} u_t$$

where u_t is a (not necessary fundamental) white noise and

$$b(L) = (1 - \mu_1) \cdots (1 - \mu_n L), \qquad |\mu_j| < 1$$
$$a(L) = (1 - \alpha_1 L) \cdots (1 - \alpha_m L).$$

Note that we assume that the zeros of $b(z)$ are outside the unit circle, but that those of $a(z)$ are unrestricted. Our problem is to find a Wold moving average representation for x_t.

The solution of this problem is simply

$$x_t = \frac{d(L)}{b(L)} \varepsilon_t \tag{76}$$

where $d(L) = (1 - \lambda_1 L) \cdots (1 - \lambda_m L)$, where $\lambda_1, \ldots, \lambda_m$ are the zeros of $a(z)a(z^{-1})$ that do not lie outside the unit circle, and where ε_t is the fundamental white noise for x_t, with variance σ_ε^2 given by

$$\sigma_\varepsilon^2 = \frac{a(1)^2 \sigma_u^2}{d(1)^2}.$$

In other words, the denominator polynomial $b(L)$ is left unaltered while the methods of the preceding section are applied to factor the numerator polynomial. The reader should convince himself that this method delivers an ε_t process that is a white noise, and that lies in the linear space spanned by $\{x_t, x_{t-1}, \ldots\}$. This can be done by constructing an argument along the lines of the one in the preceding section, by assuming $|\lambda_j| < 1$ for $j = 1, \ldots, m$ and by premultiplying (76) by $b(L)/d(L)$.

18. SIGNAL EXTRACTION PROBLEMS[29]

Let y_t be a covariance stationary stochastic process with mth order moving average representation

$$y_t = a(L)u_t,$$

where

$$a(L) = \sum_{j=0}^{m} a_j L^j,$$

where u_t is a white noise with variance σ_u^2 that is not necessarily fundamental for y_t. Suppose that x_t is the sum of y_t and an orthogonal serially uncorrelated white noise η_t with variance σ_η^2,

$$x_t = y_t + \eta_t$$

where

$$E\eta_t u_{t-s} = 0 \qquad \text{for all } s.$$

Suppose that an agent observes $\{x_t, x_{t-1}, \ldots\}$ at t, and wishes to construct linear least squares forecasts of x's on the basis of this information set. To construct the linear least squares forecast for x_{t+k} given $\{x_t, x_{t-1}, \ldots\}$, one uses the Wiener–Kolmogorov formula (62), which requires that a Wold moving average representation $x_t = d(L)\varepsilon_t$ be obtained for x_t.

To obtain the Wold representation for x_t, we simply use the method of Section 16. In particular, the covariance generating function of x_t is

$$g_x(z) = a(z)a(z^{-1})\sigma_u^2 + \sigma_\eta^2.$$

We find the zeros of $g_x(z)$, which come in reciprocal pairs, and prepare the factorization

$$g_x(z) = d(z)\,d(z^{-1})\sigma_\varepsilon^2$$

---

[29] Multivariate versions of signal extraction problems require the factorization of matrix polynomials in the lag operator, of the same kind encountered in Chapter IX, Section 10. As in the univariate case, there is an equivalence between the mathematics involved in solving linear-quadratic control problems and linear signal extraction problems. In the control literature, this equivalence is called "duality". Hansen and Sargent (1981a) describe practical methods for factoring matrix polynomials in the lag operator which arise from an optimal control or signal extraction problem. Blanchard and Kahn (1980), Whiteman (1983), and Dagli and Taylor (1984) discuss problems in which the matrix polynomial in the lag operator does not come from an optimum control or prediction problem (i.e., the matrix polynomial lacks b-symmetry in L). These three works contain results on the existence, uniqueness, and computation of solutions of linear systems generated by such nonsymmetric matrix polynomials.

where the zeros of $d(z) = (1 - \lambda_1 z) \cdots (1 - \lambda_m z)$ do not lie inside the unit circle, and σ_ε^2 solves

$$\sigma_\varepsilon^2 = \frac{g_x(1)}{d(1)^2}.$$

The Wiener-Kolmogorov formula (62) can then be used to calculate $P[x_{t+k}|x_t, x_{t-1} \cdots]$.

Moving into a richer class of examples, we now let y_t be a process with mixed moving average, autoregressive representation

$$y_t = \frac{a(L)}{b(L)} u_t$$

where u_t is a white noise with variance σ_u^2, and

$$a(L) = (1 - \alpha_1 L) \cdots (1 - \alpha_m L)$$
$$b(L) = (1 - \mu_1 L) \cdots (1 - \mu_m L), \qquad |\mu_j| < 1$$

where the α_j's can be on either side of the unit circle. Suppose that x_t is the sum of y_t and a serially uncorrelated white noise η_t with variance σ_η^2,

$$x_t = y_t + \eta_t$$

where $E\eta_t u_{t-s} = 0$ for all s. Again we desire to find $P[x_{t+k}|x_t, x_{t-1}, \ldots]$, so we need to find a Wold representation for x_t. We use the method of Section 17.

The covariance generating function of x is

$$g_x(z) = \frac{a(z)a(z^{-1})}{b(z)b(z^{-1})} \sigma_u^2 + \sigma_\eta^2.$$

Taking the right-hand side to a common denominator gives

$$g_x(z) = \frac{\sigma_u^2 a(z)a(z^{-1}) + \sigma_\eta^2 b(z)b(z^{-1})}{b(z)b(z^{-1})}. \tag{77}$$

The numerator polynomial is of order $p = \max(n, m)$, and can be factored to be of the form

$$\sigma_u^2 a(z)a(z^{-1}) + \sigma_\eta^2 b(z)b(z^{-1}) = \sigma_\varepsilon^2 d(z)d(z^{-1}) \tag{78}$$

where

$$d(z) = (1 - \lambda_1 L) \cdots (1 - \lambda_p L), |\lambda_j| \leq 1, \qquad j = 1, \ldots, p$$

and where σ_ε^2 solves

$$\sigma_\varepsilon^2 = \frac{\sigma_u^2 a(1)^2 + \sigma_\eta^2 b(1)^2}{d(1)^2}.$$

The Wold moving average representation for x_t is then

$$x_t = \frac{d(L)}{b(L)} \varepsilon_t. \tag{79}$$

The Wiener-Kolmogorov formula can be applied to (79).

A famous application of the preceding analysis is due to Muth (1960). Muth assumed that income x_t is the sum of a first order Markov process $[1/(1 - \rho L)]u_t, |\rho| < 1$, and an uncorrelated white noise η_t. The agent's problem was to predict his future income. Setting $a(L) = 1, b(L) = (1 - \rho L)$, we find that equation (78) becomes

$$\sigma_u^2 + \sigma_\eta^2(1 - \rho z)(1 - \rho z^{-1}) = \sigma_\varepsilon^2(1 - \lambda_1 z)(1 - \lambda_1 z^{-1}).$$

The expression on the left can be written

$$\rho z^{-1} \sigma_\eta^2 \left[-z^2 + \left(\frac{\sigma_u^2}{\sigma_\eta^2 \rho} + \left(\frac{1}{\rho} + \rho \right) \right) z - 1 \right].$$

Applying the quadratic formula, and setting λ_1 equal to the root that is smaller in absolute value, we have

$$\lambda_1 = \frac{1}{2} \left[\left(\frac{\sigma_u^2}{\sigma_\eta^2 \rho} \right) + \left(\frac{1}{\rho} + \rho \right) - \left\{ \left[\frac{\sigma_u^2}{\sigma_\eta^2 \rho} + \left(\frac{1}{\rho} + \rho \right) \right]^2 - 4 \right\}^{1/2} \right]. \tag{80}$$

The limiting value of λ_1 as ρ approaches 1 from below is

$$\lambda_1 = 1 + \frac{1}{2} \left(\frac{\sigma_u^2}{\sigma_\eta^2} \right) - \left\{ \frac{\sigma_u^2}{\sigma_\eta^2} \left(1 + \frac{1}{4} \frac{\sigma_u^2}{\sigma_\eta^2} \right) \right\}^{1/2}, \tag{81}$$

which is the expression obtained by Muth (1960). Thus, we have that x_t has the first-order moving average, first-order autoregressive representation

$$x_t = \left(\frac{1 - \lambda_1 L}{1 - \rho L} \right) \varepsilon_t,$$

where ε_t is a fundamental white noise for x_t with variance σ_ε^2 that solves

$$\sigma_\varepsilon^2 = \frac{\sigma_u^2 + \sigma_\eta^2(1 - \rho)^2}{(1 - \lambda_1)^2}.$$

The result from page 294 now applies with $\beta \equiv \rho$ and $\lambda_1 \equiv -a$. Thus we have

$$P_t x_{t+k} = [\rho^{k-1}(\rho - \lambda_1)/(1 - \lambda_1 L)]x_t,$$

so that projections of future x's are a geometric average of past x's.

19. PREDICTING GEOMETRIC DISTRIBUTED LEADS

It is important to know the solution of the following problem in order to use a variety of linear rational expectations models. Let x_t be a covariance stationary stochastic process with Wold moving average representation

$$x_t = c(L)\varepsilon_t, \qquad c_0 = 1 \tag{82}$$

where ε_t is a fundamental white noise for x and $c(L) = \sum_{j=0}^{\infty} c_j L^j$ is square summable. We further assume that $c(L)$ has an inverse $a(L) = c(L)^{-1}$ which is one-sided in nonnegative powers of L and square summable. Thus, x_t has the autoregressive representation

$$a(L)x_t = \varepsilon_t \tag{83}$$

where $a(L) = 1 - a_1 L - a_2 L^2 - \cdots$.

We want to calculate the following linear projection

$$y_t = P\left[\sum_{j=0}^{\infty} \lambda^j x_{t+j} \mid x_t, x_{t-1}, \ldots\right] \equiv P_t \sum_{j=0}^{\infty} \lambda^j x_{t+j} \tag{84}$$

where $|\lambda| < 1$. Projections of such geometric distributed leads occur in a variety of linear rational expectations models. We begin by noting that y_t defined by (84) satisfies the stochastic difference equation

$$y_t = \lambda P_t y_{t+1} + x_t. \tag{85}$$

That is, y_t is the stationary solution of the difference equation (84) as can be verified by repeated substitution in (85). We seek expressions for y_t of the forms

$$y_t = g(L)x_t \tag{86}$$

and

$$y_t = d(L)\varepsilon_t \tag{87}$$

where

$$d(L) = \sum_{j=0}^{\infty} d_j L^j, \qquad g(L) = \sum_{j=0}^{\infty} g_j L^j, \qquad \sum_{j=0}^{\infty} g_j^2 < +\infty, \sum_{j=0}^{\infty} d_j^2 < +\infty.$$

We know that representation (86) exists by definition, and therefore that $d(L) = g(L)c(L)$ also exists. That is, a representation of the form (87) exists because $\{x_t, x_{t-1}, \ldots\}$ and $\{\varepsilon_t, \varepsilon_{t-1}, \ldots\}$ span the same space.

We shall solve for $d(L)$ using (85) and prediction theory. Using (87), we have that

$$P_t y_{t+1} = \left[\frac{d(L)}{L}\right]_+ \varepsilon_t$$

or

$$P_t y_{t+1} = \left[\frac{d(L)}{L} - \frac{d_0}{L} \right] \varepsilon_t.$$

Substituting this and (82) and (87) into (85) gives

$$d(L)\varepsilon_t = \lambda \left[\frac{d(L)}{L} - \frac{d_0}{L} \right] \varepsilon_t + c(L)\varepsilon_t.$$

Since this equation holds for all ε_t realizations, it implies, after rearranging, that

$$(1 - \lambda L^{-1}) d(L) = c(L) - \lambda d_0 L^{-1},$$

an equation that we desire to solve for $d(L)$ as a function of $c(L)$. We determine d_0 by evaluating the above equation at $L = \lambda$, to get $c(\lambda) = d_0$. Using this value for d_0 gives

$$d(L) = \frac{c(L) - \lambda c(\lambda) L^{-1}}{1 - \lambda L^{-1}}. \tag{88}$$

Using $g(L) = d(L)c(L)^{-1}$ and $c(L)^{-1} = a(L)$, we get

$$g(L) = \frac{1 - \lambda a(\lambda)^{-1} a(L) L^{-1}}{1 - \lambda L^{-1}}. \tag{89}$$

For the case in which $a(L)$ is an rth order polynomial $a(L) = 1 - \sum_{j=1}^{r} a_j L^j$, Hansen and Sargent (1980) show by using polynomial long division that (89) can be expressed

$$g(L) = a(\lambda)^{-1} \left[1 + \sum_{j=1}^{r-1} \left(\sum_{k=j+1}^{r} \lambda^{k-j} a_k \right) L^j \right] \tag{90}$$

so that

$$g(L) = \sum_{j=0}^{r-1} g_j L^j,$$

with

$$g_0 = a(\lambda)^{-1}, \qquad g_j = a(\lambda)^{-1} \sum_{k=j+1}^{r} \lambda^{k-j} a_k$$

for $j = 1, \ldots, r - 1$. Evidently, the coefficients g_j can be computed recursively via the following formulas:

$$g_0 = a(\lambda)^{-1}$$

$$g_r = 0 \tag{91}$$

$$g_{j-1} = \lambda g_j + \lambda g_0 a_j \qquad j = r, r - 1, \ldots, 2.$$

Various versions of formulas (88), (89), and (90) were originally derived in papers by Saracoglu and Sargent (1978), Hansen and Sargent (1980), and Futia (1981).

20. THE CHAIN RULE OF FORECASTING

The law of iterated projections implies a recursion relationship that is sometimes very useful in a forecasting context. The relationship is known as Wold's "chain rule of forecasting." It shows how projections $P_t x_{t+k}$ for all $k \geq 2$ can be calculated from knowledge of the form of $P_t x_{t+1}$ alone.[30]

Suppose that $\{x_t\}$ is a linearly indeterministic covariance stationary stochastic process for which

$$P_t x_{t+1} = \sum_{j=0}^{\infty} h_j x_{t-j}, \qquad \sum_{j=0}^{\infty} h_j^2 < \infty.$$

It follows that

$$P_{t+k} x_{t+k+1} = h_0 x_{t+k} + h_1 x_{t+k-1} + \cdots + h_k x_t + h_{k+1} x_{t-1} + \cdots.$$

Projecting both sides of this equation on $(x_t, x_{t-1}, \ldots)$ gives, via the law of iterated projections,

$$P_t x_{t+k+1} = h_0 P_t x_{t+k} + h_1 P_t x_{t+k-1} + \cdots + h_{k-1} P_t x_{t+1} + \sum_{i=0}^{\infty} h_{k+i} x_{t-i}. \quad (92)$$

This recursion relationship is the "chain rule of forecasting" which shows how to build up projections of x_t arbitrarily far into the future from knowledge of the formula for the one-step-ahead projection alone.

To take an example, suppose that $\{x_t\}$ is a first-order Markov process so that

$$P_t x_{t+1} = \lambda x_t, \qquad |\lambda| < 1.$$

From application of (92) it follows that $P_t x_{t+j} = \lambda^j x_t, j \geq 1$.

21. SOME APPLICATIONS TO RATIONAL EXPECTATIONS MODELS

Let us return to the example of Cagan's portfolio balance schedule, only now we assume that m_t is a covariance stationary stochastic process and the log of the price level now expected for next period is the linear least squares projection of p_{t+1} on information available at time t. We then have the difference equation

$$m_t - p_t = \alpha P_t p_{t+1} - \alpha p_t, \qquad \alpha < 0 \quad (93)$$

---

[30] Interesting applications of the chain rule of forecasting occur in Shiller (1972).

where $P_t p_{t+1}$ is the linear least squares forecast of p_{t+1} given information available at time t. This difference equation can be rewritten as

$$p_t = \left(\frac{-\alpha}{1-\alpha}\right)P_t p_{t+1} + \left(\frac{1}{1-\alpha}\right)m_t$$

or

$$p_t = \lambda P_t p_{t+1} + (1-\lambda)m_t$$

where $\lambda = -\alpha/(1-\alpha)$, which implies that $0 < \lambda < 1$ since $\alpha < 0$. The stationary solution of the above difference equation obeys[31]

$$p_t = (1-\lambda)\sum_{j=0}^{\infty} \lambda^j P_t m_{t+j}. \tag{94}$$

Let us assume that m_t has the autoregressive representation

$$a(L)m_t = \varepsilon_t$$

where ε_t is fundamental for m, and $a(L) = 1 - a_1 L - \cdots - a_r L^r$. Then from formula (90) of the preceding section we have that (94) implies

$$p_t = (1-\lambda)a(\lambda)^{-1}\left[1 + \sum_{j=1}^{r-1}\left(\sum_{k=j+1}^{r} \lambda^{k-j}a_k\right)L^j\right]m_t \tag{95}$$

$$a(L)m_t = \varepsilon_t. \tag{96}$$

These two equations express how the stochastic process for p_t is a function of the stochastic process of m_t. Notice that p_t depends on $m_t, m_{t-1}, \ldots, m_{t-r+1}$ via coefficients that partly reflect the stochastic process (96) that governs m_t. As an example, we set $a(L) = 1 - a_1 L - a_2 L^2 - a_3 L^3$. Then (95) and (96) become

$$p_t = (1-\lambda)(1 - a_1\lambda - a_2\lambda^2 - a_3\lambda^3)^{-1}[1 + (a_2\lambda + a_3\lambda^2)L + (a_3\lambda)L^2]m_t$$

$$m_t = a_1 m_{t-1} + a_2 m_{t-2} + a_3 m_{t-3} + \varepsilon_t.$$

Let us reconsider the supply–demand example of Chapter IX where x_t is now a covariance stationary, indeterministic random process with mean zero and autoregressive representation $a(L)x_t = \varepsilon_t$, where ε_t is a fundamental white noise for x_t. Our system is naturally modified to become

$$C_t = -\beta p_t, \qquad\qquad \beta > 0$$

$$Y_t = \gamma P_{t-1}p_t + x_t, \qquad \gamma > 0$$

$$I_t = \alpha(P_t p_{t+1} - p_t), \qquad \alpha > 0$$

$$Y_t = C_t + I_t - I_{t-1},$$

---

[31] In this and the following example we set "transient terms" of the form $c\lambda^t$ to zero because we are interested in obtaining solutions that are covariance stationary processes.

where Y_t is production, C_t demand for consumption, and I_t holdings of inventories. Substituting the first three equations into the fourth gives

$$(\gamma + \alpha)P_{t-1}p_t + (\alpha + \beta)p_t = \alpha P_t p_{t+1} + \alpha p_{t-1} - x_t. \tag{97}$$

Taking projections of both sides against information available at time $t - 1$ gives

$$\alpha P_{t-1}p_{t+1} - (\gamma + \beta + 2\alpha)P_{t-1}p_t + \alpha P_{t-1}p_{t-1} = P_{t-1}x_t$$

or

$$(B^{-1} - \phi + B)P_{t-1}p_t = \alpha^{-1}P_{t-1}x_t$$

where

$$B^{-1}P_{t-1}z_t \equiv P_{t-1}z_{t+1}, \; BP_{t-1}z_t \equiv P_{t-1}z_{t-1},$$

and where

$$\phi = ((\beta + \gamma)/\alpha) + 2 > 0.$$

Multiplying by B gives

$$(1 - \phi B + B^2)P_{t-1}p_t = \alpha^{-1}P_{t-1}x_{t-1}$$

$$(1 - \lambda^{-1}B)(1 - \lambda B)P_{t-1}p_t = \alpha^{-1}P_{t-1}x_{t-1} \tag{98}$$

where $|\lambda| < 1$ satisfies $\lambda + \lambda^{-1} = \phi$. To ensure covariance stationarity of the solution, we shall insist that all lag distributions be square summable. Operating on both sides of (98) with the forward inverse of $(1 - \lambda^{-1}B)$ gives

$$(1 - \lambda B)P_{t-1}p_t = \frac{-\lambda\alpha^{-1}}{1 - \lambda B^{-1}} P_{t-1}x_t$$

or

$$P_{t-1}p_t - \lambda p_{t-1} = \frac{-\lambda}{\alpha} \sum_{i=0}^{\infty} \lambda^i P_{t-1}x_{t+i}.$$

Substituting this solution for $P_{t-1}p_t$ into (97) gives

$$p_t = \lambda p_{t-1} + \frac{1}{\alpha + \beta - \alpha\lambda}\left[\alpha^{-1}\lambda(\gamma + \alpha)\sum_{i=0}^{\infty}\lambda^i P_{t-1}x_{t+i} - \sum_{i=0}^{\infty}\lambda^i P_t x_{t+i}\right] \tag{99}$$

We have assumed that x_t has the autoregressive representation $a(L)x_t = \varepsilon_t$. Now by using methods similar to those used to derive (90), it can be established that

$$P_{t-1}\sum_{j=0}^{\infty}\lambda^j x_{t+j} = \left(\frac{L^{-1}I - L^{-1}a(\lambda)^{-1}a(L)}{1 - \lambda L^{-1}}\right)x_{t-1}.$$

Substituting this and (90) into (99) we have the following formula for the equilibrium stochastic process for price p_t as a function of the x_t process

$$p_t = \lambda p_{t-1} + \frac{1}{\alpha + \beta - \alpha\lambda}\left\{\alpha^{-1}\lambda(\gamma + \alpha)\left[\frac{L^{-1}I - L^{-1}a(\lambda)^{-1}a(L)}{1 - \lambda L^{-1}}\right]x_{t-1}\right.$$
$$\left. - \left(\frac{1 - \lambda a(\lambda)^{-1}a(L)L^{-1}}{1 - \lambda L^{-1}}\right)x_t\right\}$$

$$a(L)x_t = \varepsilon_t.$$

This is the solution to the stochastic difference equation (97) which expresses p_t as a function of current and lagged x's and p's, and which gives a covariance stationary process for p_t.

22. VECTOR STOCHASTIC DIFFERENCE EQUATIONS

Let x_t be an $(n \times 1)$-vector wide-sense stationary stochastic process that is governed by the matrix difference equation

$$C(L)x_t = \varepsilon_t \tag{100}$$

where ε_t is now an $n \times 1$ vector of white noises with means of zero and contemporaneous covariance matrix $E\varepsilon_t\varepsilon_t' = V$, an $n \times n$ matrix. We assume $E\varepsilon_t\varepsilon_{t-s}' = 0_{n \times n}$ for all $s \neq 0$. In (100), $C(L)$ is an $n \times n$ matrix of (finite order) polynomials in the lag operator L:

$$C(L) = \begin{bmatrix} C_{11}(L) & C_{12}(L) & \cdots & C_{1n}(L) \\ \vdots & & & \\ C_{n1}(L) & \cdots & & C_{nn}(L) \end{bmatrix},$$

where each $C_{ij}(L)$ is a finite order polynomial in the lag operator.

We assume that the matrix $C(L)$ has an inverse under convolution $C(L)^{-1} \equiv B(L)$; $C(L)^{-1}$ is defined as the matrix that satisfies

$$C(L)^{-1}C(L) = I_{n \times n}$$

where $I_{n \times n}$ is the $n \times n$ identity matrix. If it exists, $C(L)^{-1}$ can be found as follows. Evaluate the matrix z transform $C(z)$ at $z = e^{-i\omega}$ to get $C(e^{-i\omega})$. Then invert $C(e^{-i\omega})$, frequency by frequency, to get $C(e^{-i\omega})^{-1}$. Finally, the matrix coefficients $C(L)^{-1} = B(L) = \sum_{j=0}^{\infty} B_j L^j$, B_j being an $n \times n$ matrix, can be found from the inversion formula

$$B_j = \frac{1}{2\pi}\int_{-\pi}^{\pi} C(e^{-i\omega})^{-1}e^{i\omega i}\, d\omega,$$

where by integrating a matrix we mean to denote element-by-element integration.

A solution of (100) is found by premultiplying by $B(L)$ to obtain

$$x_t = B(L)\varepsilon_t. \tag{101}$$

The vector stochastic difference equation $C(L)x_t = \varepsilon_t$ is said to be an *autoregressive representation* for the vector process x_t. The solution $x_t = B(L)\varepsilon_t$ is said to be a vector *moving average representation* for the process x_t. The cross-spectral density matrix of the $n \times 1$ x_t process (which has the cross spectrum between the ith and jth components of x in the (i, j)th position) is given by

$$g_{xx}(e^{-i\omega}) = B(e^{-i\omega})VB(e^{+i\omega})' \tag{102}$$

where the prime denotes transposition. Formula (102) is analogous to the univariate equation (5), and can be derived by comparable methods.

Equation (102) is a very compact formula for calculating the cross spectra of the $n \times 1$ x_t process as a function of the fundamental parameters, the covariance matrix V and the coefficients in $C(L)$ (or $B(L)$). Equation (100) is quite a general representation and is flexible enough to incorporate exogenous variables and serially correlated noises.

In Equation (100) a variable x_{it} is said to be exogenous if $C_{ij}(L) = 0$ for all j not equal to i. This means that the row of Equation (100) corresponding to x_{it} becomes $C_{ii}(L)x_{it} = \varepsilon_{it}$, so that x_{it} is governed by only its own past interacting with the random shock ε_{it}. In this sense the evolution of x_{it} is not affected by interactions with other variables in x_t. This *is not* to say however that x_{it} is uncorrelated with other components of x_t since ε_{it} can be correlated contemporaneously with other ε's (i.e., V need not be diagonal). The definition of exogeneity given here turns out to be precisely the one used by econometricians in a time series context (see Section 24).

Serially correlated errors can be incorporated by suitably redefining the errors as components of x_t, and then modeling them as exogenous processes that affect but are not affected by other components of x_t.

A. A Compact Notation

It is always possible to write an mth-order difference equation in terms of a vector first-order system. For example, consider the bivariate system

$$x_{1,t+1} = \alpha_1 x_{1,t} + \cdots + \alpha_m x_{1,t-m+1} + \alpha_{m+1}x_{2,t} + \cdots$$

$$+ \alpha_{2m}x_{2,t-m+1} + \varepsilon_{1,t+1}$$

$$x_{2,t+1} = \beta_1 x_{1,t} + \cdots + \beta_m x_{1,t-m+1} + \beta_{m+1}x_{2,t} + \cdots \tag{103}$$

$$+ \beta_{2m}x_{2,t-m+1} + \varepsilon_{2,t+1}$$

where $(\varepsilon_{1,t+1}, \varepsilon_{2,t+1})$ are two serially uncorrelated white-noise processes. Equations (103) can be written as

$$x_{t+1} = Ax_t + \varepsilon_{t+1} \tag{104}$$

where

$$A = \begin{bmatrix} \alpha_1 & \alpha_2 & \cdots & \alpha_m & \alpha_{m+1} & & \cdots & \alpha_{2m} \\ 1 & 0 & \cdots & 0 & 0 & & \cdots & 0 \\ \vdots & & & & & & & \\ 0 & 0 & 1 & 0 & 0 & & \cdots & 0 \\ \beta_1 & \beta_2 & \cdots & \beta_m & \beta_{m+1} & & \cdots & \beta_{2m} \\ 0 & 0 & & 0 & 1 & 0 & \cdots & 0 \\ \vdots & & & & & & & \\ 0 & 0 & & 0 & 0 & \cdots & 0 & 1 & 0 \end{bmatrix} \begin{matrix} \\ \\ \\ \\ \leftarrow (m+1)\text{th row} \\ \\ \\ \\ \end{matrix}$$

$$\uparrow (m+1)\text{th column}$$

$$x_{t+1} = \begin{bmatrix} x_{1,t+1} \\ x_{1,t} \\ \vdots \\ x_{1,t-m+2} \\ x_{2,t+1} \\ x_{2,t} \\ \vdots \\ x_{2,t-m+2} \end{bmatrix}, \qquad \varepsilon_{t+1} = \begin{bmatrix} \varepsilon_{1,t+1} \\ 0 \\ 0 \\ \vdots \\ 0 \\ \varepsilon_{2,t+1} \\ 0 \\ 0 \\ \vdots \\ 0 \end{bmatrix} \begin{matrix} \\ \\ \\ \\ \\ \leftarrow (m+1)\text{th row} \\ \\ \\ \\ \end{matrix}$$

The solution of the vector difference equation (104) can be written

$$x_{t+\tau} = A^\tau x(t) + \varepsilon(t + \tau) + A\varepsilon(t + \tau - 1) + \cdots + A^{\tau-1}\varepsilon(t + 1). \quad (105)$$

Since $E\varepsilon(t + \tau)x(t)' = 0_{2m \times 2m}$ for all $\tau \geq 1$, multiplying the solution (105) through by $x(t)'$ and taking expected values gives the matrix Yule–Walker equation

$$Ex_{t+\tau}x_t' = A^\tau Ex_t x_t', \quad \tau \geq 1, \quad \text{or} \quad C_x(\tau) = A^\tau C_x(0), \quad \tau \geq 1, \quad (106)$$

where $C_x(\tau) = Ex(t + \tau)x(t)'$. As before, we have the result that the covariogram (this time the matrix covariogram) obeys the deterministic part of the difference equation with initial conditions given by the lagged covariances that are in $C_x(0)$.

Using the compact notation (104), it is straightforward to show that the cross-spectral density matrix $\Omega(e^{-i\omega})$ of the vector x process is given by

$$\Omega(e^{-i\omega}) = (e^{i\omega}I - A)^{-1}V(Ie^{-i\omega} - A')^{-1} \quad (107)$$

where $V = E\varepsilon_t\varepsilon_t'$ and where it is assumed that the process is stationary, which requires that the eigenvalues of A have absolute values less than unity.

Assuming that the eigenvalues of A are distinct, it is possible to represent A in the form $A = P\Lambda P^{-1}$ where the columns of P are the eigenvectors of A while Λ is the diagonal matrix whose diagonal entries are the eigenvalues of A. Then we have

$$A^{\tau} = P\Lambda^{\tau}P^{-1},$$

so that the solution (106) can be written

$$C_x(\tau) = P\Lambda^{\tau}P^{-1}C_x(0).$$

This expression shows how the eigenvalues of A govern the behavior of the solution. It also illustrates how increasing the number of variables in the system or increasing the number of lags in any particular equation increases the order of the A matrix, and thereby contributes to the potential for generating complicated covariograms. Reference to this point can be used to show, for example, that while a one-variable, first-order difference equation cannot deliver a covariogram with damped oscillations of period greater than two periods (the periodicity if the single root is negative), a multivariate, first-order (i.e., single-lag) system can have complex roots and may therefore generate oscillatory covariograms.

Formula (102) or (107) has been used to summarize and analyze the stochastic properties of linear macroeconometric models. For interesting examples of such work, the reader is referred to articles by Chow and Levitan (1969) and by Howrey (1971).

B. Optimal Prediction: Compact Notation

Using the fact that ε_t in (104) is a serially uncorrelated vector process, it is straightforward to deduce from (105) that the projection of $x_{t+\tau}$ against x_t is given by

$$P[x_{t+\tau}|x_t] = A^{\tau}x_t. \tag{108}$$

This is a compact formula for linear least squares predictors of a vector governed by a finite order stochastic difference equation. As an example illustrating the use of this formula, return to the portfolio balance example (93), which leads to a solution for the log of the price level of the form

$$p_t = (1 - \lambda) \sum_{j=0}^{\infty} \lambda^j P_t m_{t+j} \tag{109}$$

where $\lambda = -\alpha/(1 - \alpha)$, and where m_t is the log of the money supply. Suppose that m_t is the first element of a vector x_t that evolves according to $x_t = Ax_{t-1} + \varepsilon_t$ where ε_t is a vector white noise. Let e be the unit vector that validates our writing $m_t = ex_t$. Then substituting (108) into the above solution for p_t gives

$$p_t = (1 - \lambda)e\left(\sum_{j=0}^{\infty} \lambda^j A^j\right)x_t.$$

If the eigenvalues of A are bounded by $1/\lambda$ in modulus,[32] then we have that $\sum_{j=0}^{\infty} \lambda^j A^j = (I - \lambda A)^{-1}$. Therefore, our solution can be represented

$$p_t = (1 - \lambda)e(I - \lambda A)^{-1}x_t$$
$$x_t = Ax_{t-1} + \varepsilon_t. \tag{110}$$

Two comments about this derivation are in order. First, in the special case in which only lagged m's appear in the x_{t-1} vector, the above formula is equivalent with formula (90). In fact formula 90 could be derived from the above one simply by explicitly inverting $(I - \lambda A)$.

Second, we notice from (110) that not only lagged m's but also any other variables that appear in the vector x_t also enter the equation (110) for p_t. Thus, any variables that help predict future m's end up in the equation (110) expressing p_t as a function of current and lagged variables.

23. OPTIMAL FILTERING FORMULA

It is convenient to have a formula for the projection of a random variable y_t against current and past values of a covariance stationary, indeterministic random process x_t. We assume that y_t and x_t have means of zero and are jointly covariance stationary, indeterministic processes. That is, we seek the h_j that characterize the one-sided projection

$$y_t = \sum_{j=0}^{\infty} h_j x_{t-j} + u_t \tag{111}$$

where $Ex_{t-j}u_t = 0$ for all $j \geq 0$. First, suppose that x_t has the moving average representation

$$x_t = d(L)\varepsilon_t, \qquad d(L) = \sum_{j=0}^{\infty} d_j L^j$$

where $\{\varepsilon_t\}$ is a serially uncorrelated process of innovations in x, i.e., ε_t is fundamental for x. As an intermediate step,[33] think of projecting y_t on current and past ε's:

$$y_t = \sum_{j=0}^{\infty} \phi_j \varepsilon_{t-j} + u_t \tag{112}$$

where $Eu_t\varepsilon_{t-j} = 0$ for all $j \geq 0$. We assume that x_t has both a moving average and an autoregressive representation, so that it is easy to see that $\{x_t, x_{t-1}, \ldots\}$

---

[32] Nonstationarity of $\{m_t\}$ in the form of $\max|\lambda_i| > 1$ still leaves the proposed solution valid as long as $\max_i|(\alpha/(1 - \alpha))\lambda_i| < 1$.

[33] This is the method that Kolmogorov used to derive the formula we are after. See Whittle (1983, p. 42).

and $\{\varepsilon_t, \varepsilon_{t-1}, \ldots\}$ span the same space. For this reason, u_t in (111) equals u_t in (112). Since the ε's form an orthogonal process, we have that the ϕ_j are the simple least squares coefficients

$$\phi_j = Ey_t\varepsilon_{t-j}/E\varepsilon_t^2 = Ey_t\varepsilon_{t-j}/\sigma^2$$

where $\sigma^2 = E\varepsilon_t^2$. Thus we can write

$$\phi(L) = \sum_{j=0}^{\infty} \phi_j L^j, \qquad \phi(L) = \sigma^{-2}[g_{y\varepsilon}(L)]_+ \tag{113}$$

where $[\ ]_+$ again means "ignore negative powers of L" and $g_{y\varepsilon}(L)$ is the cross-covariance generating function

$$g_{y\varepsilon}(L) = \sum_{k=-\infty}^{\infty} E(y_t\varepsilon_{t-k})L^k.$$

We can relate $g_{y\varepsilon}(L)$ to the cross-covariance generating function $g_{yx}(L)$ as follows:

$$g_{yx}(z) = \sum_k (Ey_t x_{t-k})z^k$$

$$= \sum_k (Ey_t\, d(L)\varepsilon_{t-k})z^k$$

$$= \sum_k (Ey_t(d_0\varepsilon_{t-k} + d_1\varepsilon_{t-k-1} + \cdots))z^k$$

$$= d_0 \sum_k (Ey_t\varepsilon_{t-k})z^k + d_1 \sum_k (Ey_t\varepsilon_{t-k-1})z^k + d_2 \sum_k (Ey_t\varepsilon_{t-k-2})z^k + \cdots$$

$$= d_0 g_{y\varepsilon}(z) + d_1 z^{-1} g_{y\varepsilon}(z) + d_2 z^{-2} g_{y\varepsilon}(z) + \cdots$$

$$= d(z^{-1})g_{y\varepsilon}(z).$$

Thus we have $g_{y\varepsilon}(z) = g_{yx}(z)/d(z^{-1})$. Substituting this into (113), we obtain

$$\phi(L) = \frac{1}{\sigma^2}\left(\frac{g_{yx}(L)}{d(L^{-1})}\right)_+.$$

So we have

$$y_t = \frac{1}{\sigma^2}\left(\frac{g_{yx}(L)}{d(L^{-1})}\right)_+ \varepsilon_t + u_t$$

$$= \frac{1}{\sigma^2}\left(\frac{g_{yx}(L)}{d(L^{-1})}\right)_+ \frac{1}{d(L)} x_t + u_t, \tag{114}$$

so that in (111) we have

$$h(L) = \frac{1}{\sigma^2}\left(\frac{g_{yx}(L)}{d(L^{-1})}\right)_+ \frac{1}{d(L)}. \tag{115}$$

A classic application of this formula is due to Muth (1960). Suppose that income evolves according to $x_t = y_t + \varepsilon_t$ where $y_t = \rho y_{t-1} + u_t$, $|\rho| < 1$, and where u_t and ε_t are mutually orthogonal at all lags and serially uncorrelated. Here x_t is measured income, while y_t is "systematic" or permanent income. The consumer only "sees" $x_t, x_{t-1}, \ldots$ and desires to estimate systematic income y_t by a linear function $x_t, x_{t-1}, \ldots$. The consumer is assumed to know all the relevant moments. This problem can be solved quickly using formula (115), and the reader is invited to do so.

24. THE RELATIONSHIP BETWEEN WIENER–GRANGER CAUSALITY AND ECONOMETRIC EXOGENEITY

We now study the conditions under which the projection of y_t on the entire x process equals the projection of y_t on only current and all past x's, i.e., the condition under which

$$g_{yx}(z)/g_x(z) = [g_{yx}(z)/d(z^{-1})]_+ (1/d(z)\sigma^2)$$

where $g_x(z) = \sigma^2 d(z)d(z^{-1})$. Sims (1972a) proved the important result that these two projections are equal if and only if lagged y's fail linearly to help predict x, given lagged x's. We shall first prove Sims's result in a different way than he did. The method is in the spirit of Wiener's derivation of the Wiener–Kolmogorov prediction formula and has certain advantages when it comes to working Exercises 6–13.

We consider a jointly covariance stationary stochastic process $\{y_t, x_t\}$, with $Ex_t = Ey_t = 0$ and with covariance generating functions $g_x(z)$, $g_y(z)$, $g_{yx}(z)$. We assume that x possesses an autoregressive representation and that both y and x are linearly indeterministic. We now consider the projection of x_t on past values of x and past values of y:

$$x_t = \sum_{j=1}^{\infty} h_j x_{t-j} + \sum_{j=1}^{\infty} v_j y_{t-j} + u_t \tag{116}$$

where the least squares residual u_t obeys the orthogonality conditions $Eu_t x_{t-\tau} = Eu_t y_{t-\tau} = 0$ for $\tau = 1, 2, \ldots$. Solving (116) for u_t permits the orthogonality conditions to assume the form of the normal equations

$$E\left\{\left(x_t - \sum_{j=1}^{\infty} h_j x_{t-j} - \sum_{j=1}^{\infty} v_j y_{t-j}\right)x_{t-\tau}\right\} = 0, \qquad \tau = 1, 2, \ldots$$

$$E\left\{\left(x_t - \sum_{j=1}^{\infty} h_j x_{t-j} - \sum_{j=1}^{\infty} v_j y_{t-j}\right)y_{t-\tau}\right\} = 0, \qquad \tau = 1, 2, \ldots.$$

These equations can be written

$$c_x(\tau) = \sum_{j=1}^{\infty} h_j c_x(\tau - j) + \sum_{j=1}^{\infty} v_j c_{yx}(\tau - j), \tag{117}$$

$$c_{xy}(\tau) = \sum_{j=1}^{\infty} h_j c_{xy}(\tau - j) + \sum_{j=1}^{\infty} v_j c_y(\tau - j), \tag{118}$$

which are required to hold *only for positive integers* $\tau = 1, 2, \ldots$. Multiplying both sides of (117) and (118) by z^τ and summing over *all* τ, we get the following equation in terms of the z transforms

$$g_x(z) + m(z) = h(z)g_x(z) + v(z)g_{yx}(z), \tag{119}$$

$$g_{xy}(z) + n(z) = h(z)g_{xy}(z) + v(z)g_y(z), \tag{120}$$

where $m(z)$ and $n(z)$ are each unknown series in *nonpositive powers* of z only. That $m(z)$ and $n(z)$ are series in nonpositive powers of z is equivalent with Equations (117) and (118) holding only for $\tau \geq 1$. Equations (119) and (120) are the normal equations for $h(z)$ and $v(z)$.

Following Wiener, Granger (1969) has proposed the terminology that "y causes x" whenever $v(z) \neq 0$. That is, y is said to cause x if, given all past values of x, past values of y help to predict x. The conditions under which $v(z)$ does or does not equal zero turn out to be of substantial interest to econometricians and macroeconomists, which is the reason that this concept of causality is an interesting one to study.

Consider the projection of y_t on the entire x process,

$$y_t = \sum_{j=-\infty}^{\infty} b_j x_{t-j} + \varepsilon_t$$

where $E\varepsilon_t x_{t-j} = 0$ for all j. Under what conditions will the lag distribution $\{b_j\}$ be one-sided on the past and present, so that $b_j = 0$, for $j < 0$? From formula (45) we have that

$$b(z) = g_{yx}(z)/g_x(z). \tag{121}$$

Suppose that x_t has the Wold moving average representation

$$x_t = d(L)\eta_t, \qquad \eta_t = x_t - P[x_t | x_{t-1}, \ldots], \qquad \sum_{j=0}^{\infty} d_j^2 < \infty.$$

Then

$$g_x(z) = \sigma_\eta^2 \, d(z) \, d(z^{-1}). \tag{122}$$

We have assumed that x possesses an autoregressive representation so that $[d(z)]^{-1}$ is one-sided and square summable in nonnegative powers of z.

Combining (121) and (122), we have that $g_{yx}(z)$ can be expressed as

$$g_{yx}(z) = \sigma_\eta^2 b(z)\, d(z)\, d(z^{-1}).$$

Thus, if $b(z)$ is one-sided in nonnegative powers of z, then we have that $g_{yx}(z)$ can be factored as

$$g_{yx}(z) = a(z)\, d(z^{-1}) \tag{123}$$

where $a(z) = \sigma_\eta^2 b(z)\, d(z)$. Here $a(z)$ is one-sided in nonnegative powers of z.

We now prove the following important theorem that is due to Sims:

Theorem: $v(z) = 0$ if and only if $b(z)$ is one-sided in nonnegative powers of z.

Proof: First, we shall show that if $b(z)$ is one-sided in nonnegative powers of z, then $v(z) = 0$. We begin by noting that the solution of (119) and (120) for $(h(z), v(z))$ is unique. Consequently, it will suffice to show that if $b(z)$ is one-sided, then there exist $m(z)$ and $n(z)$, each one-sided in nonpositive powers of z, for which $v(z) = 0$ and (119) and (120) hold. Choose $m(z) = -d_0 \sigma_\eta^2 d(z^{-1})$ and $n(z) = -d_0 a(z^{-1})$. These are each one-sided in nonpositive powers of z, as required. Next, recall that if $b(z)$ is one-sided in nonnegative powers of z, then $g_{yx}(z) = a(z)\, d(z^{-1})$. Substituting these into (119) and (120) gives

$$\sigma_\eta^2 d(z)\, d(z^{-1}) - \sigma_\eta^2 d(z^{-1})\, d_0 = h(z)\sigma_\eta^2 d(z^{-1})\, d(z) \tag{119'}$$

$$a(z^{-1})\, d(z) - d_0 a(z^{-1}) = h(z)a(z^{-1})\, d(z). \tag{120'}$$

Dividing the first equation by $z\sigma_\eta^2 d(z^{-1})$ and the second by $za(z^{-1})$ results in the same equation, namely

$$\frac{d(z)}{z} - \frac{d_0}{z} = \frac{h(z)}{z}\, d(z). \tag{124}$$

Since $h(z) = \sum_{j=1}^{\infty} h_j z^j$, the right-hand side is one-sided in nonnegative powers of z, while d_0/z involves only negative powers of z. Applying the annihilation operator $[\ ]_+$ to both sides of (124) and rearranging gives

$$\frac{h(z)}{z} = \left[\frac{d(z)}{z}\right]_+ \frac{1}{d(z)}, \tag{125}$$

which is just the univariate Wiener–Kolmogorov prediction formula for the z-transform of the coefficients of the projection of x_t on its own infinite past. With this choice of $h(z)/z$, it is directly verified that (124) holds, and therefore that (119') and (120') also hold. Consequently, with $h(z)/z$ given by (125) and $v(z) = 0$, (119) and (120) hold. This proves that if $b(z)$ is one-sided in nonnegative powers of z, then $v(z) = 0$.

Next, we prove the other direction of implication, namely, that if $v(z) = 0$ is the solution of (119) and (120), then $b(z)$ is one-sided in nonnegative powers of z.

Suppose that (119) and (120) are satisfied with $v(z) = 0$. Then equation (119) implies that

$$h(z) = z\left[\frac{d(z)}{z}\right]_+ \frac{1}{d(z)}.$$

Substituting this into (120) with $v(z) = 0$ gives

$$g_{xy}(z) + n(z) = z\left[\frac{d(z)}{z}\right]_+ \frac{1}{d(z)}\, g_{xy}(z).$$

Dividing the above equation by $zg_{xy}(z)/d(z)$ gives

$$\frac{d(z)}{z} + \frac{n(z)\, d(z)}{zg_{xy}(z)} = \left[\frac{d(z)}{z}\right]_+.$$

But since $d(z)/z - d_0/z = [d(z)/z]_+$, the above equation implies that $-d_0 = n(z)\, d(z)/g_{xy}(z)$, or

$$n(z) = -d_0 g_{xy}(z)/d(z). \tag{126}$$

Now, $n(z)$ is a polynomial in nonpositive powers of z. Therefore, for (126) to hold, $g_{xy}(z)$ must be capable of being represented as $g_{xy}(z) = c(z^{-1})\, d(z)$, where $c(z^{-1})$ is one-sided in nonpositive powers of z. Then it follows that $g_{yx}(z) = c(z)\, d(z^{-1})$, and that the z-transform $b(z)$ of coefficients in the projection of y on the x_t process is given by $b(z) = c(z)\, d(z^{-1})/\sigma_\eta^2\, d(z)\, d(z^{-1}) = c(z)/\sigma_\eta^2\, d(z)$, which is one-sided in nonnegative powers of z. This completes the proof that if (119) and (120) are satisfied with $v(z) = 0$, then $b(z)$ is one-sided in nonnegative powers of z.

In words, Sims's theorem asserts that the projection of y on the entire x process equals the projection of y on current and past x's if and only if y *fails* to Granger cause x (i.e., y fails to help predict x).

Example: Suppose that

$$g_x(z) = (1 + 0.4z)(1 + 0.4z^{-1}), \qquad g_y(z) = (1 - 0.2z)(1 - 0.2z^{-1}),$$

$$g_{yx}(z) = \frac{(1 - 0.2z)}{1 - 0.9z^{-1}}.$$

The projection of y on the entire x process has coefficient generating function

$$\frac{g_{yx}(z)}{g_x(z)} = \frac{1 - 0.2z}{(1 - 0.9z^{-1})(1 + 0.4z)(1 + 0.4z^{-1})},$$

which has nonzero coefficients on negative powers of z (expand the polynomial in z by partial fractions to verify this). Therefore y Granger causes (helps predict) x. The projection of x on the entire y process has the coefficient generating function

$$\frac{g_{xy}(z)}{g_y(z)} = \frac{g_{yx}(z^{-1})}{g_y(z)} = \frac{1 - 0.2z^{-1}}{(1 - 0.9z)(1 - 0.2z^{-1})(1 - 0.2z)}$$

$$= \frac{1}{(1 - 0.9z)(1 - 0.2z)},$$

which involves only nonnegative powers of z. Therefore x fails to Granger cause y (i.e., given lagged y's, x fails to help predict y).

To gain additional perspective on Sims's theorem, we now undertake to indicate the proof that Sims gave. We do this not only because the theorem is very important, but because his proof provides useful practice in projection arguments and useful insights into the nature of bivariate Wold representations.

Let $\begin{bmatrix} x_t \\ y_t \end{bmatrix}$ be a bivariate, jointly covariance stationary stochastic process. Suppose that $\begin{bmatrix} x_t \\ y_t \end{bmatrix}$ is a strictly linearly indeterministic process with mean zero. Under these conditions, the bivariate version of Wold's theorem states that there exists a moving average representation of the (x_t, y_t) process

$$\begin{bmatrix} x_t \\ y_t \end{bmatrix} = \begin{bmatrix} c^{11}(L) & c^{12}(L) \\ c^{21}(L) & c^{22}(L) \end{bmatrix} \begin{bmatrix} \varepsilon_t \\ u_t \end{bmatrix}$$

where $c^{ij}(L) = \sum_{k=0}^{\infty} c_k^{ij} L^k$ are square summable polynomials in the lag operator L that are one-sided in nonnegative powers of L; ε_t and u_t are serially uncorrelated processes with $Eu_t\varepsilon_s = 0$ for all t, s; $E\varepsilon_t^2 = \sigma_\varepsilon^2$, $Eu_t^2 = \sigma_u^2$; and where the one-step-ahead prediction errors are given by

$$x_t - P[x_t | x_{t-1}, \dots, y_{t-1}, \dots] = c_0^{11}\varepsilon_t + c_0^{12}u_t,$$

$$y_t - P[y_t | x_{t-1}, \dots, y_{t-1}, \dots] = c_0^{21}\varepsilon_t + c_0^{22}u_t,$$

i.e., ε and u are "jointly fundamental for x and y."[34] Wold's theorem establishes the sense in which a vector moving average is a general representation for an indeterministic covariance stationary vector process. The theorem can be proved by pursuing the same kind of projection arguments used in proving the univariate version of the theorem. Below, we shall show how to construct a Wold representation from knowledge of the covariograms of x and y and their cross covariogram.

---

[34] The statement "$\{\varepsilon_t\}$ and $\{u_t\}$ are jointly fundamental for $\{x_t, y_t\}$" means that the one-step-ahead errors in forecasting (y_t, x_t) from past x's and y's are linear combinations of ε_t and u_t.

We now make the further assumption that the (x_t, y_t) process has an autoregressive representation. In particular, think of constructing a sequence of projections

$$\begin{bmatrix} x_t \\ y_t \end{bmatrix} = F_1^n \begin{bmatrix} x_{t-1} \\ y_{t-1} \end{bmatrix} + \cdots + F_n^n \begin{bmatrix} x_{t-n} \\ y_{t-n} \end{bmatrix} + \begin{bmatrix} a_{xt}^n \\ a_{yt}^n \end{bmatrix} \tag{127}$$

where $F_1^n, \ldots, F_n^n$ are 2×2 matrices of least squares coefficients and we have the orthogonality conditions

$$E \begin{bmatrix} x_{t-j} \\ y_{t-j} \end{bmatrix} [a_{xt}^n \quad a_{yt}^n] = \begin{bmatrix} 0 & 0 \\ 0 & 0 \end{bmatrix}$$

for $j = 1, \ldots, n$. We assume that as $n \to \infty$, the F_j^n converge to F_j for each j. This is the assumption that (x_t, y_t) possesses an autoregressive representation and is stronger than the conditions required for (x_t, y_t) to have a vector moving average representation. We can write the autoregressive representation for (x_t, y_t) as

$$\begin{bmatrix} x_t \\ y_t \end{bmatrix} = \sum_{j=1}^{\infty} F_j \begin{bmatrix} x_{t-j} \\ y_{t-j} \end{bmatrix} + \begin{bmatrix} a_{xt} \\ a_{yt} \end{bmatrix}$$

$$= F(L) \begin{bmatrix} x_{t-1} \\ y_{t-1} \end{bmatrix} + \begin{bmatrix} a_{xt} \\ a_{yt} \end{bmatrix}, \qquad F(L) = \sum_{j=1}^{\infty} F_j L^{j-1}$$

where the random variables (a_{xt}, a_{yt}) obey the least squares orthogonality conditions

$$E \begin{bmatrix} x_{t-j} \\ y_{t-j} \end{bmatrix} [a_{xt} \quad a_{yt}] = \begin{bmatrix} 0 & 0 \\ 0 & 0 \end{bmatrix}$$

for all $j \geq 1$. The random variables (a_{xt}, a_{yt}) are the one-step-ahead errors in predicting (x_t, y_t) from all past values of x and y.

Now consider obtaining the following representation for the (x_t, y_t) process:

$$A(L) \begin{bmatrix} x_t \\ y_t \end{bmatrix} = \begin{bmatrix} \varepsilon_t \\ u_t \end{bmatrix} \qquad \text{or} \qquad (A_0 - A_1 L - A_2 L^2 \cdots) \begin{bmatrix} x_t \\ y_t \end{bmatrix} = \begin{bmatrix} \varepsilon_t \\ u_t \end{bmatrix} \tag{128}$$

where A_j is a 2×2 matrix for each j, where A_0 is chosen to be lower triangular and $\begin{bmatrix} \varepsilon_t \\ u_t \end{bmatrix}$ are pairwise orthogonal processes (at all lags) that are serially uncorrelated. Can we be sure that such a representation can be arrived at, in particular one with A_0 being lower triangular and ε and u being orthogonal processes? The answer is in general yes,[35] as the following argument suggests. Think of projecting x_t against all *lagged* x's and *lagged* y's. This gives the first row of $A(L)$ and gives a least squares residual process ε_t that is by construction orthogonal to all lagged y's and all lagged x's. Next project y_t against *current* and lagged x's and all lagged y's. This gives the second row of $A(L)$ and delivers a disturbance process u_t that is by construction orthogonal to *current* and *lagged* x's and lagged y's. This procedure produces an A_0 that is lower triangular as required. Further, notice that since ε_t is orthogonal to all lagged x's and y's and since the representation (128) that we have achieved permits lagged ε's and u's to be expressed as linear combinations of lagged x's and y's, it follows that ε_t is orthogonal to lagged u's and ε's. A similar argument shows that u_t is orthogonal to lagged u's and ε's. Finally, since by construction u_t is orthogonal to current and lagged x's and lagged y's and since ε_t is by definition a linear combination of current and lagged x's and lagged y's, it follows that u_t and ε_t are orthogonal contemporaneously.

To check that he understands this construction, the reader is invited to verify that it would also be possible to choose A_0 to be upper triangular with a new and generally different error process $\begin{bmatrix} u \\ \varepsilon \end{bmatrix}$ that satisfies the same conditions on second moments that the $\begin{bmatrix} u \\ \varepsilon \end{bmatrix}$ process satisfies.

To get (128) in a form that is useful for studying prediction problems, premultiply by A_0^{-1} to get[36]

$$A_0^{-1} A(L) \begin{bmatrix} x_t \\ y_t \end{bmatrix} = A_0^{-1} \begin{bmatrix} \varepsilon_t \\ u_t \end{bmatrix}$$

or

$$\begin{bmatrix} x_t \\ y_t \end{bmatrix} = A_0^{-1} [A_1 L + A_2 L^2 + \cdots] \begin{bmatrix} x_t \\ y_t \end{bmatrix} + A_0^{-1} \begin{bmatrix} \varepsilon_t \\ u_t \end{bmatrix}$$

$$= A_0^{-1} H(L) \begin{bmatrix} x_t \\ y_t \end{bmatrix} + A_0^{-1} \begin{bmatrix} \varepsilon_t \\ u_t \end{bmatrix} \tag{129}$$

---

[35] We have remarked earlier that the vector moving average representation of a vector process z_t in terms of the vector noise n_t, $z_t = C(L)n_t$, where the components of n_t are white noises that are mutually orthogonal at all lags, is a very general representation. An autoregressive representation for z_t can be obtained by inverting the preceding equation to get $A(L)z_t = n_t$ where $A(L) = C(L)^{-1}$, which is to say $A(e^{-i\omega}) = C(e^{-i\omega})^{-1}$ for each ω between $-\pi$ and π. The autoregressive representation exists provided that $C(e^{-i\omega})$ is invertible at each frequency between $-\pi$ and π. This condition is a restriction but is one that can usually be assumed in applied work. (For an example of a $C(e^{-i\omega})$ that violates the condition, consider the univariate example $C(e^{-i\omega}) = 1 - e^{-i\omega}$—the transform of the first difference operator $1 - L$—which equals zero at $\omega = 0$ and so is not invertible there.)

[36] Notice that (129) is identical with (127) for $n = \infty$, so that we must have $F_j = A_0^{-1} A_j$,

$$\begin{pmatrix} a_{xt} \\ a_{yt} \end{pmatrix} = A_0^{-1} \begin{pmatrix} \varepsilon_t \\ u_t \end{pmatrix}.$$

Notice that (a_{xt}, a_{yt}) are by the orthogonality conditions serially uncorrelated and uncorrelated with one another at all nonzero lags.

where $H(L) = A_1 L + A_2 L^2 + \cdots$. The linear least squares prediction of the $\begin{bmatrix} x_t \\ y_t \end{bmatrix}$ process based on all lagged x's and all lagged y's (call it $P_{t-1}\begin{bmatrix} x_t \\ y_t \end{bmatrix}$) from (129) is then

$$P_{t-1}\begin{bmatrix} x_t \\ y_t \end{bmatrix} = A_0^{-1} H(L) \begin{bmatrix} x_t \\ y_t \end{bmatrix} = F(L)L \begin{bmatrix} x_t \\ y_t \end{bmatrix}$$

since by construction $P_{t-1}\begin{bmatrix} \varepsilon_t \\ u_t \end{bmatrix} = 0$. The one-step-ahead prediction errors in predicting $\begin{bmatrix} x \\ y \end{bmatrix}$ process are given by

$$A_0^{-1}\begin{bmatrix} \varepsilon_t \\ u_t \end{bmatrix}.$$

Thus x prediction errors and y prediction errors are contemporaneously correlated so long as A_0 is not diagonal. Notice that since A_0 is lower triangular, so is A_0^{-1}, so that ε_t is the one-step-ahead prediction error in predicting x from past x's and y's which is what should be expected given the way the ε_t process was constructed above.

If $A_0^{-1}A(L)$ is lower triangular (i.e., the matrix coefficient is lower triangular for *each* power of L), then given lagged x's, lagged y's do not help predict current x. That is, if $A_0^{-1}A(L)$ is lower triangular, and, therefore, so is $A_0^{-1}H(L)$, then $P_{t-1}x_t$ involves only lagged x's, lagged y's all bearing zero regression coefficients. In the language of Wiener and Granger, y is said to *cause* x if given past x's, past y's help predict current x. Thus, the lower triangularity of $A_0^{-1}A(L)$ is equivalent with y's *failing* to cause x, in the Wiener–Granger sense.

Given that A_0^{-1} is lower triangular, we now claim the following: $A_0^{-1}A(L)$ is lower triangular if and only if $A(L)^{-1}$ is lower triangular. To show this, suppose first that $A_0^{-1}A(L)$ is lower triangular. Then note

$$A(L)^{-1} = A(L)^{-1} A_0 A_0^{-1}.$$

But we know that $A(L)^{-1}A_0$, being the inverse of $A_0^{-1}A(L)$, is lower triangular, as is A_0^{-1}. Noting that the product of two lower triangular matrices is also lower triangular then proves that $A(L)^{-1}$ is lower triangular.[37]

Now suppose that $A(L)^{-1}$ is lower triangular. Since A_0 is lower triangular, it follows that $A_0^{-1}A(L)$ is lower triangular. So we have proved that $A_0^{-1}A(L)$ is lower triangular if and only if $A(L)^{-1}$ is lower triangular.

---

[37] To make the argument in terms of ordinary matrices, write $A(e^{-i\omega})^{-1} = A(e^{-i\omega})^{-1} A_0 A_0^{-1}$ and note that $A(e^{-i\omega})^{-1}A_0$ is the inverse of the lower triangular matrix $A_0^{-1}A(e^{-i\omega})$ at each frequency and so is lower triangular. It follows that $A(e^{-i\omega})^{-1}$ is lower triangular (at each frequency) being the product of two lower triangular matrices. It then follows that

$$A_j^{-1} = (1/2\pi) \int_{-\pi}^{\pi} A(e^{-i\omega})^{-1} e^{i\omega j} \, d\omega$$

is lower triangular for $j = 0, 1, 2, \ldots$.

This establishes that if $A_0^{-1}A(L)$ is lower triangular, then (128) can be "inverted" to yield the vector moving average representation

$$\begin{bmatrix} x_t \\ y_t \end{bmatrix} = C(L)\begin{bmatrix} \varepsilon_t \\ u_t \end{bmatrix} \tag{130}$$

where $A(L)^{-1} = C(L) = C_0 + C_1 L + C_2 L^2 + \cdots$, C_j being a 2×2 matrix, and where $C(L)$ is lower triangular. Recall the extensive orthogonality conditions satisfied by ε and u; the ε and u processes are orthogonal at all lags, even contemporaneously.[38] Conversely, suppose that a moving average representation of the lower triangular form (130) exists with ε_t and u_t being serially uncorrelated processes with $E\varepsilon_t u_s = 0$ for all t and s. Then assuming that $C(L)^{-1}$ exists and equals $A(L)$ gives a representation

$$C(L)^{-1}\begin{bmatrix} x_t \\ y_t \end{bmatrix} = \begin{bmatrix} \varepsilon_t \\ u_t \end{bmatrix} \quad \text{or} \quad A(L)\begin{bmatrix} x_t \\ y_t \end{bmatrix} = \begin{bmatrix} \varepsilon_t \\ u_t \end{bmatrix}$$

where $A(L)$ is lower triangular and one-sided on the present and past. It follows then that y fails to Granger cause x.

We have now proved Sims's important theorem 1 which states:

Let (x_t, y_t) be a jointly covariance stationary, strictly indeterministic process with mean zero. Then $\{y_t\}$ fails to Granger cause $\{x_t\}$ if and only if there exists a vector moving average representation

$$\begin{bmatrix} x_t \\ y_t \end{bmatrix} = \begin{bmatrix} C^{11}(L) & 0 \\ C^{21}(L) & C^{22}(L) \end{bmatrix}\begin{bmatrix} \varepsilon_t \\ u_t \end{bmatrix}$$

where ε_t and u_t are serially uncorrelated processes with means zero and $E\varepsilon_t u_s = 0$ for all t and s, and where the one-step-ahead prediction errors $(x_t - P[x_t | x_{t-1}, \ldots, y_{t-1}, \ldots])$ and $(y_t - P[y_t | x_{t-1}, \ldots, y_{t-1}, \ldots])$ are each linear combinations of ε_t and u_t (Sims, 1972a).

---

[38] Assuming that things have been normalized so that ε and u have unit variances, the spectral density matrix of the (x, y) process satisfying (130) is, as we have seen,

$$S(e^{-i\omega}) = C(e^{-i\omega})IC(e^{-i\omega})'$$

where the prime now denotes both complex conjugation and transposition. Now let U be a 2×2 unitary matrix, i.e., a 2×2 matrix satisfying $UU' = U'U = I$ where here the prime again denotes complex conjugation and transposition. Then note that $S(e^{-i\omega})$ can also be represented

$$S(e^{-i\omega}) = C(e^{-i\omega})UIU'C(e^{-i\omega})' = [C(e^{-i\omega})U]I[C(e^{-i\omega})U]'$$
$$= D(e^{-i\omega})ID(e^{-i\omega})'$$

where $D(e^{-i\omega}) = C(e^{-i\omega})U$. Thus, we have produced a new moving average representation, one with contemporaneously orthogonal disturbances. This proves that a moving average representation is unique only up to multiplication by a unitary matrix. Notice that multiplication of $C(e^{-i\omega})$ by U will, in general, destroy the lower triangularity of $C(e^{-i\omega})$ if C originally has this property.

We are now in a position to state a second theorem of Sims that character-izes the relationship between the concept of strict econometric exogeneity and Granger's concept of causality. Sims's theorem is this:

> y_t can be expressed as a distributed lag of current and past x's (with no future x's) with a disturbance process that is orthogonal to past, present, and future x's if and only if y does not Granger cause x (Sims, 1972a).

The condition that y can be expressed as a one-sided distributed lag of x with disturbance process that is orthogonal at all lags to the x process is known as the strict econometric exogeneity of x with respect to y. In applied work it is important to test for this condition since it is required if various estimators are to have good properties. It is interesting that engineers have long called a relationship in which y is a one-sided (on the present and past) distributed lag of x a "causal" relationship, and that this long-standing use of the word cause should happen to concide with the failure of y to cause x in the Wiener–Granger sense.

First we prove that y's not Granger causing x implies that y can be expressed as a one-sided distributed lag of x with a disturbance process orthogonal to x at all lags. The lack of Granger causality from y to x is equivalent with $A_0^{-1}A(L)$ being lower triangular. As we have seen, this implies that $C(L)$ in (130) is lower triangular, so that

$$x_t = C^{11}(L)\varepsilon_t, \tag{131}$$

$$y_t = C^{21}(L)\varepsilon_t + C^{22}(L)u_t, \tag{132}$$

where all polynomials in L involve only nonnegative powers of L. Inverting (131) and substituting into (132) gives[39]

$$y_t = C^{21}(L)C^{11}(L)^{-1}x_t + C^{22}(L)u_t$$

which expresses y_t as a one-sided distributed lag of x (no negative powers of L enter) with a disturbance process u_t that is orthogonal to ε_t and therefore to x_t at all lags. This proves half of the theorem.

To prove the other half, one would start with a one-sided lag distribution and a moving average representation for x_t

$$y_t = h(L)x_t + \eta_t, \qquad x_t = a(L)\varepsilon_t,$$

where by hypothesis η is orthogonal to x and therefore to ε at all lags. Then by finding the moving average representation for η_t, say $\eta_t = m(L)u_t$ where $Eu_t\varepsilon_s = 0$ for all t, s, one gets the lower triangular vector moving average representation

$$y_t = h(L)a(L)\varepsilon_t + m(L)u_t, \qquad x_t = a(L)\varepsilon_t$$

---

[39] In assuming that (x_t, y_t) has an autoregressive representation we have in effect assumed that $C^{11}(L)$ has an inverse that is one-sided in nonnegative powers of L.

or

$$\begin{bmatrix} x_t \\ y_t \end{bmatrix} = C(L) \begin{bmatrix} \varepsilon_t \\ u_t \end{bmatrix}$$

where $C(L)$ is lower triangular. Assuming that $C(L)^{-1}$ exists then gives

$$C(L)^{-1} \begin{bmatrix} x_t \\ y_t \end{bmatrix} = \begin{bmatrix} \varepsilon_t \\ u_t \end{bmatrix}$$

where $C(L)^{-1}$ is lower triangular and say equal to $A(L)$. Multiplying the above equation, which is in the form of (130), through by A_0^{-1}, which is also lower triangular then gives

$$A_0^{-1} A(L) \begin{bmatrix} x_t \\ y_t \end{bmatrix} = A_0^{-1} \begin{bmatrix} \varepsilon_t \\ u_t \end{bmatrix}$$

or

$$[I - A_0^{-1} A_1 L - A_0^{-1} A_2 L^2 - \cdots] \begin{bmatrix} x_t \\ y_t \end{bmatrix} = A_0^{-1} \begin{bmatrix} \varepsilon_t \\ u_t \end{bmatrix}.$$

The lower triangularity of the matrices on the left and the orthogonality properties of ε and u establish that in this system y does not Granger cause x, i.e., y does not help predict x given lagged x's. This proves the other half of Sims's theorem 2.

25. SIMS'S APPLICATION TO MONEY AND INCOME

Economists at the Federal Reserve Bank of St. Louis (Andersen and Jordan, 1968) have computed estimates of one-sided distributed lag regressions of (the log of) nominal income (y_t) against (the log of) money (m_t):

$$y_t = \sum_{j=0}^{\infty} h_j m_{t-j} + \eta_t, \tag{133}$$

where $E\eta_t m_{t-j} = 0$ for $j = 0, 1, 2, \ldots$. Those economists recommend that the h_j be taken seriously and be regarded as depicting the response of nominal income to exogenous impulses in the money supply. However, Keynesian economists have tended not to regard the h_j as good estimates of the response pattern (or "dynamic multipliers") of nominal income to money. Their argument has two parts. First, in the kind of macroeconometric model the Keynesians have in mind, even were it true that money had been made to behave exogenously with respect to nominal income, the "final form" for money income has many additional right-hand-side variables not included in (133), e.g.,

$$y_t = \sum_{j=0}^{\infty} v_j m_{t-j} + \sum_{j=0}^{\infty} w_j z_{t-j} + \varepsilon_t \tag{134}$$

where z_t is a vector of stochastic processes including government tax and expenditures parameters and w_j is a vector conformable to z_t; the error term ε_t is a stationary stochastic process that obeys the orthogonality conditions $E\varepsilon_t m_{t-j} = E\varepsilon_t z_{t-j} = 0$ for $j = 0, \pm 1, \pm 2, \dots$.

The strong condition that ε must be orthogonal to m and z at all leads and lags is the requirement that m and z be "strictly econometrically exogenous with respect to y" in relation (134). These orthogonality conditions characterize (134) as a "final form" relationship. In (134) the v_j are the dynamic money multipliers that depict the average response of y_t to a unit impulse in m, holding constant the z's. Applying the law of iterated projections to (134), we obtain

$$P[y_t | m_t, m_{t-1}, \dots] = \sum_{j=0}^{\infty} v_j m_{t-j} + \sum_{k=0}^{\infty} w_k P[z_{t-k} | m_t, m_{t-1}, \dots].$$

Let $P[z_{t-k} | m_t, m_{t-1}, \dots] = \sum_{j=0}^{\infty} \alpha_{kj} m_{t-j}$. Then we have[40]

$$P[y_t | m_t, m_{t-1}, \dots] = \sum_{j=0}^{\infty} v_j m_{t-j} + \sum_{k=0}^{\infty} w_k \sum_{j=0}^{\infty} \alpha_{kj} m_{t-j}$$

or

$$y_t = \sum_{j=0}^{\infty} \left(v_j + \sum_{k=0}^{\infty} w_k \alpha_{kj} \right) m_{t-j} + \eta_t \tag{135}$$

where by the orthogonality principle we have $E\eta_t m_{t-j} = 0, j = 0, 1, 2, \dots$. Now (135) is identical with (133), so that the population h_j of (133) obey

$$h_j = v_j + \sum_{k=0}^{\infty} w_k \alpha_{kj}.$$

Therefore, the h_j in general *do not* equal the money multipliers, the v_j. The h_j are "mongrel" coefficients that do not indicate the typical average response of y to exogenous inpulses, in m, everything else, namely the z's, being held constant. For this reason, Keynesians would argue, estimating Equation (133) is not a good way of estimating the dynamic multipliers, the v_j.

Now project both sides of (134) against the entire sequence $\{m_{t-j}\}_{j=-\infty}^{\infty}$ to get

$$y_t = \sum_{j=0}^{\infty} h_j m_{t-j} + \sum_{k=0}^{\infty} w_k \sum_{j=-\infty}^{\infty} \gamma_{kj} m_{t-j} + \xi_t \tag{136}$$

where $E\xi_t m_{t-j} = 0$ for all j and

$$P(z_{t-k} | \{m_{t-j}\}_{j=-\infty}^{\infty}) = \sum_{j=-\infty}^{\infty} \gamma_{kj} m_{t-j}$$

[40] This is a version of H. Theil's "omitted variable theorem." See Theil (1971, pp. 548–550).

where γ_{kj} is a vector of coefficients. We can write (136) as

$$P(y_t|\{m_{t-j}\}_{j=-\infty}^{\infty}) = \sum_{j=-\infty}^{\infty} d_j m_{t-j}$$

where

$$d_j = \begin{cases} h_j + \sum\limits_{k=0}^{\infty} w_k \gamma_{kj}, & j \geq 0. \\ \sum\limits_{k=0}^{\infty} w_k \gamma_{kj}, & j < 0. \end{cases}$$

In general, so long as the processes m_t and z_t are correlated (as we had to assume to make the argument that the St. Louis h_j are mongrel parameters), the γ_{kj} and therefore the d_j will not vanish for some $j < 0$. That is because in general future m's will help explain current and past z_t.[41] Therefore, so long as the w_k are not zero in the final form (134), i.e., so long as the z's appear in the final form for y_t, the projection of y_t on current, lagged, and future m's is predicted to be two-sided. For this reason, a test of the null hypothesis that the projection of y_t on the entire $\{m\}$ process is one-sided (i.e., it equals the projection of y_t on current and past m's alone) can be regarded as testing the null hypothesis that the w_k in (134) are zeros. But remember that the contention that the w_k are not zero is what underlies the Keynesian objection against interpreting the St. Louis equation's h_j as estimates of the dynamic money multipliers. So computing the two-sided projection

$$y_t = \sum_{j=-\infty}^{\infty} \delta_j m_{t-j} + \hat{\eta}_t \tag{137}$$

where $E\hat{\eta}_t m_{t-j} = 0$ for all j, and testing the null hypothesis that $\delta_j = 0$ for all $j < 0$ provides a means of testing the null hypothesis that the St. Louis equation is "properly specified"—i.e., that it is appropriate to set the w_k equal to zero.

Using post-World War II U.S. data, Sims estimated (137) and implemented the preceding test. He found that he could not reject with high confidence the hypothesis that future m's bear zero coefficients in (137). In general, if the Keynesian objection to the St. Louis equation were correct, in large enough samples one would expect to reject the hypothesis tested by Sims. Sims's particular statistical results have provoked much controversy. Since his tests are subject to the usual kinds of type I and type II statistical errors, there is some room for disagreement about how far his reports go in confirming using the

---

[41] Unless m_t is strictly exogenous with respect to the vector z_t or, equivalently, the vector z_t does not Granger cause m_t.

St. Louis equation to estimate money multipliers. Nevertheless, it should be recognized how much of a contribution Sims made in providing a formal statistical setting in which one could in principle subject to statistical testing the Keynesian claims made against the St. Louis approach. Before Sims's work, those claims were entirely a priori and, though they had been made repeatedly, had never been subjected to any empirical tests.

As it happens, the test implemented by Sims is also useful in discriminating against another hypothesis which has often been advanced to argue that the St. Louis equation (133) is not a legitimate final form (i.e., does not have a disturbance that obeys the requirement that it be orthogonal to past, present, and future m's). The argument is that the money supply fails to be exogenous in (133) because the monetary authority has set m via some sort of feedback rule on lagged y's. For example, it is often asserted that the Federal Reserve "leans against the wind," increasing m faster in a recession, and more slowly in a boom. If the Fed behaved this way, it could mean that the projection (133) of y on m partly reflects this feedback from past y to m as well as the effect of m on y. Furthermore, such behavior by the Fed would in general lead us to expect the projection of y on the entire m process to differ from the projection of y on current and past m's, so that the η_t in (133) would not obey the restrictions $E\eta_t m_{t-s} = 0$ for all s; i.e., (133) would not be a final form.

Now Sims's theorems assure us that if the projection of y_t on $\{m_{t-j}\}_{j=-\infty}^{\infty}$ is one-sided on the present and past (as Sims was unable to reject), then there exists a representation (i.e., a model consistent with the data) of the form

$$m_t = C^{11}(L)\varepsilon_t, \qquad y_t = d(L)m_t + C^{22}(L)u_t$$

where $Eu_t\varepsilon_s = 0$ for all t, s, and $d(L)$, $C^{11}(L)$, $C^{22}(L)$ are one-sided on the present and past. This representation is one in which there is no feedback from y to m. Thus, Sims's results are consistent with (but do not necessarily imply) the view that there was no systematic feedback from y to m in the sample period he studied.

Sims's work on money and income was important because it provided a valid framework for testing empirically some often-stated objections to interpreting St. Louis regressions as final form equations.

26. MULTIVARIATE PREDICTION FORMULAS

Continue to assume that (x_t, y_t) is a jointly covariance stationary, strictly indeterministic process with a moving average representation

$$\begin{bmatrix} x_t \\ y_t \end{bmatrix} = \begin{bmatrix} C^{11}(L) & C^{12}(L) \\ C^{21}(L) & C^{22}(L) \end{bmatrix} \begin{bmatrix} \varepsilon_t \\ u_t \end{bmatrix} = C(L) \begin{bmatrix} \varepsilon_t \\ u_t \end{bmatrix}$$

where $E\varepsilon_t u_s = 0$ for all $t, s, \{\varepsilon_t, u_t\}$ are jointly fundamental for (x_t, y_t), and where $C(L)^{-1}$ exists and is one-sided and convergent in nonnegative powers of L, so that (x_t, y_t) has an autoregressive representation

$$C(L)^{-1}\begin{bmatrix} x_t \\ y_t \end{bmatrix} = \begin{bmatrix} \varepsilon_t \\ u_t \end{bmatrix} \quad \text{or} \quad A(L)\begin{bmatrix} x_t \\ y_t \end{bmatrix} = \begin{bmatrix} \varepsilon_t \\ u_t \end{bmatrix}$$

where $A(L) = C(L)^{-1}$. Paralleling our calculations in the univariate case, it is easy to deduce that the projection of (x_{t+1}, y_{t+1}) against $\{x_t, x_{t-1}, \ldots, y_t, y_{t-1}, \ldots\}$, call it $P_t\begin{bmatrix} x_{t+1} \\ y_{t+1} \end{bmatrix}$, is

$$P_t\begin{bmatrix} x_{t+1} \\ y_{t+1} \end{bmatrix} = \left(\frac{C(L)}{L}\right)_+\begin{bmatrix} \varepsilon_t \\ u_t \end{bmatrix} = \left(\frac{C(L)}{L}\right)_+ A(L)\begin{bmatrix} x_t \\ y_t \end{bmatrix}.$$

More generally, we have

$$P_t\begin{bmatrix} x_{t+j} \\ y_{t+j} \end{bmatrix} = \left(\frac{C(L)}{L^j}\right)_+ A(L)\begin{bmatrix} x_t \\ y_t \end{bmatrix}.$$

These results extend in a natural way to n-dimensional stochastic processes. In particular, the n-variate version of Wold's theorem implies that if $\{y_t\}$ is an n-dimensional, jointly covariance stationary, strictly indeterministic stochastic process with mean zero, it has a moving average representation

$$y_t = C(L)\varepsilon_t \tag{138}$$

where $C(L) = C_0 + C_1 L + \cdots$, C_j being an $n \times n$ matrix and the C_j being "square summable," where ε_t is an $(n \times 1)$-vector stochastic process, where the components ε_{it} are serially uncorrelated and mutually orthogonal (at all lags), $E\varepsilon_{it}\varepsilon'_{js} = 0$ for all t, s where $i \neq j$; and the ε_{it} are "jointly fundamental for y_t," i.e., for each i, $y_{it} - (Py_{it}|y_{t-1}, y_{t-2}, \ldots)$ is a linear combination of $\varepsilon_{jt}, j = 1, \ldots, n$. For the process (138), we have the prediction formula

$$E_t y_{t+j} = [C(L)/L^j]_+ \varepsilon_t$$

where $E_t(x) \equiv Ex|y_t, y_{t-1}, \ldots$. Where $C(L)^{-1}$ exists, so that y_t has a vector autoregressive representation, then we also have the formula

$$E_t y_{t+j} = [C(L)/L^j]_+ C(L)^{-1} y_t.$$

To take an example, let R_{nt} be the rate of n-period bonds, and assume that (R_{nt}, R_{1t}) has moving average representation

$$R_{nt} = \alpha(L)\varepsilon_t + \beta(L)u_t, \quad n > 1, \qquad R_{1t} = \gamma(L)\varepsilon_t + \delta(L)u_t \tag{139}$$

where all lag operators are one-sided on the present and past, and

$$R_{nt} - P_{t-1}R_{nt} = \alpha_0\varepsilon_t + \beta_0 u_t, \qquad R_{1t} - P_{t-1}R_{1t} = \gamma_0\varepsilon_t + \delta_0 u_t.$$

The rational expectations theory of the term structure asserts that

$$R_{nt} = \frac{1}{n}[R_{1t} + P_t R_{1t+1} + \cdots + P_t R_{1t+n-1}]$$

$$= \frac{1}{n}\left[\gamma(L) + \frac{\gamma(L)}{L} + \cdots + \frac{\gamma(L)}{L^{n-1}}\right]_+ \varepsilon_t$$

$$+ \frac{1}{n}\left[\delta(L) + \frac{\delta(L)}{L} + \cdots + \frac{\delta(L)}{L^{n-1}}\right]_+ u_t$$

or

$$R_{nt} = \frac{1}{n}\left[\left[\frac{1-L^{-n}}{1-L^{-1}}\right]\gamma(L)\right]_+ \varepsilon_t + \frac{1}{n}\left[\left[\frac{1-L^{-n}}{1-L^{-1}}\right]\delta(L)\right]_+ u_t. \tag{140}$$

Thus, comparing (139) with (140), it is seen that the rational expectations theory of the term structure imposes the following restrictions across the equations of the moving average representation of the (R_{nt}, R_{1t}) process:

$$\alpha(L) = \frac{1}{n}\left[\left[\frac{1-L^{-n}}{1-L^{-1}}\right]\gamma(L)\right]_+, \qquad \beta(L) = \frac{1}{n}\left[\left[\frac{1-L^{-n}}{1-L^{-1}}\right]\delta(L)\right]_+.$$

These restrictions embody the content of the theory and are refutable. Hansen and Sargent (1981c) describe how to impose and test these restrictions econometrically.

Further applications of multivariant prediction formulas to rational expectations models occur in Whiteman (1983, 1984), Hansen and Sargent (1981c, 1981a), and Dagli and Taylor (1984).

27. THE EFFECTS OF FILTERING ON ONE-SIDED AND TWO-SIDED PROJECTIONS

Consider a jointly covariance stationary, linearly indeterministic process (y_t, x_t). Consider the projections

$$y_t = \sum_{j=-\infty}^{\infty} b_j x_{t-j} + \varepsilon_t,$$

$$E\varepsilon_t x_{t-j} = 0 \qquad \text{for all integer } j \tag{141}$$

$$y_t = \sum_{j=0}^{\infty} h_j x_{t-j} + v_t$$

$$Ev_t x_{t-j} = 0 \qquad \text{for integer } j \geq 0. \tag{142}$$

Assume that x_t has Wold representation $x_t = d(L)\eta_t$, where $E\eta_t^2 = 1$. We have seen that the generating functions $b(L)$ and $h(L)$ are given by the formulas

$$b(z) = \frac{g_{yx}(z)}{d(z^{-1})\,d(z)} \tag{143}$$

$$h(z) = \left[\frac{g_{yx}(z)}{d(z^{-1})}\right]_+ \frac{1}{d(z)} \tag{144}$$

where $x_t = d(L)\eta_t$ is a Wold representation for x_t.

Now consider the filtered series

$$y_t^f = f(L)y_t$$
$$x_t^f = f(L)x_t$$

where

$$f(L) = \sum_{j=-\infty}^{\infty} f_j L^j, \qquad \sum_{j=-\infty}^{\infty} f_j^2 < +\infty.$$

We have that the covariance generating functions $g_{y^f x^f}(z)$, $g_{x^f}(z)$, $g_{y^f}(z)$ are given by

$$g_{y^f}(z) = f(z)f(z^{-1})g_y(z)$$
$$g_{x^f}(z) = f(z)f(z^{-1})g_x(z) \tag{145}$$
$$g_{y^f x^f}(z) = f(z)f(z^{-1})g_{yx}(z).$$

Using these formulas, we consider the projections analogous to (141) and (142) with the filtered series, y_t^f, x_t^f:

$$y_t^f = \sum_{j=-\infty}^{\infty} b_j^f x_{t-j}^f + \tilde{\varepsilon}_t \tag{146}$$

$$E\tilde{\varepsilon}_t x_{t-j}^f = 0 \qquad \text{for all integer } j$$

$$y_t^f = \sum_{j=0}^{\infty} h_j^f x_{t-j}^f + \tilde{v}_t \tag{147}$$

$$E\tilde{v}_t x_{t-j}^f = 0 \qquad \text{for all integer } j \geq 0.$$

Let $b^f(L) = \sum_{j=-\infty}^{\infty} b_j^f L^j$, $h^f(L) = \sum_{j=0}^{\infty} h_j^f L^j$. To implement the filtering formula (144), we require a Wold representation for the filtered series x_t^f. We can obtain such a representation

$$x_t^f = c(L)a_t$$

where $c(z)$ has no zeros inside the unit circle and $Ea_t^2 = 1$; $c(z)$ satisfies

$$c(z)c(z^{-1}) = g_{x^f}(z) = f(z)f(z^{-1})\,d(z)\,d(z^{-1}). \tag{148}$$

However, in general, $f(z)\,d(z) \neq c(z)$.

Now applying the two-sided filtering formula (143) gives

$$b^f(z) = \frac{f(z)f(z^{-1})g_{yx}(z)}{f(z)f(z^{-1})g_x(z)}$$

or

$$b^f(z) = \frac{g_{yx}(z)}{d(z)\,d(z^{-1})} = b(z). \tag{149}$$

Applying the one-sided filtering formula (144) gives

$$h^f(z) = \left[\frac{f(z)f(z^{-1})g_{yx}(z)}{c(z^{-1})}\right]_+ \frac{1}{c(z)}. \tag{150}$$

Comparison of (143) and (149) shows that filtering both series by a common filter leaves unaltered the two-sided infinite projection of y on x. Comparison of (144) and (150) shows that in general, filtering y and x with a common filter alters the projection of y on the one-sided infinite past of x. However, there is an important special case in which the one-sided projection is unaltered by filtering both y and x. This special case occurs when the one-sided projection equals the two-sided projection, which we know to be unaltered by filtering. Sims's theorem establishes that this case obtains when the y process fails to Granger cause x. We thus have established the following proposition:

If y fails to Granger cause x, then filtering fails to alter the projection of y on x.

A converse of this proposition also holds:

Consider the one-sided projection of y_t on $[x_t, x_{t-1}, \ldots]$,

$$y_t = \sum_{j=0}^{\infty} h_j x_{t-j} + v_t = h(L)x_t + v_t \tag{151}$$

where $Ev_t x_{t-j} = 0$ for $j \geq 0$. Let F be the space of one-sided, square summable sequences with elements $f = \{f_j\}_{j=0}^{\infty}$, $\sum_{j=0}^{\infty} f_j^2 < +\infty$. Assume that for every $f \in F$, the one-sided projection of $f(L)y_t$ on $[f(L)x_t, f(L)x_{t-1}, \ldots]$ can be represented as

$$f(L)y_t = h(L)[f(L)x_t] + f(L)v_t \tag{152}$$

where $E[f(L)v_t] \cdot [f(L)x_{t-k}] = 0$ for $k \geq 0$, and where $h(L)$ is the same operator $h(L)$ that appears in (151). Then $\{y_t\}$ fails to be Granger-caused by $\{x_t\}$.

To prove the proposition, we begin by evaluating $E[f(L)v_t] [f(L)x_{t-j}]$, which is assumed to be zero for all $j \geq 0$ and all $f \in F$. For $j = 0$, we obtain

$$E(f_0 v_t + f_1 v_{t-1} + f_2 v_{t-2} + \cdots)(f_0 x_t + f_1 x_{t-1} + \cdots)$$
$$= \sum_{h=0}^{\infty} f_h \sum_{k=h+1}^{\infty} f_k E x_{t-h} v_{t-k}.$$

Evidently, unless $Ex_t v_{t-k} = 0$ for *all* k (that is, $k > 0$ as well as $k \leq 0$), f can be chosen to make the above expression unequal to zero. Therefore, the condition that the one-sided projection of $y_t^f \equiv f(L)y_t$ on $x_t^f \equiv f(L)x_t$ have the same generating function $h(L)$ for all $f \in F$ implies that v_t is orthogonal to all *future* x_t's $\{x_{t+k}, k \geq 0\}$, as well as current and past x_t's. Therefore, the one-sided projection of $\{y_t\}$ on current and past x_t equals the two-sided projection of $\{y_t\}$ on past, present, and future $\{x_t\}$. It follows from Sims's theorem 2 that $\{y_t\}$ fails to Granger-cause $\{x_t\}$.

These propositions provide the foundation of the result in econometrics that generalized least squares estimates of projection equations like (142) are consistent if and only if x_t fails to be Granger-caused by y_t. Under standard regularity conditions, generalized least squares estimates of $h(z)$ converge to $h^f(z)$ given by (150), where $f(z)$ is a filter that is one-sided in nonnegative powers of z and that whitens v_t.

28. PRESERVATION OF ORTHOGONALITY CONDITIONS UNDER FILTERING

Various rational expectations models often lead to restrictions that take the form of orthogonality conditions. Hayashi and Sims (1983) and Hansen and Sargent (1982a) have studied the effects that filtering an equation has on the validity of such orthogonality conditions. They were concerned with understanding the circumstances under which filtering to remove serial correlation from a set of disturbances could create a representation among filtered variables not satisfying the theoretical orthogonality conditions that characterized the original unfiltered representation.

Suppose that one is interested in the one-sided projection equation

$$y_t = \sum_{j=0}^{\infty} h_j x_{t-j} + v_t \tag{153}$$

where $Ev_t x_{t-j} = 0$ for $j \geq 0$. Suppose that v_t is serially correlated, and has covariance generating function $g_x(z)$ which can be factored as

$$g_x(z) = d(z)\, d(z^{-1}). \tag{154}$$

It follows from (154) that v_t can be represented either as

$$v_t = d(L)a_t, \qquad Ea_t^2 = 1 \tag{155}$$

or

$$v_t = d(L^{-1})\tilde{a}_t, \qquad E\tilde{a}_t^2 = 1. \tag{156}$$

where $d(L) = \sum_{j=0}^{\infty} d_j L^j$, where a_t is a white noise satisfying $a_t = v_t - P[v_t | v_{t-1}, v_{t-2}, \ldots]$ and $\tilde{a}_t$ is a white noise satisfying $\tilde{a}_t = v_t - P[v_t | v_{t+1}, v_{t+2}, \ldots]$. Let $\gamma(L) = \sum_{j=0}^{\infty} \gamma_j L^j = d(L)^{-1}$.

Consider the effects on (153) of "backward" filtering, that is, of operating with $\gamma(L)$ on both sides of equation (153). We obtain

$$\gamma(L)y_t = \sum_{j=0}^{\infty} h_j\gamma(L)x_{t-j} + (\gamma_0 v_t + \gamma_1 v_{t-1} + \cdots). \tag{157}$$

Note that the residual in (157) is not in general orthogonal to x_{t-j} for $j \geq 0$. For we have

$$E(\gamma(L)v_t)x_{t-j} = E[\gamma_0 v_t + \gamma_1 v_{t-1} + \cdots]x_{t-j}$$

$$= \sum_{k=0}^{\infty} \gamma_k E v_{t-k}x_{t-j}. \tag{158}$$

Since (153) imposes only that $Ex_{t-j}v_t = 0$ for $j \geq 0$, (158) becomes

$$E(\gamma(L)v_t)x_{t-j} = \sum_{k=j+1}^{\infty} \gamma_k E v_{t-k}x_{t-j}.$$

The orthogonality conditions imposed in (153) do not imply that $E v_{t-k}x_{t-j} = 0$ for $k > j$. Therefore, in general, the residual in (157) is not orthogonal to the set $\{x_t, x_{t-1}, \ldots\}$. For a variety of linear rational expectations models, this is important because it means that $\{x_{t-j}\}_{j\geq 0}$ cannot be used via an instrumental variables technique to estimate $\{h_j\}_{j=0}^{\infty}$ in equation (157). More precisely, equation (157) does *not* imply the restrictions

$$E(\gamma(L)y_t)x_{t-k} = \sum_{j=0}^{\infty} h_j E(\gamma(L)x_{t-j})x_{t-k}, \qquad k \geq 0,$$

which would be imposed in such an instrumental variables estimator.

The idea of Hayashi and Sims was to "forward filter" (153) to obtain

$$\gamma(L^{-1})y_t = \sum_{j=0}^{\infty} h_j\gamma(L^{-1})x_{t-j} + (\gamma_0 v_t + \gamma_1 v_{t+1} + \cdots). \tag{159}$$

The orthogonality conditions in (153) do imply that the residual in (159) is orthogonal to $\{x_{t-j}\}_{j=0}^{\infty}$. For we have

$$E(\gamma(L^{-1})v_t)x_{t-j} = \gamma_0 E v_t x_{t-j} + \gamma_1 E v_{t+1}x_{t-j} + \gamma_2 E v_{t+2}x_{t-j} + \cdots = 0,$$

since $E v_t x_{t-j} = 0$ for $j \geq 0$. Thus, the residual in (159) is a white noise $(\gamma(L^{-1})v_t = \tilde{a}_t)$, and is orthogonal to $x_{t-j}, j \geq 0$. Hayashi and Sims propose to estimate $\{h_j\}_{j=0}^{\infty}$ by imposing the orthogonality conditions

$$E(\gamma(L^{-1})y_t)x_{t-k} = \sum_{j=0}^{\infty} h_j E(\gamma(L^{-1})x_{t-j})x_{t-k}, \qquad k \geq 0.$$

Estimators along these lines can be shown to be efficient as well as consistent. The key to retaining consistency is using a filter that preserves orthogonality of the residual to the potential instruments $\{x_{t-j}\}_{j=0}^{\infty}$. The key to obtaining efficiency is to find a filter that manages to make the residual serially uncorrelated.

29. THEORIES RESTRICTING ONE-SIDED PROJECTIONS

There is a class of linear rational expectations models that give rise to a theoretical restriction on the one-sided projection of a process y on a process x, but which leave the serial correlation of the residual process unrestricted. These specifications then fit naturally into the setting analyzed in the preceding section.

These specifications are motivated by an idea of Shiller (1972), who used an iterated projections argument to show that when private agents are assumed to observe more information relevant for forecasting than does the econometrician, the error thereby induced in the equation of interest to the econometrician remains orthogonal to part of the econometrician's information set. These orthogonality conditions can restrict the variables observable to the econometrician, and provide a sufficient basis for estimating and testing the model. We illustrate Shiller's idea in the context of a rational expectations version of Cagan's model of hyperinflation.

The log of the price level p_t is assumed to be determined as the average of expected future values of the log of the money supply:

$$p_t = (1 - \lambda) \sum_{j=0}^{\infty} \lambda^j P[m_{t+j}|\Omega_t], \qquad |\lambda| < 1 \tag{160}$$

where $\Omega_t \supset \Omega_{t-1} \supset \Omega_{t-2}, \ldots$, and where Ω_t is the information set available to private agents. We assume that there is an econometrician who observes a proper subset $\phi_t \subset \Omega_t$ at each date, where $\phi_t \supset \phi_{t-1} \supset \phi_{t-2} \supset \cdots$. Thus, private agents are assumed to base their forecasts of m_{t+j} on more information than is available to the econometrician.

Shiller's idea was to define the error term

$$s_t = (1 - \lambda) \sum_{j=0}^{\infty} \lambda^j [P[m_{t+j}|\Omega_t] - P[m_{t+j}|\phi_t]]. \tag{161}$$

From the law of iterated projections, it follows that

$$P[s_t|\phi_t] = 0.$$

From the orthogonality principle that states that a projection error is orthogonal to every component in the information set used to form the projection, it follows that

$$Es_t x_{t-k} = 0, \qquad k \geq 0$$

for any $x_t \in \phi_t$. Therefore, we can represent (160) as

$$p_t = (1 - \lambda) \sum_{j=0}^{\infty} \lambda^j P[m_{t+j}|\phi_t] + s_t, \tag{162}$$

where s_t is orthogonal to ϕ_t. To be more concrete, let us suppose that the econometrician has data on $(m_t, m_{t-1}, \ldots)$ as his ϕ_t. Suppose that m_t has the moving average representation

$$m_t = c(L)\varepsilon_t$$

where $c(L) = \sum_{j=0}^{\infty} c_j L^j$, $\sum_{j=0}^{\infty} c_j^2 < +\infty$, $\varepsilon_t = m_t - P[m_t|m_{t-1}, m_{t-2}, \ldots]$. Then from formula (89) we have that

$$p_t = (1 - \lambda)\left[\frac{1 - \lambda c(\lambda)c(L)^{-1}L^{-1}}{1 - \lambda L^{-1}}\right]m_t + s_t \tag{163}$$

$$c(L)^{-1}m_t = \varepsilon_t. \tag{164}$$

Equation (163) is a projection equation, i.e., $Es_t m_{t-j} = 0$ for $j \geq 0$. However, in general, $Es_t m_{t-j} \neq 0$ for $j < 0$. Intuitively, the reason can be understood from equation (161) that defines s_t. The random variable s_t reflects information in Ω_t that is useful for predicting future variables of m and that is not reflected in ϕ_t. For this reason, s_t will in general be correlated with m_{t+k}, $k > 0$.

In addition, s_t is in general serially correlated. Equation (161) defines s_t as a linear least squares error in projecting $z_t \equiv (1 - \lambda) \sum_{j=0}^{\infty} \lambda^j P[m_{t+j}|\Omega_t]$ on ϕ_t. Because lagged values of the random variable z_t being projected are *not* included in the information set ϕ_t being projected onto, there is no reason to expect s_t to be serially uncorrelated. Compare this situation with the argument in Chapter XVI, p. 445 that implies that a forecast error is serially uncorrelated in the case in which lagged values of the variable being projected are in the information set.

Thus, (163) is an example that fits the situation analyzed in the preceding section: it is a projection equation, but the disturbance s_t is both serially correlated and correlated with future m_{t+k}'s.

Using $a(L) = c(L)^{-1} = (1 - a_1 L - a_2 L^2, \ldots)$, we can rewrite (163) and (164) as

$$p_t = \sum_{j=0}^{\infty} h_j m_{t-j} + s_t \tag{165}$$

$$m_t = \sum_{j=1}^{\infty} a_j m_{t-j} + \varepsilon_t \tag{166}$$

where

$$h(L) = (1 - \lambda)\frac{[1 - \lambda a(\lambda)^{-1}a(L)L^{-1}]}{1 - \lambda L^{-1}}. \tag{167}$$

Using the orthogonality conditions $Es_t m_{t-j} = E\varepsilon_t m_{t-j} = 0$ for $j \geq 1$, (165) and (166) imply

$$Ep_t m_{t-k} = \sum_{j=0}^{\infty} h_j Em_{t-j} m_{t-k}, \qquad k \geq 0 \tag{168}$$

$$Em_t m_{t-k} = \sum_{j=1}^{\infty} a_j Em_{t-j} m_{t-k}, \qquad k \geq 0. \tag{169}$$

Equations (167), (168), and (169) supply an extensive set of restrictions on the moments of the data that are observable to the econometrician. The restrictions (169) are sufficient to uniquely determine the a_j's (equations (169) are the univariate Yule–Walker equations for the m process). From (167), the parameters h_j in (168) are not all free to vary independently. Rather, given the a_j's, (167) restricts the h_j's to vary together only as a function of the single parameter λ.

A way of looking at the idea of Hayashi and Sims (1983) is to note that equations (168) and (169) fail to exhaust all of the implications of (165), (166), and (167). Equation (168) is the condition that s_t is orthogonal to $\{m_t, m_{t-1}, m_{t-2}, \ldots\}$. "Backward filtering" destroys the orthogonality conditions because in general s_{t-1} is *not* orthogonal to $\{m_t, m_{t-1}, m_{t-2}, \ldots\}$. However, for $k \geq 0$, s_{t+k} *is* orthogonal to $\{m_t, m_{t-1}, m_{t-2}, \ldots\}$. Therefore, "forward filtering" leaves the orthogonality conditions intact. Forward filtering can be interpreted as a measure designed to impose upon the covariance structure more of the restrictions implied by the theory. By imposing more of these restrictions, more efficient estimation procedures can be constructed.[42]

30. SEASONAL ADJUSTMENT AND FORECASTING GEOMETRIC DISTRIBUTED LEADS

A stochastic process x_t is said to have an important seasonal component if its spectral density has peaks in the vicinity of the seasonal frequencies, meaning that the process has a substantial portion of its variance occurring over the seasonal frequencies. It is a common practice to "seasonally adjust" the series in order to remove the seasonal components. Unless the seasonal components are thought mainly to reflect measurement errors that are unrelated to economic activity, seasonal adjustment is typically misleading. We briefly indicate how using seasonally adjusted data can distort analysis.

We have often encountered, and shall encounter even more often later, models in which economic agents decide to make an endogenous variable y_t a geometric sum of expected future values of a variable x_t:

$$y_t = P_t \sum_{j=0}^{\infty} \lambda^j x_{t+j}, \tag{170}$$

---

[42] See Hansen and Sargent (1982a) for a formal development of this argument.

where P_t is the linear least squares projection operator conditioned on $[x_t, x_{t-1}, \ldots]$. Now let x_t be a covariance stationary stochastic process with Wold representation

$$x_t = c(L)\varepsilon_t \qquad (171)$$

$\varepsilon_t = x_t - P_{t-1}x_t$. Let x_t have a substantial seasonal component, say reflecting weather or seasonal movements in tastes (Christmas and Easter). These seasonal movements are assumed not to be due to measurement error, but are truly occurring in the process that x_t is measuring. We have seen above that (170) and (171) imply that y_t will obey

$$y_t = \left[\frac{c(L) - \lambda c(\lambda)L^{-1}}{1 - \lambda L^{-1}}\right]\varepsilon_t. \qquad (172)$$

or

$$y_t = \left[\frac{1 - \lambda c(\lambda)c(L)^{-1}L^{-1}}{1 - \lambda L^{-1}}\right]x_t. \qquad (173)$$

Now suppose that an analyst has seasonally adjusted x_t to obtain a process x_t^a. Typically this is accomplished by taking

$$x_t^a = h(L)x_t \qquad (174)$$

where $h(L)$ is a long two-sided filter that attenuates (but does not completely eradicate) power at the seasonal frequencies. We indicated how to construct such a filter in Section 6 above. Typically, these seasonal adjustment filters are symmetric with $h_j = h_{-j}$. (See Exercise 2 and Section 6.)

If the economic agent is choosing y_t to obey (173), then y_t is related to the seasonally adjusted series x_t^a by

$$h(L)y_t = \left[\frac{1 - \lambda c(\lambda)c(L)^{-1}L^{-1}}{1 - \lambda L^{-1}}\right]h(L)x_t$$

or

$$h(L)y_t = \left[\frac{1 - \lambda c(\lambda)c(L)^{-1}L^{-1}}{1 - \lambda L^{-1}}\right]x_t^a. \qquad (175)$$

Suppose that seasonally adjusted data on y_t, denoted y_t^a, are created via the *same* filter $h(L)$ used to create x_t^a, so that

$$y_t^a = h(L)y_t. \qquad (176)$$

In view of (176), (175) becomes

$$y_t^a = \left[\frac{1 - \lambda c(\lambda)c(L)^{-1}L^{-1}}{1 - \lambda L^{-1}}\right]x_t^a \qquad (177)$$

where $c(L)$ is the Wold representation for the seasonally *unadjusted* series x_t given in (171). (In Sims (1974) and Exercise 10, the effects are studied of adjusting y_t and x_t by using *different* seasonal filters.)

If agents are behaving according to (173) or (177), the restrictions across the y_t^a and x_t^a processes cannot be computed from knowledge of the autoregression for x_t^a alone, without knowledge of the seasonal adjustment filter $h(L)$. If one routinely applies the Hansen–Sargent formula (90) based on using the moving average or autoregressive representation for the seasonally adjusted series, an error is committed, whose nature we now briefly explore.

We continue to suppose that economic agents are actually choosing y_t to satisfy (170) and therefore (173). Suppose that the economist mistakenly uses the seasonally adjusted data to create the model

$$y_t = P_t \sum_{j=0}^{\infty} \lambda^j x_{t+j}^a \tag{178}$$

where now P_t denotes the least squares projection on the space $[x_t^a, x_{t-1}^a, \dots]$. To deduce the implications of model (178), we need the Wold representation of x_t^a,

$$x_t^a = d(L)a_t, \qquad d(L) = \sum_{j=0}^{\infty} d_j L^j \tag{179}$$

$$a_t = x_t^a - P[x_t^a | x_{t-1}^a, x_{t-2}^a, \dots].$$

Now $d(L)$ of (179) is related to $c(L)$ of (171) by the spectral factorization equation

$$\sigma_a^2 d(L)\, d(L^{-1}) = \sigma_\varepsilon^2 h(L)h(L^{-1})c(L)c(L^{-1}), \tag{180}$$

where $\sigma_a^2 = Ea_t^2$, $\sigma_\varepsilon^2 = E\varepsilon_t^2$, and $d(L)$ has all of its zeros outside the unit circle. Note that in general $h(L)$ is two sided in powers of L, and that $d(L) \neq h(L)c(L)$.

Equations (178) and (179) imply that

$$y_t = \left[\frac{1 - \lambda\, d(\lambda)\, d(L)^{-1}L^{-1}}{1 - \lambda L^{-1}} \right] x_t^a. \tag{181}$$

Using $x_t^a = h(L)x_t$, we have that

$$y_t = \left[\frac{1 - \lambda\, d(\lambda)\, d(L)^{-1}L^{-1}}{1 - \lambda L^{-1}} \right] h(L)x_t. \tag{182}$$

A comparison of equations (173), (180), and (182) shows how (182) misspecifies the relationship between y_t and $\{x_t\}$ if agents are responding to forecasts of the seasonally unadjusted series while the economist attributes to agents their responding to forecasts of the seasonally adjusted series. Alternatively, a comparison of (175) with (181) shows how deducing the cross-equation restrictions on the basis of the seasonally adjusted data misspecifies the relationship between y_t^a and x_t^a. Continuing to suppose that $y_t^a = h(L)y_t$, applying $h(L)$ to both sides of (181) implies that

$$y_t^a = h(L)\left[\frac{1 - \lambda\, d(\lambda)\, d(L)^{-1}L^{-1}}{1 - \lambda L^{-1}}\right]x_t^a, \qquad (183)$$

whereas the actual value of y_t^a is determined by the right side of (175).

We illustrate these calculations as follows. For monthly U.S. money supply (M2) for the period 1959:1 to 1986:2 we constructed an 18th order autoregression for both seasonally adjusted and seasonally unadjusted M2. The spectral densities of seasonally adjusted and unadjusted M2 are reported in Figure 8. Notice the dips in the spectral density of the adjusted series at the seasonal frequencies (see Exercise 2). The autoregressive coefficients are plotted for the seasonally adjusted and unadjusted series in Figure 9. In Figure 10, we report the values of the two filters in x associated with (177) and (181); namely,

$$b^{nsa}(L) = \left[\frac{1 - \lambda c(\lambda)c(L)^{-1}L^{-1}}{1 - \lambda L^{-1}}\right]$$

$$b^{sa}(L) = \left[\frac{1 - \lambda\, d(\lambda)\, d(L)^{-1}L^{-1}}{1 - \lambda L^{-1}}\right]$$

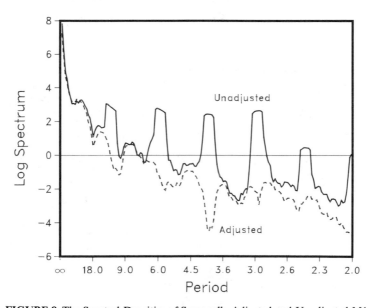

FIGURE 8 The Spectral Densities of Seasonally Adjusted and Unadjusted M1.

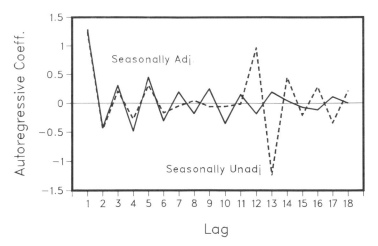

FIGURE 9 Autoregressions for M2, 1959:1–1986:12.

where we set $\lambda = 0.9$ and where we have used the estimated autoregressive representations reported in Figure 9 for $c(L)$ and $d(L)$. Note the difference in $b^{nsu}(L)$ and $b^{sa}(L)$ in the vicinity of 12 lags.

Figures 11 and 12 summarize the magnitude and phase of the transfer function from innovations in M2 to "y_t" that are associated with $b^{nsa}(L)$ and $b^{sa}(L)$. That is, let the filters associated with the autoregressive representations

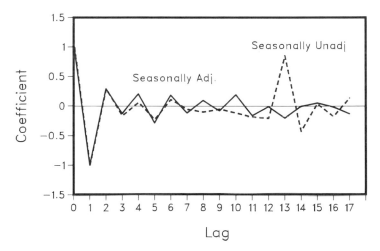

FIGURE 10 Coefficients for forecasting geometric sum of future M2, $\lambda = 0.9$.

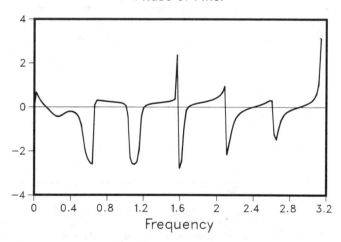

FIGURE 11 Frequency response to innovations in seasonally unadjusted M2 of forecast of geometric distributed lead of M2, $\lambda = 0.9$.

be denoted $a^{sa}(L)$ and $a^{nsa}(L)$, respectively. Then Figures 11–12 report the magnitude and phase of

$$h(e^{-iw})h(e^{+iw})$$

where $h(L)$ is given by $b^{nsa}(L)/a^{nsa}(L)$ or $b^{sa}(L)/a^{sa}(L)$, respectively. Note the substantially different responses revealed in these figures.

Some of these ideas are explored further in Exercises 22 and 23.

Amplitude of Filter

Phase of Filter

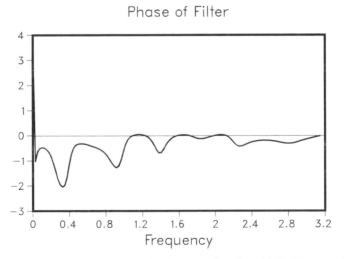

FIGURE 12 Frequency response to innovation in seasonally adjusted M2 of forecast of geometric distributed lead of M2, $\lambda = 0.9$.

31. AGGREGATION OVER TIME

This section briefly introduces Sims's (1971) framework for studying the effects of aggregation over time. The idea is to assume that there is an underlying stochastic process that is evolving in continuous time, on which the economist has observations at discrete points in time. Sims studied the question of how closely the projection of y on x in discrete time approximates the corresponding projection in continuous time. Discussing Sims's work permits us briefly to introduce the concept of a continuous time stochastic process.

We now suppose that $y(t)$, $x(t)$ is a continuous time jointly covariance stationary stochastic process. The linear structure of such a process is characterized by the covariance functions

$$c_x(\tau) = Ex_t x_{t-\tau}$$

$$c_y(\tau) = Ey_t y_{t-\tau} \qquad (184)$$

$$c_{yx}(\tau) = Ey_t x_{t-\tau}$$

where now $\tau \in \mathbf{R}$, where $\mathbf{R}$ is the set of real numbers. To be the matrix covariance function of a real-valued covariance stationary process it is necessary and sufficient that the matrix function

$$\begin{bmatrix} c_y(\tau) & c_{yx}(\tau) \\ c_{xy}(\tau) & c_x(\tau) \end{bmatrix}$$

must be nonnegative definite. This is equivalent with the requirement that for any finite n, any finite index set of times $t_1, \ldots, t_n$, and any sequence of (2×1) real-valued vectors $h_1, \ldots, h_n$, the covariance function (184) must imply that

$$Ez^2 > 0$$

where

$$z \equiv \sum_{j=1}^{n} h_j^T \begin{bmatrix} y_{t_j} \\ x_{t_j} \end{bmatrix}.$$

The projection of y_t on the entire x process is defined by

$$y_t = \int_{-\infty}^{\infty} b(s)x(t-s)\,ds + u(t) \qquad (185)$$

where $u(t)$ is a least-squares residual that satisfies the orthogonality conditions $Eu(t)x(t-s) = 0$ for all $s \in \mathbf{R}$. Multiplying (185) by $x(t-k)$ and taking expectations gives the normal equation

$$c_{yx}(k) = \int_{-\infty}^{\infty} b(s)c_x(k-s)\,ds \qquad (186)$$

for all $k \in \mathbf{R}$. The normal equation (186) determines the function $b(s)$.

Now suppose that one has observations on (y_t, x_t) only at the discrete points of time $t \in I$, where I is the set of integers $\{0, \pm 1, \pm 2, \ldots\}$. Thus, we view the discrete time process as representing a sampled version of the underlying continuous time process. Sims (1971) posed and answered the following question. Consider the discrete time projections of y_t on all past, present, and future x_t's:

$$y_t = \sum_{j=-\infty}^{\infty} B_j x_{t-j} + \varepsilon_t \qquad (187)$$

where $E\varepsilon_t x_{t-j} = 0$ for $j \in I$. What is the relationship between the sequence $\{B_j\}_{j=-\infty}^{\infty}$ in (187) and the function $(b(s), s \in \mathbf{R})$ in (185)? Under what circumstances does the B_j sequence "resemble $b(s)$," i.e., under what circumstances is B_j close to being a sampled version of $b(s)$, so that $B_j \simeq b(j), j \in I$? To answer this question, Sims derived a formula expressing B_j as a particular kind of average of $b(s)$.

Multiplying (187) by $x_{t-\tau}$, for integer τ, and taking expectations of both sides gives the normal equations

$$c_{yx}(\tau) = \sum_{j=-\infty}^{\infty} B_j c_x(\tau - j), \qquad \tau = 0, \pm 1, \pm 2, \ldots. \tag{188}$$

Since (186) holds for all $k \in \mathbf{R}$, (188) and (186) together imply that

$$\sum_{j=-\infty}^{\infty} B_j c_x(\tau - j) = \int_{-\infty}^{\infty} b(s) c_x(\tau - s)\, ds, \qquad \tau = 0, \pm 1, \pm 2, \ldots. \tag{189}$$

Multiplying both sides by z^τ and summing over τ gives

$$B(z) g_x(z) = m(z) \tag{190}$$

where

$$B(z) = \sum_{\tau=-\infty}^{\infty} B_\tau z^\tau,$$

$$g_x(z) = \sum_{\tau=-\infty}^{\infty} c_x(\tau) z^\tau,$$

and

$$m(z) = \sum_{\tau=-\infty}^{\infty} z^\tau \int b(s) c_x(\tau - s)\, ds.$$

Now let $g_x(z)^{-1} = \sum_{j=-\infty}^{\infty} \gamma_j z^j \equiv \gamma_x(z)$.[43] Operating on both sides of (190) with $\gamma_x(z)$ gives

$$B(z) = \gamma_x(z) m(z)$$

or

$$B_j = \sum_{k=-\infty}^{\infty} \gamma_x(k) \int_{-\infty}^{\infty} b(s) c_x(j - k - s)\, ds$$

or

$$B_j = \int_{-\infty}^{\infty} b(s) \sum_{k=-\infty}^{\infty} \gamma_x(k) c_x(j - k - s)\, ds. \tag{191}$$

---

[43] The sequence $\{\gamma_j\}$ is called the "inverse under convolution" of the sequence $\{c_x(\tau)\}$.

Equation (191) is a version of Sims's formula. Define

$$r_x(j - s) = \sum_{k = -\infty}^{\infty} \gamma_x(k)c_x(j - k - s).$$ (192)

Then from (191), we have

$$B_j = \int_{-\infty}^{\infty} b(s)r_x(j - s)\, ds, \qquad j = 0, \pm 1, \pm 2, \dots.$$ (193)

Formula (193) has an interpretation as a version of Theil's omitted variables theorem. Since

$$Py_t|\{x_{t-k}\}_{k=-\infty}^{\infty} = \sum_{k=-\infty}^{\infty} B_k x_{t-k},$$ (194)

use (185) and the orthogonality of $u(t)$ to $x(t - s)$ for all s to write

$$Py_t|\{x_{t-k}\}_{k=-\infty}^{\infty} = \int_{-\infty}^{\infty} b(s)Px(t - s)|\{x_{t-k}\}_{k=-\infty}^{\infty}\, ds$$

or from (194)

$$\sum_{k=-\infty}^{\infty} B_k x_{t-k} = \int_{-\infty}^{\infty} b(s) \sum_{k=-\infty}^{\infty} \delta_k^s x_{t-k}\, ds$$ (195)

where $Px(t - s)|\{x_{t-k}\}_{k=-\infty}^{\infty} = \sum_{k=-\infty}^{\infty} \delta_k^s x_{t-k}$, $s \in \mathbf{R}$. The $\{\delta_k^s\}_{k=-\infty}^{\infty}$ sequence for each $s \in \mathbf{R}$ is determined from the orthogonality conditions

$$Ex(t - s)x(t - j) = \sum_{k=-\infty}^{\infty} \delta_k^s Ex_{t-k}x_{t-j}$$

or

$$c_x(s - j) = \sum_{k=-\infty}^{\infty} \delta_k^s c_x(j - k) \qquad \text{for all integer } j.$$ (196)

Recalling that we have defined $\gamma_x(k)$ be the inverse under convolution of the sequence $c_x(k)$, convoluting each side of (196) with the sequence $\gamma_x(k)$ gives

$$\delta_h^s = \sum_{k=-\infty}^{\infty} \gamma_x(k)c_x(h - k - s),$$ (197)

which shows that $\delta_h^s = r_x(h - s)$. Now exchanging orders of integration and summation in (195) gives

$$\sum_{k=-\infty}^{\infty} B_k x_{t-k} = \sum_{k=-\infty}^{\infty} \left[\int_{-\infty}^{\infty} b(s)\delta_k^s\, ds \right] x_{t-k}.$$

This implies that

$$B_k = \int_{-\infty}^{\infty} b(s)\delta_k{}^s \, ds \qquad (198)$$

which is equivalent with (193) because $\delta_k{}^s = r_x(k - s)$. Equation (198) expresses B_k as the convolution of the function $b(s)$ with the function $\{\delta_k{}^s\}$, where $\delta_k{}^s$ is the coefficient on x_k in the projection of $x(t - s)$ on $\{x_j\}_{j=-\infty}^{\infty}$.

Equation (193) or (198) shows how B_k depends on $b(s)$ for all s, not just s close to k. Sims (1971) describes examples in which the $r_x(k - s)$ function is such that B_k is very different from $b(k)$. In general, (193) reveals that even if $b(s)$ is one-sided on the past ($b(s) = 0$ for $s < 0$), $B_k \neq 0$ for $k < 0$. This means that if y fails to Granger cause x in continuous time, in general y in discrete time will Granger cause x; how strongly y in discrete time Granger causes x depends on the function $r_x(s)$.

Sims's work was extended to a multivariate setting by Geweke (1978). Hansen and Sargent (1982) apply an approach related to Sims's in order to study the connection between vector autoregressions in continuous time and their discrete time counterparts. Methods for estimating continuous time models from discrete time observations are described by Bergstrom (1983) and Hansen and Sargent (1981b).

32. EFFECTS OF ERRORS IN VARIABLES

We have already considered some aspects of the ways that measurement errors distort the autoregressive or Wold moving average representation of an error ridden variable relative to that of the true variable. For example, the solution of the dynamic signal extraction problem described in Section 18 hinged on deducing a Wold representation for the error-ridden data from knowledge of the covariance generating functions of the true process and the measurement error process. Such a Wold representation was derived by obtaining the spectral density of the error-ridden data, then "factoring" it so that the associated moving average kernel generated a white noise contained in the space of square summable linear combinations of current and lagged values of the error-ridden variable. In interpreting autoregressions and vector autoregressions, one often traces out the "impulse response function," i.e., the coefficients of a Wold moving average representation. (For example, see the "innovation accounting" methods introduced by Sims (1980).) In interpreting such representations where some or all of the data are error-ridden, it is important to remember the signal extraction or spectral factorization problem which those autoregressions are implicitly solving.

This section briefly considers the effects of errors in variables on the nature of the projections in Sims's theorem 2. We shall show how measurement errors make error-ridden observations x on a variable X which is not Granger caused by Y appear to be Granger caused by either Y or an error-ridden measure of it, y.

Let (Y_t, X_t) be a jointly covariance stationary process of two "true" (accurately measured) variables with covariance generating functions $g_{YX}(z)$, $g_X(z)$, $g_Y(z)$. The two-sided projection of Y on the X process is given by

$$Y_t = B(L)X_t + U_t$$

where $EU_t X_{t-s} = 0$ for all s, and

$$B(z) = \frac{g_{YX}(z)}{g_X(z)}.$$

Now let (y_t, x_t) be a jointly covariance stationary process of error-ridden measured values corresponding to (Y_t, X_t). Assume that (y_t, x_t) is related to (Y_t, X_t) by

$$y_t = Y_t + \eta_t$$

$$x_t = X_t + \varepsilon_t$$

where η_t and ε_t are jointly covariance stationary stochastic processes that satisfy the orthogonality conditions

$$E\varepsilon_t \eta_{t-s} = EY_t\eta_{t-s} = EX_t\eta_{t-s} = EY_t\varepsilon_{t-s} = EX_t\varepsilon_{t-s} = 0 \qquad (199)$$

for all t and s. Let the covariance generating functions of ε and η be $g_\varepsilon(z)$ and $g_\eta(z)$. The two-sided projection of y on the x process is given by

$$y_t = b(L)x_t + u_t$$

where $Eu_t x_{t-s} = 0$ for all t and s and

$$b(z) = \frac{g_{yx}(z)}{g_x(z)}.$$

But the orthogonality conditions (199) imply that $g_{yx}(z) = g_{YX}(z)$ and $g_x(z) = g_X(z) + g_\varepsilon(z)$. Therefore, we have that

$$b(z) = \frac{g_{YX}(z)}{g_X(z) + g_\varepsilon(z)} = B(z)\frac{g_X(z)}{g_X(z) + g_\varepsilon(z)}. \qquad (200)$$

Defining $w(z) = g_X(z)/(g_X(z) + g_\varepsilon(z))$, we have

$$b(z) = B(z)w(z) \qquad (201)$$

or

$$b_k = \sum_{j=-\infty}^{\infty} w_j B_{k-j} \qquad (202)$$

where w_j is given by the inversion formula

$$w_j = \frac{1}{2\pi i} \int w(z) z^{-j-1}\, dz.$$

Equation (200), (201), or (202) shows that in general $b(z) \neq B(z)$, and that $\{b_k\}$ is the convolution of $\{B_k\}$ with a weighting function $\{w_k\}$ that is two-sided and symmetric ($w_k = w_{-k}$) and that in general is of infinite order. Therefore, b_k for a given k in general is a function of B_h for all h's. It follows from these observations, or directly from (200), that even if $B(z)$ is one-sided, $b(z)$ will in general be two-sided. By Sims's theorem, this means that even if Y fails to Granger cause X, y will Granger cause the error-ridden series x.

To take a simple example that illustrates this phenomenon, let $g_X(z) = [(1 - \rho z)(1 - \rho z^{-1})]^{-1}, |\rho| < 1, g_{yx}(z) = (1 + az)/(1 - \rho z^{-1}), g_\eta(z) = 0, g_\varepsilon(z) = \sigma_\varepsilon^2$. We have that $B(z) = (1 + az)(1 - \rho z)$, so that the projection of Y on X is one-sided, and X fails to Granger cause Y. We have that $w(z) = 1/[1 + \sigma_\varepsilon^2(1 - \rho z)(1 - \rho z^{-1})] = 1/\lambda_0(1 - \lambda_1 z)(1 - \lambda_1 z^{-1})$ where $|\lambda_1| < 1$ and $\lambda_0(1 - \lambda_1 z)(1 - \lambda_1 z^{-1}) = 1 + \sigma_\varepsilon^2(1 - \rho z)(1 - \rho z^{-1})$. We see that $b(z)$ is two-sided even though $B(z)$ is one-sided.

33. BUBBLES

Following Blanchard and Watson (1982), consider the stochastic expectational difference equation

$$y_t = \lambda P_t y_{t+1} + x_t, \qquad |\lambda| < 1 \tag{203}$$

where x_t is a stationary autoregressive process

$$x_t = \rho x_{t-1} + \varepsilon_t, \qquad |\rho| < 1 \tag{204}$$

where ε_t is a white noise that is fundamental for x_t. In (203), P_t is the linear least squares projection operator, conditioned on information known at t. An application of formula (90) shows that the *stationary* solution of (203) given (204) is

$$y_t = \frac{1}{1 - \lambda\rho} x_t. \tag{205}$$

Blanchard and Watson noted that in addition to the stationary solution (205) there are many nonstationary solutions. These nonstationary solutions can be characterized as follows. Let c_t be any martingale, that is, let c_t be any stochastic process that satisfies $P_t c_{t+1} = c_t$. Then a solution of (203) is

$$y_t = \frac{1}{1 - \lambda\rho} x_t + \left(\frac{1}{\lambda}\right)^t c_t. \tag{206}$$

That (206) is a solution of (203) can be verified directly.

Three examples of martingales c_t can usefully be given. A first is the constant $c_t = c$ for all t. This is the sort of deterministic bubble encountered in Chapter IX. A second is the one proposed by Blanchard and Watson, namely, the process

$$c_{t+1} = \begin{cases} c_t/\pi & \text{with prob } \pi, \quad 0 < \pi < 1 \\ 0 & \text{with prob } (1-\pi) \end{cases}.$$

The process c_{t+1} is readily verified to be a martingale. A third example is generated from the x_t process itself. Simply set $c_t = \rho^{-t} x_t$, which is a martingale in light of (204).

In Chapter XIV, we study a model in which a transversality condition serves to make setting $c_t = 0$ the only admissible solution for a version of equation (203). There has recently been work designed to estimate and test models in which there are insufficient boundary conditions to justify setting $c_t = 0$. (See Blanchard and Watson (1982), Meese (1986), Sargent and Wallace (1985), and Hamilton and Whiteman (1985).) Such models have been proposed as candidates for understanding the stock market, foreign exchange rates, and hyperinflations.

EXERCISES

1. (Sims's approximation error formula.) Let (y_t, x_t) be jointly covariance stationary with means of zero. Let the projection of y_t on the x process be

$$\sum_{j=-\infty}^{\infty} b_j^0 x_{t-j}.$$

Suppose a researcher fits by least squares

$$y_t = \sum_{j=-\infty}^{\infty} b_j^1 x_{t-j} + u_t$$

where u_t is a disturbance and $\{b_j^1\}$ is a constrained parameterization so that b_j^1 cannot equal b_j^0 for all j. Some examples of commonly encountered constrained parameterizations are:

    (i) truncation: $b_j^1 = 0$ for $|j| > m$, m a fixed positive integer;
    (ii) polynomial approximation: $b_j^1 = \alpha_0 + \alpha_1 j + \cdots + \alpha_m j^m$, m a fixed positive integer, α_j free;
    (iii) Pascal lag distributions (Solow)

$$b^1(L) = \frac{1}{(1 - \lambda L)^r}$$

where r is a fixed positive integer and $|\lambda| < 1$.
(a) Derive Sims's formula, which asserts that in population, least squares picks b_j^1 to minimize

$$\int_{-\pi}^{\pi} |b^0(e^{-i\omega}) - b^1(e^{-i\omega})|^2 g_x(e^{-i\omega})\, d\omega.$$

Hints: Write y_t as

$$y_t = \sum_{j=-\infty}^{\infty} b_j^0 x_{t-j} + \varepsilon_t;$$

$E\varepsilon_t x_{t-j} = 0$ for all j. Then show that

$$E\left(y_t - \sum_{j=-\infty}^{\infty} b_j^1 x_{t-j}\right)^2 = E(z_t^2)$$

where

$$z_t = \sum_{j=-\infty}^{\infty} (b_j^0 - b_j^1)x_{t-j} + \varepsilon_t.$$

(b) Apply formula (33) to calculate the spectrum of z_t. (c) Apply formula (20) to calculate the variance of z_t (see Sims, 1972b).

2. ("Optimal" seasonal adjustment via signal extraction.) Suppose that an analyst is interested in estimating x_t but only observes $X_t = x_t + u_t$ where $Ex_t u_s = 0$ for all t and s, and where x_t and u_t are both covariance stationary stochastic processes with means of zero and known (to the analyst) covariance generating functions $g_x(z)$ and $g_u(z)$ respectively; $g_u(e^{-i\omega}) > 0$ for all ω, but has most of its power concentrated at seasonal frequencies. The analyst estimates x_t by the projection

$$\hat{x}_t = \sum_{j=-\infty}^{\infty} h_j X_{t-j},$$

the projection of the unknown x_t on the X_t process.
  A. Derive a formula for the h_j (use (45)).
  B. Prove that $g_{\hat{x}}(e^{-i\omega}) < g_x(e^{-i\omega})$ for all ω.
  C. Prove that if $g_x(e^{-i\omega})$ is relatively smooth across the seasonal and nonseasonal frequencies, then since $g_u(e^{-i\omega})$ has big peaks at the seasonal frequencies, it follows that $g_{\hat{x}}(e^{-i\omega})$ will have substantial dips at the seasonal frequencies.

3. Let x_t be any covariance stationary stochastic process with $Ex_t = 0$.
  A. Prove that there exists a representation

$$x_t = \sum_{j=0}^{\infty} c_j u_{t+j} + \theta_t$$

where $c_0 = 1$, $\sum c_j^2 < \infty$, $Eu_t^2 \geq 0$, $Eu_t u_s = 0$ for $t \neq s$ and $E\theta_t u_s = 0$ for all t and s; θ_t is a process that can be predicted arbitrarily well by a linear function of only *future* values of x; and $u_t = x_t - P[x_t | x_{t+1}, x_{t+2}, \ldots]$.
  B. Prove that $c_j = d_j$ where d_j is the object in Wold's theorem.
  C. Does $u_t = \varepsilon_t$ where ε_t is the object in Wold's theorem? Does $Eu_t^2 = E\varepsilon_t^2$?
  D. Does $\theta_t = \eta_t$ where η_t is the object in Wold's theorem?

4. Consider the "explosive" first-order Markov process $y_t = \lambda y_{t-1} + \varepsilon_t$, $t = 1, 2, \ldots, \lambda > 1$, where ε_t is white noise with mean zero and variance σ_ε^2, and y_0 is given.
  A. Prove that for each realization $(\varepsilon_1, \varepsilon_2, \ldots,)$ the y_t process has the representation

$$y_t = \lambda^t \eta_0 + \frac{1}{1 - \lambda^{-1}L} u_t$$

where u_t is a white noise. Find formulas for η_0 and u_t in terms of the ε process, λ, and y_0. (*Hint*: solve the difference equation forward and impose the initial condition.)
  B. Is the u_t process "fundamental" for y_t?

5. Consider the univariate first-order mixed moving average, autoregressive process $z_t = \lambda z_{t-1} + a_t - \beta a_{t-1}$ where a_t is a fundamental white noise for z and $0 < \beta < 1$, $0 < \lambda < 1$.
  A. Write the process in the form (104). (*Hint*: try $x_t = (z_t, a_t)'$ and $\varepsilon_t = (a_t, a_t)'$.)

B. Use formula (108) to derive a formula for $P[z_{t+2}|z_t, z_{t-1}, \ldots]$. Verify that this answer agrees with the result of applying the Wiener–Kolmogorov formula (62).

6. For the processes below, determine whether x Granger causes y and whether y Granger causes x.

A.

$$g_x(z) = \sigma_\varepsilon^2 \frac{1}{1 - 0.9z}\frac{1}{1 - 0.9z^{-1}}, \qquad g_y(z) = \sigma_u^2(1 - 0.8z)(1 - 0.8z^{-1}),$$

$$g_{yx}(z) = \sigma_{u\varepsilon}(1 - 0.8z)(1 + 0.5z^{-1}).$$

B.

$$g_x(z) = \sigma_\varepsilon^2(1 + 0.99z)(1 + 0.99z^{-1}), \qquad g_y(z) = \sigma_u^2\left(\frac{1}{1 - 0.7z + 0.3z^2}\right)\left(\frac{1}{1 - 0.7z^{-1} + 0.3z^{-2}}\right),$$

$$g_{yx}(z) = \sigma_{u\varepsilon}(1 + 0.2z)(1 + 0.99z^{-1}).$$

C.

$$g_x(z) = \sigma_\varepsilon^2\left(\frac{1}{1 - 0.7z}\right)\left(\frac{1}{1 - 0.7z^{-1}}\right), \qquad g_y(z) = \sigma_u^2\left(\frac{1}{1 - 0.8z}\right)\left(\frac{1}{1 - 0.8z^{-1}}\right),$$

$$g_{yx}(z) = \sigma_{u\varepsilon}\left(\frac{1}{1 - 0.8z}\right)\left(\frac{1}{1 - 0.7z^{-1}}\right).$$

7. Consider the simple Keynesian macroeconomic model

$$c_t = \sum_{j=0}^{\infty} b_j Y_{t-j} + \varepsilon_t, \qquad \sum_{j=0}^{\infty} b_j^2 < \infty, \qquad c_t + I_t = Y_t \qquad (*)$$

where c_t, Y_t, and I_t are consumption, GNP, and investment, respectively, all measured as deviations from their means. Here ε_t is a stationary disturbance process that satisfies $E\varepsilon_t \cdot I_s = E\varepsilon_t = 0$ for all t and s and I_s is a stationary stochastic process. Assume that $(1 - b(L))$ has a one-sided, square summable inverse in nonnegative powers of L.

A. Determine whether Y Granger causes I.

B. Determine whether c Granger causes Y and whether Y Granger causes c. (*Hint*: solve for c_t and Y_t each as "reduced form" functions of I and ε, then apply formula (18) to calculate the cross spectrum and use formula (45) to investigate Granger causality.)

C. Is the consumption function (*) a projection (regression) equation?

8. Consider a (y, x) process that has a Wold moving average representation

$$y_t = a(L)\varepsilon_t + ka(L)u_t, \qquad x_t = c(L)\varepsilon_t$$

where k is a constant, $a(L)$ and $c(L)$ are each one-sided on the past and present and square summable, $Eu_t = E\varepsilon_t = Eu_t\varepsilon_s = 0$ for all t and s, and where ε_t and u_t are jointly fundamental for y and x. Finally, assume that both $a(L)$ and $c(L)$ are invertible, i.e., have square-summable inverses that are one-sided in nonnegative powers of L.

A. Determine whether y Granger causes x and whether x Granger causes y.

B. Find the coefficient generating function for the projection of y on the entire x process.

C. Find the coefficient generating function for the projection of x on the entire y process.

D. Obtain a different Wold moving average representation for the (y, x) process. (*Hint*: choose one white noise process as $\eta_{1t} \equiv \varepsilon_t + ku_t$, and choose the other as η_{2t}, the error in the projection of ε_t on $\varepsilon_t + ku_t$, $\varepsilon_t = \rho(ku_t + \varepsilon_t) + \eta_{2t}$, where η_{2t} is a least squares disturbance.)

9. Consider Lucas's aggregate supply curve

$$y_t = \gamma(p_t - P[p_t|\Omega_{t-1}]) + \lambda y_{t-1} + u_t, \qquad 0 < |\lambda| < 1, \quad \gamma > 0 \qquad (*)$$

where y is the log of real GNP, p the log of the price level, and u_t a stationary random disturbance process. Suppose that p_t follows the Markov process

$$p_t = \sum_{i=1}^{n} w_i p_{t-i} + \varepsilon_t \qquad (\dagger)$$

where $P[\varepsilon_t | \Omega_{t-1}] = 0$. Here Ω_{t-1} is an information set including *at least* lagged y's and lagged p's.

A. Suppose that $Pu_t | \Omega_{t-1} = 0$, so that u_t is serially uncorrelated. Prove that p fails to Granger cause y. (In fact, this can be proved where p follows any arbitrary stationary stochastic process and is not dependent on p following ($\dagger$).)

B. Now assume ($\dagger$) and suppose that u_t is serially correlated, and in particular that

$$u_t = \rho u_{t-1} + \xi_t, \qquad 0 < |\rho| < 1$$

where $P[\xi_t | \Omega_{t-1}] = 0$. Prove that p Granger causes y by calculating

$$P[y_t | y_{t-1}, y_{t-2}, \ldots, p_{t-1}, p_{t-2}, \ldots].$$

10. Suppose that y_t fails to Granger cause x, where both y and x are seasonally unadjusted processes. Suppose that an investigator studies seasonally adjusted processes y_t^a and x_t^a (see Sims, 1974):

$$y_t^a = f(L)y_t, \qquad x_t^a = g(L)x_t$$

where $f(L)$ and $g(L)$ are each finite-order two-sided, symmetric ($f_j = f_{-j}$, $g_j = g_{-j}$) seasonal adjustment filters chosen so that y_t^a and x_t^a have less power at the seasonal frequencies than do y_t and x_t, respectively. Assume that y_t^a and x_t^a are strictly linearly indeterministic, as are y_t and x_t.

Prove that if $f(L) \neq g(L)$, then y_t^a in general Granger causes x_t^a. (*Hint:* first calculate the coefficient generating function for the projection of y_t on the x process, then calculate the coefficient generating function for the projection of y_t^a on the x^a process.)

11. In a recent article, a macroeconomist reported a regression of the log of the price level (p_t) on current and past values of the log of the money supply (m_t):

$$p_t = a + \sum_{j=0}^{\infty} h_j m_{t-j} + \varepsilon_t, \qquad E\varepsilon_t m_{t-j} = 0 \qquad \text{for } j \geq 0 \qquad (*)$$

$$E\varepsilon_t = 0$$

where ε_t is a random disturbance. He found that the h_j were nonzero for many j's. He concluded that prices are "too sticky" to be explained by an equilibrium model. According to this economist, "classical" macroeconomics implies that $h_0 = 1$ and $h_j = 0$ for $j \neq 0$.

Now consider the following classical macroeconomic model:

$$m_t - p_t = \alpha(P_t p_{t+1} - p_t) + y_t + u_t \text{ (portfolio balance schedule)},$$

$y_t = $ constant (extreme classical full-employment assumption). Here $\alpha < 0$, and u_t is a stationary random process obeying

$$Eu_t m_s = 0 \qquad \text{for all } t, s, \qquad Eu_t = 0.$$

The money supply is exogenous and has moving average representation

$$m_t = d(L)e_t, \qquad e_t = m_t - Pm_t | m_{t-1}, m_{t-2}, \ldots, \qquad \text{and} \qquad \sum_{j=0}^{\infty} d_j^2 < \infty.$$

Derive a formula giving the $h(L) = \sum_{j=0}^{\infty} h_j L^j$ in ($*$) as a function of α and $d(L)$. Is the macroeconomist correct in his interpretation of the implications of classical theory?

12. Let the portfolio balance schedule be Cagan's

$$\mu_t - x_t = \alpha(P_t x_{t+1} - P_{t-1} x_t) + \eta_t \qquad (*)$$

where μ_t is the rate of growth of the money supply, x_t is the rate of inflation, and η_t satisfies $P_{t-1}\eta_t = 0$, where $P_t[y] \equiv P[y|\mu_t, \mu_{t-1}, \ldots, x_t, x_{t-1}, \ldots]$ in which y is any random variable. (Equation (*) is just the first difference of Equation (93) in the text.)

   A. Prove that a solution of (*) is

$$P_t x_{t+1} = \frac{1}{1-\alpha} \sum_{j=1}^{\infty} \left(\frac{-\alpha}{1-\alpha}\right)^{j-1} P_t \mu_{t+j}. \tag{†}$$

   B. Suppose that (x_t, μ_t) has the bivariate vector moving average, autoregressive representation

$$\begin{pmatrix} x_t \\ \mu_t \end{pmatrix} = \begin{pmatrix} 1 & 0 \\ 1-\lambda & \lambda \end{pmatrix} \begin{pmatrix} x_{t-1} \\ \mu_{t-1} \end{pmatrix} + \begin{pmatrix} a_{1t} - \lambda a_{1t-1} \\ a_{2t} - \lambda a_{2t-1} \end{pmatrix}$$

where $a_{1t} = x_t - P_{t-1}x_t$, $a_{2t} = \mu_t - P_{t-1}\mu_t$, $|\lambda| < 1$, and a_{1t} and a_{2t} have finite variances and nonzero covariance. Prove that Cagan's formula for the expected rate of inflation π_t,

$$\pi_t = \frac{1-\lambda}{1-\lambda L} x_t$$

is implied by the hypothesis of rational expectations, i.e., by Equation (†).

   C. Prove that μ fails to Granger cause x.

   D. Calculate the coefficients in the projection of $\mu_t - x_t$ on the x_t process. Is this projection equation the same as Cagan's equation

$$\mu_t - x_t = [\alpha(1-\lambda)/(1-\lambda L)](1-L)x_t + \xi_t, \tag{§}$$

where ξ_t is random? If not, use your formula for the projection equation to determine the biases that would emerge from mistakenly regarding Cagan's (§) as a projection equation.

13. *Depreciation, Gestation, and Delivery Lags.* Consider a firm that is a perfect competitor in the market for its one output, and a monopsonist in the market for additions to the stock of the single factor of production that it uses, capital. The firm sells its output at the price p, which is constant over time. Output in period t, $q(t)$, is produced according to the production function

$$q(t) = A_0 + A_1 K(t) - \frac{A_2}{2} K(t)^2, \qquad A_0, A_1, A_2 > 0 \tag{1}$$

where $K(t)$ is the firm's capital stock at the beginning of period t. The firm's capital stock is related to its investment decisions at t and earlier by

$$K(t) = g(L)I(t) \tag{2}$$

where $I(t)$ is investment in period t, and

$$g(L) = g_0 + g_1 L + g_2 L^2 + \cdots.$$

The polynomial $g(L)$ reflects depreciation, delivery, and possible gestation lags. (A common example is the geometrical model $g(L) = L/(1 - (1-\delta)L)$ where δ is "the" depreciation rate; (2) is designed to encompass this as well as all sorts of plausible alternative models of depreciation and gestation–delivery lags.) The firm faces a supply curve for investment of

$$J(t) = B_0 + \frac{B_1}{2} I(t) + \varepsilon(t) \qquad B_0, B_1 > 0$$

where $J(t)$ is the price of investment goods, and where $\varepsilon(t)$ is a bounded sequence of shocks to supply. There is no uncertainty.

The firm's problem is to maximize undiscounted present value

$$\sum_{t=0}^{\infty} \left\{ p\left[A_0 + A_1 g(L)I(t) - \frac{A_2}{2}[g(L)I(t)]^2 \right] - \left[B_0 + \frac{B_1}{2}I(t) + \varepsilon(t) \right]I(t) \right\} \tag{3}$$

with respect to $\{I(t): t \geq 0\}$ and taking as given $\{I(-s): s > 0\}$ and $\{\varepsilon(t): t \geq 0\}$.

A. Prove that the Euler equation for this problem is of the form

$$\{-B_0 - \varepsilon(t) + pA_1g(1)\} = \{pA_2g(L^{-1})g(L) + B_1\}I(t).$$

B. Prove that if $B_1 > 0$, then the optimal investment plan is obtained by solving "the stable roots of the characteristic polynomial $\{pA_2g(L^{-1})g(L) + B_1\}$ backwards, the unstable roots forwards."

C. Solve the special version of this problem that results when

$$g(L) = \frac{L}{1 - \mu L}$$

where $\mu = 1 - \delta$, $\delta =$ the depreciation rate, $0 < \mu < 1$.

D. Argue that the characteristic polynomial that must be factored in solving problem (C) is equivalent with the one encountered by John F. Muth in his signal extraction interpretation of the permanent income hypothesis. State a version of that signal extraction problem that leads to this same characteristic polynomial as encountered in (C).

14. Let (y_t, x_t) be a jointly covariance stationary process with mean of zero. Consider the projection equations

(i)
$$x_t = \sum_{j=-\infty}^{\infty} b_j y_{t-j} + u_t, \qquad Eu_t y_s = 0 \qquad \text{for all } t, s$$

(ii)
$$y_t = \sum_{j=-\infty}^{\infty} h_j x_{t-j} + \varepsilon_t, \qquad E\varepsilon_t x_s = 0 \qquad \text{for all } t, s.$$

Let $g_y(w)$, $g_x(w)$, $g_u(w)$, $g_\varepsilon(w)$ be the spectral densities of y, x, u, and ε, respectively.

A. Prove that the coherence satisfies

$$\text{coh}(w) = 1 - \frac{g_u(w)}{g_y(w)}$$

$$\text{coh}(w) = 1 - \frac{g_\varepsilon(w)}{g_x(w)}.$$

B. Prove that R^2 in equation (ii) (i.e., $1 - Eu^2/Ey^2$) is given by

$$R_{xy}^2 = \frac{1/2\pi \int_{-\pi}^{\pi} \text{coh}(w)g_y(w)\,dw}{1/2\pi \int_{-\pi}^{\pi} g_y(w)\,dw}.$$

C. Prove that the R^2 in equation (i) is given by

$$R_{yx}^2 = \frac{1/2\pi \int_{-\pi}^{\pi} \text{coh}(w)g_x(w)\,dw}{1/2\pi \int_{-\pi}^{\pi} g_x(w)\,dw}.$$

15. Let y_t be a mixed moving average, autoregressive process $y_t = (B(L)/A(L))\varepsilon_t$, where ε_t is a white noise with unit variance, $B(L) = \prod_{j=1}^{m}(1 - \mu_j L)$, and $A(L) = \prod_{j=1}^{n}(1 - \lambda_j L)$, $|\lambda_j| < 1$ for $j = 1, \ldots,$ n, and where $\lambda_j \neq \lambda_i$ for $i \neq j$, $\lambda_j \neq \mu_k$ for all $j = 1, \ldots, n, k = 1, \ldots, m$, and $m \le n$. The autocovariance generating function for y is $g_y(z) = B(z)B(z^{-1})/A(z)A(z^{-1})$. Use formula (25) to establish the formula

$$c_y(\tau) = \sum_{s=1}^{n} \frac{\lambda_s^{n+|\tau|-m-1}\prod_{j=1}^{m}(1 - \mu_j\lambda_s)(\lambda_s - \mu_j)}{\prod_{j=1}^{n}(1 - \lambda_j\lambda_s)\prod_{j=1, j\neq s}^{n}(\lambda_s - \lambda_j)}.$$

16. Let $b(L)$ be the polynomial in the lag operator $b(L) = (1 + \mu L)/(1 - \lambda L) = \sum_{j=-\infty}^{\infty} b_j L^j$ where $|\lambda| < 1$. Use formula (25) to establish that

$$b_j = \begin{cases} 0 & j < 0 \\ 1 & j = 0 \\ \lambda^j + \mu\lambda^{j-1} & j \ge 1 \end{cases}$$

17. Consider the generating function of the second-order Solow-Pascal lag distribution $w(z) = 1/(1 - \lambda z)^2$, $|\lambda| < 1$. Use formulas (23) and (25) to evaluate the coefficients of the lag distribution. Compare your results with equation (31) of Chapter IX.

18. Let x_t be a covariance stationary stochastic process with mean zero and covariogram

$$c(\tau) = \begin{cases} 1.25, & \tau = 0 \\ -0.5, & \tau = \pm 1 \\ 0, & |\tau| \geq 2. \end{cases}$$

A. Use a computer to calculate the projections

$$x_t = P[x_t | x_{t-1}, \ldots, x_{t-n}] = \sum_{j=1}^{n} A_j^n x_{t-j}$$

for $n = 1, 2, 3, 4, 5$. As n increases, is A_j^n for fixed j seeming to approach a limit? What value seems to be approached?

B. Use the method of Section 15 to find a Wold (fundamental) moving average representation for x_t. Invert this moving average representation to obtain the autoregressive representation

$$x_t = \sum_{j=1}^{\infty} A_j x_{t-j}.$$

Do the A_j^n calculated in A seem to be approaching A_j as $n \to \infty$?

Three inverse optimal prediction problems.

19. Suppose that x_t is a stochastic process with Wold representation

$$x_t = c(L)\varepsilon_t, \qquad \varepsilon_t = x_t - P[x_t | x_{t-1}, \ldots].$$

Suppose that x_t satisfies

$$P[x_{t+1} | x_t, x_{t-1}, \ldots] = \rho x_t, \qquad |\rho| < 1.$$

Use the Wiener-Kolmogorov formula to prove that $c(L)$ must be $1/(1 - \rho L)$.

20. Suppose that x_t is a stochastic process with Wold representation $x_t = c(L)\varepsilon_t$ where $\varepsilon_t = x_t - P[x_t | x_{t-1}, \ldots]$. Suppose that x_t is such that

$$P[x_{t+2} | x_t, x_{t-1}, \ldots] = \rho P[x_{t+1} | x_t, x_{t-1}, \ldots]$$

where $|\rho| < 1$. Use the Wiener-Kolmogorov formula to prove that $c(L)$ must be given by

$$c(L) = \frac{c_0 + (c_1 - \rho c_0)L}{1 - \rho L}.$$

21. Suppose that x_t is a stochastic process with Wold representation $x_t = c(L)\varepsilon_t$, where $\varepsilon_t = x_t - P[x_t | x_{t-1}, \ldots]$. Suppose that x_t is such that

$$P[x_{t+k} | x_t, x_{t-1}, \ldots] = \rho^k P[x_{t+1} | x_t, x_{t-1}, \ldots]$$

for all $k \geq 1$ where $|\rho| < 1$. Use the Wiener-Kolmogorov prediction formula to prove that $c(L) = (c_0 + (c_1 - \rho c_0)L)/(1 - \rho L)$.

22. *Seasonality* Consider a firm that faces the following optimum problem: to maximize

$$E_0 \sum_{t=0}^{\infty} \left\{ f_0 n_t - \frac{f_1}{2} n_t^2 - \frac{d}{2} (n_t - n_{t-1})^2 - w_t n_t \right\} \tag{1}$$

subject to n_{-1} given, and where $f_0, f_1, d > 0$; E_t is the mathematical expectation conditioned on information known at time t. Here n_t is employment at t, and w_t is the real wage at t. The firm maximizes (1) over linear contingency plans for setting n_t as a function of information available at t, which includes n_{t-1} and $\{w_t, w_{t-1}, \ldots\}$. The real wage w_t is assumed to follow the Markov process

$$(1 - \delta L^4)w_t = \varepsilon_t, \qquad 0 < \delta < 1 \tag{2}$$

where ε_t is a fundamental white noise for w_t (we shall ignore constant terms in the w_t process). The data are *quarterly*.

A. Compute the *spectrum* of the w_t process, and plot it. Argue that w_t is characterized by a strong seasonal.

B. Compute the optimal linear decision rule of the form

$$n_t = \lambda n_{t-1} + \sum_{j=0}^{3} h_j w_{t-j}, \tag{3}$$

giving explicit closed-form formulas for the h_j's. Describe the cross-equation restrictions between the parameters of the Markov process (2) for w_t and the parameters of the decision rule (3).

C. Calculate the projection of n_t against $\{w_t, w_{t-1}, \ldots\}$. Then calculate the projection of n_t against the entire w process, $\{\ldots, w_{t+2}, w_{t+1}, w_t, w_{t-1}, \ldots\}$. Argue that n fails to Granger cause w.

D. Because of the strong seasonal in real wages, an analyst forms the "seasonally adjusted" series

$$n_t^a = (1 - \delta L^4)n_t$$

$$w_t^a = (1 - \delta L^4)w_t.$$

Assuming that the economic agents look at the seasonally *un*adjusted series in forming their decisions, and so behave according to (3), calculate the projection of n_t^a on $\{w_t^a, w_{t-1}^a, \ldots\}$.

E. Suppose that economic agents care about the seasonally *un*adjusted data, and so behave according to (3). But, as often has been the practice, the econometrician uses the seasonally adjusted data. Let the econometrician construct his model by imagining that the agent is maximizing

$$E_0 \sum_{t=0}^{\infty} \left\{ f_0 n_t^a - \frac{f_1}{2}(n_t^a)^2 - \frac{d}{2}(n_t^a - n_{t-1}^a)^2 - w_t^a n_t^a \right\}$$

subject to n_{-1}^a given and the law of motion for w_t^a implied by (2) and the definition of w_t^a.

(i) Derive the decision rule of the form

$$n_t^a = \tilde{\lambda} n_{t-1}^a + \sum_{j=0}^{3} \tilde{h}_j w_{t-j}^a$$

that the econometrician attributes to the agent. Describe the cross-equation restrictions built into the econometrician's model.

(ii) Use the projection of n_t^a on w_t^a that you calculated earlier to argue that the econometrician's cross-equation restrictions will not describe the agents' behavior. Describe how the econometrician could mistakenly reject the "rational expectations hypothesis" because of his procedure of using seasonally adjusted data.

23. Consider a jointly covariance stationary, linearly indeterministic stochastic process (y_t, x_t, X_t) with means of zero. The processes y_t, x_t, X_t are connected as follows. The variable y_t is determined as

$$y_t = \alpha \sum_{j=0}^{\infty} \lambda^j P[x_{t+j}|\Omega_t], \qquad \alpha > 0, 0 < \lambda < 1 \tag{1}$$

where P is the linear least squares projection operator and $\Omega_t \supset \Omega_{t-1} \supset \Omega_{t-2} \cdots$ and $\Omega_t = (x_t, x_{t-1}, x_{t-2} \cdots)$. (In (1), y_t might be the log of the price level and x_t the log of the money supply, so that (1) becomes an implication of Cagan's portfolio balance condition.) There is available a noisy measure of x_t, namely X_t, which is governed by

$$X_t = x_t + u_t, \tag{2}$$

where u_t is a mean zero stochastic process satisfying $Eu_s x_t = 0$ for all t and s. The process u_t has covariance generating function

$$g_u(z) = \sum_{\tau = -\infty}^{\infty} z^{\tau} Eu_t u_{t-\tau} \tag{3}$$

We suppose that $g_u(z)$ is known to an econometrician. We shall think of u_t as being a seasonal noise, so that $g_u(e^{-i\omega})$ has much of its power concentrated at the seasonal frequencies (although nothing in the analytics of this problem restricts us to this interpretation). The econometrician observes the processes for y_t, X_t, but *not* x_t. In preparation for estimation, the econometrician is interested in characterizing the restrictions which his knowledge (1), (2) and (3) places on the observables y_t, X_t. In answering the following questions, assume that the econometrician knows the covariance generating functions for all of the observables, $g_X(z)$, $g_y(z)$, $g_{yX}(z)$, as well as the covariance generating function (3).

A. Given the generating functions that are known, describe how to obtain a univariate Wold representation for X_t,

$$X_t = d(L)a_t \tag{4}$$

where $a_t = X_t - P[X_t | X_{t-1}, \ldots]$, $\sum_{j=0}^{\infty} d_j^2 < +\infty$.

B. Given the known generating functions, give a formula for $\theta(L)$ in the one-sided projection

$$x_t = \theta(L)X_t + \varepsilon_t \tag{5}$$

where $E\varepsilon_t X_{t-s} = 0$ for $s \geq 0$, $\theta(L) = \sum_{j=0}^{\infty} \theta_j L^j$. Define the "one-sided seasonally adjusted" series $\tilde{x}_t$ as

$$\tilde{x}_t = \theta(L)X_t. \tag{6}$$

How does $\tilde{x}_t$ compare with $\hat{x}_t$ associated with the two-sided seasonal adjustment procedure described in Exercise 2?

C. Consider the projection of y_t on X_t, $X_{t-1}, \ldots$,

$$y_t = h(L)X_t + s_t \tag{7}$$

where $h(L) = \sum_{j=0}^{\infty} h_j L^j$ and $Es_t X_{t-j} = 0$ for $j \geq 0$. Prove that

$$h(L) = \alpha \left[\frac{\theta(L) - \lambda L^{-1}\theta(\lambda)\, d(\lambda)\, d(L)^{-1}}{1 - \lambda L^{-1}} \right]. \tag{8}$$

(Hint: at this point it might help to be familiar with pages 266–277 of "Instrumental Variables Procedures for Estimating Linear Rational Expectations Models," by Lars Hansen & Thomas Sargent, *Journal of Monetary Economics*, 1982.)

D. Using long division on (8), derive explicit formulas for the h_j's in terms of λ, the θ_j's and the parameters of $d(L)$. (Here it might help to consult Hansen & Sargent, "A Note on Wiener–Kolmogorov Formulas in Linear Rational Expectations Models," *Economics Letters*, 1982.)

E. Describe how to find a Wold representation for $\tilde{x}_t$ defined by (6). In the course of answering this question, describe special conditions on $\theta(L)$ which imply that

$$\tilde{x}_t = \theta(L)\, d(L)a_t$$

is a Wold representation for the one-sided seasonally adjusted series $\tilde{x}_t$.

F. Since the econometrician does not have data on x_t but has data on $\tilde{x}_t$, a friend recommends that you use the model

$$y_t = \alpha \sum_{j=0}^{\infty} \lambda^j P[\tilde{x}_{t+j} | \tilde{x}_t, \tilde{x}_{t-1}, \ldots] + \tilde{s}_t = f(L)\tilde{x}_t + \tilde{s}_t \tag{9}$$

where $E\tilde{s}_t\tilde{x}_{-j} = 0$ for $j \geq 0$. (This model is derived by assuming that the agents in the model are acting on the basis of forecasts of the one-sided seasonally adjusted series $\tilde{x}_t$, when in fact they are setting y_t on the basis of forecasts of x_t.) Derive an explicit formula for $f(L)$ in terms of the parameters of the Wold representation for $\tilde{x}_t$.

G. Under what circumstances is $f(L)\tilde{x}_t = h(L)X_t$, where $f(L)\tilde{x}_t$ is from (9) and $h(L)X_t$ is from (7)? Interpret these circumstances as describing conditions under which correct restrictions on the y_t, X_t process are derived by proceeding as if the agents set y_t as a function of forecasts of $\tilde{x}_t$.

H. Collect the restrictions on (y_t, x_t) as

$$X_t = d(L)a_t \tag{4}$$

$$x_t = \theta(L)X_t + \varepsilon_t \tag{5}$$

$$y_t = h(L)X_t + s_t \tag{7}$$

where $\theta(L)$, $d(L)$, $h(L)$ are given by the formulas that you have derived.

(i) Argue that in general y Granger causes X in (7). Prove that y *fails* to Granger cause x. (Hint: start by going back to equation (1).)

(ii) Argue informally (but precisely) that there is no reason to expect s_t to be serially uncorrelated.

(iii) Let s_t have a Wold representation $s_t = c(L)\eta_t$ where η_t is a fundamental white noise for s_t. Argue that in general $E\eta_t X_{t-j} \neq 0$ for $j \geq 0$. (Therefore, backward filtering in (5) designed to whiten the residual destroys the orthogonality with X_{t-j}.)

(iv) Prove that s_t has a representation $s_t = c(L^{-1})\tilde{\eta}_t$ where $\tilde{\eta}_t = s_t - P[s_t|s_{t+1}, s_{t+2}, \ldots]$. Prove that (5) implies that $E\tilde{\eta}_t X_{t-j} = 0$ for $j \geq 0$.

(v) Interpret the results in (iii) and (iv) in terms of the considerations motivating Hayashi and Sims.

I. Briefly describe an econometric strategy for estimating λ and α from the orthogonality conditions associated with (4), (5), and (7).

24. Let x_t have the Wold representation

$$x_t = c(L)\varepsilon_t, \qquad c(z) = \sum_{j=0}^{\infty} c_j z^j$$

where $\varepsilon_t = x_t - P[x_t|x_{t-1}, \ldots]$. Assume that x_t has an autoregressive representation so that $a(L)x_t = \varepsilon_t$ where $c(L)^{-1} = a(L)$.

Derive a formula for the h_j's in

$$P_t\left[\sum_{j=0}^{\infty} \lambda^j x_{t+j+1}|x_t, x_{t-1}, \ldots\right] = \sum_{j=0}^{\infty} h_j x_{t-j}, \qquad |\lambda| < 1.$$

25. Assume that the first difference of a stochastic process z_t is covariance stationary, purely linearly indeterministic, has mean zero and has Wold moving average representation

$$(1 - L)z_t = c(L)\varepsilon_t \tag{†}$$

where $c(L) = \sum_{j=0}^{\infty} c_j L^j$, $\sum_{j=0}^{\infty} c_j^2 < \infty$, and ε_t is a fundamental white noise for $(1 - L)z_t$. Beveridge and Nelson (1981) define the "permanent component" of z_t as

$$\bar{z}_t = z_t + \lim_{n \to \infty} E_t[\Delta z_{t+1} + \cdots + \Delta z_{t+n}]$$

where $\Delta = (1 - L)$.

A. Prove that

$$\lim_{n \to \infty} E_t[\Delta z_{t+1} + \cdots + \Delta z_{t+n}] = [(c(L) - c(1))/(L - 1)]\varepsilon_t.$$

Hint: use the Hansen–Sargent formula (90) or the reasoning used to derive it.

B. Prove that $\bar{z}_t$ follows the "random walk" $(1 - L)\bar{z}_t = c(1)\varepsilon_t$.

C. Prove that $\bar{z}_t$ can be obtained from z_t by "filtering" according to the formula

$$\bar{z}_t = c(1)c(L)^{-1}z_t. \tag{*}$$

D. Beveridge and Nelson define the "cyclical" part of the series as $s_t = z_t - \bar{z}_t$. Show that s_t can be obtained from z_t via the formula

$$s_t = \left[1 - \frac{c(1)}{c(L)}\right]z_t.$$

E. Note that the preceding formula and the Wold representation (†) imply that

$$s_t = \frac{c(L) - c(1)}{1 - L}\varepsilon_t. \tag{**}$$

Is (**) a Wold representation for s_t?

Hints: at this point the reader might want to consult Hansen and Sargent (1980). Note that (**) is the version of formula (88) that is obtained by solving Exercise 24, then driving λ to unity from below. Does the assumption that $c(L)$ has a square summable inverse in nonnegative powers of L imply that $[c(L) - c(1)]$ has a square summable inverse in nonnegative power of L?

F. In light of your answer to E, describe the effects of filtering a pair of time series (z_{1t}, z_{2t}), each with the univariate filter applied by Beveridge and Nelson, to obtain cyclical series (s_{1t}, s_{2t}). Suppose that z_2 fails to Granger cause z_1. Does it follow that s_2 fails to Granger cause s_1?

REFERENCES

Allen, R. G. D. (1960). *Mathematical Economics*, 2nd ed., New York: Macmillan.

Altug, S. (1986). "Time to Build and Aggregate Fluctuations: Some New Evidence." Unpublished Manuscript, Federal Reserve Bank of Minneapolis.

Anderson, L. C., and Jordan, J. L. (1968). "Monetary and Fiscal Actions: A Test of Their Relative Importance in Economic Stabilization." *Federal Reserve Bank of St. Louis Review*, Vol. 50, No. 11, pp. 11–23.

Anderson, T. W. (1971). *The Statistical Analysis of Time Series*, New York: Wiley.

Apostol, T. M. (1974). *Mathematical Analysis*, 2nd ed., Reading, Massachusetts: Addison-Wesley.

Bergstrom, A. R. (1983). "Gaussian Estimation of Structural Parameters in Higher Order Continuous Time." *Econometrica*, Vol. 51, No. 1, pp. 117–152.

Beveridge, S. and Nelson, C. R. (1981). "A New Approach to Decomposition of Economic Time Series Into Permanent and Transitory Components with Particular Attention to Measurement of the 'Business Cycle'." *Journal of Monetary Economics*, Vol. 7, No. 2, pp. 151–174.

Blanchard, O. J. and Kahn, C. M. (1980). "The Solution of Linear Difference Models Under Rational Expectations." *Econometrica*, Vol. 48, No. 5, pp. 1305–1311.

Blanchard, O. J. and Watson, M. W. (1982). "Bubbles, Rational Expectations and Financial Markets." In *Crises in the Economic and Financial Structure: Bubbles, Bursts, and Shocks* (Paul Wachtel, ed.). Lexington: Lexington Books.

Brock, W. A. (1982). "Asset Prices in a Production Economy." In *The Economics of Information and Uncertainty* (J. J. McCall, ed.). Chicago: University of Chicago Press, for the National Bureau of Economic Research.

Burns, A. and Mitchell, W. C. (1946). *Measuring Business Cycles*, New York: National Bureau of Economic Research.

Cagan, P. (1956). "The Monetary Dynamics of Hyperinflation." In *Studies in the Quantity Theory of Money* (M. Friedman, ed.). Chicago, Illinois: University of Chicago Press.

Chow, G. C., and Levitan, R. E. (1969). "Nature of Business Cycles Implicit in a Linear Economic Model." *The Quarterly Journal of Economics*, Vol. LXXXIII, No. 3, pp. 504–517.

Churchill, R. V., Brown, J. W., and Verhey, R. F. (1974). *Complex Variables and Applications*, 3rd Edition, New York: McGraw-Hill.

Dagli, C. A. and Taylor, J. B. (1984). "Estimation and Solution of Linear Rational Expectations Models Using a Polynomial Matrix Factorization." *Journal of Economic Dynamics and Control*, Vol. 8, No. 3, pp. 341–348.

Frisch, R. (1933). "Propagation Problems and Impulse Problems in Dynamic Economics." In *Economic Essays in Honor of Gustav Cassel*, London: Allen and Unwin.

Futia, C. A. (1981). "Rational Expectations in Stationary Linear Models." *Econometrica*, Vol. 49, No. 1, pp. 171–192.

Gabel, R. A. and Roberts, R. A. (1973). *Signals and Linear Systems*, New York: Wiley.

Geweke, J. (1978). "Temporal Aggregation in the Multiple Regression Model." *Econometrica*, Vol. 46, No. 3, pp. 643–662.

Geweke, J. and Singleton, K. (1981a). "Maximum Likelihood 'Confirmatory' Factor Analysis of Economic Time Series." *International Economic Review*, Vol. 22, No. 1, p. 37–54.

Geweke, J. and Singleton, K. (1981b). "Latent Variable Models for Time Series: A Frequency Domain Approach with an Application to the Permanent Income Hypothesis." *Journal of Econometrics*, Vol. 17, No. 3, pp. 287–304.

Granger, C. W. J. (1966). "The Typical Spectral Shape of an Economic Variable." *Econometrica*, Vol. 34, No. 1, pp. 150–161.

Granger, C. W. J. (1969). "Investigating Causal Relations by Econometric Models and Cross-Spectral Methods." *Econometrica*, Vol. 37, No. 3, pp. 424–438.

Hamilton, J. D. and Whiteman, C. H. (1985). "The Observable Implications of Self-Fulfilling Expectations." *Journal of Monetary Economics*, Vol. 16, No. 3, pp. 353–373.

Hansen, L. P. and Sargent, T. J. (1980). "Formulating and Estimating Dynamic Linear Rational Expectations Models." *Journal of Economic Dynamics and Control*, Vol. 2, No. 1, pp. 7–46.

Hansen, L. P. and Sargent, T. J. (1981a). "Linear Rational Expectations Models for Dynamically Interrelated Variables." In *Rational Expectations and Econometric Practice* (R. E. Lucas, Jr. and T. J. Sargent, eds.). Minneapolis: University of Minnesota Press.

Hansen, L. P. and Sargent, T. J. (1981b). "Formulating and Estimating Continuous Time Rational Expectations Models." *Staff Report No. 75, Federal Reserve Bank of Minneapolis*.

Hansen, L. P. and Sargent, T. J. (1981c). "Exact Linear Rational Expectations Models: Specification and Estimation." *Federal Reserve Bank of Minneapolis, Staff Report #71*, September.

Hansen, L. P. and Sargent, T. J. (1982a). "Instrument Variables Procedures for Estimating Linear Rational Expectations Models." *Journal of Monetary Economics*, Vol. 9, No. 3, pp. 263–296.

Hansen, L. P. and Sargent, T. J. (1982b). "Two Difficulties in Interpreting Vector Autoregressions." Working Paper, Federal Reserve Bank of Minneapolis.

Hayashi, F. and Sims, C. A. (1983). "Nearly Efficient Estimation of Time Series Models With Predetermined, but not Exogenous, Instruments." *Econometrica*, Vol. 51, No. 3, pp. 783–798.

Howrey, E. P. (1968). "A Spectrum Analysis of the Long-swing Hypothesis." *International Economic Review*, Vol. 9, No. 2, pp. 228–260.

Howrey, E. P. (1971). "Stochastic Properties of the Klein-Goldberger Model." *Econometrica*, Vol. 39, No. 1, pp. 73–88.

Koopmans, T. C. (1947). "Measurement Without Theory." *Review of Economics and Statistics*, Vol. 29, No. 3, pp. 161–172.

Kydland, F. E. and Prescott, E. C. (1982). "Time to Build and Aggregate Fluctuations." *Econometrica*, Vol. 50, No. 6, pp. 1345–1371.

Meese, R. (1986). "Testing for Bubbles in Exchange Markets: A Case of Sparkling Rates?" *Journal of Political Economy*, Vol. 94, No. 2, pp. 345–373.

Muth, J. F. (1960). "Optimal Properties of Exponentially Weighted Forecasts." *Journal of the American Statistical Association*, Vol. 55, No. 290, pp. 299–306.

Naylor, A. W. and Sell, G. R. (1971). *Linear Operator Theory in Engineering and Science*, New York: Holt.

Nerlove, M. (1967). "Distributed Lags and Unobserved Components in Economic Time Series." In *Ten Economic Studies in the Tradition of Irving Fisher* (W. Fellner, et al.). New York: Wiley.

Saracoglu, R. and Sargent, T. J. (1978). "Seasonality and Portfolio Balance Under Rational Expectations." *Journal of Monetary Economics*, Vol. 4, No. 3, 438–58.

Sargent, T. J. and Sims, C. A. (1977). "Business Cycle Modeling Without Pretending to Have Too Much A Priori Economic Theory." In *New Methods in Business Cycle Research* (C. A. Sims, ed.). Minneapolis: Federal Reserve Bank.

Sargent, T. J. and Wallace, N. (1985). "Identification and Estimation of a Model of Hyperinflation With a Continuum of 'Sunspot' Equilibria." *Discussion Paper No. 220*, Center for Economic Research, University of Minnesota.

Shiller, R. (1972). "Rational Expectations and the Structure of Interest Rates." Unpublished Ph.D. Thesis, Cambridge, Massachusetts: M.I.T.

Sims, C. A. (1971). "Discrete Approximations to Continuous Time Distributed Lags in Econometrics." *Econometrica*, Vol. 39, No. 3, pp. 545–563.

Sims, C. A. (1972a). "Money, Income, and Causality." *American Economic Review*, Vol. LXII, No. 4, pp. 540–552.

Sims, C. A. (1972b). "Approximate Prior Restrictions in Distributed Lag Estimation." *Journal of the American Statistical Association*, Vol. 67, No. 337, pp. 169–175.

Sims, C. A. (1974). "Seasonality in Regression." *Journal of the American Statistical Association*, Vol. 69, No. 347, pp. 618–626.

Sims, C. A. (1980). "Macroeconomics and Reality." *Econometrica*, Vol. 48, No. 1, pp. 1–48.

Slutzky, E. (1937). "The Summation of Random Causes as the Source of Cyclic Processes." *Econometrica*, Vol. 5, pp. 105–146.

Theil, H. (1971). *Principles of Econometrics*, pp. 548–550. New York: Wiley.

Whiteman, C. H. (1983). *Linear Rational Expectations Models: A User's Guide*, Minneapolis: University of Minnesota Press.

Whiteman, C. H. (1984). "Lucas on the Quantity Theory: Hypothesis Testing Without Theory." *American Economic Review*, Vol. 74:4, pp. 742–749.

Whittle, P. (1983). *Prediction and Regulation by Linear Least-Square Methods*, 2nd ed., revised. University of Minnesota Press: Minneapolis.

Wold, H. (1938). *The Analysis of Stationary Time Series*, 1st ed., Uppsala: Almquist and Wicksell.

CHAPTER XII

THE CONSUMPTION FUNCTION

1. INTRODUCTION

The literature on the consumption function aims to provide a theory that explains some of the time series and cross section correlations between consumption and income, and sometimes also correlations among consumption, wealth, and interest rates. The subject has served as an important laboratory for building dynamic theories that are sufficiently simple and tractable to guide interpretation of the data. Thus, important efforts in applied dynamics of Milton Friedman, John F. Muth, Robert E. Lucas, Jr. and Robert E. Hall were inspired by the subject of the consumption function. These efforts have had ramifications for applied work throughout dynamic macroeconomics.

Initial work on the subject was inspired by paradoxes that emerged from applying the early Keynesian consumption function of the form $C_t = a + bY_t$. From the cross sections came estimates of the marginal propensity to consume b that were much less than estimates from the time series, which seemed to require reconciling. In aggregate time series, consumption is a much smoother series over the business cycle than is income. To model this pattern statistically, consumption was posited to be a distributed lag of income, making consumption a smoothed version of income. Economic theories were sought to interpret this distributed lag. This led to Friedman's work on permanent income, which was inspired by the idea of using Irving Fisher's theory of intertemporal consumption allocation to account for the dynamics in the data. Friedman did not make completely tight or explicit the link between Fisher's theory and the regressions that he studied, but subsequent work has. John F. Muth soon built upon Friedman's work and discovered specifications of the stochastic process for income that assured optimality for Friedman's assumed adaptive expectations, or geometric lag distribution, for permanent income. Implicit in Muth's argument was Lucas's critique of econometric policy evaluation. In 1973 Lucas used the consumption function of Friedman and Muth as an example to illustrate his critique. By using stochastic optimization theory explicitly, Robert

Hall was able to characterize additional interesting and easily testable implications of the permanent income theory. In effect, Hall noted that the household's Euler equation restricts the projection of consumption on lagged information. Hansen and Sargent did work that obtains additional characterizations involving projections in alternative directions to the one used by Hall.

This chapter studies a version of the permanent income theory of consumption. The theory is developed by studying the intertemporal optimum problem faced by a single consumer who is confronted with an exogenous stochastic process for labor income and the opportunity to borrow or lend a limited amount at a fixed interest rate.[1] Using the tools for prediction and dynamic optimization that are described in Chapters XI and IX, we can describe precisely the restrictions that this theory places on time series data. We use these tools to compute the projections of consumption on various combinations of assets and income that are implied by the theory. In particular, we compute the projection of consumption on three subspaces. We compute the projection of consumption on current and past labor income alone, the projection of consumption on current and past values of "total income" which includes labor income plus interest on assets, and the projection of consumption on current and past labor income and current assets. These projections are the theoretical counterparts of various sample regressions that have been computed in the empirical literature on consumption.

2. THE CONSUMER'S CHOICE PROBLEM

A representative consumer is assumed to choose a strategy for consumption that maximizes

$$E_0 \sum_{t=0}^{\infty} \beta^t u(c_t), \qquad 0 < \beta < 1 \tag{1}$$

where c_t is consumption at t, E_t is the mathematical expectation operator conditioned on information known to the consumer at t, and u is a one period utility function satisfying $u' > 0$, $u'' < 0$.[2] The objective (1) is maximized with respect to $\{c_t, A_{t+1}\}_{t=0}^{\infty}$ subject to the sequence of budget constraints

$$A_{t+1} = R_t[A_t + y_t - c_t], \qquad t = 0, 1, \ldots \qquad A_0 \text{ given}, \tag{2}$$

where $R_t \geq 1$ is the gross rate of return on savings between periods t and $t + 1$, A_t is assets (or indebtedness, if negative), and y_t is noncapital or labor income at t. We assume that y_t is a given stochastic process, outside of the control of the agent, with features to be specified below. The consumer is assumed to know the

---

[1] Multiple agent equilibrium versions of the permanent income model are described in Sargent (1986). See especially the chapter and exercises on the Bewley-Townsend model.

[2] The quadratic utility function used below, $u_0 + u_1 c_t - (u_2/2)c_t^2$, satisfies these restrictions only for c_t in the interval $0 \leq c_t < u_1/u_2$.

law of motion of y_t. At time t, the consumer's information is assumed to include at least $\{y_{t-s}, s \geq 0\}$ and A_t. In the interests of obtaining a version of the permanent income model, we assume that $R_t = R > 1$ for all t. We shall assume further that $\beta R^2 > 1$. We also assume that $\{y_t\}$ is a stochastic process of mean exponential order less than β^{-1}, so that $\lim_{j \to \infty} E_t y_{t+j} \beta^j = 0$ for all t.

In this model, some device is needed to rule out indefinitely large and growing borrowing on the part of the consumer. We shall impose the condition

$$E_0 A_t \geq M > -\infty \qquad \text{for all } t \tag{3}$$

where M is a finite but possibly very large negative number. Subject to the condition (3) on borrowing, we solve the difference equation (2) with $R_t = R$ to obtain

$$\sum_{j=0}^{\infty} \left(\frac{1}{R}\right)^j E_t c_{t+j} = A_t + \sum_{j=0}^{\infty} \left(\frac{1}{R}\right)^j E_t y_{t+j}, \tag{4}$$

which states that the expected present value of consumption at t equals the expected present value at t of labor income plus initial nonlabor assets A_t.

Substituting the constraints (2) into the objective function (1), the problem is to choose a strategy for A_t to maximize

$$E_0 \sum_{t=0}^{\infty} \beta^t u(y_t + A_t - R^{-1} A_{t+1})$$

subject to the boundary conditions (3) and A_0 given. Proceeding as in Chapter IX and XIV, the Euler equations can be found to be[3]

$$E_t R \beta u'(c_{t+1}) = u'(c_t) \qquad t = 0, 1, \dots$$

or

$$E_t u'(c_{t+1}) = (\beta R)^{-1} u'(c_t) \tag{5}$$

where $c_t = y_t + A_t - R^{-1} A_{t+1}$. Notice that if a condition like (3) were not imposed, (5) could be satisfied with $u'(c_{t+1}) = u'(c_t) = 0$, which is an instruction to consume an unbounded amount each period, and to borrow at the gross real rate R to support this plan. This would imply an unbounded volume of indebtedness that would violate (3).

---

[3] Using the method of Chapter IX, the Euler equation for a nonstochastic version of the problem is found to be $R\beta u'(c_{t+1}) = u'(c_t)$. The appropriate Euler equation for the stochastic version of the problem is found formally by replacing all functions of random variables in the Euler equation for the nonstochastic version of the problem with conditional expectations, conditioned on information available at t. (Technically, this involves an exchange of order of an integration and a differentiation operation.) Stochastic Euler equations and the relationship between stochastic and nonstochastic linear-quadratic control problems are described more thoroughly in Chapter XIV.

Equation (5) is Robert Hall's (1978) result that the marginal utility of consumption follows a univariate first order Markov process, and that no other variables Granger cause the marginal utility of consumption. In the special case that $(\beta R)^{-1} = 1$, (5) predicts that the marginal utility of consumption is a "martingale."[4] For specific forms of the utility function, Hall tested this implication by estimating vector autoregressions including the marginal utility of consumption and testing the zero restrictions associated with lack of Granger causality.

To obtain tighter restrictions, we consider the special case in which utility is quadratic,

$$u(c_t) = u_0 + u_1 c_t - \frac{u_2}{2} c_t^2 \tag{6}$$

with $u_0, u_1, u_2 > 0$, so that $u'(c_t) = u_1 - u_2 c_t$. We also assume that the satiation level of consumption, u_1/u_2, is large relative to the typical value of y_t. More precisely, we assume for all $t \geq 0$, with probability arbitrarily close to one we have the condition

$$E_t \sum_{j=0}^{\infty} R^{-j} y_{t+j} < u_1/u_2.$$

Such a condition prevents simply consuming at the satiation level u_1/u_2 for $t \geq 0$.

When (6) is assumed, (5) implies that

$$E_t c_{t+1} = \alpha + (\beta R)^{-1} c_t \tag{7}$$

where

$$\alpha = \frac{u_1(1 - (\beta R)^{-1})}{u_2}.$$

Recursions on equation (7) imply that

$$E_t c_{t+j} = \alpha \left[\frac{1 - \gamma^j}{1 - \gamma} \right] + \gamma^j c_t, \tag{8}$$

where $\gamma \equiv (\beta R)^{-1}$. Substituting (8) into (4), using $\beta R^2 > 1$ and $R > 1$, and solving for c_t gives

$$c_t = \left(\frac{-\alpha}{R - 1} \right) + \left(1 - \frac{1}{\beta R^2} \right) \left[\sum_{j=0}^{\infty} \left(\frac{1}{R} \right)^j E_t y_{t+j} + A_t \right]. \tag{9}$$

---

[4] A "martingale" is a stochastic process x_t that satisfies $E_t x_{t+1} = x_t$.

Equations (9) and (8) characterize the optimal consumption plan under the borrowing limit (3) and our assumption that $\{y_t\}$ is small relative to u_1/u_2.[5]

In the special case that is often considered, it is assumed that $\beta R = 1$, in which case (8) and (9) become the consumption plan

$$E_t c_{t+j} = c_t, \qquad \text{for all } j \geq 1 \tag{10}$$

$$c_t = \left(1 - \frac{1}{R}\right)\left[\sum_{j=0}^{\infty}\left(\frac{1}{R}\right)^j E_t y_{t+j} + A_t\right]. \tag{11}$$

Equations (10) and (11) form a version of the "permanent income theory." The expression on the right side of (11) can be interpreted as the consumer's "permanent income:" it is the rate at which the consumer expects to be able to consume while leaving intact total wealth, including both the "nonhuman" part A_t and the human part $\sum_{j=0}^{\infty}\left(\frac{1}{R}\right)^j E_t y_{t+j}$. Since equation (11) is exact and involves no random disturbance, equations (10) and (11) immediately imply Hall's result that permanent income follows a "martingale."[6]

3. THE PROJECTION OF CONSUMPTION ON LABOR INCOME

Collecting results in the special case in which $\beta R = 1$, we have the structure

$$A_{t+1} = R[A_t + y_t - c_t] \tag{2}$$

$$E_t c_{t+j} = c_t \qquad \text{for } j \geq 1. \tag{10}$$

$$c_t = \left(1 - \frac{1}{R}\right)\left[\sum_{j=0}^{\infty} R^{-j} E_t y_{t+j} + A_t\right]. \tag{11}$$

[5] While the model described in the text is useful for expositing the permanent income theory of consumption, it has some undesirable limiting properties. The equilibrium law of motion for assets satisfies

$$A_{t+1} = \left(\frac{1}{\beta R}\right)A_t + \frac{\alpha R}{(R-1)} + Ry_t - \left(R - \frac{1}{\beta R}\right)\sum_{j=0}^{\infty} R^{-j} E_t y_{t+j}.$$

This equation is derived by substituting (9) into the budget constraint (2). When $\beta R > 1$, the above equation implies that $E_t A_{t+j}$ converges as $j \to \infty$. Further, from equation (8) and the definition of α, when $\beta R > 1$, $\lim_{j \to \infty} E_t c_{t+j} = u_1/u_2$. Thus, it happens that, when $\beta R > 1$, the system can be expected to converge to a level of asset holdings such that consumption varies stochastically around the bliss level of consumption u_1/u_2. This is unsatisfactory because it implies that eventually the marginal utility of consumption fluctuates about zero. Despite such undesirable limiting behavior, the model behaves sensibly at low levels of consumption.

[6] See Hall's paper (1978) for implementation of econometric tests of this martingale characterization. Further work along this line is executed by Hansen and Singleton (1982) who provide an econometric method for imposing and testing restrictions implied by Euler equations in which the econometrician faces no unobserved components. An alternative econometric approach to implementing the restrictions on a vector imposed by an Euler equation is described by Hansen and Singleton (1983). The papers by Hansen and Singleton (1982, 1983) and the references in them describe the relationship between consumption and asset prices.

We now supplement this structure with the hypothesis that y_t is a stationary stochastic process with Wold moving average representation[7]

$$y_t = \bar{y} + g(L)\varepsilon_t, \quad g(L) = \sum_{j=0}^{\infty} g_j L^j, \quad \sum_{j=0}^{\infty} g_j^2 < +\infty \tag{12}$$

where $\varepsilon_t = y_t - E_{t-1}y_t \equiv y_t - Ey_t|1, y_{t-1}, y_{t-2},\ldots$ Here $\bar{y}$ is a mean level of labor income, and ε_t is the innovation process to labor income. We shall show that the structure (2), (10), (11) and (12) implies that the projection of c_t on 1, y_t, $y_{t-1},\ldots$ assumes a simple form closely related to that studied by Muth. We shall also display a simple formula linking the innovation in consumption, $c_{t+1} - c_t$, to the innovation in labor income ε_{t+1}.

We begin by noting that (2) and (11) imply that

$$c_{t+1} - c_t = \left(1 - \frac{1}{R}\right) \sum_{j=0}^{\infty} R^{-j}\{E_{t+1}y_{t+j+1} - E_t y_{t+j+1}\}. \tag{13}$$

This equation is derived simply by subtracting the right side of (11) for c_t from the same equation for c_{t+1}, and then using (2). Now in Chapter XI it was established that for specification (12),

$$\sum_{j=0}^{\infty} R^{-j} E_{t+1}(y_{t+1+j} - \bar{y}) = \left(\frac{g(L) - R^{-1}g(R^{-1})L^{-1}}{1 - R^{-1}L^{-1}}\right)\varepsilon_{t+1}. \tag{14}$$

Using similar methods to the one used to derive the preceding formula, it can be shown that

$$\sum_{j=0}^{\infty} R^{-j} E_t(y_{t+1+j} - \bar{y}) = \left[\frac{g(L)L^{-1} - g(R^{-1})L^{-1}}{1 - R^{-1}L^{-1}}\right]\varepsilon_t. \tag{15}$$

Substituting (14) and (15) into (13) and rearranging gives

$$c_{t+1} - c_t = \left(1 - \frac{1}{R}\right)g(R^{-1})\varepsilon_{t+1}. \tag{16}$$

Equation (16) confirms that consumption c_t is a martingale, and links the innovation in c_t to the innovation ε_t in labor income via the constant of proportionality $(1 - R^{-1})g(R^{-1})$, which is seen to depend on the stochastic process for labor income, via the dependence on $g(L)$.

Use (12) to represent the innovation ε_t as

$$\varepsilon_t = g(L)^{-1}[y_t - \bar{y}].$$

---

[7] In the remainder of this chapter, and in Chapter XIII also, we take $E_t(\cdot)$ to be the linear least squares projection operator, conditioned on information available at time t. That is, we take E_t as the projection operator P_t defined in Chapter XI. A valid alternative interpretation is that E_t is the mathematical expectation operator conditioned on information available at t, and that the assumptions stated under equation (12) assure that conditional expectations are linear in the conditioning variables.

Substituting this into (16) gives

$$(1 - L)c_{t+1} = (1 - R^{-1})g(R^{-1})g(L)^{-1}(y_{t+1} - \bar{y}), \qquad (17)$$

which shows consumption to be an exact linear function of its own lagged value and a distributed lag in current and past values of labor income y_t, Notice that the coefficients in this distributed lag depend on the interest rate R and on the stochastic process generating labor income, via $g(L)$. Repeating (12) and (17), we have

$$y_t = g(L)\varepsilon_t + \bar{y}$$
$$c_t = (1 - R^{-1})g(R^{-1})g(L)^{-1}(1 - L)^{-1}(y_t - \bar{y}).$$

These two equations indicate that the distributed lag by which labor income appears to influence consumption depends on the stochastic process that is assumed to govern labor income. This is indicated by the presence of $g(L)$ in each of the preceding equations. The theory asserts that it would be fruitless to search for an income process-invariant consumption function of the distributed lag form

$$c_t = \sum_{j=0}^{\infty} h_j y_{t-j} + \text{constant}$$

with h_j's that are constant across different processes generating labor income. The theory implies that the h_j's are themselves functions of the g_j's governing the income process.

The preceding example is a version of one used by Robert E. Lucas, Jr. in his criticism of macroeconometric policy evaluation procedures as they existed before 1973. The example is consistent with the earlier argument of Gordon and Hynes (1970) that it is misdirected to seek decision rules for consumption, investment, or price setting that are independent of the laws of motion of variables impinging on agents' constraints and preferences.

4. MUTH'S SPECIAL CASE

Consider the special case of (12), studied by Muth, in which $\bar{y} = 0$ and

$$g(L) = \frac{1 - bL}{(1 - L)}, \qquad 0 < b < 1. \qquad (18)$$

In this case, (17) implies

$$c_{t+1} = \frac{(1 - bR^{-1})}{1 - bL} y_{t+1},$$

which expresses consumption as a geometric distributed lag in y, with the weights adding up to $(1 - bR^{-1})/(1 - b)$.

In the special case governed by (18), it is instructive to trace out the moving average representation depicting the responses of y and c to the innovations ε_t. Equations (18), (12), (2) and (16) imply

$$y_t = \varepsilon_t + (1 - b)[\varepsilon_{t-1} + \varepsilon_{t-2} + \cdots] \tag{19}$$

$$c_t = (1 - bR^{-1})[\varepsilon_t + \varepsilon_{t-1} + \varepsilon_{t-2} + \cdots] \tag{20}$$

$$A_{t+1} = b[\varepsilon_t + \varepsilon_{t-1} + \varepsilon_{t-2} + \cdots]. \tag{21}$$

According to (19), a fraction $(1 - b)$ of an innovation of ε_t in labor income persists forever. In this sense, $(1 - b)\varepsilon_t$ constitutes a permanent change in labor income. The effect of such an innovation in labor income is to change the value of permanent labor income, $(1 - R^{-1})[\sum_{j=0}^{\infty} R^{-j}E_t y_{t+j}]$, by the amount $(1 - R^{-1})[1 + (1 - b)R^{-1} + (1 - b)R^{-2} + \cdots]\varepsilon_t = (1 - bR^{-1})\varepsilon_t$. Equation (20) states that the response to such an innovation in labor income is a permanent change in consumption by the amount $(1 - bR^{-1})\varepsilon_t$. This change in consumption just equals the innovation in $(1 - R^{-1}) \sum_{j=0}^{\infty} R^{-j}E_t y_{t+j}$. Equation (21) shows that an innovation ε_t in labor income leads to a "permanent" change in assets of $bR^{-1}\varepsilon_t$. Notice that $b\varepsilon_t$ can be interpreted as the "transitory" part of the innovation to labor income. Current ε_t is divided in the fractions $(1 - bR^{-1})$ to consumption and bR^{-1} to saving. Lagged ε's are divided in the fractions $(1 - bR^{-1})$ to consumption and $b(R^{-1} - 1)$ to saving.

5. ANALYZING TAX CHANGES

a. A Lump Sum Tax-Subsidy

We modify the model by assuming that the consumer's problem is now to maximize (1) subject to

$$A_{t+1} = R[A_t + y_t - \tau_t - c_t]$$

$$\tau_t = h(L)\xi_t, \quad h(L) = \sum_{j=0}^{\infty} h_j L^j, \quad \sum_{j=0}^{\infty} h_j^2 < +\infty$$

$$y_t = g(L)\varepsilon_t + \bar{y}$$

where τ_t is now a lump sum tax, and ξ_t is a fundamental white noise for τ_t. We assume that ξ_t is orthogonal to ε_s for all t and s. The reader can derive by steps analogous to those leading to (17) the following equation for consumption

$$(1 - L)c_{t+1} = (1 - R^{-1})g(R^{-1})g(L)^{-1}(y_{t+1} - \bar{y})$$
$$- (1 - R^{-1})h(R^{-1})h(L)^{-1}\tau_{t+1}. \tag{22}$$

Equation (22) indicates how the distributed lag response of consumption to taxes depends on the stochastic process for taxes.

b. A Tax on Income from Savings

A tax on savings can be represented by altering the budget restraint (2) to be

$$A_{t+1} = \theta R[A_t + y_t - c_t], \qquad 0 < \theta \le 1,$$

where $(1 - \theta)$ is the gross tax rate on savings, which we assume is constant over time. With such a specification, it is evident that (17) becomes

$$(1 - L)c_{t+1} = (1 - (\theta R)^{-1})g((\theta R)^{-1})g(L)^{-1}(y_{t+1} - \bar{y}),$$

which indicates how different settings for θ would alter the relation between consumption and labor income.

6. THE PROJECTION OF CONSUMPTION ON TOTAL INCOME: FRIEDMAN'S MODEL

The preceding sections computed the projection of c_t on current and lagged values of labor income that is implied by our model with $\beta R = 1$. In the special case of the income process studied by Muth, namely, $(1 - L)y_t = (1 - bL)\varepsilon_t$, we found that consumption can be expressed as a geometric distributed lag of labor income, with the decay coefficient being b, which is thus inherited directly from the stochastic process for labor income.

Although it delivers a geometric distributed lag projection of consumption on labor income, in important respects, this setup does not reflect what Friedman seems to have had in mind in his time series empirical work, in which he fit a geometric distributed lag of consumption on income. First, Friedman's concept of measured income was different and included interest on accumulated assets. Second, Friedman (1963) conjectured that the decay parameter in the geometric lag distribution of consumption on income should equal the discount factor in consumers' preferences. In this section, we indicate that in a special case of the preceding model Friedman's conjecture is true.

We begin by repeating (11) for convenience:

$$c_t = \left(1 - \frac{1}{R}\right)\left[A_t + \sum_{j=0}^{\infty}\left(\frac{1}{R}\right)^j E_t y_{t+j}\right]. \tag{11}$$

Recall that this embodies the special assumption that $\beta R = 1$. In the interests of building a version of a model that Friedman used to study the time series, we now assume that labor income is governed by the simple stochastic process

$$y_t = \bar{y} + \varepsilon_t, \tag{23}$$

where $\bar{y}$ is a constant and ε_t is a sequence of independently and identically distributed random variables with mean zero and constant variance. For the labor income process (23), $E_t y_{t+j} = \bar{y}$ for all $j \geq 1$, so that (11) becomes $c_t = (1 - 1/R)[A_t + 1/(1 - 1/R)\bar{y} + \varepsilon_t]$ or

$$c_t = \left(1 - \frac{1}{R}\right)[A_t + \varepsilon_t] + \bar{y}. \tag{24}$$

Substituting (24) into the budget constraint (2) gives

$$A_{t+1} = A_t + \varepsilon_t. \tag{25}$$

Now let us define measured income at time t, y_{mt}, as

$$y_{mt} = \left(1 - \frac{1}{R}\right)A_t + y_t. \tag{26}$$

This definition adds to labor income the interest income on non-human assets. We suppose that the analyst has data on the measured sum of interest and labor income, y_{mt}, and seek to know how c_t and y_{mt} are related. A definition like y_{mt} is what Milton Friedman (1956), Robert Lucas (1976), Thomas Sargent (1978), and others have used when they analyzed the connections between the time series for consumption and income of an optimizing household.

We now proceed to determine the projection of c_t on $[y_{mt}, y_{mt-1}, \ldots]$. To do this, we solve (24), (25) and (26). Equations (24) and (26) imply that

$$c_t = y_{mt} - \frac{1}{R}\varepsilon_t. \tag{27}$$

Solving (25) for A_t in terms of lagged ε's and substituting the result into (26) gives

$$y_{mt} = \bar{y} + \varepsilon_t + \left(1 - \frac{1}{R}\right)(\varepsilon_{t-1} + \varepsilon_{t-2} + \cdots). \tag{28}$$

Substituting (28) into (27) then gives $c_t = (1 - 1/R)[\varepsilon_t + \varepsilon_{t-1} + \cdots] + \bar{y}$ or

$$c_t = \frac{(1 - 1/R)}{(1 - L)}\varepsilon_t + \bar{y}. \tag{29}$$

Formally, solving (28) for ε_t gives

$$\varepsilon_t = \frac{(1 - L)}{1 - (1/R)L}(y_{mt} - \bar{y}). \tag{30}$$

Finally, using (30) to eliminate ε_t from (29) gives

$$c_t = \frac{(1 - 1/R)}{1 - (1/R)L}y_{mt}. \tag{31}$$

Equation (31) expresses consumption as a geometric distributed lag of measured income y_{mt}, with a decay parameter equal to $1/R$, the reciprocal of the gross real rate of return. Recall that in deriving (11), we assumed that $\beta R = 1$, so that (31) could also be written

$$c_t = \frac{(1 - \beta)}{(1 - \beta L)} y_{mt}. \tag{32}$$

Equation (31) or (32) has the geometric form that Milton Friedman used in his empirical work (1956). Furthermore, Friedman argued that the geometric decay coefficient in discounting past measured income should equal the discount rate that agents use to discount future expected labor income in forming their permanent income. We have shown that Friedman's conclusions are delivered by the model consisting of a representative consumer who maximizes (1) with respect to (2) and the special income process (23), where $\beta R = 1$, and where utility is quadratic in consumption.

We can obtain a permanent income interpretation of this model by arguing along the following lines. Substitute (23) and (25) into (26) and rearrange to obtain

$$(1 - L)y_{mt} = (1 - \beta L)\varepsilon_t.$$

Application of the Wiener–Kolmogorov prediction formula to this process for y_{mt} gives

$$E_t y_{mt+j} = \frac{(1 - \beta)}{(1 - \beta L)} y_{mt}, \qquad j \geq 1.$$

Suppose that we define "permanent income" at t as

$$\sum_{j=1}^{\infty} \alpha_j E_t y_{mt+j}$$

for any $\{\alpha_j\}_{j=1}^{\infty}$ sequence satisfying $\sum_{j=1}^{\infty} \alpha_j = 1$. (See the discussion in Friedman (1956) about how to define permanent income in terms of current forecasts of future measured income over alternative horizons.) Then notice that for *any* sequence $\{\alpha_j\}$ obeying $\sum_{j=1}^{\infty} \alpha_j = 1$, equation (32) is equivalent with

$$c_t = \sum_{j=1}^{\infty} \alpha_j E_t y_{mt+j}.$$

The model can therefore be represented in terms of equality between consumption and permanent income defined as $\sum_{j=1}^{\infty} \alpha_j E_t y_{mt+j}$.[8]

---

[8] However, it would be a misspecification to impose the restriction

(*) $$c_t = k \sum_{j=0}^{\infty} \beta^j E_t y_{mt+j}$$

for some constant k. This restriction in conjunction with the stochastic process $(1 - L)y_{mt} = (1 - \beta L)\varepsilon_t$ implies

$$c_t = k \left[\frac{(1 - \beta) + \beta L}{1 - \beta L} \right] y_{mt},$$

which is *not* the projection of c_t on current and past y_m that is represented in (32). The misspecification (*) was committed by Sargent (1978) and corrected by Flavin (1981).

It is useful to trace out the moving average responses of c_t and y_{mt} to an innovation ε_t in labor income. From (29) and (28) we obtain

$$c_t = (1 - \beta)\varepsilon_t + (1 - \beta)\varepsilon_{t-1} + (1 - \beta)\varepsilon_{t-2} + \cdots + \bar{y}$$

$$y_{mt} = \varepsilon_t + (1 - \beta)\varepsilon_{t-1} + (1 - \beta)\varepsilon_{t-2} + \cdots + \bar{y}.$$

An innovation ε_t in labor income leads to a permanent change in subsequent measured income of $(1 - \beta)\varepsilon_t$, through the mechanism of asset accumulation. Coincidentally, a permanent change of consumption of $(1 - \beta)\varepsilon_t$ occurs.

It should be emphasized that this model of the projection of consumption on measured income depends sensitively on the specifications of the particular stochastic process (23) for labor income. Positing a different process for labor income would alter the projection of consumption on measured income via the workings of the cross-equation restrictions inherent in dynamic rational expectations models.

7. PROJECTIONS ON LABOR INCOME AND CURRENT ASSETS

We now return to equations (11) and (12):

$$c_t = (1 - R^{-1})\left[\sum_{j=0}^{\infty} R^{-j} E_t y_{t+j} + A_t \right] \tag{11}$$

$$y_t = \bar{y} + g(L)\varepsilon_t, \quad g(L) = \sum_{j=0}^{\infty} g_j L^j, \quad \sum_{j=0}^{\infty} g_j^2 < \infty. \tag{12}$$

By using the formula (88) of Hansen and Sargent that was presented in Chapter XI, we can represent (11) as

$$c_t = \bar{y} + (1 - R^{-1})A_t$$
$$+ (1 - R^{-1})\left[\frac{g(L) - R^{-1}g(R^{-1})L^{-1}}{1 - R^{-1}L^{-1}} \right]\varepsilon_t \tag{33}$$

or

$$c_t = \bar{y} + (1 - R^{-1})A_t$$
$$+ (1 - R^{-1})\left[\frac{1 - R^{-1}g(R^{-1})g(L)^{-1}L^{-1}}{1 - R^{-1}L^{-1}} \right](y_t - \bar{y}). \tag{34}$$

To specialize (34) somewhat, assume that labor income follows the mixed moving average autoregressive process

$$a(L)y_t = b(L)\varepsilon_t \tag{35}$$

where $\varepsilon_t = y_t - E[y_t|y_{t-1}, y_{t-2}, \ldots]$, $a(L) = 1 - a_1 L - \cdots - a_p L^p$, $b(L) = 1 - b_1 L - \cdots - b_p L^p$, where the zeros of $a(z)$ and $b(z)$ do not lie inside the unit circle. Then Hansen and Sargent (1981) have given a formula that implies

$$\sum_{j=0}^{\infty} R^{-j} E_t y_{t+j} = \left\{ \left[\frac{L - R^{-1} a(R^{-1})^{-1} a(L)}{L - R^{-1}} \right] \right.$$

$$\left. + R^{-1} a(R^{-1})^{-1} \left[\frac{b(L) - b(R^{-1})}{L - R^{-1}} \right] b(L)^{-1} a(L) \right\} y_t. \tag{36}$$

In the interests of getting a specification close to the geometric lag in income used by Milton Friedman, we consider the first-order case

$$(1 - a_1 L) y_t = (1 - b_1 L) \varepsilon_t, \qquad |a_1| \leq 1, \quad |b_1| < 1. \tag{37}$$

In this special case, (36) becomes

$$\sum_{j=0}^{\infty} R^{-j} E_t y_{t+j} = (1 - a_1 R^{-1})^{-1} \left[\frac{(1 - R^{-1} b_1) - (b_1 - R^{-1} b_1 a_1) L}{1 - b_1 L} \right] y_t.$$

Considering further the special case considered by Muth (1960), in which $a_1 = 1$, the consumption function and labor income process become

$$c_t = \left[\frac{(1 - R^{-1} b_1) - b_1(1 - R^{-1})L}{(1 - b_1 L)} \right] y_t + (1 - R^{-1}) A_t \tag{38}$$

$$(1 - L) y_t = (1 - b_1 L) \varepsilon_t, \qquad |b_1| < 1. \tag{39}$$

Equation (38) expresses consumption as a sum of a distributed lag in labor income that declines geometrically (after the first lag), and an interest rate times initial nonhuman wealth. For R close to unity, the lag distribution on labor income is close to being geometric.

Once again, representations (38) and (39) display the dependence of the decision rule for consumption on the parameters of the stochastic process for labor income.

8. TRANSITORY CONSUMPTION

The above setups implied that consumption is an exact (nonstochastic) function of permanent income, there being no "transitory consumption" in Milton Friedman's language. We now briefly indicate a modification designed to add such a transitory component to consumption. Adding transitory consumption stemming from preference shocks destroys the martingale charcterization of consumption, but does not alter the main methodological implications of the theory.

We modify preferences to be of the form

$$u(c_t) = u_0 + u_1 c_t - \frac{u_2}{2} c_t + c_t a_t,$$

where a_t is a serially uncorrelated random process with mean zero. We assume that $Ea_t y_s = 0$ for all t and s. We assume that at time t, the consumer knows a_t, and past values a_{t-1}, a_{t-2}, but does not know future values of a_{t+j} for $j \geq 1$. We continue to assume that R_t is constant over time, and that $R\beta = 1$. Under these circumstances, the household's optimum plan is to choose a consumption plan that satisfies the expected present value constraint (4) and the Euler equation $E_t[u_1 - u_2 c_{t+1} + a_{t+1}] = [u_1 - u_2 c_t + a_t]$ or

$$E_t c_{t+1} = c_t - \frac{1}{u_2} a_t. \tag{40}$$

Equation (40) and the white noise nature of a_t imply

$$E_t c_{t+j} = c_t - \frac{1}{u_2} a_t. \tag{41}$$

Substituting (41) into (4) and solving for c_t gives

$$c_t = \left(\frac{1}{u_2 R}\right) a_t + \left(1 - \frac{1}{R}\right) \left[A_t + \sum_{j=0}^{\infty} \left(\frac{1}{R}\right)^j E_t y_{t+j} \right]. \tag{42}$$

Here $(u_2 R)^{-1} a_t$ is "transitory consumption," that is consumption that is unrelated to permanent income, $y_{pt} \equiv (1 - 1/R)[A_t + \sum_{j=0}^{\infty} (1/R)^j E_t y_{t+j}]$. Equations (40) and (42) and the definition of y_{pt} imply that

$$E_t y_{pt+1} = y_{pt} + \frac{1}{u_2} \left[\frac{1}{R} - 1 \right] a_t, \tag{43}$$

and that

$$c_{t+1} = c_t + w_0 a_{t+1} - \frac{1}{u_2} a_t + (1 - R^{-1})g(R^{-1})\varepsilon_{t+1} \tag{44}$$

where w_0 is a constant (which we ask the reader to determine). In (44), $y_t = g(L)\varepsilon_t$ is a Wold representation for y_t, as in Section 3. Equations (40) and (44) state that the first difference of consumption is a first-order moving average process. Therefore, the presence of disturbances to preferences modifies Hall's characterization of consumption as a martingale.[9] While the marginal utility of consumption remains a martingale, consumption is not one, even with quadratic utility.

[9] More generally, the presence of random disturbances to preferences prevents one from using the method of Hansen and Singleton (1982) to estimate preference parameters and to test the restrictions imposed by the Euler equation. The reason is that the Euler equations involve processes unobservable to the econometrician. Hansen and Singleton's (1982) procedure works in situations in which Euler equations lead to exact relationships among projections and observables. For linear models such as those studied in this chapter, the econometric method described by Hansen and Sargent (1982) is able to estimate systems in which there are unobservable (to the econometrician) stationary random shocks to preferences with arbitrary serial correlations.

9. CONSUMPTION, PERMANENT INCOME, AND THE INVESTMENT ACCELERATOR: A STOCHASTIC GROWTH INTERPRETATION

We can reinterpret some of our previous results in terms of a linear quadratic version of a stochastic growth model (see Brock and Mirman (1972)). The model can be interpreted either as a single agent (Robinson Crusoe) economy, or as a "social planning model" with a representative agent.[10] In the latter interpretation, a social planner is supposed to choose a contingency plan for consumption to maximize

$$E_0 \sum_{t=0}^{\infty} \beta^t \left(u_0 + u_1 c_t^* - \frac{u_2}{2} c_t^{*2} \right), \qquad 0 < \beta < 1, \tag{45}$$

subject to k_0 given and

$$c_t^* + k_{t+1} = f k_t + \theta_t, \qquad f > 1 \tag{46}$$

$$\theta_t = g(L)\varepsilon_t, \qquad g(L) = \sum_{j=0}^{\infty} g_j L^j. \tag{47}$$

Here k_t is the level of capital, c_t^* is the level of consumption, and θ_t is a technology shock with Wold representation $g(L)\varepsilon_t$, where $\varepsilon_t = \theta_t - E\theta_t|\theta_{t-1}$, $\theta_{t-2}, \ldots$. We impose the technical condition that $\beta f^2 > 1$, and require that $E_0 k_t \geq M > -\infty$ for all t. Equation (46) is a linear production function restricting the social planner's feasible choices of (k_{t+1}, c_t^*). The planner takes the technology shock process $\{\theta_t\}$ as given, and seeks to maximize (45) over contingency plans for (c_t^*, k_{t+1}) as a function of $(k_t, \theta_{t-s}, s \geq 0)$.

Evidently, this model is equivalent with the model of Section 2, with $f^{-1}\theta_t = y_t$, $f^{-1}c_t^* = c_t$, $k_t = A_t$, $f = R$. It follows immediately that the solution of the social planning problem satisfies the appropriate version of (9), in particular,

$$c_t^* = \left(\frac{-\alpha f}{f-1} \right) + \left(1 - \frac{1}{\beta f^2} \right) \left[\sum_{j=0}^{\infty} f^{-j} E_t \theta_{t+j} + f k_t \right]. \tag{48}$$

It is of some interest to reconsider the approach of Section 6 in light of the present interpretation of the model. Let us define net output or income at time t as

$$y_{nt} = (f-1)k_t + \theta_t. \tag{49}$$

The variable y_{nt} defined by (49) has a natural interpretation as disposable or net income (notice from (46) and (49) that the constraint facing the social planner

---

[10] See Lucas, Prescott, and Stokey (forthcoming) for an interpretation of this model as describing the competitive equilibrium of a decentralized economy consisting of firms and households.

can be expressed $c_t^* + (k_{t+1} - k_t) = y_{nt}$. Notice that y_{nt} given by (49) corresponds to f times the concept of measured income defined by (26).

In parallel with Section 6, let us study the special case in which the technology shock θ_t is a white noise. Further, let us consider the special case in which $f\beta = 1$. Then the results in Section 6 immediately imply that the solution of the social planning problem can be represented as

$$c_t^* = \frac{(1 - f^{-1})}{(1 - f^{-1}L)} y_{nt} \tag{50}$$

$$y_{nt} = (f - 1)k_t + \theta_t \tag{49}$$

$$k_{t+1} - k_t = y_{nt} - c_t^*. \tag{51}$$

Equations (49), (50), and (51) imply the following representation for net investment:

$$(k_{t+1} - k_t) = \frac{f^{-1}(1 - L)}{1 - f^{-1}L} y_{nt} \tag{52}$$

or

$$(k_{t+1} - k_t) = f^{-1} \sum_{j=0}^{\infty} f^{-j}(y_{nt-j} - y_{nt-j-1}).$$

Equation (52) is a version of a "distributed lag accelerator," net investment being exactly a geometric distributed lag of the change in net income, y_{nt}.

This derivation of the investment accelerator is special in several senses. The projection of net investment on current and past net output given in (52) is not "structural" or invariant under intervention. In particular, an alteration of the stochastic process for the "technology shock" θ_t would not preserve (52), which is derived under the assumption that θ_t is a white noise.

Note that the model can be reinterpreted as describing a social planner who is maximizing (45) while facing an exogenous stochastic process for government purchases, $\bar{g}_t$, which does not enter the planner's preference function. To support this reinterpretation simply set $\theta_t = -\bar{g}_t$ in (46).[11] On this interpretation, the point of the preceding paragraph is that the projection of net investment on net income will not be invariant with respect to the stochastic process for government purchases. Thus, the preceding derivation of the accelerator does not support its use as a "demand function for investment" suitable for inclusion as one component of a macroeconometric model. Instead, the derivation depicts a set of restrictions on preferences, technology, and stochastic processes for shocks which make the investment accelerator emerge as a correct description of the comovements of the stochastic process for $(y_{nt}, k_{t+1} - k_t)$ that the social planner chooses.

---

[11] With a simple modification, a technology shock could also be retained. Just set $\theta_t = \eta_t - \bar{g}_t$ where η_t is now the technology shock.

10. CONCLUSIONS

The process of building the theory of consumption described above began as a conservative attempt to modify the Keynesian consumption function to incorporate the distributed lag needed to match the correlations in the data. This enterprise eventually led to the insight that the decision rule for consumption at t as a function of the agent's information at t—the consumption function—ought not to be regarded as invariant with respect to alterations in the processes for taxes, labor income, and the interest rate that face the agent. It followed that the formerly widespread practice of holding consumption functions invariant while simulating the effects on consumption of alternative tax and income processes contradicted the theory. This was Lucas's critique of econometric policy evaluation. This insight, which has had revolutionary consequences for the practice of macroeconomics and econometrics, emerged naturally and logically from the process of refining the Keynesian consumption function to bring it into line with dynamic theory.

Despite revealing these revolutionary consequences, the preceding presentation of the theory mostly follows the Keynesian practice of confronting agents with an exogenous process for labor income, which is not a consequence of their own choices. Alternatively, the stochastic growth interpretation adopted in Section 9 is one in which the social planner faces a trivial choice about labor supply (there is no labor supply in the preference function, and in the production process labor is present, if at all, only in fixed proportions with capital). In Chapter XVIII, we shall study theories in which households simultaneously choose consumption and labor income paths.

REFERENCES

Brock, W. A. and Mirman, L. (1972). "Optimal economic growth and uncertainty: the discounted case." *Journal of Economic Theory*, Vol. 4, No. 3, pp. 479–513.

Fisher, I. (1930). *The Theory of Interest*, New York: Macmillan.

Flavin, M. A. (1981). "The adjustment of consumption to changing expectations about future income." *Journal of Political Economy*, Vol. 89, No. 5, pp. 974–1009.

Friedman, M. (1956). *A Theory of the Consumption Function*, Princeton, New Jersey: Princeton University Press.

Friedman, M. (1963). "Windfalls, the 'horizon,' and related concepts in the permanent-income hypothesis." In *Measurement in Economics* (Christ, et al, eds.). Stanford, California: Stanford University Press.

Gordon, D. and Hynes, A. (1970). "On the theory of price dynamics." In *The New Microeconomics in Employment and Inflation Theory* (E. S. Phelps et al, eds.). New York: W. W. Norton.

Hall, R. E. (1978). "Stochastic implications of the life-cycle-permanent income hypothesis: theory and evidence." *Journal of Political Economy*, Vol. 86, No. 6.

Hansen, L. P. and Sargent, T. J. (1981). "A note on Wiener–Kolmogorov prediction formulas for rational expectations models." *Economic Letters*, Vol. 8, pp. 255–260.

Hansen, L. P. and Sargent, T. J. (1982). "Instrumental variables procedures for estimating linear rational expectations models." *Journal of Monetary Economics*, Vol. 9, pp. 263–296.

Hansen, L. P. and Singleton, K. J. (1983). "Stochastic consumption, risk aversion, and the temporal behavior of asset returns." *Journal of Political Economy*, Vol. 91, No. 2, pp. 249–265.

Hansen, L. P. and Singleton, K. J. (1982). "Generalized instrumental variables estimation of nonlinear rational expectations models." *Econometrica*, Vol. 50, No. 5, pp. 1269–1286.

Lucas, R. E. Jr. (1976). "Econometric policy evaluation: a critique." In *The Phillips Curve and the Labor Market* (K. Brunner and A. Meltzer, eds.). Vol. 1 of Carnegie-Rochester Conference in Public Policy, a supplementation series to the *Journal of Monetary Economics*, Amsterdam: North Holland Publishers.

Lucas, R. E. Jr, Prescott, E. C. and Stokey, N. L. (1988). *Recursive Methods for Economic Dynamics*, Cambridge: Harvard University Press (forthcoming).

Muth, J. F. (1960). "Optimal properties of exponentially weighted forecasts." *Journal of the American Statistical Association*, Vol. 55, No. 290, pp. 299–306.

Sargent, T. J. (1986). *Dynamic Macroeconomic Theory*, Cambridge: Harvard University Press.

Sargent, T. J. (1980). "Rational expectations, econometric exogeneity, and consumption." *Journal of Political Economy*, Vol. 86, No. 4, pp. 673–700.

CHAPTER XIII

GOVERNMENT DEBT AND TAXES

1. INTRODUCTION

This chapter reinterprets the mathematics in the preceding chapter in order to model some aspects of government finance. By renaming variables, the household budget constraint of the last chapter is reinterpreted as the budget constraint facing a government that always abstains from inflationary finance (that is, a government that doesn't print currency to finance any of its expenditures). Section 2 of this chapter describes the restrictions that are placed on time series of government purchases and tax collections by the intertemporal government budget constraint. Intuitively, this constraint seems to place only mild restrictions on the time series because it is a restriction involving infinite sequences. There is always the possibility of satisfying the budget constraint, even while running large and persistent deficits, by intending to run large surpluses later. Section 2 gives a formal description of precisely how restrictive the intertemporal budget constraint is when government expenditures are covariance stationary.

Section 3 pursues the observation of Robert Barro (1979), that there is a formal analogy between the permanent income theory of consumption and a model of "tax smoothing." A simple linear-quadratic dynamic optimal tax model is formulated which is mathematically equivalent with the permanent income model of the last chapter. This model is one in which the sequence of net-of-interest government expenditures is taken as given and as following a covariance stationary stochastic process. The idea is that tax collections are distorting and should be allocated over time to minimize the distortion. The model has the implication, stressed by Robert Barro, that in response to a large temporary increase in government expenditures, such as occurs during a short war, the government should raise taxes a little, run (potentially large) deficits during the war, and then run a large string of surpluses after the war.

2. OBSERVABLE IMPLICATIONS OF PRESENT VALUE BALANCED BUDGETS[1]

Consider the flow version of the government budget constraint

$$B_{t+1} = R[B_t + g_t - \tau_t] \tag{1}$$

where R is the gross real rate of return on government one-period debt, g_t is the level of real government expenditures, τ_t is the level of real tax collections, and B_t is the stock of real government debt, due at time t, and denominated in units of time t goods. We assume that $R > 1$ and that R is constant over time.[2] We assume that (g_t, τ_t) is a jointly covariance stationary stochastic process with moving average representation[3]

$$\begin{bmatrix} g_t \\ \tau_t \end{bmatrix} = \begin{bmatrix} \mu_g \\ \mu_\tau \end{bmatrix} + \begin{bmatrix} \sum_{k=0}^{\infty} C_k L^k \end{bmatrix} \varepsilon_t$$

or

$$\begin{bmatrix} g_t \\ \tau_t \end{bmatrix} = \begin{bmatrix} \mu_g \\ \mu_\tau \end{bmatrix} + \begin{bmatrix} c_1(L) \\ c_2(L) \end{bmatrix} \varepsilon_t. \tag{2}$$

Here, μ_g is the mean of g_t and μ_τ is the mean of τ_t. In (2), we assume that

$$\sum_{k=0}^{\infty} \operatorname{tr} C_k C_k^T < +\infty.$$

We let

$$\begin{bmatrix} c_1(L) \\ c_2(L) \end{bmatrix} \equiv \sum_{k=0}^{\infty} C_k L^k,$$

where $c_1(L)$ and $c_2(L)$ are each 1×2 vector-polynomials in the lag operator L. In (2), $\{\varepsilon_t\}$ is a (2×1) vector white noise satisfying

$$C_0 \varepsilon_t = \begin{bmatrix} g_t - E g_t | \phi_{t-1} \\ \tau_t - E \tau_t | \phi_{t-1} \end{bmatrix}$$

---

[1] The approach taken in this section is closely related to some of the ideas in Shim (1984). Shim estimated a vector autoregression and used the implied vector moving average representation to deduce the response to innovations of the discounted present value of government deficits. (He actually used a finite-horizon approximation to the present value.) Shim also used a version of restriction (6) to motivate empirical work that explored the connection between prospective government deficits and the current price level (see Shim's equation (4.4)).

[2] For extensive discussions of the government budget constraint in systems in which the real interest rate is not assumed constant, see Lucas and Stokey (1983) and Sargent (1986).

[3] Using an argument in Hansen and Sargent (1980), it can be shown that all that is required for the arguments in this section to go through is that (g_t, τ_t) be a process of mean exponential order less than R. This weak assumption would require minor modifications of the argument in several places, but would still imply restriction (6).

where E is the linear least squares projection operator and ϕ_{t-1} is the information set $\{\varepsilon_{t-1}, \varepsilon_{t-2}, \ldots\}$.

We impose on the solution to (1) the side condition that there exists an $M < +\infty$ such that

$$E_0 B_{t+1} \leq M \tag{3}$$

for all t. Condition (3) imposes an upper bound of M on the volume of government debt that is projected at time 0.

In (1), we regard B_t as predetermined at time t, being entirely determined by past decisions about g_t and τ_t. Since B_{t+1} is then known at t, we can represent (1) in the equivalent form:

$$E_t B_{t+1} = R[B_t + g_t - \tau_t]. \tag{4}$$

Subject to the condition (3), the solution to the difference equation (4) satisfies the "present value form" of the budget constraint:

$$E_t \sum_{j=0}^{\infty} R^{-j} \tau_{t+j} = B_t + E_t \sum_{j=0}^{\infty} R^{-j} g_{t+j}. \tag{5}$$

We now pose the following question: What restrictions on the time series for (g_t, τ_t) are imposed by the intertemporal budget constraint (5)? In other words, by observing time series of (g_t, τ_t), can we determine whether (5) (or equivalently (1) and (2)) is being obeyed? Given representation (2), this question is well posed. The answer is that (5) imposes upon (2) the cross-equation restriction

$$c_1(R^{-1}) = c_2(R^{-1}), \tag{6}$$

and that μ_g and μ_τ are not restricted by (5).

To prove the equality asserted in (6), we argue as follows. Since B_t is bounded, is predetermined, and is a function solely of past values of g_t and τ_t, it has a representation of the form

$$B_t = \mu_B + c_3(L)\varepsilon_t. \tag{7}$$

Here, μ_B is a constant, $c_3(L) = \sum_{j=0}^{\infty} c_{3k} L^k$, and $c_{30} = 0$ because B_t is predetermined at t, and so is only a function of information available at $t-1$. The Wiener–Kolmogorov prediction formula implies that

$$E_t B_{t+1} = \mu_B + \left(\frac{c_3(L)}{L}\right)_+ \varepsilon_t$$

or

$$E_t B_{t+1} = \mu_B + [c_{31} + c_{32}L + \cdots]\varepsilon_t. \tag{8}$$

Substituting (7), (8), and (2) into (4) and noting that the result must hold for all realizations of ε_t gives

$$(c_{31}L + c_{32}L^2 + \cdots) - R^{-1}(c_{31} + c_{32}L + \cdots) = c_2(L) - c_1(L) \tag{9}$$

and

$$\mu_B - R^{-1}\mu_B = \mu_\tau - \mu_g. \tag{10}$$

Evaluating (9) at $L = R^{-1}$ makes the left side of the equation zero, implying our result:

$$c_2(R^{-1}) = c_1(R^{-1}). \tag{6}$$

Note that (10) can be rearranged to read

$$\mu_\tau = \mu_g + \mu_B[1 - R^{-1}]. \tag{11}$$

Equation (11) states that the mean of tax collections μ_τ must equal the mean level of government expenditures plus the mean level of interest payments on the debt $[\mu_B(1 - R^{-1})]$. In other words, μ_τ and μ_g themselves are not restricted by (4) and (2), since a value of μ_B can always be found to satisfy (11).

The restriction (6) is interpretable in terms of the response of the system to innovations ε_t. Writing out restriction (6), we have

$$\sum_{k=0}^{\infty} c_{2k}R^{-k} = \sum_{k=0}^{\infty} c_{1k}R^{-k}. \tag{6'}$$

The $\{c_{jk}\}_{k=0}^{\infty}$ trace out the response of variable j ($j = 1$ for g, $j = 2$ for τ) to an innovation ε_t. Restriction (6) states that the present value of these responses has to be equal for g and τ.

It is useful to study how equality (6) can be attained as an application of the formula (90) of Hansen and Sargent (1980) of Chapter XI. Express equation (4) as

$$B_t = -d_t + R^{-1}E_tB_{t+1} \tag{12}$$

where $d_t \equiv g_t - \tau_t$. Thus, d_t is the net-of-interest government deficit. Let us use the compact notation

$$d_t = c_d(L)\varepsilon_t + \mu_d$$

where $c_d(L) \equiv c_1(L) - c_2(L)$ and $\mu_d = \mu_g - \mu_\tau$. The application of formula (88) of Chapter XI to (12) gives

$$B_t = -\left\{\frac{Lc_d(L) - R^{-1}c_d(R^{-1})}{L - R^{-1}}\right\}\varepsilon_t + \mu_B \tag{13}$$

or

$$B_t = c_3(L)\varepsilon_t + \mu_B,$$

where $c_3(L) \equiv -\{[Lc_d(L) - R^{-1}c_d(R^{-1})]/[L - R^{-1}]\}$. We impose that B_t is predetermined at time t by requiring that $c_{30} = 0$, which is equivalent with imposing that $c_3(0) = 0$. Imposing $c_3(0) = 0$ in formula (13) for $c_3(L)$ gives

$$c_3(0) = -c_d(R^{-1}).$$

We impose $c_3(0) = 0$ by requiring that $c_d(R^{-1}) = 0$, which is restriction (6).

With $c_d(R^{-1}) = 0$, (13) becomes[4]

$$B_t = \mu_B - \left\{\frac{Lc_d(L)}{L - R^{-1}}\right\}\varepsilon_t. \tag{14}$$

Expanding the polynomial in L by long division shows that the above equation is equivalent with

$$B_{t+1} = \mu_B + R\{c_0 + R[c_0 + R^{-1}c_1]L + \cdots$$
$$+ R^n[c_0 + R^{-1}c_1 + \cdots + R^{-n}c_n]L^n + \cdots\}\varepsilon_t \tag{15}$$

$$= \mu_B + R\left\{\sum_{n=0}^{\infty} R^n \left(\sum_{j=0}^{n} c_j R^{-j}\right) L^n\right\}\varepsilon_t$$

where $c_d(L) \equiv \sum_{j=0}^{\infty} c_j L^j$. Thus, the response of B_{t+1} to the lagged innovation ε_{t-n} is equal to $R^{n+1}[c_0 + R^{-1}c_1 + \cdots + R^{-n}c_n]$. The expected present value budget balance condition $c_d(R^{-1}) = 0$ is necessary in order that the response of real government debt to innovations in the deficit eventually damp out.

As an example of restriction (6), suppose that

$$\varepsilon_t = \begin{bmatrix} \varepsilon_{1t} \\ 0 \end{bmatrix}$$

and that $c_1(L) - [1/(1 - \rho_1 L), 0]$, $|\rho_1| < 1$. Suppose that τ_t is first-order autoregressive; then (6) implies that $c_2(L) = [1/(1 - \rho_2 L), 0]$ where

$$\frac{1}{1 - \rho_1 R^{-1}} = \frac{1}{1 - \rho_2 R^{-1}}.$$

This last equality implies that $\rho_1 = \rho_2$. Thus, if g_t and τ_t are each first-order autoregressive processes, then (6) is very restrictive.

However, (6) becomes progressively less restrictive as the order of the parameterization is increased. To take a second example, let

$$\varepsilon_t = \begin{bmatrix} \varepsilon_{1t} \\ 0 \end{bmatrix}, \qquad c_1(L) = \left(\frac{1}{1 - \rho_1 L}, 0\right), \qquad |\rho_1| < 1$$

and

$$c_2(L) = \left(\frac{1}{1 - \delta_1 L - \delta_2 L^2}, 0\right).$$

---

[4] Note that formally the polynomial in L in (14) equals the polynomial $(1 - RL)^{-1}Rc_d(L)L$ that would be obtained by writing (1) as $(1 - RL)B_{t+1} = Rd_t$, then inverting the polynomial $(1 - RL)$ to solve for B_{t+1}. The coefficients in the polynomial $(1 - RL)^{-1}Rc_d(L)$ diverge in positive powers of L unless $c_d(R^{-1}) = 0$. (Technically, the condition $c_d(R^{-1}) = 0$ places a zero in the numerator at $L = R^{-1}$ which cancels out the explosive effects of the pole at $L = R^{-1}$ contributed by the denominator.)

Here, τ_t is permitted to be second-order autoregressive while g_t must be first-order autoregressive. Then (6) implies that $\delta_1 + R^{-1}\delta_2 = \rho_1$. This is evidently a less restrictive condition than obtains when both processes are first-order autoregressive processes. It can be shown that (6) becomes less and less restrictive as we permit the dimensionality of the parameterization of $c(L)$ to increase.[5,6]

Compared with the cross-equation restrictions characterizing many rational expectations models,[7] the restriction $c_1(R^{-1}) = c_2(R^{-1})$ is a very weak one when $c_1(L)$ and $c_2(L)$ have high dimensional parameterizations. This stems from the weakness of the present value constraint (5) itself. This weakness relates informally to the fact that observers of governments frequently have a difficult time inferring from observed sequences for (g_t, τ_t) whether the budget is in balance in the present value sense. The government can always promise to run sufficient surpluses in the more or less distant future in order to balance the budget. The weakness of restriction (6) under high dimensional parameterizations of $c_1(L)$ and $c_2(L)$ is a precise way of formulating this weakness of the present value budget constraint, which obtains even under the restriction that (g_t, τ_t) is covariance stationary.

In the next section, we describe a simple model of government behavior which imposes additional cross-equation restrictions on the (g_t, τ_t) process.

3. TAX SMOOTHING

Robert Barro (1979) has pointed out the formal similarity of a particular dynamic optimal taxation problem to a model of consumer behavior. Barro attained a result, reminiscent of Hall's characterization of consumption, that taxes should follow a martingale. Here, we briefly describe the linear-quadratic

---

[5] If we permit $C(L)$ to have an infinite dimensional parameterization, (6) is not restrictive in a sense described precisely by Sims (1972). In particular, let $C(L)$ be generated by sequences of matrices C_j satisfying

$$\sum_{j=0}^{\infty} R^{-2j} \operatorname{tr}(C_j C_j') < +\infty$$

where "tr" denotes the trace. Then a version of Sims's approximation argument (1972) can be constructed to show that even if the true $C(L)$ does not obey (6), an arbitrarily close approximation to the true $C(L)$ can be obtained with a "false" one that obeys (6). The goodness of approximation is measured by the metric of mean squared error of prediction for the adjusted series $[R^{-t}g_t, R^{-t}\tau_t]$.

[6] Note that restriction (6) implies that det $C(z)$ has a zero at R^{-1}, which is inside the unit circle. This means that representation (2) is not a Wold representation, the ε_t process not being jointly fundamental for $[g_t, \tau_t]$.

[7] Examples of which are described in Chapters XI, XII, and XIV.

optimal taxation problem which is equivalent to the permanent income model of consumption described in Chapter XII.[8]

The idea is that taxes are distorting and that the government has an incentive to allocate taxes across time in order to minimize the distortion. The current period distortion at time t is modeled as equal to $[+u_1\tau_t + (u_2/2)\tau_t^2]$ where u_1 and $u_2 > 0$, and where τ_t is total taxes collected at time t.[9] The government has to finance a given stream of government expenditures $\{g_t\}$, where g_t is an exogenous stochastic process.[10] The government's problem is to select a strategy for choosing $\{\tau_t, B_{t+1}\}_{t=0}^{\infty}$ in order to maximize

$$E \sum_{t=0}^{\infty} \beta^t \left[-u_1\tau_t - \frac{u_2}{2}\tau_t^2 \right], \qquad 0 < \beta < 1 \tag{17}$$

subject to the budget constraint

$$B_{t+1} = R[B_t + g_t - \tau_t], \qquad R > 1 \tag{18}$$

$$B_t \le M < +\infty, \qquad \text{for all } t$$

B_0 given.

The government takes $\{g_t\}$ as a given process, and regards B_0 as a fixed initial condition. At time t, the government knows the values of $\{B_t, g_t, g_{t-1}, \ldots\}$, but must forecast future values of g. We assume that $\beta R^2 > 1$ and $R > 1$.

This problem is mathematically equivalent to the one described in Section 2 of Chapter XII. In the present problem, g_t plays the role of y_t in the previous model, τ_t plays the role of c_t, and B_{t+1} plays the role of A_{t+1}. It follows that all of the results of Chapter XII have interpretations in terms of the present model. Thus, corresponding to (7) of Chapter XII, we have

$$E_t\tau_{t+1} = -\alpha + (\beta R)^{-1}\tau_t \tag{19}$$

where

$$\alpha = \frac{u_1[1 - (\beta R)^{-1}]}{u_2}.$$

[8] In a heuristic way, such a tax smoothing model might be used to rationalize the large deficits in the government budget created during the Reagan administration. The argument would be that the advent of the Reagan administration signaled a large negative innovation in the expected present value of government expenditures, with substantial expenditure reductions to occur only in the more or less distant future. The optimal response to this innovation is to reduce taxes immediately and to run a string of government deficits while waiting for expenditures to be reduced.

[9] It is important that the distortion at time t is assumed not to depend on expected *future* tax collections.

[10] The model could be extended to have the government choose a $\{g_t\}_{t=0}^{\infty}$ stochastic process, say, by adding to the current period return a quadratic function in g_t and a random shock ε_t. This would not alter the key substantive implications of the model in the text.

In the case that $(\beta R)^{-1} = 1$, (19) states that tax collections should follow a martingale regardless of the stochastic process followed by $\{g_t\}$. Corresponding to equation (9) of Chapter XII, we have the representation for τ_t

$$\tau_t = \left(\frac{\alpha}{R-1}\right) + \left(1 - \frac{1}{\beta R^2}\right)\left[\sum_{j=0}^{\infty} R^{-j}E_t g_{t+j} + B_t\right]. \tag{20}$$

Equation (20) is a "permanent government expenditures theory" for tax collections.

We now pursue the analogy to the model in Chapter XII. First, suppose that g_t has the representation

$$g_t = \bar{g} + \tilde{g}(L)\varepsilon_t, \quad \sum_{j=0}^{\infty} \tilde{g}_j^2 < +\infty$$

where $\varepsilon_t = g_t - Eg_t|1, g_{t-1}, g_{t-2}, \ldots$. Here, $\bar{g}$ is the mean level of government expenditures, and ε_t is the innovation process to government expenditures. In the special case that $\beta R = 1$, we have, by analogy to equation (16) of Chapter XII,

$$\tau_{t+1} - \tau_t = \left(1 - \frac{1}{R}\right)\tilde{g}(R^{-1})\varepsilon_{t+1} \tag{21}$$

and

$$(1 - L)\tau_{t+1} = (1 - R^{-1})\tilde{g}(R^{-1})\tilde{g}(L)^{-1}(g_{t+1} - \bar{g}). \tag{22}$$

Equation (22) gives the projection of taxes on government expenditures (that is, net-of-interest government expenditures).[11]

The special case considered by Muth was

$$\tilde{g}(L) = \frac{(1 - bL)}{(1 - L)}, \quad 0 < b < 1. \tag{23}$$

As we saw in Chapter XII, in this case (22) implies

$$\tau_{t+1} = \frac{(1 - bR^{-1})}{1 - bL}g_{t+1}.$$

Tracing out the responses of τ_t, B_t, and g_t to innovations ε_t gives

$$g_t = \varepsilon_t + (1 - b)[\varepsilon_{t-1} + \varepsilon_{t-2} + \cdots] \tag{24}$$

$$\tau_t = (1 - bR^{-1})[\varepsilon_t + \varepsilon_{t-1} + \varepsilon_{t-2} + \cdots] \tag{25}$$

$$B_{t+1} = b[\varepsilon_t + \varepsilon_{t-1} + \varepsilon_{t-2} + \cdots]. \tag{26}$$

---

[11] Note that representation (21) obeys the restriction (6). Formally, (21) shows that when $c_1(L) = \tilde{g}(L)$, $c_2(L) = (1 - L)^{-1}(1 - R^{-1})\tilde{g}(R^{-1})$. These imply that $c_1(R^{-1}) = c_2(R^{-1}) = \tilde{g}(R^{-1})$. This merely verifies that solution (21) builds in budget balance in the sense of expected present values.

Equation (24) reveals that a fraction $(1 - b)$ of an innovation to g_t is "permanent." The effect of an innovation ε_t is to change $(1 - R^{-1}) \sum_{j=0}^{\infty} R^{-j} E_t g_{t+j}$ by the amount $(1 - R^{-1})[1 + (1 - b)R^{-1} + (1 - b)R^{-2} + \cdots]\varepsilon_t = (1 - bR^{-1})\varepsilon_t$. Equation (25) states that an innovation to government expenditures should lead to a permanent change in taxes by the amount $(1 - bR^{-1})\varepsilon_t$, which just equals the innovation to $(1 - R^{-1}) \sum_{j=0}^{\infty} R^{-j} E_t g_{t+j}$.

For values of b close to 1, an innovation ε_t is mostly transitory (see (24)). According to (25), an innovation ε_t in government expenditures is accompanied by an innovation of only $(1 - R^{-1}b)\varepsilon_t$ in tax collections. However, this change in tax collections is permanent (see (25)). According to (26), an innovation ε_t in g_t leads to a large innovation of $b\varepsilon_t$ in government borrowing B_{t+1}, which is "permanent." These responses incorporate the fashion in which transitory increases in government purchases, as occur during a short war, are optimally financed by borrowing during the war while raising taxes "permanently."

Representation (22) gives the projection of taxes on net-of-interest government expenditures. Proceeding by analogy with Section 6 of Chapter XII, it is possible also to calculate the projection of τ_t on government expenditures gross of interest, g_{mt}. Defining $g_{mt} = (1 - R^{-1})B_t + g_t$, we adopt the special stochastic structure

$$g_t = \bar{g} + \varepsilon_t \tag{27}$$

where ε_t is a white noise with mean zero and constant variance. Under this specification, and $\beta R = 1$, it follows that

$$\tau_t = \frac{(1 - \beta)}{(1 - \beta L)} g_{mt}, \tag{28}$$

as in Section 6 of Chapter XII.

4. A NOTE ON GOVERNMENT EXPENDITURES ON CAPITAL ACCOUNT

The preceding formulation assumes that all government expenditures are on "current account," in the sense that government expenditures g_t generate no prospects of future revenues for the government. We now indicate how parts of the preceding apparatus, in particular the government budget constraint, must be altered when some government expenditures are on "capital account." Capital account expenditures are defined as expenditures that lead to the accumulation of assets that yield a competitive rate of return to the government. Examples of capital account expenditures are government purchases of private capital,[12] government expenditures on welfare and public education that

---

[12] This assumes that the products of government-owned enterprises are priced correctly. If the government-owned enterprise charges too low a price, then the purchasing of that enterprise is only partly a "capital account" item. Notice that it is not durability of the purchased good alone that determines whether it is a capital account expenditure. Rather, the decisive aspect is the prospect for sufficient future income to the government stemming from the purchase.

increases the recipients' productivity by enough to increase the present value of subsequent tax collections by an amount equal to the government expenditure, and government loans to the private sector at the market rate of interest. Capital account expenditures are, by definition, self-amortizing and do not require current or subsequent taxation in order to finance them.

Let government owned "capital" be given by k_t at the beginning of period t. Government capital obeys the transition law $k_{t+1} = k_t + i_t$, where i_t is capital account government expenditures at period t.[13] In period t, the government earns net income on its capital in the amount $(R - 1)k_t$. The government budget constraint (1) is modified to become

$$B_{t+1} = R[B_t + g_t + i_t - \tau_t - (R - 1)k_t].$$ (29)

Using the transition law for k_t, we have that $i_t - (R - 1)k_t = k_{t+1} - Rk_t$. Thus, the budget constraint (29) can be rewritten as

$$B_{t+1} = R\{B_t + g_t - \tau_t + k_{t+1} - Rk_t\}.$$

The stock form of this constraint is

$$E_t \sum_{j=0}^{\infty} R^{-j}\tau_{t+j} = B_t + E_t \sum_{j=0}^{\infty} R^{-j}g_{t+j} + E_t \sum_{j=0}^{\infty} R^{-j}[k_{t+j+1} - Rk_{t+j}].$$ (30)

Writing out the sum and cancelling common terms shows that

$$E_t \sum_{j=0}^{\infty} R^{-j}[k_{t+j+1} - Rk_{t+j}] = -Rk_t.$$

Substituting this into (30) gives

$$E_t \sum_{j=0}^{\infty} R^{-j}\tau_{t+j} = (B_t - Rk_t) + E_t \sum_{j=0}^{\infty} R^{-j}g_{t+j}.$$ (31)

Note that the term Rk_t equals the capitalized value of net interest earnings on the government's holdings of capital k_t:

$$\sum_{j=0}^{\infty} R^{-j}(R - 1)k_t = Rk_t.$$

Thus, equation (31) states that the expected present value of tax collections equals the expected present value of government purchases on current account plus the government's initial net indebtedness, $B_t - Rk_t$. Note also that the stochastic process for i_t fails to appear directly in (31). Its failure to appear is a reflection of the fact that capital account expenditures do not affect the prospects for present value budget balance.

---

[13] We assume that i_t is a stochastic process such that k_t is of mean exponential order less than R.

5. CONCLUSIONS

The case for "tax smoothing" based on the model of Section 3 depends on some special features of the problem confronting the tax authority.[14] The objective function has been given a form which simplifies the problem. In particular, the "current return function" $[-u_1\tau_t - \frac{1}{2}u_2\tau_t{}^2]$ is specified to depend on current tax collections and *not* on expected future tax collections. This is a critical simplification for reasons indicated in Chapter XV. When private agents face genuinely dynamic optimum problems, their current decisions, and therefore measures of the current distortions caused by taxation, will generally depend on the entire path of current and future taxes. A framework which accommodates these effects would induce important differences in both the mathematical structure of the government's problem and the substantive nature of the results. In Chapter XV, we shall return to an optimal taxation problem that incorporates such dynamic effects of future taxes on current distortions.

REFERENCES

Barro, R. J. (1979). "On the determination of the public debt." *Journal of Political Economy*, Vol. 87, pp. 940–941.

Hansen, L. P. and Sargent, T. J. (1980), "Formulating and estimating dynamic linear rational expectations models." *Journal of Economic Dynamics and Control*, Vol. 2, No. 1, pp. 7–46.

Lucas, R. E. Jr. and Stokey, N. L. (1983). "Optimal fiscal and monetary policy in an economy without capital." *Journal of Monetary Economics*, Vol. 12, pp. 55–93.

Sargent, T. (1986). *Dynamic Macroeconomic Theory*, Cambridge: Harvard University Press.

Shim, S. D. (1984). "Inflation and the government budget constraint: international evidence," Ph.D. Thesis, University of Minnesota.

Sims, C. A. (1972). "Approximate prior restrictions in distributed lag estimation." *Journal of the American Statistical Association*, Vol. 67, No. 337, pp. 169–175.

Turnovsky, S. J. and Brock, W. A. (1980). "Time consistency and optimal government policies in perfect foresight equilibrium." *Journal of Public Economics*, Vol. 13, pp. 183–212.

---

[14] For more general models of the problem confronting the tax authority, see Lucas and Stokey (1983) and Turnovsky and Brock (1980).

CHAPTER XIV

INVESTMENT UNDER UNCERTAINTY

This chapter studies aspects of the capital accumulation process in setups where firms are uncertain about the future. Our first task is to extend our earlier study of quadratic dynamic optimization problems to the case in which there is uncertainty about future values of the exogenous processes facing agents. Then we shall present a simple version of Lucas and Prescott's model of firms' investment behavior in a competitive industry. In the process we shall be able to give a precise characterization of the concept of a rational expectations equilibrium.

1. OPTIMUM DECISION RULES UNDER A QUADRATIC OBJECTIVE[1]

We consider the problem: maximize (at each point in time t) the discounted present value

$$v_t = E_t \sum_{j=0}^{\infty} b^j g(n_{t+j-1}, n_{t+j}, z_{t+j}) \tag{1}$$

over stochastic processes for $\{n_{t+j}\}_{j=0}^{\infty}$ subject to $n_{t-1} = \bar{n}_{t-1}$ given. Here $E_t(x) = Ex|\Omega_t$ where E is the mathematical expectation operator and Ω_t is an information set to be specified. We assume that the discount factor obeys $0 < b < 1$ and that $g(n_{t+j-1}, n_{t+j}, z_{t+j})$ is concave in n_{t+j-1}, n_{t+j}. Here z_{t+j} is a vector of random variables that are exogenous to the decision maker. At time $t + j$ the decision maker will have available an information set Ω_{t+j} on which to base his decision. We assume that $\Omega_t \supset \Omega_{t-1}$ for all t. The decision-maker's problem at time t is to set n_t and to devise a strategy for setting $n_{t+1}, n_{t+2}, \ldots$ as

---

[1] The approach taken in this section originally stems from Holt et al. (1960). For a rigorous approach to some of the topics discussed here, see Telser and Graves (1972). The systems that we study are solved by engineers by solving matrix Riccati equations. See Kwakernaak and Sivan (1972). In their jargon, the systems that we study are *not* "controllable," but are "stabilizable" and "detectable," so that convergence of the Riccati equations in the infinite-time problem is assured.

functions of the information that he knows will become available in the future. In effect, to maximize (1) the decision-maker simultaneously chooses n_t and functions $\tilde{n}_{t+1}(\cdot), \tilde{n}_{t+2}(\cdot), \ldots$ giving $n_{t+1} = \tilde{n}_{t+1}(\Omega_{t+1}), n_{t+2} = \tilde{n}_{t+2}(\Omega_{t+2}), \ldots$. These functions give a complete contingency plan for setting future values of $\{n_{t+j}\}_{j=1}^{\infty}$ as based on the information that will be available when n_{t+j} must actually be set. The maximization of (1) is carried out over stochastic processes for $\{n_{t+j}\}_{j=0}^{\infty}$ which make n_{t+j} a function of information Ω_{t+j}. We shall always assume that Ω_{t+j} contains at least $\{n_{t+j-1}, n_{t+j-2}, \ldots, z_{t+j}, z_{t+j-1}, \ldots\}$.

To match the notation in (1) with one problem that interests us, let

$$g(n_{t-1}, n_t, z_t) = (f_0 + a_t)n_t - \tfrac{1}{2}f_1 n_t^2 - w_t n_t - \tfrac{1}{2}d(n_t - n_{t-1})^2 \qquad (2)$$

where $f_0, f_1, d > 0$, w_t is the real wage, n_t is employment, and a_t is a random shock to the productivity of labor. When we make w_t and a_t stochastic processes, the solution to (1) becomes a stochastic version of the demand for labor studied in Chapter IX.

Equating to zero the derivative of v_t in (1) with respect to n_t gives one first-order necessary condition for an optimum,

$$g_2(n_{t-1}, n_t, z_t) + bE_t g_1(n_t, n_{t+1}, z_{t+1}) = 0. \qquad (3)$$

Here we are assuming that n_{t-1} and z_t are all known at t, while n_{t+1} and z_{t+1} are still random. To be able to solve for n_t from (3), we must know the contingency plan for setting n_{t+1} in order to be able to evaluate the conditional expectation that appears in (3). How will n_{t+1} be determined? At time $t+1$ the decision-maker will be facing a problem of the same form as (1) with n_t and Ω_{t+1} given, namely, to maximize

$$v_{t+1} = E_{t+1} \sum_{j=0}^{\infty} b^j g(n_{t+j}, n_{t+j+1}, z_{t+j+1}) \qquad (4)$$

subject to n_t given. At $t+1$ the first-order necessary condition for n_{t+1} is given by equating to zero the derivative of (4) with respect to n_{t+1}:

$$g_2(n_t, n_{t+1}, z_{t+1}) + bE_{t+1} g_1(n_{t+1}, n_{t+2}, z_{t+2}) = 0. \qquad (5)$$

Continuing in this way, we find that since n_{t+j} must be optimal at $t+j$, the plan for setting $n_t, n_{t+1}, n_{t+2}, \ldots$ must satisfy the system of stochastic difference equations

$$g_2(n_{t+j-1}, n_{t+j}, z_{t+j}) + bE_{t+j} g_1(n_{t+j}, n_{t+j+1}, z_{t+j+1}) = 0, \qquad j = 0, 1, 2, \ldots. \qquad (6)$$

Equations (6) are the stochastic Euler equations.

The transversality condition can be obtained as in Chapter IX, by considering a finite T horizon version of problem (1), obtaining the first-order condition for n_{t+T}, and then taking the limit of this condition as $T \to \infty$. This leads to the transversality condition

$$\lim_{T \to \infty} b^T E_t g_2(n_{T-1}, n_T, z_T) n_T = 0. \tag{7}$$

The object now is to find a stochastic process $\{n_{t+j}\}_{j=0}^{\infty}$ that satisfies the Euler equations (6) and the transversality condition (7). For most problems, finding an explicit solution to (6) and (7) is an imposing, if not an intractable, task.

Where the Euler equations and transversality condition are linear equations, it is possible to solve explicitly for the optimizing decision rule. To indicate how an explicit solution can be found, we return to our demand-for-labor example where $g(\cdot, \cdot, \cdot)$ is given by (2).

The firm seeks a stochastic process for employment to maximize

$$v_t = E_t \sum_{j=0}^{\infty} b^j \{(f_0 + a_{t+j} - w_{t+j}) n_{t+j} - \tfrac{1}{2} f_1 n_{t+j}^2 - \tfrac{1}{2} d(n_{t+j} - n_{t+j-1})^2\}$$

subject to n_{t-1} given. We assume that the firm faces exogenous stochastic processes $\{a_{t+j}\}_{j=0}^{\infty}$ and $\{w_{t+j}\}_{j=0}^{\infty}$ that are of exponential order less than $1/\sqrt{b}$, by which we mean that for some $K > 0$ and $1 \leq x < 1/\sqrt{b}$,

$$|E_t w_{t+j}| < K(x)^{j+t}, \qquad |E_t a_{t+j}| < K(x)^{j+t}$$

for all t and all $j > 0$. The Euler equations are

$$f_0 + a_{t+j} - w_{t+j} - f_1 n_{t+j} - d(n_{t+j} - n_{t+j-1}) + db E_{t+j}(n_{t+j+1} - n_{t+j}) = 0,$$
$$j = 0, 1, 2, \ldots$$

or

$$b E_{t+j} n_{t+j+1} + \phi n_{t+j} + n_{t+j-1} = d^{-1}(w_{t+j} - a_{t+j} - f_0), \qquad j = 0, 1, 2, \ldots \tag{8}$$

where $\phi = [-f_1 d^{-1} - (1 + b)]$. The transversality condition is

$$\lim_{T \to \infty} E_t b^T \{f_0 + a_{t+T} - w_{t+T} - f_1 n_{t+T} - d(n_{t+T} - n_{t+T-1})\} n_{T+t} = 0. \tag{9}$$

Equations (8) and (9) will be recognized as generalizations of the Euler equations and transversality condition, respectively, for the nonstochastic problem studied in Chapter IX since in the nonstochastic case we have trivially $E_{t+j} n_{t+j+1} = n_{t+j+1}$.

Our aim now is to find a stochastic process $\{n_{t+j}\}_{j=0}^{\infty}$ that satisfies (8) and (9). For convenience, let $z_{t+j} = d^{-1}(w_{t+j} - a_{t+j} - f_0)$. In the nonstochastic case, we found that the solution was

$$n_{t+j} = \lambda_1 n_{t+j-1} - \lambda_1 \sum_{i=0}^{\infty} \left(\frac{1}{\lambda_2}\right)^i z_{t+j+i}$$

where $\lambda_1 < 1 < \lambda_2$ and where λ_1 and λ_2 solve

$$1 + \frac{\phi}{b} L + \frac{1}{b} L^2 = (1 - \lambda_1 L)(1 - \lambda_2 L).$$

It is perhaps natural to guess that a solution to (8) and (9) will be given by

$$n_{t+j} = \lambda_1 n_{t+j-1} - \lambda_1 \sum_{i=0}^{\infty} \left(\frac{1}{\lambda_2}\right)^i E_{t+j} z_{t+j+i}, \qquad j = 0, 1, 2, \ldots. \tag{10}$$

That (10) is in fact the solution can be verified directly. First, shift (10) forward one period and use the law of iterated mathematical expectations to condition both sides on Ω_{t+j} to get

$$E_{t+j} n_{t+j+1} = \lambda_1 n_{t+j} - \lambda_1 \sum_{i=0}^{\infty} \left(\frac{1}{\lambda_2}\right)^i E_{t+j} z_{t+j+1+i}. \tag{11}$$

Substituting (10) and (11) into the Euler equation (8) gives

$$b\left\{ -\lambda_1 \sum_{i=0}^{\infty} \left(\frac{1}{\lambda_2}\right)^i E_{t+j} z_{t+j+1+i} \right\}$$

$$+ \{b\lambda_1 + \phi\} \left\{ \lambda_1 n_{t+j-1} - \lambda_1 \sum_{i=0}^{\infty} \left(\frac{1}{\lambda_2}\right)^i E_{t+j} z_{t+j+i} \right\} + n_{t+j-1} = z_{t+j},$$

which must hold identically if the candidate (10) is to solve the Euler equations. But since $-\phi = b(\lambda_1 + \lambda_2)$ and $b\lambda_2 = 1/\lambda_1$, we have that $\{b\lambda_1 + \phi\}\lambda_1 = -1$, which makes the preceding equation collapse to

$$-\sum_{i=0}^{\infty} \left(\frac{1}{\lambda_2}\right)^{i+1} E_{t+j} z_{t+j+i+1} + \sum_{i=0}^{\infty} \left(\frac{1}{\lambda_2}\right)^i E_{t+j} z_{t+j+i} = z_{t+j},$$

which does hold identically. This verifies that the candidate solution satisfies the Euler equation. Under the assumption that z_t is of exponential order less than $1/\sqrt{b}$, it can be shown as in Chapter IX that the transversality condition is also satisfied.

Actually, there is no need to guess that (10) is the correct solution since the following constructive method can be used to find the solution of the Euler equation. Write the Euler equation as

$$bE_s n_{s+1} + \phi E_s n_s + E_s n_{s-1} = E_s z_s. \tag{12}$$

This equation can be expressed as

$$(bB^{-2} + \phi B^{-1} + 1)E_s n_{s-1} = E_s z_s$$

where the operator B is defined by $B^{-j}E_{s-1}n_s = E_{s-1}n_{s+j}$ for integer j.[2] The preceding equation can be expressed as

$$b(\lambda_1 - B^{-1})(\lambda_2 - B^{-1})E_s n_{s-1} = E_s z_s \tag{13}$$

where $b(\lambda_1 - B^{-1})(\lambda_2 - B^{-1}) = (bB^{-2} - b(\lambda_1 + \lambda_2)B^{-1} + b\lambda_1\lambda_2) = bB^{-2} + \phi B^{-1} + 1$. Without loss of generality, we select $|\lambda_1| < 1$ and $\lambda_2 = 1/\lambda_1 b$. Operate on both sides of the above equation with $[(\lambda_2 - B^{-1})]^{-1}$ to obtain the solution[3]

$$(\lambda_1 - B^{-1})E_s n_{s-1} = \frac{1}{b}\frac{1}{(\lambda_2 - B^{-1})}E_s z_s + c\lambda_2{}^s = \frac{1}{b\lambda_2}\frac{1}{1 - (1/\lambda_2)B^{-1}}E_s z_s + c\lambda_2{}^s$$

where c is a constant which must be set to zero to satisfy the transversality condition. Using $\lambda_2^{-1} = b\lambda_1$ and the definition of the B operator, this equation can be expressed as

$$n_s - \lambda_1 n_{s-1} = -\lambda_1 \sum_{i=0}^{\infty} (\lambda_1 b)^i E_s z_{s+i}, \tag{14}$$

---

[2] It is necessary to distinguish two operators B and L. The operator B is defined by

$$B^{-1}[Ex_{t+j}|\Omega_{t-1}] = Ex_{t+j+1}|\Omega_{t-1},$$

i.e., application of B^{-1} shifts forward by one period the date on the variables whose conditional forecast is being computed, but leaves the information set unaltered. The lag operator L is defined by

$$L^j x_t = x_{t-j}.$$

In particular, notice that this definition implies that

$$L^{-1}(Ex_{t+j}|\Omega_{t-1}) = Ex_{t+j+1}|\Omega_t,$$

so that application of L^{-1} shifts both the random variable x *and* the information set Ω forward by one period.

[3] We must be careful here because the properties of B make the forward inverse of $1 - \lambda_2 B$ the only legitimate one, apart from reasons of convergence. Operating on both sides of an equation with polynomials in nonpositive powers of B is legitimate. But it is *not* legitimate to operate with polynomials in positive powers of B. For example, $E_t x_{t+1} = E_t y_{t+1}$ does *not* imply that $BE_t x_{t+1} = BE_t y_{t+1}$, i.e., $x_t = y_t$. The operation in the text is legitimate because it involves operating only with polynomials in nonpositive powers of B.

which, as we have already verified, is a solution of the Euler equation that satisfies the transversality condition.[4]

The solution to our quadratic problem has the special characteristic that only the conditional means of the z_{t+j} appear, not any higher moments. The solution is said to exhibit the "certainty equivalence" or "separation" principle possessed by quadratic $g(\ )$'s. That is, the problem can be separated into two stages: first, get minimum mean squared error forecasts of the exogenous z_t, which are the conditional expectations $E_t z_{t+j}$; second, at time t, solve the nonstochastic optimization problem

$$\underset{n_t, n_{t+1}, \ldots}{\text{maximize}} \ V_t = \sum_{j=0}^{\infty} b^j g(n_{t+j-1}, n_{t+j}, E_t z_{t+j}), \qquad n_{t-1} \text{ fixed.}$$

Solving this separated problem gives the correct solution for n_t, and as settings for n_{t+j} the correct values of $E_t n_{t+j}, j \geq 1$. This separation of forecasting from optimization considerations is computationally very convenient and explains why quadratic objective functions are assumed in much applied work. For general functional forms for $g(\cdot, \cdot, \cdot)$, the certainty equivalence principle does not hold, so that the forecasting and optimization problems do not "separate."

2. OPTIMAL LINEAR POLICIES

The decision rule (10) sets n_t as a linear function of n_{t-1} and the conditional expectations $E_t w_{t+i}$ and $E_t a_{t+i}$, $i = 0, 1, 2, \ldots$. However, in general these conditional expectations are nonlinear functions of the information in Ω_t. Given particular stochastic processes for w_t and a_t, Equation (10) can be solved for a decision rule expressing n_t as, in general, a nonlinear function of n_{t-1} and Ω_t. This is the optimal decision rule.

Suppose that we wish to consider maximizing v_t while restricting ourselves to the class of decision rules that express n_t as linear functions of n_{t-1} and the information in Ω_t. Suppose that $g(\ )$ is given by (2), so that the optimal

---

[4] It can be verified that another stochastic process for $\{n_{t+j}\}$ that satisfies the Euler equations and the transversality condition is given by

$$n_{t+j} = \lambda_1 n_{t+j-1} - \lambda_1 \sum_{i=0}^{\infty} \lambda_2^{-i} z_{t+j+i}. \qquad (*)$$

This stochastic process is one in which values of n_{t+j} depend on future values of z_{t+j}, which we assume are not observable at time $t + j$. Consequently, equation $(*)$ is not a solution of our original problem, which is to find a plan for choosing n_{t+j} as a function of information Ω_{t+j} that is assumed to be available at time $t + j$. The stochastic process for $\{n_{t+j}\}$ that satisfies the Euler equations and the transversality conditions and that also can be expressed as a function of the information known at time $t + j$ is said to be a *realizable* or *nonanticipative* solution of the first-order conditions. Thus, a solution of our problem can be obtained by finding the realizable solution of the Euler equations and the transversality condition.

(nonlinear) decision rule obeys (10). Then the optimal linear rule can be obtained by replacing the conditional mathematical expectations in (10) with the corresponding linear least squares projections on the information set Ω_t.

In the special case where $\{z_{t+j}\}$ is a multivariate normal stochastic process, conditional mathematical expectations are linear and equal the corresponding linear least squares projections. In this case, under a quadratic objective function, linear least squares policies are optimal among the class of all decision rules making n_t a function of n_{t-1} and Ω_t.

With Gaussian (i.e., normal) exogenous processes $\{w_t\}$ and $\{a_t\}$, the decision rule n_t would, in general, with positive probability call for negative settings of employment on occasion. Therefore, with Gaussian w_t and a_t processes, the decision rule (10) does not with probability one build in the nonnegativity constraint $n_{t+j} \geq 0$ for all j. With our setup with Gaussian processes, it is usual to assume that the variances of w_t and a_t are sufficiently small relative to the pertinent constants (i.e., f_0 and the constants in the stochastic processes for w_t and a_t) that negative n's would be called for with very small probability. Alternatively, one could assume various kinds of non-Gaussian distributions of innovations for w_t and a_t that are sufficiently truncated that $\{n_t\}$ would be nonnegative with probability one. In that case it is necessary to replace $E_t w_{t+i}$ and $E_t a_{t+i}$ with linear least squares forecasts in (10) in order to retain a linear decision rule.

3. LUCAS'S CRITIQUE

In Chapter XI, we derived a formula for the linear least squares prediction of a geometric lead of the kind that appears in equation (14). In particular, suppose that z_t has the autoregressive representation

$$a(L)z_t = \varepsilon_t \tag{15}$$

where $a(L) = 1 - a_1 L - \cdots - a_r L^r$ and where $\varepsilon_t = z_t - P[z_t | z_{t-1}, \ldots]$. Then formula (90) of Chapter XI asserts that

$$E_t \sum_{i=0}^{\infty} \lambda_2^{-i} z_{t+i} = \frac{(1 - \lambda_1 ba(\lambda_1 b)^{-1} a(L) L^{-1})}{1 - \lambda_1 b L^{-1}} z_t$$

$$= a(\lambda_1 b)^{-1} \left[1 + \sum_{j=1}^{r-1} \left(\sum_{k=j+1}^{r} (\lambda_1 b)^{(k-j)} a_k \right) L^j \right] z_t \tag{16}$$

where $\lambda_1 b = \lambda_2^{-1}$.

Substituting (16) into (14) gives the *pair* of equations

$$n_t = \lambda_1 n_{t-1} - \lambda_1 \frac{(1 - \lambda_1 ba(\lambda_1 b)^{-1} a(L) L^{-1})}{1 - \lambda_1 b L^{-1}} z_t \tag{17a}$$

$$a(L)z_t = \varepsilon_t. \tag{17b}$$

Equation (17a) is an optimal linear *decision rule* for employment which expresses employment at t as a linear function of the relevant information possessed by the firm at t, namely n_{t-1} and $z_t, z_{t-1}, \ldots, z_{t-r+1}$. Equation (17a) asserts that the form of dependence on $z_t, z_{t-1}, \ldots, z_{t-r+1}$ depends on the nature of the stochastic process for $\{z_t\}$, by virtue of the appearance of the parameters of $a(L)$ in (17a). The variables $(z_t, z_{t-1}, \ldots, z_{t-r+1})$ appear in (17a) only because they are used to predict $\sum_{j=0}^{\infty} (\lambda_1 b)^j z_{t+j}$. The best predictor of this geometric sum depends on the nature of the stochastic process for $\{z_t\}$, which is why the parameters of $a(L)$ appear in (17a).

The fact that the optimal decision rule for n_t inherits parameters from the stochastic process for $\{z_t\}$ implies that one cannot in general expect to find a single decision rule that will be optimal across a range of hypothetical processes for the variables z_t that enter either the objective function or the constraints. That is, the parameters $h_2, \ldots, h_r$ in the decision rule for employment,

$$n_t = h_1 n_{t-1} + h_2 z_t + h_3 z_{t-1} + \cdots + h_r z_{t-r+1}, \tag{18}$$

depend on the law of motion (15) of z_t. In general, it is fruitless to search for a single decision rule of the form $n_t = h(n_{t-1}, \Omega_t)$ that will hold across a range of hypothetical environments (laws of motion for $\Omega_t = z_t, z_{t-1}, \ldots, z_{t-r+1}$). This principle was stated in the context of labor supply behavior by Gordon and Hynes (1970) and also underlies Robert E. Lucas's critique of econometric policy evaluation procedures as they existed in 1973 (1976). Lucas observed that those policy evaluation procedures relied on Keynesian models that assumed that decision rules like (18) were *structural* in the sense of being invariant under hypothetical interventions in the processes for z_t (or Ω_t). Keynesian models consisted of collections of decision rules for consumption, investment in capital, employment, and portfolio balance. In evaluating alternative policy rules for the government (i.e. laws of motion for components of Ω_t or z_t controlled by the government) those private decision rules were assumed to be fixed. (See Chapter XVII below for some examples of such policy control exercises.) Lucas criticized such procedures on the grounds that optimal decision theory implies that the decision rules of private agents are themselves functions of the laws of motion chosen by the government for its components of z_t or Ω_t. That is, consumption, investment, and portfolio balance schedules ought not to be regarded as structural.[5] Instead, policy evaluation procedures should take into account the dependence of private decision rules on the government's choice of a policy rule. In Section 8 and the following chapter, we study some optimal policy problems for the government that respect this dependence.

---

[5] Because of the present structure of a quadratic objective function and a linear law of motion for z_t, the decision rule (17a) is independent of the variance of the innovation (ε_t). In particular, all of the points made in this paragraph hold even if $E\varepsilon_t^2 = 0$, in which case the firm can forecast future z's perfectly from current and past z_t's. The point being made here was stated for a continuous time model of Chapter I (p. 41).

4. INVESTMENT

We now apply these dynamic optimization methods to Lucas and Prescott's (1971) model of investment under uncertainty. To be able to use our simple optimization tools, we must specialize their model by rigging the specification of demand and technology so that the optimization problems involved fit our linear–quadratic setup. Lucas and Prescott's model provides an interesting illustration of the concept of a "rational expectations equilibrium" in which the objects under study are stochastic processes that satisfy particular equilibrium conditions. The practical interest in Lucas and Prescott's model is that it provides a framework for performing econometric evaluation of the effects of alternative tax policy regimes on the rate of investment.

Our method will be first to study a "perfect foresight" model in which the exogenous variables are nonstochastic and hence reasonably posited to be perfectly predicted. It is then easy to move to a stochastic setting where the exogenous variables are stochastic processes about which agents have particular kinds of information.

We consider an industry in which n identical competitive firms use a single input, capital, to produce a single output. The industry demand curve for output at time t is

$$p_t = A_0 - A_1 Y_t + u_t, \qquad A_0, A_1 > 0, \tag{19}$$

where p_t is the price of output at t, Y_t is industry output, and u_t is a shock to demand. The output of each firm is $f_0 k_t$ where k_t is the firm's capital stock at time t and $f_0 > 1$. Industry output is then $Y_t = n f_0 k_t$.

The representative firm is competitive in the output and factor markets and thus is a price-taker with respect to the sequence of output prices $\{p_{t+j}\}_{j=0}^{\infty}$ and the sequence of prices of capital $\{J_{t+j}\}_{j=0}^{\infty}$. We begin by studying the non-stochastic case in which $\{J_{t+j}\}$ and $\{u_{t+j}\}$ are known sequences of exponential order less than $1/\sqrt{b}$. We shall also tentatively assume that the price sequence $\{p_{t+j}\}$ facing the firm is of exponential order less than $1/\sqrt{b}$, although we shall eventually solve for $\{p_{t+j}\}$ as an endogenous sequence. In the nonstochastic case currently under study, at time t the representative firm faces known sequences $\{p_{t+j}\}_{j=0}^{\infty}$, $\{J_{t+j}\}_{j=0}^{\infty}$ and chooses a sequence of capital stocks $\{k_{t+j}\}_{j=0}^{\infty}$ to maximize discounted present value

$$v_t = \sum_{j=0}^{\infty} b^j \left\{ p_{t+j}(f_0 k_{t+j}) - J_{t+j}(k_{t+j} - k_{t-1+j}) - \frac{d}{2}(k_{t+j} - k_{t-1+j})^2 \right\} \tag{20}$$

subject to k_{t-1} given. Here $d > 0$ is a coefficient that determines costs, internal to the firm, of adjusting its capital stock rapidly. The discount factor b obeys $0 < b < 1$.

The Euler equation for this problem is

$$p_{t+j} f_0 - J_{t+j} + b J_{t+j+1} - d(1+b)k_{t+j} + b \, d k_{t+j+1} + d k_{t+j-1} = 0,$$

$$j = 0, 1, \ldots. \tag{21}$$

We can rewrite this as

$$b\left(1 - \left(1 + \frac{1}{b}\right)L + \frac{1}{b}L^2\right)k_{t+j+1} = \frac{1}{d}(J_{t+j} - bJ_{t+j+1} - p_{t+j}f_0)$$

or

$$b\left(1 - \frac{1}{b}L\right)(1 - L)k_{t+j+1} = \frac{1}{d}(J_{t+j} - bJ_{t+j+1} - p_{t+j}f_0).$$

The solution of this difference equation that satisfies the transversality condition[6] is

$$(1 - L)k_{t+j+1} = \frac{-d^{-1}}{1 - bL^{-1}}(J_{t+j+1} - bJ_{t+j+2} - p_{t+j+1}f_0), \qquad (22)$$

which gives the firm's rate of investment as a function of future values of the output price and the price of capital.

While the representative firm perceives the output price as being independent of its own decisions about capital, the price is influenced by the actions of all firms together since p_t satisfies the market demand curve (19). As all firms vary their capital stocks together, the market price varies according to $p_t = A_0 - A_1 nf_0 k_t + u_t$. We now seek an *equilibrium* pair of sequences $\{\bar{p}_{t+j}\}_{j=0}^{\infty}$, $\{\bar{k}_{t+j}\}_{j=0}^{\infty}$ that satisfy the following two equilibrium conditions:

(i) Given the representative firm's equilibrium capital sequence $\{\bar{k}_{t+j}\}_{j=0}^{\infty}$, prices $\{\bar{p}_{t+j}\}_{j=0}^{\infty}$ clear the market, i.e.,

$$\bar{p}_{t+j} = A_0 - A_1 Y_{t+j} + u_{t+j} = A_0 - A_1 nf_0 \bar{k}_{t+j} + u_{t+j}.$$

(ii) When the representative firm faces the sequence $\{\bar{p}_{t+j}\}$ as a price-taker, the sequence $\{\bar{k}_{t+j}\}$ maximizes present value (20).

Thus, we seek an equilibrium in which the firm is on its demand curve (22) for capital and the market clears so that (19) is satisfied.

To find an equilibrium capital sequence, substitute $A_0 - A_1 f_0 nk_{t+j} + u_{t+j}$ for p_{t+j} in the Euler equation (21) to obtain[7]

$$A_0 f_0 + f_0 u_{t+j} - J_{t+j} + bJ_{t+j+1} - \{d(1 + b) + A_1 f_0^2 n\}k_{t+j}$$
$$+ dk_{t+j-1} + dbk_{t+j+1} = 0. \qquad (23)$$

---

[6] The transversality condition is derived by a procedure analogous to the one used in Section 1 and in Chapter IX.

[7] In order that we obtain a rational expectations competitive equilibrium, it is important that $A_0 - A_1 f_0 nk_{t+j} + u_{t+j}$ is substituted for p_{t+j} only after the Euler equation has been obtained, i.e., *after* and not before (20) has been differentiated with respect to k_{t+j}. This insures that the firm is acting as a price taker with respect to the $\{p_{t+j}\}$ sequence. If one substitutes $A_0 - A_1 f_0 nk_{t+j} + u_{t+j}$ for p_{t+j} in (20) *before* differentiating with respect to k_{t+j}, one obtains a rational expectations monopoly equilibrium.

Write this equation as

$$bk_{t+j+1} + \phi k_{t+j} + k_{t+j-1} = d^{-1}\{J_{t+j} - bJ_{t+j+1} - f_0 u_{t+j} - A_0 f_0\}$$

where

$$\phi = -\left((1+b) + \frac{A_1 f_0^2 n}{d}\right).$$

As earlier, write this equation as

$$b\left(1 + \frac{\phi}{b}L + \frac{1}{b}L^2\right)k_{t+j+1} = \frac{1}{d}\{J_{t+j} - bJ_{t+j+1} - f_0 u_{t+j} - A_0 f_0\}$$

or

$$b(1 - \lambda_1 L)(1 - \lambda_2 L)k_{t+j+1} = d^{-1}\{J_{t+j} - bJ_{t+j+1} - f_0 u_{t+j} - A_0 f_0\}$$

where

$$\left(1 + \frac{\phi}{b}L + \frac{1}{b}L^2\right) = (1 - \lambda_1 L)(1 - \lambda_2 L) \quad \text{and} \quad \lambda_1 < 1 < \frac{1}{b} < \lambda_2.$$

The solution for k_{t+j+1} that satisfies the transversality condition for the firm's problem is

$$k_{t+j+1} = \lambda_1 k_{t+j} - \frac{\lambda_1 d^{-1}}{1 - \lambda_2^{-1} L^{-1}} \{J_{t+j+1} - bJ_{t+j+2} - f_0 u_{t+j+1} - A_0 f_0\},$$

$$j = -1, 0, 1, 2, \ldots. \quad (24)$$

This gives the equilibrium $\{k_{t+j}\}$ sequence as a function of initial capital k_{t-1} and future values of the exogenous demand shock u_t and the factor price J_t.

To obtain the equilibrium output price sequence, we substitute the equilibrium k_{t+j} sequence into the market demand schedule to obtain

$$p_{t+j} = A_0 - A_1 n f_0 k_{t+j} + u_{t+j}. \quad (25)$$

By construction, we have generated sequences $\{k_{t+j}\}$, $\{p_{t+j}\}$ that satisfy our equilibrium conditions (i) and (ii).

5. A DIGRESSION ON THE RELATION BETWEEN EQUILIBRIUM AND OPTIMALITY

Suppose that we pose Lucas and Prescott's question, Is the difference equation (23) that determines the market equilibrium capital sequence the Euler equation for an interesting maximum problem? The chances for an affirmative answer look promising since (23) is in the form of an Euler equation. Consider the maximum problem: maximize

$$W_t = \sum_{j=0}^{\infty} b^j \{[A_0 f_0 n k_{t+j} - \tfrac{1}{2} A_1 (f_0^2 n^2 k_{t+j}^2) + f_0 n u_{t+j} k_{t+j}]$$

$$- n J_{t+j}(k_{t+j} - k_{t+j-1}) - \tfrac{1}{2} dn(k_{t+j} - k_{t+j-1})^2\}, \qquad (26)$$

subject to k_{t-1} given. It is readily verified that the Euler equation for this problem is exactly (23). Now the term in brackets is the area under the demand curve for output associated with the capital sequence $\{k_{t+j}\}$. For we have

$$\int_0^{Y_t} (A_0 - A_1 x + u_t) \, dx = A_0 Y_t - \tfrac{1}{2} A_1 Y_t^2 + Y_t u_t$$

$$= A_0 f_0 n k_t - \tfrac{1}{2} A_1 f_0^2 n^2 k_t^2 + f_0 n k_t u_t.$$

Thus the equilibrium that we have calculated implicitly maximizes the social welfare criterion (26), which equals the discounted consumer surplus minus producer surplus.

Lucas and Prescott used the observation that an equilibrium implicitly solves a social welfare problem to enable them to characterize the equilibrium in situations where the direct method that we were able to use to construct the equilibrium $\{p_{t+j}\}$, $\{k_{t+j}\}$ is not available. The special linear–quadratic nature of our setup is what enabled us to construct the equilibrium directly. In more general settings Lucas and Prescott's device is very handy, for it enables the model builder to replace a complicated "fixed point" problem with a maximization problem.

6. INVESTMENT UNDER UNCERTAINTY

Let us now take $\{u_{t+j}\}_{j=0}^{\infty}$ and $\{J_{t+j}\}_{j=0}^{\infty}$ to be exogenous stochastic processes of exponential order less than $1/\sqrt{b}$. The representative firm is a price-taker with respect to $\{J_{t+j}\}$ and also with respect to the output market equilibrium price stochastic process $\{p_{t+j}\}$. At time t the firm has an information set Ω_t consisting of at least $\{p_t, p_{t-1}, \ldots, J_t, J_{t-1}, \ldots, k_{t-1}, k_{t-2}, \ldots, u_t, u_{t-1}, \ldots\}$. The firm chooses a stochastic process $\{k_{t+j}\}_{j=0}^{\infty}$ to maximize

$$v_t = E_t \sum_{j=0}^{\infty} b^j \left\{ p_{t+j} f_0 k_{t+j} - J_{t+j}(k_{t+j} - k_{t+j-1}) - \frac{d}{2}(k_{t+j} - k_{t+j-1})^2 \right\}, \qquad (27)$$

subject to k_{t-1} given. Here $E_t(x) \equiv E(x)|\Omega_t$, where E is the mathematical expectation operator. Paralleling our analysis in Section 1, it is readily verified that the firm's optimum plan is to choose the following stochastic process for capital:

$$k_{t+j} = k_{t+j-1} - \frac{1}{d} \sum_{i=0}^{\infty} b^i E_{t+j} \{ J_{t+j+i} - b J_{t+j+1+i} - f_0 p_{t+j+i} \}, \qquad (28)$$

which agrees with our solution (22) in the nonstochastic case.

While the price process p_t is given to each firm, it is not given to the market as a whole. We now seek an *equilibrium* pair of stochastic processes $\{\bar{p}_{t+j}\}_{j=0}^{\infty}$ and $\{\bar{k}_{t+j}\}_{j=0}^{\infty}$ that satisfy the following two equilibrium conditions:

(i) Given the representative firm's optimal contingency plan (stochastic process) for setting $\{\bar{k}_{t+j}\}$, the stochastic process for prices $\{\bar{p}_{t+j}\}_{j=0}^{\infty}$ clears the output market, i.e.,

$$\bar{p}_{t+j} = A_0 - A_1 n f_0 \bar{k}_{t+j} + u_{t+j}.$$

(ii) When the representative firm faces the stochastic process $\{\bar{p}_{t+j}\}_{j=0}^{\infty}$ as a price-taker, the stochastic process $\{\bar{k}_{t+j}\}_{j=0}^{\infty}$ maximizes expected present value (27).

An equilibrium satisfying (i) and (ii) is said to be a "rational expectations equilibrium" because firms are being assumed to form the forecasts of the future output prices that appear in (27) by taking conditional mathematical expectations with respect to the stochastic process that actually governs prices.

We seek a pair of stochastic processes $\{k_{t+j}\}$, $\{p_{t+j}\}$ in which the firm is following its contingency plan (28) and the market clears so that (19) is satisfied.

Proceeding in complete analogy with the nonstochastic analysis, it is straightforward to show that the equilibrium processes for $\{k_{t+j}\}$ and $\{p_{t+j}\}$ satisfy

$$k_{t+j+1} = \lambda_1 k_{t+j} - \frac{\lambda_1}{d} \sum_{i=0}^{\infty} \left(\frac{1}{\lambda_2} \right)^i E_{t+j+1} \{ J_{t+j+1+i}$$

$$- b J_{t+j+2+i} - f_0 u_{t+j+1+i} - A_0 f_0 \}, \qquad (29)$$

$$p_{t+j} = A_0 - A_1 n f_0 k_{t+j} + u_{t+j}. \qquad (30)$$

Now suppose that J_t and u_t are governed by the stochastic processes

$$a(L)J_t = \varepsilon_{Jt}$$
$$g(L)u_t = \varepsilon_{ut} \qquad (31)$$

where $a(L) = 1 - a_1 L - \cdots - a_r L^r$, $g(L) = 1 - g_1 L - \cdots - g_r L^r$,

$$\varepsilon_{Jt} = J_t - P[J_t | J_{t-1}, u_{t-1}, J_{t-2}, u_{t-2}, \ldots]$$

and

$$\varepsilon_{ut} = u_t - P[u_t | J_{t-1}, u_{t-1}, J_{t-2}, u_{t-2}, \ldots].$$

We also assume that the zeros of $a(z)$ and $g(z)$ all exceed unity in absolute value.[8]

Using formula (90) of Chapter XI we have that (29) can be represented as

$$
\begin{aligned}
k_{t+j+1} = \lambda_1 k_{t+j} - \lambda_1 d^{-1}\Bigg\{ &\left[\frac{1 - \lambda_1 ba(\lambda_1 b)^{-1} a(L) L^{-1}}{1 - \lambda_1 bL^{-1}}\right] J_{t+j+1} \\
&- b\left[\frac{L^{-1}I - L^{-1}a(b\lambda_1)^{-1} a(L)}{1 - \lambda_1 bL^{-1}}\right] J_{t+j+1} \\
&- f_0\left[\frac{1 - \lambda_1 bg(\lambda_1 b)^{-1} g(L) L^{-1}}{1 - \lambda_1 bL^{-1}}\right] u_{t+j+1} - A_0 f_0/(1 - \lambda_1 b)\Bigg\}.
\end{aligned}
\tag{32}
$$

Equation (32) represents the equilibrium motion of capital.

7. SUPPLY, DEMAND AND IDENTIFICATION

We now indicate how equations (29) and (32) can be used to derive a dynamic "supply curve". By a supply curve we mean a schedule expressing the representative firm's output decision at t as a function of previous levels of output, current and lagged output prices p_t, and current and lagged factor prices J_t. After deriving such a schedule, we shall indicate why it is of limited usefulness either for econometric purposes or for analyzing policy interventions.

For convenience, we shall specialize the model by assuming that in (31) $g(L) = I$, and $a(L) = (1 - \rho L), |\rho| < 1$. Thus, u_t is a white noise, while J_t is a first order autoregressive process. These specializations will simplify the calculations without altering the main messages of our analysis.

The representative firm's stock k_t obeys (28):

$$
k_t = k_{t-1} - d^{-1} \sum_{j=0}^{\infty} b^j E_t\{J_{t+j} - bJ_{t+j+1}\} + d^{-1} f_0 \sum_{j=0}^{\infty} b^j E_t p_{t+j}.
\tag{28}
$$

For clarity, we now let K_t be the aggregate capital stock, $K_t = nk_t$. We set $\bar{f}_0 = f_0 \lambda_1 d^{-1} n$ and $\bar{A}_0 = A_0/(1 - \lambda_1 b)$. The aggregate capital stock follows the equilibrium law of motion given by (32), which in the case $a(L) = (1 - \rho L)$, $g(L) = 1$ simplifies to

$$
K_t = \lambda_1 K_{t-1} - \lambda_1 d^{-1} n \left\{\frac{1 - b\rho}{1 - \lambda_1 b\rho}\right\} J_t + \bar{f}_0(u_t + \bar{A}_0).
\tag{33}
$$

---

[8] Actually, we only need to require that the zeros of $a(z)$ and $g(z)$ all exceed $(b\lambda_1)^{-1}$ in absolute value. This condition is sufficient to guarantee that the expectation of the geometric sums in (29) converge.

Using (33) and $J_t = \rho J_{t-1} + \varepsilon_{Jt}$ we can represent the law of motion of the vector $(K_t, J_t, 1)$ as

$$
\begin{pmatrix} K_{t+1} \\ J_{t+1} \\ 1 \end{pmatrix} = \begin{pmatrix} \lambda_1 & \dfrac{-\lambda_1 \rho d^{-1} n(1-b\rho)}{(1-\lambda_1 b\rho)} & \bar{f}_0 \bar{A}_0 \\ 0 & \rho & 0 \\ 0 & 0 & 1 \end{pmatrix} \begin{pmatrix} K_t \\ J_t \\ 1 \end{pmatrix}
$$
$$
+ \begin{pmatrix} \dfrac{-\lambda_1 d^{-1} n(1-b\rho)}{(1-\lambda_1 b\rho)} \varepsilon_{Jt+1} + \bar{f}_0 u_{t+1} \\ \varepsilon_{Jt+1} \\ 0 \end{pmatrix}
$$

(34)

or

$$
x_{t+1} = A x_t + \varepsilon_{t+1} \tag{35}
$$

where $x_t = (K_t, J_t, 1)^T$, the superscript T denotes matrix transposition, and ε_{t+1} is the (3×1) white noise vector in (34). From Chapter (XI) we have the formula

$$
E_t \sum_{j=0}^{\infty} \mu^j x_{t+j} = (I - \mu A)^{-1} x_t. \tag{36}
$$

This formula holds for any scalar μ for which μ times the modulus of the eigenvalue of maximum modulus of A is less than unity in absolute value. Applying formula (36) to (34) gives

$$
E_t \sum_{j=0}^{\infty} \mu^j \begin{pmatrix} K_{t+j} \\ J_{t+j} \\ 1 \end{pmatrix}
$$
$$
= \begin{pmatrix} \dfrac{1}{1-\mu\lambda_1} K_t - \dfrac{\mu n \lambda_1 \rho d^{-1}(1-b\rho)}{(1-\lambda_1 b\rho)(1-\mu\lambda_1)(1-\rho\mu)} J_t + \dfrac{\bar{f}_0 \bar{A}_0}{(1-\mu\lambda_1)(1-\mu)} \\ \dfrac{1}{1-\rho\mu} J_t \\ \dfrac{1}{1-\mu} \end{pmatrix}
$$

(37)

We shall use this result shortly.

Returning to (28), using $a(L) = (1 - \rho L)$, we can express it as

$$
k_t = k_{t-1} - d^{-1} \left\{ J_t - f_0 \sum_{j=0}^{\infty} b^j E_t p_{t+j} \right\}.
$$

Substituting from the demand curve for p_{t+j} gives

$$k_t = k_{t-1} - d^{-1}J_t + \frac{d^{-1}f_0 A_0}{1-b} + d^{-1}f_0 u_t - d^{-1}f_0^2 A_1 \sum_{j=0}^{\infty} b^j E_t K_{t+j}. \quad (38)$$

Using formula (37) to evaluate the last term and rearranging gives

$$k_t = k_{t-1} - d^{-1}\left\{1 - \frac{f_0^2 A_1 b\lambda_1 \rho d^{-1} n}{(1-\lambda_1 b\rho)(1-b\lambda_1)}\right\}J_t$$

$$+ \left[\frac{d^{-1}f_0 A_0}{1-b} - \frac{d^{-1}f_0^2 nA_1 b\bar{f}_0 \bar{A}_0}{(1-b\lambda_1)(1-b)}\right]$$

$$+ d^{-1}f_0 u_t - \frac{d^{-1}f_0^2 A_1}{1-b\lambda_1} K_t.$$

Now use the demand curve $p_t = A_0 - A_1 f_0 K_t + u_t$ to eliminate K_t from the above equation to obtain

$$k_t = k_{t-1} - d^{-1}\left\{1 - \frac{nf_0^2 A_1 b\lambda_1 \rho d^{-1}}{(1-\lambda_1 b\rho)(1-b\lambda_1)}\right\}J_t$$

$$+ \left[\frac{d^{-1}f_0 A_0}{1-b} - \frac{d^{-1}f_0^2 A_1 b\bar{f}_0 \bar{A}_0}{(1-b\lambda_1)(1-b)} - \frac{d^{-1}f_0 A_0}{1-b\lambda_1}\right]$$

$$- \frac{d^{-1}f_0 b\lambda_1}{1-b\lambda_1} u_t + \frac{d^{-1}f_0}{1-b\lambda_1} p_t.$$

Use $y_t = f_0 k_t$ to obtain

$$y_t = y_{t-1} - d^{-1}f_0\left\{1 - \frac{f_0^2 A_1 b\lambda_1 \rho d^{-1} n}{(1-\lambda_1 b\rho)(1-b\lambda_1)}\right\}J_t$$

$$+ \left[\frac{d^{-1}f_0^2 A_0}{1-b} - \frac{d^{-1}f_0^3 A_1 b\bar{f}_0 \bar{A}_0 n}{(1-b\lambda_1)(1-b)} - \frac{d^{-1}f_0^2 A_0}{1-b\lambda_1}\right]$$

$$- \frac{d^{-1}f_0^2 b\lambda_1}{1-b\lambda_1} u_t + \frac{d^{-1}f_0^2}{1-b\lambda_1} p_t. \quad (39)$$

Equation (39) is a "dynamic supply curve," expressing supply decisions of the representative firm as a function of lagged supply decisions and current factor and output prices. If we had permitted $g(L)$ and $a(L)$ to be higher than first order Markov processes, lagged p_t's and J_t's would also have appeared in (39).

Note that all of the parameters of the demand curve appear in the dynamic supply curve (39). The parameters of the demand curve enter both directly and indirectly, via their influence upon λ_1. Further, the disturbance term u_t in the demand curve appears on the right side of the supply curve. The presence of u_t indicates a phenomenon that would be present in generalized versions of this model in which a vector of demand shifters z_t was added to the demand equation. In general, those demand shifters and any variables that help predict

("Granger cause") future values of those demand shifters would also appear in the dynamic supply schedule corresponding to (39). Thus, the forces that act on supply are not independent of those operating on demand. The economic intuition behind this circumstance is immediate. From (29) any variables that help predict future prices will appear in firms' supply curve as "information variables." In general, variables impinging on the current and future state of demand will be among such information variables.

The appearance in the supply curve of variables and parameters that appear in the demand curve subverts the exclusion restrictions that are often relied upon in econometrics to identify a supply curve. Those conditions identify a supply schedule by requiring that there exist variables impinging on demand that do not affect supply.[9] The failure of those standard conditions to apply means that if the parameters determining the supply schedule are to be identified, a different source of identification must be found. Fortunately, a source of identification is available, namely, the extensive set of restrictions across the parameters of the equilibrium law of motion of capital (32) (or the corresponding equation for supply Y_t) and the laws of motion (31) for J_t and u_t. These restrictions surface in the appearance of a common set of parameters, $a(L)$ and $g(L)$, in both (31) and (32). Methods for exploiting such restrictions for identification and estimation are discussed by John Taylor (1979, 1980) and Hansen and Sargent (1980).

Econometric work that incorporates these ideas typically aims to go beyond supply and demand curves to the parameters of preferences and technology underlying them. One reason is that the parameters of supply and demand are themselves functions of those deeper parameters. Furthermore, in order to evaluate alternative government policy rules, one needs knowledge about these deeper parameters. This point is illustrated repeatedly in Section 8 and the following chapter, where we study several problems of optimal taxation in the context of the present model of investment under uncertainty.

8. INVESTMENT UNDER UNCERTAINTY AND AN EXTERNALITY

We now modify the preceeding model by assuming that the technology is

$$y_t = (f_0 k_t + f_1 K_t), \qquad f_1 \neq 0$$

where k_t is the capital stock of the representative firm and $K_t = nk_t$ is the aggregate capital stock in the industry. When $f_1 \neq 0$, there is an externality, the aggregate capital stock helping each individual firm to produce output. This

---

[9] Put differently, Milton Friedman (1953) has argued that the concepts of "supply" and "demand" are useful analytical categories to the extent that they effectively sort the forces operating on price and quantity into mutually exclusive categories. The failure of dynamic theories to imply such a sorting is a compelling reason for going beyond supply and demand curves to the preferences, technologies, and endowment structures that underly them. See Sargent (1981, 1982) for further development of this argument. A classic article on the subject of this section is by Working (1927).

specification is a linear version of the specification of Paul Romer (1983). The remainder of the model without government intervention is the same as above.

For convenience, we define the one-period rental on capital as

$$w_t = J_t - bE_t J_{t+1}. \tag{40}$$

The motivation of definition (40) is that upon replacing $J_{t+j}(k_{t+j} - k_{t+j-1})$ with $w_{t+j}k_{t+j}$ in (27), definition (40) leads to the same marginal condition (29). (This is equivalent with a summation by parts argument, which would be the appropriate counterpart to the integration by parts argument used in Chapter III, p. 80 to motivate the definition of the cost of capital.) Alternatively, we could define the rental rate on capital as that stochastic process w_t satisfying the simple asset-pricing formula

$$J_t = \sum_{j=0}^{\infty} b^j E_t w_{t+j},$$

so that the current price of capital is the expected present discounted value of current and future rentals. This definition implies that J_t is related to w_t by the stochastic difference equation (40).

The representative firm chooses a contingency plan for k_t to maximize

$$E_0 \sum_{t=0}^{\infty} b^t \{ p_t(f_0 k_t + f_1 K_t) - w_t k_t - (d/2)(k_t - k_{t-1})^2 \}$$

subject to

$$p_t = A_0 - A_1(f_0 + nf_1)K_t + u_t$$

$$(1 - a_1 L - a_2 L^2 - \cdots - a_r L^r)w_t = \varepsilon_{wt}$$

$$(1 - c_1 L - c_2 L^2 - \cdots - c_r L^r)u_t = \varepsilon_{ut}$$

where the zeros of $(1 - a_1 z - \cdots - a_r z^r)$ and of $(1 - c_1 z - \cdots - c_r z^r)$ all exceed $\sqrt{b}$ in modulus, and $\varepsilon_{wt} = w_t - E_{t-1}w_t$, $\varepsilon_{ut} = u_t - E_{t-1}u_t$.[10] The Euler equation for the firm's problem is

$$E_t \{ p_t f_0 - w_t - d(k_t - k_{t-1}) + bd(k_{t+1} - k_t) \} = 0, \qquad t \geq 0. \tag{41}$$

---

[10] The optimization for the representative firm's problem is also subject to a perceived law of motion for the aggregate capital stock K_t,

$$K_t = H_0 + H_1 K_{t-1} + H_2 w_t + \cdots + H_{2+r-1}w_{t-r+1} + H_{2+r}u_t + \cdots + H_{2+2r-1}u_{t-r+1},$$

and subject to K_{t-1} known at t. The representative firm's optimization problem induces a mapping from the firm's perceived law of motion for K_t to the actual law of motion for K_t. A rational expectations equilibrium can be defined as a fixed point of this mapping. The rational expectations equilibrium for this model is studied using this mapping in Sargent (1981).

Substituting $p_t = A_0 - A_1(f_0 + nf_1)K_t + u_t$ into the above equation, multiplying by n, and rearranging gives

$$-bE_tK_{t+1} + [(1 + b) + A_1nd^{-1}(f_0{}^2 + nf_1f_0)]K_t - K_{t-1}$$
$$= d^{-1}[A_0 f_0 n + f_0 nu_t - nw_t]. \tag{42}$$

Equation (42) is the stochastic difference equation that the rational expectations competitive equilibrium implicitly solves.[11]

We now study the social planning problem in the context of the externality. Using $Y_t = (f_0 + nf_1)K_t$, the expected present value of consumer surplus plus producer surplus now is given by

$$E_0 \sum_{t=0}^{\infty} b^t\{A_0(f_0 + nf_1)K_t - (A_1/2)[(f_0 + nf_1)K_t]^2$$

$$+ u_t(f_0 + nf_1)K_t - w_tK_t - (d/(2n))(K_t - K_{t-1})^2\}, \tag{43}$$

which is to be maximized subject to K_{-1} given. The Euler equation for this problem is

$$-bE_tK_{t+1} + \left[(1 + b) + \frac{A_1n(f_0 + nf_1)^2}{d}\right]K_t - K_{t-1}$$

$$= d^{-1}[nA_0(f_0 + nf_1) + n(f_0 + nf_1)u_t - nw_t], \qquad t \geq 0. \tag{44}$$

Comparing equations (42) and (44), we see that when $f_1 > 0$, the stochastic difference equation (42) that is solved by the rational expectations competitive equilibrium is not the Euler equation (44) associated with the problem of maximizing the social planning welfare criterion (43). This is sufficient to establish that in the presence of the externality (i.e. $f_1 \neq 0$), the competitive equilibrium fails to be optimal relative to the welfare criterion (43).

We now describe how an intervention can be designed to correct the suboptimality stemming from the externality. The government is assumed to use a distorting tax on purchases of new capital in this industry to offset the distortion. (The tax is assumed to be rebated lump sum to the consumers of the

---

[11] Lucas and Prescott's equilibrium concept has the property that the law of motion of output price that is perceived by the representative firm prompts behavior by the firm that, in conjunction with market clearing, makes the actual law of motion of the output price equal to the perceived law. This fixed point property in the space of perceived laws of motion was something that previous researchers seemed to recognize as desirable, but had not attained. For example, both Nadiri and Rosen (1974) and Nerlove, Grether and Carvalho (1979) make remarks that can be interpreted as describing some properties of the mapping from a perceived to an actual law of motion for output prices that their models induce. In particular, see Nerlove, Grether and Carvalho's discussion of their concept of "quasi-rational expectations," and their recognition that their own equilibrium concept does not have the fixed point property of Lucas and Prescott's. Multiple input versions of Lucas and Prescott's model were studied by Hansen and Sargent (1981).

industry.) In particular, the government is supposed to collect a tax on the representative firm in the amount $\tau_t k_t$ at time t. The tax τ_t is chosen according to the schedule

$$\tau_t = (\alpha_0 + \alpha_1 u_t + \alpha_2 w_t + \alpha_3 k_t). \tag{45}$$

The schedule (45) is assumed to be known to the firm. The task of the government is to choose values of the constants $(\alpha_0, \alpha_1, \alpha_2, \alpha_3)$ that make the competitive equilibrium socially optimal, if this is possible.

Under this tax scheme, the representative firm maximizes

$$E_0 \sum_{t=0}^{\infty} b^t \{ p_t(f_0 k_t + f_1 K_t) - w_t k_t - (d/2)(k_t - k_{t-1})^2$$

$$- (\alpha_0 + \alpha_1 u_t + \alpha_2 w_t + \alpha_3 k_t) k_t \}$$

subject to k_{-1} given. The Euler equation for this problem is

$$p_t f_0 - w_t - d(k_t - k_{t-1}) + bdE_t(k_{t+1} - k_t) - \alpha_0 - \alpha_1 u_t - \alpha_2 w_t - 2\alpha_3 k_t = 0.$$

Substituting $p_t = A_0 - A_1[f_0 + nf_1]K_t + u_t$ into the above equation for p_t, and multiplying by n gives

$$-bE_t K_{t+1} + [(1 + b) + A_1 nd^{-1}(f_0^2 + nf_1 f_0) + 2\alpha_3 d^{-1}]K_t - K_{t-1}$$
$$= d^{-1}[(nA_0 f_0 - n\alpha_0) + (nf_0 - n\alpha_1)u_t - (n + \alpha_2 n)w_t]. \tag{46}$$

Equation (46) is the stochastic difference equation that is solved by the rational expectations competitive equilibrium in the presence of the tax schedule (45).

Evidently, if the government were to set $\alpha_0, \alpha_1, \alpha_2, \alpha_3$ to satisfy

$$\alpha_0 = -A_0 nf_1$$

$$\alpha_1 = -nf_1$$

$$\alpha_2 = 0 \tag{47}$$

$$\alpha_3 = (A_1 n/2)[(f_0 + nf_1)^2 - (f_0^2 + nf_1 f_0)],$$

then (46) and the Euler equation for the social planning problem (44) would be equivalent. It follows that if the parameters of the tax schedule is set according to (47), then the rational expectations competitive equilibrium with distorting taxes is socially optimal with respect to social welfare criterion (43).

Equations (47) display the information that the government needs in order to carry out an optimal intervention via a distorting tax schedule. The government needs to know parameters of preferences (A_0, A_1), technology (f_0, f_1), and of industry structure (n). The reason that rational expectations econometrics aims to estimate the "deep" parameters determining preferences and technologies is precisely because these are the parameters that are needed in order to derive optimal government policy interventions.

The current example is one in which there is a case for the government to intervene upon a rational expectations competitive equilibrium. This example illustrates one of the two main justifications for intervention: the presence of externalities. The second main reason is the need to collect government revenues and the nonavailability of nondistorting taxes. We move on to study this second reason in the next chapter.

9. CONCLUSIONS

The concept of a rational expectations competitive equilibrium which we have studied has the attractive property that firms in the industry are forecasting the output price optimally. The firms in the model forecast prices as well as the economist who is modelling them. The output price is endogenous, being influenced by firms' behavior in the light of their forecasts of the price. There is a mapping from firms' *perceived* law of motion for the output price to the *actual* law of motion. A rational expectations equilibrium is a fixed point of this mapping.

Linear versions of the Lucas–Prescott model, like those studied in this chapter, have served as the basis for a variety of applications. Econometric implementation of such models is described by Sargent (1981), and Hansen and Sargent (1980). Equilibrium linear models with multiple factors of production were studied by Hansen and Sargent (1981) and applied by Eichenbaum (1983)[12] to study inventory investment. Townsend (1983) studied two-industry versions of a linear Lucas–Prescott model in which the two industries are linked together by a signal extraction problem stemming from the structure of demand.[13]

Linear Lucas–Prescott models have been useful for studying the effects of government interventions on the equilibrium stochastic process for an industry or economy. Eckstein and Eichenbaum (1985a, 1985b) describe some examples. Hansen, Epple, and Roberds (1985) use a version of a Lucas–Prescott model to study a variety of non-competitive rational expectations equilibria in the context of a market for an exhaustible resource. Some of Hansen, Epple and

[12] Lucas and Prescott's equilibrium concept was fruitfully applied by Martin Eichenbaum (1983) in his study of inventories and sales. Eichenbaum observed that the solution of the social planning (market equilibrium) problem caused market-wide sales and inventories to interact dynamically according to an interrelated factor demand model. This was so even though Eichenbaum adopted precisely the same technology at the level of the firm which had caused earlier researchers to puzzle over an apparent "decomposition" (lack of dynamic cross-effects) of inventory and sales decisions. Other interesting applications of the Lucas–Prescott equilibrium concept can be found in Eckstein and Eichenbaum (1985).

[13] Townsend (1983) linked together two Lucas–Prescott industries by positing an "unobservable index structure" for their demand shock and by endowing them with one of several possible information structures. The firms in Townsend's models face signal extraction problems which are well posed only in light of the equilibrium law of motion for state variables in the other industry.

Roberds' methods can be used to model the optimal choice of government tax policy for a government that must raise revenues by taxing an industry that is in a rational expectations competitive equilibrium. The next chapter applies some of their methods to model taxation.

EXERCISES

1. Assume that

$$J_{t+1} = \alpha J_t + \eta_{t+1}, \qquad |\alpha| < 1/b,$$

$$u_{t+1} = \beta u_t + \varepsilon_{t+1}, \qquad |\beta| < 1/b,$$

where $E_t \eta_{t+1} = \bar{\eta}$ and $E_t \varepsilon_{t+1} = \bar{\varepsilon}$. Use this information and (29) to calculate a "reduced form" for investment of the form

$$k_{t+j+1} - \lambda_1 k_{t+j} = \gamma_0 + \gamma_1 J_{t+1+j} + \gamma_2 u_{t+1+j}$$

giving explicit formulas for γ_0, γ_1, and γ_2 in terms of λ_1, d, λ_2, α, β, $\bar{\eta}$, and $\bar{\varepsilon}$.

2. (Certainty equivalence principle). Let x be a random variable with probability density $g(x)$, and let α, a parameter, be set by a decision-maker. Let $f(x, \alpha)$ be concave and twice continuously differentiable. Consider *Problem 1*: choose α to maximize $Ef(x, \alpha) = \int f(x, \alpha) g(x) \, dx$.

   A. Find the first-order necessary condition for choosing α.

   B. Suppose that $f(x, \alpha) = (x, \alpha) A(x, \alpha)' + (x, \alpha) B$ where B is a 2×1 matrix, (x, α) is a 1×2 vector, and A is a 2×2 negative definite matrix. Prove that in this special case, choosing α to solve Problem 1 gives the same α as choosing α to solve the following *Problem 2*: choose α to maximize $f(Ex, \alpha)$. The equivalence of these answers in the special case of a quadratic objective function is known as the "certainty equivalence" or separation principle.

3. (Eckstein (1983)). There is a large number n of identical farms producing corn. Each farm maximizes

$$E_0 \sum_{t=0}^{\infty} b^t \left\{ p_{t+1} y_{t+1} - c_0 a_t - \frac{c_1}{2} a_t^2 - c_2 a_t a_{t-1} - w_t a_t \right\} \tag{1}$$

subject to a_{-1} given. Here $c_0, c_1, c_2 > 0$, $0 < b < 1$, a_t is acres planted at t, y_{t+1} is output at time $t + 1$, p_{t+1} is the price of corn at $t + 1$, and w_t is the cost of fertilizer applied per acre. Output is produced subject to the constant returns to scale production function

$$y_{t+1} = f a_t, \qquad f > 0. \tag{2}$$

The demand curve for corn is

$$p_{t+1} = \beta_0 - \beta_1 Y_{t+1} + u_{t+1} \tag{3}$$

where β_0, $\beta_1 > 0$, Y_{t+1} is total output at $t + 1$, $(Y_{t+1} \equiv n y_{t+1})$ and u_{t+1} is a random shock to demand. Assume that u_t follows the Markov process

$$u_t = \rho u_{t-1} + \varepsilon_t$$

$|\rho| < 1$, where ε_t is a "white noise", with $E\varepsilon_t = 0$, $E\varepsilon_t^2 = \sigma_\varepsilon^2$, $E\varepsilon_t \varepsilon_{t-j} = 0$ for $j \neq 0$. Assume that the fertilizer cost w_t follows the moving average process

$$w_t = d_0 \eta_t + d_1 \eta_{t-1}$$

where η_t is a serially uncorrelated random variable with mean zero. The farm is assumed to maximize (1) by choosing a linear contingency plan for setting a_t. At time t, the farm is assumed to see $w_t, w_{t-1}, \ldots, u_t, u_{t-1}, \ldots, a_{t-1}$, and industry-wide initial acreage $A_{t-1} (\equiv n a_{t-1})$

A. Carefully *define* a rational expectations equilibrium for this industry.

B. Describe how to compute a rational expectations equilibrium. Get as far as you can in computing the equilibrium for the following parameter values:

$$\beta_1 = 10^{-6} \qquad c_1 = 16$$

$$n = 10^6 \qquad c_2 = 4$$

$$f = 1 \qquad b = 1$$

(Find the equilibrium in terms of the unspecified parameters, i.e., d_0, d_1, etc.)
NOTE: These calculations should work out simply. If you have trouble, don't waste time on the arithmetic, but describe analytically the proper way to calculate the equilibrium.

C. Describe the effect on the equilibrium law of motion of A_t of a change in the fertilizer-cost process to the form

$$w_t = g_0 \varepsilon_t + g_1 \varepsilon_{t-1} + g_2 \varepsilon_{t-2}.$$

where ε_t is a white noise.

4. A small country produces one good, bananas, under competitive conditions. There is free entry into the industry within the country. The price of bananas, p_t, is determined exogenously to the country and is a stochastic process with Wold moving average representation

$$p_t = c(L)\varepsilon_t, \tag{1}$$

where $c(L) = \sum_{j=0}^{\infty} c_j L^j$, ε_t is fundamental for p_t and $c(L)^{-1}$ exists as square summable in nonnegative powers of L. Output of bananas at t, y_t, is determined via the single-factor production function

$$y_t = f(L)n_t \tag{2}$$

where $f(L) = \sum_{j=0}^{\infty} f_j L^j$, where $\sum_{j=0}^{\infty} f_j^2 < +\infty$, and n_t is employment. Each competitive firm faces a wage rate w_t, which it takes parametrically. For the country (industry) as a whole, however, the wage rate obeys the upward sloping supply schedule

$$w_t = \beta_0 + \beta_1 N_t, \qquad \beta_0, \beta_1 > 0, \tag{3}$$

where N_t is total employment of labor in the country's banana industry. (Either of the following specifications for N_t will do. First, $N_t = mn_t$, where m is the number of firms, and n_t is the employment of a representative firm, "fractional" values of n_t and m being acceptable. Second, there is a continuum of firms with $N_t = \int n_t(w) \, du(w)$, where $u(\cdot)$ is a measure over firms' employment). The representative firm faces p_t and w_t parametrically, and solves the following optimum problem

$$\max E_0 \sum_{t=0}^{\infty} \{p_t f(L)n_t - w_t n_t\} \tag{4}$$

subject to (1) with $\{p_t, p_{t-1}, \ldots\}$ being known at time t. Here E_t is conditional expectation given information at time t. Notice that there are constant returns to scale.

A. Find the "marginal expected present value" of employing an additional worker at time t.

B. Close the model by appealing to free entry and impose the equilibrium condition that wages adjust, via (3), to ensure zero expected present value. Derive the equilibrium condition restricting the wage process w_t in a form

$$w_t = E_t \sum_{j=0}^{\infty} h_j p_{t+j}$$

giving an explicit expression for the h_j's.

C. Assume that

$$f(L) = \frac{1}{1 - \lambda L}, \qquad |\lambda| < 1 \tag{*}$$

$$c(L) = \frac{1}{1 - \rho_1 L - \rho_2 L^2} \tag{**}$$

where the zeros of $(1 - \rho_1 z - \rho_2 z^2)$ lie outside the unit circle. Under these special specifications, derive a representation for the equilibrium wage process of the form

$$w_t = \sum_{j=0}^{\infty} g_j p_{t-j}, \tag{5}$$

giving explicit formulas for the g_j's as functions of $(\lambda, \rho_1, \rho_2)$.

D. Describe how representation (5) would change if a banana cartel were formed (one that excluded our country as a competitive fringe producer) that changed $c(L)$ from the form (**) to the form

$$c(L) = 1 + 0.99L.$$

How does this experiment illustrate Lucas's critique of pre-1973 econometric policy evaluation procedures?

5. (Stabilizing Prices vs. Quantities). Consider an industry consisting of n identical firms that produce a single good. Output y_t of the representative firm is related to its capital k_t by $y_t = f k_t$, $f > 0$. The representative firm maximizes

$$E_0 \sum_{t=0}^{\infty} \beta^t \{ p_t y_t - (w_t + \tau_t)k_t - (d/2)(k_t - k_{t-1})^2 \}, \qquad 0 < \beta < 1$$

where E_t is the expectations operator conditional on observations known at t, p_t is the price of the good, w_t is the rental rate on capital, τ_t is a specific tax-subsidy on capital, and $d > 0$ reflects costs of rapid adjustment. The demand curve is given by

$$p_t = A_0 - A_1 Y_t + u_t; \qquad A_0, A_1 > 0$$

where $Y_t = n y_t = n f k_t = f K_t$, and where u_t is a random shock to demand. Assume that w_t is a random process

$$w_t = \bar{\omega} + \varepsilon_{wt}$$

where ε_{wt} is a serially independent random variable with mean zero and constant variance. Assume that u_t is a serially independent random variable with mean zero and constant variance. At time t, the representative firm knows

$$\{ k_{t-1}, K_{t-1}, w_t, w_{t-1}, \ldots, u_t, u_{t-1}, \ldots, \tau_t, \tau_{t-1}, \ldots \}.$$

A. Initially assume that $\tau_t = 0$ for all t, so that capital is neither taxed nor subsidized. Define a *rational expectations competitive equilibrium*, and display the equilibrium law of motion for K_t.

B. Now suppose that the government sets τ_t as a linear function of

$$\{ u_{t-1}, u_{t-2}, \ldots, \varepsilon_{wt-1}, \varepsilon_{wt-2}, \ldots \}.$$

with a constant term of zero (this makes the subsidy-tax average out to zero over long periods of time). First, find a linear feedback law for τ_t that minimizes the variance of the *stationary* distribution of industry output Y_t (i.e., assume that the linear feedback rule has been operating forever to calculate the variance of Y). Second, find a linear feedback law for τ_t that minimizes the stationary variance of p_t.

(*Hint*: Write the equilibrium law of motion for K_t in the form $K_t = g_0 + g_1(L)u_t + g_2(L)\varepsilon_{wt}$ and proceed.)

    C. Under what more general assumption about the serial correlation pattern of the demand shock $\{u_t\}$ would the "objective" of minimizing the stationary variance of price lead to a different decision rule for τ_t than the objective of minimizing the stationary variance of quantity?

    D. Is it a good goal for policy to minimize the stationary variance of price? Of quantity?

6. An industry consists of a large number of n firms, produces a single good, and faces a demand schedule

$$p_t = A_0 - A_1 Y_t + u_t, \qquad A_0, A_1 > 0 \tag{1}$$

where p_t is the price at t, Y_t is total industry output at t, and u_t is a serially uncorrelated random process with mean zero. There are n identical firms, each with cost function

$$c_t = c_0 + c_1 y_t + \frac{c_2}{2} y_t^2 + \frac{c_3}{2}(y_t - y_{t-1})^2 + \frac{c_4}{2}(Y_t - Y_{t-1})^2 + J_t y_t + \tau_t y_t. \tag{2}$$

$$c_0, c_1, c_2, c_3, c_4 > 0$$

Here y_t is a representative firm's output, and $Y_t = n y_t$; J_t is a stochastic process representing the effects of factor prices on costs, and τ_t is a tax-subsidy rate set by the government. Assume that

$$J_t = \lambda J_{t-1} + \varepsilon_t, \qquad |\lambda| < 1 \tag{3}$$

where ε_t is a serially uncorrelated random process with mean zero. The tax parameter τ_t is set by the government according to the feedback rule

$$\tau_t = \delta_0 + \delta_1 y_t + \delta_2 y_{t-1} \tag{4}$$

where $\delta_0, \delta_1, \delta_2$ are constants. Each firm's tax rate thus depends on the firm's own output, a dependence recognized by the firm. In (2), the term $(c_4/2)(Y_t - Y_{t-1})^2$ reflects costs of adjusting industry-wide output over and above those taken into account by individual firms. There is thus an externality.

    A representative firm maximizes

$$E \sum_{t=0}^{\infty} \beta^t \{p_t y_t - c_t\}, \qquad 0 < \beta < 1 \tag{5}$$

with y_{-1} and Y_{-1} given.

    A. Define a rational expectations competitive equilibrium.

    B. Compute the rational expectations competitive equilibrium.

    C. Consider the "social planning" problem of maximizing the expected value of discounted consumer surplus minus producer surplus. (In formulating the social costs of production, omit the term $\tau_t y_t$ from the cost function (2)). For arbitrary settings of $(\delta_0, \delta_1, \delta_2)$ does the rational expectations competitive equilibrium solve this social planning problem?

    D. Find values of $(\delta_0, \delta_1, \delta_2)$ (if they exist) that make the rational expectations competitive equilibrium solve the social planning problem.

7. The duck decoy industry is under investigation by the Anti-Trust Division of the Justice Department. One group of economists in the division thinks that there is a conspiracy among the n firms in the industry to set price and quantity as though the industry were a monopoly. A second group argues that the industry is competitive. For $s = 1, \ldots, T$, time series data are available on industry output, Y_s, the price of duck decoys, p_s, aggregate capital at time s, K_s, and the rental rate on capital, w_s.

The industry consists of a fixed number of n identical firms. Duck decoys are produced according to the production function

$$y_t = fk_t, \qquad f > 0 \tag{1}$$

where y_t is output of the representative firm, and k_t is the capital stock of the representative firm at t. Aggregate output is

$$Y_t = fK_t \tag{2}$$

where

$$Y_t = ny_t, \qquad K_t = nk_t. \tag{3}$$

The demand for duck decoys obeys

$$p_t = A_0 - A_1 Y_t + u_t, \qquad A_0 > 0, \quad A_1 > 0 \tag{4}$$

where u_t is a random shock to demand with Wold moving average representation

$$u_t = \frac{1}{1 - \rho L} \varepsilon_{ut}, \qquad |\rho| < 1 \tag{5}$$

where ε_{ut} is a white noise with mean zero and variance σ_u^2. The rental rate on capital w_t is governed by the upward sloping supply curve to the industry

$$w_t = B_0 + B_1 K_t, \qquad B_0 > 0, \quad B_1 > 0. \tag{6}$$

The net cash flow at time t of the representative firm is

$$\pi_t = p_t y_t - w_t k_t - (d/2)(k_t - k_{t-1})^2. \tag{7}$$

The present value of the representative firm's cash flow is

$$E \sum_{t=0}^{\infty} b^t \pi_t, \qquad 0 < b < 1. \tag{8}$$

At time t, the firm takes $k_{t-1}, u_t, u_{t-1}, \ldots$, as given.

    A. Define a rational expectations competitive equilibrium.

    B. Compute the rational expectations competitive equilibrium.

    C. What "social planning problem" does the rational expectations equilibrium implicitly solve?

    D. Define a collusive or monopolistic rational expectations equilibrium.

    E. Compute the monopolistic rational expectations equilibrium.

    F. Show that the "feedback coefficient" of K_t on K_{t-1} is *smaller* in the monopolistic than in the competitive equilibrium. (Hint, a graphical argument will suffice.)

    G. Suppose that the Justice Department economists know the values of f, n, b, d. However, they do not know the values of (B_0, B_1, A_0, A_1) and would have to estimate them econometrically from observations on $(Y_s, K_s, s = 1, \ldots, T)$. (The Justice Department has no reliable data on P_s or w_s.) Given the information available to the economists, is it possible for them to determine whether the industry is behaving competitively or monopolistically?

    H. Suppose that the Justice Department economists know the values f, n, b, d. However, they do not know the values of (B_0, B_1, A_0, A_1) and would have to estimate them econonometrically from observations on $(Y_s, K_s, p_s, w_s, s = 1, \ldots, T)$. Given the information now assumed to be available to the economists, is it possible for them to determine whether the industry is behaving competitively or monopolistically?

REFERENCES

Eckstein, Z. (1984). "A rational expectations model of agricultural supply." *Journal of Political Economy*, Vol. 92, No. 1, pp. 1-19.

Eckstein, Z. and Eichenbaum, M. S. (1985a). "Inventories and quantity-constrained equilibria in regulated markets: the U.S. petroleum industry 1947-1972." In *Energy, Foresight and Strategy* (T. J. Sargent, ed.) Washington, D.C.: Resources for the Future.

Eckstein, Z. and Eichenbaum, M. S. (1985b). "Oil supply disruptions and the optimal tariff in a dynamic stochastic equilibrium model." In *Energy, Foresight, and Strategy*, (T. J. Sargent, ed.) Washington, D.C.: Resources for the Future.

Eichenbaum, M. S. (1983). "A rational expectations equilibrium model of inventories of finished goods and employment." *Journal of Monetary Economics*, Vol. 12, No. 2, pp. 259-278.

Eichenbaum, M. S. (1984). "Rational expectations and the smoothing properties of inventories of finished goods." *Journal of Monetary Economics*, Vol. 14, No. 1, pp. 71-96.

Friedman, M. (1953). "The methodology of positive economics." In *Essays in Positive Economics* (Milton Friedman). Chicago: University of Chicago Press.

Gordon, D. F. and Hynes A. (1970). "On the theory of price dynamics." In *Microeconomic Foundations of Employment and Inflation Theory* (Edmund S. Phelps et al., eds.). New York: Norton.

Hansen, L. P. and Sargent, T. J. (1980). "Formulating and estimating dynamic linear rational expectations models." *Journal of Economic Dynamics and Control*, Vol. 2, No. 1, pp. 7-46. (Reprinted in: *Rational Expectations and Econometric Practice*, R. E. Lucas Jr. and T. J. Sargent, eds., University of Minnesota Press, 1981).

Hansen, L. P. and Sargent, T. J. (1981). "Linear rational expectations models for dynamically interrelated variables." In *Rational Expectations and Econometric Practice*, (R. E. Lucas Jr. and T. J. Sargent, eds.). Minneapolis: University of Minnesota Press.

Hansen, L. P., Epple, D. and Roberds, W. (1985). "Linear-quadratic duopoly models of resource depletion." In *Energy, Foresight and Strategy* (T. J. Sargent, ed.). Washington, D.C. Resources for the Future.

Holt, C. C., et al. (1960). *Planning Production, Inventories, and Work Force* (with contributions by C. P. Bonini and P. R. Winter), Englewood Cliffs, New Jersey: Prentice-Hall.

Kwakernaak, H. and Sivan, R. (1972). *Linear Optimal Control Systems*, New York: Wiley.

Lucas, R. E. Jr. (1976). "Econometric policy evaluation: a critique." *The Phillips Curve and the Labor Market* (K. Brunner and A. Meltzer, eds.) Vol. 1 of Carnegie-Rochester Conferences in Public Policy, a supplementary series to the *Journal of Monetary Economics*, Amsterdam: North-Holland.

Lucas, R. E. Jr. and Prescott, E. C. (1971). "Investment under uncertainty." *Econometrica*, Vol. 39, No. 5, pp. 659-681.

Nadiri, M. I. and Rosen, S. (1974). *A Disequilibrium Model of Demand for Factors of Production*, New York: National Bureau of Economic Research.

Nerlove, M., Grether, D. M. and Carvalho, J. (1979). *The Analysis of Economic Time Series*, New York: Academic Press.

Romer, P. M. (1983). "Externalities and Increasing Returns in Dynamic Competitive Analysis." *Working Paper No. 8319*, Department of Economics, University of Rochester.

Sargent, T. J. (1981). "Interpreting economic time series." *Journal of Political Economy*, Vol. 89, No. 2, pp. 213-248.

Sargent, T. J. (1982). "Beyond supply and demand curves in macroeconomics." *American Economic Review*, Vol. 72, No. 2, pp. 382-389.

Taylor, J. B. (1981). "Estimation and control of a macroeconomic model with rational expectations." *Econometrica*, Vol. 47, No. 5, pp. 1267-1286 (Reprinted in *Rational Expectations and Econometric Practice*, R. E. Lucas Jr. and T. J. Sargent, eds., University of Minnesota Press).

Taylor, J. B. (1980). "Output and price stability: an international comparison." *Journal of Econometric Dynamics and Control*, Vol. 2, No. 1, pp. 109–132.

Telser, L. G. and Graves, R. L. (1972). *Functional Analysis in Mathematical Economics*, Chicago, Illinois: University of Chicago Press.

Townsend, R. (1983). "Forecasting the forecasts of others." *Journal of Political Economy*, Vol. 91, No. 4, pp. 546–588.

Working, E. J. (1927). "What do statistical 'demand curves' show?" *Quarterly Journal of Economics*, Vol. 41, No. 1, pp. 212–235. (Reprinted in *Readings in Price Theory*, ed. by the AEA, Homewood, IL: Irwin, 1952.)

CHAPTER XV

DYNAMIC OPTIMAL TAXATION

1. INTRODUCTION

This chapter uses the model of Chapter XIV to study aspects of the problem of optimal dynamic taxation. It is assumed that there is an industry whose equilibrium is described by the model of Chapter XIV. A government authority is required to raise revenue of a given present value by taxing investment in this industry. The tax is distorting. The government's problem is to choose a strategy for taxing that maximizes discounted consumer surplus net of costs of production. The government authority acts as a "leader" in a dynamic game with the market. The "market" takes the government's tax strategy as given, and chooses capital according to a version of equation (22) of Chapter XIV, a version in which a function of expected future values of the tax rate τ_t is added to the right hand side. The government chooses a strategy for taxes taking into account its knowledge of the dependence of market equilibrium k_t upon its choice of $\{\tau_t\}$.

This optimal taxation example is a useful vehicle for illustrating features that arise in a wide class of dominant player dynamic games. Such games are of interest to macroeconomists since it is widely believed that descriptions of optimal government macroeconomic policy should emerge from the analysis of a dynamic game, in which the government is dominant with respect to a competitive private sector.

Our example possesses interesting features with respect to the feature of "time inconsistency" which can sometimes characterize the optimal plan of the dominant player in a dynamic game. We also use our example to illustrate a different equilibrium concept in which there is assumed to be no single "government," only a sequence of administrations, each incapable of committing its successors.

419

2. EQUILIBRIUM WITH THE GOVERNMENT AS DOMINANT PLAYER AND NO TAXATION OF INITIAL CAPITAL

We modify the model of Chapter XIV to include a government that is taxing capital. The demand curve for industry output continues to be given by equation (19) of Chapter XIV. Now (20) is modified by deducting tax payments in the amount $\tau_t k_t$ from cash flow at time t. Here τ_t is a tax rate that is chosen by the government. We consider a version of the model under certainty, so that the government chooses a sequence $\{\tau_t\}_{t=0}^{\infty}$. The representative firm acts as a perfect competitor with respect to the sequence for $\{\tau_t\}_{t=0}^{\infty}$. The firm's problem is to maximize

$$v_0 = \sum_{t=0}^{\infty} b^t \{ p_t f_0 k_t - J_t(k_t - k_{t-1}) - (d/2)(k_t - k_{t-1})^2 - \tau_t k_t \} \qquad (1)$$

subject to k_{-1} given and known sequences for J_t, τ_t, and p_t, $t = 0, 1, \ldots$. Proceeding as in Chapter XIV, the rational expectations competitive equilibrium can be shown to satisfy the following augmented version of (29) of Chapter XIV:

$$k_t = \lambda k_{t-1} - \frac{\lambda}{d} \frac{1}{1 - \lambda b L^{-1}} \{ J_t - b J_{t+1} - f_0 u_t - A_0 f_0 + \tau_t \}, \qquad (2)$$

where $\lambda_1 = \lambda$ and $\lambda_2^{-1} = \lambda b$. Equation (2) describes how the equilibrium volume of capital in the industry depends on the sequence of tax rates $\{\tau_t\}_{t=0}^{\infty}$.

We now describe a model in which the government chooses a sequence for tax rates $\{\tau_t\}_{t=0}^{\infty}$ by acting as a dominant player in a game with the industry. In particular, taking as given the market's equilibrium behavior as reflected in (2), the government is assumed to choose a tax sequence that maximizes the present value of consumer surplus net of production costs, subject to a sequence of intertemporal budget restraints for the government. Imposing this sequence of budget constraints is equivalent to requiring that the tax sequence raise a preassigned present value of revenue. The government's budget constraints are

$$B_{t+1} = b^{-1}(g_t + B_t - \tau_t k_t), \qquad t \geq 0 \qquad (3)$$

$$\lim_{t \to \infty} B_{t+1} b^t = 0 \qquad (4a)$$

$$B_0 = 0 \qquad (4b)$$

In (3), $\{g_t\}_{t=0}^{\infty}$ is a given nonnegative sequence of government purchases per firm of exponential order less than $1/\sqrt{b}$. B_t is the amount of one-period debt per firm that is due at the beginning of period t. Equations (3) and (4) hold if and only if

$$\sum_{t=0}^{\infty} b^t \tau_t k_t = \sum_{t=0}^{\infty} b^t g_t \equiv G. \qquad (5)$$

Equation (5) states that the present value of government receipts $\tau_t k_t$ equals the present value of the sequence g_t.

The idea here is that the government has decided to raise a certain present value of revenues by taxing this particular industry. Its problem now is how to collect these revenues in an optimal manner.

The government's problem is to maximize (26) of Chapter XIV at $t = 0$, subject to (2) and the revenue constraints (3) and (4). The maximization is over sequences for $\{k_t, \tau_t, B_{t+1}\}_{t=0}^{\infty}$, with $k_{-1} > 0$ and $B_0 = 0$ given. To solve this problem, we form the Lagrangian

$$
\begin{aligned}
L = \sum_{t=0}^{\infty} b^t \Big\{ & [A_0 f_0 n k_t - \tfrac{1}{2} A_1 (f_0^2 n^2 k_t^2) \\
& + f_0 n u_t k_t - n J_t (k_t - k_{t-1}) - \tfrac{1}{2} n d (k_t - k_{t-1})^2] \\
& + \theta_t \Big[\lambda k_{t-1} - \frac{\lambda}{d} \frac{1}{1 - \lambda b L^{-1}} (J_t - b J_{t+1} - f_0 u_t - A_0 f_0 + \tau_t) - k_t \Big] \\
& + \mu_t [b B_{t+1} - (g_t + B_t - \tau_t k_t)] \Big\}.
\end{aligned} \tag{6}
$$

Here $\{\theta_t\}_{t=0}^{\infty}$ and $\{\mu_t\}_{t=0}^{\infty}$ are sequences of nonnegative multipliers. The Euler equations for this problem with respect to k_t, τ_t and B_{t+1} are, respectively,[1]

$$
\begin{aligned}
\{ -A_1 f_0^2 n^2 k_t - nd(k_t - k_{t-1}) + bnd(k_{t+1} - k_t) + \lambda b \theta_{t+1} - \theta_t + \mu_t \tau_t \} \\
= [-A_0 f_0 n - f_0 n u_t + n J_t - n b J_{t+1}], \qquad t \geq 0 \quad (7)
\end{aligned}
$$

$$
-\frac{\lambda}{d} \frac{1}{1 - \lambda L} \theta_t + \mu_t k_t = 0, \qquad t \geq 0 \tag{8}
$$

$$
\mu_{t+1} - \mu_t = 0, \qquad t \geq 0. \tag{9}
$$

Using the factorization of the polynomial in L operating on k_t, equation (7) can be represented as

$$
\mu_t \tau_t - \frac{nd}{\lambda} (1 - \lambda b L^{-1})(1 - \lambda L) k_t - (1 - \lambda b L^{-1}) \theta_t = s_t \tag{10}
$$

where

$$
s_t \equiv \{ -A_0 f_0 n - f_0 n u_t + n J_t - n b J_{t+1} \}. \tag{11}
$$

Using the above definition of s_t, the market equilibrium condition (2) can be expressed as

$$
\frac{\lambda}{d} \frac{1}{1 - \lambda b L^{-1}} \tau_t + (1 - \lambda L) k_t = \frac{-\lambda}{dn} \frac{1}{1 - \lambda b L^{-1}} s_t. \tag{12}
$$

---

[1] Here we are using the formula for differentiating quadratic forms in polynomials in L that was described in Chapter IX, p. 213

We seek a solution $(\tau_t, k_t, \theta_t, \mu_t)_{t=0}^{\infty}$ of (8), (9), (10), and (12) subject to the given initial condition for k_{-1} and equation (5).

We first note that solutions to (9) satisfy $\mu_t = \mu$ for all $t \geq 0$. Substituting this equality into (8) and (10), we have

$$\mu k_t - \frac{\lambda}{d} \frac{1}{1 - \lambda L} \theta_t = 0 \tag{13}$$

$$\mu \tau_t - \frac{nd}{\lambda}(1 - \lambda b L^{-1})(1 - \lambda L) k_t - (1 - \lambda b L^{-1}) \theta_t = s_t. \tag{14}$$

Equations (12), (13), and (14) represent, respectively, the market equilibrium condition, and the Euler equations for the government with respect to τ_t and k_t. For given $\mu > 0$, our task is to solve (12), (13), and (14) for $(\tau_t, k_t, \theta_t)_{t=0}^{\infty}$ that satisfy the initial condition for k_{-1}. This solution will define a $\{\tau_t\}_{t=0}^{\infty}$ sequence as a function of μ. Our final step will be to select μ so that the government budget constraint (5) holds.

It is revealing to present (12), (13), and (14) as the system

$$\begin{bmatrix} 0 & \mu & -\dfrac{\lambda}{d}\dfrac{1}{1-\lambda L} \\[2ex] \mu & -\dfrac{nd}{\lambda}(1-\lambda b L^{-1})(1-\lambda L) & -(1-\lambda b L^{-1}) \\[2ex] -\dfrac{\lambda}{d}\dfrac{1}{1-\lambda b L^{-1}} & -(1-\lambda L) & 0 \end{bmatrix} \begin{bmatrix} \tau_t \\[2ex] k_t \\[2ex] \theta_t \end{bmatrix}$$

$$= \begin{bmatrix} 0 \\[2ex] s_t \\[2ex] \dfrac{\lambda}{dn}\dfrac{1}{1-\lambda b L^{-1}} s_t \end{bmatrix}. \tag{15}$$

One way to solve system (15) hinges on recognizing that it is in the form of a matrix Euler equation of the sort studied in Chapter IX. In particular, note that equation (15) can be written in the form

$$W(L) \begin{pmatrix} \tau_t \\ k_t \\ \theta_t \end{pmatrix} = \bar{s}_t \tag{16}$$

where $\bar{s}_t$ is the (3×1) vector of sequences on the right side of (15), and $W(L)$ is the (3×3) matrix polynomial on the left side of (15). A solution of the government's optimal tax problem is a value for μ and a sequence for

$(\tau_t, k_t, \theta_t)_{t=0}^{\infty}$ that satisifes (5) as well as the difference equation (16) together with the boundary conditions of given k_{-1}, and the standard transversality conditions. Evidently, the value of the nonnegative multiplier μ depends on G in (5), and will rise with increases in G. Note that for $G = 0$, $(\mu = 0, \tau_t = 0$ for all $t \geq 0)$ solves system (15) and satisfies the budget constraint (5). Also, it is true that there exist values of G sufficiently large that no μ exists for which system (15) and (5) has a solution. There is only so much revenue that can be raised by taxing this industry.

Note from (15) and the definition of $W(L)$ that $W(bL^{-1})^T = W(L)$. From this fact it follows that it is possible to factor $W(L)$ as

$$W(L) = C(bL^{-1})^T C(L)$$

where $C(L)$ is one-sided in nonnegative powers of L, where the zeros of det $C(z)$ exceed $\sqrt{b}$ and the zeros of det $C(bz^{-1})$ are less than $\sqrt{b}$ in absolute value. (See Chapter IX, p. 208 for a related result.) It then follows that the solution that satisfies the boundary conditions is given by

$$C(L)\begin{pmatrix} \tau_t \\ k_t \\ \theta_t \end{pmatrix} = C(bL^{-1})^{-1^T}\bar{s}_t.$$

This solution expresses the tax rate τ_t and the Lagrange multiplier θ_t in terms of previous values of θ, τ and capital k, and expected future values of the components of $\bar{s}_t$, namely, J_t and u_t.

An alternative method is available for solving the present problem, which involves reducing (15) to one equation in k_t by a process of substitution. Repeating (12), (13), and (14) for convenience, we want to solve

$$\frac{\lambda}{d} \frac{1}{1 - \lambda b L^{-1}} \tau_t + (1 - \lambda L)k_t = \frac{-\lambda}{dn} \frac{1}{1 - \lambda b L^{-1}} s_t, \qquad t \geq 0 \qquad (12)$$

$$\mu k_t - \frac{\lambda}{d} \frac{1}{1 - \lambda L} \theta_t = 0, \qquad t \geq 0 \qquad (13)$$

$$\mu \tau_t - \frac{nd}{\lambda}(1 - \lambda b L^{-1})(1 - \lambda L)k_t - (1 - \lambda b L^{-1})\theta_t = s_t, \qquad t \geq 0. \qquad (14)$$

We shall proceed in three steps: First, we shall solve (12), (13), and (14) for $t \geq 1$, conditional on a value for μ. Second, conditional again on the same value for μ, we solve (12), (13), and (14) for $t = 0$. Third, we choose μ so that the budget restraint (5) is satisfied, given the $(k_t, \tau_t)_{t=0}^{\infty}$ processes chosen in the previous two steps. The reason for using a solution strategy that treats $t \geq 1$ separately from $t = 0$ will be evident soon.

For $t \geq 1$, we proceed as follows. Solving (12) for τ_t and (13) for θ_t gives

$$\tau_t = -(1/n)s_t - \frac{d}{\lambda}(1 - \lambda bL^{-1})(1 - \lambda L)k_t, \qquad t \geq 0 \qquad (17)$$

$$\theta_t = \frac{d}{\lambda}\mu(1 - \lambda L)k_t, \qquad t \geq 1. \qquad (18)$$

In moving from (13) to (18), we have operated on both sides of (13) by $(1 - \lambda L)$. For this to be a valid operation, it is required that (13) hold for both dates t *and* $t - 1$. This is true for $t \geq 1$, but *not* for $t = 0$. This is the reason that the dates $t \geq 1$ are being treated differently than $t = 0$ in our solution procedure. Now, substituting (17) and (18) for τ_t and θ_t, respectively, into (14) and solving for k_t gives

$$(1 - \lambda L)k_t = \frac{-(1 + \mu/n)\,\lambda}{(2\mu + n)}\frac{1}{d}\frac{1}{1 - \lambda bL^{-1}}s_t, \qquad t \geq 1. \qquad (19)$$

Substituting (19) into (17) and (18), respectively, and solving for τ_t and θ_t gives

$$\tau_t = -\left\{\frac{\mu/n}{(2\mu + n)}\right\}s_t, \qquad t \geq 1 \qquad (20)$$

$$\theta_t = \frac{-\mu(1 + \mu/n)}{2\mu + n}\frac{1}{1 - \lambda bL^{-1}}s_t, \qquad t \geq 1. \qquad (21)$$

Substituting from the definition of s_t in (11) into (19), (20), and (21) finally gives

$$(1 - \lambda L)k_t = \frac{-(1 + \mu/n)\,\lambda}{(2\mu + n)}\frac{1}{d}\frac{1}{1 - \lambda bL^{-1}}\{-A_0 f_0 n - f_0 nu_t$$
$$+ nJ_t - nbJ_{t+1}\}, \qquad t \geq 1 \qquad (22)$$

$$\tau_t = \frac{-\mu/n}{(2\mu + n)}\{-A_0 f_0 n - f_0 nu_t + nJ_t - nbJ_{t+1}\}, \qquad t \geq 1 \quad (23)$$

$$\theta_t = \frac{-\mu(1 + \mu/n)}{2\mu + n}\frac{1}{1 - \lambda bL^{-1}}\{-A_0 f_0 n - f_0 nu_t$$
$$+ nJ_t - nbJ_{t+1}\}, \qquad t \geq 1. \qquad (24)$$

We note that

$$\frac{\partial}{\partial \mu}\left(\frac{1 + \mu/n}{2\mu + n}\right) = \frac{-1}{(2\mu + n)^2} < 0.$$

Therefore, from (22), say, with $(A_0 f_0 n + f_0 n u_t - n J_t + n b J_{t+1})$ constant and positive, an increase in the multiplier μ drives the path of capital downward for $t \geq 1$. Note also that

$$\frac{\partial}{\partial \mu}\left(\frac{\mu/n}{2\mu + n}\right) = \frac{1}{(2\mu + n)^2} > 0.$$

Therefore, from (23), say, with $(A_0 f_0 n + f_0 n u_t - n J_t + b n J_{t+1})$ constant and positive, an increase in μ increases taxes for $t \geq 1$. Also, in (24), an increase in μ tends to increase the sequence of multipliers θ_t for $t \geq 1$ The multiplier θ_t gives the marginal value of λk_{t-1} to the planner. An increase in G increases θ_t. This reflects the higher value that λk_{t-1} bears for the planner when more taxes must be raised to cover a higher G. Note that if $\mu = 0$, then $\theta_t = 0$ and $\tau_t = 0$ for all $t \geq 1$ and that the solution (22) for k_t agrees with (2).

We now solve for k_0, τ_0, θ_0, given a value of μ. For $t \geq 0$, (13) becomes

$$\mu k_0 = (\lambda/d)\theta_0 \tag{25}$$

because $\theta_{-1} = \theta_{-2} = \cdots = 0$ are the appropriate initial conditions for θ at time 0. Zero values for these initial θ_{t-j}'s reflect the fact that the planner is taking $k_{-1}, k_{-2}, \ldots$ as given and not as being influenced by his choice of $\{\tau_0, \tau_1, \ldots\}$.

Now (12) and (14) hold for $t \geq 0$. Operate on both sides of (12) by $(nd/\lambda)(1 - \lambda b L^{-1})$ and add the resulting equation to (14) to obtain

$$\tau_t = \frac{1}{\mu + n}(1 - \lambda b L^{-1})\theta_t, \qquad t \geq 0. \tag{26}$$

Substitute (26) for τ_t in (12) and evaluate at $t = 0$ to obtain

$$\frac{\lambda}{d}\frac{1}{n + \mu}\theta_0 + k_0 - \lambda k_{-1} = \frac{-\lambda}{dn}\frac{1}{1 - \lambda b L^{-1}}s_0.$$

Use (25) to eliminate θ_0 from the above equation and to solve for k_0,

$$k_0 = \left(\frac{n + \mu}{n + 2\mu}\right)\lambda k_{-1} - \frac{\lambda}{dn}\left(\frac{n + \mu}{n + 2\mu}\right)\frac{1}{1 - \lambda b L^{-1}}s_0. \tag{27}$$

Substituting (25) into (27) and solving for θ_0 gives

$$\theta_0 = d\mu\left(\frac{\mu + n}{n + 2\mu}\right)k_{-1} - \frac{\mu}{n}\left(\frac{n + \mu}{n + 2\mu}\right)\frac{1}{1 - \lambda b L^{-1}}s_0. \tag{28}$$

Finally, substituting (21) for θ_t, $t \geq 1$, and (28) for θ_0 into (26) for $t = 0$ gives

$$\tau_0 = \left(\frac{d\mu}{n + 2\mu}\right)k_{-1} - \frac{\mu(1 + \mu/n)}{(n + \mu)(n + 2\mu)}s_0$$

or

$$\tau_0 = \left(\frac{d\mu}{n + 2\mu}\right)k_{-1} - \frac{\mu}{n}\left(\frac{1}{n + 2\mu}\right)s_0. \tag{29}$$

Collecting our results, we have for fixed μ the following solution:

$$k_0 = \left(\frac{n + \mu}{n + 2\mu}\right)\lambda k_{-1} - \frac{\lambda}{dn}\left(\frac{n + \mu}{n + 2\mu}\right)\frac{1}{1 - \lambda bL^{-1}}s_0 \tag{27}$$

$$k_t = \lambda k_{t-1} - \frac{\lambda}{d}\frac{(1 + \mu/n)}{(2\mu + n)}\frac{1}{1 - \lambda bL^{-1}}s_t, \qquad t \geq 1 \tag{22}$$

$$\tau_0 = \left(\frac{d\mu}{n + 2\mu}\right)k_{-1} - \frac{\mu/n}{(n + 2\mu)}s_0 \tag{29}$$

$$\tau_t = \frac{-\mu/n}{(2\mu + n)}s_t, \qquad t \geq 1 \tag{23}$$

$$\theta_0 = d\mu\left(\frac{\mu + n}{n + 2\mu}\right)k_{-1} - \frac{\mu}{n}\left(\frac{n + \mu}{n + 2\mu}\right)\frac{1}{1 - \lambda bL^{-1}}s_0 \tag{28}$$

$$\theta_t = \frac{-\mu(1 + \mu/n)}{2\mu + n}\frac{1}{1 - \lambda bL^{-1}}s_t, \qquad t \geq 1 \tag{24}$$

$$s_t = \{-A_0 f_0 n - f_0 n u_t + n J_t - n b J_{t+1}\}. \tag{11}$$

The final step of the solution is to set μ so that $(k_t, \tau_t)_{t=0}^{\infty}$ implied by (27), (22), (29), and (23) satisfies the budget constraint (5). Note that if $G = 0$ in (5), then $\mu = 0$ is a solution. No taxes are levied, and the equilibrium equals the one with no government that we studied in Chapter XIV. With $G > 0$, μ must be set equal to a positive number if an equilibrium is to exist. Provided that G is not too large, a value of μ will exist which ensures that (5) is satisfied.

The optimal decision rules given by (27), (22), and (29), (23) are time-dependent in a special way. In particular, for setting k_t and τ_t as functions of k_{t-1}, $\{s_{t+j}\}_{j=0}^{\infty}$, different functions are used for $t = 0$, on the one hand, and for $t \geq 1$, on the other hand. (For $t \geq 1$, the *same* functions are used.) Focusing on (29) and (23), we note when $G > 0$, and therefore $\mu > 0$, that $(d\mu)/(n + 2\mu) > 0$. For simplicity consider the case in which $s_0 - s_t$ for all t. Then the optimal plan involves setting a higher tax rate τ_0 at $t = 0$ and lower tax rates τ_t for $t \geq 1$. The reason for this pattern is that at $t = 0$, the government takes k_{-1} as given, and unaffected by settings for τ_t, $t \geq 0$. However, the government takes into account the discouraging effects of τ_t, $t \geq 0$, upon k_t, $t \geq 0$. These effects prompt it to plan to tax at lower rates in the future than in the present.

The time dependency of the functions (or decision rules) (27), (22), (29), and (23) is a symptom of the *time inconsistency* of the optimal solution to the government planning problem associated with the Lagrangian (6). The time inconsistency phenomenon can be explained by studying the following "remainder" of the problem associated with (6). At time $t = 1$, we form the Lagrangian

$$L = \sum_{t=s}^{\infty} b^{t-s} \left\{ [A_0 f_0 n k_t - \tfrac{1}{2} A_1 (f_0^2 n^2 k_t^2) \right.$$

$$+ f_0 n u_t k_t - n J_t (k_t - k_{t-1}) - \tfrac{1}{2} n d (k_t - k_{t-1})^2]$$

$$+ \theta_t \left[\lambda k_{t-1} - \frac{\lambda}{d} \left(\frac{1}{1 - \lambda b L^{-1}} \right) (J_t - b J_{t+1} - f_0 u_t - A_0 f_0 + \tau_t) - k_t \right] \quad (30)$$

$$\left. + \mu_t [b B_{t+1} - (g_t + B_t - \tau_t k_t)] \right\}$$

for $s = 1$, subject to k_0 and B_1 implied by the solution for (27), (29), and (3) for $t = 0$, starting from the given initial values k_{-1} and $B_0 = 0$. This Lagrangian is associated with the problem of maximizing the "remainder" of our criterion function at $t = 1$, starting from the values of B_1 and k_0 passed on from the optimal solution at $t = 0$. This problem is to be solved with initial conditions for θ of $\theta_0 = \theta_{-1} = \cdots = 0$, since the planner is now to take k_0 as given and uninfluenced by $(\tau_1, \tau_2, \ldots)$. We want to know whether the solution of the problem associated with (30) is simply to continue the plan given by solving (6) for $t \geq 1$, namely to continue to follow (22), (23), and (24) for $t \geq 1$. It can be verified directly that so long as $G > 0$, the maximizer of (30) is *not* to continue the plan that optimizes (6). By observing the formal similarity between Lagrangians (6) and (30), it follows directly that the optimizer of (30) is given by

$$k_1 = \left(\frac{n + \mu}{n + 2\mu} \right) \lambda k_0 - \frac{\lambda}{dn} \left(\frac{n + \mu}{2\mu + n} \right) \frac{1}{1 - \lambda b L^{-1}} s_1, \quad (27')$$

$$\tau_1 = \left(\frac{d\mu}{n + 2\mu} \right) k_0 - \frac{(\mu/n)}{(n + 2\mu)} s_1, \quad (29')$$

and by (22) and (23) for $t \geq 2$. Since (27') and (29') do not agree with (22) and (23) for $t = 1$ for any $\mu > 0$, it follows that the plan (27), (22), (29), and (23) that optimizes (6) fails to optimize the Lagrangian (30) associated with the remainder. Note that relative to (23) for $t = 1$, (29') involves a *higher* setting for τ_1. This occurs because in deriving (29'), k_0 is taken as fixed and unaffected by taxes. The failure of the optimal plan for (6) to optimize the remainder problem for any $t \geq 1$ is termed the "time inconsistency" of the optimal plan associated with (6). Had it been optimal in terms of the remainder problem to continue the optimal plan associated with the original problem (6), the original plan would be said to be "time consistent."

The source of the time inconsistency can be described as follows. In the problem associated with the remainder Lagrangian (30), we have "reinitialized" by setting $\theta_0 = 0$. This step was taken by way of presenting the planner at $t = 1$ with a situation in which k_0 is given, and therefore unaffected by his choice of the sequence $\{\tau_1, \tau_2, \ldots\}$. This reinitialization of θ_0 reflects the discarding of one constraint on the government's choice at $t = 0$ and accounts for the failure of the plan that optimizes (30) to optimize the remainder problem (6) at $s = 1$.[2]

Criterion (6) is one in which the government's choice of a "control" at time t, namely τ_t, influences "current returns" dated $0, 1, \ldots, t - 1, t$.[3] Here the "current return" is the consumer surplus net of social costs of production at t. In general, a necessary condition for time consistency is that controls dated t must *not* influence returns dated earlier than t. The reader will note that in Chapter XIV we in effect utilized the time consistency of the firm's optimal plan (see Section 1). For either the firm's or the social planner's problem, controls at t (namely $k_t - k_{t-1}$) influenced returns (current period net revenue or consumer surplus net of social costs of production) dated t and later, but *not* earlier. That feature of the firm's problem is what permitted time consistency to prevail in Chapter XIV, but to fail in the present context.

3. EQUILIBRIUM WITH THE GOVERNMENT AS DOMINANT PLAYER AND TAXATION OF INITIAL CAPITAL

We now alter our problem by giving the government the ability to impose a tax τ_{-1} on the initial capital stock k_{-1} at time $t = 0$. We accomplish this by replacing (4b) with

$$B_0 = -(\tau_{-1}k_{-1}), \tag{4b'}$$

where τ_{-1} is the tax rate applied to k_{-1}. The implication of (3), (4a), and (4b') is

$$\sum_{t=0}^{\infty} b^t \tau_t k_t + \tau_{-1} k_{-1} = \sum_{t=0}^{\infty} b^t g_t \equiv G. \tag{5'}$$

The government's problem is to maximize (26) of Chapter XIV at $t = 0$, subject to (2) and the revenue constraints (3) and (4b'). The maximization is over

---

[2] Hansen, Epple and Roberds (1985) describe examples in which the optimal plan is time inconsistent and in which the time inconsistency is symptomized by the dependence of the multipliers θ_t on previous θ's.

[3] Taking account of such effects is the source of time inconsistency in the examples of Calvo (1978) and Kydland and Prescott (1977).

sequences for $\{k_t\}_{t=0}^{\infty}$, $\{B_{t+1}, \tau_t\}_{t=-1}^{\infty}$. Again k_{-1} is given as an initial condition. The Lagrangian associated with this problem is

$$L = \sum_{t=0}^{\infty} b^t \Big\{ [A_0 f_0 n k_t - \tfrac{1}{2} A_1 (f_0^2 n^2 k_t^2)$$

$$+ f_0 n u_t k_t - n J_t(k_t - k_{t-1}) - \tfrac{1}{2} n d (k_t - k_{t-1})^2]$$

$$+ \theta_t [\lambda k_{t-1} - \frac{\lambda}{d} \left(\frac{1}{1 - \lambda b L^{-1}} \right) (J_t - b J_{t+1} - f_0 u_t - A_0 f_0 + \tau_t) - k_t]$$

$$+ \mu_t [b B_{t+1} - (g_t + B_t - \tau_t k_t)] \Big\} + \mu_{-1}[B_0 + \tau_{-1} k_{-1}]. \tag{31}$$

The first order conditions for this problem with respect to k_t, τ_t and B_{t+1}, $t \geq 0$, are again (7), (8), and (9). The first order conditions for B_0 and τ_{-1} are

$$\mu_{-1} - \mu_0 = \mu_{-1} k_{-1} = 0. \tag{32}$$

Since $k_{-1} > 0$, (32) and (9) imply that the solution is given by $\mu_t = \mu = 0$ for all $t \geq -1$. The solution for $\{k_t, \tau_t, \theta_t\}_{t=0}^{\infty}$ continues to be given by (27), (22), (29), (23), (28), and (24). Evidently, the solution is to set τ_{-1} to satisfy (5'), i.e.,

$$\tau_{-1} k_{-1} = \sum_{t=0}^{\infty} b^t g_t, \qquad \tau_t = 0 \quad \text{for} \quad t \geq 0. \tag{33}$$

The solution (33) reflects the fact that at time 0, τ_t for $t \geq 0$ are distorting taxes, while τ_{-1} acts like a lump sum tax because k_{-1} is given. Since there is no restriction on the amount of the lump sum tax that can be imposed, the optimal thing to do is to use it to raise all required revenues. The government raises the entire present value $\sum_{t=0}^{\infty} b^t g_t$ with the tax on initial capital k_{-1}. For $g_t > 0$ for all t, this means that B_0 is negative, and also that $B_t < 0$ for all $t \geq 0$. The government invests the proceeds of the tax $\tau_{-1} k_{-1}$ at the gross interest rate b^{-1} and uses the interest to finance its expenditures stream $\{g_t\}_{t=0}^{\infty}$. This solution is time consistent, for this policy implies a $B_t < 0$ sequence that makes it possible to satisfy the constraints (3) with $\tau_s = 0$ for each subsequent $s \geq t$. This implies that if the "remainder problem" is posed at s starting from the B_s implied by (33), then it remains optimal to set $\mu = 0$ for the remainder problem.

4. EQUILIBRIUM WITH LIMITED TAXATION OF INITIAL CAPITAL

We now suppose that the government can impose a tax on the initial capital stock, but only within limits. In particular, we impose that

$$\tau_{-1} k_{-1} \leq R,$$

and more generally, that

$$\tau_t k_t \leq R, \qquad t \geq -1.$$

The idea here is that the parameter R is large relative to the one period tax collection $\tau_t k_t$ implied by the solution (27), (22), (29), and (23) to the original problem of Section 2, but that it is small relative to G; i.e., $\tilde{\tau}_t \tilde{k}_t < R \ll G$, where $\tilde{\tau}_t \tilde{k}_t$ is the solution of (27), (22), (29), and (23). So the restriction R on $\tau_t k_t$ would not have altered the solution of the original problem of Section 2, had it been imposed. However, the restriction will impinge on the problem once we permit taxation of the initial capital stock.

To solve the augmented problem, we now form the Lagrangian

$$
L = \sum_{t=0}^{\infty} b^t \bigg\{ [A_0 f_0 n k_t - \tfrac{1}{2} A_1 (f_0{}^2 n^2 k_t{}^2)
$$

$$
+ f_0 n u_t k_t - n J_t (k_t - k_{t-1}) - \tfrac{1}{2} n d (k_t - k_{t-1})^2]
$$

$$
+ \theta_t \bigg[\lambda k_{t-1} - \frac{\lambda}{d} \bigg(\frac{1}{1 - \lambda b L^{-1}} \bigg) (J_t - b J_{t+1} - f_0 u_t - A_0 f_0 + \tau_t) - k_t \bigg]
$$

$$
+ \mu_t [b B_{t+1} - (g_t + B_t - \tau_t k_t)] + \phi_t [R - \tau_{t-1} k_{t-1}] \bigg\}
$$

$$
+ \mu_{-1} [B_0 + \tau_{-1} k_{-1}] \tag{34}
$$

where ϕ_t is a sequence of nonnegative multipliers. The first order condition for k_t remains (7). For τ_t and B_t the first order conditions become

$$
\partial L / \partial \tau_t = -\frac{\lambda}{d} \bigg(\frac{1}{1 - \lambda L} \bigg) \theta_t + \mu_t k_t - b \phi_{t+1} k_t = 0, \qquad t \geq 0 \tag{35}
$$

$$
\frac{\partial L}{\partial \tau_{-1}} = -\phi_0 k_{-1} + \mu_{-1} k_{-1} = 0 \tag{36}
$$

$$
\frac{\partial L}{\partial B_t} = -\mu_t + \mu_{t-1} = 0, \qquad t \geq 0. \tag{37}
$$

There also is obtained the following restriction on the multiplier ϕ_t:

$$
\phi_{t+1}(R - \tau_t k_t) = 0, \qquad t \geq -1. \tag{38}
$$

Given our assumption about the magnitude of R—that it is large relative to $\{\tau_t k_t\}$ implied by (27), (22), (29), and (23) but small relative to G—the solution of this problem will involve setting, from (36),

$$
\mu_{-1} = \phi_0 > 0 \tag{39}
$$

where the last inequality reflects the occurrence that the constraint $\tau_t k_t \leq R$ will be binding for $t = -1$. For $t \geq 0$, $\phi_{t+1} = 0$. Thus (7), (8), and (9) will hold for $t \geq 0$.

The equilibrium is computed as follows: τ_{-1} is set to satisfy the constraint $\tau_{-1} k_{-1} = R$. From time $t = 0$ onward, the government must raise a stream of revenues whose present value at $t = 0$ is $\sum_{t=0}^{\infty} b^t g_t - R$. To accomplish this, $\mu_0 = \mu_{-1}$ is set so that the $(\tau_t, k_t)_{t=0}^{\infty}$ solution implied by the solution (27), (22), (29), and (23) raises revenues whose present value is $\sum_{t=0}^{\infty} b^t g_t - R$. This value of μ_{-1} determines ϕ_0 via (39).

Notice that this solution has the property that, relative to the original problem of Section 2, a lower tax rate will be imposed for $t \geq 0$. This is because fewer revenues must be raised, R having been raised by taxing k_{-1}.

Evidently, in general, the solution to the current problem is *not* time consistent. In particular, time consistency will fail to be obtained so long as the optimal plan for $\{\tau_{t-1}\}_{t=0}^{\infty}$ involves setting τ_0 so that $\tau_0 k_0 < R$.[4] When the "remainder problem" is posed at $t = 0$, the optimal thing to do is to raise τ_0 and set it so that the constraint $\tau_0 k_0 \leq R$ is binding. In solving the original problem at $t = 0$, the government views τ_0 as a distorting tax, because it affects investment. Therefore the government limits its use of this tax. However, for the "remainder problem" at $t = 1$, the government regards k_0 as fixed, converting τ_0 into a lump sum tax. The government would want to raise τ_0 vis-à-vis its setting in the optimal plan calculated at $t = 0$.

The upshot of these considerations is that the solution of the problem associated with Lagrangian (34) is not self-enforcing and cannot be expected to be implemented by "decentralizing across time" and entrusting the power to set τ_t to a sequence of administrations for $t = 0, 1, \ldots$, each facing the "remainder problem" associated with (34). To enforce the optimal solution of problem (34), it is necessary that there be some institution or mechanism that precludes the option of reconsidering the plan. That is, the process for $\{\tau_t\}_{t=-1}^{\infty}$ must be chosen once and for all at $t = 0$. Where such precommitment is in force, we obtain a model of the $\{k_t, \tau_t\}$ process. Hansen and Sargent (1980) and Hansen, Epple, and Roberds (1985) describe how such a model can be tested econometrically.

The time inconsistency of the optimal plan can be interpreted as a force for the equilibrium to break down. If it is assumed that this force cannot be checked by some sort of arrangements guaranteeing precommitment to a plan for $\{\tau_t\}_{t=-1}^{\infty}$, some other model for determining a tax process is required.

One way to obtain time consistency for the Section 4 equilibrium is to remove the restriction on the rate of taxation of initial capital, thereby implementing the Section 3 equilibrium.

An alternative way to induce time consistency is to alter the nature of the game. The source of time inconsistency is that the government at $t = 0$ plans to set τ_t, $t \geq 1$ in a way that takes into account the effect of τ_t on $k_0, k_1, \ldots, k_{t-1}$. A game in which the government is prevented from taking these effects into account in setting τ_t seems to have the potential for achieving time consistency.

---

[4] Technically, time inconsistency manifests itself in the fact that it is optimal to reset μ vis-à-vis the time 0 optimal plan when the remainder problem is solved at $t = 1$. This is true even though the government accepts the value of B_1 implied by the time 0 optimal plan as a given initial condition.

Furthermore, it has been argued (see Sims (1982) and Hansen, Epple and Roberds (1985)) that it is unrealistic to think of a single infinitely-lived government as choosing a strategy of infinite duration once and for all. As a more realistic assumption, it has been proposed to model the government's decisions as being decentralized over time. There is a sequence of "administrations." Each administration only sets controls while it is in office and is incapable of committing its successors. In the next section, we study the equilibrium for our model of investment under such a mechanism for determining the government's behavior.

5. A GAME WITH A SEQUENCE OF "ADMINISTRATIONS"

Hansen, Epple and Roberds (1985) describe an equilibrium concept in which no single infinitely lived government agent chooses once and for all a strategy for $\{\tau_t\}_{t=0}^{\infty}$. Instead, there is a sequence of "administrations" at dates $t = 0$, 1, 2, ... The administration at t views itself as taking $\{\tau_s\}_{s=t+1}^{\infty}$ as given. Thus, the administration at t views itself as being free to choose (τ_t, k_t), but as being powerless to commit its successors. At each date t, an administration predicts that future τ's will be selected by subsequent administrators with objective functions appropriate for the "remainder problem," and with similar views about their ability to commit successor administrations. We further assume that the administration in office at t believes that administrations at $t + s$ will set taxes in a way that does not feed back on capital stocks predating $t + s$. The tax at $t + s$, τ_{t+s}, is believed to depend on $\{s_k\}_{k=-\infty}^{\infty}$ but not on $k_{t+s-1}, k_{t+s-2}, \ldots$. (We verify in equation (51) below that this assumption turns out to be valid in this equilibrium.) This means that the administration at t correctly believes that it does not even have an indirect influence on τ_{t+s} through the influence of τ_t on the initial capital stock at $t + s$.

To formalize this concept of equilibrium, consider the same Lagrangian that we encountered in (6)

$$L = \sum_{t=0}^{\infty} b^t \left\{ [A_0 f_0 n k_t - \tfrac{1}{2} A_1 (f_0^2 n^2 k_t^2) \right.$$
$$+ f_0 n u_t k_t - n J_t (k_t - k_{t-1}) - \tfrac{1}{2} n d (k_t - k_{t-1})^2]$$
$$+ \theta_t \left[\lambda k_{t-1} - \frac{\lambda}{d} \left(\frac{1}{1 - \lambda b L^{-1}} \right) (J_t - b J_{t+1} - f_0 u_t - A_0 f_0 + \tau_t) - k_t \right]$$
$$+ \mu_t [b B_{t+1} - (g_t + B_t - \tau_t k_t)] \right\}$$
(40)

with k_{-1} given and $B_0 = 0$. The sense of the present equilibrium concept is that in choosing τ_t, the administration at t ignores the effect of τ_t on $k_0, \ldots, k_{t-1}$. The first order condition for τ_t becomes:

$$-\frac{\lambda}{d} \theta_t + \mu_t k_t = 0, \qquad t \geq 0.$$
(41)

The first order conditions for k_t and B_t remain (7) and (9). Again, condition (21) also holds. Condition (41) is to be compared with the first order condition for the original problem of Section 2

$$-\frac{\lambda}{d}\frac{1}{1-\lambda L}\theta_t + \mu_t k_t = 0, \qquad t \geq 0 \qquad (8)$$

or

$$-\frac{\lambda}{d}(\theta_t + \lambda\theta_{t-1} + \lambda^2\theta_{t-2} + \cdots) + \mu_t k_t = 0.$$

The difference between (41) and (8) is the absence of lagged θ's from the former. This reflects the situation that in deriving (41), the government is assumed to be ignoring the effects of τ_t on $k_0, \ldots, k_{t-1}$. Ignoring these effects accounts for the absence of lagged multipliers in (41).

Once again, condition (9) implies that $\mu_t = \mu_{t-1} = \mu$ for all $t \geq 1$. Substituting this into (7) and (41) and using (2) again gives the system

$$\mu k_t - \frac{\lambda}{d}\theta_t = 0, \qquad t \geq 0 \qquad (42)$$

$$\mu\tau_t - \frac{nd}{\lambda}(1 - \lambda bL^{-1})(1 - \lambda L)k_t - (1 - \lambda bL^{-1})\theta_t = s_t, \qquad t \geq 0 \qquad (43)$$

$$-\frac{\lambda}{d}\left(\frac{1}{1-\lambda bL^{-1}}\right)\tau_t - (1 - \lambda L)k_t = \frac{\lambda}{dn}\left(\frac{1}{1-\lambda bL^{-1}}\right)s_t, \quad t \geq 0 \qquad (44)$$

where s_t is defined by (11). Representing (42), (43) and (44) as a system in matrix notation, we have

$$\begin{bmatrix} 0 & \mu & \frac{-\lambda}{d} \\ \mu & \frac{-nd}{\lambda}(1 - \lambda bL^{-1})(1 - \lambda L) & -(1 - \lambda bL^{-1}) \\ \frac{-\lambda}{d}\left(\frac{1}{1-\lambda bL^{-1}}\right) & -(1 - \lambda L) & 0 \end{bmatrix}\begin{bmatrix} \tau_t \\ k_t \\ \theta_t \end{bmatrix}$$

$$= \begin{bmatrix} 0 \\ s_t \\ \frac{\lambda}{dn}\left(\frac{1}{1-\lambda bL^{-1}}\right)s_t \end{bmatrix}. \qquad (45)$$

Let $Y(L)$ be the (3×3) matrix polynomial on the left side of (45). We note that $Y(bL^{-1})^T \neq Y(L)$. Furthermore, there is no way of rewriting the system by redefining variables so that the resulting matrix playing the role of Y satisfies this b-symmetry condition. The consequence is that the zeros of det $Y(z)$ fail to come in b-reciprocal pairs. This means that the solution method described in Section 10 of Chapter IX, which exploits this symmetry, is not applicable.[5]

To solve for the equilibrium, we use the approach of reducing the system to one equation in k_t. Solving (42) for θ_t and (44) for τ_t gives

$$\theta_t = \frac{\mu d}{\lambda} k_t \tag{46}$$

$$\tau_t = -\frac{1}{n} s_t - \frac{d}{\lambda}(1 - \lambda b L^{-1})(1 - \lambda L)k_t. \tag{47}$$

Substituting (46) and (47) into (43) and solving for k_t gives

$$\left\{ -\lambda b L^{-1} + \left[\left(\frac{\mu + n}{2\mu + n} \right)(\lambda^2 b + 1) + \frac{\mu}{2\mu + n} \right] - \left(\frac{\mu + n}{2\mu + n} \right)\lambda L \right\} k_t$$
$$= -\frac{\lambda (\mu/n + 1)}{d (2\mu + n)} s_t. \tag{48}$$

To find the solution of (48) that satisfies the transversality condition, we factor the polynomial on the left

$$\left\{ -\lambda b L^{-1} + \left[\left(\frac{\mu + n}{2\mu + n} \right)(\lambda^2 b + 1) + \frac{\mu}{2\mu + n} \right] - \left(\frac{\mu + n}{2\mu + n} \right)\lambda L \right\}$$
$$= h_0(1 - h_1 L)(1 - h_2 L^{-1}), \tag{49}$$

where we require that $|h_1| < 1/\sqrt{b}$ and $|h_2| < \sqrt{b}$. It may occur that μ is so large in absolute value that h_1 and h_2 cannot satisfy these inequalities. In that case, no equilibrium exists.[6] When $\mu = 0$, we have $h_1 = \lambda$, $h_2 = \lambda b$, and $h_0 = 1$. In that case, the solution of (48) agrees with that given in (2). However, when $\mu > 0$, $h_2 \neq b h_1$: the zeros of (49) fail to be b-inverses of one another.

If $|h_1| < 1/\sqrt{b}$ and $|h_2| < \sqrt{b}$, the solution for k_t is given by

$$(1 - h_1 L)k_t = -\frac{\lambda (\mu/n + 1)}{d h_0 (2\mu + n)}\left(\frac{1}{1 - h_2 L^{-1}} \right)s_t. \tag{50}$$

Substituting (50) into (47) gives the following solution for taxes:

$$\tau_t = \left\{ -\frac{1}{n} + \frac{(1 - \lambda b L^{-1})(1 - \lambda L)}{(1 - h_2 L^{-1})(1 - h_1 L)} \frac{1}{h_0} \frac{(\mu/n + 1)}{(2\mu + n)} \right\} s_t. \tag{51}$$

Note that when $\mu = 0$, $\tau_t = 0$.

[5] A related but more general matrix factorization approach is applicable. See Hansen, Epple, and Roberds (1985).

[6] That is, the difference equation has no solution that satisfies the transversality condition and the initial condition for capital. See Whiteman (1983, Ch. 5) for a statement of conditions for the existence of solutions of generalizations of (48).

The computation of the equilibrium is completed by choosing μ so that the solution for $\{k_t, \tau_t\}_{t=0}^{\infty}$ satisfying (50) and (51) also satisfies (5).

Hansen, Epple, and Roberds (1985) used the equilibrium concept in this section in a model of dynamic duopoly. They were attracted to this equilibrium concept because it is by construction time consistent, and therefore self-enforcing. Sims (1982) has also described government policy-making in terms that can be interpreted as a version of this equilibrium concept.

6. CONCLUSIONS

Models of the kind studied in this chapter have several potential uses. One is as a vehicle for making recommendations for improving policy decisions. Here the vision can be illustrated with our model as follows. It is supposed that historically, say, during $t = -T, \ldots, 0$, the government was setting taxes according to some given strategy, say, $\tau_t = v(L)z_t$, where z_t was the government's information set. This strategy for setting $\{\tau_t\}$ is presumed to be improvable, that is, suboptimal relative to the criterion function (6).[7] A method for making suggestions for improving policy is available. The method proceeds as follows. Using observations from $t = -T, \ldots, 0$, an econometrician is supposed to deduce estimates of the parameters that appear in the government's objective function (6). Then the optimal policy (27), (22), (29), and (23) is deduced. This optimal policy is the economist's recommendation for improving the government's performance. This method for generating quantitative policy recommendations respects Lucas's critique (1976).

A distinct use of the model (27), (22), (29), (23), or (51) is to regard it simply as a positive or descriptive model of how taxes have actually been set historically. This view implies that the historical data were not generated by a process that can readily be improved upon by choosing a different government strategy. See Barro (1979) for an application of such reasoning.

The former view analyzes the historical data by imposing an asymmetry between the performance of private agents (which is purposeful and optimizing) and that of government agents (which is arbitrary). That asymmetry leaves scope for suggesting improvements. The latter view imposes symmetry of purposes between private and government agents, in modeling the historical time series, thereby eliminating the scope for recommending improvements of government policy strategy. Each of these views respects the "Lucas critique," and each relies heavily on the structure of restrictions imposed by the hypothesis of rational expectations. There is a big gap between these views in terms of the scope for and the nature of the "advice" which economists give the government.

---

[7] Thus, the view here is that while private agents were optimizing during $t = -T, \ldots, 0$, leading the market to behave according to (2), the government was not optimizing. The assumption that the market behaved according to (2) plays an important role because it would be used econometrically to deduce estimates of the parameters of preferences (A_0, A_1) and technology (f_0, f_1, d) to be used for estimating the optimal government policy. For example, see Hansen and Sargent (1980), and Taylor (1979).

Sims (1982) can be interpreted as asserting that the same dynamic game that governed the historical process will continue to be played during the future. Therefore, the stochastic process that prevailed historically will also describe the future. This perspective underlies Sims's interest in estimating vector autoregressions without imposing restrictions from dynamic economic theory. Sims does not propose to use vector autoregressions to study "regime changes," not only because he does not purport to identify parameters of preferences and technologies that would enable him to do so, but because he doesn't want to try to model the future in terms of a game different than the one played in the past.[8]

EXERCISES

1. (Interpretation of the model of Section 2 as permitting only a tax on new investment.)

Modify the example of Section (2) so that the goverment now imposes a tax only on new investment. The tax collected at t is $\gamma_t(k_t - k_{t-1})$.

A. Show that the market equilibrium now satisfies the following counterpart of (2):

$$k_t = \lambda k_{t-1} - \frac{\lambda}{d}\left(\frac{1}{1-\lambda bL^{-1}}\right)\{J_t - bJ_{t+1} - f_0 u_t - A_0 f_0 + \gamma_t - b\gamma_{t+1}\}. \tag{2'}$$

B. The government's problem is to choose a $\{\gamma_t\}_{t=0}^{\infty}$ sequence maximizing

$$\sum_{t=0}^{\infty} b^t[A_0 f_0 n k_t - \tfrac{1}{2}A_1(f_0{}^2 n^2 k_t{}^2) + f_0 n u_t k_t - nJ_t(k_t - k_{t-1}) - \tfrac{1}{2}nd(k_t - k_{t-1})^2]$$

subject to (2'), (3), and (4). Formulate the Lagrangian associated with this problem and show that the first-order necessary conditions are given by the system

$$\begin{bmatrix} 0 & \mu(1-L) & \dfrac{-\lambda}{d}\left(\dfrac{1-L}{1-\lambda L}\right) \\ \mu(1-bL^{-1}) & \dfrac{-nd}{\lambda}(1-\lambda bL^{-1})(1-\lambda L) & -(1-\lambda bL^{-1}) \\ \dfrac{-\lambda}{d}\left(\dfrac{1-bL^{-1}}{1-\lambda bL^{-1}}\right) & -(1-\lambda L) & 0 \end{bmatrix}\begin{bmatrix} \gamma_t \\ k_t \\ \theta_t \end{bmatrix}$$

$$= \begin{bmatrix} 0 \\ s_t \\ \dfrac{\lambda}{dn}\left(\dfrac{1}{1-\lambda bL^{-1}}\right)s_t \end{bmatrix} \tag{*}$$

where μ and $\{\theta_t\}_{t=0}^{\infty}$ are nonnegative multipliers.

[8] These matters are discussed in greater detail by Sims (1982) and Sargent (1984). The dynamic systems under study are full of self-referential aspects, which threaten to draw the analyst into the system. A consequence of such self-reference is that neither of the views mentioned in the text is free of logical contradictions. The view that there is a difference between the historical and future period in terms of the game played by the government is subject to the criticism that it amounts to assuming that in the historical period the system was not really in a rational expectations equilibrium. The view that the same game is in place historically and in the future raises a question of why we study a system that we cannot influence.

C. Show that the solution of this problem for $t \geq 1$ is given by (22), (27), (29), (23), and $\gamma_t = (1 - bL^{-1})\tau_t$, where τ_t is given by (23) and (29). Show that the present scheme raises an identical stream of revenue as the scheme in Section 2.

2. (Tax-smoothing)

Consider a model in which private agents maximize

$$\sum_{t=0}^{\infty} b^t \{u_1 c_t - \tfrac{1}{2} u_2 c_t - u_3 n_t - \tfrac{1}{2} u_4 n_t^2 - \tau_t n_t\} \qquad u_1, u_2, u_3, u_4 > 0, \qquad 0 < b < 1$$

subject to

$$c_t = f n_t, \qquad f > 0, \qquad u_1 f - u_3 > 0. \tag{2}$$

Here c_t is consumption, n_t is employment, and τ_t is a tax rate on employment.

A government chooses τ_t to maximize the welfare of the representative private agent

$$\sum_{t=0}^{\infty} b^t \{u_1 c_t - \tfrac{1}{2} u_2 c_t - u_3 n_t - \tfrac{1}{2} u_4 n_t^2\}$$

subject to (2), and

$$B_{t+1} = b^{-1}(B_t + g_t - \tau_t n_t), \qquad t \geq 0, \quad B_0 = 0.$$

Here $\{g_t\}_{t=0}^{\infty}$ is a known sequence of exponential order less than $1/\sqrt{b}$. The government also takes as given private agents' rules for selecting (n_t, c_t) as a function of $\{\tau_s\}_{s=0}^{\infty}$.

A. Formulate and solve the government's optimal taxation plan.

B. Show that if an optimal plan exists, it involves setting $\tau_t = \tau$ for all $t \geq 0$.

3. Show that if $d = 0$, the solution of the problem of Section 2 is time consistent.

REFERENCES

Barro, R. J. (1979). "On the determination of the public debt." *Journal of Political Economy*, Vol. 87, No. 5, Part 1, pp. 940–971.

Calvo, G. (1978). "On the time consistency of optimal policy in a monetary economy." *Econometrica*, Vol. 46, No. 6, pp. 1411–1428.

Friedman, M. (1953). "The methodology of positive economics." In *Essays in Positive Economics* (M. Friedman), University of Chicago Press.

Hansen, L. P. and Sargent, T. J. (1980). "Formulating and estimating dynamic linear rational expectations models." *Journal of Economic Dynamics and Control*, Vol. 2, No. 1, pp. 7–46.

Hansen, L. P., Epple, D. and Roberds, W. (1985). "Linear-quadratic duopoly models of resource depletion." In *Energy, Foresight and Strategy* (T. J. Sargent, ed.), Washington, DC: Resources for the Future.

Kydland, F. E. and Prestcott, E. (1977). "Rules rather than discretion: The inconsistency of optimal plans." *Journal of Political Economy*, Vol. 85, No. 3, pp. 473–491.

Lucas, R. E. (1976). "Econometric policy evaluation: a critique." In *The Phillips Curve and Labor Markets* (K. Brunner and A. Meltzer, eds.), Amsterdam: North-Holland.

Lucas, R. E. and Stokey, N. (1983). "Optimal fiscal and monetary policy in an economy without capital." *Journal of Monetary Economics*, Vol. 12, No. 1, pp. 55–93.

Sargent, T. J. (1984). "Autoregressions, expectations, and advice." *American Economic Review*, Vol. 74, No. 2, pp. 408–415.

Sims, C. (1982). "Policy analysis with econometric models." *Brookings Papers on Economic Activity*, Vol. 1, pp. 107–152.

Taylor, J. B. (1979). "Estimation and control of a macroeconomic model with rational expectations." *Econometrica*, Vol. 47, No. 5, pp. 1267–1286.

Whiteman, C. (1983). *Linear Rational Expectations Models: A User's Guide*, University of Minnesota Press.

CHAPTER XVI
THE PHILLIPS CURVE

The term *Phillips curve* refers to a negative correlation between wage inflation and unemployment often thought to have been originally spotted by Phillips in British data, though Irving Fisher and business cycle analysts at the National Bureau of Economic Research and elsewhere had made remarks about the correlation long before. From the point of view of the nonrandom classical model, the observed Phillips curve is a paradox since this model asserts that things causing inflation, such as growing deficits and high rates of money creation, will leave "real" variables such as unemployment and real GNP unaffected. Any evidence that suggests an influence running from higher aggregate demand to higher real GNP and lower unemployment (rather than to higher prices only) seems to contradict the classical model as we have formulated it. More generally, such evidence seems to contradict any general equilibrium model in which agents' decisions about real economic variables are homogeneous of degree zero in nominal magnitudes, as a large body of economic theory predicts.

The initial response of macroeconomists to Phillips' findings was to accept the correlation that Phillips had found as a relation suitable for including in a macroeconometric model—a big jump without first having a well-developed theory of that relation. The Phillips curve, expressing the rate of change of wages as a function of unemployment, fit very well into the Keynesian model because it seemed to provide a convenient device for making wages endogenous to the Keynesian model over time, although perhaps still fixed at a point in time (think of the Phillips curve in continuous time as reading $\dot{w}/w = f(U)$, so that $\dot{w}$ is endogenous at each moment, even while the level of w is fixed). The Phillips curve was widely interpreted as depicting a tradeoff between inflation and unemployment along which policy makers could select a point through suitable monetary and fiscal policy.

The early 1970's saw an increasing amount of dissatisfaction with the preceding use of the Phillips curve. One source of that dissatisfaction was the failure of estimated Phillips curves to remain stable over time. The apparent tradeoff between inflation and unemployment worsened in most western countries in the 1970's, as inflation rates rose.[1] Largely in response to this phenomenon, a body of theoretical work emerged in an attempt to explain how a Phillips curve could arise and to what extent it represents a tradeoff that policy makers can exploit. Important work in this area was done by Friedman (1968), Phelps *et al.* (1970), and Lucas and Prescott (1974).

1. LUCAS'S MODEL

These pages describe Lucas's model of the Phillips curve (see Lucas, 1973). Lucas's model, and much of the other work in this field, embodies the "natural rate hypothesis," which amounts merely to asserting that agents' decisions depend only on relative prices. Within the confines of such a hypothesis, if one is to explain why high inflation and high nominal aggregate demand seem to induce high aggregate output, it is necessary to construct an operational model of "money illusion." Lucas, in effect, constructed a simple model of "money illusion," one compatible with rational, optimizing behavior. As Lucas put it: "All formulations of the natural rate hypothesis postulate rational agents whose decisions depend on relative prices only, placed in an economic setting where they cannot distinguish relative from general price movements."

Lucas supposes that suppliers of a single good are located in a large number of physically separated competitive markets. Demand is distributed unevenly across markets, so prices of the one good vary across markets; the good is perishable and there is no trading across markets. All markets are identical in their behavioral parameters. The *state* of one market is differentiated from the others in only two ways. First, in each market at time t there is a relative demand shock z_t, which is serially independent and has mean zero and a finite variance. The variable z_t has density $g(z_t)$, and the sequence $(z_t, z_{t-1}, \ldots)$ has joint density $g(z_t)g(z_{t-1}) \cdots$ by virtue of the assumption of serial independence of z_t.

Second, each market has its own particular value of once lagged output y_{t-1}, which itself will turn out to be a function of the lagged values of z's that the market has drawn. Since the z_t are serially independent, it will turn out that y_{t-1} is statistically independent of the current z_t. We assume that y_{t-1} has probability density function $f(y_{t-1})$, so that the joint density of y_{t-1} and z_t is $f(y_{t-1})g(z_t)$. (Below we shall verify that y_{t-1} is statistically independent of z_t.)

Since z_t and y_{t-1} are the only aspects of the state that vary across markets, we can index markets by their values of (z_t, y_{t-1}) at time t. If two markets "draw" the same (z_t, y_{t-1}), they behave identically.

---

[1] For the United States, this fact has been well documented by R. J. Gordon in a sequence of papers dating back to 1970 in *Brookings Papers on Economic Activity*, edited by Perry and Okun (1970, 71, 77).

Agents are assumed to know the first and second moments of all probability distributions. This gives them the information needed to form linear least squares projections of random variables they do not know on the random variables they do know. We implement the hypothesis of rational expectations by assuming that agents' expectations about unknown random variables equal the linear least squares projections on certain information sets to be specified.

Supply in market (z_t, y_{t-1}) is assumed to be governed by

$$y_t(z_t, y_{t-1}) = \gamma(p_t(z) - P[p_t|I_t(z)]) + \lambda y_{t-1}, \qquad \gamma > 0, \quad 0 < \lambda < 1 \qquad (1)$$

where

$$y_t(z_t, y_{t-1}) = \text{logarithm of supply in market } (z_t, y_{t-1}),$$
$$p_t(z) = \text{logarithm of price in market with demand shock } z$$
$$\text{(assumed given to the suppliers, who are price-takers),}$$
$$p_t = \text{average economy-wide logarithm of price, the aver-}$$
$$\text{age across markets of the } p_t(z),$$
$$P[p_t|I_t(z)] = \text{the projection of } p_t \text{ on information available in}$$
$$\text{market } (z_t, y_{t-1}) \text{ at time } t,$$
$$I_t(z) = \text{information available at time } t \text{ in market } (z_t, y_{t-1}).$$
$$\text{For convenience, we follow Lucas and index this}$$
$$\text{information set only by } z, \text{ even though in general it}$$
$$\text{depends on } y_{t-1} \text{ too.}$$

According to (1), supply in market (z_t, y_{t-1}) responds directly to the gap between the current price in market (z_t, y_{t-1}) and the forecast $P[p_t|I_t(z)]$ of average economy-wide price made by agents in market (z_t, y_{t-1}). Agents in (z_t, y_{t-1}) are assumed not to know p_t because at time t they see only the price in their own market $p_t(z)$. For that reason, they have to forecast p_t by projecting it on information they do have, an information set to be specified shortly. Equation (1) depicts agents as responding to what they perceive to be increases in the relative price $p_t(z) - P[p_t|I_t(z)]$, but as failing to respond to what are perceived as general increases in the price level, i.e., those that leave $p_t(z) - P[p_t|I_t(z)]$ unaltered. The term λy_{t-1} is added to account for the possibility that supply responds also to lagged perceived relative price changes. We shall say more about this presently.

To complete the model, we have to specify the information set $I_t(z)$. We initially assume that $I_t(z)$ consists of two components. First, $I_t(z)$ of course includes $p_t(z)$ since agents in market (z_t, y_{t-1}) see the price facing them at t. We assume that $p_t(z)$ is the only current information that agents receive. Second, $I_t(z)$ includes a set Ω_{t-1}, which is information on a set of variables dated $t-1$ and earlier. We can specify Ω_{t-1} in a variety of ways. For example, Lucas assumed that Ω_{t-1} included information on all *lagged* values of $p_t(z)$ and lagged values of y_t in all markets.[2] One could equally well conceive of less comprehensive definitions of Ω_{t-1}. As we shall see, the definition of Ω_{t-1} has some important consequences. For now, along with Lucas we suppose that Ω_{t-1} includes a comprehensive list of variables including lagged outputs and prices in all markets. We do not index Ω_{t-1} by z_t or y_{t-1} since all markets are assumed to share the information in Ω_{t-1}.

Thus we have $I_t(z) = (\Omega_{t-1}, p_t(z))$. We shall find it convenient to use the recursive projection formula in getting an expression for $P[p_t|I_t(z)]$. By way of doing this, we first obtain the decomposition

$$p_t = P[p_t|\Omega_{t-1}] + \xi_t \tag{2}$$

where ξ_t is a random variable (a least squares disturbance) that by the orthogonality principle obeys $E(\xi_t P[p_t|\Omega_{t-1}]) = 0$ and $E\xi_t = 0$. Let the variance of ξ_t be denoted $E\xi_t^2 = \sigma^2$. The disturbance ξ_t is the "surprise" part of the aggregate price level, which cannot be predicted from information Ω_{t-1}.

Next, suppose that demand is distributed so that

$$p_t(z) = p_t + z_t \tag{3}$$

where $Ez_t p_t = 0$, $Ez_t \xi_t = 0$, and $Ez_t z_s = 0$ for $t \neq s$. We assume that z_t is orthogonal to all variables in Ω_{t-1}. Equation (3) expressed $p_t(z)$ as the sum of the economy-wide price p_t and a random term z_t, which is uncorrelated with p_t and previous information and which measures relative price movements. We assume that $Ez_t = 0$ and $Ez_t^2 = \tau^2$. The specification $Ez_t = 0$ merely means that relative price movements average out across markets.

Substituting (2) into (3) gives

$$p_t(z) = P[p_t|\Omega_{t-1}] + \xi_t + z_t \tag{4}$$

where again $E\xi_t z_t = 0$, so that $E\{(\xi_t + z_t)^2\} = \sigma^2 + \tau^2$. Now what is the linear least squares forecast of $p_t(z)$ given Ω_{t-1}? Since by construction ξ_t is orthogonal to Ω_{t-1} and since by assumption z_t is orthogonal to Ω_{t-1}, we have that (4) is a projection equation with disturbance $\xi_t + z_t$, so that

$$P[p_t(z)|\Omega_{t-1}] = P[p_t|\Omega_{t-1}]. \tag{5}$$

We are now in a position to apply the recursive projection formula to get an expression for $P[p_t|I_t(z)]$:

$$P[p_t|\Omega_{t-1}, p_t(z)]$$
$$= P[p_t|\Omega_{t-1}] + P[(p_t - P[p_t|\Omega_{t-1}])|(p_t(z) - P[p_t(z)|\Omega_{t-1}])]. \tag{6}$$

---

[2] Under that assumption, the information sets in different markets are differentiated only by different drawings of z_t, and not y_{t-1} since every market sees every other market's y_{t-1}. That was why Lucas indexed information sets by z_t only.

Using (2), (4), and (5) we know that

$$p_t - P[p_t|\Omega_{t-1}] = \xi_t, \qquad p_t(z) - P[p_t(z)|\Omega_{t-1}] = \xi_t + z_t$$

and also that $E\xi_t z_t = 0$. The projection of $p_t - P[p_t|\Omega_{t-1}]$ on $p_t(z) - P[p_t(z)|\Omega_{t-1}]$ is therefore given by

$$\phi(p_t(z) - P[p_t(z)|\Omega_{t-1}])$$

where the least squares regression coefficient ϕ is given by

$$\phi = E\xi_t(\xi_t + z_t)/E[(\xi_t + z_t)^2] = \sigma^2/(\sigma^2 + \tau^2).$$

Using the above and recalling that $P[p_t(z)|\Omega_{t-1})] = P[p_t|\Omega_{t-1}]$, we can write (6) as

$$P[p_t|I_t(z)] = P[p_t|\Omega_{t-1}] + (\sigma^2/(\sigma^2 + \tau^2))[p_t(z) - P[p_t|\Omega_{t-1}]]$$

or

$$P[p_t|I_t(z)] = \theta P[p_t|\Omega_{t-1}] + (1 - \theta)p_t(z) \tag{7}$$

where $\theta = \tau^2/(\tau^2 + \sigma^2)$ and $1 - \theta = \sigma^2/(\tau^2 + \sigma^2)$. The parameter θ is the fraction of the conditional variance in $p_t(z)$ due to relative price variation. The larger is this fraction, the smaller is the weight placed on $p_t(z)$ in revising $P[p_t|\Omega_{t-1}]$ to form $P[p_t|I_t(z)]$. This makes sense since the larger is θ, the more likely it is that a change in $p_t(z)$ reflects a relative rather than a general price change.

Substituting (7) into (1) gives

$$y_t(z_t, y_{t-1}) = \gamma[p_t(z) - \theta P[p_t|\Omega_{t-1}] - (1 - \theta)p_t(z)] + \lambda y_{t-1}$$

or

$$y_t(z_t, y_{t-1}) = \gamma\theta(p_t(z) - P[p_t|\Omega_{t-1}]) + \lambda y_{t-1}. \tag{8}$$

Recall that $g(z_t)f(y_{t-1})$ is the joint density of z_t, y_{t-1}. An index of average output is then given by

$$\bar{y}_t = \iint y_t(z_t, y_{t-1})g(z_t)f(y_{t-1}) \, dz_t \, dy_{t-1}$$

which is simply the mean of the distribution of $y_t(z_t, y_{t-1})$. The average price level is given by

$$p_t = \int p_t(z)g(z) \, dz.$$

Integrating both sides of (8) with respect to $g(z_t)f(y_{t-1}) \, dz_t \, dy_{t-1}$ (i.e., averaging (8) over all markets) gives[3]

$$\iint y_t(z_t, y_{t-1})g(z_t)f(y_{t-1}) \, dz_t \, dy_{t-1}$$

$$= \gamma\theta\left(\int p_t(z) \, g(z) \, dz - P[p_t|\Omega_{t-1}]\right)\int g(z) \, dz\right)\int f(y_{t-1}) \, dy_{t-1}$$

$$+ \lambda \int y_{t-1}f(y_{t-1}) \, dy_{t-1}\int g(z_t) \, dz_t$$

or

$$\bar{y}_t = \gamma\theta(p_t - P[p_t|\Omega_{t-1}]) + \lambda\bar{y}_{t-1}. \tag{9}$$

Since $\gamma > 0$ and $0 < \theta = \tau^2/(\sigma^2 + \tau^2) < 1$, Equation (9) is a version of a Phillips curve relating output directly to the gap between the average price level p_t and agents' prior forecast of the price level $P[p_t|\Omega_{t-1}]$. To write (9) in an alternative way, solve (9) for $p_t - P[p_t|\Omega_{t-1}]$ to get

$$p_t - P[p_t|\Omega_{t-1}] = (\gamma\theta)^{-1}\bar{y}_t - \lambda(\gamma\theta)^{-1}\bar{y}_{t-1}.$$

Adding and subtracting p_{t-1} gives

$$p_t - p_{t-1} = (\gamma\theta)^{-1}\bar{y}_t - \lambda(\gamma\theta)^{-1}\bar{y}_{t-1} + (P[p_t|\Omega_{t-1}] - p_{t-1}), \tag{10}$$

which is in the form of a standard natural rate Phillips curve relating inflation $p_t - p_{t-1}$ directly to output and to expected inflation $P[p_t|\Omega_{t-1}] - p_{t-1}$. According to (10), the Phillips curve shifts up in the $(p_t - p_{t-1}, \bar{y}_t)$ plane by the exact amount of any increase in expected inflation $P[p_t|\Omega_{t-1}] - p_{t-1}$. This characteristic of (10) is often taken as the hallmark of the natural unemployment rate hypothesis. It seems to offer an explanation for why the Phillips curve tradeoff worsened as average inflation rates increased over the 1970's in many western countries.

Notice that since $p_t(z) - P[p_t|\Omega_{t-1}] = \xi_t + z_t$, Equation (8) can be written

$$y_t(z_t, y_{t-1}) = \gamma\theta(\xi_t + z_t) + \lambda y_{t-1}$$

or

$$y_t = \gamma\theta\sum_{i=0}^{\infty}\lambda^i(\xi_{t-i} + z_{t-i}), \tag{8'}$$

which shows how y_t depends on current and all previous values of the relative demand shock z_t, and of the "aggregate demand" shock ξ_t.[4] It immediately

---

[3] Remember that since $g(\cdot)$ and $f(\cdot)$ are probability densities, $\int g(z) \, dz = \int f(y_{t-1}) \, dy_{t-1} = 1$.

[4] That is, ξ_t is the part of the average price level that cannot be predicted from past data.

follows that since z_t is serially independent, y_{t-1} is statistically independent of z_t, as claimed earlier. Notice that an alternative way to derive (9) would be to integrate (8') with respect to $g(z_t)g(z_{t-1}) \cdots dz_t \, dz_{t-1} \cdots$ to get

$$\bar{y}_t = \gamma\theta \sum_{i=0}^{\infty} \lambda^i \xi_{t-i}, \tag{9'}$$

which is equivalent with (9). Thus, markets can be indexed either by the sequence $(z_t, z_{t-1}, \ldots)$ or by the pair (z_t, y_{t-1}) as we have done.

It is important to note that the slope parameter $\gamma\theta$ of (9) depends on the ratio of the variances of the random terms ξ_t and z_t, since $\theta = \tau^2/(\sigma^2 + \tau^2)$. The larger is the variance of z_t $(Ez_t^2 = \tau^2)$, relative to the variance of ξ_t $(E\xi_t^2 = \sigma^2)$, the larger is θ and, therefore, the larger is $\theta\gamma$. So the more variable is z_t relative to ξ_t, the larger is the response of aggregate output y_t to unexpected aggregate price changes $(p_t - P[p_t|\Omega_{t-1}])$. That is, the larger is the variance of z_t relative to that of ξ_t, the greater is the tendency of rational agents to view a given unexpected increase in price as a relative price change to which their output decision should respond.

An implication of the dependence of the slope of (9) on the ratio of variances of relative to aggregate price movements is that (9) is *not* predicted to remain unchanged across different aggregate demand regimes. That is, a "favorable" tradeoff between output and unexpected inflation (that is, a large value of $\gamma\theta$) will exist only when σ^2 is small relative to τ^2. An attempt by the authorities to exploit the tradeoff more fully by changing aggregate demand regimes might increase the variance σ^2 relative to τ^2, and thus change the slope $\gamma\theta$. This is yet another example of how agents' optimal decision rules change in response to changes in the random processes governing the exogenous variables they base their decisions on.

For empirical support of his model, Lucas pointed to evidence that the slope parameter in (9) does indeed seem to be much smaller in regimes with very high variance in nominal aggregate demand than in regimes with low variance of nominal aggregate demand.

2. SERIAL CORRELATION IN OUTPUT

It is a fact that the unemployment rate and deviations of real GNP from its trend are highly serially correlated, i.e., strongly and positively correlated with their own lagged values. How can this fact be accounted for within the context of the preceding model? The answer depends delicately on how we specify the information set Ω_{t-1}. To begin, suppose that Ω_{t-1} includes enough information for agents to be able to know lagged values of the aggregate price index p_{t-1}, $p_{t-2}, \ldots$. This could happen if lagged values of the price index were published or if agents received with a one-period lag prices in all other markets so that they could form $p_{t-1}, p_{t-2}, \ldots$ for themselves. Further, it is obviously not restrictive at all to assume that agents' information includes their own lagged forecasts $P[p_{t-1}|\Omega_{t-2}], P[p_{t-2}|\Omega_{t-3}], \ldots$ Since both lagged forecasts and lagged prices are assumed to be included in Ω_{t-1}, it follows that the lagged forecast errors

$$p_{t-1} - P[p_{t-1}|\Omega_{t-2}], \quad p_{t-2} - P[p_{t-2}|\Omega_{t-3}], \quad \ldots$$

are included in Ω_{t-1}. The least squares orthogonality condition then implies

$$E\{(p_t - P[p_t|\Omega_{t-1}])(p_{t-j} - P[p_{t-j}|\Omega_{t-j-1}])\} = 0 \tag{11}$$

for all $j \geq 1$ since $p_{t-j} - P[p_{t-j}|\Omega_{t-j-1}]$ is included in Ω_{t-1} (remember the orthogonality principle: the least squares projection $P[p_t|\Omega_{t-1}]$ is uniquely determined by the condition that the forecast error be orthogonal to all components of Ω_{t-1}). According to Equation (11), the forecast error is uncorrelated with its own lagged values, i.e., it is serially uncorrelated. This is a direct implication of our having assumed that lagged p's are included in Ω_{t-1}.

In the context of (9), (11) has the implication that if $\lambda = 0$, $\bar{y}_t$ itself will be serially uncorrelated since then $\bar{y}_t$ equals a scalar $\gamma\theta$ times the serially uncorrelated forecast error $p_t - P[p_t|\Omega_{t-1}]$. However, if $\lambda > 0$, the effects of forecast errors that are themselves serially uncorrelated will persist and make y_t serially correlated. Since it is a fact that y_t is strongly serially correlated, it is necessary to permit λ to exceed zero (and by a healthy amount) if the facts are to be accounted for in the context of (9). An objection (see Modigliani, 1977) which has been made to this procedure is that it is ad hoc and not derived from any explicitly stated theory. From what has been presented so far, the theoretical content of (9) is entirely reflected in the relative price parameter γ and the signal extraction parameter θ. In Chapter XVIII it will be shown that costs of adjustment can lead to the presence of lagged $\bar{y}$'s in (9).

An alternative way of explaining serial correlation in output while retaining (9) is to relax the assumption that Ω_{t-1} includes lagged aggregate prices. If Ω_{t-1} does not include lagged p's, the orthogonality condition no longer implies (11), so that the forecast errors can themselves be serially correlated and can account for serially correlated output even with $\lambda = 0$ in (9). One way to think of having Ω_{t-1} exclude lagged p's is by supposing that the price indexes appropriate to agents' decisions are never collected, so that the published price indexes are error-ridden. Another device, which has been implemented by Lucas (1975), is to interpret p_t in all of the preceding as "nominal aggregate demand" rather than price, which, as above, is composed of relative and aggregate movements. If agents never observe nominal aggregate demand but know its second movements, so that they can calculate the least squares projections studied above, serially correlated output can be accounted for within the context of a version of (9) with $\lambda = 0$.

EXERCISE

Supply in an individual market that gets relative demand shock z_t is governed by

$$y_t(z) = \gamma(p_t(z) - Ep_t | I_t(z)), \qquad \gamma > 0$$

where $p_t(z) = p_t + z_t$,

$$p_t = \sum_{j=0}^{\infty} v_j \varepsilon_{t-j} = \int p_t(z) g(z_t) \, dz_t, \qquad v_0 = 1, \qquad \sum_{j=0}^{\infty} v_j^2 < \infty$$

where $Ez_t \varepsilon_s = 0$ for all t and s, and ε and z are serially independent processes with means of zero. Here $y_t(z)$ is the log of supply in market z, $p_t(z)$ is the log of price in market z, p_t is the average log price level, and $g(z_t)$ is the probability density of z_t. We assume that z and ε are each normal random variates with means of zero. Information in market z, $I_t(z)$, consists of the following three elements: Ω_{t-1}, observations on all lagged prices and quantities in *all* markets; $p_t(z)$, the current own-market price; and the current market price $p_t(z')$ in one other market. Assume that different markets have statistically independent and identically distributed z's.

A. Derive a Phillips curve of the form

$$y_t = \phi(p_t - Ep_t | \Omega_{t-1})$$

where $y_t = \int y_t(z_t) g(z_t) \, dz_t$. Give a formula for ϕ in terms of γ and the variances of ε_t and z_t.

B. Is your value for ϕ larger or smaller than the value that Lucas derived by assuming that $I_t(z)$ consisted only of the two bits of information Ω_{t-1} and $p_t(z_t)$? Can you guess what would happen to the slope ϕ if agents in market z were permitted to see current prices in n markets, as n becomes larger and larger? Heuristically explain what is going on here to affect the slope ϕ.

REFERENCES

Friedman, M. (1968). "The role of monetary policy." *The American Economic Review*, Vol. LVIII, No. 1, pp. 1–17.

Gordon, R. J. (1970). "The recent acceleration of inflation and its lessons for the future." *Brookings Papers on Economic Activity* (G. Perry and A. Okun, eds.), No. 1, pp. 8–41.

Gordon, R. J. (1971). "Inflation in recession and recovery." *Brookings Papers on Economic Activity* (G. Perry and A. Okun, eds.) No. 1, pp. 105–158.

Gordon, R. J. (1977). "Can the inflation of the 1970's be explained?" *Brookings Papers on Economic Activity* (G. Perry and A. Okun, eds.), No. 1, pp. 253–276.

Lucas, R. E. Jr. (1973). "Some international evidence on output-inflation tradeoffs." *The American Economic Review*, Vol. LXIII, No. 3, pp. 326–334.

Lucas, R. E. Jr. (1975). "An equilibrium model of the business cycle." *Journal of Political Economy*, Vol. 83, No. 6, pp. 1113–1144.

Lucas, R. E. Jr. and Prescott, E. C. (1974). "Equilibrium search and unemployment." *Journal of Economic Theory*, Vol. 7, No. 2, pp. 188–209.

Modigliani, F. (1977). "The monetarist controversy or, should we forsake stabilization policies?" *The American Economic Review*, Vol. 67, No. 2, pp. 1–19.

Phelps, E. S. *et al.* (1970). *Microeconomic Foundations of Employment and Inflation Theory*, New York: Norton.

CHAPTER XVII

OPTIMAL MONETARY POLICY

The central practical issue separating Keynesian from non-Keynesian economists is the nature of the optimal feedback rules for setting monetary and fiscal policy instruments.[1] Keynesian economists have advocated "activist" policies, which incorporate feedback from current and past observations on the state of the economy to future settings of fiscal and monetary instruments (e.g., the deficit and the money supply). Usually, these feedback rules are thought to imply that policy ought to "lean aginst the wind," calling for increases in taxes and lower rates of growth in the money supply in the boom, and lower taxes and higher growth in money when a recession is in the offing.

On the other hand, non-Keynesian economists such as Simons (1936) and Friedman (1948, 1959) have advocated that the government follow rules without feedback in setting fiscal and monetary policy. In essence, Simons and Friedman's advice to the government is threefold. First, set government expenditures on the basis of cost–benefit considerations and do not manipulate government expenditures to try to combat the business cycle. Second, keep tax rates fixed at levels that, given the rate of government expenditures, make the rate of growth of government debt average out over the business cycle to some desired level. Third, make the money supply grow at a constant rate of x percent per year, regardless of the state of business conditions. The rate x should be set with a view to the average rate of inflation desired.

---

[1] This chapter serves as an introduction to the macroeconomic literature on what Bennett McCallum (1979) called "the policy ineffectiveness proposition." A general equilibrium model emphasizing the distinct effects associated with expected and unexpected changes in the stock of currency was introduced by Lucas (1972). By grafting the aggregate supply schedule of Lucas (1973) onto a linear version of a standard Keynesian model, Sargent (1973) and Sargent and Wallace (1975, 1976) constructed simple macroeconomic models that served to emphasize this distinction. This chapter describes a version of the Sargent–Wallace model. Barro (1977, 1978) contains some closely related theoretical developments and reports some empirical tests. The macroeconomic literature on "policy ineffectiveness" was surveyed by McCallum (1979). Taylor (1979, 1980a, 1980b) has worked with a class of models in which policy is "effective" but is subject to a set of cross-equation restrictions that render inappropriate analyses in the style of Section 1 of this chapter.

The differences between the prescriptions of the two schools do not seem to be attributable to any differences over the goals each of them would like policy to achieve. Each would like to keep the economy as close as possible to "full employment," hopefully with a stable price level. Neither can the difference between policy prescriptions be traced to any differences over how to derive a feedback rule for a given economic model and a given objective function: that is essentially a technical matter about which there is no room for disagreement. Rather, the disagreement stems from fundamental differences on the question of what is the correct macroeconomic model. In particular, a great deal hinges on the question of how to model the manner in which agents form their expectations about future events.

These pages first state the case for using rules with feedback. The argument for using rules with feedback assumes that the economy can be described as a set of stochastic difference equations (i.e., an econometric model), which, when written in a particular form, has coefficients that are invariant across alternative feedback rules that the authority might use. Given this setup, rules with feedback will be shown to dominate rules without feedback. This setup displays the intellectual foundations of the Keynesian "activist" policy strategy.

We next explore the parts of the preceding setup that a non-Keynesian economist might question. In particular, it will be seen that the form of the model that must remain invariant across changes in feedback rules is one that embodies the public's rule for forecasting future prices. As we have seen repeatedly, if agents optimize, the forms of such forecasting rules depend on the nature of the exogenous stochastic processes facing them. Since changes in the government's feedback rules alter those processes, the forecasting rules and therefore the parameters of the model will change with each change in the policy feedback rule. We shall see that a defense of the Simons–Friedman rules without feedback can be erected on the foundations of this observation.

1. OPTIMAL CONTROL WITH FIXED EXPECTATIONS

Suppose that the economy is governed by the following simple macroeconomic model:

$$y_t = \gamma(p_t - {}_t p_{t-1}^*) + \lambda y_{t-1} + u_t, \qquad \gamma > 0, \tag{1}$$

$$m_t - p_t = y_t + \varepsilon_t, \tag{2}$$

$$_t p_{t-1}^* = v(L)p_{t-1} \quad \left(\equiv \sum_{i=0}^{\infty} v_i p_{t-i-1} \right) \tag{3}$$

where y_t = log of real GNP, p_t = log of the GNP deflator, m_t = log of the money supply, and ${}_t p_{t-1}^*$ is the public's expectation of the log of the price level at time t, the expectation being formed at time $t - 1$. We assume that u_t and ε_t are each serially independent, stationary random processes with means of zero and finite variances. For simplicity, we assume that ε and u are uncorrelated, so that $Eu_t\varepsilon_t = 0$. Equation (1) is a simple Phillips curve embodying the natural unemployment rate hypothesis since only unexpected increases in the price level are posited to boost aggregate supply. Equation (2) is a simple portfolio balance schedule that excludes the interest rate, for simplicity only. Equation (3) describes how expectations are formed as a weighted sum of past prices with fixed weights v_i. The model (1)–(3) determines stochastic processes for y_t, p_t, and $_t p_{t-1}^*$ as functions of the disturbance processes, u_t, ε_t, and the money supply process m_t.

The goal of the monetary authority is to choose a stochastic process for the money supply that in some sense optimizes the performance of the economy. To illustrate this problem in the simplest context,[2] we assume initially that the object of the monetary authority is to minimize the mean squared error of real GNP around some fixed target level y^*,

$$\text{M.S.E.} = E(y_t - y^*)^2. \tag{4}$$

As we shall indicate in more detail later, this criterion is a sensible one for comparing rules that have been in effect for a long time, or else in comparing the eventual performances of alternative rules after they will have been in effect for a long time. It is convenient to decompose the mean squared error as follows:

$$E[(y_t - y^*)^2] = E[((y_t - Ey_t) + (Ey_t - y^*))^2]$$
$$= E((y_t - Ey_t)^2) + E((Ey_t - y^*)^2) + 2E(y_t - Ey_t)(Ey_t - y^*).$$

Since $Ey_t - y^*$ is not random and since $E(y_t - Ey_t) = Ey_t - Ey_t = 0$, we have the decomposition

$$\text{M.S.E.} = E[(y_t - Ey_t)^2] + (Ey_t - y^*)^2, \tag{5}$$

which expresses the mean squared error as the sum of the variance of y and the "bias squared" around y^*.

To derive an optimal monetary policy rule, it is convenient first to solve for a "final form" for y_t expressing y_t as a function of current and lagged u's, ε's, and m's. Substituting (3) into (1) gives

$$(1 - \lambda L)y_t = \gamma(1 - Lv(L))p_t + u_t.$$

Solving (2) for p_t and substituting into the above equation gives

$$(1 - \lambda L)y_t = \gamma[1 - Lv(L)](m_t - y_t - \varepsilon_t) + u_t$$

or

$$[1 + \gamma - (\lambda + \gamma v(L))L]y_t = \gamma[1 - Lv(L)](m_t - \varepsilon_t) + u_t.$$

---

[2] Think of y_t as being measured in deviations from trend, so that we abstract from considerations of growth.

Assuming that $1 + \gamma - (\lambda + \gamma v(L))L$ has a stable inverse that is one-sided in nonnegative powers of L, we have

$$y_t = \frac{\gamma(1 - Lv(L))}{(1 + \gamma) - (\lambda + \gamma v(L))L}(m_t - \varepsilon_t) + \frac{1}{(1 + \gamma) - (\lambda + \gamma v(L))L}u_t$$

or

$$y_t = H(L)m_t + G(L)\varepsilon_t + F(L)u_t \tag{6}$$

where

$$H(L) = \frac{\gamma(1 - Lv(L))}{(1 + \gamma) - (\lambda + \gamma v(L))L} = \sum_{i=0}^{\infty} h_i L^i, \qquad G(L) = -H(L) = \sum_{i=0}^{\infty} g_i L^i,$$

$$F(L) = \frac{1}{1 + \gamma - (\lambda + \gamma v(L))L} = \sum_{i=0}^{\infty} f_i L^i.$$

Since $H(L)$, $G(L)$, and $F(L)$ are each one-sided, (6) is equivalent with

$$y_t = \sum_{i=0}^{\infty} h_i m_{t-i} + \sum_{i=0}^{\infty} g_i \varepsilon_{t-i} + \sum_{i=0}^{\infty} f_i u_{t-i}. \tag{6'}$$

Equation (6) is the final form for y_t.

The monetary authority is assumed to consider linear feedback rules of the form[3]

$$m_t = k + A(L)\varepsilon_{t-1} + \beta(L)u_{t-1} \tag{7}$$

where $A(L) = \sum_{i=0}^{\infty} a_i L^i$ and $\beta(L) = \sum_{i=0}^{\infty} b_i L^i$. Through (7), the monetary authority permits itself to react to unexpected changes in the position of the economy, which are completely described by the disturbances u_t and ε_t. The authority is assumed to know the structure of the economy (it knows the parameters of (1)–(3), and therefore of (6)). It also has data on all lagged values of y_t, p_t, and m_t, so that it can calculate the lagged disturbances u_t and ε_t by using its knowledge of the parameters of (1)–(3), together with its data on p_t, y_t, and m_t. The monetary authority is required to set m_t before it receives information on current y_t and p_t, which explains why it is permitted only to feedback on lagged ε's and u's in (7).

The goal of the monetary authority is to choose k, $A(L)$, and $\beta(L)$ to minimize the mean squared error (5), subject to the structure of the economy (6). The authority assumes that the parameter values in (6) remain unchanged as it contemplates the effects of alternative choices of k, the a's, and the b's in (7).

---

[3] Where the disturbances follow a normal distribution or where the objective function is quadratic and the model is linear, it is known that linear feedback rules of the form (7) are the optimal ones to follow.

To determine the effects of operating under the feedback rule (7), substitute (7) into (6) to obtain

$$y_t = H(L)[A(L)L\varepsilon_t + \beta(L)Lu_t + k] + G(L)\varepsilon_t + F(L)u_t$$
$$= kH(1) + [H(L)A(L)L + G(L)]\varepsilon_t + [H(L)\beta(L)L + F(L)]u_t. \tag{8}$$

By substituting (7) into (6), we in effect assume that (7) has been operating forever. For convenience let

$$H(L)A(L)L = \phi(L) = \sum_{i=1}^{\infty} \phi_i L^i, \qquad H(L)\beta(L)L = \psi(L) = \sum_{i=1}^{\infty} \psi_i L^i.$$

Since $E\varepsilon_t = Eu_t = 0$ for all t, we have that

$$Ey_t = kH(1).$$

The bias squared term in (5) is minimized by choosing k so that $Ey_t = y^*$:

$$Ey_t = y^* = kH(1).$$

This is accomplished by setting $k = y^*/H(1)$. Since the variance of y turns out not to depend on k, the mean squared error is minimized by minimizing the variance and bias squared separately.

From (8), the variance of y_t is given by

$$\operatorname{var} y_t = \operatorname{var} \varepsilon_t \left[g_0^2 + \sum_{j=1}^{\infty} (g_j + \phi_j)^2 \right] + \operatorname{var} u_t \left[f_0^2 + \sum_{j=1}^{\infty} (f_j + \psi_j)^2 \right].$$

To find the minimizing values of ϕ_i, for example, we require

$$\partial \operatorname{var} y_t / \partial \phi_i = (\operatorname{var} \varepsilon_t) 2(g_i + \phi_i) = 0$$

so that we set $\phi_i = -g_i$. Similarly, we set $\psi_j = -f_j$. It is readily verified that the second-order conditions for a minimum are satisfied. Thus, we are instructed to set $\phi(L)$ and $\psi(L)$ so that

$$\phi(L) = H(L)A(L)L = -\sum_{i=1}^{\infty} g_i L^i, \qquad \psi(L) = H(L)\beta(L)L = -\sum_{i=1}^{\infty} f_i L^i.$$

Solving for $A(L)$ and $\beta(L)$ gives

$$A(L) = \left(-\sum_{i=1}^{\infty} g_i L^i \right) \bigg/ H(L)L, \qquad \beta(L) = \left(-\sum_{i=1}^{\infty} f_i L^i \right) \bigg/ H(L)L, \qquad k = y^*/H(1). \tag{9}$$

Choosing $A(L)$, $\beta(L)$, and k according to (9) minimizes the mean squared error of y_t around y^*. Notice that under the rule we have that $H(L)A(L)L + G(L) = g_0$, $H(L)\beta(L)L + F(L) = f_0$, so (8) becomes

$$y_t = H(1)k + g_0 \varepsilon_t + f_0 u_t = y^* + g_0 \varepsilon_t + f_0 u_t. \tag{10}$$

Under the optimal rule (9), once it has been in effect for a long time, y equals y^* plus an irreducible, serially uncorrelated noise $f_0 u_t + g_0 \varepsilon_t$. The mean squared error under the rule equals $g_0^2 \, \text{var} \, \varepsilon_t + f_0^2 \, \text{var} \, u_t$. Notice that under the optimal rule, all serial correlation in y has been eliminated. Strong positive serial correlation in y is what most economists mean when they refer to the "business cycle." Under the optimal rule, the business cycle, then, has been eradicated.

The fact that there exists a rule that eliminates serial correlation in output underlies the Keynesian economist's practice of assigning the blame for recessions to inappropriate monetary and fiscal policy. Given the kind of setup employed here, that practice is entirely justified.

It is useful to work out the optimal monetary rule under slightly different conditions. In particular, suppose that at time $t - 1$ it is desired to set m_t so as to minimize $E_{t-1}(y_t - y^*)^2$ where $E_{t-1}(\cdot)$ is the mathematical expectation operator conditioned on information known at time $t - 1$. The authority desires to minimize $E_{t-1}(y_t - y^*)^2$, taking as given the (possibly very unwise) monetary policy that was pursued in the past. As before, it is possible to decompose the mean squared error:

$$E_{t-1}(y_t - y^*)^2 = E_{t-1}((y_t - E_{t-1}y_t)^2) + (E_{t-1}y_t - y^*)^2 \qquad (11)$$

where the first term is the conditional variance around the conditional mean and the second term is the conditional bias squared.

The final form (6) can be written

$$y_t = h_0 m_t + H_1(L)m_{t-1} + g_0 \varepsilon_t + G_1(L)\varepsilon_{t-1} + f_0 u_t + F_1(L)u_{t-1} \qquad (12)$$

where

$$H_1(L) = \sum_{i=1}^{\infty} h_i L^{i-1} = \left[\frac{H(L)}{L} \right]_+, \qquad G_1(L) = \sum_{i=1}^{\infty} g_i L^{i-1} = \left[\frac{G(L)}{L} \right]_+,$$

$$F_1(L) = \sum_{i=1}^{\infty} f_i L^{i-1} = \left[\frac{F(L)}{L} \right]_+.$$

Since ε_t and u_t are serially independent, we have $E_{t-1}u_t = E_{t-1}\varepsilon_t = 0$. Then using (12) we have

$$E_{t-1}y_t = h_0 E_{t-1}m_t + H_1(L)m_{t-1} + G_1(L)\varepsilon_{t-1} + F_1(L)u_{t-1}.$$

To minimize the bias squared, we equate $E_{t-1}y_t$ to y^* to get

$$E_{t-1}m_t = \frac{1}{h_0} y^* - \frac{H_1(L)}{h_0} m_{t-1} - \frac{G_1(L)}{h_0} \varepsilon_{t-1} - \frac{F_1(L)}{h_0} u_{t-1}.$$

Under any rule, we have

$$y_t - E_{t-1}y_t = h_0(m_t - E_{t-1}m_t) + g_0 \varepsilon_t + f_0 u_t.$$

So long as m_t must be set independently of ε_t and u_t (i.e., it must be set on the basis of information at time $t - 1$), the variance $E_{t-1}((y_t - E_{t-1}y_t)^2)$ is therefore minimized by setting $m_t = E_{t-1}m_t$. Thus, the optimal rule for setting m_t is

$$m_t = \frac{1}{h_0} y^* - \frac{H_1(L)}{h_0} m_{t-1} - \frac{G_1(L)}{h_0} \varepsilon_{t-1} - \frac{F_1(L)}{h_0} u_{t-1}. \tag{13}$$

Notice that under this rule y_t obeys

$$y_t = y^* + g_0\varepsilon_t + f_0 u_t,$$

which is derived by substituting (13) into (12). Thus, the rule succeeds in setting y_t to the target y^* plus the irreducible noise $g_0\varepsilon_t + f_0 u_t$.

To find out what happens if this rule is followed for a long time, we have only to solve the difference equation (13) for an m_t process that satisfies it for all t. To do this, write (13) as

$$h_0 m_t + H_1(L)m_{t-1} = y^* - G_1(L)\varepsilon_{t-1} - F_1(L)u_{t-1}$$

or

$$H(L)m_t = y^* - \left(\sum_{i=1}^{\infty} g_i L^i\right)\varepsilon_t - \left(\sum_{i=1}^{\infty} f_i L^i\right)u_t.$$

Operating on the above equation $H(L)^{-1}$ (*this* is where the assumption that the rule has been operating forever comes in since we are in effect eliminating lagged m's by substituting appropriately lagged versions of (13) for them) gives

$$m_t = \frac{y^*}{H(1)} - \frac{\sum_{i=1}^{\infty} g_i L^i}{H(L)}\varepsilon_t - \frac{\sum_{i=1}^{\infty} f_i L^i}{H(L)}u_t,$$

which is exactly the rule given by (9).

To summarize, we have that the final form for y_t is

$$y_t = h_0 m_t + H_1(L)m_{t-1} + g_0\varepsilon_t + G_1(L)\varepsilon_{t-1} + f_0 u_t + F_1(L)u_{t-1}.$$

We consider feedback rules of the form

$$m_t = k + \alpha(L)\varepsilon_{t-1} + \beta(L)u_{t-1} + \delta(L)m_{t-1}$$

where $\alpha(L) = \sum_{j=0}^{\infty} \alpha_j L^j$, $\beta(L) = \sum_{j=0}^{\infty} \beta_j L^j$, and $\delta(L) = \sum_{j=0}^{\infty} \delta_j L^j$. Substituting the feedback rule into the final form for y_t and rearranging gives

$$y_t = h_0 k + [H_1(L) + h_0\delta(L)]m_{t-1} + [G_1(L) + h_0\alpha(L)]\varepsilon_{t-1}$$
$$+ [F_1(L) + h_0\beta(L)]u_{t-1} + g_0\varepsilon_t + f_0 u_t.$$

Given the monetary rule (i.e., the α's, β's, and δ's), this equation determines the stochastic process for y_t. The authority is supposed to choose the parameters of the rule in order to get the most desirable possible stochastic process for y_t, e.g., to minimize $E_{t-1}(y_t - y^*)^2$.

It bears repeating that the assumption under which the optimal rule is calculated is that the parameters of the final form will remain invariant when the authority departs from its previous rule and implements any new one. As we shall see, this is exactly the point at which rational expectations theorists would question the relevance of the preceding calculations.

A. An Example

Suppose that the reduced form for real GNP is

$$y_t = \lambda y_{t-1} + b_0 m_t + b_1 m_{t-1} + \varepsilon_t$$

where ε_t is a serially independent process with mean zero and finite variance. It follows that $E_{t-1}\varepsilon_t = 0$. We assume that the authority desires to minimize $E_{t-1}(y_t - y^*)^2$. The optimal rule must satisfy

$$E_{t-1}y_t = y^*$$

so that

$$E_{t-1}y_t = \lambda y_{t-1} + b_0 E_{t-1}m_t + b_1 m_{t-1} = y^*.$$

Solving for $E_{t-1}m_t$ gives the optimal rule

$$E_{t-1}m_t = m_t = \frac{1}{b_0}y^* - \frac{\lambda}{b_0}y_{t-1} - \frac{b_1}{b_0}m_{t-1}.$$

2. THE INFORMATION VARIABLE PROBLEM

Following Kareken et al. (1973), consider the following problem. The monetary authority desires to set its instrument m_t to minimize $E_{t-1}((y_t - y^*)^2)$, which is the projection of $(y_t - y^*)^2$ on the authority's information at time $t - 1$. Its information set at time $t - 1$ consists of a set of variables Ω_{t-1}. Since the authority makes policy almost continuously, we should think of increments in t as being very small units of time, e.g., days or hours. For this reason, it becomes important to recognize that the authority receives information about some variables (e.g., interest rates, about which it receives information daily) much more often than other variables (e.g., the average quarterly value of GNP, about which it receives information only quarterly). The monetary authority is assumed to have a *model* of the economy. The important thing about this model is that it supplies the monetary authority with a complete account of the first and second moments of *all* variables of interest (whether observed or unobserved) conditional on current and lagged settings of the money supply. Further, the model is supposed to tell the monetary authority the effect of alternative settings of the variable m_t given past random variables. In effect, then, the model supplies the authority with all of the information that it needs to calculate the linear least squares projection of y_t against m_t and Ω_{t-1}:

$$P[y_t|\Omega_{t-1}, m_t] = \beta m_t + \alpha\Omega_{t-1} \qquad (14)$$

where α is a vector conformable with Ω_{t-1}. The authority will minimize $E_{t-1}\{y_t - y^*\}^2$ over the class of linear decision rules by setting

$$P[y_t|\Omega_{t-1}, m_t] = y^*$$

or

$$m_t = \frac{y^*}{\beta} - \frac{\alpha}{\beta}\Omega_{t-1}. \tag{15}$$

Now according to the optimal rule (15), what information should the authority respond to in setting m_t? In general, it should "look at everything." More precisely, it should make m_t feedback upon any component of Ω_{t-1} bearing a nonzero component of α, i.e., any component of Ω_{t-1} that helps predict the variable y_t that it is interested in controlling.

A. An Example

Suppose that the reduced form for real GNP is

$$y_t = \lambda y_{t-1} + b(L)m_t + c(L)r_{t-1} + \varepsilon_t, \qquad 0 < \lambda < 1, \tag{16}$$

where ε_t is a serially independent stationary random process that obeys the least squares orthogonality conditions $E\varepsilon_t y_{t-s} = 0$ for $s \geq 1$ and $E\varepsilon_t m_{t-s} = E\varepsilon_t r_{t-s} = 0$ for *all* s. The lag operators $b(L) = \sum_{i=0}^{\infty} b_i L^i$ and $c(L) = \sum_{i=0}^{\infty} c_i L^i$ are one-sided on the present and past. By virtue of the least squares orthogonality conditions, Equation (16) is a regression equation. Assume that the object of the monetary authority is to minimize the mean squared error $E_{t-1}((y_t - y^*)^2)$. However, while the authority wants to control y_t, it never receives reliable data on y or any lagged values of y. Instead, its information set Ω_{t-1} consists only of lagged values of m and the interest rate r. So the best that the authority can do is to pursue the rule implied by setting

$$P[y_t|\Omega_{t-1}, m_t] = y^*.$$

To calculate $P[y_t|\Omega_{t-1}, m_t]$ from (16), eliminate lagged y's from (16):

$$(1 - \lambda L)y_t = b(L)m_t + c(L)r_{t-1} + \varepsilon_t,$$

$$y_t = \frac{b(L)}{1 - \lambda L}m_t + \frac{c(L)}{1 - \lambda L}r_{t-1} + \frac{1}{1 - \lambda L}\varepsilon_t. \tag{17}$$

By virtue of the strong orthogonality conditions imposed on ε, in particular that ε_t be orthogonal to r_s and m_s for *all* s, it follows that the composite disturbance $(1 - \lambda L)^{-1}\varepsilon_t$ in (17) is orthogonal to m_s and r_s at all lags. Therefore (17) is a regression equation, so that

$$P[y_t|\Omega_{t-1}, m_t] = \frac{b(L)}{1 - \lambda L}m_t + \frac{c(L)}{1 - \lambda L}r_{t-1}.$$

Assuming that the above projection is invariant with respect to changes in the feedback rule for m, the optimal feedback rule is then

$$\frac{b(L)}{1 - \lambda L} m_t + \frac{c(L)}{1 - \lambda L} r_{t-1} = y^*$$

or

$$b_0 m_t = (1 - \lambda)y^* - c(L)r_{t-1} - \left(\sum_{i=1}^{\infty} b_i L^i\right)m_t. \tag{18}$$

Under the optimal rule (18) output moves according to

$$y_t = \lambda y_{t-1} + (1 - \lambda)y^* + \varepsilon_t, \tag{19}$$

which is derived by substituting (18) into (16). Notice that output is serially correlated under the optimal rule, this being a consequence of the information set not including observations on lagged y's.

In the context of this example, any information that will help predict y_t ought to be included in the feedback rule determining the money supply.

This example exhibits the logic underlying the Keynesian case for "activist" monetary and fiscal policy. The notion that the economy can be described by presumably a large system of stochastic difference equations with fixed parameters underlies the standard Keynesian objections to the monism of monetarists who argue that the monetary authority should ignore other variables such as interest rates and concentrate on keeping the money supply on a steady growth path. The Keynesian view that, on the contrary, the monetary authority should "look at (and respond to) everything" including interest rates, rests on the following propositions[4]: (a) the economic structure is characterized by extensive simultaneity, so that shocks that impinge on one variable, e.g., an interest rate, impinge also on most others; (b) due to lags in the system, the effects of shocks on the endogenous variables are distributed over time, and so are serially correlated and therefore somewhat predictable; and (c) the "structure" of these lags is constant over time and does not depend on how the monetary authority is behaving. These propositions imply that variables that the authority observes very frequently (e.g., daily, such as interest rates) carry information useful for revising its forecasts of future value of variables that it cannot observe as often, such as GNP and unemployment. This follows because the same shocks are affecting both the observed and the unobserved variables, and because those shocks have effects that persist. It follows then from (c) that the monetary authority should in general revise its planned setting for its policy instruments each time it receives some new and surprising reading on a variable that is determined simultaneously with a variable like GNP or unemployment that it is interested in controlling.

[4] See Kareken *et al.* (1973) for an extended statement of this argument.

Such an argument eschewing a simple x-percent growth rate rule in favor of "looking at everything" has been made by Samuelson

> when I learned that I had been wrong in my beliefs about how fast M was growing from December 1968 to April 1969, this news was just one of twenty interesting items that had come to my knowledge that week. And it only slightly increased my forecast for the strength of aggregate demand at the present time. That was because my forecasts, so to speak, do not involve "action at a distance" but are loose Markov processes in which a broad vector of current variables specify a "phase space" out of which tomorrow's vector develops. (In short, I knowingly commit that most atrocious of sins in the penal code of the monetarists—I pay a great deal of attention to all dimensions of "credit conditions" rather than keeping my eye on the solely important variable $\dot{M}/M$.)

> often, I believe, the prudent man or prudent committee can look ahead six months to a year and with some confidence predict that the economy will be in other than an average or "ergodic" state. Unless this assertion of mine can be demolished, the case for a fixed growth rate for M, or for confining M to narrow channels around such a rate, melts away.

> These general presumptions arise out of what we know about plausible models of economics and about the findings of historical experience.

> [Samuelson (1970)]

3. OPTIMAL CONTROL UNDER RATIONAL EXPECTATIONS

The preceding pages provide a simple but accurate representation of circa 1973 procedures for macroeconometric policy evaluation. First, a macroeconometric model was estimated. Then, final form equations of the form of Equation (6) were derived from the estimated model expressing each of the endogenous variables that enter the authority's objective function as functions of the policy instrument and current and lagged exogenous variables and disturbances. Those equations were assumed invariant as changes in the rule were assumed and their effects on the objective function were evaluated.

A critical aspect of the above procedure is the implicit assumption that agent's decision rules, which are impounded, for example, in the estimated investment schedule, the consumption function, and so on, remain unchanged in the face of alternative stochastic processes for the control variable that different feedback rules imply. As we have repeatedly seen, however, optimal decision rules invariably respond to changes in the stochastic processes governing the exogenous variables facing agents. Thus, the invariance assumption needed to validate the preceding case for rules with feedback will not in general hold where agents use optimal decision rules. We propose to illustrate how taking this into account can drastically change the implied optimal control rule.

Return to the model formed by (1)–(3), but replace (3) with the assumption that the public's expectations are rational, so that $_tp^*_{t-1} = Ep_t|\Omega_{t-1}$, where Ω_{t-1} is the public's information set. Making this change has the very important consequence of introducing a dependence of the parameters of the final form upon the parameters of the rule chosen by the authority. As mentioned above, the preceding calculations assumed that there were no such dependencies. As will be seen, the fact that assuming rational expectations induces such dependencies has very important policy implications.

The model under rational expectations becomes

$$y_t = \gamma(p_t - _tp^*_{t-1}) + \lambda y_{t-1} + u_t, \tag{1}$$

$$m_t - p_t = y_t + \varepsilon_t, \tag{2}$$

$$_tp^*_{t-1} = E(p_t|\Omega_{t-1}), \tag{3'}$$

where the only change in the model has been to replace the assumption of fixed autoregressive expectations in (3) with the rational expectations hypothesis embodied in (3'). Let us assume that the public and the monetary authority share the same information set Ω_{t-1}, which consists of (at least) lagged values of y, p, and m.

From (2) and the serial independence of ε_t it follows that

$$Ep_t|\Omega_{t-1} = Em_t|\Omega_{t-1} - Ey_t|\Omega_{t-1},$$

an expression which makes clear the dependence of the parameters characterizing expectations formation on the parameters of the money feedback rule. From (1) we have

$$Ey_t|\Omega_{t-1} = \lambda y_{t-1}.$$

Substituting the preceding two equations and Equation (2) into (1) gives

$$y_t = \gamma(m_t - y_t - \varepsilon_t - Em_t|\Omega_{t-1} + Ey_t|\Omega_{t-1}) + \lambda y_{t-1} + u_t$$
$$(1 + \gamma)y_t = \gamma(m_t - Em_t|\Omega_{t-1}) - \gamma\varepsilon_t + (\gamma + 1)\lambda y_{t-1} + u_t$$

or

$$y_t = \frac{\gamma}{1 + \gamma}(m_t - Em_t|\Omega_{t-1}) - \frac{\gamma}{1 + \gamma}\varepsilon_t + \frac{1}{1 + \gamma}u_t + \lambda y_{t-1}. \tag{20}$$

Equation (20) is an analogue for this model of the reduced form equation (6) in our ad hoc expectations model. The difference is that the parameters of the money control rule explicitly appear in (20) by virtue of the presence of the term $Em_t|\Omega_{t-1}$. Thus, although versions of (20) will "resemble" (6), those versions are now predicted to have parameters that depend on the choice of monetary rule.

To find the optimal rule under (20), we can try to continue to follow our old advice: set $Ey_t|\Omega_{t-1} = y^*$. But from (20), we have that

$$Ey_t|\Omega_{t-1} = \lambda y_{t-1},$$

regardless of the parameters of the money supply rule. So in this model, the bias squared is *independent* of the parameters of the money supply rule. From (20) it follows that the variance of y_t around its conditional mean of λy_{t-1} is minimized by setting

$$m_t = Em_t|\Omega_{t-1},$$

as before. (Policy rules should be deterministic and involve no surprises, a result which emerges in both this section and the previous one.) We have therefore established the following stochastic neutrality theorem that characterizes our model: one deterministic feedback rule on the basis of the information set Ω_{t-1}, which is common to the public and to the authority, is as good as any other deterministic feedback rule. That is, the mean squared error is simply not a function of the parameters determining the systematic (forecastable) part of the money supply. Via deterministic feedback rules, the monetary authority is powerless to combat the business cycle (the serial correlation in y_t). This result is the antithesis of our earlier results rationalizing activist Keynesian policy rules.

The reader is invited to verify that the truth of the neutrality theorem is not dependent on the particular information set assumed. It will continue to hold for any specification of Ω_{t-1} so long as the public and the authority share the same information set.

The preceding results provide a (weak) defense for following rules without feedback. Simple *x*-percent growth rules do as well as any deterministic feedback rules, and dominate rules with a stochastic component.

Two features of the model formed by (1), (2), and (3′) account for the neutrality result. The first is the assumption that the public's expectations are "rational" and that the public and the policy authority share the same information set. The second feature is that the system embodies the natural rate hypothesis, which is to say, supply decisions are homogeneous of degree zero in prices and expected prices.[5] Abandoning either of these hypotheses will cause the conclusions of the neutrality theorem to fail.[6]

4. WHICH VIEW DOES THE EVIDENCE FAVOR?

We have set out two logically consistent arguments, one in favor of rules with feedback, one arguing that rules with feedback are no better than rules without feedback and may be worse if they introduce into policy what agents

[5] Fischer (1977) and Phelps and Taylor (1977) describe in detail how sensitively policy ineffectiveness propositions depend on the form taken by Lucas's aggregate supply schedule.

[6] John Taylor (1980b) estimates a rational expectations model in which staggered wage contracts render nontrivial the government's choice among money supply rules. Taylor shows how an optimal money supply rule can be chosen, taking into account the cross-equation restrictions that the hypothesis of rational expectations imposes on the equilibrium of his model. While differing in substantive detail, Taylor's work affirms the methodological point made in the text: that the assumption of rational expectations renders inappropriate the invariance assumption used in the Section 1 model to compute optimal government policies.

perceive as noise from the point of view of their information sets. What evidence permits one to choose between these two views? Various kinds of naïve arguments that economists often bring to bear will not resolve the matter. A good example is the argument often heard, that from empirical observation we "know" tax cuts are a good countercyclical device because, say, a sustained boom followed the tax cut of 1964. The reason this argument does not settle anything is that souped-up versions of the model formed by (1), (2), and (3') can explain such correlations, say, between tax cuts and subsequent booms in output.[7] Even further, it can be shown quite generally that both "neutral" and "nonneutral" forms of econometric models are compatible with literally any observed patterns of the correlation in the data (see Sargent, 1976b).

From the point of view of evaluating the case for rules with feedback it is essential to verify the invariance assumption that is so critical to the argument. To have confidence in the argument there should be evidence that reduced forms of estimated macroeconometric models of the form (6) have remained invariant across changes in policy regimes in the past. Such tests have been performed too rarely in the past, but usually with results pointing to failure of the invariance assumption for various key reduced form equations.[8] More tests of this kind are needed to settle the issue. In the other direction, it can be shown that the neutrality argument in effect assumes invariance across regimes of the parameters of the reduced form as written in a different form than (6)—in the case of our little model, Equation (20). To assign any relevance to the neutrality theorem, evidence for the invariance of the reduced form as written in this way should be available.

The evidence on this issue is still fragmentary and somewhat mixed.

5. SHOULD THE MONETARY AUTHORITY USE INTEREST OR MONEY AS ITS INSTRUMENT?[9]

Consider the following macroeconomic model:

$$y_t = \gamma(p_t - {}_tp^*_{t-1}) + \lambda y_{t-1} + u_t \qquad \text{(Phillips curve)}, \gamma > 0 \qquad (21)$$

$$m_t - p_t = y_t + br_t + \varepsilon_{1t} \qquad \text{portfolio balance curve}, b < 0 \qquad (22)$$

$$y_t = c(r_t - ({}_{t+1}p^*_{t-1} - p_t)) + \varepsilon_{2t} \qquad \text{"IS curve,"} \ c < 0. \qquad (23)$$

---

[7] For an example of such a model, see Sargent (1976a).

[8] A good example of this kind of work is the paper by Muench *et al.* (1974). A scrap of evidence along these lines is reported by Neftci and Sargent (1978). Proper and improper ways of testing for neutrality are discussed by Lucas (1972b, 1973), Sargent (1971, 1976b). For a variety of time series tests, see Mishkin (1983, 1982).

[9] The issue considered in this section was considered under adaptive expectations by Bailey (1971), Poole (1970), and Kareken, Muench and Wallace (1973). Sargent and Wallace (1975) treated the issue under rational expectations. McCallum (1981, 1984) reconsidered the issue under rational expectations. A very different perspective on the issue was arrived at in the context of a general equilibrium model by Sargent and Wallace (1982).

Here r_t is the interest rate ; u_t, ε_{1t}, and ε_{2t} are each serially independent stationary random processes with means of zero. Thus, $Eu_t|\Omega_{t-1} = E\varepsilon_{1t}|\Omega_{t-1} = E\varepsilon_{2t}|\Omega_{t-1} = 0$. We assume that u, ε_1, and ε_2 have finite variances.

The monetary authority has the option of using a feedback rule on previous information for setting r_t and letting m_t be whatever it must be to achieve portfolio balance at that r_t; or alternatively of setting m_t via a feedback rule on previous information and letting r_t be whatever it must to equilibrate the system. Which of these two alternatives should the authority choose? There has been a tendency for monetarists to advocate choosing a feedback rule on m, while some (though not all) Keynesians advocate using a feedback rule on r. Previously in our study of nonstochastic models we have seen that in some classical models if the authority pegged the interest rate the price level became indeterminate (Wicksell's observation) and that in Keynesian models and other classical models with suitable definitions of disposable income, the authority could peg the interest rate, but the choice between interest and money had no consequence for the value of real GNP. That is, in the nonstochastic Keynesian model, a given level of real GNP could be achieved as well by having the authority choose a suitable money supply as by having it choose a suitable interest rate.

In the context of the preceding stochastic model, however, the authority does have a choice between using r or m as its instrument, a choice with substantive implications for the probability distribution of y. For the case of ad hoc expectations, we leave the details to be worked out in Exercise 3 at the end of the chapter.

So in the presence of uncertainty and under fixed-weight expectations, the choice between use of r and m as instruments has content. Notice that if the variances of the random variables u, ε_1, and ε_2 are set to zero, the choice no longer makes a difference, which agrees with our earlier remarks about the irrelevance of the choice between using r and m as instruments in a nonrandom Keynesian model.

Now let us turn to the choice of instruments under rational expectations. We supplement (21)–(23) with

$$_tp^*_{t-1} = E[p_t|\Omega_{t-1}], \tag{24}$$

$$_{t+1}p^*_{t-1} = E[p_{t+1}|\Omega_{t-1}], \tag{25}$$

where Ω_{t-1} includes the same variables in the information set of the authority, namely all lagged endogenous and exogenous variables. Using (24) and taking conditional expectations in (21), we have

$$Ey_t|\Omega_{t-1} = \lambda y_{t-1}. \tag{26}$$

Taking conditional expectations in (22) and (23) gives

$$Em_t|\Omega_{t-1} - Ep_t|\Omega_{t-1} = Ey_t|\Omega_{t-1} + bEr_t|\Omega_{t-1}, \tag{27}$$

$$Ey_t|\Omega_{t-1} = c(Er_t|\Omega_{t-1} - E(p_{t+1} - p_t)|\Omega_{t-1}). \tag{28}$$

Under a money supply rule, $Em_t|\Omega_{t-1}$ is given. Of course, from (26) we know that one deterministic money supply rule is as good as any other from the point of view of the mean squared error of output. But the money rule will influence the distribution of prices. To see how the distribution of prices is determined, solve (27) and (28) for $Ep_t|\Omega_{t-1}$ to get

$$Ep_t|\Omega_{t-1} = \frac{1}{1-b} Em_t|\Omega_{t-1} - \frac{1+bc^{-1}}{1-b} Ey_t|\Omega_{t-1} - \frac{b}{1-b} Ep_{t+1}|\Omega_{t-1}. \quad (29)$$

Since $b < 0$, we have that $0 < -b/(1-b) < 1$.

We can solve this difference equation in $Ep_t|\Omega_{t-1}$ in the forward direction to get

$$Ep_t|\Omega_{t-1} = \frac{1}{1-b} \sum_{j=0}^{\infty} \left(\frac{-b}{1-b}\right)^j Em_{t+j}|\Omega_{t-1}$$

$$- \frac{1+bc^{-1}}{1-b} \sum_{j=0}^{\infty} \left(\frac{-b}{1-b}\right)^j Ey_{t+j}|\Omega_{t-1}. \quad (30)$$

(We could substitute $\lambda^{j+1} y_{t-1}$ for $Ey_{t+j}|\Omega_{t-1}$.) Here we are imposing the terminal condition

$$\lim_{n \to \infty} \left(\frac{-b}{1-b}\right)^n Ep_{t+n}|\Omega_{t-1} = 0,$$

which has the effect of asserting that in the absence of money supply changes, agents will not expect accelerating inflation or deflation. Provided that the rule is such that

$$\sum_{j=0}^{\infty} \left(\frac{-b}{1-b}\right)^j Em_{t+j}|\Omega_{t-1}$$

converges, Equation (30) determines a finite expected price level $Ep_t|\Omega_{t-1}$. Presumably, then, the money supply rule can be tailored to set $Ep_t|\Omega_{t-1}$ at some desired level.

In sum, there exists a money supply rule that delivers a finite (conditionally expected) price level. While the money supply rule is powerless for affecting the probability distribution of real output (which is again a consequence of our having assumed the natural rate hypothesis together with rational expectations), the money rule does influence the distribution of prices.

Now consider an interest rate rule, which determines $Er_t|\Omega_{t-1}$. Since $Ey_t|\Omega_{t-1} = \lambda y_{t-1}$ from (21) we have that (22) determines $Em_t|\Omega_{t-1} - Ep_t|\Omega_{t-1}$ since both $Er_t|\Omega_{t-1}$ and $Ey_t|\Omega_{t-1}$ are determined. Then (23) must determine $Ep_t|\Omega_{t-1}$. Write the conditional expectation of (23) as

$$Ep_t|\Omega_{t-1} = Ep_{t+1}|\Omega_{t-1} + c^{-1}Ey_t|\Omega_{t-1} - Er_t|\Omega_{t-1}. \quad (31)$$

The solution of this difference equation is

$$Ep_t|\Omega_{t-1} = \frac{1}{c} \sum_{j=0}^{n} Ey_{t+j}|\Omega_{t-1} - \sum_{j=0}^{n} Er_{t+j}|\Omega_{t-1} + Ep_{t+n+1}|\Omega_{t-1}.$$

To solve this equation for $Ep_t|\Omega_{t-1}$ requires a terminal condition in the form of an exogenously given expected price level $Ep_{t+n+1}^{\cdot}|\Omega_{t-1}$. An increase in the value that is assigned to this terminal condition results in a one-for-one increase in $Ep_t|\Omega_{t-1}$. Thus, the expected price $Ep_t|\Omega_{t-1}$ is underdetermined by the model itself, being dependent on our having to supply a very strong terminal condition that in effect determines the price level. That is, the model itself as characterized by Equation (31) is incapable of restricting the price level. Another way to put this is by observing that under an interest rate rule, the terminal condition that we have to impose to determine the $Ep_t|\Omega_{t-1}$ is very much stricter than what we had to impose under the money supply rule.

The economics behind the underdetermined expected price level is this: under the interest rate rule, the public correctly expects that the authority will accommodate whatever quantity of money is demanded at the pegged interest rate. The public therefore expects that, *ceteris paribus*, any increase in p_t will be met by an increase in m_t. But that means that one $Ep_t|\Omega_{t-1}$ is as good as any other one from the point of view of being rational. There is nothing to anchor the expected price level. And this is not simply a matter of choosing the "wrong" level or rule for the interest rate. There is no interest rate rule that is associated with a determinate price level.

The preceding indeterminacy is the counterpart in this model of the nonstochastic, statics result that in a full-employment model with wages and prices that are instantaneously flexible, it can happen (under suitable restrictions on the IS curve) that the price level is indeterminate if the monetary authority pegs the interest rate.

EXERCISES

1. Consider the system formed by (1), (2), and (3') where (1) is replaced by

$$y_t = \gamma(p_t - {}_tp_{t-1}^*) + \lambda y_{t-1} + \alpha({}_tp_{t-1}^* - p_{t-1}) + u_t$$

where $\alpha > 0$ and where u_t and ε_t have the same properties assumed in the text. Calculate the optimal feedback rule for m_t, using the objective function in the text. Show that the neutrality theorem fails.

2. Consider the system formed by (1), (2), and (3') with (3') replaced by

$${}_tp_{t-1}^* = E[p_t|\Omega_{t-1}] + \xi_t$$

where ξ_t is a term reflecting random deviations from rationality and satisfying $E[\xi_t|\Omega_{t-1}] = 0$. Assume that the public and the government share the same information set. Find the optimal control rule for m_t. Does the neutrality theorem hold?

3. Complete the model on page 460 by assuming the fixed-weight expectations schemes

$${}_tp_{t-1}^* = vp_{t-1}, \qquad {}_{t+1}p_{t-1}^* = wp_{t-1},$$

where v and w are parameters that remain fixed in the face of variations in the rule. Assume that the authority is interested in minimizing $E_{t-1}(y_t - y^*)^2$ by choosing a feedback rule *either* of the form

$$r_t = H\Omega_{t-1} \quad or \quad m_t = G\Omega_{t-1}$$

where H and G are vectors conformable to the authority's information set Ω_{t-1}, which consists of observations on all *lagged* endogenous and exogenous variables (and therefore on lagged values of the disturbances, too, since the authority knows the model). You may assume that u_t, ε_{1t} and ε_{2t} are pairwise uncorrelated. Then prove that:

A. Whether the authority should use the interest rate rule or the money supply rule depends on the variances of u, ε_1, and ε_2 and the slopes of the IS and LM curves.

B. The more stable is the IS curve relative to the LM curve and the steeper is the IS relative to the LM curve, the more likely is it that the authority will want to use the interest rate as its instrument.

(Poole (1970) and Bailey (1971) are useful references on the problem addressed in this exercise.)

4. Let m_t be the log of the money supply and y_t be the level of real output. To test whether "money is a veil" in the long run, a researcher proposes to estimate the final form

$$y_t = \sum_{j=0}^{\infty} h_j m_{t-j} + \text{residual}_t$$

and to test whether $\sum_{j=0}^{\infty} h_j = 0$. If this sum is zero, he plans to conclude that "money is a veil." Otherwise, he will conclude that in the long run "money matters." Critically discuss the virtues and defects of this research strategy from the standpoint of economic theory. (Feel free to introduce sample models to make your case.)

5. Consider an economy described by the following equations:

$$C_t = \left(\frac{1.80}{\sqrt{2}} - 0.81\right) Y_{t-1} + 100. \qquad I_t = 0.81(Y_{t-1} - Y_{t-2}) + \varepsilon_t + 10.$$

$$Y_t = C_t + I_t + G_t,$$

where C, I, Y, and G are consumption, investment, GNP, and government purchases, respectively; and $\{\varepsilon_t\}$ is a "white-noise" process with mean $E[\varepsilon_t] = 0$ and variance $\sigma^2 = E[\varepsilon_t^2]$. The units of time are quarters. Suppose that the government sets G_t at the constant level $\bar{G}$ every period.

A. Is the economy one with a business cycle? If so, what is the average period of the cycle as measured by the period of the cycles in the covariogram of GNP?

B. Suppose now that G_t is set so that fiscal policy leans against the wind. In particular, the government employs the "feedback rule":

$$G_t = 10 - \lambda(Y_{t-1} - Y_{t-2}), \qquad \lambda > 0.$$

Show how variations in λ will affect the behavior of GNP. Can λ be set so that there are no "business cycles," defined as cycles in the covariogram of GNP?

C. Suppose that the government uses the feedback rule:

$$G_t = 10 + \lambda_1 Y_{t-1} + \lambda_2 Y_{t-2}.$$

What values of λ_1 and λ_2 minimize the variance of GNP? (*Hint*: write Y_t in the form:

$$Y_t = \text{constant} + \sum_{i=0}^{\infty} w_i \varepsilon_{t-i}$$

and see how the w_i depends on λ_1 and λ_2.)

6. Consider the macroeconomic model

$$m_t - p_t = \tau y_t + u_t \qquad \text{portfolio balance,}$$

$$y_t = \gamma(p_t - E_{t-1}p_t) + \lambda y_{t-1} + \varepsilon_t \qquad \text{aggregate supply,}$$

$$\gamma > 0, \quad 0 < \lambda < 1,$$

where m is the log of money, p is the log of the price level, y is real GNP, τ is one minus the marginal income tax rate, and $\{u_t\}$ and $\{\varepsilon_t\}$ are serially uncorrelated and mutually uncorrelated covariance stationary random processes. Here $E_{t-1}p_t$ is the linear least squares projection of p_t on lagged p's, y's, and m's.

A. Prove that in this model, Friedman's "no-feedback" rule for setting m is as good as any other rule from the point of view of the objective: minimize $E_{t-1}(y_t - y^*)^2$ where y^* is given.

B. Determine whether the tax parameter τ influences $E_{t-1}(y_t - y^*)^2$. If it does, what value of τ minimizes this objective?

C. Determine whether the tax parameter τ influences $E_{t-1}y_t$. Would your answer change if τ were permitted to depend on time and say be determined via a feedback rule?

7. An economy is described by the following equations:

$$C_t = c_1 Y_{t-1} + u_{1t} \qquad\qquad 0 < c_1 < 1$$

$$I_t = a_0 + a_1(Y_{t-1} - Y_{t-2}) + a_2 r_t + u_{2t} \qquad a_1 > 0 > a_2$$

$$m_t = b_1 r_t + b_2 Y_{t-1} + v_t \qquad\qquad b_1 < 0, \quad b_2 > 0$$

$$C_t + I_t = Y_t$$

where C_t is consumption at t, I_t is investment, Y_t is GNP, r_t is the interest rate, and m_t is the money supply: u_{1t}, u_{2t}, and v_t are serially uncorrelated random variables (white noises) that are mutually independent (i.e., u_{1t}, u_{2t}, and v_t are pairwise uncorrelated), with variances σ_{u1}^2, σ_{u2}^2, and σ_v^2.

The monetary authority desires to minimize the mean squared error: $E(Y_t - Y^*)^2$ where Y^* is the target level of GNP. To achieve this end, the monetary authority considers two alternative strategies. The first is to peg the money supply via the feedback rule

$$m_t = \Lambda_0 + \lambda_1 Y_{t-1} + \lambda_2 Y_{t-2} + \lambda_3 Y_{t-3} \qquad\qquad (*)$$

where Λ_0, λ_1, λ_2, and λ_3 are parameters to be chosen. The second is to peg the interest rate via the feedback rule:

$$r_t = \Delta_0 + \delta_1 Y_{t-1} + \delta_2 Y_{t-2} + \delta_3 Y_{t-3}. \qquad\qquad (\dagger)$$

A. Compute the optimal values of Λ_0, λ_1, λ_2, and λ_3. What is the mean squared error attained under this rule?

B. Compute the optimal values of Δ_0, δ_1, δ_2, and δ_3 assuming that the interest rate rule $(\dagger)$ is used. What is the mean squared error attained under this rule?

C. What should the monetary authority do, peg r or peg m? What feature of the above model is critical in accounting for this result?

REFERENCES

Bailey, M. (1971). *National Income and the Price Level*, 2nd ed., pp. 175–186. New York: McGraw-Hill.

Barro, R. J. (1977). "Unanticipated money growth and unemployment in the United States." *American Economic Review*, Vol. 67, No. 2, pp. 101–115.

Barro, R. J. (1978). "Unanticipated money, output, and the price level in the United States." *Journal of Political Economy*, Vol. 86, No. 4, pp. 549–580.

Fischer, S. (1977). "Long-term contracts, rational expectations, and the optimal money supply rule." *Journal of Political Economy*, Vol. 85, No. 1, pp. 191-205.

Friedman, M. (1948). "A monetary and fiscal framework for economic stability." *American Economic Review*, Vol. 38, pp. 245-264.

Friedman, M. (1959). *A Program for Monetary Stability*, New York: Fordham University Press.

Kareken, J. A., Muench, T., and Wallace, N. (1973). "Optimal open market strategy: the use of information variables." *The American Economic Review*, Vol. LXIII, No. 1, pp. 156-172.

Lucas, R. E. Jr. (1972a). "Econometric testing of the natural rate hypothesis," In *The Econometrics of Price Determination Conference* (O. Eckstein, ed.), Washington, DC: Board of Governors of the Federal Reserve System.

Lucas, R. E. Jr. (1972b). "Expectations and the neutrality of money." *Journal of Economic Theory*, Vol. 4, No. 2, pp. 103-124.

Lucas, R. E. Jr. (1973). "Some international evidence on output-inflation trade-offs." *American Economic Review*, Vol. 63, No. 5, pp. 326-334.

McCallum, B. T. (1979). "The current state of the policy-ineffectiveness debate." *American Economic Review*, Vol. 69, No. 2, pp. 240-245.

McCallum, B. T. (1981). "Price level determinacy with an interest rate policy rule and rational expectations." *Journal of Monetary Economics*, Vol. 8, No. 3, pp. 319-329.

McCallum, B. T. (1984). "Some issues concerning interest rate pegging, price level determinacy, and the real bills doctrine." *Working Paper No. 1294*, National Bureau of Economic Research.

Mishkin, F. S. (1982) "Does anticipated aggregate demand policy matter? further econometric results." *American Economic Review*, Vol. 72, No. 4, pp. 788-802.

Mishkin, F. S. (1983). *A Rational Expectations Approach to Macroeconometrics: Testing Policy Ineffectiveness and Efficient-Markets Models*, Chicago: University of Chicago Press, for the National Bureau of Economic Research.

Muench, T., Rolnick, A., Wallace, N., and Weiler, W. (1974). "Tests for structural change and prediction intervals for the reduced forms of two structural models of the U. S., the FRB-MIT and Michigan Quarterly Models." *Annals of Economic and Social Measurement*, Vol. 3, No. 3. pp. 491-520.

Neftci, S. and Sargent, T. J. (1978). "A little bit of evidence on the natural rate hypothesis from the U.S." *Journal of Monetary Economics*, Vol. 4, No. 2, pp. 315-319.

Phelps, E. S. & Taylor, J. B. (1977). "Stabilizing powers of monetary policy under rational expectations." *Journal of Political Economy*, Vol. 85, No. 1, pp. 163-190.

Poole, W. (1970). "Optimal choice of monetary policy instruments in a simple stochastic macro model." *Quarterly Journal of Economics*, May issue, pp. 197-216.

Samuelson, P. (1970). "Reflections on recent federal reserve policy." *Journal of Money, Credit and Banking*, Vol. 2, No. 1, pp. 33-44.

Sargent, T. J. (1971). "A note on the accelerationist controversy." *Journal of Money, Credit and Banking*, Vol. 3, No. 3, pp. 721-725.

Sargent, T. J. (1973). "Rational expectations, the real rate of interest, and the natural rate of unemployment." *Brookings Papers on Economic Activity*, Vol. 2, pp. 429-472. (Correction in *BPEA*, 1973:3).

Sargent, T. J. and Wallace, N. (1975). "Rational expectations, the optimal monetary instrument, and the optimal money supply rule." *Journal of Political Economy*, Vol. 83, No. 2, pp. 241-254.

Sargent, T. J. and Wallace, N. (1976). "Rational expectations and the theory of economic policy." *Journal of Monetary Economics*, Vol. 2, No. 2, pp. 169-183.

Sargent, T. J. (1976a). "A classical macroeconometric model for the United States." *Journal of Political Economy*, Vol. 84, No. 2, pp. 207-238.

Sargent, T. J. (1976b). "Observational equivalence of natural and unnatural rate theories of macroeconomics." *Journal of Political Economy*, Vol. 84, No. 3.

Sargent, T. J. and Wallace, N. (1982). "The real bills doctrine vs. the quantity theory: a reconsideration." *Journal of Political Economy*, Vol. 90, No. 6, pp. 1212-1236.

Simons, H. C. (1936). "Rule versus authorities in monetary policy." *Journal of Political Economy*, Vol. 44, pp. 1–30.

Taylor, J. B. (1979). "Estimation and control of a macroeconomic model with rational expectations." *Econometrica*, Vol. 47, No. 5, pp. 1267–1286.

Taylor, J. B. (1980a). "Output and price stability: an international comparison." *Journal of Economic Dynamics and Control*, Vol. 2, No. 1, pp. 109–132.

Taylor, J. B. (1980b). "Aggregate dynamics and staggered contracts." *Journal of Political Economy*, Vol. 88, No. 1, pp. 1–23.

CHAPTER XVIII

ASPECTS OF THE NEW CLASSICAL
MACROECONOMICS

1. INTRODUCTION

The textbook classical macroeconomic model is commonly regarded as a bad model because the time series data are generally thought to be inconsistent with the classical doctrine that employers and employees are continuously operating on their supply and demand schedules. Prominent among the empirical patterns thought to cast doubt on the classical model are these three:[1]

(1) the persistence from one business cycle to another of positive output–price and positive money–output correlations, which apparently contradicts the classical neutrality propositions:

(2) the Dunlop–Tarshis observations alleging the failure of real wages to move countercyclically (as both Keynes and various classical economists predicted they would); and

(3) the procyclical movement of output per man-hour, which apparently contradicts the law of diminishing returns to employment.

Observations (2) and (3) have often been interpreted as evidence that employers are not always on their demand schedule for employment. Observation (1) has been taken as an indication that the data are not well described by the joint assumption that the demand for labor always equals the supply and that both demand and supply depend on the real wage.

That these important phenomena seem to be paradoxes from the viewpoint of the textbook classical model has led to a search for alternative models. For example, the Dunlop–Tarshis observation about the alleged failure of real wages to move countercyclically has often been cited by those advocating abandoning equilibrium theories in favor of "disequilibrium theories." For example, see

---

[1] There are other paradoxes as well, for example, the Gibson paradox, which is the tendency for the price level and the interest rate to be positively correlated both over long periods of time and over the business cycle, which Keynes thought contradicted classical neutrality of money theorems.

Barro and Grossman (1971) and Solow and Stiglitz (1968). However, as Phelps (1969) has observed, the econometric studies on which such judgments about employment and real wages have been based are not sophisticated; and few of the equilibrium theories that the empirical studies have sought to test embody anything resembling modern dynamic factor demand and factor supply theories.

This chapter describes elements of a simple dynamic equilibrium model and its potential for explaining the paradoxes above. Essentially, our task is to provide a structure for studying whether, once costs of adjustment and uncertainty about the future are introduced, an equilibrium model of aggregate employment and real wages contradicts the time series data. The model that we construct is in a fundamental sense a direct descendent of the textbook classical model, being an equilibrium model *and* tending to bear "classical" policy implications. The model originated in the works of Lucas and Rapping (1969). We have already encountered some of the elements of the model earlier in our study of the investment schedule, the dynamic demand schedule for employment, and Lucas's model of the Phillips curve.

One thing that we noted in discussing Lucas's theory of the Phillips curve is that, with Lucas's original specification of agents' information sets, the theory contains no endogenous theory of why aggregate-demand-induced movements in output and employment persist (i.e., are serially correlated). True, the theory *accounts* for such movements through the presence of the lagged term λy_{t-1} in the Phillips curve, but it does not provide an explanation for the presence of that term. It is shown here that an endogenous theory of persistence emerges when a fuller "classical" model is constructed. In effect, this construction provides a rationalization for the inclusion of terms like λy_{t-1} on the right-hand side of the Phillips curve that Lucas estimated.

The subject of these pages in a sense takes us back to a very old topic in business cycle theory, namely, the comparative merits of "real" and "monetary" theories of the business cycle. As we shall see, once the requirement that expectations be rational is imposed on Lucas and Rapping's setup, one obtains a "real" theory of the business cycle in the sense that stochastic processes for employment and real wages are predetermined with respect to stochastic processes for the money supply and price level. One purpose of these pages is to highlight the role of Lucas's disparate-information model of the Phillips curve in restoring to the system some interaction between the "real" and purely nominal parts.

2. THE CLASSICAL THEORY OF LABOR SUPPLY AND CONSUMPTION

This section briefly describes the classical theory of the household's allocation of consumption and labor over time. The theory originated in the work of Irving Fisher (1930). The discussion here summarizes the formulation of Lucas and Rapping.

At time t the household is assumed to face exogenous sequences of money wages $\{w_{t+j}\}_{j=0}^{\infty}$, the price of "the" consumption good $\{p_{t+j}\}_{j=0}^{\infty}$, and the discount factor $\{\beta_{t+j}\}_{j=0}^{\infty}$, where $\beta_t = 1$. The household faces the budget constraint

$$A_t + \sum_{j=0}^{\infty} \beta_{t+j} w_{t+j} n_{t+j} - \sum_{j=0}^{\infty} \beta_{t+j} p_{t+j} c_{t+j} = 0 \tag{1}$$

where A_t is the given nominal quantity of (nonhuman) assets held by the household at time t. Subject to this budget constraint, the household chooses sequences $\{n_{t+j}\}_{j=0}^{\infty}, \{c_{t+j}\}_{j=0}^{\infty}$ of labor supply and consumption that maximize[2] the utility functional $U(\{c_{t+j}\}_{j=0}^{\infty}, \{n_{t+j}\}_{j=0}^{\infty})$. We assume that $U(\cdot,\cdot)$ is increasing in consumption and decreasing in employment at each point in time and is concave. The household displays diminishing marginal utility of consumption and increasing marginal disutility of work at each point in time.

Lucas and Rapping (1969) showed that the results of this constrained optimization can be summarized in a pair of consumption, labor supply plans

$$n_{t+k} = \tilde{n}_k(A_t, w_t, \beta_{t+1} w_{t+1}, \beta_{t+2} w_{t+2}, \ldots, p_t, \beta_{t+1} p_{t+1}, \beta_{t+2} p_{t+2}, \ldots),$$

$$c_{t+k} = \tilde{c}_k(A_t, w_t, \beta_{t+1} w_{t+1}, \beta_{t+2} w_{t+2}, \ldots, p_t, \beta_{t+1} p_{t+1}, \beta_{t+2} p_{t+2}, \ldots),$$

$$k = 0, 1, 2, \ldots,$$

where each schedule is homogeneous of degree zero in

$$A_t, \qquad \{\beta_{t+j} p_{t+j}\}_{j=0}^{\infty}, \qquad \{\beta_{t+j} w_{t+j}\}_{j=0}^{\infty}.$$

By virtue of this zero-degree homogeneity, we can write

$$n_{t+k} = \tilde{n}_k\left(\frac{A_t}{p_t}, \frac{w_t}{p_t}, \beta_{t+1} \frac{w_{t+1}}{p_t}, \beta_{t+2} \frac{w_{t+2}}{p_t}, \ldots, 1, \beta_{t+1} \frac{p_{t+1}}{p_t}, \beta_{t+2} \frac{p_{t+2}}{p_t}, \ldots\right). \tag{2}$$

Following Lucas and Rapping (1969), consider the logarithmic version of (2) for $k = 0$:

$$\ln n_t = \alpha_0 + \alpha_1 \ln \frac{A_t}{p_t} + \sum_{j=0}^{\infty} h_j \ln\left(\beta_{t+j} \frac{w_{t+j}}{p_t}\right) + \sum_{j=1}^{\infty} v_j \ln\left(\beta_{t+j} \frac{p_{t+j}}{p_t}\right).$$

From our discussion of the term structure of interest rates we recall that the discount factor can be written

$$\beta_{t+k} = [(1 + r_{1t})(1 + r_{1t+1}) \cdots (1 + r_{1t+k-1})]^{-1}$$

---

[2] $U(\cdot,\cdot)$ maps sequences $\{c_{t+j}\}, \{n_{t+j}\}$ into the real line.

where r_{1t} is the rate of interest on one-period loans extending between period t and $t + 1$. Using the approximation (good for small x) that $\ln(1 + x) = x$, we have for $j \geq 1$,

$$h_j \ln \frac{w_{t+j}}{p_t(1 + r_{1t}) \cdots (1 + r_{1t+j-1})}$$

$$= h_j \ln \left[\frac{w_{t+j}}{p_{t+j}} \frac{p_{t+j}}{p_{t+j-1}} \frac{p_{t+j-1}}{p_{t+j-2}} \cdots \frac{p_{t+1}}{p_t} \frac{1}{(1 + r_{1t}) \cdots (1 + r_{1t+j-1})} \right]$$

$$= h_j \{\ln w_{t+j} - \ln p_{t+j} + (\ln p_{t+j} - \ln p_{t+j-1} - r_{1t+j-1})$$

$$+ (\ln p_{t+j-1} - \ln p_{t+j-2} - r_{1t+j-2}) + \cdots + (\ln p_{t+1} - \ln p_t - r_{1t})\}$$

$$= h_j(\ln w_{t+j} - \ln p_{t+j}) + h_j \sum_{k=1}^{j} (\ln p_{t+k} - \ln p_{t+k-1} - r_{1t+k-1}). \qquad (3)$$

Similarly, we have

$$v_j \ln \frac{p_{t+j}}{p_t} \frac{1}{(1 + r_{1t}) \cdots (1 + r_{1t+j-1})}$$

$$= v_j \{(\ln p_{t+j} - \ln p_{t+j-1} - r_{1t+j-1}) + \cdots + \ln p_{t+1} - \ln p_t - r_{1t}\}. \qquad (4)$$

Substituting (3) and (4) into the logarithmic version of (2) gives

$$\ln n_t = \alpha_0 + \alpha_1 \ln \left(\frac{A_t}{p_t} \right) + \sum_{j=0}^{\infty} h_j(\ln w_{t+j} - \ln p_{t+j})$$

$$+ \sum_{j=1}^{\infty} h_j \sum_{k=1}^{j} (\ln p_{t+k} - \ln p_{t+k-1} - r_{1t+k-1})$$

$$+ \sum_{j=1}^{\infty} v_j \sum_{k=1}^{j} (\ln p_{t+k} - \ln p_{t+k-1} - r_{1t+k-1}).$$

This can be rearranged to the more compact form

$$\ln n_t = \alpha_0 + \alpha_1 \ln \left(\frac{A_t}{p_t} \right) + \sum_{j=0}^{\infty} h_j(\ln w_{t+j} - \ln p_{t+j}) + \sum_{j=0}^{\infty} z_j(r_{1t+j} - \pi_{t+j}) \quad (5)$$

where $\pi_{t+j} = \ln p_{t+j+1} - \ln p_{t+j}$ and where

$$z_j = - \sum_{k=j+1}^{\infty} (h_k + v_k).$$

The household's labor supply decision at t is predicted to depend on the entire future sequences of real wages and of (one-period) real rates of interest.

In a stochastic setting the "natural" counterpart to (5) would be

$$
\ln n_t = \alpha_0 + \alpha_1 \ln\left(\frac{A_t}{p_t}\right) + \sum_{j=0}^{\infty} h_j E_t\left\{\ln \frac{w_{t+j}}{p_{t+j}}\right\}
$$

$$
+ \sum_{j=0}^{\infty} z_j E_t\left(r_{1t+j} - \ln \frac{p_{t+j+1}}{p_{t+j}}\right) + \varepsilon_t \tag{6}
$$

where ε_t is a random process, and $E_t\{x\}$ is the linear least squares projection of x on some information set available at t. This is the kind of labor-supply schedule that we shall incorporate in later sections.

Lucas and Rapping (1969) made the plausible argument that for low j's, h_j would be positive, while for high j's, h_j would be negative. This pattern implies that households respond to a temporary increase in the real wage by working more now, but that they respond less to what they perceive to be a permanent increase in the real wage. If $\sum_{j=0}^{\infty} h_j = 0$, then there is no current response to a current increase in the real wage that is perceived as permanent (or once-and-for-all), so that labor supply is perfectly inelastic to permanent changes in the real wage. If $\sum h_j < 0$, then labor supply is backward-bending in a certain sense.

The reader will immediately notice that we could have applied the same sequence of approximations to obtain a consumption schedule of the form

$$
\ln c_t = \alpha'_1 \ln\left(\frac{A_t}{p_t}\right) + \sum_{j=0}^{\infty} h'_j E_t \ln\left\{\frac{w_{t+j}}{p_{t+j}}\right\} + \alpha'_0
$$

$$
+ \sum_{j=0}^{\infty} z'_j E_t\left\{r_{1t+j} - \ln \frac{p_{t+j+1}}{p_{t+j}}\right\} + u_t \tag{7}
$$

where u_t is a random process. This is truly "classical" consumption function as opposed to the Keynesian one. Notice that it envisions the household as being confronted with sequences of (or, in the case of uncertainty, stochastic processes for) wages, prices, and interest rates at which the household is free to trade. This is to be contrasted with the Keynesian consumption function, which in effect confronts households with exogenous *incomes* (which are sums of factor prices times factor quantities) which are not viewed as subject to choice by the household. Clower and Barro and Grossman have usually emphasized that a cornerstone of the Keynesian model is the assumption that households are not free to trade whatever quantities they want at going wages and prices.

3. AN EQUILIBRIUM MODEL OF THE LABOR MARKET

In this section we study a special version of Lucas and Rapping's (1969) model that is simple enough for us to construct an explicit solution for the household's contingency plan for its labor supply. Our setup is adopted mainly for its tractability. But partly we also take our cue from Lucas and Rapping's empirical results, in which it is hard to detect much of a role for A_t/p_t and the real interest rate terms in (6). We shall place the consumer in a special setting in which he is cut off from the loan market, being constrained to consume today his current income today. The resulting labor supply schedule is a version of (6) in which real interest rates and the real asset term A_t/p_t are absent.

Our plan is then to combine the representative household's labor-supply plan with the labor-demand plan for a representative firm like the one studied in Chapters IX and XIV. By insisting that the labor supply always equal labor demand, we obtain a dynamic "classical" model that determines stochastic processes for employment and the real wage.

A. The Household

The representative household[3] faces the problem of calculating a contingency plan for its labor supply n_t and consumption c_t so as to maximize

$$E_t \sum_{j=0}^{\infty} b^j \left[u_0 c_{t+j} - [\delta_0 + \varepsilon_{t+j}] n_{t+j} - \frac{\delta_1}{2} n_{t+j}^2 - \frac{\delta_2}{2} (n_{t+j} + \gamma n_{t+j-1})^2 \right] \quad (8)$$

subject to

$$c_{t+j} = w_{t+j} n_{t+j} + \Pi_{t+j}, \qquad n_{t-1} \text{ given,}$$

$$u_0, \delta_0, \delta_1, \delta_2 > 0; \quad 0 < b < 1; \quad 0 < \gamma < 1.$$

Here c_t is consumption, n_t employment, w_t the *real* wage, and Π_t dividends that the household receives from firms at time t; ε_t is a random shock to preferences.[4] One-period utility of the household at t depends directly on its consumption at t, and inversely on its labor supply both at t and at $t-1$. The term $\frac{1}{2}\delta_2(n_t + \gamma n_{t-1})^2$ is deducted from one-period utility to capture the idea that sustained periods of especially high employment tire the household and reduce one-period utility by more than can be reflected by the terms in current employment alone. The representative household is a price-taker and maximizes (8) over alternative contingency plans for labor supply, taking as given the stochastic processes $\{w_{t+j}\}_{j=0}^{\infty}$, $\{\Pi_{t+j}\}_{j=0}^{\infty}$, and $\{\varepsilon_{t+j}\}_{j=0}^{\infty}$ which it faces.

---

[3] In this section and the next we assume that all exogenous stochastic processes are of exponential order less than $1/b$.

[4] Rather than carrying along the number of firms and the number of households as additional parameters, which is a nuisance, we use the standard device of "representative" agents. The substantive aspect of this device is to build in the assumption that all firms are alike and all households are alike, while technically it serves to eliminate the need to carry along the numbers of each kind of unit. See our treatment of Lucas and Prescott's investment model in Chapter XIV for an example where the numbers of units are carried along explicitly. Likewise, the reader can easily carry along m_1 firms and m_2 households in the present analysis.

Using the constraint to eliminate c_t from (8), the household's problem becomes to choose a contingency plan for $\{n_{t+j}\}$ to maximize

$$E_t \sum_{j=0}^{\infty} b^j \left[u_0(w_{t+j} n_{t+j} + \Pi_{t+j}) - (\delta_0 + \varepsilon_{t+j}) n_{t+j} \right.$$

$$\left. - \frac{\delta_1}{2} n_{t+j}^2 - \frac{\delta_2}{2} (n_{t+j} + \gamma n_{t+j-1})^2 \right] \tag{9}$$

subject to n_{t-1} given. The Euler equation for this problem is

$$\gamma b \delta_2 E_{t+j} n_{t+j+1} + (\delta_1 + \delta_2 + \delta_2 \gamma^2 b) n_{t+j} + \delta_2 \gamma n_{t+j-1}$$

$$= u_0 w_{t+j} - \delta_0 - \varepsilon_{t+j}, \qquad j = 0, 1, 2, \dots. \tag{10}$$

This can be written

$$[1 + \psi B + b^{-1} B^2] E_{t+j} n_{t+j+1} = (\gamma b \delta_2)^{-1} [u_0 w_{t+j} - \delta_0 - \varepsilon_{t+j}],$$

$$j = 0, 1, 2, \dots \tag{11}$$

where $\psi = (\delta_1/\gamma \delta_2 b) + (1/\gamma b) + \gamma > 0$, and where B is the operator defined by $B E_t x_{t+j} = E_t x_{t+j-1}$. As usual, we seek a factorization

$$1 + \psi B + b^{-1} B^2 = (1 - \lambda_1 B)(1 - \lambda_2 B).$$

Equating like powers of B gives

$$-(\lambda_1 + \lambda_2) = \psi, \qquad \lambda_1 \lambda_2 = 1/b.$$

So λ_1 solves $b \lambda_1 + \lambda_1^{-1} = -b\psi$. Since $\psi > 0$, the solution values of λ_1 and λ_2 occur in the third quadrant of Figure 1 and are negative. By an argument analogous to the one used in Section 8, Chapter IX, we can show that one root, say λ_1, is strictly less than unity in absolute value, while the other root λ_2 exceeds unity in absolute value. For assume that $\delta_1 = 0$, so that

$$1 + \left(\frac{1}{\gamma b} + \gamma \right) B + \frac{1}{b} B^2 = (1 + \gamma B)\left(1 + \frac{1}{\gamma b} B \right).$$

So in this case, $\lambda_1 = -\gamma > -1$ and $\lambda_2 = -1/\gamma b < -1/b < -1$. Inspection of Figure 1 shows that introduction of a strictly positive δ_1, by lowering $-b\psi$, serves to increase λ_1 and decrease λ_2, so that the bounds $|\lambda_1| < 1 < 1/b < |\lambda_2|$ hold.

The solution of the Euler equation that satisfies the transversality condition is

$$n_{t+j+1} = \lambda_1 n_{t+j} - \frac{\lambda_1}{\gamma \delta_2} \sum_{i=0}^{\infty} \left(\frac{1}{\lambda_2} \right)^i \{ u_0 E_{t+j+1} w_{t+j+1+i} - E_{t+j+1} \varepsilon_{t+j+1+i} - \delta_0 \},$$

$$j = -1, 0, 1, 2, \dots. \tag{12}$$

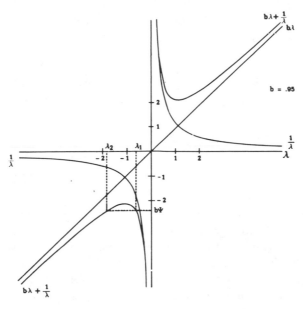

FIGURE 1

Since λ_1 and λ_2 are negative, the household's contingency plan makes employment vary inversely with respect to once-lagged employment, directly with respect to the current wage, inversely with respect to the wage expected for one-period ahead, and so on. The contingency plan (12) is the counterpart of Lucas and Rapping's labor-supply schedule (6).

B. The Firm

The representative firm is identical with the one described in Section 1, Chapter XIV. The firm is a perfect competitor that chooses a stochastic process for its employment $\tilde{n}_t$ to maximize

$$v_t = E_t \sum_{j=0}^{\infty} b^j \Pi_{t+j}, \tag{13}$$

$$\Pi_{t+j} = (f_0 + a_{t+j})\tilde{n}_{t+j} - \frac{f_1}{2}\tilde{n}_{t+j}^2 - \frac{d}{2}(\tilde{n}_{t+j} - \tilde{n}_{t+j-1})^2 - w_{t+j}\tilde{n}_{t+j},$$

where $f_0, f_1, d > 0$, $\tilde{n}_{t-1}$ is given, $\tilde{n}_{t+j}$ is the firm's demand for employment, and $\{a_{t+j}\}$ is a sequence of random shocks to technology. The firm is a price-taker and faces stochastic processes for $\{w_{t+j}\}$ and $\{a_{t+j}\}$ which are beyond its control. As we have seen, the Euler equation for this problem is

$$bE_{t+j}\tilde{n}_{t+j+1} + \phi\tilde{n}_{t+j} + \tilde{n}_{t+j-1} = d^{-1}(w_{t+j} - a_{t+j} - f_0), \qquad j = 0, 1, 2, \ldots.$$

where $\phi = -((f_1/d) + (1 + b))$. The optimal contingency plan for the representative firm is

$$\tilde{n}_{t+j+1} = \tilde{\lambda}_1 \tilde{n}_{t+j} - \frac{\tilde{\lambda}_1}{d} \sum_{i=0}^{\infty} \left(\frac{1}{\tilde{\lambda}_2}\right)^i \{E_{t+j+1} w_{t+j+1+i}$$

$$- E_{t+j+1} a_{t+j+1+i} - f_0\}, \qquad j = -1, 0, 1, 2, \ldots$$

where

$$\left(1 + \frac{\phi}{b} B + \frac{1}{b} B^2\right) = (1 - \tilde{\lambda}_1 B)(1 - \tilde{\lambda}_2 B) \qquad \text{and} \qquad 0 < \tilde{\lambda}_1 < 1 < \frac{1}{b} < \tilde{\lambda}_2.$$

C. Equilibrium

We have constructed a demand schedule and a supply schedule for labor, in each case an entire "contingency plan" giving desired employment as a function of initial employment and the stochastic process for the real wage. We now assume that the labor market clears at all points in time and solve for the stochastic processes for employment and the real wage that always clear the market. Our model is thus a dynamic, stochastic version of the classical labor market model studied in Chapter I.

Formally, an *equilibrium* is a pair of stochastic processes

$$\{\bar{w}_{t+j}\}_{j=0}^{\infty}, \qquad \{\bar{n}_{t+j}\}_{j=0}^{\infty}$$

that satisfies the following conditions, given n_{t-1}:

(i) When the representative household takes $\{\bar{w}_{t+j}\}_{j=0}^{\infty}$ as given, the process $\{\bar{n}_{t+j}\}_{j=0}^{\infty}$ maximizes the utility functional (9).

(ii) When the representative firm takes $\{\bar{w}_{t+j}\}_{j=0}^{\infty}$ as given, the process $\{\bar{n}_{t+j}\}_{j=0}^{\infty}$ maximizes the firm's expected present value (13).

In other words, an equilibrium is a stochastic process for the real wage $\{w_{t+j}\}$ such that the household is always on its supply schedule (12), the firm is always on its demand schedule, and the supply of labor always equals the demand,

$$n_{t+j} = \tilde{n}_{t+j}, \qquad j = 0, 1, 2, \ldots.$$

To construct an equilibrium, write the Euler equation for the household as

$$A^c E_{t+j} n_{t+j+1} + B^c n_{t+j} + C^c n_{t+j-1} = w_{t+j} - \frac{\delta_0}{u_0} - \frac{1}{u_0} \varepsilon_{t+j}, \qquad j = 0, 1, 2, \ldots,$$

$$\tag{14}$$

where $A^c = \gamma b \delta_2 / u_0$, $B^c = (\delta_1 + \delta_2 + \delta_2 \gamma^2 b)/u_0$, and $C^c = \delta_2 \gamma / u_0$. Set $\tilde{n}_{t+j} = n_{t+j}$ and write the Euler equation for the firm as

$$A^f E_{t+j} n_{t+j+1} + B^f n_{t+j} + C^f n_{t+j-1} = w_{t+j} - a_{t+j} - f_0, \qquad j = 0, 1, 2, \ldots \tag{15}$$

where $A^f = db$, $B^f = -(f_1 + d(1 + b))$, $C^f = d$.

Our object is to find stochastic processes $\{n_{t+j}\}_{j=0}^{\infty}$ and $\{w_{t+j}\}_{j=0}^{\infty}$ that satisfy the transversality conditions of the firm and household problems and that satisfy the Euler equations (14) and (15). To proceed, eliminate w_{t+j} by subtracting (15) from (14) to get

$$A^s E_{t+j} n_{t+j+1} + B^s n_{t+j} + C^s n_{t+j-1} = a_{t+j} + f_0 - \frac{\delta_0}{u_0} - \frac{1}{u_0} \varepsilon_{t+j}$$

where $A^s = A^c - A^f$, $B^s = B^c - B^f$, $C^s = C^c - C^f$. By substituting their definitions for A^s, B^s, and C^s, the preceding equation can be written

$$b(u_0 d - \gamma \delta_2) E_{t+j} n_{t+j+1} + (-u_0(f_1 + d(1 + b)) - \delta_1 - \delta_2 - \gamma^2 \delta_2 b) n_{t+j}$$
$$+ (u_0 d - \delta_2 \gamma) n_{t+j-1} = \varepsilon_{t+j} + \delta_0 - u_0 f_0 - u_0 a_{t+j} \qquad (16)$$

or

$$b E_{t+j} n_{t+j+1} + W n_{t+j} + n_{t+j-1} = \frac{1}{u_0 d - \delta_2 \gamma} [\varepsilon_{t+j} + \delta_0 - u_0 f_0 - u_0 a_{t+j}]$$
$$(17)$$

where

$$W = (-u_0(f_1 + d(1 + b)) - \delta_1 - \delta_2 - \gamma^2 \delta_2 b)/(u_0 d - \delta_2 \gamma).$$

From the definition of ψ, write

$$b\psi = \frac{\delta_1 + \delta_2 + \delta_2 \gamma^2 b}{\delta_2 \gamma} = \frac{\psi_n}{\psi_d}.$$

From the definition of ϕ, write

$$\phi = -\frac{u_0(f_1 + d(1 + b))}{u_0 d} = \frac{\phi_n}{\phi_d}.$$

Then notice that W can be written

$$W = \frac{W_n}{W_d} = \frac{\phi_n - \psi_n}{\phi_d - \psi_d} = \phi \frac{\phi_d}{\phi_d - \psi_d} - b\psi \frac{\psi_d}{\phi_d - \psi_d}.$$

Since $\phi < 0$, $\psi > 0$, $\psi_d > 0$, $\phi_d > 0$, it follows that

$$|W| \geq \min(|\phi|, |b\psi|) \qquad \text{and} \qquad \text{sign } W = \text{sign}(\psi_d - \phi_d). \qquad (18)$$

Condition (18) and our previous studies of Equations (14) and (15) via Figure 1 combine to ensure that the solution of Equation (16) can be obtained by the same techniques applied to the Euler equations (14) and (15), and that the roots of the characteristic polynomial are real.

In particular, we seek the factorization

$$1 + \frac{W}{b} B + \frac{1}{b} B^2 = (1 - \mu_1 B)(1 - \mu_2 B).$$

By proceeding as in our earlier analyses of the Euler equations (14) and (15), and using the conditions (18), it is straightforward to establish that, choosing μ_1 to be the smaller in absolute value, $|\mu_1| < 1 < 1/b < |\mu_2|$. Further, using condition (18) and Figure 1,

$$\text{sign } \mu_1 = \text{sign } \mu_2 = \text{sign } (\phi_d - \psi_d) = \text{sign}(u_0 d - \delta_2 \gamma)$$

for from Figure 1, we know that the sign of the μ's equals minus the sign of the W.

Having achieved this factorization, we can compute the solution of (16) that satisfies the transversality condition of the representative firm as being

$$n_{t+j+1} = \mu_1 n_{t+j} - \frac{\mu_1}{u_0 d - \delta_2 \gamma} \sum_{i=0}^{\infty} \left(\frac{1}{\mu_2}\right)^i E_{t+j+1}\{\varepsilon_{t+j+i+1}$$

$$+ \delta_0 - u_0 f_0 - u_0 a_{t+j+i+1}\}, \qquad j = -1, 0, 1, 2, \ldots \qquad (19)$$

This gives the solution stochastic process for $\{n_{t+j}\}_{j=0}^{\infty}$ as a function of the stochastic process of the exogenous preference and technology shock processes $\{\varepsilon_{t+j}\}$ and $\{a_{t+j}\}$.

To determine the equilibrium stochastic process for $\{w_{t+j}\}_{j=0}^{\infty}$, we can use the solution (19) to eliminate $E_{t+j} n_{t+j+1}$, n_{t+j}, and n_{t+j-1} from the firm's Euler equation (15). The result is an expression for $\{w_{t+j}\}$ in terms of constants and the exogenous processes $\{a_{t+j}\}$ and $\{\varepsilon_{t+j}\}$. (Of course, we could just as well use the Euler equation for the household in this last step of calculating the $\{w_{t+j}\}_{j=0}^{\infty}$ process.)

D. A Digression on Long-Term Contracts

Some recent work is directed at establishing the claim that assuming long-term contracts vitiates the kind of stochastic neutrality results that hold in some rational expectations models (Fischer, 1977; Modigliani, 1977). As we shall see, even stronger neutrality properties characterize the present model, but they really have nothing to do with the "length" of contracts per se.

Consider the equilibrium stochastic process for the real wage, which can be written

$$w_{t+j} = f_0 + a_{t+j} - \frac{\mu_1 A^f}{u_0 d - \delta_2 \gamma} \sum_{i=0}^{\infty} \left(\frac{1}{\mu_2}\right)^i E_{t+j}\{\varepsilon_{t+j+i+1}$$

$$+ \delta_0 - u_0 f_0 - u_0 a_{t+j+i+1}\} + [(\mu_1 A^f + B^f) + C^f L]n_{t+j}$$

where $\{n_{t+j}\}$ obeys (19). There are two ways to think of the above equation for the real wage. The first interpretation is as above, namely, as describing the real wage turned out by a competitive labor market that clears each period. The second interpretation, which should be familiar from our study of Arrow–Debreu contingent claims, is as a contingency plan or rule for setting the real wage at $t + j$, contingent on all relevant information available up through time $t + j$. It would be a standard application of the Arrow–Debreu analysis to regard the above equation as a rule for setting the real wage that is written into an infinitely lived labor contract at time t and then executed forever. So the above equation can be regarded as a *model* of a long-term labor contract.

E. Equilibrium and Optimality

Our study of Lucas and Prescott's model of investment and the resemblance of Equation (16) to an Euler equation lead us to ask if there is an interesting optimum problem that the competitive equilibrium solves. The answer is yes. In words, it is the social planning problem: choose a stochastic process for employment that maximizes the household's expected utility (8) subject to the technology of the economy. That is, the "planner" is supposed to maximize

$$v_t = E_t \sum_{j=0}^{\infty} b^j \left\{ u_0 c_{t+j} - [\delta_0 + \varepsilon_{t+j}] n_{t+j} - \frac{\delta_1}{2} n_{t+j}^2 - \frac{\delta_2}{2} (n_{t+j} + \gamma n_{t+j-1})^2 \right\} \tag{20}$$

subject to

$$c_{t+j} = (f_0 + a_{t+j}) n_{t+j} - \tfrac{1}{2} f_1 n_{t+j}^2 - \tfrac{1}{2} d(n_{t+j} - n_{t+j-1})^2, \qquad n_{t-1} \text{ given.}$$

By using the constraint to eliminate c_{t+j} from (20) it is straightforward to show that the Euler equation for this problem is exactly (16). Further, the transversality condition for this problem matches up with those for the representative firm and household. It therefore follows that the competitive equilibrium employment process does maximize the "social welfare" criterion (20).

That the equilibrium employment process maximizes the representative household's welfare subject to the technology is interesting because the model is one that can easily possess a business cycle in the sense of serially correlated fluctuations in employment. To take a simple example, suppose that $\{\varepsilon_{t+j}\}$ and $\{a_{t+j}\}$ are serially independent exogenous processes so that $E_t \varepsilon_{t+1} = E_t a_{t+1} = 0$ for all t. Then the solution (19) becomes

$$n_{t+j+1} = \mu_1 n_{t+j} - \frac{\mu_1}{u_0 d - \delta_2 \gamma} (\varepsilon_{t+j+1} - u_0 a_{t+j+1}) + \text{constant}, \tag{21}$$

which says that employment follows a first-order Markov process with "decay" parameter μ_1.

In the context of the present model it is easy to think of tax schemes that can effectively combat the business cycle in the sense of reducing both the variance and serial correlation of employment. It is also clear that so long as the technology remains unaltered, such policies will in general lower the level of social welfare produced by the competitive equilibrium employment process.

The interested reader can study this further in Exercise 1 at the end of the chapter.

F. Serial Correlation in Employment and the Phillips Curve

From the preceding calculations, it is evident that the model is capable of generating serially correlated movements in employment in response to serially uncorrelated shocks. The existence of serially correlated movements in employment is no paradox from the viewpoint of equilibrium models of the class represented by (14) and (15).[5] However, the model formed by (14) and (15) is inconsistent with the notion that movements in "aggregate demand" or "money" are sources of the shocks impinging on employment. That is, the model cannot account for positive price–employment or money–employment correlations that originate from the action of aggregate demand on employment. To show this formally, notice that the two equations (14) and (15) are sufficient to determine the bivariate stochastic process for (n_t, w_t). From this fact it follows that the model is a "real" model of business fluctuations in the following very strong sense: the vector stochastic process for (n_t, w_t) can be determined analytically before the stochastic process for the price level p_t has been determined. In this model monetary policy is powerless to affect employment. Indeed, even unexpected movements in money are asserted to have no effects on n_t or w_t. The strong real property is a consequence of two features of the system. First, there is the specification of the structural equations (14) and (15) with their exclusion of "money illusion." Second, there is the imposition of rational expectations, which enters by way of our having assumed that agents' expectations are linear least squares forecasts formed with reference to the probability distribution generated by the solution to (14) and (15). The strong real property will not in general prevail where agents' expectations are posited to be arbitrary functions of, say, own past values.

The tendency of economists to regard real models of this type as incomplete or wrong is due to the fact that positive output–price and output–money correlations have characterized business cycles for a long time, coupled with a widespread belief that those correlations reflect a reality in which both the price level and aggregate output and employment are responding sympathetically to a common causal force such as "aggregate demand" or "money." Many economists have desired to explain the positive price–output correlations with a model in which the price level and aggregate output and employment are simultaneously determined; this desideratum is to be contrasted with the

---

[5] It is not necessary to rely on costs of adjustment to produce serially correlated movements in output in an equilibrium model. Stochastic versions of the Cass–Koopmans optimal growth model, which can be interpreted as models of a competitive economy, exhibit serially correlated output. See Brock and Mirman (1972). Also inspect the solution for capital in Exercise 5 of Chapter IX.

preceding real model in which a complete theory of employment and the real wage is obtained without any theory of the price level having been advanced.

4. DISPARATE INFORMATION SETS

It was to explain demand-induced price–output correlations while retaining the hypothesis of rational expectations that Lucas resorted to a setup with dispersed markets and information discrepancies. That setup can be adapted to generate demand-induced price–employment correlations in the present model while delivering the added dividend that there emerges an endogenous theory of the persistence of effects of aggregate-demand shocks.

Firms and households are assumed to be dispersed over a continuum of markets. Both firms and workers are forever stuck in the market where they happen to be, a simplification that rules out interesting search problems. The logarithm of the price in a particular market at time t obeys

$$p_t(z_t, x_t) = p_t + z_t - \alpha x_t, \qquad \alpha > 0, \tag{22}$$

where p_t is the logarithm of the economy-wide average price level, z_t is a serially independent stationary relative demand shock with probability density $g(z_t)$, and x_t is a serially independent, stationary, market-specific technology shock with probability density $f(x_t)$. The average log price p_t follows a stochastic process to be described below. We assume that $Ex_t = Ez_t = 0$ for all t and that p, z, and x are mutually independent at all leads and lags, so that the price in a particular market is the sum of the average price level, an orthogonal market-specific relative demand component z_t and an orthogonal (relative) technology shock $-\alpha x_t$.

The state of a particular market relative to the average economy-wide state at time t is entirely determined by the sequences of relative demand shocks $\{z_t, z_{t-1}, z_{t-2}, \ldots\}$ and relative technology shocks $\{x_t, x_{t-1}, x_{t-2}, \ldots\}$ that it has received up to the present time. That is, all markets are identical in their behavioral parameters and face environments differentiated only by the different sequences $\{z_t, z_{t-1}, \ldots\}$ and $\{x_t, x_{t-1}, \ldots\}$ that they face. This fact permits us to index individual markets by the sequences $\{z_t, z_{t-1}, \ldots\}$, $\{x_t, x_{t-1}, \ldots\}$ that they have faced: if two markets have drawn identical z and x sequences over the past, they will have behaved in identical fashion. From the assumptions that z_t and x_t are mutually and serially independent, it follows that the sequence $(z_t, z_{t-1}, \ldots)$ has joint density $g(z_t)g(z_{t-1})\cdots$; the sequence $(x_t, x_{t-1}, \ldots)$ has joint density $f(x_t)f(x_{t-1})\cdots$; and $(z_t, x_t, z_{t-1}, x_{t-1}, z_{t-2}, x_{t-2}, \ldots)$ has joint density $g(z_t)f(x_t)g(z_{t-1})f(x_{t-1})\cdots$. We shall let $\bar{z}_t$ denote the sequence $(z_t, z_{t-1}, \ldots)$ and $\bar{x}_t$ denote the sequence $(x_t, x_{t-1}, \ldots)$.

It will turn out that at time t employment and the money wage in market $(\bar{z}_t, \bar{x}_t)$ will depend on $(\bar{z}_t, \bar{x}_t)$ as well as the other state variables that influence all markets. We denote the logarithm of the equilibrium money wage and the level of employment in market $(\bar{z}_t, \bar{x}_t)$ as $w_t(\bar{z}_t, \bar{x}_t)$ and $n_t(\bar{z}_t, \bar{x}_t)$, respectively. We denote the economy-wide averages of $w_t(\bar{z}_t, \bar{x}_t)$ and $n_t(\bar{z}_t, \bar{x}_t)$ as $\bar{w}_t$ and $\bar{n}_t$, so that

$$\bar{w}_t = \iint \cdots \int w_t(\bar{z}_t, \bar{x}_t) g(z_t) f(x_t) g(z_{t-1}) f(x_{t-1}) \cdots dz_t \, dx_t \, dz_{t-1} \, dx_{t-1} \ldots,$$

$$\bar{n}_t = \iint \cdots \int n_t(\bar{z}_t, \bar{x}_t) g(z_t) f(x_t) g(z_{t-1}) f(x_{t-1}) \cdots dz_t \, dx_t \, dz_{t-1} \, dx_{t-1} \ldots.$$

Let $n_t(\bar{z}_t, \bar{x}_t)$ or for short n_t be employment in market $(\bar{z}_t, \bar{x}_t)$ at time t. We shall assume that in market $(\bar{z}_t, \bar{x}_t)$, the representative firm's contingency plan for setting its employment solves the "Euler equation"

$$A^f E n_{t+1} | I_t(\bar{z}_t, \bar{x}_t) + B^f n_t + C^f n_{t-1} = w_t(\bar{z}_t, \bar{x}_t) - p_t(z_t, x_t) + (u_{1t} + x_t) \quad (23)$$

where $A^f = bC^f$ and $I_t(\bar{z}_t, \bar{x}_t)$ is information available at t in market $(\bar{z}_t, \bar{x}_t)$, to be specified below. Here $u_{1t} + x_t$ is a shock to technology composed of the sum of an economy-wide term u_{1t} that affects all markets and a market-specific term x_t. The operator E is the linear least squares projection operator.

Equation (23) will be regarded as a version of the Euler equation (15) of Section 3C, in which we have replaced the real wage with the log of the real wage in market $\bar{z}_t, \bar{x}_t$.[6]

We assume that in market $(\bar{z}_t, \bar{x}_t)$, the representative household's contingency plan for setting its labor supply n_t satisfies the Euler equation[7]

$$A^c E n_{t+1} | I_t(\bar{z}_t, \bar{x}_t) + B^c n_t + C^c n_{t-1} = w_t(\bar{z}_t, \bar{x}_t) - E p_t | I_t(\bar{z}_t, \bar{x}_t) + u_{2t} \quad (24)$$

where $A^c = bC^c$, and where u_{2t} is an economy-wide random shock to labor supply. Equation (24) will be regarded as a version of the Euler equation (14) of Section 3C with the real wage having been replaced by the logarithm of the real wage that is pertinent to labor suppliers. We have deflated the money wage in market $(\bar{z}_t, \bar{x}_t)$ by the (expected) average economy-wide price level to reflect that an employee cares about his prospective wage measured not in terms of own-market goods but in terms of an economy-wide average bundle of goods. As in

---

[6] One way to think about this is by supposing that units have been chosen to make the real wage, say, W_t/P_t, equal unity on average. Then let $w_t = \ln W_t$ and $p_t = \ln P_t$, and use the approximation

$$W_t/P_t = 1 + \ln(W_t/P_t) = 1 + w_t - p_t,$$

which comes from the first two terms of a Taylor's series expansion of $\exp(\ln(W/P))$ about $W/P = 1$. Our choice of linear functional forms in the variables of interest is motivated by the desire to build a model for which an explicit solution can be obtained. A cost of replacing the real wage with its logarithm in (23) is that the link between (23) and the maximum problem of Section 3, for which it is the Euler equation, has been broken, and the formal justification for using the transversality condition to select the correct or "stable" solution of (23) has been lost. However, we shall continue to solve (23) by imposing what looks like the transversality condition, solving "stable" roots backward and "unstable" roots forward. Maybe the approximation argument above is the best formal justification for this procedure.

the setup of Lucas described in Chapter XVI the assumption is that the labor supplier works in one market but shops in many other markets. In what follows, E will be the linear least squares projection operator. The decision rules that we derive are thus optimal linear rules.

For the purposes of this section, we shall assume that the shocks u_{1t} and u_{2t} are serially independent and mutually independent stochastic processes with means of zero. The processes u_{1t} and u_{2t} correspond to constants times the a_t and ε_t processes, respectively, of the previous section. We have also omitted the constants from the right-hand sides of the demand and labor supply schedules since the interesting aspects of our calculations will not involve them.

To complete the model in the simplest way, we assume that p_t is governed by the exogenous stochastic process

$$p_t = v(L)u_{3t} \tag{25}$$

where $v(L)$ is a square-summable polynomial in the lag operator that is one-sided on the present and past. We assume that $u_{1t}, u_{2t}, u_{3t}, z_t$, and x_t are serially independent and mutually independent random processes with means of zero and finite variances. We thus assume that $Ex_t u_{js} = Ez_t u_{js} = 0$ for all t, j, and s. We assume that $Eu_{js}u_{kt} = 0$ for all j and k, and all t and s except where $j = k$ and $t = s$. Thus, the u_{jt} are orthogonal at all leads and lags.

Combining (22) and (25) we also have

$$p_t(z_t, x_t) = v(L)u_{3t} + z_t - \alpha x_t. \tag{26}$$

An *equilibrium* is a solution of the stochastic difference equations (23), (24), and (26) and is a stochastic process that has a moving-average representation

$$n_t(\bar{z}_t, \bar{x}_t) = a(L)u_{1t} + b(L)u_{2t} + c(L)u_{3t} + d(L)z_t + r(L)x_t, \tag{27}$$

$$w_t(\bar{z}_t, \bar{x}_t) = e(L)u_{1t} + f(L)u_{2t} + g(L)u_{3t} + k(L)z_t + s(L)x_t \tag{28}$$

where all polynomials in the lag operator are square-summable and one-sided on the present and past. Imposing square summability on the distributed lags amounts to imposing the transversality condition. Our object now is to construct the polynomials in L that appear in (27) and (28).[8]

It remains to specify the information set $I_t(\bar{z}_t, \bar{x}_t)$. We assume that agents in market $(\bar{z}_t, \bar{x}_t)$ at time t know *lagged* values of all economy-wide aggregates $u_{1t-1}, u_{1t-2}, \ldots, u_{2t-1}, u_{2t-2}, \ldots, u_{3t-1}, u_{3t-2}, \ldots$, as well as all lagged values of own-market variables. Knowing all lagged values of u_1, u_2, and u_3 is equivalent with knowing all lagged values of the economy-wide aggregates $\bar{n}, \bar{w}$, and p. In

---

[7] Using the same symbol n_t for labor demand and labor supply means that we have imposed market clearing at all t.

[8] The algorithm used to compute an equilibrium for the model of this section is usefully compared to the algorithms used by Townsend (1983) to compute equilibria for his models.

addition, we assume that agents in market $(\bar{z}_t, \bar{x}_t)$ see the current variables $p_t(z_t, x_t)$, $w_t(\bar{z}_t, \bar{x}_t)$, u_{2t} and $(u_{1t} + x_t)$. Thus, in each market, agents see the own-market money wage, the shock to preferences, and the own-market shock to technology. Knowledge of economy-wide aggregates other than u_{2t} is obtained only with a one-period lag. It is convenient to partition the information set $I_t(\bar{z}_t, \bar{x}_t)$ as follows:

$$I_t(\bar{z}_t, \bar{x}_t) = \{w_t(\bar{z}_t, \bar{x}_t), p_t(z_t, x_t), u_{1t} + x_t, \theta_t\},$$

$$\theta_t = \{u_{1t-1}, u_{1t-2}, \ldots; x_{t-1}, x_{t-2}, \ldots; u_{2t}, u_{2t-1}, \ldots;$$

$$u_{3t-1} u_{3t-2}, \ldots; z_{t-1}, z_{t-2}, \ldots\}.$$

Let us write Equations (23) and (24) as

$$A^f E_t n_{t+1} + B^f n_t + C^f n_{t-1} = (w_t(\bar{z}_t, \bar{x}_t) - p_t(z_t, x_t)) + u_{1t} + x_t, \tag{29}$$

$$A^c E_t n_{t+1} + B^c n_t + C^c n_{t-1} = (w_t(\bar{z}_t, \bar{x}_t) - p_t(z_t, x_t))$$
$$+ (p_t(z_t, x_t) - Ep_t | I_t(\bar{z}_t, \bar{x}_t)) + u_{2t}, \tag{30}$$

where $E_t y \equiv Ey | I_t(\bar{z}_t, \bar{x}_t)$. Subtracting (29) from (30) gives

$$A^s E_t n_{t+1} + B^s n_t + C^s n_{t-1} = u_{2t} - u_{1t} - x_t + (p_t(z_t, x_t) - Ep_t | I_t(\bar{z}_t, \bar{x}_t)) \tag{31}$$

where $A^s = A^c - A^f$, $B^s = B^c - B^f$, $C^s = C^c - C^f$. Our goal is to find a stochastic process $n_t(\bar{z}_t, \bar{x}_t)$ that satisfies the "Euler equation" (31) and the "transversality condition." To apply the methods of Section 3, we have only to determine $p_t(z_t, x_t) - Ep_t | I_t(\bar{z}_t, \bar{x}_t)$ in terms of the exogenous processes $u_{1t}, u_{2t}, u_{3t}, z_t$, and x_t.

Given their information set $I_t(\bar{z}_t, \bar{x}_t)$, agents' expectations are formed optimally. Therefore, we can use the recursive projection (Kalman filter) formula to write

$$Ep_t | I_t(\bar{z}_t, \bar{x}_t) = Ep_t | \theta_t + E\{(p_t - Ep_t | \theta_t) | (w_t(\bar{z}_t, \bar{x}_t) - Ew_t(\bar{z}_t, \bar{x}_t) | \theta_t),$$
$$(p_t(z_t, x_t) - Ep_t | \theta_t), u_{1t} + x_t\}. \tag{32}$$

From (25)–(28), it is straightforward to calculate

$$p_t - Ep_t | \theta_t = v_0 u_{3t},$$

$$w_t(\bar{z}_t, \bar{x}_t) - Ew_t(\bar{z}_t, \bar{x}_t) | \theta_t = e_0 u_{1t} + g_0 u_{3t} + k_0 z_t + s_0 x_t,$$

$$p_t(z_t, x_t) - Ep_t | \theta_t = v_0 u_{3t} + z_t - \alpha x_t.$$

The regression (32) then becomes

$$Ep_t | I_t(\bar{z}_t, \bar{x}_t) = Ep_t | \theta_t + \phi_1(e_0 u_{1t} + g_0 u_{3t} + k_0 z_t + s_0 x_t)$$
$$+ \phi_2(v_0 u_{3t} + z_t - \alpha x_t) + \phi_3(u_{1t} + x_t) \tag{33}$$

where (ϕ_1, ϕ_2, ϕ_3) satisfies the least squares normal equations,

$$M\begin{bmatrix} \phi_1 \\ \phi_2 \\ \phi_3 \end{bmatrix} = \begin{bmatrix} v_0 g_0 E u_3{}^2 \\ v_0{}^2 E u_3{}^2 \\ 0 \end{bmatrix}, \tag{34}$$

where M is a 3×3 symmetric matrix with $M_{11} = e_0{}^2 E u_1{}^2 + g_0{}^2 E u_3{}^2 + k_0{}^2 E z^2 + s_0{}^2 E x^2$, $\quad M_{12} = v_0 g_0 E u_3{}^2 + k_0 E z^2 - \alpha s_0 E x^2$, $\quad M_{13} = e_0 E u_1{}^2 + s_0 E x^2$, $M_{22} = v_0{}^2 E u_3{}^2 + \alpha^2 E x^2 + E z^2$, $M_{23} = -\alpha E x^2$, $M_{33} = E u_1{}^2 + E x^2$.

Subtracting (33) from $p_t(z_t, x_t)$ gives

$$p_t(z_t, x_t) - E p_t | I_t(\bar{z}_t, \bar{x}_t) = p_t(z_t, x_t) - E p_t | \theta_t$$
$$- \phi_1 \{ e_0 u_{1t} + g_0 u_{3t} + k_0 z_t + s_0 x_t \}$$
$$- \phi_2 \{ v_0 u_{3t} + z_t - \alpha x_t \} - \phi_3 \{ u_{1t} + x_t \}.$$

Using $p_t(z_t, x_t) - E p_t | \theta_t = v_0 u_{3t} + z_t - \alpha x_t$ gives

$$p_t(z_t, x_t) - E p_t | I_t(\bar{z}_t, \bar{x}_t) = -(\phi_1 e_0 + \phi_3) u_{1t} + (v_0 - \phi_2 v_0 - \phi_1 g_0) u_{3t}$$
$$+ (1 - \phi_1 k_0 - \phi_2) z_t - (\alpha + \phi_1 s_0 - \phi_2 \alpha + \phi_3) x_t. \tag{35}$$

Substituting the right-hand side of (35) for $p_t(z_t, x_t) - E p_t | I_t(\bar{z}_t, \bar{x}_t)$ in (31) gives

$$A^s E_t n_{t+1} + B^s n_t + C^s n_{t-1} = -(1 + \phi_1 e_0 + \phi_3) u_{1t}$$
$$+ u_{2t} + (v_0 - \phi_2 v_0 - \phi_1 g_0) u_{3t}$$
$$+ (1 - \phi_1 k_0 - \phi_2) z_t$$
$$- (1 + \alpha + \phi_1 s_0 + \phi_3 - \phi_2 \alpha) x_t$$

or

$$A^s E_t n_{t+1} + B^s n_t + C^s n_{t-1} = \alpha_1 u_{1t} + \alpha_2 u_{2t} + \alpha_3 u_{3t} + \alpha_4 z_t + \alpha_5 x_t \tag{36}$$

where

$$\alpha_1 = -(1 + \phi_1 e_0 + \phi_3), \qquad \alpha_2 = 1,$$
$$\alpha_3 = v_0 - \phi_2 v_0 - \phi_1 g_0, \qquad \alpha_4 = 1 - \phi_1 k_0 - \phi_2, \tag{37}$$
$$\alpha_5 = -(1 + \alpha + \phi_1 s_0 + \phi_3 - \phi_2 \alpha).$$

As earlier, we seek a factorization

$$A^s\left(1 + \frac{B^s}{A^s} L + \frac{C^s}{A^s} L^2\right) = A^s(1 - \lambda_1 L)(1 - \lambda_2 L).$$

Since we are assuming that A^s, B^s, and C^s are the same parameters as in Section 3C, it follows that such a factorization exists with

$$|\lambda_1| < 1 < 1/b < |\lambda_2|.$$

It therefore follows that the solution of (36) that satisfies our square summability or transversality condition is

$$n_t - \lambda_1 n_{t-1} = -\frac{1}{\lambda_2 A^s} \sum_{i=0}^{\infty} \left(\frac{1}{\lambda_2}\right)^i E_t\{\alpha_1 u_{1t+i} + \alpha_2 u_{2t+i}$$

$$+ \alpha_3 u_{3t+i} + \alpha_4 z_{t+i} + \alpha_5 x_{t+i}\}.$$

Since $(u_{1t}, u_{2t}, u_{3t}, z_t, x_t)$ are assumed to be serially independent and mutually independent at all leads and lags, this becomes

$$n_t - \lambda_1 n_{t-1} = -\frac{1}{\lambda_2 A^s}(\alpha_1 u_{1t} + \alpha_2 u_{2t} + \alpha_3 u_{3t} + \alpha_4 z_t + \alpha_5 x_t) \qquad (38)$$

or

$$n_t(\bar{z}_t, \bar{x}_t) = -\frac{1}{\lambda_2 A^s}\frac{1}{1 - \lambda_1 L}(\alpha_1 u_{1t} + \alpha_2 u_{2t} + \alpha_3 u_{3t} + \alpha_4 z_t + \alpha_5 x_t). \qquad (39)$$

This is the solution stochastic process for $n_t(\bar{z}_t, \bar{x}_t)$ in terms of A^s, λ_1, and the as yet undetermined parameters α_1, α_2, α_3, α_4, and α_5.

From (38) we have $E_t n_{t+1} = \lambda_1 n_t$. Substituting this into the representative firm's Euler equation (23) gives

$$(A^f \lambda_1 + B^f) n_t + C^f n_{t-1} = w_t(\bar{z}_t, \bar{x}_t) - p_t(z_t, x_t) + u_{1t} + x_t$$

or

$$w_t(\bar{z}_t, \bar{x}_t) = p_t(z_t, x_t) - u_{1t} - x_t + [(A^f \lambda_1 + B^f) + C^f L] n_t$$

$$= v(L) u_{3t} + z_t - \alpha x_t - u_{1t} - x_t$$

$$- \frac{1}{\lambda_2 A^s}\left[\frac{D^f + C^f L}{1 - \lambda_1 L}\right](\alpha_1 u_{1t} + \alpha_2 u_{2t} + \alpha_3 u_{3t} + \alpha_4 z_t + \alpha_5 x_t)$$

where $D^f \equiv A^f \lambda_1 + B^f$. Collecting common terms gives the following solution for $w_t(\bar{z}_t, \bar{x}_t)$:

$$w_t(\bar{z}_t, \bar{x}_t) = -\left(I + \frac{\alpha_1}{\lambda_2 A^s}\left(\frac{D^f + C^f L}{1 - \lambda_1 L}\right)\right)u_{1t} - \frac{\alpha_2}{\lambda_2 A^s}\left(\frac{D^f + C^f L}{1 - \lambda_1 L}\right)u_{2t}$$

$$+ \left[v(L) - \frac{\alpha_3}{\lambda_2 A^s}\left(\frac{D^f + C^f L}{1 - \lambda_1 L}\right)\right]u_{3t} + \left[I - \frac{\alpha_4}{\lambda_2 A^s}\left(\frac{D^f + C^f L}{1 - \lambda_1 L}\right)\right]z_t$$

$$- \left[(1 + \alpha) + \frac{\alpha_5}{\lambda_2 A^s}\left(\frac{D^f + C^f L}{1 - \lambda_1 L}\right)\right]x_t. \qquad (40)$$

Matching up leading coefficients in (28) and (40) and using the definitions (37) of the α_j gives

$$-1 - \frac{\alpha_1}{\lambda_2 A^s} D^f = -1 + \frac{1 + \phi_1 e_0 + \phi_3}{\lambda_2 A^s} D^f = e_0,$$

$$- \frac{\alpha_2}{\lambda_2 A^s} D^f = \frac{-1}{\lambda_2 A^s} D^f = f_0,$$

$$v_0 - \frac{\alpha_3}{\lambda_2 A^s} D^f = v_0 - \frac{v_0 - \phi_2 v_0 - \phi_1 g_0}{\lambda_2 A^s} D^f = g_0. \quad (41)$$

$$1 - \frac{\alpha_4}{\lambda_2 A^s} D^f = 1 - \frac{1 - \phi_1 k_0 - \phi_2}{\lambda_2 A^s} D^f = k_0.$$

$$-(1 + \alpha) - \frac{\alpha_5}{\lambda_2 A^s} D^f = -(1 + \alpha) + \frac{1 + \alpha + \phi_1 s_0 + \phi_3 - \phi_2 \alpha}{\lambda_2 A^s} D^f = s_0.$$

Equations (41) are five equations that given (ϕ_1, ϕ_2, ϕ_3) determine the leading coefficients e_0, f_0, g_0, k_0, and s_0. The normal equations (34) and the Equations (41) form a system of eight nonlinear equations in e_0, f_0, g_0, k_0, s_0, ϕ_1, ϕ_2, and ϕ_3. Given a solution, we can calculate $\alpha_1, \alpha_2, \alpha_3, \alpha_4$, and α_5 from Equations (37) and then obtain the solution for $n_t(\bar{z}_t, \bar{x}_t)$ from Equation (38) and the solution for $w_t(\bar{z}_t, \bar{x}_t)$ from Equation (40).

For several sets of parameter values, we have calculated the solutions to (34) and (41). These are shown in Table 1. Even with $\alpha = 0$, enough confusion is present that agents cannot disentangle relative from absolute price changes, so that $-\alpha_3/\lambda_2 A^s > 0$. This means that surprise increases in the aggregate price level increase employment (see the solution for employment (38)). With $\alpha = 0$, it may seem at first glance that agents have enough information to disentangle z_t and u_{3t} perfectly. Thus, consider the projection equation

$$v_0 u_{3t} = \phi_1(e_0 u_{1t} + g_0 u_{3t} + k_0 z_t + s_0 x_t)$$
$$+ \phi_2(v_0 u_{3t} + z_t - \alpha x_t) + \phi_3(u_{1t} + x_t) + \xi_t \quad (42)$$

where ξ_t is a least squares residual and the ϕ_i satisfy the normal equations (34). Rearranging the above equation we can write

$$-\xi_t = (\phi_1 e_0 + \phi_3)u_{1t} + (\phi_1 s_0 + \phi_3 - \phi_2 \alpha)x_t$$
$$+ (\phi_1 g_0 + \phi_2 v_0 - v_0)u_{3t} + (k_0 \phi_1 + \phi_2)z_t. \quad (43)$$

We now ask whether it is possible to choose ϕ_1, ϕ_2, and ϕ_3 to make ξ_t identically zero, which requires that the coefficients on u_{1t}, u_{3t}, x_t, and z_t in the above equation be zero. If $\alpha = 0$, then reference to (41) shows that we must have $e_0 = s_0$, so that if the coefficient on u_{1t} in (43) is driven to zero, so is the

TABLE 1

Solutions of Equations (34) and (41)

Set	α	σ_x^2	σ_z^2	$-\dfrac{\alpha_1}{\lambda_2 A^s}$	$-\dfrac{\alpha_2}{\lambda_2 A^s}$	$\dfrac{\alpha_3}{\lambda_2 A^s}$	$\dfrac{\alpha_4}{\lambda_2 A^s}$	$-\dfrac{\alpha_5}{\lambda_2 A^s}$	e_0	f_0	g_0	k_0	s_0	ϕ_1	ϕ_2	ϕ_3
1	0	0	0	−0.074	0.074	0	0	−0.074	−0.052	−0.948	1.000	1.000	−0.052	0	1.000	0
2	0	0.2	0.2	−0.074	0.074	0.0123	0.0123	−0.074	−0.052	−0.948	0.842	0.842	−0.052	0.712	0.234	−0.037
3	0	0.5	0.5	−0.074	0.074	0.0250	0.0250	−0.074	−0.052	−0.948	0.684	0.684	−0.052	−34.650	24.370	−1.810
4	0.5	0.5	0.5	−0.082	0.074	0.0270	0.0270	−0.095	0.048	−0.948	0.651	0.651	−0.278	0.693	0.180	0.072
5	0	0	0.5	−0.074	0.074	0.0250	0.0250	−0.074	−0.052	−0.948	0.684	0.684	−0.052	−15.620	11.350	−0.816

Common solution values: $\lambda_1 = 0.731$, $\lambda_2 = 1.44$; $1/\lambda_2 A^s = -0.074$; $D^f/\lambda_2 A^s = 0.9478$. Common parameter values: $u_0 = 1$; $\delta_1 = 0.25$; $\delta_2 = 0.25$; $\gamma = 0.5$; $f_1 = 0.25$; $d = 10$; $b = 0.95$; $v_0 = 1$; $\sigma_{\mu_1}^2 = 1$; $\sigma_{\mu_3}^2 = 1$.

coefficient on x_t. This looks promising because in general it is possible to solve the following three equations for ϕ_1, ϕ_2, and ϕ_3, given e_0, v_0, g_0, and k_0:

$$e_0\phi_1 + \phi_3 = 0,$$

$$g_0\phi_1 + v_0\phi_2 - v_0 = 0,$$

$$k_0\phi_1 + \phi_2 = 0.$$

However, inspection of Equations (41) shows that $g_0 = v_0 k_0$, so that the last two equations are inconsistent. This implies that it is *not* possible to find values of ϕ_1, ϕ_2, and ϕ_3 that simultaneously solve the three preceding equations. In words, even if $\alpha = 0$, perfect extraction of the "signal" $v_0 u_{3t}$ is not possible on the basis of the three noisy observations that appear in (42).

With $\alpha = 0$, z is the sole source of "confusion." In Table 1, compare values of the slope $-\alpha_3/\lambda_2 A^s$ for sets 1, 3, and 5, and notice that the addition of variance in x leaves parameter values unchanged between sets 3 and 5. However, given $Ex^2 > 0$, an increase in α adds to confusion and raises the parameter $-\alpha_3/\lambda_2 A^s$, as evidenced by comparing sets 3 and 4. Most important, holding the other parameters fixed, $-\alpha_3/\lambda_2 A^s$ increases as the variance of the relative demand parameter z_t increases. This is the same effect captured in the version of Lucas's model of the Phillips curve that we studied earlier.

5. BEHAVIOR OF ECONOMY-WIDE AVERAGES

By averaging (27) and (28) across markets (i.e., integrating both sides with respect to $g(z_t)f(x_t)g(z_{t-1})f(x_{t-1})\cdots dz_t\, dx_t\, dz_{t-1}\, dx_{t-1}\cdots)$, we obtain

$$\bar{n}_t = a(L)u_{1t} + b(L)u_{2t} + c(L)u_{3t}, \tag{44}$$

$$\bar{w}_t = e(L)u_{1t} + f(L)u_{2t} + g(L)u_{3t}. \tag{45}$$

Subtracting (25) from (45) gives

$$(\bar{w}_t - p_t) = e(L)u_{1t} + f(L)u_{2t} + (g(L) - v(L))u_{3t}. \tag{46}$$

Equations (44)–(46) form a moving average representation for the economy-wide averages $\bar{n}_t$, $\bar{w}_t$, $\bar{w}_t - p_t$. Here $a(L)$, $b(L)$, $c(L)$, $e(L)$, $f(L)$, and $g(L)$ are the same polynomials in L that appear in the solutions (27) and (28) for the individual-market solutions.

Notice that, in contrast to our results in Section 3, the solutions (44) and (46) for $\bar{n}_t$ and $\bar{w}_t - p_t$ involve polynomials in the price level innovation u_{3t} as well as the economy-wide labor supply and labor demand shocks u_{1t} and u_{2t}. This fact establishes that the strong real property of the Section 3 model does not obtain here, a direct result of the information discrepancies in the present setup. That is, the price level shock u_{3t} in general appears in the solutions for $\bar{n}_t$ and $\bar{w}_t - p_t$, in contrast to the model of Section 3 in which stochastic processes for employment and real wage were completely predetermined with respect to the stochastic process for p_t.

By averaging both sides of (39) over markets we obtain

$$\bar{n}_t = -\frac{1}{\lambda_2 A^s}\frac{1}{1-\lambda_1 L}(\alpha_1 u_{1t} + \alpha_2 u_{2t} + \alpha_3 u_{3t}).$$

Note that $v_0 u_{3t} = p_t - Ep_t|\Omega_{t-1} = p_t - Ep_t|p_{t-1}, p_{t-2}, \ldots$, where Ω_{t-1} is any information set including at least $\{p_{t-1}, p_{t-2}, p_{t-3}, \ldots\}$. Then the above equation can be written

$$\bar{n}_t = -\frac{\alpha_3}{v_0 \lambda_2 A^s}[p_t - Ep_t|\Omega_{t-1}] + \lambda_1 \bar{n}_{t-1} + \eta_t \tag{47}$$

where $\eta_t \equiv -(1/\lambda_2 A^s)[\alpha_1 u_{1t} + \alpha_2 u_{2t}]$. Equation (47) is identical with Lucas's aggregate-supply schedule, except that it determines employment instead of output. (It would be easy to use a production function to get closer to Lucas's schedule by eliminating $\bar{n}_t$ from (47) in favor of output.) In Chapter XVII we analyzed some of the policy implications of the supply schedule (47) under the assumption of rational expectations. That analysis indicated that even though surprise changes in the price level cause output (or employment) to move, systematic countercyclical monetary policy was impossible because, under rationality, systematic movements in the aggregate price level fool no one. Thus, while introducing information discrepancies across markets has destroyed the strong real property of the model in Section 3, the model remains quite classical in that it implies that one feedback rule for the money supply is equivalent with any other from the viewpoint of the distribution of aggregate employment.

6. THE PROCYCLICAL BEHAVIOR OF "LABOR PRODUCTIVITY" AND "REAL HOURLY EARNINGS"

Of the observations that cast doubt on classical theory, two important ones are, first, the alleged failure of the employment–capital ratio to move inversely with real wages;[9] and second, the tendency of time series production functions to display constant or slightly increasing returns to labor and zero or negative returns to capital, i.e., the widely known procyclical behavior of output per man-hour.[10] Lucas (1970) has advanced an ingenious theory that potentially accounts for these observations. This section sets out an explanation along the lines of Lucas's with one modification introduced, namely increasing costs of increasingly rapid adjustment of straight-time labor are postulated. This amendment is a natural one and has the virtue of permitting Lucas's model potentially

---

[9] This evidence is reviewed by Bodkin (1969).

[10] This empirical regularity is summarized succinctly by the regressions presented by Bodkin and Klein (1967) and Lucas (1970).

to explain the data with much less stringent restrictions on the form of the production function than are required in Lucas's setup.[11]

To focus things narrowly on how Lucas's theory works, in this section we assume that the firm faces an exogenous real wage rate and takes its capital stock as fixed over time. These assumptions can be relaxed with some effort.

Suppose that the firm faces the instantaneous production function

$$y(t + \tau) = f(n(t + \tau), k(t + \tau)), \qquad f_n, f_k, f_{nk} > 0; f_{nn}, f_{kk} < 0$$
$$t = 0, 1, 2, 3, \ldots; \qquad \tau \in [0, 1).$$

Here $y(t + \tau)$ is the rate of output per unit time at instant $t + \tau$, $n(t + \tau)$ is the number of employees at instant $t + \tau$, and $k(t + \tau)$ is the stock of capital at $t + \tau$. The length of the "day" is 1, so that t indexes days and τ indexes moments within the day. The firm is assumed to have a constant capital stock over the day so that

$$k(t + \tau) = k(t) \equiv k_t \qquad \text{for} \quad \tau \in [0, 1).$$

The firm is assumed to be able to hire workers for a straight-time shift of fixed length $h_1 < 1$ at the real wage w_t during day t. During the overtime shift of length $h_2 = 1 - h_1$, the firm can hire all the labor it wants during day t at the real wage aw_t, where $a \approx 1.5$ is an overtime premium.[12] Thus, for the first h_1 moments of day t the firm must pay workers w_t while for the remaining h_2 moments it must pay aw_t. Confronted with these market opportunities, it is optimal for the firm to choose to set $n(t + \tau) = n_{1t}$ for $\tau \in [0, h_1]$ and $n(t + \tau) = n_{2t}$ for $\tau \in (h_1, 1)$. That is, it is optimal for the firm to choose a single level of straight-time employment n_{1t} during t, and a single level of overtime employment of n_{2t} during day t.

The firm's output over the "day" is then

$$y_t = \int_0^1 y(t + \tau) \, d\tau = h_1 f(n_{1t}, k_t) + h_2 f(n_{2t}, k_t).$$

The firm is assumed to be a competitor in the output market and the market for labor.

The firm is assumed to bear daily costs of adjusting its straight-time labor force of $(d/2)(n_{1t} - n_{1t-1})^2$ and to bear daily costs of adjusting its overtime labor force of $(e/2)(n_{2t} - n_{2t-1})^2$. We assume that $d \gg e$, so that it is substantially more expensive to adjust the straight-time than the overtime labor force.

---

[11] Those restrictions were discussed by Sargent and Wallace (1974).

[12] Hansen and Sargent (1986) construct an equilibrium model of the shift premium which extends the approach described in this section.

The firm chooses contingency plans for n_{1t} and n_{2t} to maximize its expected real present value

$$v_t = E_t \sum_{j=0}^{\infty} b^j \left[(f_0 + a_{t+j} - w_{t+j}) h_1 n_{1t+j} - \frac{f_1}{2} h_1 n_{1t+j}^2 \right.$$

$$- \frac{d}{2} (n_{1t+j} - n_{1t+j-1})^2 + (f_0 + a_{t+j} - aw_{t+j}) h_2 n_{2t+j} - \frac{f_1}{2} h_2 n_{2t+j}^2$$

$$\left. - \frac{e}{2} (n_{2t+j} - n_{2t+j-1})^2 \right]$$

where $f_0, f_1, d, e > 0, a > 1, 0 < b < 1$, and n_{1t-1} and n_{2t-1} are given. Here $\{a_t\}$ is a shock to productivity. As in Chapter XIV, $\{w_t\}$ and $\{a_t\}$ are stochastic processes of exponential order less than $1/\sqrt{b}$ and are taken as given by the firm.

The Euler equations for n_{1t} and n_{2t} are

$$bE_{t+j} n_{1t+j+1} + \phi_1 n_{1t+j} + n_{1t+j-1} = \frac{h_1}{d} (w_{t+j} - a_{t+j} - f_0), \qquad j = 0, 1, 2, \ldots$$

$$bE_{t+j} n_{2t+j+1} + \phi_2 n_{2t+j} + n_{2t+j-1} = \frac{h_2}{e} (aw_{t+j} - a_{t+j} - f_0), \qquad j = 0, 1, \ldots$$

where

$$\phi_1 = -\left(\frac{f_1 h_1}{d} + (1+b) \right), \qquad \phi_2 = -\left(\frac{f_1 h_2}{e} + (1+b) \right).$$

Obtain the factorizations

$$1 + \frac{\phi_1}{b} L + \frac{1}{b} L^2 = (1 - \lambda_1 L)(1 - \lambda_2 L),$$

$$1 + \frac{\phi_2}{b} L + \frac{1}{b} L^2 = (1 - \mu_1 L)(1 - \mu_2 L).$$

Given the assumptions on the parameters, as in Chapters IX and XIV, factorizations exist with $0 < \lambda_1 < 1 < 1/b < \lambda_2$ and $0 < \mu_1 < 1 < 1/b < \mu_2$. Having obtained these factorizations, it follows as in Chapter XIV that the optimal contingency plans for n_1 and n_2 are

$$n_{1t} = \lambda_1 n_{1t-1} - \frac{\lambda_1 h_1}{d} \sum_{i=0}^{\infty} \left(\frac{1}{\lambda_2} \right)^i E_t(w_{t+i} - a_{t+i} - f_0), \tag{48}$$

$$n_{2t} = \mu_1 n_{2t-1} - \frac{\mu_1 h_2}{e} \sum_{i=0}^{\infty} \left(\frac{1}{\mu_2} \right)^i E_t(aw_{t+i} - a_{t+i} - f_0). \tag{49}$$

From $f_1 h_1/d < f_1 h_2/e$, it follows that $-\phi_1 < -\phi_2$, which implies that $\lambda_1 > \mu_1$ and $1/\lambda_2 > 1/\mu_2$ (refer to Figure 4 of Chapter IX). So where the straight-time adjustment cost parameter d is sufficiently greater than the overtime adjustment cost parameter e, it is optimal for straight-time employment to adjust more sluggishly than overtime employment to real wage and technology signals in the sense that $\lambda_1 > \mu_1$ and $1/\lambda_2 > 1/\mu_2$ in (48) and (49).

To take a specific example, suppose that $\{w_t\}$ follows a first-order Markov process for which

$$E_t w_{t+i} = w_t \qquad \text{for all} \quad i \geq 0.$$

Suppose that the technology shock a_t follows a first-order Markov process that is orthogonal to w_t at all leads and lags. Then (48) becomes

$$n_{1t} = \lambda_1 n_{1t-1} - \frac{\lambda_1 h_1}{d}\left(\frac{1}{1-(1/\lambda_2)}\right)w_t + \text{constant} + \beta_1 a_t$$

where β_1 is a constant. Using $\lambda_1 \lambda_2 = 1/b$ (see p. 201), we can write

$$n_{1t} = \lambda_1 n_{1t-1} - \frac{h_1}{d}\left(\frac{1}{b(\lambda_2 - 1)}\right)w_t + \text{constant} + \beta_1 a_t. \tag{50}$$

Similarly, we can write

$$n_{2t} = \mu_1 n_{2t-1} - \frac{ah_2}{e}\left(\frac{1}{b(\mu_2 - 1)}\right)w_t + \text{constant} + \beta_2 a_t \tag{51}$$

where β_2 is a constant. On the above assumptions, (50) and (51) are regression equations. For d sufficiently larger than e, the slope coefficient on w_t in (50) is smaller than the one in (51).

Now in this model the firm operates in the region of diminishing returns to both straight-time and overtime labor. But when the real wage decreases, it changes the mix of straight-time and overtime labor, on average hiring relatively more overtime labor if d is high enough. What does this do to output per man measured as an average over the entire "day"—as the time series data typically have been measured? Output per man-hour over the day is

$$A_t = \frac{h_1 f(n_{1t}, k_t) + h_2 f(n_{2t}, k_t)}{h_1 n_{1t} + h_2 n_{2t}}.$$

How does this statistic vary as a function of $h_1 n_{1t} + h_2 n_{2t}$ (man-hours over the day)? If d is high enough relative to e, when w_t decreases, on average the firm hires relatively more high marginal-product, overtime labor. This creates the possibility that the statistic A_t varies directly with man-hours, despite there being diminishing returns to additional labor on each shift. In this manner Lucas's model is potentially able to reconcile the procyclical behavior of output per man-hour (i.e., the positive correlation between A_t and $(h_1 n_{1t} + h_2 n_{2t})$ with diminishing returns to employment.

Now consider the statistic "average hourly real earnings"

$$B_t = \frac{w_t(h_1 n_{1t} + a h_2 n_{2t})}{h_1 n_{1t} + h_2 n_{2t}},$$

which is the measure of real earnings studied in most of the Dunlop–Tarshis literature. While the regressions (50) and (51) imply that both n_{1t} and n_{2t} vary inversely on average with w_t, it is possible that the statistic B varies *directly* with "daily" man-hours $h_1 n_{1t} + h_2 n_{2t}$. This can happen if the firm's response to a lower real wage is to change the mix of man-hours toward relatively highly paid overtime hours, thus inflating the statistic B even in the face of increases in total man-hours. In this way Lucas's theory potentially explains the anomalous Dunlop (1938)-Tarshis (1939) observations about procyclical real-wage movements while retaining both the assumption that firms operate continuously on their demand schedules and the assumption of diminishing returns to employment.

To illustrate how the model works, we generated artificial data and computed regressions of average productivity on measures of output and man-hours. We assumed that real wages followed the second-order Markov process

$$w_t = 1.6 w_{t-1} - 0.8 w_{t-2} + \alpha + \xi_{1t}$$

where $E_{t-1}\xi_{1t} - 0$ and where α is chosen to make the mean of w_t equal 3. The process a_t is chosen to follow the Markov process

$$a_t = 0.8 a_{t-1} + \xi_{2t}$$

where $E_{t-1}\xi_{2t} = 0$, and ξ_{2t} and ξ_{1s} are statistically independent at all lags and leads. The other parameters are as reported in Table 2. For these parameters, the optimal decision rules for n_{1t} and n_{2t} turn out to be[13]

$$n_{1t} = 0.9242 n_{1t-1} - 0.0872 w_t + 0.0613 w_{t-1} + 0.0621 a_t + 0.5322,$$

$$n_{2t} = 0.1468 n_{2t-1} - 2.7796 w_t + 0.3102 w_{t-1} + 1.6528 a_t + 13.6712.$$

Notice that overtime employment is much more responsive to real wage movements than is straight-time employment.

We defined the two output series

$$Y_t = h_1[(f_0 + a_t)n_{1t} - \tfrac{1}{2} f_1 n_{1t}^2] + h_2[(f_0 + a_t)n_{2t} - \tfrac{1}{2} f_1 n_{2t}^2],$$

$$X_t = Y_t - \tfrac{1}{2} d(n_{1t} - n_{1t-1})^2 - \tfrac{1}{2} e(n_{2t} - n_{2t-1})^2.$$

We also defined corresponding average productivity variables

$$A_t = Y_t/MH_t, \qquad AA_t = X_t/MH_t,$$

---

[13] It is a useful exercise for the reader to verify that these are the correct decision rules, (48) and (49). *Hint*: use the method of Chapter XIV.

TABLE 2

$f_0 = 6.0$	$a = 1.5$
$f_1 = 0.5$	$\sqrt{\operatorname{var} w_t} = 0.75$
$b = 0.95$	$Ew_t = 3$
$h_1 = 1.0$	$\sqrt{\operatorname{var} a_t} = 0.1$
$h_2 = 0.5$	$d = 50$
	$e = 0.05$

ξ_{1t}, ξ_{2t} are normal, random deviates.

where manhours $MH_t \equiv h_1 n_{1t} + h_2 n_{2t}$. For a simulation of length 350, we computed the following least squares regressions, with estimated standard errors in parentheses beneath each coefficient,

$$A_t = \underset{(0.038)}{4.58} + \underset{(0.0011)}{0.0015\,Y_t} + \text{residual}_t,$$

$$A_t = \underset{(0.038)}{4.69} - \underset{(0.0050)}{0.0074\,MH_t} + \text{residual}_t,$$

$$AA_t = \underset{(0.0037)}{4.57} + \underset{(0.0011)}{0.0016\,X_t} + \text{residual}_t.$$

$$AA_t = \underset{(0.038)}{4.68} - \underset{(0.0051)}{0.0069\,MH_t} + \text{residual}_t.$$

The artificial data thus indicate approximately constant returns to increasing employment. Notice that for a one-shift model (set $h_2 = 0$) we would have

$$\frac{Y_t}{MH_t} = (f_0 + a_t) - \frac{f_1}{2}\frac{1}{h_1}(MH_t).$$

With the parameter values in Table 2 the coefficient $-\frac{1}{2}f_1(1/h_1)$ is -0.25. The difference between this value and the estimates in the above regressions, which are zeros to two digits, measures the effects of the systematic changes in relative importance of the two shifts as output varies.[14]

7. CONCLUSIONS

This chapter has formulated a simple linear-quadratic optimal growth model and has used a decentralized version of it to model real wages and employment. We have also experimented in sections 4 and 5 with trying to graft

---

[14] In this example, $h_1 + h_2 = 1.5$, instead of having $h_1 + h_2 = 1$ above. This normalization obviously does not affect the argument.

a signal-extraction version of the Phillips curve onto the model in order to permit correlations to emerge between real variables and purely nominal variables. Kydland and Prescott (1982) have advocated the view that for many purposes, real versions of the stochastic growth model are sufficient. Kydland and Prescott (1982) show how the technology and preferences of the Brock-Mirman (1972) model can be altered so as to match some of the second moments of U.S. time series data on real aggregates. On the basis of that work, Kydland and Prescott argue that for understanding real economic fluctuations, there is no need to resort to the sort of Phillips curve mechanism described in Chapter XVI. Further, Kydland and Prescott work with a version of the stochastic growth model which can readily be decentralized into a competitive equilibrium. Like the model of Section 3 of this chapter, Kydland and Prescott's equilibrium is optimal.

At this time, within the equilibrium approach to studying economic fluctuations two aspects of the sort of model used in this chapter and in Kydland and Prescott (1982) remain open and controversial. One is the role of purely nominal magnitudes in affecting the dynamics of real variables. The second and related aspect is whether it is sufficient to understand business cycles by using a model whose equilibrium is optimal, or whether one wants to use a model like the ones studied in Chapters XIV and XV, whose equilibria are susceptible to improvement through nontrivial government action.

EXERCISE

Consider the following modified version of the model of Section 3 of Chapter XVIII. The representative firm continues to maximize $v_t = E_t \sum_{j=0}^{\infty} b^j \Pi_{t+j}$ where Π_{t+j} remains defined as

$$\Pi_{t+j} = (f_0 + a_{t+j})\tilde{n}_{t+j} - \frac{f_1}{2}\tilde{n}_{t+j}^2 - \frac{d}{2}(\tilde{n}_{t+j} - \tilde{n}_{t+j-1})^2 - w_{t+j}\tilde{n}_{t+j}.$$

The firm maximizes v_t by choosing a contingency plan for $\tilde{n}_t$ as a function of $\tilde{n}_{t-1}$ and current and lagged values of w and a.

The representative household's problem is modified by the presence of a government that taxes or subsidizes it. The household's problem is to maximize

$$E_t \sum_{j=0}^{\infty} b^j \left[u_0 c_{t+j} - (\delta_0 + \varepsilon_{t+j})n_{t+j} - \frac{\delta_1}{2} n_{t+j}^2 - \frac{\delta_2}{2}(n_{t+j} + \gamma n_{t+j-1})^2 \right]$$

subject to

$$c_{t+j} = w_{t+j}n_{t+j} + \Pi_{t+j} - \tau_{t+j}n_{t+j} - \theta n_{t+j}^2 + T_{t+j}.$$

Here the government is imagined to collect an employment tax-subsidy in the amount

$$T_{t+j} = \tau_{t+j}n_{t+j} + \theta n_{t+j}^2$$

and to remit the proceeds back to workers in a lump sum fashion. Thus, the tax is devised solely to induce or correct distortions in marginal conditions. The government is imagined to choose a contingency plan for τ_{t+j}, given its information, and to set θ in order to obtain its objectives.

Assume that $\{\varepsilon\}$ and $\{a\}$ are mutually uncorrelated white noises.

A. Suppose that the government desires to minimize the stationary variance of employment, and that it constrains itself to choosing among stationary contingency plans for τ_{t+j}. Then determine the optimal rule for taxes and characterize the variance and serial correlation properties of equilibrium employment under the following alternative assumptions.

(i) Assume that θ is constrained to be zero (a constitutional amendment prohibits "quadratic taxation"). Further assume that the government has an information lag relative to private agents, and must select its contingency plan for τ_{t+j} as a linear function of *lagged* a's and ε's,

$$\tau_{t+j} = v_1(L)a_{t+j-1} + v_2(L)\varepsilon_{t+j-1},$$

where $v_1(L)$ and $v_2(L)$ are each one-sided in nonnegative powers of L. The government aims to minimize the stationary variance of $\{n\}$ over choices of $v_1(L)$ and $v_2(L)$.

(ii) Assume that θ is constrained to be zero, but that there is no information lag, so that now

$$\tau_{t+j} = w_1(L)a_{t+j} + w_2(L)\varepsilon_{t+j}$$

where $w_1(L)$ and $w_2(L)$ are chosen by the government to minimize the variance of n and are both one-sided in nonnegative powers of L.

(iii) Assume now that the government is constrained to set $\tau_{t+j} = 0$ for all $t + j$, but that it is free to set θ at any value it wants in order to minimize the stationary variance of $\{n\}$.

B. Prove that all three optimal tax schemes that you derived in (i), (ii), and (iii) eradicate the "business cycle."

C. Now suppose that the government's objective is to maximize welfare of the representative agent in the economy. Derive the optimal setting for θ and the optimal contingency plan for τ_{t+j}. Under this plan, might there still be a business cycle?

REFERENCES

Barro, R. J. and Grossman, H. I. (1971). "A general disequilibrium model of income and employment." *American Economic Review*, Vol. LXI, No. 1, pp. 82–93.

Bodkin, R. G. (1969). "Real wages and cyclical variation in employment: a re-examination of the evidence." *The Canadian Journal of Economics*, Vol. II, No. 3, pp. 353–374.

Bodkin, R. G. and Klein, L. R. (1967). "Nonlinear estimation of aggregate production functions." *Review of Economics and Statistics*, Vol. 49, pp. 28–44.

Brock, W. A., and Mirman, L. J. (1972). "Optimal economic growth and uncertainty: the discounted case." *Journal of Economic Theory*, Vol. 4, No. 3, pp. 479–513.

Clower, R. W. (1965). "The keynesian counterrevolution: a theoretical appraisal," In *The Theory of Interest Rates* (F. H. Hahn and F. P. R. Brechling, eds.), London: Macmillan, and New York: St. Martin's.

Dunlop, J. T. (1938). "The movement of real and money wage rates." *Economic Journal*, Vol. XLVIII, pp. 413–434.

Fischer, S. (1977). "Long-term contracts, rational expectations, and the optimal money supply Rule." *Journal of Political Economy*, Vol. 85, No. 1, pp. 191–206.

Fisher, I. (1930). *Theory of Interest*, New York, Macmillan.

Hansen, G. and Sargent, T. J. (1986). "Straight-time and overtime in equilibrium." *Journal of Monetary Economics* (forthcoming).

Keynes, J. M. (1939). "Relative movements of real wages and output." *Economic Journal*, Vol. XLIX, pp. 34–51.

Kydland, F. E. and Prescott, E. C. (1982). "Time to build and aggregate fluctuations." *Econometrica*, Vol. 50, No. 6: 1345–1371.

Lucas, R. E. Jr. (1970). "Capacity, overtime, and empirical production functions." *American Economic Review, Papers and Proceedings*, Vol. LX, No. 2, pp. 23–27.

Lucas, R. E. Jr. (1973). "Some international evidence on output-inflation tradeoffs." *American Economic Review*, Vol. 63, pp. 326-34.

Lucas, R. E. Jr. and Rapping, L. (1969). "Real wages, employment, and inflation." *Journal of Political Economy*, Vol. 77, No. 5, pp. 721-754.

Modigliani, F. (1977). "The monetarist controversy or, should we forsake stabilization policies?" *American Economic Review*, Vol. 67, No. 2, pp. 1-19.

Phelps, E. S. (1969). "A note on short-run employment and real wage rate under competitive commodity markets." *International Economic Review*, Vol. 10, pp. 220-232.

Sargent, T. J., and Wallace, N. (1974). "The elasticity of substitution and cyclical behavior of productivity, wages, and labor's share." *American Economic Review, Papers and Proceedings*, Vol. LXIV, No. 2, pp. 257-263.

Solow, R. M., and Stiglitz, J. E. (1968). "Output, employment and wages in the short run." *Quarterly Journal of Economics*, Vol. LXXXII, pp. 537-560.

Tarshis, L. (1939). "Changes in real and money wage rates." *Economic Journal*, Vol. XLIX, pp. 150-154.

Townsend, R. E. (1983). "Forecasting the forecasts of others." *Journal of Political Economy*, Vol. 91, No. 4, pp. 546-588.

FORMULAS FROM TRIGONOMETRY

Here we briefly state all of the trigonometric identities that are used in Chapters IX and XI. Allen (1956) contains a helpful chapter on complex numbers to which the reader seeking more details is referred.

We can write the complex number z (see Figure A1) in the alternative forms

$$z = x + iy \qquad \text{(rectangular coordinates)}$$

$$= re^{i\theta} \qquad \text{(polar coordinates)}$$

$$= r(\cos\theta + i\sin\theta)$$

where

$$r = \sqrt{x^2 + y^2}, \qquad \theta = \tan^{-1}\left(\frac{y}{x}\right),$$

$$\cos\theta = \frac{e^{i\theta} + e^{-i\theta}}{2} = \frac{x}{r}, \qquad \sin\theta = \frac{e^{i\theta} - e^{-i\theta}}{2i} = \frac{y}{r}.$$

We can immediately obtain de Moivre's theorem from

$$(re^{i\theta})^n = r^n e^{in\theta} = r^n(\cos n\theta + i\sin n\theta)$$

which gives

$$(r\cos\theta + ir\sin\theta)^n = r^n(\cos n\theta + i\sin n\theta).$$

We also obtain

$$1 = e^{i\theta}e^{-i\theta} = (\cos\theta + i\sin\theta)(\cos\theta - i\sin\theta)$$

$$= \cos^2\theta + \sin^2\theta,$$

which is Pythagoras's theorem. Notice that since $\cos\theta = x/r$, and $\sin\theta = y/r$, the above equation can be rearranged to read

$$r^2 = x^2 + y^2.$$

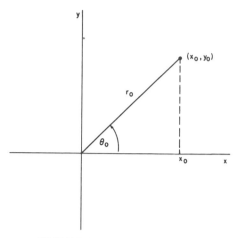

FIGURE A1 The complex plane.

We can obtain all the trigonometric identities that we need from

$$e^{i(\theta + w)} = e^{i\theta}e^{iw},$$

$$\cos(\theta + w) + i\sin(\theta + w) = (\cos\theta + i\sin\theta)(\cos w + i\sin w)$$

$$= (\cos\theta\cos w - \sin w\sin\theta)$$

$$+ i(\sin\theta\cos w + \sin w\cos\theta).$$

Therefore we have

$$\cos(\theta + w) = \cos\theta\cos w - \sin w\sin\theta,$$

$$\sin(\theta + w) = \sin\theta\cos w + \sin w\cos\theta.$$

Using $\cos w = \cos(-w)$, $\sin(-w) = -\sin w$, we obtain from the preceding equations

$$\cos(\theta - w) = \cos\theta\cos w + \sin w\sin\theta,$$

$$\sin(\theta - w) = \sin\theta\cos w - \sin w\cos\theta.$$

Adding the appropriate pairs of the preceding equations gives

$$\cos(\theta + w) + \cos(\theta - w) = 2\cos\theta\cos w,$$

$$\sin(\theta + w) + \sin(\theta - w) = 2\sin\theta\cos w.$$

Finally, setting $\theta = w$ in the above equations gives

$$\cos 2\theta = \cos^2\theta - \sin^2\theta, \qquad \sin 2\theta = 2\sin\theta\cos\theta.$$

REFERENCE

Allen, R. G. D. (1956). *Mathematical Economics*, London: Macmillan.

AUTHOR INDEX

Numbers in italics refer to the pages on which complete references are listed.

A

Ackley, G., 114, *116*
Agnew, R., 38, *48*
Alchian, A. A., 94, *95*
Allen, R. G. D., 176, *221*, 242, *359*, 499, *500*
Altug, S., 284, *359*
Andersen, L. C., 324, *359*
Anderson, B. D. O., *238*
Anderson, T. W., 285, 286, 288, *359*
Apostol, T., 249, *359*
Archibald, G. C., 107, *116*
Arrow, K. J., 137, *140*, 141, 144, 148, 151, *163*, 172, 479
Azariadis, C., 141, 165, *175*

B

Baily, M., 165, *175*
Bailey, M. J., 114, *116*, 460, 464, *465*
Barro, R., 18, 41, *48*, 380, 385, *390*, 453, *437*, 447, *465*, 469, 472, *497*
Bartle, R. G., 117, *131*
Baumol, W., 157, *163*, 176, 189, *221*
Beneveniste, L. M., 139, *140*
Bergstrom, A. R., 346, *359*
Beveridge, S., 358, *359*
Bewley, T., 363
Blanchard, O. J., 300, 348, 349, *359*
Bodkin, R. G., 74, *77*, 490, *497*
Boulding, K., 141, *164*

C

Cagan, P., 34, 37, *48*, 117, *131*, 195, 196, 211, 216, 219, *221*, 231, *238*, 293, 305, 334, 352–356, *359*
Calvo, G., 87, *95*, 428, *437*
Carvalho, J., 409, *417*
Cass, D., 218, 480
Chipman, J. S., 153, *163*
Chow, G., 311, *360*
Christ, C., 112, 115, *116*
Churchill, R. V., 242, 254, 255, *360*
Clower, R., 18, *48*, 71, *77*, 73, 94, 472, *497*

D

Dagli, C. A., 300, 329, *360*
Debreu, G., 148, 479
Dunlop, J. T., 468, 494, *497*

E

Eckstein, Z., 411, 412, *417*
Eisner, R., 132, *140*

Brock, W., 284, *359*, 376, *378*, *390*, 480, 496, *497*
Brown, J. W., 242, 254, 255, *360*
Burns, A., 283, 284, *359*

SUBJECT INDEX

ECONOMIC THEORY, ECONOMETRICS, AND MATHEMATICAL ECONOMICS

Edited by Karl Shell, Cornell University

Recent titles

Haim Levy and Marshall Sarnat, editors, *Financial Decision Making under Uncertainty*

Yasuo Murata, *Mathematics for Stability and Optimization of Economic Systems*

Alan S. Blinder and Philip Friedman, editors, *Natural Resources, Uncertainty, and General Equilibrium Systems: Essays in Memory of Rafael Lusky*

Jerry S. Kelly, *Arrow Impossibility Theorems*

Peter Diamond and Michael Rothschild, editors, *Uncertainty in Economics: Readings and Exercises*

Fritz Machlup, *Methodology of Economics and Other Social Sciences*

Robert H. Frank and Richard T. Freeman, *Distributional Consequences of Direct Foreign Investment*

Elhanan Helpman and Assaf Razin, *A Theory of International Trade under Uncertainty*

Edmund S. Phelps, *Studies in Macroeconomic Theory. Volume 1: Employment and Inflation. Volume 2: Redistribution and Growth*

Marc Nerlove, David M. Grether, and José L. Carvalho, *Analysis of Economic Time Series: A Synthesis*

Jerry Green and José Alexander Scheinkman, editors, *General Equilibrium, Growth and Trade: Essays in Honor of Lionel McKenzie*

Michael J. Boskin, editor, *Economics and Human Welfare: Essays in Honor of Tibor Scitovsky*

Carlos Daganzo, *Multinomial Probit: The Theory and Its Application to Demand Forecasting*

L. R. Klein, M. Nerlove, and S. C. Tsiang, editors, *Quantitative Economics and Development: Essays in Memory of Ta-Chung Liu*

Giorgio P. Szegö, *Portfolio Theory: With Application to Bank Asset Management*

M. June Flanders and Assaf Razin, editors, *Development in an Inflationary World*

Thomas G. Cowing and Rodney E. Stevenson, editors, *Productivity Measurement in Regulated Industries*

Robert J. Barro, editor, *Money, Expectations, and Business Cycles: Essays in Macroeconomics*

Ryuzo Sato, *Theory of Technical Change and Economic Invariance: Application of Lie Groups*

Iosif A. Krass and Shawkat M. Hammoudeh, *The Theory of Positional Games: With Applications in Economics*

Giorgio Szegö, editor, *New Quantitative Techniques for Economic Analysis*

John M. Letiche, editor, *International Economic Policies and Their Theoretical Foundation: A Source Book*

Murray C. Kemp, editor, *Production Sets*

Andreu Mas-Colell, editor, *Noncooperative Approaches to the Theory of Perfect Competition*

Jean-Pascal Benassy, *The Economics of Market Disequilibrium*

Tatsuro Ichiishi, *Game Theory for Economic Analysis*

David P. Baron, *The Export-Import Bank: An Economic Analysis*

Real P. Lavergne, *The Political Economy of U.S. Tariffs: An Empirical Analysis*

Halbert White, *Asymptotic Theory for Econometricians*

Thomas G. Cowing and Daniel L. McFadden, *Microeconomic Modeling and Policy Analysis: Studies in Residential Energy Demand*

Svend Hylleberg, *Seasonality in Regression*

Jean-Pascal Benassy, *Macroeconomics: An Introduction to the Non-Walrasian Approach*

C. W. J. Granger and Paul Newbold, *Forecasting Economic Time Series, Second Edition*

Marc Nerlove, Assaf Razin, and Efraim Sadka, *Household and Economy: Welfare Economics of Endogenous Fertility*

Jean-Michel Grandmont, editor, *Nonlinear Economic Dynamics*

Thomas Sargent, *Macroeconomic Theory, Second Edition*